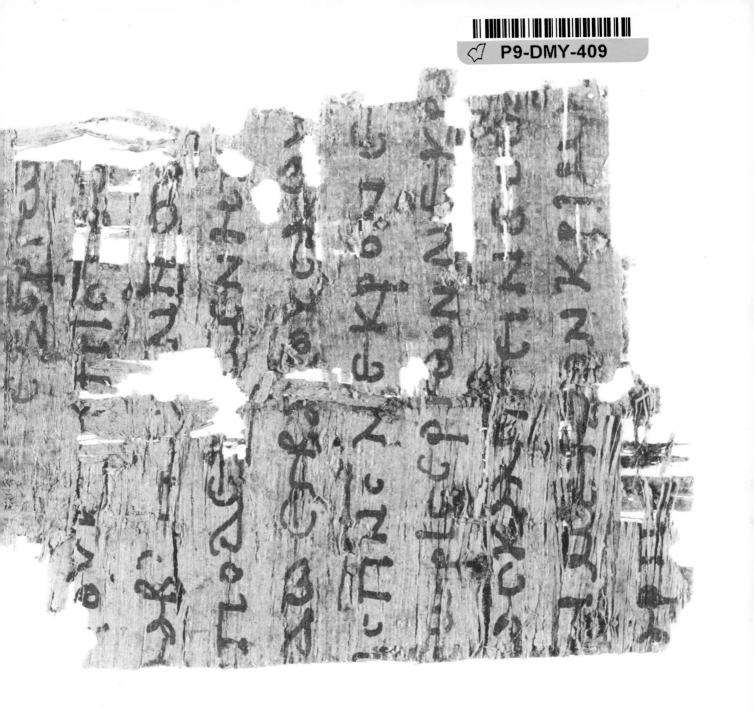

**Hermeneia
—A Critical
and Historical
Commentary
on the Bible**

James

A Commentary on
the Epistle of James

by Martin Dibelius†

Revised by
Heinrich Greeven

Translated by
Michael A. Williams

Edited by
Helmut Koester

**Fortress
Press**   Philadelphia

Translated from the German *Der Brief des Jakobus*
by Martin Dibelius†; eleventh, revised edition
prepared by Heinrich Greeven. Kritisch-
Exegetischer Kommentar über das Neue Testament
begründet von Heinrich August Wilhelm Meyer,
Fünfzehnte Abteilung—11. Auflage. © Vandenhoeck & Ruprecht, Göttingen, 1964.

**Library of Congress Catalog Card Number 74–80428
ISBN 0–8006–6006–4**

20–6006 Printed in the United States of America

Type set by Fyldetype, Ltd., the United Kingdom

Martin Dibelius, 1881–1947, was for thirty–two years
Professor of New Testament Exegesis and Criticism at
the University of Heidelberg, Germany. A contributor
to both the *Handbuch zum Neuen Testament* and the
Meyer Kommentar, he is remembered for his contributions
to the *Formgeschichtliche* studies. His major work, *From
Tradition to Gospel*, appeared in English in 1935.
Dibelius' *The Pastoral Epistles*, revised after his death
by Hans Conzelmann, has already been published in
Hermeneia.

Heinrich Greeven, born in 1906, is presently Professor
at Ruhr University in Bochum, West Germany, having
previously served on theological faculties in Greifswald,
Heidelberg, Bethel, and Kiel. He has written several
important studies, particularly in the area of early
Christian community and worship, including numerous
contributions to Kittel's *Theological Dictionary of the
New Testament* and *Die Religion in Geschichte und
Gegenwart*. Greeven also revised Dibelius' commentary
on Colossians, Ephesians, and Philemon in the
Handbuch zum Neuen Testament, and edited Dibelius'
well-known collection, *Studies in the Acts of the Apostles*,
translated into English in 1956.

Contents

The name *Hermeneia*, Greek ἑρμενεία, has been chosen as the title of the commentary series to which this volume belongs. The word *Hermeneia* has a rich background in the history of biblical interpretation as a term used in the ancient Greek–speaking world for the detailed, systematic exposition of a scriptural work. It is hoped that the series, like its name, will carry forward this old and venerable tradition. A second, entirely practical reason for selecting the name lay in the desire to avoid a long descriptive title and its inevitable acronym, or worse, an unpronounceable abbreviation.

The series is designed to be a critical and historical commentary to the Bible without arbitrary limits in size or scope. It will utilize the full range of philological and historical tools including textual criticism (often ignored in modern commentaries), the methods of the history of tradition (including genre and prosodic analysis), and the history of religion.

Hermeneia is designed for the serious student of the Bible. It will make full use of ancient Semitic and classical languages; at the same time, English translations of all comparative materials—Greek, Latin, Canaanite, or Akkadian—will be supplied alongside the citation of the source in its original language. Insofar as possible, the aim is to provide the student or scholar with full critical discussion of each problem of interpretation and with the primary data upon which the discussion is based.

Hermeneia is designed to be international and interconfessional in the selection of its authors; its editorial boards were also formed with this end in view. Occasionally the series will offer translations of distinguished commentaries which originally appeared in languages other than English. Published volumes of the series will be revised continually, and, eventually, new commentaries will replace older works in order to preserve the currency of the series. Commentaries are also being assigned for important literary works in the categories of apocryphal and pseudepigraphical works of the Old and New Testaments, including some of Essene or Gnostic authorship.

The editors of *Hermeneia* impose no systematic–theological perspective upon the series (directly, or indirectly by its selection of authors). It is expected that authors will struggle to lay bare the ancient meaning of a biblical work or pericope. In this way the text's human relevance should become transparent, as is always the case in competent historical discourse. However, the series eschews for itself homiletical translation of the Bible.

The editors are heavily indebted to Fortress Press for its energy and courage in taking up an expensive, long–term project, the rewards of which will accrue chiefly to the field of biblical scholarship.

The present volume is the translation of a "classic" of biblical interpretation. When it was first published more than half a century ago, it was a pioneering work in the application of form and literary critical methods to the interpretation of a writing from the New Testament, and it has lost little, if any, of its freshness and acumen. Indeed, this commentary on James also remains unsurpassed with respect to thoroughness of investigation, depth of insight, consistency of method, and presentation of relevant historical materials. Martin Dibelius' student, Professor Heinrich Greeven, has updated the work of his teacher so that it has stayed abreast of the more recent scholarly debate. This, the editors hope, fully justifies its inclusion in a series that wants to be a useful tool for the understanding of the Bible in our time.

We are grateful to Professor Thomas L. Budesheim of the Central Baptist Theological Seminary (Kansas City, Kansas) for a first draft of the translation of a part of this volume. Michael A. Williams of Harvard University produced the final translation of the whole volume, including most Greek and Latin texts. He also assisted in the editing of the manuscript, updated the bibliography, undertook the task of copyediting with great skill, and composed the indices. His scholarly competence, his masterful control of languages, his penetrating understanding of the subject–matter, his respect for detail and accuracy, and his ability to accomplish a task quickly, thoroughly, and seemingly without effort have been of immeasurable value. If this volume proves to be helpful, all thanks are due to him. Natalie A. Petrochko of Harvard Divinity School gave most valuable help in the composition of the indices.

The editor responsible for this volume is Helmut Koester of Harvard University.

June 1975

Frank Moore Cross, Jr.
For the Old Testament
Editorial Board

Helmut Koester
For the New Testament
Editorial Board

This commentary endeavors to understand the Letter of James as evidence for early Christian paraenesis and to explicate the problems of the letter in terms of the particular presuppositions of this paraenesis, the way in which it was transmitted, and the way in which it combines Christian, Jewish, and Hellenistic elements. I hope, of course, that even those readers who reject this approach to the letter will still find this book useful. Only the commentary itself can justify my point of view, which is set forth briefly in the Introduction. The following comments should help to understand how I arrived at this view.

The study of the Catholic Epistles is encumbered with a difficulty inherent in the literary and religious character of this sort of document. The person who has dealt extensively with the Pauline epistles is accustomed to expecting in early Christian letters a living witness to concrete circumstances within a specific church as well as original ideas and statements produced by a creative personality. The Catholic Epistles, with the possible exception of the Johannine letters, greatly disappoint these expectations, and the Letter of James in particular meets up to neither one. Deducing from admonitions and warnings what historical situations actually existed is a method often used with splendid success in the letters of Paul, but it leads nowhere in James. If one attempts this with real seriousness in James, the result is a picture of a church in which there is a curious and unlikely mixture of an original freshness and at the same time an undeniable decay—instead of a picture that is animated and has clear-cut features. And this is precisely because the Letter of James does not deal with the actual situation of a specific church, but with possible problems of early Christianity in general. Therefore its statements cannot be taken as allusions to specific incidents within an individual church. Even the individuality of the writer (which the letters of Paul vividly display) recedes into the background, for he is neither an "author" nor a prophet. Instead, he is a teacher and as such he does not strive to fashion new thoughts but rather to give life to ancient wisdom in order to revive it for a new period and new problems.

Essential to the cultural perspective of the Letter of James, it seems to me, is that which is typical rather than that which is particular. Furthermore, it seems to me that when the individual statements in the epistle are understood in the context of the developing paraenetic tradition, as surely as they are devoid of any direct historical reference, they do relate to actual history. To be sure, the letter manifests thoughts and admonitions of the most divergent origins. But at the same time, the choice and variation of these thoughts and admonitions give indication of those areas of Christian life which most urgently needed direction and regulation. These needs and the paraenetic tradition which is utilized are the primary focus of my investigation.

In this effort two requirements had to be met. First, sayings material had to be dealt with as such; thus, in the interpretation of unconnected sayings I had to disregard arguments based upon a merely postulated connection of the individual sayings. I have discussed these problems in an "Analysis" which precedes each section, because I did not want to interrupt repeatedly the interpretation of each section with a discussion of the connection of the sayings. In doing so, I also emphasize that such an analysis of an entire section must precede the interpretation of each individual passage.

A second requirement resulted from an attempt to understand the individual admonition in terms of the history of the ethical tradition. Here the task was not primarily the compilation of parallels from the most diverse quarters, but rather collection from specific circles of particular evidence in which some kind of genealogy could be observed. Therefore the reader will discover many quotations from Sirach and the *Sayings of the Fathers (Pirke Aboth)*, from *Pseudo-Phocylides* and Philo, from the *Testaments of the Twelve Patriarchs*, from the *Shepherd of Hermas*, from Epictetus and Marcus Aurelius, Seneca and Plutarch. I have had to omit a great deal of material in the interest of space. However, I am grateful to the publishers for their sensitivity to the extraordinary nature of the problems and for allowing me to exceed by one sheet the planned length of the commentary, which now has the same number of sheets as its predecessor in this series, the commentary by Beyschlag. After all that has already been said, I hardly need to emphasize that this present volume has nothing in common with its predecessor except for its place in the Meyer *Kommentar* series.

The Letter of James is in no way impoverished when understood, as I attempt to do here, as a deposit of tradition and a writing which contains admonitions for the daily life of Christians. For in the history of ethics the task is as much the channeling of creative forces into a mass movement as it is the unleashing of these forces. The author of James has lent and still lends his efforts to the first of these tasks. As one nameless man among the many, he speaks to the many about the Christianization of life for himself and for them. This view of James as a book of popular slogans is in complete accord with some most important and current questions. In order to prevent misunderstandings, however, I want to make it absolutely clear that I had this basic view of the letter prior to assuming the responsibility for the revision of the commentary in 1910, long before the War and the Revolution. The completion of the manuscript was so long delayed primarily because my varied war time activities kept me for three years from research and writing. The working conditions at the university library in Heidelberg during the past several winters were a further hindrance. For example, in 1917 it was the only German university library which had to be closed as the result of a coal shortage and it remained closed until April 1, 1918. The coal delivered for its use was confiscated by the governmental agency which regulated the distribution of coal.

It goes without saying that a commentary on the Letter of James is not the place to discuss the full range of the enormous problem which scholarship faces in the matter of the emergence of primitive Christian ethics. Yet the study of this letter may help to sharpen the student's insight into the problem which is directly connected with essential questions not only of our scholarship but also of our lives. The primary task of this commentary, it seems to me, is to lead its readers to that insight.

Heidelberg   *Martin Dibelius*
September, 1920.

After the eighth through tenth editions of this commentary appeared with a separate supplement, the publishers and editor decided in response to frequent requests to issue a new edition in which the addenda are inserted into the commentary, mostly in the form of footnotes. My addenda are frequently identified in that they refer to the author in the third person. Those additions which derive from Dibelius himself are not specifically identified. More exact information on these is found in the eighth through tenth editions.

Typographical reasons necessitate the discontinuance of printing the "Analyses" in special type as was done in the earlier editions. Nevertheless, these sections should be commended to the reader for special consideration. For in them, the form–critical methodology which gives this commentary its unique character is, as it were, crystallized.

I wish to express my appreciation to my colleagues in Marburg, Prof. Rudolf Bultmann and Prof. Werner Georg Kümmel, for allowing the use of comments and information which they sent to Dibelius by letter.

That this commentary has gone into its eleventh edition and with this edition into its fourth printing demonstrates that it is as much as ever a welcome stimulus to and counsellor in theological endeavours with regard to the Letter of James. Preparations are being made for an English edition.

I am grateful to Mrs. Ilse Heuck, Mr. Hauke Heuck and Vicar Dieter Müller for conscientious assistance in reading the proofs.

Kiel
June, 1964.

Heinrich Greeven

1. Abbreviations

Abbreviations used in this volume for sources and literature from antiquity are the same as those in the *Theological Dictionary of the New Testament*, ed. Gerhard Kittel, tr. Geoffrey W. Bromiley, vol. 1 (Grand Rapids, Michigan, and London: Eerdmans, 1964), xvi–xl. Some abbreviations are adapted from that list and can be easily identified.

In addition, the following abbreviations have been used:

ad loc.	*ad locum*, at the place or passage discussed
Arist.	*Letter of Aristeas*
b.	Babylonian Talmud, followed by the title, or abbreviated title, of the tractate
2 Bar.	*2 Baruch* (Syriac Apocalypse of Baruch)
BFTh	Beiträge zur Förderung der christlichen Theologie
BSF	Biblische Studien, Freiburg
BWANT	Beiträge zur Wissenschaft vom Alten und Neuen Testament
BZ	*Biblische Zeitschrift*
BZAW	Beihefte zur Zeitschrift für die alttestamentliche Wissenschaft
BZNW	Beihefte zur Zeitschrift für die neutestamentliche Wissenschaft und die Kunde der älteren Kirche
c.	*circa*, approximately
CD	The Cairo Genizah Damascus Document
CG	Cairensis Gnosticus, i.e., the Coptic Gnostic library from Nag Hammadi
cf.	confer, compare with
Con Neot	*Coniectanea Neotestamentica*
Corp. Herm.	*Corpus Hermeticum*, ed. A. D. Nock, tr. A.-J. Festugière, 4 vols. (Paris: Société d'édition "Les Belles Lettres," 1945–54; vol. 1, ²1960)
CSCO	Corpus scriptorum christianorum orientalium
[Ed.]	Editor of this volume of Hermeneia
ed(s).	editor(s), edited by
e.g.	for example
1 En.	*1 Enoch* (Ethiopic Enoch)
2 En.	*2 Enoch* (Slavonic Enoch)
ET	English translation
ET	*Expository Times*
et al.	and others
et passim	and here and there (in other passages)

FRLANT	Forschungen zur Religion und Literatur des Alten und Neuen Testaments
GCS	Die griechischen christlichen Schriftsteller der ersten drei Jahrhunderte (Leipzig and Berlin: Hinrichs and Akademie-Verlag, 1897ff)
GGA	*Göttingische Gelehrte Anzeigen*, 1839ff
GThT	*Gereformeerd Theologisch Tijdschrift*
HCNT	Hand-Commentar zum Neuen Testament, ed. H. J. Holtzmann, *et al.*
HNT	Handbuch zum Neuen Testament, ed. Hans Lietzmann and Günther Bornkamm
HTR	*Harvard Theological Review*
ibid.	in the same place
ICC	International Critical Commentary, ed. S. R. Driver, A. Plummer, C. A. Briggs
idem	the same (person)
i.e.	that is, namely
Iren., *Adv. haer.*	Irenaeus, *Adversus haereses*
j.	Jerusalem Talmud or Palestinian Talmud, followed by abbreviated title of the tractate
JBL	*Journal of Biblical Literature*
JPTh	*Jahrbücher für protestantische Theologie*
Jub.	*Book of Jubilees*
KEK	Kritisch-exegetischer Kommentar über das Neue Testament, founded by Heinrich August Wilhelm Meyer
lit.	literally
Loeb	The Loeb Classical Library, founded by James Loeb, ed. E. H. Warmington (Cambridge, Mass., and London: Harvard University Press and Heinemann, 1912ff)
LXX	The Septuagint
MPG	Migne, J. P.: Patrologiae cursus completus. Series Graeca
MPL	Migne, J. P.: Patrologiae cursus completus. Series Latina
n.	note, footnote
N.F.	Neue Folge
NGG	*Nachrichten von der königlichen Gesellschaft der Wissenschaften zu Göttingen, Philologisch-historische Klasse*
NJDTh	*Neue Jahrbücher für Deutsche Theologie*
NKZ	*Neue kirchliche Zeitschrift*
no.	number
Nov Test	*Novum Testamentum*

NTAbh	Neutestamentliche Abhandlungen		*ThQ*	*Theologische Quartalschrift*
NTD	Das Neue Testament Deutsch, ed. Paul Althaus and Johannes Behm		*ThStKr*	*Theologische Studien und Kritiken*
NThT	*Nieuw Theologisch Tijdschrift*		*ThT*	*Theologisch Tijdschrift*
NTS	*New Testament Studies*		*ThZ*	*Theologische Zeitschrift*
op. cit.	in the work cited		tr.	translator, translated by
p. (pp.)	page(s)		[Trans.]	translator of this volume of Hermeneia
par	and the parallel(s) in the other Synoptic Gospels		[trans. by Ed.]	translated by editor of this volume of Hermeneia
pl.	plural		TS	Texts and Studies; Contributions to Biblical and Patristic Literature
PrM	*Protestantische Monatshefte*		TTL	Theological Translation Library
Q	Qumran documents:		TU	Texte und Untersuchungen zur Geschichte der altchristlichen Literatur
1 QH	Hodayot, Thanksgiving Hymns			
1 QpHab	Pesher Habakkuk, the Commentary on Habakkuk		*TZTh*	*Tübinger Zeitschrift für Theologie*
1 QM	Milḥamah, the War of the Children of Light Against the Children of Darkness		UNT	Untersuchungen zum Neuen Testament
			v(vv)	verse(s)
1 QS	Serek hay-yaḥad, the Rule of the Community		VFVRUL	Veröffentlichungen des Forschungsinstituts für vergleichende Religionsgeschichte an der Universität Leipzig
4 QpPs 37	Pesher Psalm 37, the Commentary on Psalm 37		viz.	*videlicet,* that is to say
Rec.	Recension		vol(s).	volume(s).
REJ	*Revue des Etudes Juives*		*ZAW*	*Zeitschrift für die alttestamentliche Wissenschaft*
RGG	*Die Religion in Geschichte und Gegenwart: Handwörterbuch für Theologie und Religionswissenschaft*		*ZKG*	*Zeitschrift für Kirchengeschichte*
			ZKTh	*Zeitschrift für katholische Theologie*
RHPhR	*Revue d'Histoire et de Philosophie Religieuses*		*ZLThK*	*Zeitschrift für die gesamte lutherische Theologie und Kirche*
RHR	*Revue de l'Histoire des Religions*		*ZNW*	*Zeitschrift für die neutestamentliche Wissenschaft und die Kunde der älteren Kirche*
RSV	Revised Standard Version of the Bible			
RVV	Religionsgeschichtliche Versuche und Vorarbeiten, ed. Richard Wünsch and Ludwig Deubner		*ZRGG*	*Zeitschrift für Religions- und Geistesgeschichte*
SAB	*Sitzungsberichte der Deutschen (to 1944: Preussischen) Akademie der Wissenschaften zu Berlin*		*ZThK*	*Zeitschrift für Theologie und Kirche*
			ZWL	*Zeitschrift für kirchliche Wissenschaft und kirchliches Leben*
SAH	*Sitzungsberichte der Heidelberger Akademie der Wissenschaften*		*ZWTh*	*Zeitschrift für wissenschaftliche Theologie*
sc.	*scilicet,* namely			
SchrNT	Die Schriften des Neuen Testaments, neu übersetzt und für die Gegenwart erklärt, 3rd edition edited by Wilhelm Bousset and Wilhelm Heitmüller			
ser.	series			
sing.	singular			
SJT	*Scottish Journal of Theology*			
StGGB	*Studien der evangelisch-protestantischen Geistlichen des Grossherzogthums Baden*			
StTh	*Studia Theologica*			
s.v.	*sub verbo* or *sub voce,* under the word (entry)			
TDNT	*Theological Dictionary of the New Testament,* ed. Gerhard Kittel and Gerhard Friedrich, tr. Geoffrey W. Bromiley, vols. 1–9 (Grand Rapids, Michigan: Eerdmans, 1964–74)			
ThLBl	*Theologisches Literaturblatt*			
ThLZ	*Theologische Literaturzeitung*			

2. Short Titles of Frequently Cited Literature

When a commentary on James is cited with only the short title, and no indication of page number, etc., the reference is *ad loc.*—that is, to the place in that commentary where the verse(s) in question is discussed.

Aland, "Der Herrenbruder"
Kurt Aland, "Der Herrenbruder Jakobus und der Jakobusbrief: Zur Frage eines urchristlichen Kalifats," *ThLZ* 69 (1944): 97–104.

Bauer, *Lexicon*
Walter Bauer, *A Greek-English Lexicon of the New Testament and Other Early Christian Literature*, tr. and ed. William F. Arndt and F. Wilbur Gingrich (Chicago: University of Chicago Press, 1957).

Bede
Bede, *Super divi Jacobi epistolam*, MPG 93, 9–42.

Beer, *Leben Abraham's*
B. Beer, *Leben Abraham's nach Auffassung der jüdischen Sage* (Leipzig: Leiner, 1859).

Belser
Johannes Evang. Belser, *Die Epistel des heiligen Jakobus* (Freiburg: Herder, 1909).

Bernays, "Phokylideische Gedicht"
Jacob Bernays, "Über das Phokylideische Gedicht," *Gesammelte Abhandlungen von Jacob Bernays*, ed. H. Usener, vol. 1 (Berlin: Hertz, 1885), 192–261.

Bertholet
Alfred Bertholet and Bernhard Stade, *Biblische Theologie des Alten Testaments* (Tübingen: Mohr [Siebeck], 1905–11).

Beyschlag
Willibald Beyschlag, *Kritisch-exegetisches Handbuch über den Brief des Jacobus*, KEK 15 (Göttingen: Vandenhoeck & Ruprecht, ⁶1897).

Blass-Debrunner
F. Blass and A. Debrunner, *A Greek Grammar of the New Testament and Other Early Christian Literature*, tr. and ed. Robert W. Funk (Chicago: University of Chicago Press, 1961).

Bonhöffer, *Epiktet und das NT*
Adolf Bonhöffer, *Epiktet und das Neue Testament*, RVV 10 (Giessen: Töpelmann, 1911).

Bousset, *Kyrios Christos*
Wilhelm Bousset, *Kyrios Christos: A History of the Belief in Christ from the Beginnings of Christianity to Irenaeus*, tr. John E. Steely (New York: Abingdon, 1970).

Brückner, *Chronologische Reihenfolge*
Wilhelm Brückner, *Die chronologische Reihenfolge in welcher die Briefe des Neuen Testaments verfasst sind* (Haarlem: Bohn, 1890).

Brückner, "Kritik"
Wilhelm Brückner, "Zur Kritik des Jakobusbriefs," *ZWTh* 17 (1874): 530–41.

Bultmann, *Stil*
Rudolf Bultmann, *Der Stil der paulinischen Predigt und die kynisch-stoische Diatribe*, FRLANT 13 (Göttingen: Vandenhoeck & Ruprecht, 1910).

Burger
Karl Burger and G. Chr. Luthardt, *Die katholischen Briefe*, Kurzgefasster Kommentar zu den heiligen Schriften Alten und Neuen Testaments sowie zu den Apokryphen, eds. Hermann Strack und Otto Zöckler, part B, vol. 4 (Nördlingen: Beck, 1888), 209–31.

Calvin
John Calvin, *Commentaries on the Catholic Epistles*, tr. John Owen (Edinburgh: Calvin Translation Society, 1855).

Cassiodorus
Flavius Magnus Aurelius Cassiodorus, *Complexiones canonicarum epistularum septem*, MPL 70, 1377–80.

Catena (= the so-called "Catena of Andreas")
J. A. Cramer, ed. *Catenae Graecorum Patrum in Novum Testamentum*, vol. 8 (Oxford: University Press, 1840).

catenae and scholia
This designation indicates the agreement of all or several of the ancient commentaries listed in the Bibliography of this commentary under the section "The Ancient Church."

Charles, *APOT*
R. H. Charles, ed., *The Apocrypha and Pseudepigrapha of the Old Testament in English*, with Introduction and Critical and Explanatory Notes to the Several Books, 2 vols. (Oxford: Clarendon, 1913).

Cladder, "Die Anlage des Jakobusbriefes"
H. J. Cladder, "Die Anlage des Jakobusbriefes," *ZKTh* 28 (1904): 37–57.

Danby
Herbert Danby, tr., *The Mishnah, Translated from the Hebrew with Introduction and Brief Explanatory Notes* (Oxford: Clarendon, 1933).

Deissmann, *Bible Studies*
Adolf Deissmann, *Bible Studies*, tr. Alexander Grieve (Edinburgh: Clark, 1901).

Deissmann, *LAE*
Adolf Deissmann, *Light from the Ancient East: The New Testament Illustrated by Recently Discovered Texts of the Graeco-Roman World*, tr. and ed. Lionel R. M. Strachen (New York: Doran, 1927).

Deissmann, *Urgeschichte*
Adolf Deissmann, *Die Urgeschichte des Christentums im Lichte der Sprachforschung* (Tübingen: Mohr [Siebeck], 1910).

Dibelius, "Ἐπίγνωσις ἀληθείας"
Martin Dibelius, "Ἐπίγνωσις ἀληθείας," in *idem*, *Botschaft und Geschichte*, vol. 2 (Tübingen: Mohr [Siebeck], 1956), 1–13.

Dibelius, *From Tradition to Gospel*
Martin Dibelius, *From Tradition to Gospel*, tr. Bertram Lee Woolf (New York: Scribner, 1935).

Dibelius, *Der Hirt des Hermas*
  Martin Dibelius, *Der Hirt des Hermas*, HNT Ergänzungsband, part 4 (Tübingen: Mohr [Siebeck], 1923).

Dibelius–Conzelmann, *The Pastoral Epistles*
  Martin Dibelius and Hans Conzelmann, *The Pastoral Epistles*, Hermeneia, tr. Philip Buttolph and Adela Yarbro, ed. Helmut Koester (Philadelphia: Fortress, 1972).

Dibelius–Greeven, *Kolosser, Epheser, Philemon*
  Martin Dibelius and Heinrich Greeven, *An die Kolosser, Epheser, an Philemon*, HNT 12 (Tübingen: Mohr [Siebeck], ³1953).

Didymus
  Didymus Alexandrinus, *In epistulas catholicas enarratio*, MPG 39, 1749–54.

Dionysius Bar Ṣalibi
  Dionysius Bar Ṣalibi, *In Apocalypsim, Actus et epistulas catholicas*, ed. and tr. (Latin) I. Sedlacek, Corpus scriptorum christianorum orientalium, Scriptores Syri, series 2, vol. 101 (Rome: Karolus de Luigi, 1909).

Dupont–Sommer, *Essene Writings*
  A. Dupont–Sommer, *The Essene Writings from Qumran*, tr. G. Vermes (Cleveland, Ohio and New York: World Publishing Co., 1962).

Eisler
  Robert Eisler, *Orphisch–dionysische Mysterien–Gedanken in der christlichen Antike*, Vorträge der Bibliothek Warburg 2, 2, ed. Fritz Saxl (Leipzig and Berlin: Teubner, 1925).

Epstein
  I. Epstein, ed., *The Babylonian Talmud* [ET] (London: Soncino, 1935–52).

Erasmus
  Desiderius Erasmus, *Opera Omnia*, vol. 6 (Leiden: Vander, 1705; reprint London: Gregg Press, 1962), 1025–38 (his commentary on James).

Ewald
  H. Ewald, *Das Sendschreiben an die Hebräer und Jakobus' Rundschreiben* (Göttingen: Dieterich, 1870).

Feine, *Jakobusbrief*
  Paul Feine, *Der Jakobusbrief nach Lehranschauungen und Entstehungsverhältnissen* (Eisenach: Wilckens, 1893).

Freedman–Simon
  H. Freedman and Maurice Simon, eds., *Midrash Rabbah* [ET], 10 vols. (London: Soncino, 1939).

Gaugusch
  Ludwig Gaugusch, *Der Lehrgehalt der Jakobusepistel*, Freiburger Theologische Studien 16, eds. G. Hoberg and G. Pfeilschifter (Freiburg: Herder, 1914).

Gebser
  August Rudolph Gebser, *Der Brief des Jakobus* (Berlin: Rücker, 1828).

Geffcken, *Kynika*
  Johannes Geffcken, *Kynika und Verwandtes* (Heidelberg: Winter, 1909).

Grafe, *Stellung und Bedeutung*
  Ed. Grafe, *Die Stellung und Bedeutung des Jakobusbriefes in der Entwicklung des Urchristentums* (Tübingen and Leipzig: Mohr [Siebeck], 1904).

Gregory, *Einleitung*
  Caspar René Gregory, *Einleitung in das Neue Testament* (Leipzig: Hinrichs, 1909).

Harnack, *Expansion of Christianity*
  Adolf Harnack, *The Mission and Expansion of Christianity in the First Three Centuries*, tr. and ed. James Moffatt (London: Williams & Norgate, 1908; reprint New York: Harper, 1961).

Hauck
  Friedrich Hauck, *Die Briefe des Jakobus, Petrus, Judas und Johannes*, NTD 10 (Göttingen: Vandenhoeck & Ruprecht, ⁸1957).

Haupt, review of Erdmann, *Der Brief des Jakobus*
  Erich Haupt, review of D. David Erdmann, *Der Brief des Jakobus*, and of W. Beyschlag, *Kritisch-exegetisches Handbuch über den Brief des Jakobus*, in *ThStKr* 56 (1883): 177–94.

Haupt, review of Spitta, *Der Brief des Jakobus*
  Erich Haupt, review of F. Spitta, *Der Brief des Jakobus*, and of G. Wandel, *Der Brief des Jakobus*, in *ThStKr* 69 (1896): 747–77.

Heitmüller, "*Im Namen Jesu*"
  Wilhelm Heitmüller, "*Im Namen Jesu*": *Eine sprach– und religionsgeschichtliche Untersuchung zum Neuen Testament speziell zur altchristlichen Taufe*, FRLANT 1, 2 (Göttingen: Vandenhoeck & Ruprecht, 1903).

Hennecke–Schneemelcher
  Edgar Hennecke, *New Testament Apocrypha*, ed. Wilhelm Schneemelcher, tr. and ed. R. McL. Wilson, 2 vols. (Philadelphia: Westminster, 1963–5).

Herder
  Johann Gottfried Herder, *Briefe zweener Brüder Jesu in unserem Kanon*, in *Herders sämmtliche Werke*, ed. Bernhard Suphan, vol. 7 (Berlin: Weidmann, 1884), 471–573.

Hilgenfeld, "Jakobus"
  A. Hilgenfeld, "Der Brief des Jakobus," *ZWTh* 16 (1873): 1–33.

Hirzel, *Dialog*
  Rudolf Hirzel, *Der Dialog* (Leipzig: Hirzel, 1895).

Hofmann
  J. Chr. Hofmann, *Der Brief Jakobi*, in *idem*, *Die heilige Schrift neuen Testaments* 7, 3 (Nördlingen: Beck, 1875–6).

Hollmann
  Georg Hollmann and Wilhelm Bousset, *Der Jakobusbrief*, in SchrNT 3 (Göttingen: Vandenhoeck & Ruprecht, ³1917), 218–47.

Holtzmann, *Theologie*
  Heinrich Julius Holtzmann, *Lehrbuch der neutestamentlichen Theologie*, 2nd edition by A. Jülicher and W. Bauer (Tübingen: Mohr [Siebeck], ²1911).

O. Holtzmann, *Berakot*

 G. Beer and O. Holtzmann, eds. *Die Mischna*: *Text, Übersetzung, und ausführliche Erklärung*, vol. 1, part 1: *Berakot* (Giessen: Töpelmann [Ricker], 1912).

Hort

 F. J. A. Hort, *The Epistle of St. James: The Greek Text with Introduction, Commentary as far as chapter IV, verse 7, and Additional Notes* (London: Mac-Millan, 1909).

Huther

 Joh. Ed. Huther, *Critical and Exegetical Handbook to the General Epistles of James, Peter, John, and Jude*, tr. Paton J. Gloag, *et al.*, Meyer's Commentary on the New Testament 10 (New York: Funk & Wagnalls, ²1887).

Kawerau

 Gustav Kawerau, "Die Schicksale des Jakobusbriefes im 16. Jahrhundert," *ZWL* 10 (1889): 359–70.

Kittel, "Der geschichtliche Ort"

 Gerhard Kittel, "Der geschichtliche Ort des Jakobusbriefes," *ZNW* 41 (1942): 71–105.

Kittel, *Probleme*

 Gerhard Kittel, *Die Probleme des palästinischen Spätjudentums und das Urchristentum*, BWANT 37 (Stuttgart: Kohlhammer, 1926).

Kittel, review of Dibelius, *Der Brief des Jakobus*

 Gerhard Kittel, review of Martin Dibelius, *Der Brief des Jakobus*, in *ThLBl* 44 (1923): 3–7.

Kittel, "Die Stellung des Jakobus"

 Gerhard Kittel, "Die Stellung des Jakobus zu Judentum und Heidenchristentum," *ZNW* 30 (1931): 145–57.

Knopf, *Briefe Petri und Judä*

 Rud. Knopf, *Die Briefe Petri und Judä*, KEK 12 (Göttingen: Vandenhoeck & Ruprecht, ⁷1912).

Köhler, *Glaube und Werke*

 Albert Köhler, *Glaube und Werke im Jakobusbrief*, Beilage zum Jahresberichte des Gymnasiums zu Zittau, Easter 1913 (Zittau: Menzel, 1913).

Könnecke, *Emendationen*

 C. Könnecke, *Emendationen zu Stellen des Neuen Testaments*, BFTh 12, 1 (Gütersloh: Bertelsmann, 1908).

Kühl, *Stellung*

 Ernst Kühl, *Die Stellung des Jakobusbriefes zum alttestamentlichen Gesetz und zur Paulinischen Rechtfertigungslehre* (Königsberg i. Pr.: Koch, 1905).

Lauterbach

 Jacob Z. Lauterbach, ed. and tr., *Mekilta de–Rabbi Ishmael*, 3 vols. (Philadelphia: Jewish Publication Society of America, 1933–5).

Liddell-Scott

 Henry George Liddell and Robert Scott, *A Greek-English Lexicon*, revised by Henry Stuart Jones (Oxford: Clarendon, ⁹1940; reprint with Supplement, 1968).

Luther's Works

 American Edition of *Luther's Works*, ed. Jaroslav Pelikan and Helmut T. Lehmann, 55 vols. (St. Louis, Mo.: Concordia; Philadelphia: Fortress, 1955–).

Massebieau

 L. Massebieau, "L'Épître de Jacques est–elle l'oeuvre d'un Chrétien," *RHR* 32 (1895): 249–83.

Mayor

 Joseph B. Mayor, *The Epistle of St. James* (London: MacMillan, ³1910).

Meinertz, *Jakobusbrief*

 Max Meinertz, *Der Jakobusbrief und sein Verfasser in Schrift und Überlieferung*, BSF 10, 1–3 (Freiburg: Herder, 1905).

Ménégoz, "Justification par la foi"

 Eugène Ménégoz, "Étude comparative de l'enseignement de saint Paul et de Saint Jacques sur la justification par la foi," *Études de théologie et d'histoire* (Paris: Fischbacher, 1901), 121–50.

Meyer, *Rätsel*

 Arnold Meyer, *Das Rätsel des Jacobusbriefes*, BZNW 10 (Giessen: Töpelmann, 1930).

Meyer, *Ursprung und Anfänge*

 Eduard Meyer, *Ursprung und Anfänge des Christentums* (Stuttgart and Berlin: Cotta, 1921–3).

Moulton, *Prolegomena*

 James Hope Moulton, *A Grammar of the New Testament Greek*, vol. 1: *Prolegomena* (Edinburgh: Clark, ³1919; reprint 1957).

Nägeli, *Wortschatz*

 Theodor Nägeli, *Der Wortschatz des Apostels Paulus* (Göttingen: Vandenhoeck & Ruprecht, 1905).

Norden, *Kunstprosa*

 Eduard Norden, *Die Antike Kunstprosa vom VI. Jahrhundert v. Chr. bis in die Zeit der Renaissance* (Berlin: Teubner, ⁴1923; reprint Darmstadt: Wissenschaftliche Buchgesellschaft, 1958).

Oec

 Oecumenius, *Jacobi Apostoli epistola catholica*, MPG 119, 451–510.

Pfleiderer, *Primitive Christianity*

 Otto Pfleiderer, *Primitive Christianity: Its Writings and Teachings in their Historical Connections*, tr. W. Montgomery, ed. W. D. Morrison, TTL 22, 26, 27, 31 (New York: Putnam, 1906–1911).

Preisendanz

 Karl Preisendanz, *Papyri Graecae Magicae: Die griechischen Zauberpapyri* (Leipzig and Berlin: Teubner, 1928–31).

Preuschen, *Antilegomena*

 Erwin Preuschen, *Antilegomena: Die Reste der ausserkanonischen Evangelien und urchristlichen Ueberlieferungen* (Giessen: Ricker [Töpelmann], 1901).

Radermacher, *Grammatik*

 Ludwig Radermacher, *Neutestamentliche Grammatik*, HNT 1, 1 (Tübingen: Mohr [Siebeck], ²1925).

Reitzenstein, *Historia*

Richard Reitzenstein, *Historia Monachorum und Historia Lausiaca*, FRLANT 24 (Göttingen: Vandenhoeck & Ruprecht, 1916).

Reitzenstein, *Mysterienreligionen*

R. Reitzenstein, *Die Hellenistischen Mysterienreligionen nach ihren Grundgedanken und Wirkungen* (Leipzig: Teubner, ³1927; reprint Darmstadt: Wissenschaftliche Buchgesellschaft, 1956).

Ropes

James Hardy Ropes, *A Critical and Exegetical Commentary on the Epistle of St. James*, ICC (Edinburgh: Clark, 1916).

Rossbroich

M. Rossbroich, *De Pseudo-Phocylideis*, Diss. Münster (Münster: Theissing, 1910).

Schlatter

Adolf Schlatter, *Der Brief des Jakobus* (Stuttgart: Calwer Vereinsbuchhandlung, ²1956).

Schlatter, *Chronograph*

Adolf Schlatter, *Der Chronograph aus dem zehnten Jahre Antonins*, TU 12, 1 (Leipzig: Hinrichs, 1894).

Schlatter, *Glaube*

Adolf Schlatter, *Der Glaube im Neuen Testament* (Stuttgart: Calwer Vereinsbuchhandlung, ⁵1963).

Schmidt, *Lehrgehalt*

Woldemar Gottlob Schmidt, *Der Lehrgehalt des Jacobus-Briefes: Ein Beitrag zur neutestamentlichen Theologie* (Leipzig: Hinrichs, 1869).

Scholion

Christian Friedrich Matthaei, *SS. Apostolorum Septem Epistolae Catholicae* (Riga, 1782), 183–95.

Schürer, *Jewish People*

Emil Schürer, *A History of the Jewish People in the Time of Jesus Christ*, tr. John MacPherson, Sophia Taylor, and Peter Christie (New York: Scribner, ²1896).

Schwarz, "Jak. 2, 14–26"

G. Schwarz, "Jak. 2, 14–26," *ThStKr* 64 (1891): 704–37.

Schwegler

Albert Schwegler, *Das nachapostolische Zeitalter in den Hauptmomenten seiner Entwicklung*, vol. 1 (Tübingen: Fues, 1846).

Shepherd

Massey H. Shepherd, "The Epistle of James and the Gospel of Matthew," *JBL* 75 (1956): 40–51.

von Soden

H. von Soden, *Hebräerbrief, Briefe des Petrus, Jakobus, Judas*, HCNT 3, 2 (Freiburg: Mohr [Siebeck], ³1899).

von Soden, "Der Jacobusbrief"

H(ermann) von Soden, "Der Jacobusbrief," *JPTh* 10 (1884): 137–92.

von Soden, *Schriften*

Hermann Freiherr von Soden, *Die Schriften des Neuen Testaments in ihrer ältesten erreichbaren Textgestalt* (Göttingen: Vandenhoeck & Ruprecht, 1902–13).

Spitta

Friedrich Spitta, "Der Brief des Jakobus," in *idem*, *Zur Geschichte und Litteratur des Urchristentums*, vol. 2 (Göttingen: Vandenhoeck & Ruprecht, 1896), 1–239.

Theoph

Theophylactus, *Epistola catholica Sancti Jacobi apostoli*, MPG 125, 1131–90.

Tischendorf

Constantin Tischendorf, ed., *Novum Testamentum Graece*, vol. 2 (Leipzig: Giesecke & Devrient, 1872).

Ward, *Communal Concern*

Roy Bowen Ward, *The Communal Concern of the Epistle of James*, Unpub. Diss. (Harvard, 1966).

Weiffenbach, *Jak 2, 14–26*

Wilhelm Weiffenbach, *Exegetisch-theologische Studie über Jak 2, 14–26* (Giessen: Ricker, 1871).

Weinel, *Biblische Theologie*

H. Weinel, *Biblische Theologie des Neuen Testaments: Die Religion Jesu und des Urchristentums*, Grundriss der theologischen Wissenschaft 3, 2 (Tübingen: Mohr [Siebeck], ⁴1928).

B. Weiss, *Jakobusbrief*

Bernhard Weiss, *Der Jakobusbrief und die neuere Kritik* (Leipzig: Deichert, 1904).

B. Weiss, *NT Handausgabe*

Bernhard Weiss, *Das Neue Testament, Handausgabe*, vol. 3 (Leipzig: Hinrichs, ²1902).

Weiss, *Primitive Christianity*

Johannes Weiss, *The History of Primitive Christianity*, tr. and ed. Frederick C. Grant (New York: Wilson-Erickson, 1937).

Wendland, *Anaximenes*

Paul Wendland, *Anaximenes von Lampsakos: Studien zur ältesten Geschichte der Rhetorik* (Berlin: Weidmann, 1905).

Wendland, *Hellenistische Kultur*

Paul Wendland, *Die hellenistisch-römische Kultur in ihren Beziehungen zu Judentum und Christentum, Die urchristlichen Literaturformen*, HNT 1, 2–3 (Tübingen: Mohr [Siebeck], ²,³1912).

Wendland, "Philo und die kynisch-stoische Diatribe"

Paul Wendland, "Philo und die kynisch-stoische Diatribe," in Paul Wendland and Otto Kern, *Beiträge zur Geschichte der griechischen Philosophie und Religion* (Berlin: Reimer, 1895), 1–75.

de Wette

W. M. L. de Wette, *Kurze Erklärung der Briefe des Petrus, Judas und Jakobus*, 3rd edition by Bruno Brückner, in his *Kurzgefasstes exegetisches Handbuch zum Neuen Testament* 3, 1 (Leipzig: Hirzel, ³1865).

Wettstein

Johann Jakob Wettstein, *Novum Testamentum Graecum etc.*, vol. 2 (Amsterdam: Ex Officina Dommeriana, 1752).

Windisch, *Barnabasbrief*

Hans Windisch, *Der Barnabasbrief*, HNT Ergänzungsband, part 3 (Tübingen: Mohr [Siebeck], 1920).

Windisch, *Katholische Briefe* (1911)

Hans Windisch, *Die katholischen Briefe*, HNT 4, 2 (Tübingen: Mohr [Siebeck], 1911).

Windisch-Preisker

Hans Windisch, *Die katholischen Briefe*, 3rd edition by Herbert Preisker, HNT 15 (Tübingen: Mohr [Siebeck], ³1951).

Winer-Schmiedel

Georg Benedikt Winer, *Grammatik des neutestamentlichen Sprachidioms*, 8th edition by Paul Wilh. Schmiedel (Göttingen: Vandenhoeck & Ruprecht, ⁸1894).

Wordsworth, "The Corbey St. James"

John Wordsworth, "The Corbey St. James (*ff*), and its relation to other Latin versions, and to the original language of the Epistle," *Studia Biblica*, vol. 1 (Oxford: Clarendon, 1885), 113–50.

Zahn, *Forschungen*

Theodor Zahn, *Forschungen zur Geschichte des neutestamentlichen Kanons und der altkirchlichen Literatur* (Erlangen and Leipzig: Deichert [Böhme], 1881–1904).

Zahn, *Introduction*

Theodor Zahn, *Introduction to the New Testament*, tr. John Moore Trout, *et al.* (New York: Scribner, 1909).

Zahn, *NT Kanon*

Theodor Zahn, *Geschichte des neutestamentlichen Kanons*, vol. 1 (Erlangen and Leipzig: Deichert [Böhme], 1888–9).

The English translation of the Greek text of the Epistle of James printed in this volume was made by translator and editor on the basis of the Greek text, incorporating all text–critical decisions of the author. The author's exegetical considerations are reflected consistently in this translation. If the reader frequently finds "brothers and sisters" as the translation of the Greek address ἀδελφοί, (usually translated as "brothers" or "brethren"), it does not merely reflect our awareness of adequate English expressions which are not offensive to female readers. It should also be recognized that this Greek term in fact has this meaning (using the purely grammatical masculine plural as a generic term). This is particularly evident in James 2:14–15 where the Greek text uses only the masculine form in the plural as a generic, but *both* the masculine *and* feminine in the singular. We are painfully aware of the difficulties which still exist with respect to the use of the personal pronoun ("he," "his," "him") which is almost always generic in Greek; but we wanted to avoid the awkwardness of saying repeatedly "his/her" and we refused to utilize the plural for the Greek singular as this would have destroyed some of the peculiar features of the style of paraenesis in the Epistle of James.

The translator is responsible for all translations of other biblical texts, but he has followed the Revised Standard Version whenever possible.

Translations of ancient Greek and Latin texts are taken from the *Loeb Classical Library* in all instances in which no particular source for the translation is identified. In all other cases, the source of the translation is given in brackets [ ]; or it is noted that the translator has rendered the text into English [Trans.].

Whenever available, recent scholarly works are cited in their published English versions. Quotations from literature not available in English have been rendered by the translator.

With respect to all scholarly publications which are available in the English language, we have not preserved the author's references to the original publications in other languages, except in the bibliography. Though it seemed desirable to maintain such references, it would have overburdened the footnotes considerably.

The bibliography has been brought up to date by the translator, including the additional entries provided by Professor Greeven for the most recent German edition; but we do not claim to have listed completely all recent publications.

The endpapers to this volume are reproductions of fragments from a third century papyrus, listed among New Testament manuscripts as p[20]. The front endpaper is James 2:19–3:20; the back endpaper is James 3:4–9. The reproduction on p. v is a fragment of a fifth century codex of the Catholic Epistles, listed among New Testament manuscripts as p[5]. The text is of James 2:21–22. These reproductions are reprinted with the permission and courtesy of the Rare Book Reading Room of the Princeton University Library, Princeton, New Jersey.

"If the Epistle is 'of straw,'
then there is within that straw
a very hearty, firm, nourishing,
but as yet uninterpreted and unthrashed,
grain"
Johann Gottfried Herder[1]

1. The Literary Genre of the Letter of James (= Jas)

A clear concept of a document's literary character is necessary in order to understand it as a whole. Otherwise a novel might be confused with a historical account, or an official decree confused with a private letter. Most genres in contemporary writings are recognized by the manner of their publication. But this criterion cannot be used for primitive Christian writings—and thus, for Jas—for we know nothing for certain about the publication of these "books" which are preserved only as parts of the Bible. Nor does it help that Jas is to be regarded as a "letter" by virtue of its beginning, its placement in the corpus of the "Catholic" Epistles, the heading and the colophon contributed by the compiler, and by ecclesiastical tradition. For the question of literary genre is not resolved by the recognition of epistolary form, especially in a writing from that period. Admittedly, men like Epicurus and Paul gave instructions by means of letters which were actually sent, which were therefore genuine "letters." The same form, however, also served merely as a literary veneer.[2] "Letters" from philosophers and princes were contrived because of an interest in the biography of a person as well as in the service of scholarship.[3] The "letters" of *Barnabas* and *2 Clement* ex-

emplify how documents lacking even the most remote resemblance to a letter could be so designated.

Only the document itself can provide the necessary information as to its genre. Therefore one must determine the content and purpose of Jas, its literary technique and its "style"—i.e., we must analyze the document. So in this commentary, each section is preceded by an Analysis and in what follows I will summarize the results of these individual Analyses. Jas 2:1–3:12, the core of the writing, is composed of three expositions, each having characteristics of a treatise. One discerns in this section the style of the diatribe (excepting the isolated saying in 2:13) as it is known especially from Epictetus, and in another form, e.g., from the writings of Philo:[4] the readers are sometimes apostrophized; sometimes the opponents are addressed; sometimes the style is that of a learned discourse.

But these *treatises* in Jas are framed by material of a different sort: in 3:13–5:6 there are both smaller, self-contained units (3:13–17; 4:1–6; 4:13–16) but also less unified texts and even isolated sayings like 3:18 and 4:17. Here one may speak of *groups of sayings* in the same very general sense in which the transmission of prophetic speeches and of Jesus' logia combined larger and smaller units into groups. On the other hand, the character of 1:1–27 and 5:7–20 is clear. Here the form of the brief or expanded saying predominates, and these sayings are usually strung together quite loosely, requiring their designation as *series of sayings* as opposed to groups of sayings.

The results of this analysis are indeed complex, but

---

1 From Johann Gottfried Herder, *Briefe zweener Brüder Jesu in unserem Kanon*, in *Herders sämmtliche Werke*, ed. Bernhard Suphan, vol. 7 (Berlin: Weidmann, 1884), 500, n. 2.

2 See Rudolf Hirzel, *Der Dialog*, vol. 1 (Leipzig: Hirzel, 1895), 300ff, 353ff.

3 In addition to Hirzel, *Dialog*, vol. 1, pp. 300ff, 353ff, see Wilhelm von Christ, *Geschichte der griechischen Litteratur*, part 2, 5th edition by Wilhelm Schmid, Handbuch der klassischen Altertumswissenschaft 7, 2, ed. Iwan von Müller (München: Beck, ⁵1909), 365–7, as well as section 2 of the Introduction to James Hardy Ropes, *A Critical and Exegetical Commentary on the Epistle of St. James*, ICC (Edinburgh: Clark, 1916).

4 See below, section 5 of the Introduction. In addition to Ropes (see above, n. 3), see Eduard Norden, *Die*

Antike Kunstprosa vom VI. Jahrhundert v. Chr. bis in die Zeit der Renaissance, vol. 1 (Berlin: Teubner, ⁴1923; reprint Darmstadt: Wissenschaftliche Buchgesellschaft, 1958), 129f; Albrecht Bonhöffer, *Epiktet und das Neue Testament*, RVV 10 (Giessen: Töpelmann, 1911); Rudolf Bultmann, *Der Stil der paulinischer Predigt und die kynisch–stoische Diatribe*, FRLANT 13 (Göttingen: Vandenhoeck & Ruprecht, 1910); Paul Wendland, "Philo und die kynisch–stoische Diatribe," in Paul Wendland and Otto Kern, *Beiträge zur Geschichte der griechischen Philosophie und Religion* (Berlin: Reimer, 1895); idem, *Die hellenistisch–römische Kultur in ihren Beziehungen zu Judentum und Christentum, Die urchristlichen Literarformen*, HNT 1, 2–3 (Tübingen: Mohr [Siebeck], ²,³1912), 75ff.

they do lead to the recognition of one consistent feature of Jas: *the entire document lacks continuity in thought.* There is not only a lack of continuity in thought between individual sayings and other smaller units, but also between larger treatises. That is not to say that the letter has no coherence of any sort.[5] Rather it simply emphasizes the basic difference between this text and the coherent discussions which make up most of the Pauline letters.[6]

To be sure, the question of the epistolary nature of Jas has not yet been answered, for there are sections in the letters of Paul and Ignatius which closely resemble Jas. However, these are framed by other sections of a decidedly epistolary character, and thus they occur in documents growing out of epistolary situations and which are meant to be correspondence. Thus one must look for indications which point to such an *epistolary situation* if one is to decide whether Jas is a letter or at least intentionally simulates an actual letter (as do the Pastoral Epistles).

There is not the slightest hint in the text of Jas that there were personal or other reasons which forced the author to compose this writing at that particular moment. The person of the author does not stand out in the letter, and when he does mention himself, it is with reticence in a passage that has no significance for our question (3:1; the first person singular of 2:18 is purely rhetorical).

At first glance, the writing seems to reveal much more about the circumstances of the readers. At least, many interpreters have drawn inferences about the readers based upon the various warnings and admonitions in the letter. The merits of such judgments will be discussed later.[7] Suffice it to say that even those warnings and admonitions do not reveal a specific occasion for

the letter and, consequently, do not disclose an actual epistolary situation. Usually, interpreters[8] call attention to the trials mentioned in 1:2 and assert that 2:6f also suggests the idea that the readers of Jas were suffering persecution. However, the theme touched upon in 1:2 is abandoned immediately thereafter, and with respect to 2:6f the commentary will show that these verses do not refer to persecution, but rather to the familiar ill-treatment which had become the order of the day for the Christian "common people." Similarly, other statements in Jas against the rich do not permit one to infer an epistolary situation, because they express only typical contrasts and prevailing attitudes.[9] The author nowhere states that he is writing to the readers because he has heard this or that about them. The author's excitement about and elaboration of pressing dangers are never so great as to allow us to view those concerns as the actual occasion for his "letter."

Not only are there no indications of an epistolary situation in Jas, there are also no *epistolary remarks* of any sort. There is no news, no messages, no greetings. We also look in vain for an epistolary introduction (or proem) in which the correspondence between letter writer and readers is kept up or resumed. Nor is there any sort of epistolary ending; any of the admonitions in Jas would be as good a conclusion as 5:19f. In view of this, the prescript in 1:1 is the only epistolary element in the entire document.

All these observations make it impossible to consider Jas an actual letter. The form of a letter—intimated only in 1:1—does not characterize the writing. Indeed, its formal characteristics assign Jas to another genre. To be sure, the closest formal parallels to Jas in the New Testament are certain sections in the letters of Paul, but these sections are the least epistolary in

---

5   See below, section 8 of the Introduction.

6   The absence of continuity, the scarcity of continuous trains of thought, distinguishes Jas even from diatribe. Therefore I cannot concur with Ropes (section 2 of his Introduction), who attempts to characterize Jas as a diatribe. The presence of brief diatribes (see above) and the occasional use of devices common in diatribe style do not make a text as a whole a diatribe (see below, section 5 of the Introduction).

7   See below, section 7 of the Introduction.

8   Willibald Beyschlag, *Kritisch–exegetisches Handbuch über den Brief des Jacobus,* KEK 15 (Göttingen: Van-

denhoeck & Ruprecht, [6]1897); H. von Soden, *Hebräerbrief, Briefe des Petrus, Jakobus, Judas,* HCNT 3, 2 (Freiburg: Mohr [Siebeck], [3]1899); Bernard Weiss, *Der Jakobusbrief und die neuere Kritik* (Leipzig: Deichert, 1904).

9   See below, section 6 of the Introduction.

10   For the following discussion, see Martin Dibelius, *From Tradition to Gospel,* tr. Bertram Lee Woolf (New York: Scribner's, 1935), 238ff.

11   See the Analysis to 3:13–4:12.

12   For the following, see Paul Wendland, *Anaximenes von Lampsakos: Studien zur ältesten Geschichte der Rhetorik* (Berlin: Weidmann, 1905), 81ff; Rudolf Vetschera,

character in the entire Pauline corpus.[10] In 1 Thess 4:1–12; 5:1ff; Gal 5:13ff; 6; Rom 12; 13; Col 3; 4, there are texts in which—just as in Jas 1; 3:13ff; 4; 5—are found sayings and groups of sayings very diverse in content, lacking any particular order, and containing no emphasis upon a special thought of pressing importance for a particular situation. These paraenetic sections of the Pauline letters do not possess the charm and individuality found in the other parts of his letters. For in paraenesis Paul produces very little which is new, but rather transmits older sayings material. As a result, for these chapters in the Pauline corpus many more parallels from early Christian literature may be adduced than for others. Besides Jas, one may point especially to Heb 13, to parts of the *Epistle of Barnabas* and of the *Didache*; in all these instances, what one finds is *paraenesis* in the form of unconnected sayings which have no real relationship to one another. The sayings of Jesus also belong in this category. For the "speeches" of Jesus in Matthew and Luke consist of sayings loosely joined together, and these collections are extraordinarily similar in form to the first and final sections of Jas. This is understandable, for the sayings of Jesus were also initially collected, not from a historical, but from a paraenetical interest.

Finally, there is one other early Christian text which has rightly been adduced again and again as a parallel to Jas: the center section of the *Shepherd of Hermas*, the so-called *Mandates*. To be sure, the formal similarity is not obvious at first glance, for in *Hermas* one finds extended admonitions, not short sayings. But closer consideration and comparison with corresponding parallels (cf., e.g., *Herm. mand.* 2.4ff with *Did.* 4.7; 1.5) demonstrate that *Hermas* sets forth and argues more extensively that which is taught elsewhere in the form of sayings. Hence, the *Mandates* contain *expanded paraenesis*. They delineate—mostly in dialogical form—that which an early Christian teacher would want to say for the explication and application of paraenetic sayings.

This also leads to an understanding of the three treatises which comprise the central section of Jas. For, as the Analysis indicates, they contain nothing other than expansions of paraenetic sayings, either generalizations or specializations. These treatises however are not in dialogue—in contrast to the *Mandates*—but in diatribe form (it is well-known that diatribe itself can include dialogical elements; see Jas 2:14ff). The inclusion of an isolated saying (2:13) between the first and second diatribe is further indication that the treatises themselves are not unrelated in character to the surrounding sayings and groups of sayings; as is noted in the Analysis, the saying is attached exactly as though it were in a series of sayings. A first step toward an expanded paraenesis is found in the annotated saying 4:11f[11]—again evidence that this amplified form is not alien to Jas.

Having examined the various parts of the document with respect to its literary character *we may designate the "Letter" of James as paraenesis.* By paraenesis we mean a text which strings together admonitions of general ethical content.[12] Paraenetic sayings ordinarily address themselves to a specific (though perhaps fictional) audience, or at least appear in the form of a command or summons. It is this factor which differentiates them from the *gnomologium*, which is merely a collection of maxims.

By classifying Jas as paraenesis, the letter becomes part of a long and significant history. For the early Christian paraenesis is not conceivable outside the larger context of Greek and Jewish paraenetical traditions.[13] To begin with, since Christians were living in expectation of the end of the world, they had neither the inclination nor the ability to initiate an ethical renewal of a world which seemed to be doomed for destruction. As the years passed, however, everyday problems required with ever increasing urgency a Christian answer from the churches. However, the ethical directives of Jesus—the only materials of their own with which the Christians could supply the need—

Zur griechischen Paränese, Programm des Staatsgymnasiums zu Smichow (Smichow: Rohliček & Sievers, 1912). These authors also deal with the distinction between *protrepticus*, *paraenesis*, and *gnomologium*. Ropes, who denies a close relationship of Jas to paraenesis (p. 18), ignores this distinction.

13   This larger context has been sketched by Martin Dibelius also in his history of early Christian literature, first published in 1926, translated under the title *A Fresh Approach to the New Testament and Early Christian Literature* (New York: Scribner, 1936).

by no means covered all the areas of life and culture for which decisions had to be made. Quite understandably the Christian churches availed themselves of the praxis of Diaspora Judaism, in this matter as in others. In its missionary activities, Judaism in the Diaspora had produced just that which the young Christian churches were lacking: ethical directives for new converts. The Jewish text used in *Did.* 1ff and *Barn.* 19–20, the so–called "Two Ways," clearly indicates both the fact that and the manner in which Christians availed themselves of such Jewish aids.

Christian writings and Jewish authors such as Philo and Josephus allow us only to guess at the wealth of Jewish paraenesis available. But this conjecture gains support when one observes how extensive and rich a history lies behind the popular Wisdom teaching of Judaism. Many maxims of different origins and varied content have been collected in the didactic poetry of Wisdom literature. Paraenesis in the sense in which we are talking about it arose with the transformation of this poetry into prose. Thus the two paraenetic chapters in the book of Tobit (4:5–19; 12:6–10) provide a parallel to Jas. Occasionally, this paraenesis once again assumes a special literary dress; in keeping with the practice of Hellenistic Judaism, the paraenesis is dressed up as Greek poetry: the verses of Pseudo-Phocylides[14] and perhaps the sayings of Pseudo-

Menander[15] provide a clear picture of this kind of Jewish moral teaching in the form of sayings. A sort of expanded paraenesis, united with legendary and apocalyptic elements, seems to be present in the *Test. XII*.[16] The Talmudic tractate *Pirke Aboth* and later collections mark the revival of the sayings tradition among the rabbis.

Yet the rich sayings material of Judaism itself is neither homogeneous nor entirely original. The influence of the Hellenistic world is clearly visible in the later Wisdom literature, and may have played an even greater role in the instruction of proselytes, since with the presentation of Hellenistic sayings material Judaism could lay claim to certain universal thoughts and ideals. Moreover, the above–mentioned pseudepigraphical writings, which attempt to appeal to Greeks in Greek fashion, are openly Hellenistic in language and terminology. It is characteristic that for Pseudo–Menander either a Greek or a Jewish provenance could be argued, and for Pseudo–Phocylides either a Jewish or a Greek or a Christian provenance.

Therefore, at least through the agency of Judaism, nascent Christian paraenesis was subject to Greek and Hellenistic influence. In this respect Chrisitanity is also the heir of a long literary development which—as one can observe in Judaism—leads from poetry to prose.[17] After the didactic poems of Hesiod come the parae-

---

14　For the text of Pseudo-Phocylides see *Theognis* etc., ed. Douglas Young, Bibliotheca Teubneriana (Leipzig: Teubner, 1961), 95–112. Jacob Bernays, "Über das Phokylideische Gedicht," *Gesammelte Abhandlungen von Jacob Bernays*, ed. H. Usener, vol. 1 (Berlin: Hertz, 1885), 192–261, had published an earlier critical edition of this poem which bears the name of Phocylides of Miletus, the ancient composer of didactic poetry, and, in my opinion, Bernays proved the poem to be a product of Hellenistic Judaism. But against Bernays, see Arthur Ludwich, "Über das Spruchbuch des falschen Phokylides," *Verzeichnis der auf der königlichen Albertus–Universität zu Königsberg im Sommer–Halbjahre vom 15. April 1904 an zu haltenden Vorlesungen und der öffentlichen akademischen Anstalten* (Königsberg: Hartung, 1904); Albrecht Dieterich, *Nekyia: Beiträge zur Erklärung der neuentdeckten Petrusapokalypse* (Leipzig & Berlin: Teubner, ²1913), 180ff; on the whole question see M. Rossbroich, *De Pseudo-Phocylideis*, Diss. Münster (Münster: Theissung, 1910).

15　J. P. N. Land, *Anecdota Syriaca*, vol. 1, part 2 (Leiden:

Brill, 1862), 64–73, has published a Syriac document entitled "The Wise Menander Has Said." In all likelihood this is a book of sayings which was attributed to the Greek comedy writer Menander because he was well-known for his maxims. The kinship with Jewish Wisdom sayings is certain, but it is not as certain that the Menander sayings are of purely Jewish origin. See Antonius Baumstark, "Lucubrationes Syro-Graecae," *Jahrbuch für classische Philologie*, Supplementband 21 (1894): 473–90; Wilhelm Frankenberg, "Die Schrift des Menander (Land, *anecd. syr.* I, S. 64ff) ein Produkt der jüdischen Spruchweisheit," *ZAW* 15 (1895): 226–77.

16　I consider the framework of the document to be Jewish. But see Nils Messel, "Über die textkritisch begründete Ausscheidung vermeintlicher christlicher Interpolationen in den Testamenten der Zwölf Patriarchen," *Abhandlungen zur semitischen Religionskunde und Sprachwissenschaft* (Festschrift für Wolf Wilhelm Grafen von Baudissin) BZAW 33 (Giessen: Töpelmann, 1918), 355–74.

17　On the following, see Wendland, *Anaximenes*, 81ff.

netical writings in prose. The oldest of these which are preserved are the writings *Ad Nicoclem* and *Nicocles* of Isocrates. The most characteristic is *Ad Demonicum* of Pseudo-Isocrates. The wisdom sayings of popular philosophy are blended with the wealth of maxims from comedy. These are then richly enlarged by Hellenistic popular–philosophy and are recorded in independent literary works as well as in *florilegia*. Christianity has profited from all of this, indirectly at first through the agency of Hellenistic Judaism, but later on certainly directly. In this manner Christian writings have become the transmitters of popular ethics of antiquity. Jas is to be counted as one of these writings, even though its role in passing on this tradition by no means exhausts its importance.

When one examines the Letter of James in this context, the features which are most characteristic of the literary genre of paraenesis as well as of the sayings material preserved in the paraenesis are, in fact, clearly discernable. The first feature is a pervasive *eclecticism* which is a natural consequence of the history and nature of paraenesis, since the concern is the transmission of an ethical tradition that does not require a radical revision even though changes in emphasis and form might occur.[18] Hopefully, this commentary will demonstrate that this is also applicable to most sections of Jas. One would do well not to overestimate the author's part in the development of thought in the writing. With this recognition, the question of the identity of the author naturally loses in importance. If one asks where in the document the style and purpose of the author are most likely to be found, one must first of all point to the "treatises," especially to the sections 2:1–12 and 2:14–16, where the structure and lines of thought were apparently shaped by the author himself. Furthermore, the way in which the various ideas within the groups of sayings are strung together in chapter 4 gives an impression of the author's design. And finally, one may gain an impression of this design

by observing what the author selects[19] from the tradition: repetitions of the same motifs (see below) are a sure witness as to what was on his mind. But he does not claim that these thoughts were original with him.

On the other hand, the author should not be reproached for his eclectic style and he should not be accused of "parading the fruits of his studies."[20] For this eclecticism is an inherent aspect of paraenesis. Paul, too, in the paraenetical sections of his letters, is more interested in transmission than in originality. The historical significance and effectiveness of Jas is certainly not depreciated by the identification of this eclecticism. The document in itself is very modest, but it becomes a witness to a significant development when one hears in its words the echo of ancient thoughts and admonitions to which Jas has given a Christian emphasis and which he has popularized among Christians past and present. From this point of view one must also evaluate the parallels to statements in Jas which I have cited in this commentary, drawing upon the collection of other scholars and adding some texts on the basis of my own studies. In citing these parallels, I was not aiming at completeness, but at a demonstration of the phenomenon of eclecticism. The reader should know just how widespread were the thoughts which have gained lasting influence by means of Jas' writing, though Jas may not have been the first Christian to express them.

A second, often noted characteristic of Jas is the *lack of continuity*. This, too, is explained by the literary character of paraenesis. Often enough a continuity of thought cannot be demonstrated in the above–mentioned paraenetic literature of varied origins: chapters in the book of *Tobit*; Pseudo-Isocrates, *Ad Demonicum*; the paraenetic sections of Paul's letters; and the "Two Ways." Jas is no different.[21] Of course, already the ancient editors have made emendations in the text of Jas in an effort to provide connections between the individual sayings. Older and more recent

---

18 Isoc., *Ad Nicoclem* 41: "Certainly it is not necessary to search for something new in these words" (ἀλλὰ γὰρ οὐκ ἐν τοῖς λόγοις χρὴ τούτοις ζητεῖν τὰς καινότητας).

19 I.e., within a given series of sayings; see the Analysis of 1:19–27, and throughout Jas.

20 Ed. Grafe, *Die Stellung und Bedeutung des Jakobusbriefes in der Entwicklung des Urchristentums* (Tübingen

and Leipzig: Mohr [Siebeck], 1904), 11.

21 Indeed, Luther said of Jas in his "Preface to the Epistles of St. James and St. Jude": "he throws things together so chaotically" (trans. Charles M. Jacobs in *Luther's Works*, vol. 35, ed. E. Theodore Bachmann [Philadelphia: Muhlenberg, 1960], 397). Similar opinions appear several times in the 16th century: Erasmus Alberus, *Dialogus vom Interim*;

commentators, too, have repeatedly tried to point out a unified arrangement throughout the document, or at least an intentional progression of thought.[22] *It seems to me that the literary evaluation of Jas depends completely upon the resolution of this question.* In order not to burden the exegesis with the investigation of possible connections in thought, each section in the commentary is introduced by an Analysis. In these Analyses I hope to have demonstrated that large portions of Jas reveal no continuity in thought whatsoever. The supposition that changes in theme were required by the needs of the readers[23] can in no way alter this insight. In the first place, there is no mention of these needs in the text. Moreover, whenever correspondence has to meet such needs one might find a treatment of various un-connected themes in successive sections, as in 1 Corinthians, but not a disorderly change of theme from saying to saying such as we find in Jas. Only a comparison with other documents of the same literary genre can explain this, for it reveals that the stringing together of saying after saying is the most common form of paraenesis.

Although there is no continuity in thought in such a string of sayings, there are formal connections. The best known device for an external connection in paraenetic literature is the *catchword*: one saying is attached to another simply because a word or cognate of the same stem appears in both sayings. Originally, this was a mnemonic device. The memory finds its way more easily from one statement to another when aided

Petrus Palladius, *Isagoge ad libros propheticos et apostolicos* (the quotations are found in Gustav Kawerau, "Die Schicksale des Jakobusbriefes im 16. Jahrhundert," *ZWL* 10 [1889]: 368f).

22 Arrangements have been inferred upon the basis of Jas 1:19 by Ernst Pfeiffer, "Der Zusammenhang des Jakobusbriefes," *ThStKr* 23 (1850): 163–80, and H. J. Cladder, "Die Anlage des Jakobusbriefes," *ZKTh* 28 (1904): 37–57 (see below, in the Analysis of 1:19–27). An intentional progression in thought is also defended by Th. Tielemann, "Versuch einer neuen Auslegung und Anordnung des Jakobusbriefes," *NKZ* 5 (1894): 580–611; B. Weiss, *Jakobusbrief*, 41ff; Reginald St. John Parry, *A Discussion of the General Epistle of St. James* (London: Clay, 1903) —Dibelius notes that he is familiar with this volume only by way of *Theologischer Jahresbericht* (1903): 306. C. F. Georg Heinrici, *Der literarische Charakter der neutestamentlichen Schriften* (Leipzig: Dürr, 1908), 75, even though he recognizes the kinship of Jas to the books of sayings in the Old Testament, still finds in Jas 3:13–18 a thought which is supposed to give unity to the whole document.

Continuity and intentional progression of thought in Jas are explicitly contested by Carl von Weizsäcker, *The Apostolic Age of the Christian Church*, vol. 2, tr. James Millar, TTL 5 (New York: Putnam, 1895), 28f; Adolf von Harnack, *Geschichte der altchristlichen Litteratur bis Eusebius*, part 2, vol. 1 (Leipzig: Hinrichs, 1897, ²1958), 487; Hermann von Soden, *The History of Early Christian Literature: The Writings of the New Testament*, tr. J. R. Wilkinson, ed. W. D. Morrison, Crown Theological Library 13 (New York: Putnam, 1906); Grafe, *Stellung und Bedeutung*, 10ff; Paul Feine and Johannes Behm, *Introduction to the New Testament*, completely reedited by Werner Georg Kümmel, tr. A. J. Mattill, Jr. (New York and Nashville: Abingdon, 1966), 287.

Older attempts at tying together individual sayings are cited occasionally in the Analyses.

M. Rustler, *Thema und Disposition des Jakobusbriefes: Eine formkritische Studie*, Unpub. Diss. (Wien, 1952), is one of the more recent attempts at elaborating the arrangement of Jas, and this study carries the systematization to the extreme. The author asserts that the encompassing theme is "the problem of social tensions between rich and poor." The author believes that Jas pursues this theme "in a well-organized manner, thought through to the smallest detail" (p. 84). "The Christian solution for social tensions" is set forth in three major sections: 1) fundamental dogmatics 1:2–27; 2) practical ethics 2:1–3:12; 3) eschatology 3:13–5:20. Each of these major sections can be divided into three sub-sections: thesis (1:2–11; 2:1–13; 3:13–4:10), antithesis (1:12–18; 2:14–26; 4:11–5:6), and synthesis (1:19–27; 3:1–12; 5:7–20). In this process, Rustler has noted the undeniable presence of issues in some sections of the letter and has elevated these to the position of cardinal ideas for the entire letter, thereby cramming it into the confines of a rigid scheme. That cannot be done without doing violence to the text. For example, Rustler's connection of the sins of the tongue in 3:1–12 (pp. 68–73) with the social problem is remarkably feeble and strained. It is questionable whether such schematization contributes to the deeper understanding of the individual "pericopes."

23 So Beyschlag, in section 3 of his Introduction.

24 See below in the individual Analyses.

25 This differentiation between thematic, associative (effected either by antithesis or synonymity) and

by these catchwords. But this device has become literary and its use cannot serve as evidence that the statements in question were already juxtaposed in the oral tradition. For example, the sayings of Jesus could have been fitted together in this way either by the pre–Gospel tradition or by the Gospel writers. One must reckon with the possibility that the author of a paraenesis may have slightly changed a traditional saying in order to adapt it for such a connection.

The frequent use of this favorite device of formal connection is further evidence of the paraenetic character of Jas. I believe that catchword connection can be observed in the following instances:[24] 1:4 and 5; 1:12 and 13; (1:15 and 16-18?); 1:26 and 27; 2:12 and 13; (3:11f and 13f?); 3:17 and 18; 5:9 and 12; 5:13ff, 16ff and 19f.

Some examples from Greek, Jewish and Christian paraenesis will demonstrate how frequently paraenetic literature employed the technique of catchword connection. I have not considered those instances in which the catchword also represents a connection in thought (e.g. Pseudo–Isoc., *Ad Demonicum* 24-26, where both the catchword and the theme is "friends" [φίλοι]). Nor are those cases considered in which it is only a matter of associative connections (e.g., Gal 6:5: the thought "everyone will have to bear his own load" has evoked the other thought in 6:6 "let him who is taught . . . share etc."; likewise, "measure" [μέτρον] in Mk 4:24 is perhaps prompted by the mention of "bushel" [μόδιος] in 4:21). Only such examples are listed in which similarity of word or cognate leads to a uniting of elements which are unrelated in their subject–matter:[25]

Pseudo-Isoc., Ad Demonicum

16:
μηδὲν αἰσχρόν

15:
ἃ ποιεῖν αἰσχρὸν ταῦτα νόμιζε μηδὲ λέγειν εἶναι καλόν
"nothing *shameful* (remains hidden)"
"What is *shameful* to do deem it dishonorable even to speak of."

22:
τοῖς πονηροῖς ἀπιστεῖν, τοῖς χρηστοῖς πιστεύειν
τρόπον ὅρκου πιστότερον παρέχεσθαι
"Consider it right to *distrust* wicked men, as it is to *trust* honorable men."
"For good men must show their conduct to be more *trustworthy* than an oath."
Then, connected to the latter of these sayings is 23, which refers to an "administered *oath*" (ὅρκος ἐπακτός).

37:
μηδενὶ πονηρῷ πράγματι μήτε παρίστασο μήτε συνηγόρει
μηδενὶ χρῶ πονηρῷ
"If a cause is *evil* do not support it or plead for it."
"Do not associate with an *evil* man."

40:
πειρῶ τῷ σώματι μὲν εἶναι φιλόπονος, τῇ δὲ ψυχῇ φιλόσοφος
μέγιστον γὰρ ἐν ἐλαχίστῳ νοῦς ἀγαθὸς ἐν ἀνθρώπου σώματι
"Try to be in your *body* a lover of toil, and in your soul a lover of wisdom."
"For a sound mind in a man's *body* is the greatest thing in the smallest compass."

43:
ἐὰν δέ ποτέ σοι συμβῇ κινδυνεύειν
μᾶλλον εὐλαβοῦ ψόγον ἢ κίνδυνον
"but if it should ever fall your lot to incur *danger* . . ."
"Beware of blame more than of *danger*."

Tob

4:13b:
"For in *arrogance* (ὑπερηφανία) there is ruin and great confusion."

4:13a:
"Do not be so *arrogant* (ὑπερηφανεύου) as to refuse to take a wife from among your brethren and the sons and daughters of your own people."

---

purely formal catchword connections is not taken into consideration by Thaddaeus Soiron, *Die Logia Jesu: Eine literarkritische und literargeschichtliche Untersuchung zum synoptischen Problem*, NTAbh 6, 4 (Münster: Aschendorff, 1916). Soiron's collection of examples from the Synoptic Gospels is very profitable, but clearly fails to prove that source–hypotheses are unacceptable. For it is not necessary to trace the origin of every catchword connection to the oral tradition.

Tob   **4:17:**
"Place *your bread* (τοὺς ἄρτους σου) on the grave of the righteous, but give none to sinners."
4:16:
"Give of *your bread* (ἐκ τοῦ ἄρτου σου) to the hungry, and of your clothing to the naked."

Tob   **4:19:**
"Ask [God] that your ways may be made straight and that all your paths and *counsels* (βουλαί) may prosper."
4:18:
"Seek *counsel* (συμβουλίαν) from every wise man, and do not despise any useful *counsel* (συμβουλίας)."

Tob   **12:7:**
It is good to guard the secret of a king, but gloriously to reveal *the works of God* (ἔργα τοῦ θεοῦ)."
12:6:
"It is good to praise God and to exalt his name, worthily declaring *the works of God* (τοὺς λόγους τῶν ἔργων τοῦ θεοῦ)."

Tob   **12:9:**
"For *almsgiving* (ἐλεημοσύνη) delivers from death, and it will purge away every sin."
12:8:
"Prayer is good when accompanied by fasting, *almsgiving* (ἐλεημοσύνης), and righteousness."

Wisd   **6:21:**
"Therefore if you delight in thrones and scepters, O monarchs over the people, honor wisdom, that *you may reign* (βασιλεύσητε) forever."
6:20:
"So the desire for wisdom leads to a *reign* (βασιλείαν)."
This is an example of connection by means of a catchword if, as I think is probable, the word "reign" (βασιλεία) in 6:20 means something quite different than the verb in 6:21—namely, the "reign" or "kingdom of God" (βασιλεία τοῦ θεοῦ).

Matt   **6:34:**
"Therefore *do not be anxious* (μὴ οὖν μεριμνήσητε) about tomorrow, for tomorrow will be anxious for itself."
6:31-33:
"Therefore *do not be anxious* (μὴ οὖν μεριμνήσητε), saying, 'What shall we eat?' or 'What shall we drink?' or 'What shall we wear?'"

Matt   **10:31:**
"*Fear not*, therefore (μὴ οὖν φοβεῖσθε); you are of more value than many sparrows."
10:28:
"And *do not fear* (καὶ μὴ φοβεῖσθε) those who kill the body but cannot kill the soul . . ."
10:26:
"Therefore *do not fear* (μὴ οὖν φοβηθῆτε) them; for nothing is covered that will not be revealed, or hidden that will not be known."

Matt   **10:37:**
"He who loves *father or mother* (πατέρα ἢ μητέρα) more than me is not worthy of me; and he who loves *son or daughter* (υἱὸν ἢ θυγατέρα) more than me is not worthy of me."
10:35:
"For I have come to set a man against his *father*, and a *daughter* against her *mother* (κατὰ τοῦ πατρὸς αὐτοῦ καὶ θυγατέρα κατὰ τῆς μητρὸς αὐτῆς)."

Matt   **12:36:**
"I tell you, on the day of judgment people will render account for every careless word they *speak* (λαλήσουσιν)."
12:34:
"For out of the abundance of the heart the mouth *speaks* (λαλεῖ)."

Matt   **13:12:**
"For to him who has more *will be given* (δοθήσεται), and he will have abundance."
13:11:
"To you it *has been given* (δέδοται) to know the secrets of the kingdom of heaven, but to them it *has not been given* (οὐ δέδοται)."

Matt   **18:12-14:**
"If someone has a hundred sheep, and one of them has gone astray. . . . So it is not the will of my Father who is in heaven that *one of these little ones* (ἓν τῶν μικρῶν τούτων) should perish."
18:10:
"See that you do not despise *one of these little ones* (ἑνὸς τῶν μικρῶν τούτων); for I tell you that in heaven their angels. . . ."
18:6-9:
"But whoever causes *one of these little ones* (ἕνα τῶν μικρῶν τούτων) who believe in me to sin, it would be better for him to have a great millstone fastened round his neck. . . ."

Matt **18:19f:**
"For where *two or three* (δύο ἢ τρεῖς) are gathered in my name. . . ."

18:15–18:
"But if he does not listen, take one or two others along with you, that every word may be confirmed by the evidence of *two or three* witnesses (δύο μαρτύρων ἢ τριῶν)."

Matt **23:29:**
"Woe to you, scribes and Pharisees, hypocrites! for you build the *tombs* (τάφους) of the prophets. . . ."

23:27f:
"Woe to you, scribes and Pharisees, hypocrites! for you are like whitewashed *tombs* (τάφοις). . . ."

Mk **9:38:**
"Teacher, we saw a man casting out demons *in your name* (ἐν τῷ ὀνόματί σου), and we forbade him. . . ."

9:37:
"Whoever receives one such child *in my name* (ἐπὶ τῷ ὀνόματί μου) receives me."

Mk **9:43:**
"And if your hand *causes you to sin* (σκανδαλίσῃ), cut it off."

9:42:
"Whoever *causes* one of these little ones *to sin* (σκανδαλίσῃ). . . ."

Mk **9:49:**
"For everyone will be salted with *fire* (πυρί)."

9:48:
". . . where the worm does not die, and the *fire* (πῦρ) is not quenched."

Mk **9:50b:**
"Have *salt* (ἅλα) in yourselves, and be at peace with one another."

9:50a:
"*Salt* (ἅλας) is good; but if the *salt* (ἅλας) has lost its saltness, how will you season it?"

9:49:
"For everyone *will be salted* (ἁλισθήσεται) with fire."

Mk **11:25:**
"And whenever you stand *praying* (προσευχόμενοι), forgive. . . ."

11:24:
"Therefore I tell you, whatever *you ask in prayer* (προσεύχεσθε), believe that you will receive it. . . ."

Mk **12:38–40:**
"Beware of the *scribes* (γραμματέων), who like to go about in long robes. . . ."

12:35–37:
"How can the *scribes* (γραμματεῖς) say that the Christ is the son of David?"

12:28–34:
"And *one of the scribes* (εἷς τῶν γραμματέων) came up and heard them disputing . . . and . . . asked him, 'Which commandment is the first of all?' "

Lk **11:34:**
"Your eye is the *lamp* (λύχνος) of your body. . . ."

11:33:
"No one after lighting a *lamp* (λύχνον) puts it in a cellar or under a bushel. . . ."

Lk **12:10:**
"And every one who speaks a word against *the Son of man* (εἰς τὸν υἱὸν τοῦ ἀνθρώπου) will be forgiven. . . ."

12:8f:
"And I tell you, every one who acknowledges me before men, *the Son of man* (ὁ υἱὸς τοῦ ανθρώπου) also will acknowledge. . . ."

Lk **12:11f:**
". . . for *the Holy Spirit* (τὸ ἅγιον πνεῦμα) will teach you in that very hour what you ought to say."

12:10:
". . . but he who blasphemes against *the Holy Spirit* (εἰς τὸ ἅγιον πνεῦμα) will not be forgiven."

Lk **13:25:**
"When once the householder has risen up and shut the *door* (τὴν θύραν). . . ."

13:24:
"Strive to enter by the narrow *door* (διὰ τῆς στενῆς θύρας)."

Lk **16:13:**
"You cannot serve God and *mammon* (μαμωνᾷ)."

16:10–12:
"If then you have not been faithful in the *unrighteous mammon* (ἐν τῷ ἀδίκῳ μαμωνᾷ). . . ."

16:9:
"And I tell you, make friends for yourselves by means of *unrighteous mammon* (ἐκ τοῦ μαμωνᾶ τῆς ἀδικίας). . . ."

Lk **16:17:**
"But it is easier for heaven and earth to pass away, than for one dot of *the law* (τοῦ νόμου) to become void."

16:16:
"*The law* (ὁ νόμος) and the prophets were until John."

Lk **17:5f:**
". . . you could say to this sycamine tree, 'Be rooted up, and be planted *in the sea* (ἐν τῇ θαλάσσῃ).'"
17:1–4:
". . . better for him if a millstone were hung round his neck and he were cast *into the sea* (εἰς τὴν θάλασσαν). . . ."

Lk **17:22f:**
"And they will say to you, '*Lo there!*' or '*Lo here!*' (ἰδοὺ ἐκεῖ, ἰδοὺ ὧδε) Do not go, do not follow them."
17:21:
"Nor will they say, '*Lo here!*' or '*There!*' (ἰδοὺ ὧδε ἢ ἐκεῖ) for behold, the kingdom of God is in the midst of you."

Lk **18:9–14:**
"He also told this parable to some who trusted in themselves that they were righteous and despised others: 'Two men went up into the temple *to pray* (προσεύξασθαι). . . .'"
18:1–8:
"And he told them a parable, to the effect that they ought always *to pray* (προσεύχεσθαι) and not lose heart."

Lk **19:41–44:**
"For the days shall come upon you, when your enemies . . . will not leave *one stone upon another* (λίθον ἐπὶ λίθον) in you."
19:40:
"I tell you, if these were silent, the very *stones* (οἱ λίθοι) would cry out."

Rom **12:14a:**
"Bless those who *pursue* you with oppression (τοὺς διώκοντας)."
12:13:
"*Pursue* hospitality" (τὴν φιλοξενίαν διώκοντες).

Rom **12:14b:**
"*Bless* (εὐλογεῖτε) and do not curse."
12:14a:
"*Bless* (εὐλογεῖτε) those who pursue you with oppression."

Rom **12:16c:**
"Do not esteem yourselves to be 'great *minds*'" (μὴ γίνεσθε φρόνιμοι παρ' ἑαυτοῖς).
12:16b:
"Do not *set your minds* on proud thoughts (τὰ ὑψηλὰ φρονοῦντες), but associate with the lowly."
12:16a:
"Be of the same *mind* (τὸ αὐτὸ φρονοῦντες) with one another."

Rom **12:18:**
". . . live peaceably with *all people* (μετὰ πάντων ἀνθρώπων)."
12:17:
". . . take thought for what is noble in the sight of *all people* (ἐνώπιον πάντων ἀνθρώπων)."

Rom **13:8:**
"*Owe* (ὀφείλετε) no one anything, except to love one another."
13:7:
"Pay to all *that which is owed* (τὰς ὀφειλάς) to them, taxes to whom taxes are due, etc."

Gal **6:3–5:**
". . . let each one test his own work. . . . For each one will have to *bear* (βαστάσει) his own load."
6:2:
"*Bear* (βαστάζετε) one another's burdens, and so fulfil the law of Christ."

Gal **6:9:**
"And let us not grow weary in well-doing, for at the proper occasion *we shall reap* (θερίσομεν), if we do not lose heart."
6:8:
"For the one who sows to his own flesh *will* from the flesh *reap* (θερίσει) corruption; but the one who sows to the Spirit *will* from the Spirit *reap* (θερίσει) eternal life."

Gal **6:10:**
"Therefore, whenever we have *occasion* (καιρόν) let us do good to all people. . . ."
6:9:
". . . at the proper *occasion* (καιρῷ) we shall reap. . . ."

Eph **4:29:**
"Let no evil talk come out of your mouths, but only that which edifies where there is a *need* (χρείας) for edification. . . ."
4:28:
"Let the thief no longer steal, but rather let him labor . . . so that he may be able to give to those in *need* (χρείαν)."

Col **3:12:**
"*Put on* (ἐνδύσασθε) . . . compassion, kindness, lowliness, etc."
3:9–11:
". . . you have put off the old nature with its practices and have *put on* (ἐνδυσάμενοι) the new nature. . . ."

Col **3:17:**
". . . do everything in the name of the Lord Jesus, *giving thanks* (εὐχαριστοῦντες) to God the Father through him."
3:16:
". . . as you sing psalms and hymns and spiritual songs with *thankfulness* (ἐν τῇ χάριτι) in your hearts to God."
3:15:
"And be *thankful* (εὐχάριστοι)."

Of course, such purely external connection results in a certain lack of design. Associated with this feature is yet another characteristic of paraenetic literature: *the repetition of identical motifs in different places within a writing.* The purely formal principle of arrangement sometimes, but not always, prevents arrangement according to thought. Moreover, a certain conditioning of the tradition, in most instances no longer recognizable, may play a role: what was transmitted combined was left combined, and therefore, there were certain obstacles to the arrangement of the materials according to thought. For example, in the short paraenesis in Tob 4, the admonition to be merciful is found in v 7 as well as in v 16; in the paraenetic section of Romans, one finds the warning against haughtiness in 12:3 and in 12:16b, the admonition to unity in 12:4 and 12:16a, an exhortation to love in 12:9 and in 13:9f. Similar instances are often noted with regard to Jas and are occasionally used in attempts to establish that there is an arrangement:[26] an admonition to meekness in 1:21 and in 3:13ff; a warning about the tongue in 1:26 and in 3:3ff; perserverence in suffering is preached in 1:2–4, 12 and again in 5:7ff; work is enjoined as a duty in 1:22ff and in 2:14ff; the rich are dealt with in 1:9ff, in 2:1ff and in 5:1ff; and the prayer of faith is discussed in 1:5–8 and in 5:16ff.

Finally, there is one other feature which Jas shares with other paraenetic literature: the admonitions in Jas do not apply to a single audience and a single set of circumstances; *it is not possible to construct a single frame into which they will all fit.* The rich people addressed in 5:1ff and the tradesmen addressed in 4:13ff are certainly not the addressees in the discourses of 2:1ff. Nor may one simply take for granted that the people addressed in 5:7f are threatened by the dangers set forth in 3:1ff and in 4:1ff. Such inconsistencies are not at all unusual in paraenetic materials. The sayings collected in the Sermon on the Mount in Matthew and the Sermon on the Plain in Luke cannot all be made to fit a single audience. Nor do the regulations in 1 Timothy suit the epistolary situation which the letter presupposes. Again, the sayings in Tob 4 are supposed to be the farewell admonition of a father to his son, but the selection of these admonitions does not seem to confirm this at all. The ultimate cause for such inconsistencies is stated in Pseudo–Isoc., *Ad Demonicum* 44 (cf. also Isoc., *Ad Nicoclem* 40f): the addressee, he says, should not wonder if some of the author's statements did not apply to him (Demonicus) at his present age; for he wanted to give Demonicus both advice for the present and instruction for the future. In this way his words would be a storehouse from which Demonicus could draw whatever he needed. To be a ταμιεῖον, a treasury—that is also the intention of Jas.

2. The Author of the Letter of James

Among the Catholic Epistles, there are only two which bear in their prescripts the name of a person of high reputation who is immediately identifiable—1 and 2 Peter. Three others, according to their superscriptions, derive from yet another authority from early Christianity—1, 2 and 3 John. Therefore, from the outset it is natural to assume that Jas also wants to appear as the writing of a famous person when, in the prescript, it mentions James, the slave of God and of the Lord Jesus Christ. This assumption is apparently confirmed by the Letter of Jude, which refers in its prescript to our letter or to its author: the author calls himself "Jude, a slave of Jesus Christ, the brother of James"; hence, this James must be a well–known person.

Our writing itself offers further evidence that this is the case: the admonitions in the letter give the impression of authority, and yet the author's right to speak in this way is never explicitly justified. It follows, therefore, that either the Letter of James does in fact come from a man named James—but in this case he would not have written in such a way if he were not sure of his own reputation—, or the letter is falsely attributed to

---

26   See above, n. 22.

someone named James—but an obscure person with this name would not have been chosen as the patron for this authoritative paraenesis.

Our sources know only *one* person of reputation in primitive Christianity who could have been suggested by the way in which his name appears in the prescript of our letter: *James, the brother of Jesus*. One must, of course, exclude James the younger (Mk 15:40) and the James who is called the father of Jude (Lk 6:16). The apostle James, "the son of Alphaeus," must also be disregarded, for he is mentioned only in the catalogues of the apostles and then only with this additional identifying phrase (his mention in several textual witnesses to Mk 2:14 is a harmonizing emendation). James the son of Zebedee, also, was not particularly important in early Christianity. He was executed at too early a date to have become an authoritative figure for the churches outside of Palestine; he was also executed much too early to have been the author of Jas, especially if this writing already presupposes the preaching of Paul.[27] On the other hand, the leader of the Jerusalem church is introduced simply as "James" in Acts 12:17; 15:13 and 21:18, as well as in 1 Cor 15:7 and in Gal 2:12—and according to Gal 1:19 this is "the Lord's brother." Along with Peter and John he is one of the "pillars" of the church (Gal 2:9).[28] He alone can be the person of authority whom the pre-

script in Jas 1:1 had in mind. Now we see why he can be mentioned without further title in Jude 1. All efforts to identify James the brother of the Lord with one of the other persons of the same name can be disregarded. Ever since Jerome, the Catholic tradition had equated the Lord's brother with James the Apostle, the son of Alphaeus.[29] But that position runs aground, because according to Mk 3:21, 31ff (Jn 7:5) Jesus did not have a brother among the twelve disciples.

Both within the writings of the New Testament and elsewhere, there are a number of *reports about James the brother of the Lord*. To be sure, the riddles they pose are nearly as many as the data they report. James and his brothers and sisters, mentioned in Mk 6:3, were younger siblings of Jesus who evidently were in no way kindly disposed toward his ministry (Mk 3:21, 31ff; Jn 7:5). And yet not only are these brothers and their mother included with the disciples in Acts 1:14 as believers in Christ, but from Gal 2; Acts 12:17; 15:13 and 21:18, it becomes evident that James was one of the persons of authority in the Jerusalem church; in fact he emerged as the real leader of that church.

Nothing is known about the time and circumstance of James' conversion. However, in 1 Cor 15:7, Paul intimates that an appearance of Christ played a role in the life of James. The *Gospel of the Hebrews*, fragments of which are cited by Jerome in *De viris inlustribus* 2,

27 See below, section 4 of the Introduction. Actually, Jas has seldom been attributed to the son of Zebedee; see the postscript in Codex Corbeiensis (*ff*): "the letter of James, the son of Zebedee" (explicit epistola Jacobi filii Zaebedei); see further Gottfried Jäger, "Der Verfasser des Jakobusbriefes," *ZLThK* 39 (1878): 420–6; see below, section 9 of the Introduction, on Martin Luther, and section 10 on sy^vg. Joh. Mader, "Apostel und Herrenbrüder," *BZ* 6 (1908): 398, has expressed the opinion that the author was the son of Alphaeus, not the same as the brother of the Lord.

28 On the other hand, Karl Heussi, "Gal 2 und der Lebensausgang der jerusalemischen Uraposter," *ThLZ* 77 (1952): 67–72, identifies the James of Gal 2:9 with the son of Zebedee. But even if that were the case, the leadership position of the Lord's brother would be sufficiently proven by Gal 1:19 and 2:12.

29 Jerome, *De perpetua virginitate B. Mariae (Adversus Helvidium)*, 13ff (MPL 23, 205). See on this text Theodor von Zahn, *Forschungen zur Geschichte des ur, neutestamentlichen Kanons und der altkirchlichen Literat*

vol. 6 (Leipzig and Erlangen: Deichert [Böhme], 1900), 320ff; see also below, n. 50. Most Catholic scholars today also accept this identification (but see K. Endemann, "Zur Frage über die Brüder des Herrn," *NKZ* 11 [1900]: 833–65). They appeal to three factors: 1) James is called an apostle in Gal 1:19—but the text can be interpreted differently; and besides, for Paul the term "apostle" (ἀπόστολος) is not equivalent to one of the twelve disciples. 2) James is introduced in Acts with no identifying comment, which makes it necessary to equate him with the only other James mentioned in Acts (1:13)—but this abrupt manner of introducing a person is also found in Acts 8:5 with regard to Philip. 3) According to the *Gospel of the Hebrews*, the Lord's brother was present at the last supper—but that does not prove that he was one of the twelve disciples; moreover, this information appears in a legend which has reshaped an older tradition in order to honor James (see below).

The view held by Jerome, that James was only a cousin of Jesus, has almost supplanted another view

contained a description of this Christophany. But this is the first time that we find a *legendary modification of the tradition about James*: Whereas Paul mentions this as the fourth appearance of Christ, in the *Gospel of the Hebrews* James is apparently the first, or at least the most important witness of the resurrection. According to the *Gospel of the Hebrews*, after the Lord's Supper in which he participated, James had sworn to abstain from all nourishment until he should see the resurrected Jesus. Now the Lord appears to him and personally offers him bread.[30] The affinity of this motif to Jn 20:24–29 is clear, but so is the difference: In John 20 a disciple is doubtful about this news even though the resurrection has already occurred; but in the *Gospel of the Hebrews* James, even before the event, insists that he experience the resurrection which has evidently been predicted. This indicates stubborn faith[31] rather than doubt. But it is not made clear whether James' attitude differed from that of the other disciples, who also must have known the same prediction. The original version of this tradition probably had to do with doubt, that is, doubt about the resurrection which had already occurred and had been testified to by others. The oath,

therefore, must have had a function similar to the vow of Jn 20:25, and the tradition must have contained appearances which took place before the appearance to James. That this was the case is shown by Paul in 1 Cor 15. But a tradition intent on the glorification of the Lord's brother would not have much use for a doubting James. So it shifted the whole picture: It moved the oath back before the events of Easter, and thus transformed a statement of doubt into a statement of faith which is reminiscent of Mk 14:25. This opened up the possibility of making James the principal witness to the resurrection.

The conversion of James may indeed have been connected with an appearance of Christ (not in the *Gospel of the Hebrews* itself, but in older tradition). But the *position of leadership which James held* apparently was dependent upon other events and it was only on the basis of this leadership that then the tradition about him was reshaped.[32] A position of honor was accorded by the church to this relative of Jesus. When Peter (and the other apostles?) left Jerusalem, probably during a persecution (Acts 12), James remained behind and became the most respected member of the church;

according to which James was a son of Joseph by his first marriage. Both views assume the chastity of Mary; the view of Jerome also assumes Joseph's chastity. See Zahn, *Forschungen*, vol. 6, pp. 306ff.

30 Jerome, *De viris inlustribus* 2: "And when the Lord had given the linen cloth to the servant of the priest, he went to James and appeared to him [James is therefore the principal witness!]. For James had sworn that he would not eat bread from that hour in which he had drunk the cup of the Lord until he should see him risen from among them that sleep" (dominus autem cum dedisset sindonem servo sacerdotis, ivit ad Jacobum et apparuit ei. Juraverat enim Jacobus se non comesurum panem ab illa hora, qua biberat calicem domini [the conjecture *dominus* is unnecessary and contradicts the point of the oath: the Lord's supper was James' last meal before the voluntary fast], donec viderat eum resurgentem a dormientibus). Jerome continues the quotation: "And shortly thereafter the Lord said: Bring a table and bread!" (afferte ait Dominus, mensam et panem). This implies that others were present, probably the disciples. Jerome concludes the quotation: "he took the bread, blessed it and brake it and gave it to James the Just and said to him: My brother [hence, it is certainly the brother of the Lord], eat your bread, for the Son of Man is risen from among

them that sleep" (Tulit panem et benedixit, ac fregit et dedit Jacobo Justo et dixit ei: Frater mi, comede panem tuum, quia resurrexit Filius hominis a dormientibus) [text from MPL 22, 642f; reprinted in Erwin Preuschen, *Antilegomena: Die Reste der ausserkanonischen Evangelien und urchristlichen Ueberlieferungen* (Giessen: Ricker [Töpelmann], [2]1905), 7f; ET from Edgar Hennecke, *New Testament Apocrypha*, ed. Wilhelm Schneemelcher, tr. and ed. R. McL. Wilson, vol. 1 (Philadelphia: Westminster, 1963), 165].

31 A similar instance of stubborn faith is narrated in *Historia Lausiaca* 22 (ed. Butler, in TS 6, 2, pp. 69ff) and by Rufinus in *Historia monachorum* 31 (MPL 21, 457ff): Paul the Innocent used the threat of a hunger strike to constrain the Lord to heal a demoniac. So also in Acts 23:12 the oath is an expression of the obdurate resolution of those who swore it.

32 Gerhard Kittel, "Der geschichtliche Ort des Jakobusbriefes," *ZNW* 41 (1942): 73f, argues that the relatives of Jesus (δεσπόσυνοι) held no special position before the year 50 (but see Kurt Aland, "Der Herrenbruder Jakobus und der Jakobusbrief: Zur Frage eines urchristlichen 'Kalifats,'" *ThLZ* 69 [1944]: 99. On the question of the establishment by James, the Lord's brother, of an early Christian caliphate, see also Hans von Campenhausen, "Die Nachfolge des Jakobus," *ZKG* 63 (1950/51): 133–

from this patriarchal position of honor developed his position as the leading authority. Still another circumstance may have contributed to this change in the situation. According to all available information, especially from Gal 2:12, also from Acts 21:18ff, and finally from Hegesippus (see below), James was an advocate of a praxis which demanded that Christians fulfill the Jewish Law. At about the same time, nomistic tendencies appear, first in the Jewish–Christian communities and later also elsewhere in the form of the Judaizing movement. The words of Rom 15:31 indicate what kind of difficulties a man like Paul might expect in Jerusalem. James, though himself not a "Judaizer," was far more equipped than Peter to meet the demands of the Law, and therefore it is no wonder that in such a period he prevailed as the leader. Thus the patriarchal position of honor and nomistic tendencies were the ultimate sources of his authority. That other influential men were absent from Jerusalem favored such a development. This state of affairs seems still to be reflected in later writers who, faithful to their conception of succession and episcopacy, speak of a specific communication of gnosis by the Lord to James the Just,

John and Peter, and at the same time of a sort of renunciation by the Apostles of the position of honor, whereupon it is accorded to James.[33]

James the brother of the Lord was martyred. But the *reports of his death* are contradictory. The least elaborate report is found in Josephus, *Ant.* 20.200. According to this account, during the period of the interregnum between the death of Festus and the assumption of office by Albinus (A.D. 62) the high priest Ananus the Younger, using Jewish court procedures, condemned several people because of alleged transgressions of the Law and had them stoned. Among them, Josephus recounts, was "a man named James, the brother of Jesus who was called the Christ." These events caused the Pharisees to voice complaints against the Sadducee Ananus and resulted in his removal from office.

The view that this report about James is a Christian interpolation can really appeal only to the fact that the text of Josephus has been altered elsewhere by Christian hands and that a reference to the death of James was apparently inserted somewhere into the *Antiquities* or into the *Jewish War* and that the reference

44; reprinted in *idem, Aus der Frühzeit des Christentums: Studien zur Kirchengeschichte des ersten und zweiten Jahrhunderts* (Tübingen: Mohr [Siebeck], 1963), 135–51; Ethelbert Stauffer, "Zum Kalifat des Jacobus," *ZRGG* 4 (1952): 193–214; *idem*, "Petrus und Jakobus in Jerusalem," *Begegnung der Christen: Studien evangelischer und katholischer Theologen* (Festschrift Otto Karrer), ed. Maximilian Roesle and Oscar Cullmann (Stuttgart: Evangelisches Verlagswerk, 1959), 361–72.

William K. Prentice, "James the Brother of the Lord," in *Studies in Roman Economic and Social History* (Festschrift Allan Chester Johnson), ed. P. R. Coleman–Norton (Princeton: University Press, 1951), 144–51, would like to identify "James the Lord's brother" with James the Lesser (Mk 15:40) and with James the son of Alphaeus (in all the lists of the apostles). Prentice assumes, as do others, that Alphaios = Halphai = Clopas. He interprets the Mary of Jn 19:25 as the *wife* of Clopas and he identifies her with the mother of James (the Lesser) and Joses (Matt 27:56; Mk 15:40), thus she would be a sister–in–law of Jesus' mother rather than a sister—having the same name! According to Hegesippus (in Eus., *Hist. eccl.* 3.11), Clopas was the brother of Jesus' father Joseph. Hegesippus also reports that the successor of James the Lord's brother was James' broth-

er Simon. Thus there would be a group of three brothers: James (the Lesser), Joses, and Simon. Finally, Prentice finds these brothers in Matt 13:55 and Mk 6:3, and his conclusion is that James, Joses (Joseph), Simon, and Judas were not brothers of Jesus but rather his cousins. Yet Prentice's entire construction collapses in light of one consideration: It is hardly possible that James the brother of the Lord, who was such an important figure in the early church, could be mentioned in passing as "James the Lesser" (Mk 15:40). And even if that were acceptable, what tendency could have been at work in the tradition so that all four catalogues of the apostles consistently call him "James the son of Alphaeus"?

33 Clem. Alex., *Hypotyposes*, in Eus., *Hist. eccl.* 2.1.3ff. Clement himself seems to be dependent upon Hegesippus; see Zahn, *Forschungen*, vol. 6, pp. 271ff, against Adolf Schlatter, *Der Chronograph aus dem zehnten Jahre Antonins*, TU 12, 1 (Leipzig: Hinrichs, 1894), 31f.

34 Origen apparently read this interpolation (*Cels.* 1.47; 2.13; *Comm. in Matt.* 13:55, tome 10, 17), and perhaps Eusebius (*Hist. eccl.* 2.23.20); but both writers quote it without reference to its location. Of uncertain origin is a more exact quotation in the *Passover Chronicle* (MPG 92, 596). The passage is missing in the manuscript tradition of Josephus.

characterized the fall of Jerusalem as the divine punishment for the execution of that "just man."[34] But that is not a convincing argument, since the words of this passage contain nothing which would mark them as a Christian interpolation, i.e., there is no glorification of either James or Christianity. Furthermore, even about Christ himself they speak in a very indifferent tone, quite unlike the tone with which we are familiar in the Christian forgeries of the Greek and Slavonic texts of Josephus.

If we now consider the Christian tradition about the death of James as preserved by Hegesippus (in Eus., *Hist. eccl.* 2.23.4–8),[35] we see that it does not agree at all with the report from Josephus. To be sure, one may doubt whether the text of this fragment is intact,[36] but the central motifs of the narration are clear in any case. James is pictured as a true saint. He lives as a Nazirite and prays with such persistence for the forgiveness of the people's sins that his knees become calloused like those of a camel. He is surnamed "the Just" and Oblias—the latter term is translated "rampart" ($\pi\epsilon\rho\iota\omega\chi\dot{\eta}$) of the people.[37] The Jews, who ac-

---

This interpolation is not necessarily dependent upon Hegesippus, for it might be explained as a transference of the divine retribution motif as the genuine Josephus employs it in the story of John the Baptist (*Ant.* 18.116). See Schlatter, *Chronograph*, 66ff, who considers Origen's quotation from Josephus to be unreliable; Emil Schürer, *A History of the Jewish People in the Time of Jesus Christ*, Division 1, vol. 2, tr. John MacPherson (New York: Scribner, [2]1896), 186f; Zahn, *Forschungen*, vol. 6, pp. 301ff, who considers both texts in Josephus to be Christian forgeries; Eduard Schwartz, "Zu Eusebius Kirchengeschichte, I. Das Martyrium Jakobus des Gerechten," *ZNW* 4 (1903): 59f; Johannes Weiss, *The History of Primitive Christianity*, tr. and ed. Frederick C. Grant, vol. 2 (New York: Wilson–Erickson, 1937), 709ff; both Schwartz and Weiss believe that *Ant.* 20.200 is genuine.

35 Apparently dependent upon Hegesippus are Clem. Alex., *Hypotyposes* (in Eus., *Hist. eccl.* 2.1.4f) and Epiphanius, *Haer.* 78.14. (Objections to this derivation are found in Schlatter, *Chronograph*, 75ff.) On the other hand, Eusebius' own account, in *Hist. eccl.* 2.23.1f, strives to integrate the reports of Josephus and Hegesippus. The statements about James in the Infancy Gospels and in the Pseudo–Clementine literature will not be considered here, since they are of no consequence for the question of authorship. See the brief collection of materials in Ropes, 69ff. On the derivation of the Naassene secret tradition about James the Lord's brother, see Hippolytus, *Ref.* 5.7.1; 10.9.3.

36 Extensive criticism of the text is given by Schwartz, *op. cit.* (above, n. 34), 48ff; other suggestions are given by Schlatter, *Chronograph*, 75ff, and Weiss, *Primitive Christianity*, vol. 2, pp. 711ff. The following seem to be the most serious reservations: 1) The report in Eus., *Hist. eccl.* 2.23.6 that James alone was allowed to enter the sanctuary or the Holy of Holies is added in order to justify the subsequent report that James prayed in the temple. 2) In 2.23.8–10, there

is a competition between the identification of James' opponents as Jewish sectarians on the one hand and as scribes and Pharisees on the other. 3) The question about the "gate of Jesus" ($\theta\acute{\upsilon}\rho\alpha\ \tau o\hat{\upsilon}\ {}^{\prime}I\eta\sigma o\hat{\upsilon}$ 2.23.8,12) grows out of a misunderstanding of a Semitic expression; the "Torah of Jesus" was probably intended. 4) The three acts of violence in 2.23.15–18 (the fall from the temple, the stoning, the assault by a fuller) constitute a juxtaposing of elements which is scarcely tolerable in a legend; one tradition is probably combined here with another, or with a motif inferred from scripture, to form a network of events which it is now difficult to disentangle. See further, Ernst von Dobschütz, *Christian Life in the Primitive Church*, tr. George Bremner, ed. W. D. Morrison, TTL 18 (New York: Putnam, 1904), 392ff; F. C. Burkitt, *Christian Beginnings* (London: University of London Press, 1924), 57–63, thinks that it is possible to deduce several character traits of the historical James from Hegesippus' narrative; Gerhard Kittel, "Die Stellung des Jakobus zu Judentum und Heidenchristentum," *ZNW* 30 (1931): 145, rejects Hegesippus as a source of historical value, referring to Eduard Meyer, *Ursprung und Anfänge des Christentums*, vol. 3 (Stuttgart and Berlin: Cotta, 1923), 73, n. 2.

37 The traditional text in Eus., *Hist. eccl.* 2.23.7 reads: "So from his excessive righteousness he was called the Just and Oblias, that is in Greek, 'Rampart of the people and righteousness,' as the prophets declare concerning him" ($\delta\iota\dot{\alpha}\ \gamma\acute{\epsilon}\ \tau o\iota\ \tau\dot{\eta}\nu\ \dot{\upsilon}\pi\epsilon\rho\beta o\lambda\dot{\eta}\nu\ \tau\hat{\eta}\varsigma\ \delta\iota\kappa\alpha\iota o\sigma\acute{\upsilon}\nu\eta\varsigma\ \alpha\dot{\upsilon}\tau o\hat{\upsilon}\ \dot{\epsilon}\kappa\alpha\lambda\epsilon\hat{\iota}\tau o\ \dot{o}\ \delta\acute{\iota}\kappa\alpha\iota o\varsigma\ \kappa\alpha\dot{\iota}\ \dot{\omega}\beta\lambda\acute{\iota}\alpha\varsigma,\ \ddot{o}\ \dot{\epsilon}\sigma\tau\iota\nu\ {}^{\prime}E\lambda\lambda\eta\nu\iota\sigma\tau\dot{\iota}\ \pi\epsilon\rho\iota o\chi\dot{\eta}\ \tau o\hat{\upsilon}\ \lambda\alpha o\hat{\upsilon}\ \kappa\alpha\dot{\iota}\ \delta\iota\kappa\alpha\iota o\sigma\acute{\upsilon}\nu\eta,\ \dot{\omega}\varsigma\ o\dot{\iota}\ \pi\rho o\phi\hat{\eta}\tau\alpha\iota\ \delta\eta\lambda o\hat{\upsilon}\sigma\iota\nu\ \pi\epsilon\rho\dot{\iota}\ \alpha\dot{\upsilon}\tau o\hat{\upsilon}$). Those who have attempted to explain the curious designation "Oblias" include: Hans Joachim Schoeps, "Jacobus $\dot{o}$ $\delta\acute{\iota}\kappa\alpha\iota o\varsigma\ \kappa\alpha\grave{\iota}\ {}^{\prime}\Omega\beta\lambda\acute{\iota}\alpha\varsigma$: Neuer Lösungsvorschlag in einer schwierigen Frage," *Biblica* 24 (1943): 398–403; reprinted in *idem, Aus frühchristlicher Zeit: Religionsgeschichtliche Untersuchungen* (Tübingen: Mohr [Siebeck], 1950), 120–5, 301 (Nachtrag); Charles C.

knowledge James' righteousness, ask that he testify against Jesus. He is to do so from the pinnacle of the temple, in the hearing of all the people, on the day of Passover. But from the pinnacle James instead confesses Jesus as the Son of man and that he will come again, whereupon the Jews cast him down from the pinnacle. Since James is still not dead, they stone him, and even as he is dying he prays for his enemies. Finally, a fuller uses his fuller's club to finish him off. His gravestone may still be seen. The fragment concludes by saying that immediately after the martyrdom of James Vespasian began the siege of Jerusalem.

The narrative of Hegesippus reveals a large number of typical legendary motifs (not to mention some problems with regard to content), so that in itself this narrative must already be viewed with skepticism as to its reliability. One must be all the more careful not to play this report off against that of Josephus. I call attention to the following details:

1) That the Jews seriously expect the leader of the Christian community to give the people anti–Christian instruction is a legendary exaggeration. The author wants to glorify the righteousness—in the Jewish technical sense of the term—of his hero by making James an authority figure for the Jews, also.

2) One basis for the legend's formation is the Old Testament. In *Hist. eccl.* 2.23.15, the author himself cites Isa 3:10 in the wording "Let us take the just man, etc." ($\mathring{\alpha}\rho\omega\mu\epsilon\nu$ $\tau\grave{\text{o}}\nu$ $\delta\acute{\imath}\kappa\alpha\iota\text{o}\nu$ $\kappa\tau\lambda$.), and he has the opponents expressly cry out, "Let us stone James the Just" ($\lambda\iota\theta\acute{\alpha}\sigma\omega\mu\epsilon\nu$ '$I\acute{\alpha}\kappa\omega\beta\text{o}\nu$ $\tau\grave{\text{o}}\nu$ $\delta\acute{\imath}\kappa\alpha\iota\text{o}\nu$), obviously to demonstrate the fulfillment of the prophecy. Apparently, other texts about the "righteous man" have exerted an influence, such as Wisd 2:15: "because his manner of life is unlike that of others" ($\mathring{\text{o}}\tau\iota$ $\mathring{\alpha}\nu\acute{\text{o}}\mu\text{o}\iota\text{o}\varsigma$ $\tau\text{o}\hat{\imath}\varsigma$ $\mathring{\alpha}\lambda\lambda\text{o}\iota\varsigma$ $\acute{\text{o}}$ $\beta\acute{\imath}\text{o}\varsigma$ $\alpha\mathring{\upsilon}\tau\text{o}\hat{\upsilon}$), and perhaps also LXX Ps 33:16, which speaks of the "prayer" ($\delta\acute{\epsilon}\eta\sigma\iota\varsigma$) of the righteous.

3) This is one of the oldest martyr–legends in early Christianity. It is not surprising that it borrows motifs, and indeed, motifs out of the Jesus–tradition (pinnacle of the temple, witness to the Son of man, the dying prayer for the enemy). But in other ways as well the author has furnished the life of his hero with motifs customarily used in connection with saints. Of these motifs, the most prominent are the practices of the Nazirite, which the author has intensified (and at the same time has distorted) by means of other characteristics of cultural nonconformity: abstinence from eating flesh, from anointing with oil, and from bathing. Significantly, during the execution it is a Rechabite who intervenes in James' behalf. The prayer for the people is probably another of these motifs, for the calloused knees may have had their prototype in some stories

Torrey, "James the Just, and his Name 'Oblias,'" *JBL* 63 (1944): 93–8; Harald Sahlin, "Noch einmal Jacobus 'Oblias,'" *Biblica* 28 (1947): 152f; Klaus Baltzer and Helmut Köster, "Die Bezeichnung des Jakobus als '$\Omega B\Lambda IA\Sigma$," *ZNW* 46 (1955): 141f.

Both Schoeps and Sahlin presuppose a shift in meaning or a reinterpretation of a Hebrew text in their effort to explain the origin of the surname Oblias (Schoeps) or "rampart of the people and righteousness" ($\pi\epsilon\rho\iota\text{o}\chi\grave{\eta}$ $\tau\text{o}\hat{\upsilon}$ $\lambda\alpha\text{o}\hat{\upsilon}$ $\kappa\alpha\grave{\iota}$ $\delta\iota\kappa\alpha\iota\text{o}\sigma\acute{\upsilon}\nu\eta$ [Sahlin]). Torrey conjectures that "Oblias" ($\Omega B\Lambda IA\Sigma$) derived from "Obdias" ($\Omega B\Delta IA\Sigma$), but he ignores the phrase, "that is in Greek" ($\mathring{\text{o}}$ $\mathring{\epsilon}\sigma\tau\iota\nu$ '$E\lambda\lambda\eta\nu\iota\sigma\tau\acute{\imath}$), and he is not thinking of the Biblical prophet Obadiah. Schoeps had already called attention to the LXX of Obad 1, where "and a *messenger* has been sent among the nations" (וְצִיר בַּגּוֹיִם שֻׁלָּח) is rendered: "and he sent a *rampart* unto the nations" ($\kappa\alpha\grave{\iota}$ $\pi\epsilon\rho\iota\text{o}\chi\grave{\eta}\nu$ $\epsilon\mathring{\imath}\varsigma$ $\tau\grave{\alpha}$ $\mathring{\epsilon}\theta\nu\eta$ $\mathring{\epsilon}\xi\alpha\pi\acute{\epsilon}\sigma\tau\epsilon\iota\lambda\epsilon\nu$), and Schoeps had traced the remarkable translation back to a confusion of the stems צִיר ("messenger") and צוּר ("to enclose"; מָצוֹר "rampart, enclosure"). But

Baltzer and Köster were the first to observe that—without resorting to a hypothetical Hebrew text which Hegesippus would have read or perhaps would himself have written—the LXX of Obad 1 is all that is needed to explain Hegesippus' interpretation of '$\Omega\beta\delta\acute{\imath}\alpha\varsigma$, the traditional honorary name of the Lord's brother. Moreover, reference to the prophets then becomes both understandable and significant. Furthermore, in Jas 1:1 there could be an allusion to Obdias ('$\Omega\beta\delta\acute{\imath}\alpha\varsigma$) meaning "servant of the Lord." At present, only the words "and righteousness" ($\kappa\alpha\grave{\iota}$ $\delta\iota\kappa\alpha\iota\text{o}\sigma\acute{\upsilon}\nu\eta$) which follow "rampart of the people" ($\pi\epsilon\rho\iota\text{o}\chi\grave{\eta}$ $\tau\text{o}\hat{\upsilon}$ $\lambda\alpha\text{o}\hat{\upsilon}$) remain without a satisfactory explanation.

A. Böhlig, "Zum Martyrium des Jakobus," *Nov Test* 5 (1962): 207–13 (reprinted in his *Mysterion und Wahrheit: Gesammelte Beiträge zur spätantiken Religionsgeschichte*, Arbeiten zur Geschichte des späteren Judentums und des Urchristentums 6 [Leiden: Brill, 1968], 112–8), reports on a further development of the James legend in the *Second Apocalypse of James* (CG V, 4: 44, 10–63, 32) in the Nag

about ascetics. In his version of Hegesippus' report, Epiphanius (*Haer.* 78.14) added a motif which is developed out of Jas 5:18—the phrase "the prayer of a *just* man" (δέησις δικαίου) in Jas 5:16 probably occasioned this development: "and when there came a drought, he raised his hands unto heaven and prayed; and immediately heaven gave forth rain" (καί ποτε ἀβροχίας γενομένης, ἐπῆρε τὰς χεῖρας εἰς οὐρανόν, καὶ προσηύξατο, καὶ εὐθὺς ὁ οὐρανὸς ἔδωκεν ὑετόν).

This legend from Hegesippus cannot be considered a serious rival to the short, clear, and prosaic statement of Josephus. However, it is valuable as evidence of Jewish–Christian piety, and moreover it sketches the image of the "just" James which was current in certain circles of Jewish Christianity.

One has to form a mental picture of the image of this James, the historical image as well as the legendary image, before it is possible to decide the *question of the authorship* of our document. According to the tradition, James appears as an advocate of hidebound Jewish–Christian piety to the very end of his life. The title "the Just" must be understood in the legalistic sense: the advocates of strict ritualistic praxis who are mentioned in Gal 2:12 are acting on commisison from James. The question now is whether the Letter of James can be understood as the work of this man.

In making this judgment, it is necessary to guard against illusory arguments. Among these is the argument which appeals to the relationship between our text and the dominical sayings in order to prove that our text was written by the Lord's brother. For this relationship is not due primarily to characteristics shared exclusively by the Letter of James and the sayings of Jesus, but rather it corresponds to the fact that they belong to a common literary genre: our text and the collections of sayings in the Gospels both belong to the genre of paraenesis.[38] But, on the other hand, it is just as invalid to argue that James the brother of the Lord is not the author on the grounds that the

writing lacks any of the detailed comments about Jesus which are to be expected from a brother. For a paraenesis is an impersonal writing, not a confession in which reminiscences would be expressed. Also, the absence in the prescript of the title "the brother of the Lord" can be explained either as the restraint of an unknown epigone or as the self–evident confidence of the actual James.

More serious objections against this James as the author arise from the chronology, even if we forego at the outset any attempt to reconstruct from the text the situation of the Christian communities: Jas 2:14ff, in any case, cannot be comprehended without the previous activity of Paul, as is shown in the commentary.[39] Therefore, our document could have been composed only in the last years of James' life. Yet the letter presupposes not only Paul's formulation of the question about the Law, but also the resolution of Paul's struggles regarding the Law. Only in this way can the innocent manner with which 1:25 and 2:12 refer to the "law of freedom" be explained. This takes us considerably beyond the lifetime of James.

Nor does the language of our text point to an author who spent his life as a Jew in Palestine. The author writes Greek as his mother tongue. He employs rhetorical devices[40] and catchword links[41] so often that any hypothesis that the Greek is a translation is untenable. Furthermore, he uses the Greek Bible.[42]

The decisive argument against James as the author arises from the position of our document with regard to the Law. For the most authenticated element in the tradition about the Lord's brother is his legalistic piety and the report in Gal 2:12 that in the struggles over the justification of ritualism within Christianity James stood on the side of tradition.[43] Admittedly, our author says nothing against ritualism. But in 1:27 he does enjoin purity from the world without even intimating the difficult problems (e.g., food laws) which were connected with this injunction in the period and en-

---

Hammadi Library. James is also characterized as "the Just" in the *Gospel of Thomas* (logion 12): it is for his sake that heaven and earth came into being.

38   See further, section 4 of the Introduction.

39   See the second Excursus on 2:26.

40   See below, section 5 of the Introduction.

41   See above, section 1 of the Introduction.

42   See below, section 4 of the Introduction. Some of

the force of this argument is lost if one agrees with Dalman, Zahn, and Schlatter that the Palestinians during the early Christian period were bilingual. On this question see Gerhard Kittel, *Die Probleme des palästinischen Spätjudentums und das Urchristentum,* BWANT 37 (Stuttgart: Kohlhammer, 1926), 38f and 58f.

43   That the absence of a ritualism in the letter is an

vironment in which the historical James lived. These problems appear to be non–existent for our author. But that means—since he did not write prior to Paul—that they had already disappeared from the scope of his concern. Indeed, using a Jewish regulation (2:10), the author even dares to demand the fulfillment of the entire Law, apparently without in any way considering the application of this injunction to the sabbath, circumcision and purification laws—the sense which it had within Judaism. The expression "law of freedom" (1:25 and 2:12) is also a clear indication that in his ritual and moral injunctions the author does not have the Mosaic Law in mind at all. But neither does he need any longer to protest against the old Law in the name of this new law, for apparently the danger of a ritualistic reaction no longer exists.[44] That is indicated by the innocence with which he speaks of law and, in 2:14ff, "works"—as though no one could associate these statements with ritual injunctions.[45] *Jas 2:10 was hardly written by someone who is Paul's exact opposite; Jas 1:25 and 2:12 were obviously not written by a Christian who was a strict legalist; Jas 1:27 was surely not written by a Christian ritualist—and finally, the entire letter was certainly not written by someone who spoke Aramaic.* This realization seems to me to exclude James the brother of Jesus as the composer of the document.

But then, from the outset, was this James claimed as

the author of the text? In light of the observations which were made at the beginning of this section, it is hardly credible that an obscure man by the name of James wrote the document. But also, the hypothesis that Jas 1:1 is a later addition—a hypothesis which because of its very nature can never be completely refuted—must be considered incapable of proof and, for that reason, improbable. The document's late appearance in the canon leads von Harnack to assume that the text must have existed for some time without the name of James attached to it.[46] But the silence of the church fathers can be interpreted differently, and the eclecticism of the author which is likewise stressed by von Harnack is capable of a much better explanation.[47] And what leads Johannes Weiss to separate the prescript from the rest of the letter is only the difficulty which these words offer for the interpreter.[48] But against this must be noticed the fact that the play on words $\chi\alpha\iota\rho\epsilon\iota\nu$—$\chi\alpha\rho\acute{\alpha}\nu$ ("greeting"—"joy") binds 1:1 to 1:2 very firmly, and that the author employs such rhetorical devices elsewhere.[49] Moreover, whoever around A.D. 200 would have made his paraenetic text a "Letter of James" by attaching Jas 1:1 to it would presumably have heroized his patron James accordingly in the title of the document—"brother of the Lord."[50]

Therefore, we are dealing with a *pseudonymous document.*[51] To some this assumption seems objectionable

important argument against the brother of the Lord being the author is even admitted by Gerhard Kittel, review of Martin Dibelius, *Der Brief des Jakobus,* in *ThLBl* 44 (1923): 6f. On the other hand, in "Die Stellung des Jakobus," 148–54, and in "Der geschichtliche Ort," 99, Kittel states that Jas (in contrast to the caricature of the raving, wild Judaizer) preserves only the attitude of the devout Jews which in the beginning was the accepted thing for the first Christians in Jerusalem. But that is reason enough (and consequently there is no need for a preliminary discussion in this connection about the events at Antioch mentioned in Gal 2:12ff) to insist upon the question as to why the controversies which are so frequent in the Synoptic tradition (e.g., Sabbath healings, rules for purification, honoring of vows, divorce) have no echo in Jas, at least none which even intimates the conservative Jewish position. Cf. also Aland, "Der Herrenbruder," 100–2.

44 The absence of any kind of differentiation along this line is a decisive argument against the hypothesis that James had changed his viewpoint at a later

time (as argued by Ludwig Lemme, "Das Judenchristenthum der Urkirche und der Brief des Clemens Romanus," *NJDTh* 1 [1892]: 342, n. 1). But this hypothesis also conflicts with the report from Josephus (the complaints of the Pharisees!) and the legend from Hegesippus.

45 This innocence would be far more understandable in a Jew of the Diaspora than in a Palestinian Jewish Christian of Paul's day (on this, cf. section 3 of the Introduction).

46 Adolf von Harnack, *Geschichte der altchristlichen Litteratur bis Eusebius,* part 2, vol. 1 (Leipzig: Hinrichs, 1897), 487f.

47 Cf. sections 1 and 9 of the Introduction.

48 Weiss, *Primitive Christianity,* vol. 2, p. 743, n. 4; see below in the commentary on 1:1.

49 See below, section 5 of the Introduction.

50 The designation of the author as "a servant of God and of the Lord Jesus Christ" ($\theta\epsilon o\hat{u}$ $\kappa\alpha\grave{\iota}$ $\kappa\upsilon\rho\acute{\iota}o\upsilon$ $\mathrm{'}I\eta\sigma o\hat{u}$ $X\rho\iota\sigma\tau o\hat{u}$ $\delta o\acute{u}\lambda o\varsigma$) is taken by Kittel, "Der geschichtliche Ort," 75, as proof that at the time of composition kinship to the Lord was still of no importance,

because of the fact that except for 1 : 1 the text nowhere tries to prove that its author was the well–known James; hence, the document is apparently making no effort at all at pretence. A further objection involves the refusal to believe such a Christian teacher capable of the immorality of a deliberate fraud. Both arguments must be examined upon the basis of what is known about literary custom in the ancient world and in early Christianity.

With regard to the question of authenticity, the Letter of James and those of Paul have to be evaluated differently from the outset. With the latter, what is involved is an original writer, a number of whose genuine letters were known and a number of whose letters had been lost. It was natural that someone should equip a document with the authenticating characteristics of some such lost letter and, at the same time, approximate the diction and style of the "letter" as closely as possible by imitating the major prototype. The Letter to the Ephesians seems to have originated in this manner; such procedure had been common for some time. But even someone who did not engage in such literary artistry, when writing in a situation which

approximated that of Paul and which perhaps was intentionally somewhat camouflaged, could still produce pseudonymous Pauline letters. The Pastoral Epistles bear witness to this practice. This method of literary imitation could not be used in the case of the other classical figures within early Christianity, since nothing written by them was available. In addition, the imitation of the historical figure of an author could be carried out only in those cases where certain data from his life were generally known (cf. 2 Petr 1 : 18).

Pseudonymity of this sort is not what is involved either in the Letter of James or in the Epistles of Jude and *Barnabas*. Their character is explicable only by the circumstance that epistolary form has already become literary.[52] This form was no longer taken seriously; it could be toyed with by employing epistolary motifs here and there but without following the form of a letter all the way through or fully developing an epistolary situation. In this way a long perfected technique comes into play within Christianity.[53] To this technique must be accounted the fact that the author of the *Epistle of Barnabas*—a treatise containing instruction and paraenesis, but bearing none of the

---

and therefore that an early date for the letter must be assumed. On the other hand, Meyer, *Ursprung und Anfänge*, vol. 1, p. 73, believes that at the time of the writing of our document, as well as of the Letter of Jude, James and Jude already were no longer viewed as brothers of Jesus, but rather as sons from a first marriage of Joseph's; accordingly, he assigns a late date to Jas: the first half of the second century (*ibid.*, vol. 3, p. 227, n. 2, and p. 610). However, Kittel, "Der geschichtliche Ort," 75, n. 12, suggests that at any time after A. D. 66, not only as late as A. D. 200, one would expect a pseudonymous document attributed to James to designate him as the brother of the Lord: The reason for the year 66 (the year of the migration of the primitive community ιo Pella in Bashan/Batanea) is the report of Julius Africanus (Eus., *Hist. eccl.* 1.7.14) that the relatives of the Lord (δεσπόσυνοι) had carried on missionary activity from Nazareth and Cochaba (near Pella!) —Kittel, "Der geschichtliche Ort," 73f.

51 Among those who would argue for pseudonymity are: Friedrich Heinrich Kern, "Der Charakter und Ursprung des Briefs Jakobi," *TZTh* (1835, 2. Heft): 3–132 (but he takes a different position in his commentary, *Der Brief Jakobi* (Tübingen: Fues, 1838]); A. Hilgenfeld, "Der Brief des Jakobus," *ZWTh* 16 (1873): 27; Wilhelm Brückner, "Zur Kritik des

Jakobusbriefs," *ZWTh* 17 (1874): 539; Grafe, *Stellung und Bedeutung*, 48; Heinrich Julius Holtzmann, *Lehrbuch der historisch–kritischen Einleitung in das Neue Testament* (Freiburg: Mohr [Siebeck], ³1892); Adolf Jülicher, *An Introduction to the New Testament*, tr. Janet Penrose Ward (London: Smith, Elder, and Co., 1904); and the commentaries of von Soden and Ropes (on pp. 8ff in the latter are found useful observations about pseudonymity in general). Otto Pfleiderer, *Primitive Christianity: Its Writings and Teachings in their Historical Connections*, tr. W. Montgomery, ed. W. D. Morrison, vol. 4, TTL 26 (New York: Putnam, 1911), 311, n. 1, assumes an unknown author named James who later was falsely identified with the brother of the Lord; Hans Windisch, *Die katholischen Briefe*, HNT 4, 2 (Tübingen: Mohr [Siebeck], 1911), thinks that both this hypothesis as well as that of pseudonymity are worthy of consideration.

52 See above, section 1 of the Introduction.

53 Further evidence of such a technique can be seen in fixed rhetorical introductory statements which are not meant to be taken seriously: thus, Heb 5:11ff declares the readers to be immature in order immediately thereafter, in 6:1ff, to make extremely difficult demands of them. In *Barn.* 1.18, the author does not want to speak as a teacher, and yet in 9.9

characteristics of correspondence—speaks in 1.5 of the dispatching of the document. The same explanation is called for when, with "Hail in peace" ($\chi\alpha\acute{\iota}\rho\epsilon\tau\epsilon\ \acute{\epsilon}\nu\ \epsilon\acute{\iota}\rho\acute{\eta}\nu\eta$) at the beginning of the document and with "I was zealous to write to give you gladness" ($\acute{\epsilon}\sigma\pi o\acute{\upsilon}\delta\alpha\sigma\alpha\ \gamma\rho\acute{\alpha}\psi\alpha\iota\ \epsilon\acute{\iota}s\ \tau\grave{o}\ \epsilon\acute{\upsilon}\phi\rho\hat{\alpha}\nu\alpha\iota\ \acute{\upsilon}\mu\hat{\alpha}s$) and the benediction at the end of the document, he employs various epistolary motifs but never shifts completely into epistolary style. The epistolary orientation of Heb 13:22–25, and yet the totally non–epistolary beginning of Hebrews, should also be mentioned in this connection.

To this category of texts belongs the paraenesis of Jas, which never alludes to an epistolary situation, which with the address "brothers" is imitating oratory style rather than epistolary style, and which, finally, does not sound at all like a letter. And yet at the beginning of the document the epistolary motif of the pre-script is employed. Indeed, it is the usual secular pre-script, not one with a religious coloring. The author cannot name a particular church as the addressee, so he "writes," using apocalyptic terminology, to the twelve tribes in the Diaspora, i.e., to the Christians.[54] Naming the sender, and a sender who is in fact a classical figure, is also an epistolary motif. This sort of fictitious labeling is especially favored in religious and philosophical communities which are concerned with harmonizing their views with those of the classical period. The custom is particularly familiar to us from Neo–Pythagorean circles, and 1 Jn 2:7 may be claimed as in indication of the motive for such fictitious labeling: "I am writing you no new commandment, but an old commandment which you had from the beginning."

The innocent labeling of our text is far removed from the previously mentioned art of literary imitation or disguise. Nowhere in the text does the author attempt to make authorship by James credible by alluding to, or by mentioning the names of, individuals.[55] There-fore, any *moral condemnation* of this method would right away have to be limited by the fact that the fraud is

not carried through at all, and 1:1 constitutes the only mark of the pseudonymity. Yet even such limited con-demnation is inadmissable here, since a disguise which follows the literary custom of the day cannot be re-garded as a fraudulent attempt to deceive.

The complete *innocence of this pseudonymity* is also shown by the choice of the name. We, of course, believe that we can perceive on the basis of historical criticism that James could not have written in this manner. But such critical considerations were foreign to the author. He was conscious only of serving the law of freedom and of aspiring after an ideal of practical Christianity which could really be called righteousness (2:23ff). In the mind of the author, to whom the actual struggles over the Law in the first generation were foreign, James the "Just," who was zealous for the Law, seemed the appropriate literary patron for such a document. In choosing this name, the author did not have in mind some special purpose such as those behind the artistic fictions of style or situation in the pseud-epigraphical literature. Those who gave to the "*Epistle*" *of Barnabas*—which in its text nowhere alludes to the famous missionary and companion of Paul—the title which it bears today acted with the same innocence. To us, of course, it is incredible that a document with such an anti–Semitic tendency could be assigned to the Levite Barnabas (Acts 4:36). But a period which no longer had a feeling for the actual concerns of the apostolic generation might have recognized among the classical witnesses Barnabas the Levite as the suitable patron for just such a text, with its utilization of laws governing fasting and foods.

What can be inferred from the text about the *actual author of Jas*[56] is next to nothing. He is included among the "teachers" according to 3:1 and, as is shown in the commentary, he has at his disposal a rich tradition. In part, this tradition is of Jewish provenance, and even where its origin is to be sought within Hellenism it still may have been mediated to the Christians

---

he boasts of the gift of teaching with which God has endowed him!

54   See below in the commentary on Jas 1:1.

55   It goes without saying that the expression "greeting" ($\chi\alpha\acute{\iota}\rho\epsilon\iota\nu$) in 1:1 is not an imitation of the epistolary greeting attributed to James in Acts 15:23 (as sug-gested by W. Brückner, "Die nach Petrus, Jakobus und Judas sich nennenden Briefe," *StGGB* 5 (1897):

168; *idem, Die chronologische Reihenfolge in welcher die Briefe des Neuen Testaments verfasst sind* [Haarlem: Bohn, 1890], 292), since $\chi\alpha\acute{\iota}\rho\epsilon\iota\nu$ is the normal epis-tolary greeting.

56   The abbreviation "Jas" will be used in this com-mentary both to signify the author and to signify his writing.

through the propaganda and literature of Greek–speaking Judaism. But that cannot be used as an argument for the supposition that the author himself was a Jew by birth. The text is—at the earliest—second generation, and by that time the Jewish heritage had already become the secure possession of these Christians, especially in those churches which evolved directly out of Diaspora Judaism without any fundamental break. For them, Abraham is "our father" (2:21), without their having to justify that claim in some way. Therefore, the search for more specific knowledge about the author will have to be abandoned, especially when one considers that his writing is paraenesis and is therefore dependent upon tradition. In this sort of material there is no room for the presentation of original thoughts. So the author properly remains for us one unknown person among the many, more a witness than a creator. What *is* clear to us are his general convictions, and these are of a homogeneous character in spite of his eclecticism.

3. Religio–Historical Relationships

Jas is paraenesis. That is also to say that the writing makes use of much traditional material. The author often discloses his belief and his intention more indirectly than directly, more by his selection and arrangement of traditional thought and by the new emphasis which he gives to it than by the creation and formulation of new ideas. Consequently, the endeavour to determine the place of the writing within the history of religions runs up against two difficulties.

First, *Jas has no "theology."* For even though, in spite of his eclecticism, the world of ideas and values to which his writing bears witness is relatively homogeneous, still paraenesis provides no opportunity for the development and elaboration of religious ideas. At best they are only touched upon, and in most instances they are merely presupposed. Yet we cannot determine with certainty either how much Jas presupposes or what is the precise nature of the religious property with which he credits his readers. Compare this with the paraenetic sections of the Pauline letters: It would be difficult for someone to distill from them any "theology" at all, and quite certainly the theology of Paul cannot be gathered from them.

Secondly, *it is not always possible to deduce from adopted concepts the intellectual environment of the author who appropriates them.* Though individual statements have the ring of antiquity, it does not necessarily follow that the entire document is of great age. The situation is similar with technical expressions. In the commentary on Jas 1:18 it will be shown that Jas speaks there of the "new birth." But it would be erroneous to assume upon the basis of this that he is also part of the mystical thought–world from which this idea ultimately derives. Even if "the implanted word" ($\check{\epsilon}\mu\phi\upsilon\tau\sigma\varsigma\ \lambda\acute{o}\gamma\sigma\varsigma$) in 1:21 should actually prove to be an echo of Stoic terminology, the expression as Jas used it had obviously already been given a new meaning by the Christians.[57] And if the "wheel of becoming" in 3:6 is originally an Orphic expression, that does not make Jas an Orphic. Nor can Jas be considered either a Gnostic or a combatant against Gnosticism because of the term "psychical" ($\psi\upsilon\chi\iota\kappa\acute{o}\varsigma$) in 3:15, a technical expression used by Gnostics. He has used various materials whose provenance was unknown to him, or even intrinsically alien to him.

A certain internationalism and interconfessionalism is characteristic of paraenesis, for ethical imperatives have no need whatsoever to specify in every case which faith they serve. It is no accident that with a number of paraenetic texts the question of the religious sphere from which they actually originate can and has been raised. That is true, for example, of the *Testaments of the Twelve Patriarchs*, the *Mandates* in the *Shepherd of Hermas*, Pseudo–Phocylides, and Pseudo–Menander. And it is not surprising that Spitta and Massebieau have posed the question regarding Jas.[58] Their thesis, viz., that

---

57 See below in the commentary on 1:21.

58 Friedrich Spitta, "Der Brief des Jakobus," in his *Zur Geschichte und Litteratur des Urchristentums*, vol. 2 (Göttingen: Vandenhoeck & Ruprecht, 1896), 1–239; this work has also been reprinted in a separate edition, and I cite the latter. L. Massebieau, "L'Épitre de Jacques est–elle l'oeuvre d'un Chrétien?" *RHR* 32 (1895): 249–83. Both works were produced at about the same time, but independently of one another. For a criticism, cf. in addition to the commentaries, Theodor Zahn, *Introduction to the New Testament*, tr. John Moore Trout *et al.*, vol. 1 (New York: Scribner, 1909), section 8; and the reviews of Spitta's work by Erich Haupt, review of F. Spitta, *Der Brief des Jakobus*, and of G. Wandel, *Der Brief des Jakobus*, in *ThStKr* 69 (1896): 747–77, and by R.

Jas is a Jewish document which has undergone a quite superficial Christianization by some later hand through the addition of two references to Christ in 1:1 and 2:1, has at the outset a certain plausibility. For Spitta's book, which was epoch–making in this connection, has pointed out that at least in part Jas contains concepts which are of an earlier, non–Christian, and largely Jewish origin—and expositions in this commentary will reconfirm this. It is only a question of whether the Christianization of this material was the work of our author, himself incorporating these sayings into his writing (which then would have been a Christian writing from the very beginning),[59] or whether it was the work of an interpolator who improperly introduced two references to Christ into a Jewish text.

Of course, the interpolation hypothesis recommended by Spitta and Massebieau can provide no proof for the resolution of this question. There is nothing at all in 1:1 to suggest the deletion of "and of the Lord Jesus Christ" (καὶ κυρίου Ἰησοῦ Χριστοῦ so Spitta) or of "Jesus Christ" (Ἰησοῦ Χριστοῦ so Massebieau).[60] In 2:1, the text is certainly smoother if one reads simply "of the Lord of glory" (τοῦ κυρίου τῆς δόξης so Spitta) or "of our Lord of glory" (τοῦ κυρίου ἡμῶν τῆς δόξης so Massebieau). But though the text is awkward, it is comprehensible, and this sort of heaping up of phrases is more tolerable in technical expressions of cultic or liturgical language than elsewhere. And even if the deletion should be appropriate here, the later interpolation need not be explained as a covert Christianization of a Jewish text. If someone were intending such a thing, he would scarcely have constructed such an odd expression.

Instead, I would ascribe an interpolation in this case to the desire to characterize the nature of the faith with greater clarity and richness. This is a desire which could also be gathered from other variants in New Testament writings (Gal 1:6, 15). Perhaps the hypothesis that only the phrase "of glory" (τῆς δόξης) is an interpolation could be defended in the same way. In any event, if 1:1 cannot be disputed, an interpolation in 2:1 would then appear quite innocent; but there are no compelling reasons to assume an interpolation at all.[61]

The resolution of the question must be sought in another area. Massebieau apparently finds the most difficulty in what he sees to be the non–Christian character of the theology of Jas, and in the fact that where Jas does allude to the words of Jesus they are not properly identified. But thereby he totally misunderstands the essence of paraenesis, which by its very nature cannot at all bring together a coherent structure of theological thought. The sketch which Massebieau draws of such a structure and labels non–Christian is a scheme which he himself has created. In the commentary on 5:12, I have attempted to show both the fact that such paraeneses do not identify the sayings of Jesus which they contain, and also the reason why this is the case. Massebieau's consternation over this passage could be aimed just as well against Rom 12:14. The absence of a quotation formula in such a case still does not prove the pre–Christian origin of the writing; of course, neither does a saying like Jas 5:12 guarantee its Christian character.

For both Spitta and Massebieau are doubtless correct in their observation that the unbiased reader of Jas senses in some passages the lack of decisively Christian references. The models are Abraham, Rahab, Job and Elijah; a reference to the suffering of Jesus cannot even be gleaned from 5:11. We seek in vain for traces of a Christ–cult, of preaching about the cross and the resurrection, indeed, of any relatively enthusiastic emphasis of particularly Christian sentiments. Jas seems to lie completely in line with pre–Christian Jewish literature. Yet all these observations still cannot decide the provenance of the writing. For what is involved is still for the most part adopted paraenesis, and Christianization of such texts took place slowly and gradually, as may be seen in the "Two Ways" and by a comparison of the "rules for the household" (*Haustafeln*) in Colossians, Ephesians, and 1 Peter. Therefore, is it surprising that certain sections of Jas give such an impression of being pre–Christian? From this one can infer only that Jas had access to the same traditional material as did the Jewish authors, but not that he belonged to the same religious circles.

Steck, "Die Konfession des Jakobusbriefes," *Theologische Zeitschrift aus der Schweiz* 15 (1898): 169–88.

59   It would change nothing in the formulation of this

question if Christian predecessors of Jas who are unknown to us had already similarly incorporated these sayings into writings of theirs which are now

Of course, in certain instances Spitta wants to assume a still closer connection between Jas and Jewish literature. Individual transitions from one saying to another are said to be explicable only in terms of literary reminiscences, which Spitta seeks to demonstrate by marshalling an abundance of materials from Jewish literature. This collection of Spitta's has greatly advanced the understanding of Jas, but it seems to me that proof that genuine literary reminiscences were the controlling factor for the transitions in Jas has not been produced in the decisive cases. For Spitta searches for connecting links in places where the literary style of paraenesis does not allow us to expect any connection at all; thus, he is led to assume that the author is employing highly intricate associations in places where in reality Jas is merely attaching one admonition to another in accordance with his own judgment or in adherence to a traditional sequence.[62]

Therefore, the kinship with Jewish concepts does not prove the Jewish provenance of the writing as a whole. Moreover, it can be shown that the interpretation of Jas as a Jewish text encounters substantial difficulties. Of course, the absence of legal concepts which are properly Jewish may not be stressed, for the utterances of Diaspora Judaism were by no means in tune with ritualism. Precisely in the mission among the Gentiles, these Jews stayed with the more important concepts of their faith, not the lesser ones, and they attempted to interpret allegiance to the Law in terms of Hellenistic philosophy. Therefore, I would be more inclined to credit the statements about the law of freedom in 1:25 and 2:12 to a Jew of the Diaspora for whom the question of the Law was not a burning one, than to a ritualistic Jewish–Christian like James the brother of the Lord, who stood directly in the midst of struggles over this question. Therefore, 1:27 and 2:8 would also have to be understood in terms of a more liberally oriented Diaspora Judaism, and in the interpretation of 5:12 and 5:14 one would have to get by

without considering the gospel or the Christian community.

But there are still *indications of Christian faith* in the writing which cannot be explained away by an interpolation hypothesis. They make it impossible to interpret the text as a witness from Judaism and they prohibit the acceptance of the hypothesis of Spitta and Massebieau. So far as I can see, there are three such passages.[63]

A. It is impossible to interpret 1:18 as a reference to mankind (as "first fruits") vis-à-vis creation. But then the verse can only be understood as a reference to the small group of the reborn in whose footsteps all creatures soon should follow—and that would be the Christians.

B. A Jewish understanding of the passage in 2:7 is out of the question. The addressees are readers over whom the "honorable name" is invoked. In contrast to them stand the rich over whom this name is obviously not invoked. If Jas were a Jewish writing, then these ungodly rich people would have to be sought among the ranks of the Jews. One may confidently draw this conclusion from the "literature of the Poor."[64] But then the "honorable name" would have to be a designation of Judaism, and the rich also would have to be reckoned among those who bear that name. But such is not the case. So the "honorable name" cannot be a designation for Judaism at all, but must refer to a far more limited group which does not include the rich—thus it must refer to the Christians.

C. In the second Excursus on 2:26, I attempt to show that the contrast "faith—works" which is presupposed and contested in 2:14ff is not conceivable prior to Paul, since Paul's struggle over this matter would make no sense if Jewish circles prior to him had established this antithesis. So the section in 2:14ff is a sign of Christian formulation.[65]

Now if the Christianity of the author is displayed in these other passages, then one may with certainty

lost to us.

60 See below in the commentary on 1:1.

61 See below in the commentary on 2:1.

62 Cf. below in the commentary on 1:5; 1:9 (in the Analysis); 1:13; 1:18; 1:19; 2:8.

63 In addition to the passages discussed above, 2:5 also offers a characterization which is difficult to relate to Jews; yet this passage cannot serve as definite

proof.

64 See below, section 6 of the Introduction.

65 Cf. further the Excursus on 2:10.

retain the traditional text of 1:1, and with great probability that of 2:1. Nor does one need to resort to a complicated literary hypothesis for the production of the text as it now stands.[66] The incontestable juxtaposition of Christian and Jewish elements is adequately explained by the eclectic style of paraenesis. But once it is admitted that Jewish materials were adopted and passed on within Christianity, then there is even less reason for maintaining that the author must be a *Jewish*–Christian.[67] For this adoption activity extended far beyond the limits of Jewish–Christian circles. In those Christian communities which were not under the influence of Paul and his struggles, the break with Judaism evidently did not come so sharply as a rule. Instead, these churches grew out of Diaspora Judaism, and their Christianity must be characterized as a Diaspora Judaism which has been liberated to complete universalism.[68] So it should not be surprising if writings coming out of these churches pass on Jewish materials in only superficially Christianized form. But, on the other hand, there is no reason to assume that the authors of these writings—the author of Jas and the author of the *Mandates* in the *Shepherd of Hermas*—

were themselves of Jewish extraction. The most one can conclude from the absence of anti–Gentile warnings is that Jas does not have in mind recently converted Gentile–Christians, but it is not necessary to transfer the author and readers to a place among the Jewish–Christians of Palestine. It is also self–evident that the converse cannot be proven conclusively, either.

It is really a question of whether it is possible to specify a well–defined religio–historical compartment to which our writing belongs. It has already been mentioned that these kinds of inferences cannot be drawn from the occurrence of isolated technical terms. And beyond such isolated elements, relatively little material is ever found in paraenesis which makes possible such a delineation. Essene influences have been inferred, but only because Jas appears to reflect upon mercy, oathes, riches and commercial activity in a manner similar to the Essenes.[69] But Jas also shares these thoughts with paraenetic writers who were not Essenes, and our text lacks all the positive characteristics of Essenism. Likewise, a conscious—either friendly or hostile—consideration of Gnosticism is lacking apart from the use of the term "psychical"

---

66   Such a hypothesis is proposed by Hermann von Soden, in section 4 of the Introduction to his commentary; cf. *idem*, *The History of Early Christian Literature: The Writings of the New Testament*, tr. J. R. Wilkinson, ed. W. D. Morrison, Crown Theological Library 13 (New York: Putnam, 1906), 467f.

67   That the author was a Jewish Christian is maintained by (excluding those who unconditionally maintain that the author was the Lord's brother): Hilgenfeld, "Jakobus," 26f; Brückner, *Chronologische Reihenfolge*, 291ff; Carl von Weizsäcker, *The Apostolic Age of the Christian Church*, vol. 2, tr. James Millar, TTL 5 (New York: Putnam, 1895), 395f; Jean Réville, *Les origines de l'Épiscopat: Étude sur la formation du gouvernement ecclésiastique au sein de l'église chrétienne dans l'Empire romain* (première partie), Bibliothèque de l'école des hautes études sciences religieuses 5 (Paris: Leroux, 1894), 229f; Gustav Hoennicke, *Das Judenchristentum im ersten und zweiten Jahrhundert* (Berlin: Trowitzsch, 1908), 90f; Heinrich Julius Holtzmann, *Lehrbuch der neutestamentlichen Theologie*, vol. 2, 2nd edition by A. Jülicher and W. Bauer (Tübingen: Mohr [Siebeck], ²1911), 388f; Ropes; and, cautiously, Windisch, *Katholische Briefe* (1911), Excursus on 5:20.

68   The best evidence for this is that early Christian ethics as well as certain parts of the cult were heavily

dependent upon the synagogue, and also that Christianity was conceived as a new law. In addition to Jas, the witnesses to this are: *1 Clement*, the *Shepherd of Hermas*, *Barnabas*, and Matthew. On this whole concept, cf. Wilhelm Bousset, *Kyrious Christos: A History of the Belief in Christ from the Beginnings of Christianity to Irenaeus*, tr. John E. Steely (New York: Abingdon, 1970), 350–84.

69   W. M. L. de Wette, *Kurze Erklärung der Briefe des Petrus, Judas, und Jakobus*, 3rd edition by Bruno Brückner, in de Wette's *Kurzgefasstes exegetisches Handbuch zum Neuen Testament* 3, 1 (Leipzig: Hirzel, ³1865), 193; Hilgenfeld, "Jakobus," 26; Brückner, *Chronologische Reihenfolge*, 291ff.

70   See above in section 3. The term "perfect" (τέλειος) is used in an innocuous and by no means Gnostic fashion in 1:4 and 3:2; indeed, an admission of human weakness is found beside this term in 3:2. The "malcontents" (μεμψίμοιροι) of Jude 16 can be connected with Jas 1:13 only if one is convinced to begin with of a religio–historical relationship between that which Jas reproves and that which Jude struggles against, and if one overlooks the purely practical, and not at all anti-Gnostic tendency of the saying in Jas 1:13.

71   Albert Schwegler, *Das nachapostolische Zeitalter in den Hauptmomenten seiner Entwicklung*, vol. 1 (Tübingen:

($\psi \nu \chi \iota \kappa \acute{o} s$), the provenance of which was perhaps not at all clear to the author.[70] But from 3:1ff some have wanted to infer a struggle against Gnosis.[71] In the commentary on 3:17, I have attempted to show that what appears at first glance to be very similar to the depiction of the false prophet in *Herm. mand.* 11.8 is basically only a formal parallel, and that, consequently, nothing may be inferred from this parallel alone. In the commentary on 3:16 are noted various things which might have evoked such warnings against false wisdom from Jas and from other paraenetic writers. Gnosis is but one of these possibilities and since no other characteristics point to it, it is not even the most likely one. For one cannot seriously consider the words "he judges the Law, etc." ($\kappa \rho \acute{\iota} \nu \epsilon \iota \ \nu \acute{o} \mu o \nu$) in 4:11 to be an allusion to Cerdo and Marcion, since this formulation is only a rhetorical antithesis to "he who judges his brother" ($\kappa \rho \acute{\iota} \nu \omega \nu \ \tau \grave{o} \nu \ \acute{\alpha} \delta \epsilon \lambda \phi \grave{o} \nu \ \alpha \grave{\upsilon} \tau o \hat{\upsilon}$).[72]

Therefore, it is necessary to guard against unwarranted exactitude in the religio–historiacl classification of our text.[73] This judgment is not altered by the fact that Jas represents a religious type of a distinct and relatively homogeneous character.[74] For his religiosity is consistently oriented toward the practical and betrays no definite "theology." He appropriates certain theological formulations, just as he utilizes other technical expressions. But he does not explain the new birth in 1:18, the righteousness of God in 1:20, the implanted word in 1:21, the perfect law in 1:25, the pure worship in 1:27, the heavenly wisdom in 3:17, or the parousia of the Lord in 5:7; indeed, not once does he betray a clear consciousness of the extent of the range of ideas to which he alludes in these passages.

Only 2:14–26 seems to be an exception, a section which seems theological at first glance. Yet even this section is motivated by essentially practical concerns and contains a protest against the improper application of certain theological formulations rather than a replacement of rejected concepts with different ones. Only *one* religio–historical fact can be inferred from this section:[75] The actual meaning of the Pauline slogans has faded away for Jas; his religion is a practical Christianity which with regard to the terms "law" and "works" no longer thinks about disputed religious truths, but about self–evident moral demands of the Christian life. Jas has used the word "law" in this context not in conscious contrast to the statements of others, but innocuously, without definition, as the summation of that which is the self–evident content of his practical piety. And he is not unique in this regard, either. In the Excursus on 1:25,[76] I attempt to show that the expression "the perfect law of freedom" refers to a Christianity of the new spiritual nomism, which did not first originate as a synthesis of Paulinism and Judaism, but which must be conceived as a creation of "liberated Diaspora Judaism." Involved here are the same circles and churches which are also responsible, for example, for the collection of the sayings of Jesus. Here too, therefore, Jas is not a thinker, a prophet, or an intellectual leader, but rather a pedagogue, one among many, who appropriates and distributes from the property common to all.

Fues, 1846), 442; Pfleiderer, *Primitive Christianity*, vol. 4, pp. 301f; Grafe, *Stellung und Bedeutung*, 44; H. Weinel, *Biblische Theologie des Neuen Testaments: Die Religion Jesu und des Urchristentums*, Grundriss der theologischen Wissenschaft 3, 2 (Tübingen: Mohr [Siebeck], [4]1928), section 91; most recently also Hermann Schammberger, *Die Einheitlichkeit des Jacobusbriefes im antignostischen Kampf* (Gotha: Klotz, 1936), and Hans Joachim Schoeps, *Theologie und Geschichte des Judenchristentums* (Tübingen: Mohr [Siebeck], 1949), 343–9.

72   See below in the commentary on 4:11.

73   Ernst Lohmeyer, *Galiläa und Jerusalem*, FRLANT, N.F. 34 (Göttingen: Vandenhoeck & Ruprecht, 1936), 66f, interprets Jas "as the product of a Nazarean or even Galilean primitive Christianity," just as he also assigns the brother of the Lord himself—

the life-long Nazirite, the vegetarian, the one who is tireless in prayer, and yet who did not pay the tithe and did not participate in the sacrifices—to the Galilean roots of the early church. Consequently, it is not accidental that he is considered the author of the letter. On the other hand, Arnold Meyer, *Das Rätsel des Jacobusbriefes*, BZNW 10 (Giessen: Töpelmann, 1930), 286–97, has suggested the Hellenistic synagogue in the Diaspora as the place of origin for the Jewish writing which underlies Jas, despite certain elements which it shares in common with the Essenes.

74   See below, section 8 of the Introduction.

75   Cf. the second Excursus on 2:26.

76   Cf. also the Excursus on 2:10.

In forming an opinion as to the sphere in which this writing took shape, one must also keep in mind that Jas is dependent upon tradition in many ways. To be sure, it can be discerned from the language and style that the author is at home in relatively good Greek diction.[77] However, the appropriation of materials from the tradition has evidently resulted in much linguistic unevenness as well as unevenness in subject matter. This dependence must not immediately be interpreted as evidence that the author himself was quite well–read. Of course, that the Christian teacher knows and uses the Old Testament goes without saying, but the especially strong reminiscences of Jewish Wisdom literature need by no means be due to the author's reliance upon anthologies which he has previously collected.[78] The situation would be sufficiently explained by the fact that Jas, as a Christian teacher, had to pass on moral admonitions to the communities, and that a part of these admonitions had originated in Jewish paraenesis used for the instruction of proselytes. One may infer, especially from the witnesses to this paraenesis which are mentioned above in section 1, that the Hellenistic Jews usually communicated to their proselytes the inherited sayings of Jewish Wisdom in the form of Greek prose. It is not surprising, therefore, that the Christian missionaries continued this procedure. But also the content of Jewish proselyte–paraenesis had already become thoroughly Hellenized. This was partially the result of the great process of amalgamation into which the national cultures of the East were drawn by the force of fate, and partially a direct effect of the mission which required a certain accommodation to the intellectual world of those to be converted. Therefore, when Christians borrowed from Jewish paraenesis or developed it to their liking, they could, without being aware of it, appropriate Hellenistic material at the same time.

It should not be surprising, therefore, to find in Jas metaphors whose origins can be traced back into Greek philosophy.[79] Characteristic of the fact that Jas has received such material second– or third–hand, it seems to me, is the way in which he juxtaposes technical and non-technical expression in 1:17b. Moreover, one who is aware of how profusely writers of this period quoted aphorisms from poetry cannot be surprised at quotations such as that which can most probably be perceived in 1:17, and another which can perhaps be found in 3:8b. In the less literary paraenesis, especially in that of Judaism and Christianity, the disappearance of both the name of the poet and any quotation formula was frequently accompanied by the disappearance of any consciousness that the material being used was a quotation. The Book of Acts has Paul use an explicit quotation in 17:28; but the quotation formula is lacking in the Menander quotation in 1 Cor 15:33, and in its place stands the phrase, "Do not be deceived" ($\mu\grave{\eta}\ \pi\lambda\alpha\nu\hat{\alpha}\sigma\theta\epsilon$), the same formula which we find also in Jas 1:16 before the verse which is to be quoted.[80]

Therefore, in none of these cases can it be demonstrated that James himself has read the Greek author in question.[81] Certainly he borrows, but he does so primarily because he stands right in the middle of the transmission of Jewish–Christian paraenesis. We are unable to say what role is played in this by his own preference and by his own reading, factors which indeed cannot be ruled out in the case of an author of such diction.

4. Literary Relationships

In a paraenetic text, which to a large extent hands down tradition, it is difficult to prove with certainty any dependence upon other writers. For no literary conclusions at all can be drawn from many of the parallels—even from the late Jewish passages collected by Spitta. At the outset they guarantee only the fact that during those periods and within those circles the concepts in question were cherished and the formulations in question were fixed; this is especially the case with those parallels which themselves belong to texts that are traditional in their formulation. These concepts and formulations could have come to the author just as easily through propaganda, preaching, teaching, and instruction intended for catechumens or missionaries as through books. Therefore, one must guard against far–reaching conclusions. Nevertheless, it is worthwhile to keep certain facts in mind and to con-

---

77 Cf. below, section 5 of the Introduction.
78 This is the view of Grafe, *Stellung und Bedeutung*, 11.
79 See below in the commentary on 3:3ff.
80 But cf. below in the commentary on 1:16.
81 Cf. the fundamental considerations discussed below in the commentary on 1:27.

sider some definite possibilities.

Undoubtedly, Jas used the LXX as his *Bible*. Of the few actual quotations in Jas, the passage in 2:23 = Gen 15:6 has the passive "it was reckoned" (ἐλογίσθη) in agreement with the LXX as opposed to the active found in the original Hebrew; Jas 4:6 = Prov 3:34 also follows the Greek Bible, which in this passage deviates considerably from the Hebrew. Of those passages which are only allusions to Old Testament texts, Jas 1:10f; 3:9; 5:4 and 5:7 all suggest the language of the LXX. If Jas 2:23 seems to connect the words "and he was called 'Friend of God'" (καὶ φίλος θεοῦ ἐκλήθη) with the quotation from Gen 15:6, one must at least reckon with the possibility that Judaism also had already expanded the Gen 15:6 saying in this way.[82] In that case, these last words in Jas 2:23 would no longer be classified as a quotation from the Bible.

Only in one passage does Jas appear to offer a Greek translation of the original which deviates from the LXX: Jas 5:20 = Prov 10:12. Yet this is not a word–for–word translation at all, but rather it seems to be a saying such as was already current within Christian (and already within Jewish?) paraenesis.[83] Perhaps it was formulated in imitation of the words in Proverbs, but if its formulation was earlier than Jas then even this passage constitutes no reason to ascribe to Jas the use of the Hebrew Old Testament.

It is more difficult to determine whether or not Jas had read the *Book of Sirach*. Numerous statements in our writing are in accord with passages from Sirach,[84] but nowhere is the similarity so unequivocal that a relationship of literary dependence must be inferred. Moreover, these agreements can be explained in another way: In paraenesis, ideas from Wisdom literature are often transmitted in prose form. Therefore, one who stood within the paraenetic tradition was also at home in the thought–world of Wisdom literature, although he himself need not have studied it. Nevertheless, it is probable *a priori* that a Christian teacher

such as our author was acquainted with the book which provided Jews as well as Christians with a classic collection of Wisdom sayings.

To a significantly lesser degree, the author's acquaintance with *Wisdom of Solomon* may also be considered likely. The agreements here are less numerous, but Wisd 2 contains an important piece of evidence for the religious antithesis between rich and poor which is so significant for Jas.[85]

Among the writings of Jewish literature, the *Test. XII* is the book which, next to Sirach, offers the most points of agreement with Jas. But this book itself contains paraenesis, and therefore for the most part it can be regarded only as evidence of the fact that a particular motif, a particular formulation, existed within the paraenetic tradition. A relationship of direct literary dependence cannot be deduced from these agreements.[86]

We must also increasingly come to regard *Philo* as a witness to, and transmitter of, tradition. For example, although Philo shares a number of metaphors in common with Jas, I believe that I have demonstrated in the interpretation of 3:1ff that Philo himself is not writing with creative originality in these cases. Rather, he is borrowing these similes from the propaganda of the moral philosophy of his day, a propaganda which we in turn can often infer only from the writings of Plutarch, who wrote at a later time. In such an instance, one cannot always determine with certainty the source from which Jas drew, whether from Jewish paraenesis (which, in that case, Philo also might have used), or from Cynic–Stoic diatribe in general, or from a specific writer such as Philo. In addition to moral philosophy, Philo is also a valuable witness for Diaspora Judaism, its use of the Bible, its cultic language, and its piety. It goes without saying that everything which Philo shares in common with Jas in this area must be regarded chiefly as a parallel, not as the source used by the Christian author. Anyone who reads this com-

---

82   See the first Excursus on 2:26.
83   See below in the commentary on 5:20.
84   See below in the commentary on various passages, and also the collection of passages printed in pp. cxvif in the Introduction to Joseph B. Mayor, *The Epistle of St. James* (London: MacMillan, ³1910).
85   See below, section 6 of the Introduction.
86   Examples are cited below in the commentary on

1:3, 4, 5; 4:5, 7b, 8a, 8b; 5:11.

mentary will see for himself the variety of the agreements between Philo and Jas, agreements which are to be explained in various ways.[87]

The kinship between Jas and the *Sayings of Jesus* has frequently been emphasized. So far as I can see, what is involved here is a three–fold similarity:

1) In the first place, there is a purely formal similarity: In part, Jas contains paraenesis made up of sayings, and the words of Jesus were collected in the same way, connected to one another only externally (by means of catchword association) or not connected at all. Thus, these collections of sayings which are incorporated into the Gospels of Matthew and Luke have the same literary character as, for example, Jas 1 and 5.

2) But beyond this, one can also speak of a similarity of style. The use of short, pointed imperatives by both Jesus and Jas warrants this; but it is especially warranted by the kinship involving fixed groups of metaphors: the metaphors of the soil and the plants (5:7; 3:12), of the moths and rust (5:2f) and points of contact with the Watching and Waiting group of metaphors (5:9) are encountered in Jas as well as in the Gospels. The address "adulteresses" (4:4) and the drawing of attention to the prophets (5:10; 5:17f) also remind one of the language of Jesus.

3) But finally, the Gospels and Jas share the same general convictions. In both places we breath the atmosphere of an ethical rigorism whose pithy injunctions warn against the world and a worldly attitude, and exhort to peace, meekness and humility.[88] We gaze here into the realm of prayer which rejoices in the granting of its request, and of faith which works miracles.[89] Also, the piety of the Poor is dominant in both cases,[90] combined with the admonition to be merciful (Jas 2:13) and the threat against the rich; to be sure, in Jas this threatening occasionally falls into the level of the sub–Christian.[91]

Certainly many of these common features can be explained as a relationship consisting of similarities in intuition. As is shown in the commentary on 1:27, this spirit, which reduces all religious obligations to a demonstration of morality in the individual's life, also has its parallels elsewhere in the waning era of antiquity. But the preaching of Jesus and the paraenesis of Jas both exhibit this spirit in Jewish–Christian form. Of course, much of this common material undoubtedly has come into both the Gospel tradition and Jas as a heritage from Israelite–prophetic religion as well as from Judaism.

But even closer connections exist. The sayings of Jesus were collected for a paraenetic purpose, and community paraenesis made use of such sayings, although frequently without identifying them by means

---

87 A list is found in Mayor, p. cxxi, although admittedly it is far from complete and even occasionally in error. Discussions of the relationship between Philo and Jas are found in Carl Siegfried, *Philo von Alexandria als Ausleger des Alten Testaments* (Jena: Dufft, 1875), 310–4, and in Paul Feine, *Der Jakobusbrief nach Lehranschauungen und Entstehungsverhältnissen* (Eisenach: Wilckens, 1893), 142–6.

88 Especially noteworthy are the following points of contact: The man who is making his plans in Jas 4:13 reminds one of the parable of the rich farmer in Lk 12:16ff; the admonition to action rather than mere hearing in Jas 1:22 is similar to the parable at the conclusion of the Sermon on the Mount; Jas 3:18 reminds one of Matt 5:9; the warning against judging in Jas 4:11 calls to mind Matt 7:1; the admonition to humility in Jas 4:10 resembles Matt 23:12 = Lk 14:11, 18:14. Cf. further Karl Werner, "Ueber den Brief Jacobi," *ThQ* 54 (1872): 263ff; H. von Soden, "Jacobusbrief," *JPTh* 10 (1884): 169; Brückner, *Chronologische Reihenfolge*, 290; Paul Feine, *Der Jakobusbrief nach Lehranschauungen und*

Entstehungsverhältnissen (Eisenach: Wilckens, 1893), 133; Spitta, 158ff; Adolf Schlatter, *Der Brief des Jakobus* (Stuttgart: Calwer, 1932), 9–19; Kittel, "Der geschichtliche Ort," 84–94, no longer attaches particular importance (as he did in Kittel, review of Dibelius, *Der Brief des Jakobus*, 6) to the fact that the reminiscences involve chiefly the Sermon on the Mount. Instead, he especially stresses the fact that these sayings or reminiscences are never "quoted" as dominical sayings. Kittel believes that this assures for Jas, as well as for the "Two Ways" in the *Didache*, a date of composition prior to the development from quotation of "words of the Lord" to quotation of "scripture." But Kittel is overlooking the fact that this anonymity is easily explained from the very nature of paraenesis (cf. above, toward the end of section 3). The formal analogies (Gerhard Kittel, *TDNT* 4, p. 108, n. 151) cannot be ignored. Cf. also Aland, "Der Herrenbruder," 103f.

89 Cf. below in the commentary on 1:5ff, 4:3, and 5:16ff.

90 See below in the Introduction, section 6.

of explicit quotation.[92] Whoever taught the paraenesis of the Christian communities passed on to these communities the sayings of Jesus whether he was aware of it or not. Jas himself provides evidence for this with the saying about swearing in 5:12. In the commentary it is shown that there is in that verse an extra–canonical form of the saying, a form which is also attested elsewhere, and that we have no reason to regard the saying as not genuine simply because it is not specifically quoted as a dominical saying.

Therefore, upon the basis of this particular case as well as more general considerations it must be assumed that Jas is familiar with the Jesus–tradition. Moreover, the communities in which this tradition was collected—this would not in the first instance have been the Pauline churches—disseminated among themselves the spirit which is expressed in the sayings of Jesus and applied it to new life situations. In the process, this spirit was frequently constricted, to be sure. Yet even then the seriousness of the resolve and the intensity of the demand were still strong enough to have their effects and to generate new resolve and new demand. It is also through this indirect route that a correspondence between our document and the gospel of Jesus could have come about.

But it cannot be proven that Jas has used one of our Gospels.[93] In fact, Jas 5:12 is evidence for, not a knowledge of the Gospel of Matthew, but rather knowledge of another tradition. The saying in 4:3 is a correction to Matt 7:7 rather than an echo of it; yet even here it is not exactly the wording of the saying of Jesus which is presupposed, but rather, as in Jas 1:5, only the Christian hope that prayer will be answered. I have argued in the commentary that also the metaphorical language of 3:12 is not to be explained from the parallel saying in the Gospels, and that finally even 2:8 does not quote a saying of Jesus but rather the Old Testament.

The connections between Jas and the letters of Paul[94] ought not at the outset to be overrated. For though the section in Jas 2:14–26 seems to me to presuppose an acquaintance with definite Pauline slogans,[95] it also demonstrates precisely the fact that any penetrating reading of the letters of Paul upon the part of Jas is out of the question. He is familiar with only the slogans, not the concepts, and one would think that such a familiarity was rather caused by transmission through non–literary channels. Nor does the evidence of other passages conflict with this hypothesis. In the Excursus on 1:15, I have attempted to demonstrate that, as to their form and content, the concatenations in Jas 1:2–4 and Rom 5:3–5 are to be explained upon the basis of common presuppositions. In the commentary on 2:10, I have attempted to show that there and in Gal 5:3 a Jewish principle is being used. Furthermore, if Jas 2:8 is not a reference to the summing up of the Law in the commandment of love,[96] then Rom 13:9 and Gal 5:14 are no more to be considered parallels than the saying of Jesus. The "Yes" and "No" (ναὶ ναί—οὖ οὖ) of 2 Cor 1:17–19, should there exist any connections here at all, has been influenced by the dominical saying about swearing and

---

91 See below in the Introduction, section 8.

92 Cf. Dibelius, *From Tradition to Gospel*, 240ff.

93 Aland, "Der Herrenbruder," 99f, 104, argues that because of Jas 5:17 (cf. Lk 4:25) the use of the Gospels by Jas is open to discussion. Kittel, "Der geschichtliche Ort," 84–90 does not include this passage among his list of 26 reminiscences in Jas of dominical sayings; instead, this passage is used (p. 81) in his argument for the Palestinian provenance of Jas. A careful presentation of the arguments for viewing Jas as dependent upon a tradition of dominical sayings precisely such as that offered by Matthew can be found in Massey H. Shepherd, "The Epistle of James and the Gospel of Matthew," *JBL* 75 (1956): 40–51.

94 Cf. H. Holtzmann, "Die Zeitlage des Jakobusbriefes," *ZWTh* 25 (1882): 292; Feine, *Jakobusbrief*,

100–21; for the opposite position, see Michael Zimmer, "Das schriftstellerische Verhältnis des Jacobusbriefes zur paulinischen Literatur," *ZWTh* 36 (1893): 481–503; and against Zimmer, Paul Feine, "Ueber literarische Abhängigkeit und Zeitverhältnisse des Jakobusbriefes," *NJDTh* 3 (1894): 322–34; in a number of cases a mediating position ("the domination of the language of the church of that period by Pauline expressions") is assumed by von Soden, "Der Jacobusbrief," 162ff.

95 See below in the second Excursus on 2:26.

96 See below in the commentary on 2:8.

not by Jas 5:12.

Some parallel terms in Paul and Jas require more serious consideration. For here there exists the possibility that certain of Paul's formulations became a part of the common Christian vocabulary and in this way came to be used in Jas. Perhaps in the term "righteousness of God" ($\delta\iota\kappa\alpha\iota o\sigma\acute{\upsilon}\nu\eta$ $\theta\epsilon o\hat{\upsilon}$) in 1:20 a reflection of the Pauline expression can be recognized; in that case, of course, its original meaning of "righteousness apart from works" has been completely stripped away and it has become a designation for lawful conduct in the sense in which our document understands the notion "lawful." Perhaps also the image of the strife of the "passions" ($\dot{\eta}\delta o\nu\alpha\acute{\iota}$) among our members in Jas 4:1 had already become popular among Christians by means of Rom 7:23.[97]

On the other hand, it does not seem to me to be possible to appeal to the term "partiality" ($\pi\rho o\sigma\omega\pi o-\lambda\eta\mu\psi\acute{\iota}\alpha$) as a Pauline formulation.[98] And the expression "to those who love him" ($\tau o\hat{\iota}\varsigma$ $\dot{\alpha}\gamma\alpha\pi\hat{\omega}\sigma\iota\nu$ $\alpha\dot{\upsilon}\tau\acute{o}\nu$) in 1:12 and 2:5 is a repetition of a Jewish–Christian formula, not of the Pauline saying in 1 Cor 2:9, which itself is a quotation. Likewise, the contrast of hearing and doing in 1:22 is Jewish and does not originate from Rom 2:13. And the ardor of the Poor which is found in Jas is so certainly a part of a large religio–historical context that Jas 2:5 cannot be derived from 1 Cor 1:27.

All things considered, one can say that Jas obviously writes after Paul, but that he is not writing under the sort of Pauline influence which could be explained as resulting from the reading of Paul's letters.

The relationship of Jas to *1 Peter* has received much attention,[99] and the similarity of the writings has often been overrated. A certain kinship in style is clear at the outset, for, in part, 1 Peter also contains paraenesis.[100] That in the prescripts of both writings the Christians are designated as those who dwell in the Diaspora is symbolic of their kinship of style, but it is not a mark of literary borrowing.

The most important parallels are Jas 1:2f: 1 Petr 1:6f and Jas 4:6–10: 1 Petr 5:5–9. The first pair of passages, which deal with the "various trials" ($\pi o\iota\kappa\acute{\iota}\lambda o\iota$ $\pi\epsilon\iota\rho\alpha\sigma\mu o\acute{\iota}$), are examined in the Excursus on 1:4. The conclusion there is that a general kinship of thought is present, and that there is a partial agreement in terminology which, however, is only noteworthy when considered within the too narrowly defined framework of the vocabulary of the New Testament. The second pair contain paraenesis: an admonition to be humble, then the quotation from Prov 3:34, and finally the call to resist the Devil. However, in the commentary it is demonstrated that these motifs are applied in an entirely different way in 1 Peter, and that the great difference between these points of reference makes literary dependence in either direction improbable. Thus, the similarity between these pairs of passages could go back to the perfectly understandable kinship among paraenetic materials.[101]

The saying, "Love covers a multitude of sins" ($\dot{\alpha}\gamma\acute{\alpha}\pi\eta$ $\kappa\alpha\lambda\acute{\upsilon}\pi\tau\epsilon\iota$ $\pi\lambda\hat{\eta}\theta o\varsigma$ $\dot{\alpha}\mu\alpha\rho\tau\iota\hat{\omega}\nu$) in 1 Petr 4:8 is obviously used in Jas 5:20, but the saying is older than 1 Peter. And the concept of the rebirth, which in the context

---

97   But cf. the objections discussed below in the commentary on 4:1.

98   See below in the commentary on 2:1.

99   Brückner, "Kritik," 530–41; *idem*, "Die nach Petrus, Jakobus und Judas sich nennenden Briefe," *StGGB* 5 (1879): 163ff; *idem*, *Chronologische Reihenfolge*, 60ff; von Soden, "Der Jacobusbrief," 167ff. Too many parallels are cited in Mayor, pp. cii–cvii, and even more in Spitta, 184ff. The length of these lists is misleading, since "putting away" ($\dot{\alpha}\pi o\theta\acute{\epsilon}\mu\epsilon\nu o\iota$ Jas 1:21; 1 Petr 2:1), "look into" ($\pi\alpha\rho\alpha\kappa\acute{\upsilon}\pi\tau\omega$ Jas 1:25; 1 Petr 1:12), and "good conduct" ($\kappa\alpha\lambda\grave{\eta}$ $\dot{\alpha}\nu\alpha\sigma\tau\rho o\phi\acute{\eta}$ Jas 3:13; 1 Petr 2:12) are mentioned as parallels. If the term "partiality" ($\pi\rho o\sigma\omega\pi o\lambda\eta\mu\psi\acute{\iota}\alpha$) was already in use (see below in the commentary on Jas 2:1), then "impartially" ($\dot{\alpha}\pi\rho o\sigma\omega\pi o\lambda\acute{\eta}\mu\pi\tau\omega\varsigma$) in 1 Petr 1:17 is not remarkable. Cf. also Albert Wif-

strand, "Stylistic Problems in the Epistles of James and Peter," *StTh* 1 (1948): 170–82.

100   Cf. Eduard Lohse, "Paränese und Kerygma im 1. Petrusbrief," *ZNW* 45 (1954): 68–89. On the kinship with Jas (stringing together items by means of catchwords!), see especially pp. 80f, 86.

101   Here, as in the Excursus on Jas 1:4, it must be stressed that in 1 Peter the continuity is better and the execution of the author's scheme is more unified. But when dealing with paraenetic texts, that is not a sign of priority; to the contrary, if any text would have the appearance of being earlier it would be one which presents the paraenetic material without reworking it. But in reality what is involved here is not a difference in age, but merely a greater or lesser degree of the literary reworking of paraenesis.

in 1 Petr 1:23 is described but in Jas 1:18 is only touched upon, also cannot be considered a proof of literary dependence, especially since the terminology in the two passages is different. 1 Petr 2:11 uses the same metaphor of the warring passions as does Jas 4:1, but the metaphor is older. The portrayal in Jas 1:10f inclines toward the wording of the Deutero–Isaiah passage which is quoted in 1 Petr 1:24f, although there in a totally different sense. But it is precisely the style of the LXX, not that of a Christian author, which here produces the kinship.

Consequently, the thesis of a demonstrable literary relationship between Jas and 1 Peter, together with its literary–historical conclusions, seems to me to be unfounded. And this is chiefly because it does not take into account the extent to which paraenetic formulations become common material and elude one–sided literary evaluation.

The relationship of Jas to the *Shepherd of Hermas*

requires still greater attention.[102] Here there is found a kinship which goes beyond lexical and conceptual agreements. Extensive and coherent discussions in *Hermas* could be placed alongside isolated admonitions in Jas and could serve as a commentary on the latter. This is especially the case with regard to the sphere of thought related to faith and doubt. *Herm. mand.* 9 is the best interpretation of Jas 1:5–8 imaginable.[103] Nevertheless, the terms used are not the same in every case. In both, the doubter is called δίψυχος,[104] but Jas uses διακρίνεσθαι for "to doubt," while Hermas uses διστάζειν.

---

102 Cf. Theodor Zahn, *Der Hirt des Hermas* (Gotha: Perthes, 1868), 396ff; C. Taylor, "The Didache Compared with the Shepherd of Hermas," *Journal of Philology* 18 (1890): 320f; Feine, *Jakobusbrief*, 136ff; Mayor, pp. lxxivff; and *The New Testament in the Apostolic Fathers by a Committee of the Oxford Society of Historical Theology* (Oxford, 1905), 108ff, an extremely useful work for such studies. While most scholars believe *Hermas* to be dependent upon Jas, Heinrich Julius Holtzmann, *Lehrbuch der historisch-kritischen Einleitung in das Neue Testament* (Freiburg: Mohr [Siebeck], ³1892), 336, and Pfleiderer, *Primitive Christianity*, vol. 4, pp. 296f, argue that Jas is dependent upon *Hermas* (see also below, n. 162). Oscar J. F. Seitz, "Relationship of the Shepherd of Hermas to the Epistle of James," *JBL* 63 (1944): 131–40 (and again in his "Antecedents and Signification of the Term ΔΙΨΥΧΟΣ," *JBL* 66 [1947]: 211–9), upon the basis of an examination of the contexts in which the word "double–minded" (δίψυχος) appears in Jas 1:8; 4:8; *1 Clem.* 23.3; *2 Clem.* 11.2 and *Herm. mand.* 9, seeks to prove that all these writings draw in the same manner upon a "current book" (so, before him, Ropes, 89) which is called in Jas 4:5 "the scripture" (ἡ γραφή), in *1 Clem.* 23.3 "this scripture" (ἡ γραφὴ αὕτη), and in *2 Clem.* 11.2 "the prophetic word" (ὁ προφητικὸς λόγος); cf. further, Shepherd, 41, n. 3. Following the study of Wallace I. Wolverton, "The Double–Minded Man in the Light of Essene Psychology," *Anglican Theological Review* 38 (1956): 166–75 (among other comparisons made by Wolverton are: Jas 1:6, 8 with 1 QH VII, 2–5; Jas

4:1–3 with 1 QS V, 4–5; Jas 4:6–8 with 1 QS III, 8, X, 21, 24, and 1 QH VII, 2–5), Oscar J. F. Seitz, "Afterthoughts on the Term 'Dipsychos,'" *NTS* 4 (1957–8): 327–34, once again expressed his view on the provenance of the word group δίψυχος, –ία, –εῖν, and he conjectured that the source was the *Book of Eldad and Modad* which is quoted in *Herm. vis.* 2.3.4 (cf. below in the commentary on 4:6, n. 82).

103 In fact, *Herm. mand.* 9.1–3 was already cited as an explanation of Jas 1:7 or 8 in the commentaries of Oecumenius and Theophylactus as well as in the so–called Catena of Andreas (in J. A. Cramer, ed., *Catenae Graecorum Patrum in Novum Testamentum*, vol. 8 [Oxford: University Press, 1840]); the latter text states where the *Hermas* passage was found. Then Johann Ernst Grabe, *Spicilegium ss. patrum ut et haereticorum seculi post Christum natum I. II. & III.*, vol. 1 (Oxford: Sheldon, ²1700), 303, extracted the *Hermas* passage from the Catena and thus it was introduced into editions of *Hermas* even before the discovery of Greek texts of that work. One can also compare the citation of this same passage (without any quotation formula) in Pseudo–Athanasius, *Doctrina ad Antiochum ducem*, MPG 28, 565ff, and in the 85th homily of Antiochus Monachus, MPG 89, 1692. But note that August Rudolph Gebser, *Der Brief des Jakobus* (Berlin: Rücker, 1828), 30, quotes the passage as if it were original with Oecumenius.

104 Cf. also *Herm. sim.* 6.1.2; 9.21.3.

The second sphere of thought in which the two documents are related is that of rich and poor.[105] With words which are reminiscent of Jas 5:1–6, the brief paraenesis in *Herm. vis.* 3.9.1–6 (and similarly in *Herm. sim.* 1.8ff) admonishes the rich, and *Herm. sim.* 2 attempts to provide the churches with as fundamental a solution as possible to the problem of riches. But in these passages it is presupposed that rich people—and apparently in considerable number—belong to the church. Therefore this paraenesis is calculated for a set of circumstances which are more advanced than those for which Jas writes. Thus, if Jas were dependent upon *Hermas*, he would still have to be considered as a transmitter of a paraenetic formulation which is earlier than *Hermas*.

But upon the basis of the passages which have been mentioned, no conclusion about literary dependence can be drawn with any certainty at all. Moreover, the kinship with regard to the concept of spirits (see *Herm. mand.* 3.1; 5.2.5; 10.2.6; 10.3.2), treated in the Excursus on Jas 4:5, provides no further help here but rather makes the evidence more complicated. For in *Hermas* the concept appears far less Christianized than in Jas. Therefore, it can hardly be imagined that *Hermas* was influenced here by our writing.

In fact, it is probably the case that both writings have at their disposal a relatively large store of parae-netic material which *Hermas* generally passes on in a reworked condition ("expanded paraenesis"),[106] and Jas in the form of sayings. And the agreement between individual concepts, sayings, and expressions confirms this conclusion.[107] Yet we are not able to say how this common store was transmitted to each of them. Therefore, there exist between Jas and *Hermas* the same sort of connections—though to a greater extent—which we have established between our author and 1 Peter.

The supposed or actual relatives of our writing do yield, when they are compared with Jas, all sorts of profits for the history of paraenesis, but they yield no sort of criteria for the dating of Jas. The only thing which can be said with certainty is that the struggles of Paul with regard to the Law were already a past event by the time of Jas. Yet it still remains to be asked whether other writings, less closely related to Jas, do not allow us to determine something about the chronology.

1 Clement comes first into consideration. In most respects, it, like the Letter to the Hebrews, has only certain paraenetic connections in common with our writing.[108] However, in the opinion of some scholars,[109] there is one place in *1 Clement* (30.3) where the document clearly presupposes Jas. This passage is a paraenesis which is largely admonitory in character and in which the passage from Prov 3:34, familiar to

---

105 See below in the Introduction, section 6. A more detailed discussion of rich and poor in *Hermas*, and the traditio–historical relationship to Jas, is found in Martin Dibelius, *Der Hirt des Hermas*, HNT Ergän-zungsband, part 4 (Tübingen: Mohr [Siebeck], 1923), in the Excursus on *Herm. sim.* 2.5 (pp. 555f).

106 See above in the Introduction, p. 3.

107 The same statements are found in *Herm. mand.* 12.4.7 and 12.5.2 (the devil "will flee from you" [φεύξεται ἀφ' ὑμῶν]; and in 12.5.2, "resist him" [ἀντιστάθητε αὐτῷ]) as in Jas 4:7; these statements could be of Jewish origin (see below in the commentary on Jas 4:7). Cf. further *Herm. mand.* 2.2 ("speak evil of no one" [μηδενὸς καταλάλει]) and Jas 4:11. The following passages express the same concepts: *Herm. vis.* 2.2.7 and Jas 1:12 (blessed is he who endures affliction); *Herm. mand.* 8.10; *sim.* 1.8 and Jas 1:27 (care for widows and orphans); *Herm. vis.* 1.1.8; *mand.* 4.1.2 and Jas 1:15 (desire brings death); these passages have also been influenced directly or in-directly by Jewish tradition. In addition to these, one can mention points of contact which are purely

formal in nature. I attempt to demonstrate in the commentary that this is the case with the similarity between Jas 3:17 and *Herm. mand.* 11.8; Jas 4:12 and *Herm. mand.* 12.6.3 agree in the use of a predica-tion of God which comes from Judaism; "fruit of righteousness" (καρπὸς δικαιοσύνης) is found in both Jas 3:18 and *Herm. sim.* 9.19.2, but with different meanings; the name named over the Christians is mentioned in *Herm. sim.* 8.6.4 and Jas 2:7; "to live in pleasure and luxury" (τρυφᾶν καὶ σπαταλᾶν) oc-curs in *Herm. sim.* 6.1.6 and Jas 5:5; in *Herm. mand.* 2.3 slander is called a "restless demon" (ἀκατάστα-τον δαιμόνιον), and in Jas 3:8 the tongue is called a "restless evil" (ἀκατάστατον κακόν). But in these instances it is probably merely a matter of familiar expressions.

108 Especially striking is the mention of Abraham and Rahab in Jas, Hebrews, and *1 Clement*. Below in the commentary on 2:25 and in the first Excursus on 2:26, I have attempted to show the likelihood that this and similar examples come from Judaism. Simi-larities with regard to paraenetic forms can be seen

us from Jas and 1 Peter, is quoted in reference to the term "pride" ($\dot{\upsilon}\pi\epsilon\rho\eta\phi\alpha\nu\dot{\iota}\alpha$). The texts continue: "Let us then join ourselves to those to whom is given grace from God; let us put on concord in meekness of spirit and continence, keeping ourselves far from all gossip and evil speaking, and be *justified by works, not by words*. For he says (Job 11:2), 'He that speaks much shall also fear much, or does the talkative person think that he is righteous?'" ($\dot{\epsilon}\nu\delta\upsilon\sigma\dot{\omega}\mu\epsilon\theta\alpha$ $\tau\dot{\eta}\nu$ $\dot{\delta}\mu\dot{\delta}\nu o\iota\alpha\nu$ $\tau\alpha\pi\epsilon\iota\nu o$-$\phi\rho o\nu o\hat{\upsilon}\nu\tau\epsilon\varsigma$, $\dot{\epsilon}\gamma\kappa\rho\alpha\tau\epsilon\upsilon\dot{\delta}\mu\epsilon\nu o\iota$, $\dot{\alpha}\pi\dot{\delta}$ $\pi\alpha\nu\tau\dot{\delta}\varsigma$ $\psi\iota\theta\upsilon\rho\iota\sigma\mu o\hat{\upsilon}$ $\kappa\alpha\dot{\iota}$ $\kappa\alpha\tau\alpha\lambda\alpha\lambda\iota\hat{\alpha}\varsigma$ $\pi\dot{\delta}\rho\rho\omega$ $\dot{\epsilon}\alpha\upsilon\tau o\dot{\upsilon}\varsigma$ $\pi o\iota o\hat{\upsilon}\nu\tau\epsilon\varsigma$, $\ddot{\epsilon}\rho\gamma o\iota\varsigma$ $\delta\iota\kappa\alpha\iota o\dot{\upsilon}\mu\epsilon\nu o\iota$ $\kappa\alpha\dot{\iota}$ $\mu\dot{\eta}$ $\lambda\dot{\delta}\gamma o\iota\varsigma$. $\lambda\dot{\epsilon}\gamma\epsilon\iota$ $\gamma\dot{\alpha}\rho$: $\dot{\delta}$ $\tau\dot{\alpha}$ $\pi o\lambda\lambda\dot{\alpha}$ $\lambda\dot{\epsilon}\gamma\omega\nu$ $\kappa\alpha\dot{\iota}$ $\dot{\alpha}\nu\tau\alpha\kappa o\dot{\upsilon}$-$\sigma\epsilon\tau\alpha\iota\cdot$ $\ddot{\eta}$ $\dot{\delta}$ $\epsilon\ddot{\upsilon}\lambda\alpha\lambda o\varsigma$ $o\ddot{\iota}\epsilon\tau\alpha\iota$ $\epsilon\hat{\iota}\nu\alpha\iota$ $\delta\dot{\iota}\kappa\alpha\iota o\varsigma$;). Many sense so strongly that there is a disagreement with Paul here that they believe the author, a devoted admirer of Paul, would have been capable of such a disagreement only if in making the statement he could rely upon another authority, viz., Jas. Others see in these words a conscious reconciliation between Paul and Jas. But the "devoted admirer of Paul" is by no means a Pauline student; rather, he talks past Paul just as naively as does this whole generation of the "new law." If he had wished to call upon Jas as a patron or for the purpose of a reconciliation, then he would have mentioned Jas' antithesis: works—faith. For what actually appears in *1 Clem.* 30.3 (works, not words) is not a quotation of Jas 2:14: "if someone should say he has faith" ($\dot{\epsilon}\dot{\alpha}\nu$ $\pi\dot{\iota}\sigma\tau\iota\nu$ $\lambda\dot{\epsilon}\gamma\eta$ $\tau\iota\varsigma$ $\ddot{\epsilon}\chi\epsilon\iota\nu$), but rather it is the familiar (Matt 7:21!) contrast between doing and saying which also crops up in *1 Clem.* 38.2. But in 30.3 it has its own special meaning. That is, if one reads the passage in context, it will be observed that the words in question ("justified by works, not by words") are supposed to form a bridge from the paraenesis to the quotation. The author has spoken of humility and of sins of the

tongue. Now he intends to attach the saying from Job, and to that end he grabs hold of the words, "the talkative person thinks he is righteous" ($\dot{\delta}$ $\epsilon\ddot{\upsilon}\lambda\alpha\lambda o\varsigma$ $o\ddot{\iota}\epsilon\tau\alpha\iota$ $\delta\dot{\iota}\kappa\alpha\iota o\varsigma$), from the second sentence in that saying. The term "be justified" ($\delta\iota\kappa\alpha\iota o\dot{\upsilon}\mu\epsilon\nu o\iota$) is included for the sake of a connection with this term "righteous" ($\delta\dot{\iota}\kappa\alpha\iota o\varsigma$)! What the author intends to say is: "It is through works (the works about which I am advising you) and not through *words* that one is *justified*, for Job says, 'The babbler will have to listen in turn, or does the *braggart* think that he is *justified*?'" It can be seen that precisely the most important word, "justified" ($\delta\iota\kappa\alpha\iota o\dot{\upsilon}\mu\epsilon\nu o\iota$), can be understood exclusively from the context. Therefore, there is no allusion to Jas here.

Finally, a quick look at the *Letter of Jude*! If the letter is to be considered pseudonymous as I believe it should be,[110] then the obvious question is, why did its author not choose a better known figure for his patron? Since he does not venture to designate him as "the brother of Jesus," the one thing he can say about him is that he is the "brother of James." That lends little importance to such a pseudonymous document if James is merely the leader of the early church, for a brother would not share in that honor. However, if James was already known as the author of a letter, the claim to be the brother of James would have been very significant, for then it would be a likely possibility that the brother of this James had also written a letter. Therefore, it seems to me very probable that the author of the Lèter of Jude would not have chosen this obscure brother of the Lord as his patron unless the more well–known brother of the Lord already had a reputation as the author of a letter. The heading of the Letter of Jude appears to presuppose Jas.[111]

---

in a comparison of *1 Clem.* 3.2, 46.5 with Jas 4:1. The "double–minded" ($\delta\dot{\iota}\psi\upsilon\chi o\iota$) are mentioned in the apocryphal quotation in *1 Clem.* 23.3 (and *2 Clem.* 11.2); the admonition to the wise in *1 Clem.* 38.2 resembles Jas 3:13 more in form than in content. On a parallel from Hebrews (12:11), see below in the commentary on 3:18.

109 E.g., Spitta; Mayor; Theodor Zahn, *Geschichte des neutestamentlichen Kanons*, vol. 1 (Erlangen and Leipzig: Deichert [Böhme], 1888–9), 962; *idem, Introduction*, vol. 1, p. 134, n. 4; Feine, *Jakobusbrief*, 135; Hans Windisch, review of Willem Lodder, *De godsdienstige en zedelijke denkbeelden van 1 Clemens*, in *ThLZ*

41 (1916): 199.

110 See Rud. Knopf, *Die Briefe Petri und Judä*, KEK 12 (Göttingen: Vandenhoeck & Ruprecht, [7]1912), in section 3 of his Introduction to Jude.

111 In this connection I might mention the remarkable fact that Hippolytus, in the Arabic version of his commentary on the Book of Revelation, offers the following quotation: "as is demonstrated by what Jude says in his first letter to the twelve tribes: 'who are scattered in the world'" (Hippolytus, *Exegetische und homiletische Schriften*, ed. G. Nath. Bonwetsch and Hans Achelis, part 2, in GCS 1 [Leipzig: Hinrichs, 1897], 231). Were Jas (whose prescript is surely in-

But beyond this all the evidence yields nothing.[112] If one takes into account the possibility that the Jewish tradition before James had already combined the designation of Abraham as the friend of God with Gen 15:6,[113] then naturally the same form of the quotation in Irenaeus cannot prove that he knew Jas: "(Abraham) believed God, and it was reckoned to him for righteousness and he was called the friend of God" (credidit deo et reputatum est illi ad iustitiam et amicus dei vocatus est; *Adv. haer.* 4.16.2). The texts which only mention Abraham's title of honor have no significance whatsoever.[114] Nor do these authors otherwise provide conclusive parallels. For example, Irenaeus, in *Adv. haer.* 4.34.4, took over the expression "law of freedom" (libertatis lex) from a well–established linguistic usage just as Jas (1:25) acquired his: "the perfect law, the law of freedom" (εἰς νόμον τέλειον τὸν τῆς ἐλευθερίας).[115] And the passage in Iren., *Adv. haer.* 5.1.1: "and made doers of his words" (factores autem sermonum eius facti) can be said with any degree of probability to derive from Jas 1:22 only if one finds a reminiscence of Jas 1:18 in the statement a few lines later: "and made the beginning of creation" (facti autem initium facturae). However, it is doubtful whether the discussion there is about rebirth, and what the original Greek wording was is uncertain to begin with. In Clement of Alexandria, the statement "you shall not be kingly" (οὐκ ἔσεσθε βασιλικοί *Strom* 6.164.2) cannot be linked with Jas 2:8. Rather, it is to be explained as a variation of Matt 5:20. Tertullian, in *De orat.* 29, is indeed in harmony with the paraenesis

on prayer in Jas 5:16f, but he says nothing that could only come from Jas. The same applies to the relationship of *De orat.* 8 to Jas 1:13. And that is the overall impression with which we leave these investigations: Virtually nowhere can it be shown that an author is dependent upon Jas, for the simple reason that the concepts contained in Jas are so unoriginal, and so very much the common property of primitive Christianity. In this the essence of paraenesis shows itself once more.

5. Language and Style

In large measure, Jas contains collected tradition, and yet its linguistic dress impresses the reader as being relatively homogeneous. The author either exercised a completely free hand with regard to diction—as must be assumed for chapter 2[116]—or he made a conscious effort to express his own feeling for language in the way he formed and framed the tradition—which could be true of chapter 1—or he acquired these admonitions and similes themselves from a certain *niveau* of linguistic cultivation to begin with. For Jas writes in relatively *polished Greek*. This is demonstrated by the rhetorical elements of his style, which will be discussed later, and also by certain preferences in his syntax which distinguish him from other early Christian authors. There are no actual anacolutha in the letter,[117] and for the most part the discussion is arranged in obvious groupings[118] using a large number of participles. Although in general longer sentences are not predominant in Jas, but brief sentences which are often sharply separated from one another (4:1ff), still this is a natural

tended in this passage) and the Epistle of Jude coupled together so closely at that time that they could be quoted as 1 Jude and 2 Jude and be confused with one another? Yet the tradition, and precisely the Roman tradition (the Muratorian Canon), was more propitious to Jude than to Jas, and Jas and Jude are also confused at a later period (Cassiodorus, *De institutione divinarum litterarum* 8, MPG 70, 1120). Moreover, the conclusion of the Hippolytus fragment mentioned above should put us on guard against drawing any hasty inferences from it: "Now Hippolytus . . . defends this viewpoint in his exposition of this point in the vision, and it is the correct one." Hence, great importance cannot be placed upon the exact wording of the fragment (see also Zahn, *NT Kanon*, vol. 1, p. 323, n. 3).

112 On alleged reminiscences of Jas in Justin, cf. below

in the commentary on 2:19 and 5:12; on Theophilus and Jas, cf. on 2:18; on a parallel in the *Pseudo–Clementine Homilies*, cf. on 1:13.

113 Cf. below in the first Excursus on 2:26.

114 Iren., *Adv. haer.* 4.13.4; Clem. Alex., *Paed.* 3.12.4; 3.42.3; *Strom.* 2.20.2; 2.103.2; 4.105.3; 4.106.1; Tertullian, *Adv. Jud.* 2.

115 Cf. below in the commentary on 1:25.

116 Cf. above, p. 5.

117 But see below in the commentary on 4:13.

118 But note the absence of μέν—δέ in 1:19 and the problematic μέντοι ("indeed," "to be sure") in 2:8.

119 Less striking are
2:15
γυμνοὶ ὑπάρχωσιν καὶ λειπόμενοι
3:14
εἰ δὲ ζῆλον πικρὸν ἔχετε καὶ ἐριθείαν and possibly

result of the kind of material he passed on: A person collecting sayings material is not tempted to move into literary sentence structure. The word order, too, betrays a feeling for emphasis and rhythm; the instances in which correlated elements are separated by interposing another part of the sentence are relatively numerous.[119]

The vocabulary of Jas also reveals a certain linguistic cultivation. The lists of New Testament *hapax legomena* in Jas—as well as other such catalogues—are misleading.[120] For it is, of course, merely accidental that the noun γέλως "laughter" (but not the verb γελᾶν "to laugh"), the adjective ταχύς "quick" (but not the adverb ταχύ "quickly"), and the terms ἁπλῶς "without reserve" and πικρός "bitter" occur in the New Testament only in Jas.[121] Other elements which seem within the confines of the New Testament to be curious turn out to be ingredients of good, and in some cases even literary, Koine:

4:9	κατήφεια
	sorrow, dejection
1:15, 18	ἀποκυέω
	bring forth
1:14	δελεάζομαι
	entice
3:10	χρή[122]
	it is necessary
2:16	ἐπιτήδεια τοῦ σώματος[123]
	things needed for the body

One should also mention here those terms which derive from a technical usage in the "world," and whose actual meaning is either not understood or only half-understood by Jas, and which, consequently, are used in a modified sense:

3:6	τροχὸς τῆς γενέσεως
	cycle of becoming
3:15	ψυχικός
	psychical

and perhaps also

1:21	ἔμφυτος λόγος
	implanted word
1:17	τροπή
	turning (of the solstice)
1:17	ἀποσκίασμα
	shadow (= eclipse?)

Sometimes the Greek in Jas appears not to conform to the Hellensitic development, especially insofar as that development exerted a leveling and softening influence on the language. This, too, warrants notice as an indication of a certain linguistic cultivation. Thus, in Jas one finds the gnomic aorist in 1:11, 24,[124] which apparently was unfamiliar to the Hellenistic *vernacular*. One also encounters the rather strong use of the genitive with adjectives: ἀπείραστος κακῶν "unable to be tempted with evil" in 1:13 and πάντων ἔνοχος "guilty of all of them" in 2:10; the dative of advantage (*dativus commodi*) in 3:18 and probably in 2:5; the accusative with ὀμνύαι "to swear" in 5:12, when ἐν "by" or κατά "by" is more frequently used with it elsewhere.[125] The strict use of ὅστις "whoever" in its proper meaning is found in 2:10 and 4:14, as well as in other early Christian documents. More significant is the phrase ἀπαρχήν τινα "a kind of first fruits" in

---

5:11

τὴν ὑπομονὴν Ἰὼβ ἠκούσατε καὶ τὸ τέλος κυρίου (if there is supposed to be a full stop after κυρίου; see below in the commentary on this verse).
More noteworthy are
1:2
πειρασμοῖς περιπέσητε ποικίλοις
5:10
ὑπόδειγμα λάβετε, ἀδελφοί, τῆς κακοπαθείας.
The word order in 4:6 is probably influenced by the wording of the quotation. Intentional separation is very clear in
3:8
οὐδεὶς δαμάσαι δύναται ἀνθρώπων.
Among the examples of striking word order, cf. also
3:3
τῶν ἵππων τοὺς χαλινοὺς εἰς τὰ στόματα (see below in

the commentary on 3:3).
120 Cf. the lists in Joseph Henry Thayer, tr. and ed., *A Greek–English Lexicon of the New Testament*, being Grimm's Wilke's *Clavis Novi Testamenti* (New York: Harper, 1887), and in Mayor, pp. ccxlvff.
121 Cf. for πικρός *Hermas*, and for ἁπλῶς *Hermas* and *2 Clement*.
122 The isolated occurrence of this word within the New Testament is surely no accident.
123 On the last three examples, cf. below in the commentary on those verses.
124 On 2:4 and 2:6, cf. below in the commentary.
125 Cf. also below in the commentary on 1:5, n. 36.

1:18, in which the indefinite pronoun has the force of a qualification.

These conclusions appear to contradict certain observations which point in another direction. No importance can be ascribed to such details as the Hellenistic form εἰσελήλυθαν "have reached" in 5:4 and the apparently vernacular use of ὅδε to mean "such and such"; nor can any evidence of an unschooled and barbaric Greek usage be confirmed. But what *can* be established, and what from the outset is to be expected in light of the provenance of the tradition Jas uses, are Semitic influences. To be sure, the present state of the question regarding Hebraisms does not permit a certain judgment in every case. All too frequently, the presence of alleged Semitisms has been noted in texts which have no connection whatsoever with the Hebrew language.[126] Nevertheless, it can be established beyond any doubt that the LXX served to introduce Biblical expressions into the Christian vocabulary, and especially into paraenesis, where tradition exerted an influence. Among these Biblicisms are:

2:1	προσωπολημψία
	partiality
2:9	προσωπολημπτέω
	show partiality

(Both of these are derivatives of the LXX expression πρόσωπον λαμβάνειν "to show partiality")

2:13	ποιεῖν ἔλεος
	to show mercy
1:22	ποιητὴς λόγου
	doer of the word
4:11	ποιητὴς νόμου
	doer of the law
1:23	πρόσωπον τῆς γενέσεως
	natural appearance
1:8	ἐν πάσαις ταῖς ὁδοῖς αὐτοῦ
	in all his ways
1:11	ἐν ταῖς πορείαις αὐτοῦ
	in his ways

and probably also

3:18	ποιεῖν εἰρήνην
	to make peace
5:18	διδόναι ὑετόν
	to give rain
2:16	ὑπάγετε ἐν εἰρήνῃ
	go in peace

The realtively frequent use of ἰδού "behold," and perhaps also the pleonastic use of ἄνθρωπος "human being" and ἀνήρ "man" (1:7f, 12, 19), should be added here. Of course, the abrupt style of the imperatives in 4:7ff and the accusations in 5:5f also manifest Biblical influence. It is quite natural that the expressions and style of the Biblical language were preferred in paraenesis which was made up of sayings, even when this paraenesis did not consist of sayings which had been translated. For in this way, even the external elements emphasized the continuity with the past, a continuity upon which the paraenetic tradition depended.

Greater caution is called for in the consideration of certain syntactical peculiarities which can be explained in terms of the internal development of the Greek language, but which have their parallels in the Semitic languages. If these peculiarities appear more frequently in early Christian texts than elsewhere, then the Semitic influences which are self–evident among the circles of all LXX readers—but which are also probable elsewhere among the early Christian communities—are to a certain degree responsible for this, even though we still may not brand the individual phenomenon as being contrary to Greek usage. There are a number of phenomena in Jas which fall into this category. Jas uses the genitive of abstract nouns as a substitute for adjectives. For example:

1:25	ἀκροατὴς ἐπιλησμονῆς
	forgetful hearer
2:1	τοῦ κυρίου ἡμῶν Ἰησοῦ Χριστοῦ τῆς δόξης
	our glorious Lord Jesus Christ

126 On what follows, cf. Adolf Deissmann, *Die Urgeschichte des Christentums im Lichte der Sprachforschung* (Tübingen: Mohr [Siebeck], 1910), 5f; James Hope Moulton, *A Grammar of the New Testament Greek*, vol. 1: *Prolegomena* (Edinburgh: Clark, ³1919; reprint 1957); F. Blass and A. Debrunner, *A Greek Grammar of the New Testament and Other Early Christian Literature*, tr. and ed. Robert W. Funk (Chicago: University of Chicago Press, 1961), especially § 4; Ludwig Radermacher, *Neutestamentliche Grammatik*, HNT 1, 1 (Tübingen: Mohr [Siebeck], ²1925); Bonhöffer, *Epiktet und das NT*, 193f; Mayor, pp. ccviff; Ropes, 24ff; also, cf. below in this commentary, in the remarks about καί in 1:5, εὐπρέπεια τοῦ προσώπου in 1:11, and τῷ κόσμῳ in 2:5.

2:4 κριταὶ διαλογισμῶν πονηρῶν
judges with wicked motives

3:13 πραΰτης σοφίας
wise meekness (= meek wisdom)

and probably also

5:15 ἡ εὐχὴ τῆς πίστεως
believing prayer[127]

There is also the use of the periphrastic conjugation with εἶναι "to be" (1:17; 3:15), the use of the dative with the sense of the Hebrew infinitive absolute in the phrase προσευχῇ προσηύξατο "he prayed fervently" (5:17), and the infinitive with τοῦ after προσεύχεσθαι "to pray" (5:17). All of these are phenomena which are not contrary to Greek usage, but their frequent appearance or particular application probably cannot be explained apart from Semitic influence. This sort of influence on the Christian churches resulted from association with the oral or written Greek used among the Jews. Therefore, it is a matter of general forces to which Christians were exposed and not a matter of individual influence on the author of Jas.

As is evident from the preceding, there are no Semitisms in Jas which are to be explained exclusively as linguistic slips of Jas into a Hebraic or Aramaic manner of expression. Consequently, there is no linguistic evidence whatsoever to support the hypothesis that the letter was originally written in Aramaic.[128] What finally excludes this hypothesis is the recognition of the *rhetorical character* of our writing. The plays on words and the onomatopoetic elements clearly attest that this Greek is no translation. We find in Jas a series of in-

stances where paronomasia is obviously intentional:

1:1, 2 χαίρειν—χαράν
2:4 διεκρίθητε—κριταί
2:20 ἔργων—ἀργή
3:17 ἀδιάκριτος—ἀνυπόκριτος
4:14 φαινομένη—ἀφανιζομένη

The parechesis, i.e., the similarity in the sound of words of quite different derivation, in ἀπελήλυθεν—ἐπελάθετο "he goes away—he forgets" (1:24) seems to be intentional.[129] Other rhetorical embellishments in the writing are

3:6 φλογίζουσα—φλογιζομένη
3:7 δαμάζεται—δεδάμασται

and possibly also

1:25 παρακύψας—παραμείνας

I would not venture any definite judgment about whether the following instances of alliteration are a matter of accident or design:

3:2 πολλά, πταίομεν,
ἅπαντες, πταίει
3:5 μικρὸν, μέλος, μεγάλα
3:8 δαμάσαι, δύναται

But the alliteration in 1:2: πειρασμοῖς περιπέσητε ποικίλοις is surely deliberate. Also, it seems to me that the following instances of rhyme (homoioteleuton) are probably intentional:

1:6 ἀνεμιζομένῳ—ῥιπιζομένῳ
1:14 ἐξελκόμενος—δελεαζόμενος
2:12 λαλεῖτε—ποιεῖτε
4:8 καθαρίσατε—ἁγνίσατε

And the similarity of sound in the list of words in

---

127 Cf. further "the evil world" (ὁ κόσμος τῆς ἀδικίας) in the corrupt text of 3:6.

128 So, following a few predecessors, John Wordsworth, "The Corbey St. James (*ff*), and its Relation to Other Latin Versions, and to the Original Language of the Epistle," *Studia Biblica*, vol. 1 (Oxford: Clarendon, 1885), 142ff. Among the arguments adduced for this hypothesis, the most significant is the appeal to the Latin Codex Corbeiensis (*ff*); Wordsworth argues that this Latin version gives a different rendering of the Aramaic original than does our Greek text. But for the most part, the places where *ff* deviates from the Greek can be explained in a much simpler way (cf. below in section 10 of the Introduction, and in the commentary on 2:25; 4:5; 5:2; and 5:4). The thesis that an Aramaic document underlies Jas recurs again in F. C. Burkitt, *Christian Be-*

ginnings (London: University Press, 1924), 69f. To be sure, Burkitt assumes a free Greek rendering of the Aramaic. He thinks that the expression κόσμος τῆς ἀδικίας ("world of unrighteousness") might possibly go back to a confusion of the Aramaic עלמא ("world") with מעלנא ("entrance"): The tongue is that member by which "unrighteousness" enters (cf. 3:10). But both Friedrich Hauck, *Die Briefe des Jakobus, Petrus, Judas und Johannes*, NTD 10 (Göttingen: Vandenhoeck & Ruprecht, [8]1957), 20, as well as Meyer, *Rätsel*, 108f, reject the hypothesis that an Aramaic document underlies Jas.

129 Cf. below in the commentary on 1:24.

3:17 is certainly no accident: ἁγνὴ εἰρηνική, ἐπιεικὴς εὐπειθής ... ἀδιάκριτος ἀνυπόκριτος, though perhaps this was not the doing of Jas either, but rather was taken over along with the entire series. We are familiar with similar rhetorical (although they are popular–rhetorical) devices from the related catalogues of virtues and vices in early Christian paraenesis. The concatenations in 1:3–4 and 1:5[130] are also artistic devices, and the play upon the different nuances of the term ἔλεος ("mercy") in 2:13 indicates a certain finesse.

If Jas is actually quoting a piece of poetic verse in 1:17, he is following thereby a rhetorical usage which is customary in *diatribes*. The stylistic peculiarities of this genre are not infrequent in his writing in general, especially in chapters 2 and 3 where James composes treatises instead of simply transmitting sayings. In this connection, particular mention must be made of the dialogic elements of the diatribe: the objection raised by an imaginary opponent,[131] the rhetorical apostrophes in 4:13 and 5:1[132] which are in no way aimed at the reader, the invectives in 2:20 and 4:4, the numerous rhetorical questions, and—to be distinguished from rhetorical questions—paratactical constructions with a conditional sense, as found in 5:13f. Nor is irony absent from the work (2:19; cf. also 1:9f). Finally, among the characteristics of the diatribe belong the various kinds of metaphors and similes; their stylistic nature and provenance is examined in detail in the commentary. A few of them in Jas have not turned out too well. For example, it is not initially clear that the author's simile in 3:3f refers to the

tongue; again, 3:6 and the conclusion of 3:12 actually obstruct a clear understanding, though the text of these two verses is admittedly uncertain. But just such occasional irregularities in the application of metaphors are ever–present reminders that, at many places, Jas was not an originator but a transmitter of materials. Jas was tied more closely to his tradition than were the popular philosophers to the thoughts and metaphors of their schools. Consequently, despite the stylistic kinship, Jas cannot be classified without further ado as a diatribe.[133] Moreover, in various places the writing is too much a collection of sayings and too little a treatise.

This dependence of Jas upon tradition naturally makes it difficult to judge his linguistic capabilities, for there may be many figures and constructions for which he was not responsible. And yet his style may be inferred with certainty from the treatises and from the composition also of other traditional elements of the letter. He was himself responsible for the formation of the sections in 2:1ff; 2:14ff and 4:13–16; and the connection of 1:1 with 1:2; 1:13–15 with 1:16, 17f, as well as many other connections, are clearly his work. Consequently, there is ample justification for the opinion that he wrote a relatively good Greek, with Biblical reminiscences and a few expressions which, though not contrary to Greek usage, call to mind Semitic expressions, and that he was inclined to use the artistic devices of a rhetoric that had become popular.[134]

---

130 The technique of concatenation is discussed below in the Excursus on 1:5.

131 This is discussed in detail in the commentary on 2:18.

132 The general address to the "brethren" is, as a rule, used by Jas in transitions to new sayings (1:2; 1:16; 4:11; 5:9; 5:12; 5:19) or to new sections (1:19; 2:1; 2:14; 3:1; 5:7), or in the transition from an example to its further elaboration (2:5). 3:10, 12 are exceptions to this.

133 See above, n. 3.

134 Kittel, review of Dibelius, *Der Brief des Jakobus*, 5, at this point criticizes Dibelius for failure to examine more closely the individual style which is visible in Jas, despite all the ways in which Jas is tied to the tradition: Kittel speaks of "a certain disconnectedness in the style," "a way of thinking which ad-

mittedly is saturated with both thoughts original with the author as well as those acquired from elsewhere, but which frequently finds no need whatsoever to express the thought fully or to carry out the metaphor completely" (example: 1:23ff). It must be asked whether the stylistic peculiarity of paraenesis (e.g., the use of catchword connections) does not provide far too much of an occasion for such instances of incompleteness to allow us to use them in drawing inferences about the individuality of the author. An attempt is made below in section 8 of the Introduction to bring into relief whatever can be perceived about the author's individuality. Hartwig Thyen, *Der Stil der Jüdisch–Hellenistischen Homilie*, FRLANT 65 (Göttingen: Vandenhoeck & Ruprecht, 1955), places Jas, which he considers an originally Jewish writing which has undergone only

6. Poor and Rich

There are three instances where Jas speaks in behalf of the poor and against the rich: 1:9–11; 2:5–12; 5:1–6. Moreover, the use of the two illustrations in 2:2–4 and 2:15, 16 gives unmistakable evidence of his deep sympathy for the poor. On one occasion, Jas bases his animosity toward the rich upon unpleasant experiences which not he himself, but apparently the Christian communities had had with the rich (2:5ff). At another point, he uses a most threatening tone in prophesying the punishment of the rich for their abhorrent life–style (5:1ff)—and all rich people appear to be guilty of such conduct. And at the beginning of his letter (1:9–11) Jas speaks of the self–evident destruction of the rich, as though everyone with possessions were on the brink of perdition! It is apparent that the animosity of God toward the rich is more presupposed by Jas than substantiated, and that this view presents itself here in much too universal a way to have originated only from the unpleasant experiences cited in 2:5ff. However, the motives for this animosity—whether a patriarchal, a proletarian, or an apocalyptic pride of the Poor—can be clarified only through a historical investigation which goes further back.[135]

In Israel, as in every healthy human society, poverty was originally considered a disadvantage, not something good. Only when Israel no longer possessed her national strength did the idea win acceptance that the poor man was close to God in a special way. This was expressed in two ways. The populace itself had become "poor" since the downfall of the nation; hence, the prophet in the exile could speak of the whole people as the needy (Isa 41:17; 49:13). Other writings, especially the Psalms, distinguished the poor as a special group distinct from the people as a whole; and precisely at this juncture a most momentous development of a religious and social nature came into play. On the one hand, the opposition of the great prophets to the proud authorities who were all too sure of their power and resources; on the other hand, the prophets' social injunctions, which then in Deuteronomy were partially accomplished by way of the Law—all these ideas received new impetus because of the catastrophe. The rich had estranged the people from God, so it must be the poor to whom the divine favor belonged. The more piety was understood as humbling oneself before God's will, the more poverty could function as intrinsically fertile soil for piety. As a result, "poor" and "pious"[136] appear as parallel concepts (Ps 86:1f; 132:15f), and the typical enemy of the poor is also the enemy of God (Ps 109:31). The concept of theodicy requires that this enemy should come to a frightening end but that the poor man should be exalted. The pious man prays for this to happen, trusting in the

---

slight Christian revision (pp. 15f), alongside Hebrews, Acts 7, *1 Clement, Hermas*, 1 Maccabees, *3* and *4 Maccabees*, the *Test. XII*, Philo, and other writings in which he tries to demonstrate the ongoing influence of the synagogue homily, using stylistic features as the criteria.

135　Cf. Isidore Loeb, "La littérature des pauvres dans la Bible," *REJ* 20 (1890): 161–98; 21 (1890): 1–42, 161–206; S. R. Driver, "Poor," *A Dictionary of the Bible*, ed. James Hastings, vol. 4 (Edinburgh: Clark, 1909), 19f; Wolf Wilhelm Graf Baudissin, "Die alttestamentliche Religion und die Armen," *Preussische Jahrbücher* 149 (1912): 193–231; Max Weber, "Die Wirtschaftsethik der Weltreligionen. Das antike Judentum," *Archiv für Sozialwissenschaft und Sozialpolitik* 44 (1917–18): 52–138. On the continuation of the "ardor of the Poor" (mediated by the ascetic ideal of monasticism) within Islam, cf. Hans Heinrich Schaeder, "Das Individuum im Islam," in *Die Biologie der Person*, ed. Th. Brugsch and F. H. Lewy, vol. 4 (Berlin: Urban & Schwarzenburg, 1929), 938ff: The just poor man.

136　On the connection which the term for submission to God (ענו) came to have with the designation for the socially humble (עני), cf. Alfred Rahlfs, עָנִי *und* עָנָו *in den Psalmen* (Leipzig: Dieterich, 1892), especially p. 89. Cf. also Hans Bruppacher, *Die Beurteilung der Armut im Alten Testament* (Gotha and Stuttgart: Perthes, 1924); Harris Birkeland, *ʿĀnî und ʿānāw in den Psalmen*, tr. Eugen Ludwig Rapp, Skrifter utgitt av det Norske videnskaps–akademie: Oslo. II. Hist.-filos. Klasse 1932, no. 4 (Oslo: Dybwad, 1933). The philosopher Friedrich Nietzsche has sketched (and, as he intended, stigmatized) this development with his characteristic force and one–sidedness in his parable of the lambs and the birds of prey (*The Genealogy of Morals* 1.13), where the lambs say, "These birds of prey are evil, and he who is as far removed as possible from being a bird of prey, who is rather its opposite, a lamb—is he not good?" Cf. also in *Beyond Good and Evil* 195, where it is said of the Jews: "Their prophets fused into one the expressions 'rich,' 'godless,' 'wicked,' 'violent,' 'sensual,' and for the first time coined the word 'world' as a term of re-

righteousness of God. But that which is longed for and extolled in prayers of petition and thanksgiving *appears as doctrine in the Wisdom literature*: For the moment, the devout man indeed is in want, while the ungodly man enjoys good fortune. But in the future the tables will be turned.[137] The admonition not to be upset by the good fortune of the sinner echoes again and again in the sayings of the teachers (Prov 3:31; 24:19; Sir 11:21), as does also the idea that riches lead to sin (Prov 15:16f; Sir 20:21; 34:5) and the prophecy of the destruction of riches (Prov 23:4f; Sir 11:18f; Eccl 5:12ff). But the exaltation of the poor man and the ruin of the rich man also appears as an illustration of God's power apart from the concept of theodicy (Ps 113:7f; 1 Sam 2:7f).

Thus, the motives connected with theodicy are not the only ones from which the dissemination of these ideas is explained. If these devout people had their own special religious community, which is probable,[138] then the motivating forces involved were above all a pietistic criticism of secularization and a "proletarian" protest against unrighteousness and insincerity among the rich, as well as the nationalistic–religious opposition to the Hellenistic invasion which drove the "Pious" to fight on the side of the Maccabees during the struggles for liberation in the second century before Christ. However, the ardent self–consciousness of the pious "Poor" which began in this way and was nourished in the language of the Psalms outlived the political circumstances. For even when the connection with the Maccabees was dissolved and the pious, having now become the "Pharisees," had withdrawn from the political arena,[139] this ardor of the Poor was maintained. The Maccabees and the Sadducees are the "Rich" who are so sharply accused, especially in the section of woes in *1 En.* 94ff, which has so many points of contact with Jas; and they are the "Rich" who are so bitterly depicted in *Ps. Sol.* 1.4ff. In an archaicizing manner, the name and character of the pious of an earlier period are transferred to the Pharisees, who now (*Ps. Sol.* 5.2; 10.6; 15.1) appear as the poor. That may have corresponded generally to the actual social circumstances; but even if exceptions are found, they do not alter the main point: The pious thought of themselves as the poor because *poverty had become a religious concept.*[140]

And this concept was a continuing heritage. Just as it passed from the poor of the Psalms to the Pharisees, so from these, when they became ecclesiastical authorities,[141] to yet another group whose existence can be inferred from the Synoptic reports. The followers of Jesus were made up of people from different social classes. One such group is characterized in Mk 2:15 with the phrase "tax collectors and sinners" (τελῶναι καὶ ἁμαρτωλοί). Because "sinners" in this connection

---

proach. In this inversion of valuations (in which is also included the use of the word 'poor' as synonymous with 'saint' and 'friend') the significance of the Jewish people is to be found: it is with them that the slave–insurrection in morals commences" (trans. from *The Complete Works of Friedrich Nietzsche*, ed. Oscar Levy [New York: Macmillan, 1924]).

137 The transition can be seen clearly in Ps 37, which is actually a didactic poem arranged according to the alphabet and not in accordance with some sort of progression in thought. Precisely because of this it contains several features which are related to Jas. It portrays the devout in 37:3ff, 30ff; they are patient sufferers (ענוים, LXX πραεῖς v 11) who wait for the Lord (קוי יהוה, ὑπομένοντες τὸν κύριον v 9), they are the poor (עני ואביון, πτωχὸς καὶ πένης v 14) who walk uprightly (ישרי דרך, εὐθεῖς τῇ καρδίᾳ v 14). They will possess the land (37:9, 11, 22, 29, 34). Consequently, the little which the pious man now possesses is better than the wealth of the ungodly (37:16), for the latter will wither like the grass and herbs (LXX ὡσεὶ χόρτος ταχὺ ἀποξηρανθήσονται, καὶ

ὡσεὶ λάχανα χλόης ταχὺ ἀποπεσοῦνται cf. Jas 1:10f). But all problems of theodicy are solved by the thought naively proposed in 37:25: "I have never seen the righteous forsaken."

138 Rahlfs, *op. cit.* (above, n. 136), 80–8; there Rahlfs also rejects the thesis of H. Graetz, that ענוים refers to the Levites (H. Graetz, *Kritischer Commentar zu den Psalmen nebst Text und Uebersetzung* [Breslau: Schottlaender, 1882–3], 17ff).

139 Julius Wellhausen, *Die Pharisäer und die Sadduzäer* (Greifswald: Bamberg, 1874; reprint Göttingen: Vandenhoeck & Ruprecht, 1967), 78–86; Schürer, *Jewish People*, Division 2, vol. 2, pp. 26–8.

140 Isidore Loeb, "La littérature des pauvres dans la Bible," *REJ* 20 (1890): 179f: "the destitution of the Poor Man is not the real essense of his poverty."

141 Cf. how the Pharisees are depicted in the Gospels, and the remark in Josephus, *Ant.* 18.17, that the Sadducees in their official praxis had to conform to the Pharisees, since otherwise the people would not follow them.

must naturally designate a certain group as much as "tax collectors" does, it probably is not erroneous to suppose that the "sinners" of the Gospels are the same class of people who are called the 'am ha'areṣ ("people of the land") in the Talmud.[142] For the Talmud, this part of the populace is outside the Law because of ignorance, and they are unclean because life and occupation constantly bring them into conflict with the laws governing ceremonial purity. But "sinners" were not the only ones who followed Jesus. The later development of the Christian community in Jerusalem, which assumed some of the features of legalistic Judaism (Acts 21 : 18ff), shows that this community obtained recruits from other circles. The words of Jesus provide further information. When he greets the poor as the heirs of the Kingdom (Lk 6 : 20—the older form of the Beatitudes, in my opinion), and when he speaks about the preaching to the poor (Matt 11 : 5; Lk 7 : 22), he is presupposing the faith which Isa 61 : 1ff so vividly depicts—viz., that the messianic era will bring salvation to the needy (ענו). At the heart of Jesus' preaching stands the apocalyptic conception of the Kingdom of God. But as a result he directed himself first of all to the people who yearned for the appearance of the Kingdom of God; not to defiant and recalcitrant "sinners," but to people who wanted to be pious but whose sins prevented their hope for salvation from

becoming confidence in salvation. This was the group whose frame of mind is expressed in *4 Ezra* 8.31ff and whose thought–world in general is most clearly reflected in the apocalypses.[143] *These messianic pietists were the heirs of the ardor of the Poor at the time of Jesus.*[144]

It goes without saying that along with religious factors there were economic factors involved in this' development. The agrarian culture had to yield to a certain extent to the urban culture; the increase of commerce resulted in the accumulation of capital on the one side and the growth of poverty on the other side. The appropriate context for such an advanced development would be a city like Tiberias. The population of this new settlement was, in part, people who were forced to settle there, many of whom were needy (Josephus, *Ant.* 18.36ff). However, just as the inhabitants of Tiberias had to ignore religious considerations—because their residence was the site of a graveyard—, so a certain lack of scruples in general was necessary for the Jew if he wanted to keep in step with the economic development. Besides the Herodians and Hellenists, and perhaps the rich Sadducees, the 'am ha'areṣ were best able to accommodate themselves to the new circumstances. Therefore, the "tax collectors and sinners" were not among the needy in terms of material possessions, even though from the "ec-

142 Cf. Wilhelm Bousset, *Die Religion des Judentums im späthellenistischen Zeitalter*, ed. Hugo Gressmann (Tübingen: Mohr [Siebeck], ³1966), 187f; Martin Dibelius, *An die Thessalonicher I, II, an die Philipper*, HNT 11 (Tübingen: Mohr [Siebeck], ³1937), on Phil 3 : 7; A. Frövig, *Das Selbstbewusstsein Jesu als Lehrer und Wundertäter nach Markus und der sogenannten Redequelle untersucht* (Leipzig: Deichert, 1918), 117f; Ernst Würthwein, *Der 'amm ha'arez im Alten Testament*, BWANT 4, 17 (Stuttgart: Kohlhammer, 1936).

143 Possibly similar groups are also mentioned in the Mishnah: In *Demai* 6.6 the assertion of the school of Shammai that one may sell his olives only to an Associate (חבר) is contrasted with the concession of the school of Hillel: "Even to one who regularly pays tithes." Hence, here also is a group which belongs neither to the Pharisees nor to the 'am ha'areṣ. To identify this pious lay group with the 'am ha'areṣ is out of the question. M. Friedländer's arguments to the contrary (*Die religiösen Bewegungen innerhalb des Judentums im Zeitalter Jesu* [Berlin: Reimer, 1905],

78ff) are based upon erroneous identifications; he includes among the 'am ha'areṣ the author of the *Assumption of Moses*, who in reality is an apocalyptic pietist (according to others, an Essene), and he also includes in that group the disciples of John the Baptist and Jesus, as well as the learned Hellenistic Jews.

144 Also, the sons of light in the War Scroll from Qumran are sometimes designated as "the poor": 1 QM XI, 9, 13; XIII, 14. Likewise, in 1 QH V, 13–22; 1 QpHab XII, 3, 6, 10; 4 QpPs 37 II, 9f; III, 10. Cf. on this Karl Elliger, *Studien zum Habakuk–Kommentar vom Toten Meer*, Beiträge zur historischen Theologie 15, ed. Gerhard Ebeling (Tübingen: Mohr [Siebeck], 1953), 221–3.

clesiastical" point of view they were despised and excluded.[145]

The pious poor, however, that group of laymen strongly inclined toward apocalyptic, were probably shielded by religious considerations from an economic development which could have led to the violation of the Law and which in general contradicted the traditional life-style. The piety handed down from the fathers bound them to the vocations handed down from the fathers—small holder and craftsman; religious and economic traditionalism, as is frequently the case, went hand in hand. Jesus is at home in these circles, not in those of the 'am ha'areṣ. The historical and legendary narratives about his environment and his origins place Jesus in a patriarchal–pietistic context. His parables have arisen out of the perspective of the small businessman and the lot experienced by the common people.[146]

Here we have before us the true heirs of the ardor of the Poor from the Psalms. The pride of the Poor was their inheritance from the pietistic partiarchalism of those ancient pious. It was revived again because the economic contrasts increased and the reasons for protest against the rich multiplied. One can speak here of a proletarian protest[147] only if it is remembered at the same time that the protestors themselves were not caught up in the large-scale economic affairs, and hence they did not all know from experience the difficulties under which the economically declassed "proletarian ragamuffins" of the urban centers suffered at that time: in the sayings of Jesus on anxiety in Matt 6:25ff and Lk 12:22ff, mention of anxiety over housing is significantly lacking.

The *preaching of Jesus* and the movement it stirred up supplied new strength to this pauperism by revitalizing the eschatological hope. Whereas the eschatology of salvation in the time of the exile proclaimed the overthrow of the national order—"poor" Israel would be exalted and her enemies destroyed—, the gospel of Jesus proclaimed the overthrow of the social order, in the manner of the Jewish apocalyptic literature of the Poor (*1 En.* 94ff): salvation to the poor and destruction for the rich (Lk 6:20ff).[148] In Lk 12:16ff and 16:19ff, the rich man is considered the person who lives without God. For this reason, upon the occasion of a particular encounter Jesus states the general verdict which is couched in the enigmatically pointed—hence, exagger-

---

145 Therefore, depending upon the milieu of the one making the judgment, tax collectors could be considered distinguished persons or people of a low social status. Significant evidence for this is provided by some of the recensions of the Jewish story which Hugo Gressmann, *Vom reichen Mann und armen Lazarus*, Abhandlungen der Königl. preuss. Akademie der Wissenschaften, 1918, Phil.-Hist. Klasse, Nr. 7 (Berlin: Reimer, 1918), has shown to be a parallel to the parable of Jesus about the rich man and Lazarus. The story involves the burial of a distinguished citizen and of a despised citizen upon the same day. In recension B (in Rashi's commentary on *b. Sanhedrin* 44b) a distinguished Israelite is contrasted with the tax collector who is buried in poverty and who is therefore the despised man. The same is the case in recension C (Adolph Jellinek, ed., *Bet ha-Midrasch*, vol. 1 [Leipzig: Vollrath, 1853], 89). But in recension F (in the *Baraita de-Niddah*; see Chaim M. Horowitz, ed., תוספתא עתיקתא, vol. 5 [Frankfurt a. M.: Horowitz, 1890], 15) the pious Talmudic disciple is buried by only ten men, while the tax collector (or the son of the tax collector) has a large funeral procession. To be sure, the differing estimation of the tax collector is tied together with the differing formulation of the motif of retribution. Yet both valuations must be possible, depending upon whether one is applying social or religious standards.

146 Cf. Max Maurenbrecher, *Von Nazareth nach Golgatha: Untersuchungen über die weltgeschichtlichen Zusammenhänge des Urchristentums* (Berlin-Schöneberg: Buchverlag der "Hilfe," 1909), 174f; Adolf Deissmann, *Das Urchristentum und die unteren Schichten* (Göttingen: Vandenhoeck & Ruprecht, ²1908), 24f, 30ff; Georg Adler, *Geschichte des Sozialismus und Kommunismus von Plato bis zur Gegenwart*, part 1, Hand- und Lehrbuch der Staatswissenschaften 1, 3, ed. Max von Heckel (Leipzig: Hirschfeld, ³1923), 60. On the other hand, Theodor Sommerlad, *Das Wirtschaftsprogramm der Kirche des Mittelalters* (Leipzig: Weber, 1903), in his first chapter, which deals with early Christianity, has neglected the necessary determination of the social stratum out of which the sayings of Jesus arise.

147 The one-sided "proletarian" interpretation of the beginnings of Christianity was advocated by Karl Kautsky, *Foundations of Christianity: A Study in Christian Origins*, ET of the 13th German edition (New York: International Publishers, 1925).

148 The genuineness of these woes naturally cannot be disputed with the observation that other people are addressed in what precedes and in what follows, for the apostrophe here is purely rhetorical, just as in *1 En.* 96ff and in Jas 5:1. The only thing which

ated in its formation—metaphor of the camel and the needle's eye (Mk 10:25). But the hope of overthrow as articulated by Jesus was not based upon proletarian revolutionary ideas. For Jesus and his followers expect everything to be accomplished by God, and not by the strength of their own hatred or the might of their own arms. The world is not going to be changed by humans. Rather the Kingdom of God will come from heaven. The proclamation of the Kingdom of God is not revolutionary, because it is apocalyptic.

If the proclaimer of this message and those who followed him lived in poverty, it was not because of thoroughgoing asceticism or strict proletarian consciousness, for Jesus consents to support from others and to being invited as a guest. The decisive element, again, is the apocalyptic expectation. He lives apart from active involvement in the economic functions of the world because he foresees the end of this world. Thanks to the situation in Galilee and the hospitality of his followers, this life of poverty never becomes penurious and proletarian.

It was not possible for the first church in Jerusalem to retain this life-style of the wandering rabbi, but the apocalyptic and patriarchal–pietistic motives continued to operate with undiminished force. Also involved was the social opposition to the rich, for it is known from the reports about Paul's collection that many people in the church actually were destitute. The care for these poor people was conducted upon the basis of communal living, at least this is indicated from the summary statements in Acts 2:44f and 4:32ff which are not integral to the sources but are inserted by the author. Yet one cannot characterize this naive sharing of goods in order to supply daily needs as organized communism, because three elements of the latter are missing: 1) compulsion, which is ruled out by 4:36 and 5:4; 2) equality, for the passages in 2:45 and 4:35 speak expressly of distribution in proportion to need;[149] 3) finally, the cessation of private earnings, for the whole existence based upon offering and aid presupposes that earnings continue. With this "religious communism of love,"[150] therefore, the persistence of the Christians within the economic circumstances of this world is acknowledged. But again, we discover nothing to indicate large–scale industry and advanced methods of production. Instead, we are still within patriarchal circumstances among "common people." Here the attitude of the Poor which belonged to those ancient Jewish pious lives on, here "Mammon" is considered "unrighteous," here wealth is preceived as a part of the world, and ordained for destruction as is the world itself.

Paul and his churches did not necessarily fit into this development, for his mission was conducted in the midst of the advanced economic circumstances of Hellenistic urban cultures. According to 1 Cor 7:20ff, a certain activism appears to have asserted itself within the Pauline churches, and according to 1 Cor 1:26ff, most of the Christians at Corinth belonged to the despised classes. In spite of that, Paul's letters seldom raised questions regarding the proletarian way of life, and, as far as can be seen, the overthrow of the social order currently in force played no decisive role even in eschatological currents of thought. Indeed, when Paul can conclude the prophecy that "those who buy" ($\dot{\alpha}\gamma o\rho\dot{\alpha}\zeta o\nu\tau\epsilon\varsigma$) shall become "as though they had no goods" ($\dot{\omega}\varsigma \mu\dot{\eta} \kappa\alpha\tau\dot{\epsilon}\chi o\nu\tau\epsilon\varsigma$) with the admonition "I want you to be free from anxieties" ($\theta\dot{\epsilon}\lambda\omega \delta\dot{\epsilon} \dot{\upsilon}\mu\tilde{\alpha}\varsigma \dot{\alpha}\mu\epsilon\rho\dot{\iota}\mu\nu o\upsilon\varsigma \epsilon\tilde{\iota}\nu\alpha\iota$ 1 Cor 7:32), we think we are listening to a philosopher instead of an apocalypticist.

The most likely place where the traditional attitude of the Poor would have survived was in *those* churches which very gradually outgrew Judaism and its bounds. To their form of Christianity, which is best characterized as "*liberated Diaspora Judaism*,"[151] the resolute consistency of Paul is alien. In its stead, there flourished the cultivation of both the literary and religious Jewish heritage. Thus, in the community prayer in *1 Clem.*

---

raises doubts, it seems to me, is the mechanical antithesis to the beatitudes; but this argument speaks only against the originality of the four–part formulation.

149 Cf. Sommerlad, *op. cit.* (above, n. 146), 22ff. Hence, what is involved is a regular benevolence which is as extensive as possible. Legalistic motives—almsgiving purges away sin (Tob 12:9)—may also have played a role.

150 Ernst Troeltsch, *The Social Teaching of the Christian Churches*, tr. Olive Wyon, vol. 1 (New York: Mac-Millan, 1931), 62f.

151 Bousset, *Kyrios Christos*, 367ff.

59ff, which is a witness to this kind of piety, we find expressed the idea that God exalts the humble and overthrows the haughty, that it is he who makes poor and makes rich. All of this, however, is combined with other predications of God without there being any visible trace of a burning apocalyptic expectation. A similar situation can be observed in the paraenesis of the Pastoral Epistles: It is only false trust in possessions which 1 Tim 6:17ff rebukes, just as shortly before in 6:7ff—in words which are reminiscent of the preaching of the philosophers—sufficiency, not poverty, is set forth as the ideal.

We can perhaps detect a more lively pauperistic–apocalyptic strain among these Christians in the way they formed and arranged many of the sayings of Jesus, especially as they are found in *Luke*, but above all in the *Letter of James*. Looking back over the development outlined in this sketch, it is easy to recognize the extent to which the statements of Jas about poor and rich strike notes which had sounded for a long time. Most in line with the old tradition from the Psalms and the Wisdom literature is Jas 1:9–11. But more is involved in this proclamation of the exaltation of the poor and the destruction of the rich than the mere repetition of inherited concepts. Jas can express his sympathy with the poor with so little reserve because for him being poor and being Christian were coincidental concepts, not only by virtue of his archaizing dependence on the literature, but also by virtue of his own personal conviction. This can be stated with all confidence because the entire document bears witness to a pietistic–patriarchal thought–world which was especially propitious for the revitalization of the attitude of the Poor: antipathy toward the world, mistrust of "secular" affairs, warning against arrogance, humble submission before God (4:1–4; 1:27; 4:13–16; 4:6, 10).

Together with these, to be sure, appears the threat in 5:1–6. Here, too, the archaizing tone is clear;[152] one is reminded of the threats and woes in the literature of the Poor. In this case, the proletarian hatred of the rich can be seen as the immediate factor which awakens the old notes.[153] Not one word, however, indicates the circumstances of large–scale industry and the diffi-

culties of the urban proletariat. There is absolutely no evidence of a revolutionary activism such as a genuine proletarian hatred would of necessity engender. Atonement for all the crimes of the rich was expected to come from God's righteousness, not from a revolution devised by men. Thus, the concept of theodicy is surely more determinative than the proletarian idea; and the apocalyptic conviction that the end was near gave to the former its strength.

Of course, one may not suppose that Jas himself had experienced at the hands of the rich everything with which he reproaches them in 5:1–6. The archaizing assimilation to the ancient cries of woe is no doubt operative here. What he accuses them of on the basis of his own experience is stated in 2:6f: The rich had proven themselves to be the enemies of the Christians. But Jas first had to remind his readers of this fact. According to 2:1ff, they were in greater danger of showing *too much* regard for the rich. Admittedly, the illustration in 2:2–4 may be flagrant and pointed; nevertheless, Jas is obviously alarmed at the advances made by the rich in the Christian churches. The social position of the rich man makes him suspect; therefore, our author considers this social identity to be more important than a friendly attitude toward the Christians which an individual rich person might display. Perhaps the further thoughts of Jas can be inferred: He would have trusted a rich man only if that person had aligned himself—with regard to his possessions and his way of thinking—unequivocally on the side of the poor. This is conceived in terms of pauperage, not in terms of the proletariat, for Jas was not spokesman for the masses. On the contrary: The Christians of his day were far more inclined to cooperate with the rich. James wants to oppose this development which he holds to be contrary to God's will.[154] Hence, we can see (in summary) the reason for his *patriarchal–pietistic* ethic of the Poor, his *pauperistic* animosity toward the rich, and his *apocalyptic* expectation of imminent punishment for the rich—who, just as in the "literature of the Poor," are *a priori* considered to be ungodly.

The development which Jas feared could not be halted. The churches grew and the rich also became

---

152 See below in the commentary on 5:1–6.
153 Weinel, *Biblische Theologie*, section 78.2.
154 The essay by Theodor Zahn, "Die soziale Frage und

die Innere Mission nach dem Brief des Jakobus," *ZWL* 10 (1889): 295–307, proceeds upon the presupposition that this development had already been

members; Christianity was consolidated and assumed closer contact with the world. The *Shepherd of Hermas* sheds light on these processes. Its author considers himself one of the common people, as especially his metaphorical language indicates;[155] but even he himself had been mixed up in shady transactions (*Herm. vis.* 2.3; *Herm. mand.* 3.3). However, it is primarily the rich who must be apostrophized with all the seriousness of the prophetic call to repentence (*Herm. vis.* 3.9.4ff). The words are reminiscent of Jas 5:1ff, but there is a very significant difference between the two texts. Jas shouted his threats out the window for all the world to hear; no doubt he still did not have in his own house very many of these rich who are attacked. Hermas, on the other hand, is to speak his warning "into the ears of the saints" so that they may "act in accordance with it and be cleansed from their wickedness" (*Herm. vis.* 3.8.11). The parable of the elm and the vine in *Herm. sim.* 2 is the clearest indication that rich people were actually among the members of the Christian communities: As the elm, which in itself bears no fruit, must give support to the vine that it might produce fruit, so should rich people remedy the difficulty of the poor so that the latter might pray for the rich. For the strength of the poor is prayer, "in which he is rich" ($\dot{\epsilon}\nu$ $\hat{\eta}$ $\pi\lambda o\upsilon\tau\epsilon\hat{\iota}$ *Herm. sim.* 2.7)! Therefore, the poor are still the first–class pious people, but already it could be said: "Blessed are they who have possessions and understand that their wealth is from the Lord" (*Herm. sim.* 2.10). It can be seen that the naturalization of the rich within the church is on the way.

The extent to which it was fully carried out is clearly shown to us by the sermon of Clement of Alexandria, *Quis dives salvetur* ("Who is the Rich Man who is Saved?"). The second section of the sermon recommends that the rich man use his wealth to enlist an "army" of old men, orphans and widows; these are to instruct him, admonish him and, above all, pray for him (34f). That is the theory of mutual benefit which was seen in *Hermas*. Here, however, the mutuality is far more advanced, as indicated by the first section of the sermon which reinterprets the Gospel story of the rich young man—"sell what you possess" is interpreted as cleansing the soul of the passion for wealth (11:2)—and sets far aside the notion that merely being poor bestows a religious superiority.

That is the context in which the statements in Jas about the rich and the poor are to be considered. They show our author to be an energetic representative of the ancient, recently revitalized pride of the Poor; but they also reveal that within the Christendom of his period and environment this pride began to yield to an estimation of wealth which was more compatible with the world.

7. The Circumstances of the Origin of the Letter of James

We may now draw the final conclusions from the preceding investigations. If Jas is not the work of the brother of Jesus,[156] and if it does not presuppose the preaching of Paul himself, but only the repetition of the Pauline watchwords as half–understood slogans,[157] then we ought not to place its composition too close to Paul's missionary activities.[158] On the other hand, it is probable that the author of the Letter of Jude presupposes the existence of a letter attributed to James, which therefore is probably our writing.[159] For this reason, the time of composition for Jas must not be placed too late in the second century. So we are left with the approximate time span A.D. 80–130, which

completed; but cf. against this the extensive discussion below in the commentary on 2:1ff.

155 So H. Weinel in the first German edition of Edgar Hennecke, ed., *Neutestamentliche Apokryphen* (Tübingen und Leipzig: Mohr [Siebeck], 1904), 223; cf. also Ernst von Dobschütz, *Christian Life in the Primitive Church*, tr. George Bremner, ed. W. D. Morrison, TTL 18 (New York: Putnam, 1904), 306ff.

156 See above in section 2.

157 See above in section 4.

158 On the other hand, K. Deissner, in a review of Dibelius, *Der Brief des Jakobus*, in *Theologie der Gegenwart* 15 (1921): 225f, asserts that Paul was immediately misunderstood, as his own letters demonstrate; therefore, argues Deissner, Jas 2:14ff cannot prove that there is a chronological distance between Paul and Jas. Rather, the lively polemic and the use of Gen 15 as a proof–text speak in favor of chronological proximity to Paul, says Deissner (but see the second Excursus to 2:26 in this commentary).

159 See the discussion of Jude above in section 4.

of course could be substantially reduced if it were possible to prove that *1 Clement* is dependent upon Jas.[160]

All further judgments regarding the circumstances of the origin of Jas must take their departure from the paraenetic character of the writing. Paraenesis is presented in Jas in relatively unrevised form, with little expansion and little Christianization, as is shown in the commentary, and as is seen in the comparison with *Hermas*.[161] Now this sort of paraenesis could undoubtedly be preserved in the tradition for a long time. Generally speaking, however, as the *Shepherd of Hermas* and the *Didache* illustrate, the circumstances of the second century exerted sufficient pressures to produce amplifications of the paraenesis, its application to specifically Christian situations, and at least the Christianization of the framework and arrangement of the traditional material. This consideration, too, commends the dating suggested above.[162]

In the case of Jas, one should not try to find the allusions which an actual letter might make to its milieu, to missionary activity, to the life of the community, to controversies over matters of faith, or to divisions in the community. Nor can one ask about the addressees. Since more specific information is lacking,[163] one can deal only with the question of what sort of Christians Jas expected and wished to read his letter. He obviously presupposes that his readers are "poor" Christians—as the term is interpreted above in section 6—, "little people," who were oppressed and ill-treated by the rich, especially by those rich who were hostile toward Christians. But there is not a word about a period of persecution.[164] On the contrary, what Jas thinks he must fear regarding these Christians is precisely that they would give in to favoritism and partiality in order to please the rich.

Just how much this concern was based upon actual circumstances cannot be determined from the document, for Jas 2:2–4 depicts only a hypothetical and flagrant case.[165] Jas is fearful, in any event, that the development of matters could lead to a secularization of the churches, and consequently he does not tire of warning against this development. That not every admonition in Jas is prompted by a concrete situation in the life of the church follows from the nature of paraenesis itself. Moreover, in the commentary I have attempted to prove the impossibility of this assumption with regard to numerous passages.[166] On the other hand, the selection and the amplification of admonitions naturally indicate that the circumstances of Christianity tended in general toward an adaptation to the life-style and disposition of the "world." The fundamental hostility which existed between the Christianity of the early decades and the "world" began to

---

160 But cf. to the contrary the discussion of *1 Clement* above in section 4.

161 Cf. above in section 3.

162 On the other hand, Kittel, "Der geschichtliche Ort," 81–4, removes Jas so far from the circumstances and concepts of the second century (namely, because of the author's expectation of an imminent parousia, and because of the social situations visible from the letter) that he arrives at a very early dating: before the first missionary journey of Paul. Aland, "Der Herrenbruder," 102ff, has taken issue with this, pointing to passages from the *Shepherd of Hermas* which indicate a certain proximity between *Hermas* and Jas precisely in their stance with regard to poor and rich and in their eschatological concepts. Kittel's response to this was published posthumously: "Der Jakobusbrief und die Apostolischen Väter," *ZNW* 43 (1950–51): 54–112. In this study, Kittel compares, in addition to reminiscences of dominical sayings, primarily the eschatological statements in the Apostolic Fathers with those in Jas (only the brief remarks on pp. 111f are devoted to the social situation). His conclusions: Together with the *Didache*, Jas stands at a distinct distance from the Apostolic Fathers and, indeed, both writings represent an *earlier* stage. Essentially in agreement with this conclusion, but without accepting the early date advocated by Kittel, is Leonhard Goppelt, *Christentum und Judentum im ersten und zweiten Jahrhundert* (Gütersloh: Bertelsmann, 1954), 189, n. 1.

163 Cf. above in section 3.

164 See above, p. 2.

165 Cf. the basic discussion of this in the Excursus on 2:1, as well as the observations on 1:11 and 4:16.

166 This view stands in fundamental opposition to the attempts to infer from the admonitions in the letter a picture of the community or communities to which Jas is addressed; when this latter methodology is employed, then naturally the resultant picture is going to make the addressees look very bad. Brückner, "Kritik," 540, wants to take 1:2ff, 13ff; 2:1ff; 3:1ff, 13ff; 4:1ff, 13ff; 5:1ff and 14 *all* as references to circumstances within *one* church! Von Soden "Der Jacobusbrief," 175f, speaks of neighbourly love

to ease. This alone was reason enough for the author to reprove in his paraenesis the abuses which *could* have resulted from such a development. That these abuses had in fact already appeared and presented their full danger is not usually stated; if this were the case it would have been stated—and indeed in tones of sharpest reproof. Hence, historical conclusions based upon these admonitions may be made only with regard to the overall state of affairs and may not be extended to individual cases.[167]

One form—to be sure, a completely different form—of the adaptation to the "world" appears in the emphasis on the new Christian law.[168] For this nomistic tendency of thought actually emerged from a confrontation with day to day situations, and it signifies a domestication within the world in spite of all the pietistic enmity toward the world. Admittedly, it is difficult to make use of this pheomenon in determining chronology, since the nomistic development in primitive Christianity may have begun very early.

An approximate dating can be deduced, however, from the allusion to the constitution of the churches in 5:14: The power of healing through prayer, originally a pneumatic power, has already been transferred to the officials, the elders. What we are being told here points to the second or third generation. However, in view of the timeless character of paraenesis one must avoid overly precise datings.

This same caution applies in determining the geographical localization of Jas—for paraenesis is not interested in locale. Some have suggested Palestine,[169]

using as a criterion the metaphors in Jas, especially the metaphor of early and late rains in 5:7. The good Greek in Jas does not support this hypothesis, and in the commentary on 5:7 it is shown that precisely this use of the metaphor is based not upon exact knowledge of local conditions but upon literary tradition. Other metaphors, such as the scorching heat in 1:11, and the similes in 3:1ff, are also traditional and permit no inferences about the place of composition. If one interprets the kinship with 1 Peter, *1 Clement* and the *Shepherd of Hermas* as literary dependence,[170] then the author of Jas might be sought in Rome. But since the presupposition of literary dependence is dubious, the conclusion drawn from it cannot stand. We cannot say whether or not the paraenetic material common to Jas and *Hermas* circulated only in Rome. So the attempt to fix the place of the composition of Jas must be abandoned.

8. Ethos

The manner in which Jas is tied so closely to the tradition makes it difficult to recognize what he himself believed, intended and taught. And yet it is precisely when Jas is understood as the eclectic that he is that one can recognize his interests and intentions by observing the way he used, arranged, formed and composed the tradition.[171]

---

which has grown cold, pursuit of riches, and intellectual arrogance; Grafe, *Stellung und Bedeutung*, 5, sketches a similar picture: "Thus, the sins of the tongue in all their degenerate forms had gained vast territory within the life of the community. Strife and dissension were the necessary consequences and they infected the church's entire existence with mutual discontent." Also, Wilhelm Michaelis, *Einleitung in das Neue Testament* (Bern: Haller, ²1954), 275, interprets 2:2ff; 3:1f; 4:13ff; and 5:1ff as allusions to concrete situations within the church. But then he completely forgoes sketching the picture of such a community or communities. The only concrete thing which he says about them is that they are Jewish Christians, not far from Palestine ("possibly in Syria or Cilicia" [p. 278], in agreement with Kittel).

167 Cf. below in the commentary on 4:16 and 5:6.

168 Cf. the Excursus on 1:25 and 2:10.

169 Further arguments for Palestine–Syria are adduced by Shepherd, 49–51.

170 Brückner, "Kritik," 541; von Soden, "Der Jacobusbrief," 191f; Grafe, *Stellung und Bedeutung*, 45.

171 See the discussion of this eclecticism above in section 1.

But given this presupposition, one must also forgo any attempt to bring into relief a "theology" of Jas.[172] To begin with, many motifs of primitive Christian piety are not mentioned at all—which is not surprising in a paraenetic writing—, and yet this does not justify the assertion that they had no value for Jas. His "letter" is not at all intended to reproduce his entire Christianity. Various matters are only touched upon in Jas. That this happens in so casual a way need not indicate a lack of interest; on the other hand, it could be accidental that a matter is mentioned in Jas at all. Hence, it is necessary to guard against ascribing fundamental significance to such texts and even more necessary to guard against combining them with other equally isolated texts for the purpose of constructing a theology. The saying about rebirth in 1:18, in particular, has been both overestimated and unjustifiably combined with other passages.[173] But also the presentation of sin and its consequences in the form of a catena in 1:14f must, precisely because of its form, not be theologically burdened. The comments about wisdom in 3:13–17 are meant to be paraenetic and not dogmatic; human perfection in 1:4 and 3:2 is spoken of without any theological reflection; and even in the designation of Christ in 2:1 perhaps a cultic, but no Christological, interest is to be detected.

What Jas talks about in several passages, or what at least resonates as an overtone in several of his admonitions—this alone can provide some characterization of him. To be sure, this characterization will be incomplete, since it is based upon paraenesis. As a result, whatever *can* be ascertained has to be called an "ethos" rather than a piety, for it is impossible for us to reproduce the complete range of the author's piety. But if we consider his writing in light of the presupposition described above, then clearly some trains of thought emerge which—without any artificial construction—combine to form an animated and characteristic unity.

Without doubt, what is stressed the most is the *piety of the Poor*, and the accompanying opposition to the rich and to the world. The distinctive marks and the motives of this concept have already been characterized above in section 6, and there it was indicated how tradition and the author's own inclination come together at this point. Jas wanted to be a "poor man," i.e., he wanted to be a pious man who did not participate in the world. Further, he wanted all Christians to continue to belong to the "poor"—although obviously he did not expect to be successful. He wanted to barricade every door through which the spirit of the world might enter. For this reason he warned against too many becoming teachers (3:1f, to which is joined the treatise on the tongue in 3:3–12), against obliging the rich (2:1–12), and against allowing dissension to prevail in the churches (3:13–18).[174]

His distrust of the world made him quick to spot all the excuses and self-deceptions with which a Christianity which had become unfit *could* conceal its lack of concrete evidence for its piety. The indignation at such evasions can be detected both in the traditional concepts which Jas incorporated—in 1:13ff; 1:22ff and 1:26 such self-deception is opposed—as well as in his own polemical statements in 2:14–26. For this seems to me to be the sense of this much–debated polemic:[175] A fundamentally (despite Jas' calling as teacher!) laic–practical piety is indignant about a theological slogan whose force and depth is no longer understood, and which might possibly be used to justify a Christianity which in its practice is barren. It is deeds alone which display the genuineness of the faith. The patri-

---

172 On what follows, cf. in addition to the various handbooks on "New Testament Theology," and the literature cited in the second Excursus on 2:26, also Woldemar Gottlob Schmidt, *Der Lehrgehalt des Jacobus–Briefes: Ein Beitrag zur neutestamentlichen Theologie* (Leipzig: Hinrichs, 1869); von Soden, "Der Jacobusbrief," 137ff; Ernst Vowinkel, *Die Grundgedanken des Jakobusbriefes verglichen mit den ersten Briefen des Petrus und Johannes*, BFTh 6 (Gütersloh: Bertelsmann, 1899), 6. Almost all such studies, even when they do not examine Jas from the standpoint of various dogmatic positions, still attribute too much significance to ideas which in Jas are only touched upon in passing.

173 If 1:17f is considered an isolated saying, as it must be, then in the first place the association of the "word of truth" (λόγος ἀληθείας) with the "implanted word" (λόγος ἔμφυτος 1:21) is not entirely certain; but even more, one cannot extract some sort of doctrine of the Spirit from 4:5 and then combine "Spirit" with "word," since Jas is not responsible for the concepts which are alluded to in the quotation in 4:5 (against Massebieau, 250f).

174 Also, cf. below in the commentary on 3:16.

175 Cf. above, p. 25.

archal–pietistic attitude of the Poor and of enmity toward the world gives birth to an *active, practical piety* which is closely related to the disposition of Jesus' gospel,[176] a piety out of which the entire undertaking of this paraenesis can be understood.

But this active piety has its limits, and these consist in its restriction to the Christian community. What is set forth here is a conventicle–ethic. Of course, —as in all of primitive Christianity—no program of reform is proposed whereby the world is to be transformed. But also lacking are the watchwords and motifs for dealing thoroughly with the world in terms of morals. The eschatological hope is the basis for this limitation of practical Christianity. The great cataclysm will come. For the period until the End, the Christian's watchword is perseverance—in spite of all opposition, all suffering, and despite the apparent contrary evidence of the course of the world (5:7ff; 1:2ff, 12). The Christian must only be careful to keep himself pure from the world and to leave everything else to God (1:27; 4:7, 10). One may also include in this connection, being cognizant of the necessary caution, the obviously high estimation of the prayer of faith which is certain of its being heard (1:5ff; 4:3; 5:16ff): Expect everything from God and nothing from self!

The attitude of enmity toward the world, therefore, is also the source of a *passive piety* which limits all activity to one's own existence and that of one's brother, and which, in view of the parousia, leaves the evil world to its own devices until the End—an End which will have frightening consequences for this world. This conventicular self–limitation differed, not to its advantage, from the inner freedom with which Jesus proclaimed repentance and forgiveness, from the missionary zeal of Paul and from the universal tendencies of early Catholicism. Jas proclaims the end of the ungodly rich people using both didactic as well as prophetic patterns, obviously not without satisfaction, and at any rate without expressing a missionary desire for their conversion. To the contrary, our author's disposition is in fact to abandon the rich people to their destruction rather than to give them a welcome invitation to the Christian community, for their entrance into the community might corrupt its attitude of hostility toward the world and its pride amidst poverty. In this conventicular narrowness is found the sub–Christian element occasionally perceived in the letter—specifically in 2:1–12 and 5:1–6.[177]

These sub–Christian statements, however, emanated from an essentially Christian ethos. In such efforts at determining what is essential, one can always learn from Friedrich Nietzsche's remarkable ability to penetrate to that which is authentically Christian—an ability gained through personal antipathy and an inherited Christian faith.[178] And it is here that Nietzsche would find the most characteristic feature of that which he depicts as Christianity and resists: the resentment of the masses, the revolt of those who have not fared well,[179] the slave–rebellion in morality which began in Judaism and was completed in Christianity.[180] It is the distinguishing mark of this element that all values are turned upside down by desecularization:[181]

---

176 Cf. the discussion of the sayings of Jesus above in section 4.

177 Cf. Adolf Schlatter, *Die Theologie des Neuen Testaments*, vol. 1 (Calw and Stuttgart: Vereinsbuchhandlung, 1909), 51: "a harsher impression clings to the statements in Jas than to those in the Gospels . . ." Cf. also Holtzmann, *Theologie*, vol. 2, p. 386, n. 1; Weinel, *Biblische Theologie*, section 78.2.

　　[But cf. also Roy Bowen Ward, *The Communal Concern of the Epistle of James*, Unpub. Diss. (Harvard, 1966), who gives special attention precisely to Jas 2:1–13. Ward argues that the emphasis in Jas 2 (hence, in a section where the author's own creative work shows itself the most) is more on the well–being of the elect community (cf. 1:1) than on a personal, practical piety (cf. below on 2:2, 3, n. 64)—Trans.].

178 Cf. Ernst Bertram, *Nietzsche: Versuch einer Mythologie* (Bonn: Bouvier, [8]1965), who strongly emphasizes the importance of this heritage for the "successor of long generations of Christian clergymen," and on the strength of that he ventures to exhibit the polarity in Nietzsche's nature—for the characterization of which he also makes use of the term "double–minded man" ($\dot{\alpha}\nu\dot{\eta}\rho \ \delta\dot{\iota}\psi\nu\chi os$) from Jas.

179 Nietzsche, *The Genealogy of Morals* 1.10; *Antichrist* 43; *The Will to Power* 106.

180 *Beyond Good and Evil* 195 (see above, n. 136); *The Genealogy of Morals* 1.7.

181 *Beyond Good and Evil* 62.

Jas 2:5ff can serve as a typical document of the "Chandala morality" in Nietzsche's sense,[182] and Jas 3:16[183] manifests the completely one-sided evaluation which says, "every *other* principle is simply 'world.'"[184] But Nietzsche had also correctly felt the milieu of our writing when he perceived in Christianity the reaction of the common people and smelled the "wretched plainness and hovel smoke" of their existence.[185] And finally, he was justified in connecting all of this historically with the small Jewish families of the Diaspora, with their "readiness to help, responsibility for each other, with the secret pride they had as the 'elect' which was cloaked in humility, with their secret denial—although without envy—of everything which was uppermost and possessed attraction and power."[186] All of these judgments of Nietzsche regarding Christianity are more characteristic of the ethos of Jas than of Christian piety in general.[187] But even for Jas, the reverse assessment is a valid one, for Christianity never could have become (and ought never to have become) a world religion had it not given expression to "the common people." In Jas they find a spokesman, for the paraenesis is intended to speak—without a personal ring—to all people about their obligations. And here the attitude of the common people is expressed more one-sidedly than in any other early Christian text, since it is dominated by a conscious protest against a different development. Consequently, one may call this ethos typical of early Christianity, but it must not be confused with the religion of early Christianity. For early Christian faith was able to penetrate other depths, and mount other heights, besides the paraenesis found in Jas.

If this is recognized, then it is possible to concede that the protest in Jas against faith without works is not without justification. The heights of Pauline faith are foreign to Jas. He sees only the dangers which dead faith can bring to the daily lives of Christians, his "common people"–Christians, and he addresses himself to these dangers. And in that regard, he is in the right—to the extent to which common people must be permitted to be in the right within the context of a world religion. For the masses must constitute the foundation of a world religion. Therefore, a world religion must accept the responsibility for directing the daily affairs of the masses with clear instructions. Yet it is also intrinsic to a world religion that it provide mankind with great leaders who are able to proclaim encompassing aims in terms which are new and unfamiliar to the masses. Consequently, the conception of the masses which was just mentioned characterizes only one aspect of a world religion, and therefore what Jas has said about faith and works does not represent the final word Christianity has to say on the subject. It is *one* Christian word on the matter, however, and therefore it has its proper place in the New Testament collection.[188]

The same thing is true for the writing of Jas in general. What receives shape within it is Christian ethos; nothing more: it is the Christian ethos which united and held together in the early Christian communities countless people who were of the petty bourgeois and were timorous of the world. It is the Christian spirit which also in subsequent periods has sustained entire generations and classes and fired them to perseverance in the world and to labor in the community. It is in accord with the gospel of Jesus, even though lacking its force and scope; but it is essentially alien to the spirit manifested in the letters of Paul and in the writing of "John." Yet as little as Jas may be compared with such eminent figures, just as certainly do the writings of all of them belong among the classical documents of Christianity. For this juxtaposition symbolizes both the tendency toward heights as well as the expanding breadth within Christianity, and in the coexistence of these two tendencies lies imbedded the mysterious power of Christianity as a world–conquering religion.

---

182 *Antichrist* 45; there 1 Cor 1:20ff is specifically cited; the related passage in Jas 2:5ff could have served his argument just as well.
183 See below in the commentary on 3:16.
184 *Antichrist* 46.
185 *The Will to Power* 115; *Antichrist* 52.
186 *The Will to Power* 114.
187 For criticism with regard to the characterization of Christianity as resentment in bloom, cf. Max Scheler, "Die christliche Moral und das Ressentiment," in his *Abhandlungen und Aufsätze*, vol. 1 (Leipzig: Verlag der Weissen Bücher, 1915), 116–68; however, Scheler does not do justice to Nietzsche's penetrating insight.
188 On the fundamental question, cf. Martin Dibelius, "*Επίγνωσις ἀληθείας*," reprint in *idem*, *Botschaft und*

9. The Lot of the Letter of James

If the examination of the literary relationships of Jas is undertaken with the kind of skepticism especially necessary in this area, then the alleged witnesses from the first and second centuries prove to be misleading.[189] Here and there an acquaintance with Jas could perhaps exist, but nowhere is one forced to assume that Jas was used by another author. Apart from the lack of allusions and quotations, there are some other facts which seem to warrant a skeptical judgment. In the West: Jas is missing in the Muratorian Canon even though the latter does mention Jude and 1 and 2 John. In the East: The fragments of Hegesippus preserved in Eusebius, which otherwise have so much to say about the brother of the Lord,[190] say nothing at all about his writing. Furthermore, in his *Hypotyposeis*, so far as they have been preserved, Clement of Alexandria commented upon only 1 Peter, Jude and 1 and 2 John, and the absence of Jas from this series is corroborated by what Clement seems to know in other passages.[191]

Yet the silence on the part of the witnesses extends even beyond the year A.D. 200. This is certainly true among the Syrians, where according to the *Doctrine of Addai*, according to Aphraates, and according to the Sinai Catalogue there was still no corpus at all of the Catholic Epistles;[192] the Peshitta is the first Syrian witness to vouchsafe the inclusion of Jas, 1 Peter and 1 John, but that did not enable them to gain uncontested authority.[193] The circumstances in the West are debatable. There is that remarkable quotation combining Jas and Jude which is found in Hippolytus.[194] These two, Jas and Jude (among others), are not mentioned by Cyprian as being in the canon, and at least in the traditional text of the Canon Mommsenianus these two are again missing—and just these two.[195] The canon of Pope Damascus I of A.D. 382 and the African synods of around A.D. 400 first accomplished the acceptance of the seven Catholic Epistles.

The earliest incontrovertible quotation of Jas[196] is perhaps offered by the passage from the Pseudo–Clementine tractate *De virginitate* 1.11.4:[197] "Nor did they [i.e., many people] heed what the scripture says: '*Let not many among you be teachers, brethren*, nor let all be prophets. *He who does not transgress in his speech is a perfect man*, able to tame and to subjugate his whole body*' [Jas 3:1f]" (neque attendunt ad id, quod dicit [Scriptura]: *Ne*

Geschichte, vol. 2, ed. Günther Bornkamm (Tübingen: Mohr [Siebeck], 1956), 1–13.

189 See above in section 4.

190 See above in section 2.

191 To be sure, the testimony of both Eusebius and Photius seems to speak to the contrary, since they both assert that Clement commented upon "the Catholic Epistles": Eus., *Hist. eccl.* 6.14.1: "not passing over even the disputed writings, I mean the Epistle of Jude and the remaining Catholic Epistles" (μηδὲ τὰς ἀντιλεγομένας παρελθών, τὴν Ἰούδα λέγω καὶ τὰς λοιπὰς καθολικὰς ἐπιστολάς); Photius, *Bibliotheca cod.* 109 (MPG 103, 384): "the epistles of St. Paul and the Catholic Epistles" (τοῦ θείου Παύλου τῶν ἐπιστολῶν καὶ τῶν καθολικῶν). But in view of the witnesses mentioned above in the text, there are serious objections against taking these statements of Eusebius and Photius literally (as is done by Zahn, *Forschungen*, vol. 3, pp. 150ff; idem, *NT Kanon*, vol. 1, pp. 321ff; and also Max Meinertz, *Der Jakobusbrief und sein Verfasser in Schrift und Überlieferung*, BSF 10, 1–3 [Freiburg: Herder, 1905], 100f). Therefore, they must be understood as imprecise summary statements. It cannot be proven that the information about James the brother of the Lord in Clement's *Hypotyposeis* (preserved in Eusebius; see above, n. 33 and n. 35) must come from a commentary by Clem-

ent on Jas (Adolf Harnack, *Das Neue Testament um das Jahr 200* [Freiburg i. B.: Mohr (Siebeck), 1889], 79f, 85; Johannes Leipoldt, *Geschichte des neutestamentlichen Kanons*, vol. 1 [Leipzig: Hinrichs, 1907], 233; Caspar René Gregory, *Einleitung in das Neue Testament* [Leipzig: Hinrichs, 1909], 311f).

192 Cf. on this Walter Bauer, *Der Apostolos der Syrer in der Zeit von der Mitte des vierten Jahrhunderts bis zur Spaltung der syrischen Kirche* (Giessen: Ricker [Töpelmann], 1903), 40ff, and especially 44ff, regarding alleged points of contact between Ephraem and Jas, points of contact which in fact are totally uncertain.

193 Bauer, *op. cit.* (above, n. 192), 68f.

194 See above, n. 111.

195 On the text and the interpretation of the words *una sola*, cf. Zahn, *NT Kanon*, vol. 1, pp. 324f; Adolf Jülicher, *An Introduction to the New Testament*, tr. Janet Penrose Ward (London: Smith, Elder, & Co., 1904), section 40; Gregory, *Einleitung*, 366f.

196 Meyer, *Rätsel*, 33, n. 8.

197 Text in *Patres apostolici*, ed. Franz Xaver Funk, 3rd edition by Franz Diekamp, vol. 2 (Tübingen: Laupp, 1913), 19f.

multi inter vos sint doctores, fratres, neque omnes sitis prophetae. Qui in verbis suis non praevaricatur, hic homo perfectus est, potens domare et subigere totum corpus suum) [Trans.]. If the document De virginitate actually belongs in the third century,[198] then this text—whose evidence is strengthened by further allusions—witnesses to the use of Jas as a canonical writing at that time in southern Syria or Palestine.

In Origen as well we find definite traces of the acceptance of Jas into the New Testament, although, to be sure, it is not an uncontested acceptance. A series of incontrovertible texts in Origin prove that for his own use he quotes Jas as canonical.[199] He also mentions Jas among the Biblical authors.[200] On the other hand, his scholarly conscience obliges him to admit some doubt regarding Jas (and other writings). He is aware that not all Christian churches have Jas in their New Testament. He probably has this situation in mind when he characterizes the document somewhat cautiously with the phrase, "in the letter of James which is current" ($\dot{\epsilon}\nu$ $\tau\hat{\eta}$ $\phi\epsilon\rho o\mu\acute{\epsilon}\nu\eta$ $'I\alpha\kappa\acute{\omega}\beta o\upsilon$ $\dot{\epsilon}\pi\iota\sigma\tau o\lambda\hat{\eta}$).[201] In his familiar three-fold classification of writings as recognized, spurious, or disputed, Origen evidently assigns Jas to the third class. However, this is more a statistic than his own judgment. He simply intends to establish that other churches did not have Jas, and he explains this lack as being due to doubts on the part of these Christians about the authenticity of Jas, not—as would probably have been correct—as being due to their ignorance of the document's existence.

Further witnesses to Jas, and ones which also come from the third century, are the oldest of those papyrus fragments which contain portions of Jas: P. Oxy. X, 1229 and IX, 1171.[202] These fragments, of course, confirm only that Jas was known and read in Egypt.

Eusebius of Caesarea adopted the classification of Origen, though perhaps not entirely in the same sense, and he counts Jas among the disputed works. Yet it is clear from his own statements that he and his churches harbored no reservations about the letter. Rather, this classification is primarily intended to make allowances for the opinions of others.[203] In the course of the fourth century, then, Jas apparently gained more and more acceptance.

In this history of Jas in the ancient church, a history which for the most part has been traced here in com-

198 On this, cf. Adolf Harnack, "Die pseudoclementinischen Briefe de virginitate und die Entstehung des Mönchthums," SAB (1891): 361–85.

199 In Comm. in Ps. 30 (12, 129 Lommatzsch), Origen quotes Jas 2:26 with the words "according to James" ($\dot{\omega}s$ $\pi\alpha\rho\dot{\alpha}$ $'I\alpha\kappa\acute{\omega}\beta\omega$); and Jas 5:13 in Comm. in Ps. 65 (12, 395 Lommatzsch) with "the apostle says" ($\phi\eta\sigma\grave{\iota}\nu$ $\dot{o}$ $\dot{\alpha}\pi\acute{o}\sigma\tau o\lambda os$); Jas 2:10 in Comm. in Ps. 118 (13, 70 Lommatzsch) with "well is it written" ($\kappa\alpha\lambda\hat{\omega}s$ $\gamma\acute{\epsilon}\gamma\rho\alpha\pi\tau\alpha\iota$); Jas 4:10 in Comm. in Ps. 118 (13, 100 Lommatzsch) with "for James says" ($\phi\eta\sigma\grave{\iota}$ $\gamma\grave{\alpha}\rho$ $'I\acute{\alpha}\kappa\omega\beta os$); Jas 5:13 in Comm. in Ps. 118 (13, 106 Lommatzsch) with "he says" ($\phi\eta\sigma\acute{\iota}\nu$); Jas 1:13 in Selecta in Exodum 15 (8, 324 Lommatzsch) with "it was said" ($\dot{\epsilon}\lambda\acute{\epsilon}\chi\theta\eta$); Jas 1:17 in Comm. in Joh. Frag. 6 (p. 488 Preuschen) with the comment, "which I think the scripture says" ($\ddot{o}\pi\epsilon\rho$ $\dot{\eta}\gamma o\hat{\upsilon}\mu\alpha\iota$ $\epsilon\dot{\iota}\rho\hat{\eta}\sigma\theta\alpha\iota$ $\dot{\upsilon}\pi\grave{o}$ $\tau\hat{\eta}s$ $\gamma\rho\alpha\phi\hat{\eta}s$); Comm. in Joh. Frag. 126 (p. 570 Preuschen): "as James the Apostle says" ($\kappa\alpha\theta\acute{\omega}s$ $\phi\eta\sigma\iota$ $'I\acute{\alpha}\kappa\omega\beta os$ $\dot{o}$ $\dot{\alpha}\pi\acute{o}\sigma\tau o\lambda os$), and so on. The quotations preserved only in Latin are cited by Meinertz, Jakobusbrief, 109, n. 2.

200 Hom. in Gen. 13.2 (8, 244 Lommatzsch); Hom. in Jos. 7.1 (11, 63 Lommatzsch).

201 Comm. in Joh. 19.23.152 (Preuschen): "If faith is claimed, and yet it has no works, then this sort of faith is 'barren,' as we read in the letter of James which is current" ($\dot{\epsilon}\grave{\alpha}\nu$ $\delta\grave{\epsilon}$ $\lambda\acute{\epsilon}\gamma\eta\tau\alpha\iota$ $\mu\grave{\epsilon}\nu$ $\pi\acute{\iota}\sigma\tau\iota s$, $\chi\omega\rho\grave{\iota}s$ $\delta\grave{\epsilon}$ $\ddot{\epsilon}\rho\gamma\omega\nu$ $\tau\upsilon\gamma\chi\acute{\alpha}\nu\eta$, $\nu\epsilon\kappa\rho\acute{\alpha}$ $\dot{\epsilon}\sigma\tau\iota\nu$ $\dot{\eta}$ $\tau o\iota\alpha\acute{\upsilon}\tau\eta$, $\dot{\omega}s$ $\dot{\epsilon}\nu$ $\tau\hat{\eta}$ $\phi\epsilon\rho o\mu\acute{\epsilon}\nu\eta$ $'I\alpha\kappa\acute{\omega}\beta o\upsilon$ $\dot{\epsilon}\pi\iota\sigma\tau o\lambda\hat{\eta}$ $\dot{\alpha}\nu\acute{\epsilon}\gamma\nu\omega\mu\epsilon\nu$) [Trans.]. Because of its context, the passage in Comm. in Joh. 20.10.66 (Preuschen): "a point which would not be conceded by those who accept the statement that 'Faith apart from works is barren'" ($o\dot{\upsilon}$ $\sigma\upsilon\gamma\chi\omega\rho\eta\theta\grave{\epsilon}\nu$ $\dot{\alpha}\nu$ $\dot{\upsilon}\pi\grave{o}$ $\tau\hat{\omega}\nu$ $\pi\alpha\rho\alpha\delta\epsilon\chi o\mu\acute{\epsilon}\nu\omega\nu$ $\tau\grave{o}$ $\Pi\acute{\iota}\sigma\tau\iota s$ $\chi\omega\rho\grave{\iota}s$ $\ddot{\epsilon}\rho\gamma\omega\nu$ $\nu\epsilon\kappa\rho\acute{\alpha}$ $\dot{\epsilon}\sigma\tau\iota\nu$), should probably be considered a rather harmless comment as far as the history of the canon is concerned. It is not clear why in a passage in which Origen mentions the brothers James and Jude together (Comm. in Matt. 10.17 [3, 46 Lommatzsch]) it is only the latter whom he mentions as the author of a letter. Could it be that Origen did not ascribe the Letter of James to the brother of Jesus? In view of the quotations from it which he sometimes introduces with rather solemn formulae, it is not plausible that he considered the letter to be pseudonymous.

202 See below in section 10 of the Introduction.

203 Eus., Hist. eccl. 2.23.24f: "Such is the story of James, whose is said to be the first of the Epistles called Catholic. It is to be observed that its authenticity is denied, since few of the ancients quote it, as is also the case with the Epistle called Jude's, which is itself one of the seven called Catholic; nevertheless we

pletely or partially negative witnesses, there are two striking things: First, Jas was recognized in the West about 150 years[204] later than it was in the East (with the exception of the Syrians, who rejected the Catholic Epistles in general). Second, even in the East there is not much evidence that Jas was accepted into the canon—indeed, that it enjoyed any sort of wide circulation—prior to Origen. This late and gradual emergence of Jas in the history of the canon[205] requires explanation. Harnack attempts to give an explanation with his hypothesis that the prescript is secondary:[206] the document existed originally as an anonymous writing and, consequently, did not achieve respect. However, a play on words in 1:1 and 1:2 firmly connects these two verses, making this hypothesis unlikely from the outset. Of course, it is possible to point out that the Catholic Epistles were brief, that copies of them had less value and, as a result, it is possible that they were less frequently copied or were more likely to be overlooked.[207] But these observations apply to all the Catholic Epistles and do not explain the unkind fate which fell upon the longer Epistle of James even more than upon the shorter Epistle of Jude. However, the

assumption that Jas was at first current only among Jewish–Christians because of its sender, its "address" and its contents[208] is very doubtful. Even if Jas is supposed actually to have originated in Jewish–Christian circles,[209] the Gentile–Christians were not so reticent about appropriating Jewish (or Jewish–Christian) paraenesis.

The solution to the puzzle must be sought precisely in the unique position which James occupied as a purely paraenetic text. The absence of frequent quotations can perhaps—though only to a certain degree— be regarded as fortuitous, since a paraenesis contains fewer religious and theological proof–texts than do other writings. But in addition to that, the paraenetic character of Jas accounts for its late and gradual dissemination and its initially uncertain position in the New Testament. For paraenetic tradition is an evolving and growing thing. Its materials must be expanded and applied if it is to be adequate for the needs of new generations. Each new formation and arrangement of such sayings material means the antiquating of previous compilations. To a certain extent, therefore, every new form of the paraenesis cloaks the old form.

---

know that these letters have been used publicly with the rest in most churches" (τοιαῦτα καὶ τὰ κατὰ Ἰάκωβον, οὗ ἡ πρώτη τῶν ὀνομαζομένων καθολικῶν ἐπιστολῶν εἶναι λέγεται· ἰστέον δὲ ὡς νοθεύεται μέν, οὐ πολλοὶ γοῦν τῶν παλαιῶν αὐτῆς ἐμνημόνευσαν, ὡς οὐδὲ τῆς λεγομένης Ἰούδα, μιᾶς καὶ αὐτῆς οὔσης τῶν ἑπτὰ λεγομένων καθολικῶν· ὅμως δ' ἴσμεν καὶ ταύτας μετὰ τῶν λοιπῶν ἐν πλείσταις δεδημοσιευμένης ἐκκλησίαις). In *Hist. eccl.* 3.25.3, Eusebius includes Jas among the disputed writings. Reference is made to this judgment of Eusebius at the beginning of the Catena commentary on Jas, as well as in the beginning of the commentary by Ishoʿdad (*The Commentaries of Ishoʿdad of Merv, bishop of Hadatha [c. 850 A.D.] in Syriac and English*, ed. and tr. Margaret Dunlop Gibson, vol. 4, Horae Semiticae 10 [Cambridge: University Press, 1913]).

204 Adolf von Harnack made the following casual remark to Dibelius in a postcard dated January 29, 1930: ". . . Besides, it would be a rewarding task to show how much the Letter of James was considered a godsend (in spite of and including chapter 2) in the West, once it had become known. If my admittedly deficient memory serves me correctly, the letter immediately had great success in seizing the hearts of Westerners. The study might begin with 'Augustine and the Letter of James.'" Such a study

is now provided by Paulus Bergauer, *Der Jakobusbrief bei Augustinus und die damit verbundenen Probleme der Rechtfertigungslehre* (Wien: Herder, 1962). Statistics which Bergauer compiles (p. 43) from Augustine's *Expositions of the Psalms*, his *Epistles*, his *Sermons* on texts from the Old Testament, and his *City of God* reveal that though Jas is not quoted by Augustine as copiously as are the major Pauline letters, nevertheless it is cited comparatively more often than 1 and 2 Thessalonians, Titus, Philemon, Hebrews, 2 Peter, 2 and 3 John, and Jude.

205 Whoever is less skeptical than I am about the alleged attestations mentioned above toward the end of section 4 has to construct a very fluctuating development (emergence, disappearance, emergence), which is not probable *a priori*. This applies, for example, to Meinertz, *Jakobusbrief*, 129, who hypothesizes that in the beginning Jas was highly regarded in the West but then later was forgotten.

206 See above, n. 46.

207 Gregory, *Einleitung*, 276.

208 Gregory, *Einleitung*, 277.

209 But see above, section 3.

One does not disseminate older paraenetic writings; rather one passes on (and in doing so alters) *their content.*[210] That began to change only when the unqualified veneration of the "apostolic" records gained the ascendency in the church. Then the decisive question was whether or not the document bore a classical name and whether or not this authorship was undisputed. If so, then it was entitled to dissemination and authority. And this, it seems to me, was the lot of Jas. At first, its paraenesis—in its terse, unexpanded style and with its futile opposition to the entrance of the rich into the church, an entrance which in the meantime had been accomplished[211]—quickly became obsolete. But then the document acquired respect because of the great authority of its patron. Certainly no one in the early church stirred up a controversy as to its authenticity. The allusion to such a controversy by Origen and Eusebius was evidently an effort on their part to explain the limited circulation of the letter.[212]

It is impossible to say how large a role was played in the earliest history of Jas by doubts about the apostolicity of this James. As was mentioned above,[213] Jerome identified the brother of the Lord with the son of Alphaeus. Where that opinion prevailed there was no hesitation about apostolicity. The authority of the letter and the apostolicity of its author, which together were accepted in the West during the Middle Ages,[214]

were together challenged by the criticism of the sixteenth century, a criticism which is so well–known because of Luther's energetic participation.[215] By and large the criticism was a humanistic one. On stylistic grounds, Erasmus doubted the authorship by the brother of the Lord,[216] and Luther took up this doubt because he wanted to shake the authority of Jas for dogmatic reasons.[217] He set forth his own arguments in 1522 in the "Preface to the New Testament"[218] and in the "Preface to the Epistles of St. James and St. Jude."[219] The statement about the "epistle of straw" is found in the first of these.[220] In the second he set out in detail his arguments against the apostolicity of Jas. The point of departure for his criticism of the epistle is the recognition that "in the first place it is flatly against St. Paul and all the rest of Scripture in ascribing justification to works."[221] To this purely religious argument is added the religio–historical consideration which Luther elsewhere emphasized, viz., that the letter does not contain enough of that which is specifically Christian.[222] There is also a literary argument—the relationship with 1 Peter was interpreted by Luther as dependency—and a stylistic argument, namely the absence of continuity.[223] But these arguments evidently only confirmed for him the verdict which his religious perception had long since expressed. Modern historical reflection needs neither to defend nor to deplore these

---

210 The adaptation of dominical sayings to changing circumstances, clearly perceptible in the tradition, shows that in paraenesis (for even the dominical sayings were collected at first for paraenetic purposes) the dominant concern initially was a practical one, involving the utility of the sayings. Cf. Dibelius, *From Tradition to Gospel*, 242f.

211 See above, toward the end of section 6.

212 Cf. above, in this section.

213 See above, n. 29.

214 On the Byzantine witnesses, see Meinertz, *Jakobusbrief*, 193–203, and on the Western witnesses, 203–15.

215 On what follows, cf. in addition to Meinertz, *Jakobusbrief*, 216–36, also Kawerau, 359ff.

216 Erasmus, *Opera Omnia*, vol. 6 (Leiden: Vander, 1705; reprint London: Gregg Press, 1962), col. 1038 (at the end of his commentary on Jas): "For neither does it seem to bear anywhere that apostolic majesty and dignity, nor the large number of Hebraisms one would expect from James, who was bishop of Jerusalem."

217 In the Leipzig Debate Jas 2:26 had been used against Luther. He then defends himself in the *Resolutiones super propositionibus Lipsiae disputatis*: "The style of that epistle is far beneath the apostolic majesty, nor does it compare in any way with that of Paul" (*D. Martin Luthers Werke: Kritische Gesammtausgabe*, vol. 2 [Weimar: Böhlau, 1884], 425).

218 English translation in *Luther's Works*, vol. 35, p. 362.

219 *Ibid.*, 395–7.

220 After commending those books "that show you Christ" (John, 1 John, Romans, Galatians, Ephesians, 1 Peter), Luther says, "Therefore St. James' epistle is really an epistle of straw, compared to these others, for it has nothing of the nature of the gospel about it" (*Luther's Works*, vol. 35, p. 362).

221 *Ibid.*, 396.

222 "In the second place its purpose is to teach Christians, but in all this long teaching it does not once mention the Passion, the resurrection, or the Spirit of Christ" (*Luther's Works*, vol. 35, p. 396). That is evidence against its apostolicity, since "it is the office of a true apostle to preach of the Passion and resur-

judgments. Rather it understands that out of the depth of his experience of faith Luther had to criticize this Christianity of righteousness,[224] even though he was in no way blind to its ethos.[225] However, it is precisely historical criticism which will have to guard against allowing Luther's essentially religious criticism of the apostolicity of Jas to become a factor in answering the question of authorship.

Luther, by the way, thought that the son of Zebedee was the author: "And yet, in point of time, St. James was put to death by Herod in Jerusalem, before St.

Peter."[226] Thus Luther handed on a tradition which is only meagerly attested, namely in Spain where there was national interest at stake in assigning Jas to the saint of Santiago de Compostela, i.e., the son of Zebedee,[227] and then in Dante who probably adopted this Spanish tradition.[228] It is not known, however, how Luther learned of this tradition.

rection and office of Christ." Cf. Luther's remark in *Table Talk* (*Luther's Works*, vol. 54, p. 424 modified): "It contains not a syllable about Christ. Not once does it mention Christ, except at the beginning. I maintain that some Jew wrote it who probably heard about Christ but never encountered him."

223 He says that James "throws things together so chaotically that it seems to me he must have been some good, pious man, who took a few sayings from the disciples of the apostle and tossed them off on paper. Or it may perhaps have been written by someone on the basis of his preaching" (*Luther's Works*, vol. 35, p. 397). Cf. the passage from *Table Talk* mentioned above in n. 222: "Besides, there is no order or method in the epistle. Now he discusses clothing and then he writes about wrath and is constantly shifting from one to the other" (*Luther's Works*, vol. 54, p. 425).

224 Cf. above in section 8.

225 "Though this epistle of St. James was rejected by the ancients, I praise it and consider it a good book, because it sets up no doctrines of men but vigorously promulgates the law of God" (*Luther's Works*, vol. 35, p. 395). At the conclusion of this Preface to Jas (p. 397) he says, "for there are otherwise many good sayings in him."

226 *Luther's Works*, vol. 35, p. 397.

227 Isidore of Seville, *De ortu et obitu patrum* 71.125 (MPG 83, 151): "James the son of Zebedee . . . wrote to the twelve tribes scattered among the nations, and he also preached the gospel to the people in Spain and places in the West" (Iacobus filius Zebedaei . . . duodecim tribus quae sunt in dispersione gentium scripsit atque Hispaniae et occidentalium locorum gentibus evangelium praedicavit) [Trans.]; the genuineness of the writing has been challenged precisely because of this passage. Cf. also the *Liturgia Mozarabica*, MPL 85, 540f and notes, and the references given by Henschen in *Acta Sanctorum Maii*, ed. Godfried Henschen and Daniel Papenbroech (Antwerp: Knobb, 1680), 22c, d, and by Meinertz, *Jakobusbrief*, 212, n. 8.

228 In the *Divine Comedy* 25.17f, James is presented as the Baron on whose account people are drawn to (Spanish) Galicia (where Santiago is located). This James is addressed in 25.29f (ET by I. C. Wright, *The Divine Comedy of Dante Alighieri* [London: Bell, 1883], 407ff):

O glorious soul, by whom the riches stowed
In this our palace are described!

That is probably an allusion to Jas 1:5. And in 25.67ff, Dante says to James:

'Hope,' said I, 'is an expectation sure
Of future glory—the effect of Grace
And previous merit . . .'

But for this understanding of hope Dante confesses that he must thank—next to the psalmist of Ps 9:11 —this same James (the saint of Galicia, hence, the son of Zebedee); and so he addresses him in 25.76ff:

His drops on thy Epistle thou didst then
On me sprinkle, that, embued with these,
To others I dispense the precious rain.

Regarding the question of the source of this conception of Dante's, Alfred Bassermann in Schwetzingen points out to me first of all the possibility that Dante is dependent upon Isidore (*Paradiso* 8.67ff goes back to Isidore, *Etymologiae* 14.8.14, MPL 82, 522); but secondly, and above all, Bassermann has called my attention to Dante's teacher Brunetto Latini, who in 1260 was a Florentine envoy to Alfonso X of Castile and who possibly adopted the Spanish tradition while he was there. At any rate, in Brunetto Latini's *Trésor* (written after the stay in Spain) we find the statement: "This James wrote an epistle to the twelve tribes which are in the dispersion in various lands"; admittedly, in manuscript F, and consequently in the edition by P. Chabaille, *Li livres dou Trésor par Brunetto Latini*, Collection de documents inédits sur l'histoire de France (Paris: Imprimerie Impériale, 1863), 69, this statement is found in the section on James the son of Alphaeus (1.67); but in all the other manuscripts it is found in 1.70, which deals with James the son of Zebedee

Precisely because Luther's judgment regarding Jas[229] was a matter of religious criticism, it is understandable that he could not be confused by Karlstadt's counter–arguments and Melanchthon's attempt to reconcile the two positions.[230] Examples of his criticism from a later period are his commentary on Genesis with the phrase "as James raves" (ut Iacobus delirat),[231] and the spirited marginal comments in his personal copy of the New Testament.[232] Many of his adherents followed him in this. Andreas Althamer, in his first, Latin commentary on Jas in 1527, made the most caustic judgment (he was far more conciliatory in the second, German edition of 1533). But Jas was also criticized by opponents of the Reformation.[233] Thomas de Vio (Cajetan) questions the authenticity of the letter, calling attention to, among other things, the secular form of the letter's greeting. He also denies that a reference to extreme unction is found in Jas 5:14,[234] whereas Protestant opponents of the *Augsburg Interim* attack Jas precisely because this sacrament is vouchsafed by that passage.[235] For Catholics, all doubt about the letter was allayed by the Council of Trent which unreservedly includes Jas in its index of canonical writings. And for Lutherans, the *Formula of Concord* harmonized the contraditions between Jas and Paul in the manner of Melanchthon's *Apology*.[236]

The new historical criticism of the Age of the Enlightenment was, for the most part, less concerned with the problem of authenticity than with the question of the "brother of the Lord." Now it became possible to express unabashedly the opinion that it was a question of the physical children of Joseph and Mary, and Herder was the most eminent spokesman for this position.[237] There are three important stages through which the critical research of the nineteenth century passed. In 1826, de Wette[238] declared the letter to be spurious, even using linguistic arguments to support his contention that James, the brother of Jesus, could

---

(Chabaille, p. 71; cf. p. 69, n. 4), and this is also the case in the Italian translation *Il Tesoro di Brunetto Latini*, tr. Bono Giamboni, ed. Luigi Gaiter, vol. 1 (Bologna: Romagnoli, 1878), 251.

229 In his lecture on the Letter to the Galatians (ed. Hans von Schubert, *Luthers Vorlesung über den Galaterbrief 1516/17*, Abhandlungen der Heidelberger Akademie der Wissenschaften, Philosophisch–historische Klasse 5 [Heidelberg: Winter, 1918], 37f), Luther proposes Jerome's view regarding Jas (see above in section 2), but without mentioning the letter. At that period, Luther seems not yet to have thought so critically about the letter, for in his lecture on the Letter to the Romans in 1515/16 (ed. Johannes Ficker, *Anfänge reformatorischer Bibelauslegung*, vol. 1, part 2 [Leipzig: Dieterich, 1908], 84f) he still treats Paul and Jas as though they are in harmony: Paul is speaking of "works of the Law," Jas is speaking of "works of faith."

230 On Karlstadt, see Kawerau, 361. Melanchthon, in the first edition of his *Loci Communes*, had already made use of the distinction between a living and a dead faith: Jas is opposing only the latter, but a living faith justifies: "That is indeed a living faith which spends itself in works" (trans. Charles Leander Hill, *The Loci Communes of Philip Melanchthon* [Boston: Meador, 1944], 207).

231 *Luther's Works*, vol. 4, p. 134.

232 Cf. the collection of these in Joh. Georg Walch, ed. *Dr. Martin Luthers Sämmtliche Schriften*, vol. 9 (St. Louis, Mo.: Concordia, ²1893), 1888ff, and W.

Walther, "Zu Luthers Ansicht über den Jakobusbrief," *ThStKr* 66 (1893): 595–8. For example, on Jas 1:25 Luther remarks, "You see, he teaches nothing about faith, only mere law"; on 2:12: "Oh what a chaos!"; on the comparison in 2:26, which is also criticized in the *Table Talk* passage mentioned above: "O, what a nice parable; freedom, you can turn away," and on 3:1: "Indeed; you should have observed that yourself!" [Trans.].

233 On the other hand, Luther's criticism drew Catholic defenders of Jas out onto the battlefield, such as the physician Philipp Mencel, who composed in Latin a "Poem on the canonical Epistle of St. James, which Luther called a straw epistle" (printed in the Preface of the commentary by Petrus Stewart, *In canonicam D. Jacobi epistolam brevis commentarius* [Ingolstadt: Sartorius, 1591]; printed again by M. Meinertz in *Der Katholik*, series 3, 27 [1903], 191f).

234 Thomas de Vio Caietanus, *Epistulae Pauli et aliorum apostolorum ad Graecam veritatem castigate* (Paris: apud J. Badium Ascensius, J. Parvum & J. Roigny, 1532), 207G and 212B.

235 Cf. Kawerau, 368f.

236 *Solida declaratio* 3.42f.

237 Herder, 476: "Was it not the angel who permitted the marriage of Joseph, indeed, *commanded* it in the name of God: Was God . . . a less capable judge in matters of propriety than are we? But of course, neither God, nor the angel, nor the evangelists were —monks."

238 W. M. L. de Wette, *Lehrbuch der historisch–kritischen*

not have written such fluent Greek. In 1835, Kern extensively supported this same position,[239] though he later argued for the authenticity of the letter in his 1838 commentary.[240] The second stage of the criticism was reached when Ferdinand Christian Baur and his students assigned the letter a late but secure place in their outline of early Christianity.[241] Now the letter was taken to be a document of post–Pauline Christianity with a mediating Jewish–Christian character. Finally, the hypothesis of Spitta and Massebieau[242] constituted the third stage. Even though his thesis found little agreement, Spitta's work nevertheless stimulated among later commentators a new examination of the problems,[243] and through the wealth of material which he adduced he significantly advanced the interpretation of Jas.

10. The Text
a) The Witnesses[244]

P[23] *P. Oxy.* X, 1229; Urbana, Ill. (early 3rd cent.):[245] Jas 1:10–12, 15–18. In accord with their provenance, both this papyrus fragment and the others listed below rep-

P[20] resent for the most part the "Egyptian" text–type.[246]

P. Oxy. IX, 1171; Princeton (3rd cent.): Jas 2:19–3:2; 3:4–9 (fragmentary).

B (δ 1)[247] Vaticanus; Rome (4th cent.). This is undoubtedly the best witness of the best text–type, viz., the Egyptian text–type; but that does not mean that it is infallible. Apart from the scribal errors, it also offers in 4:14 a reading which is obviously an emendation. In addition, the cases where B has peculiarities in common with the valuable Latin manuscript Corbeiensis (= *ff*) arouse suspicion (e.g., 2:3, 4; 5:20), or at least uncertainty (cf. 2:19).

ℵ (δ 2) Sinaiticus; now in London; until 1933, in Leningrad (4th cent.). This manuscript is quite closely related to B and is a very valuable witness, but it manifests more obvious mistakes than does B. In addition, traces of the so–called "Koine" text-type[248] are found in it (2:3; 2:20); and among its peculiarities are readings which are clearly

---

Einleitung in die kanonischen Bücher des Neuen Testaments (Berlin: Reimer, 1826).

239 Friedrich Heinrich Kern, "Der Charakter und Ursprung des Briefs Jakobi," *TZTh* (1835, 2. Heft): 3–132.

240 Friedrich Heinrich Kern, *Der Brief Jakobi* (Tübingen: Fues, 1838).

241 Ferdinand Christian Baur, *Paul: The Apostle of Jesus Christ*, 2nd edition by Eduard Zeller, tr. A. Menzies, vol. 2 (London: Williams & Norgate, 1875), 297ff; Schwegler, pp. 413ff.

242 See above in section 3.

243 Beyschlag, von Soden, Mayor.

244 A presentation of the value of these witnesses for the textual criticism of the entire New Testament cannot be given here. In what follows I intend no more than to sharpen the reader's vision for such observations related to the text of Jas as are significant for the character of the witnesses. [Incorporated into the main text of the English translation of this section are revisions noted on p. 86, n. 1 of the 11th German edition. This includes the listing of two additional papyrus fragments (P[54] and P[74]), and the reclassification of two witnesses as parchment framents (**0166** and **0178**) rather than as papyrus fragments. In accordance with what seems to have been Dibelius' intention, the Greek witnesses are

listed here in approximate chronological order—Trans.]

245 [This earlier dating of P[23] is proposed by K. Aland, "Neue neutestamentliche Papyri II," *NTS* 9 (1963): 307. A later dating, in the 4th century, had been suggested in Bernard P. Grenfell and Arthur S. Hunt, *The Oxyrhynchus Papyri*, part 10 (London: Egypt Exploration Fund, 1914), 16—Trans.].

246 See below in part (b).

247 In the parentheses are the manuscript designations used by Hermann Freiherr von Soden, *Die Schriften des Neuen Testaments in ihrer ältesten erreichbaren Textgestalt* (Göttingen: Vandenhoeck & Ruprecht, 1902–13). The designations with α (= ἀπόστολος) appear in von Soden's apparatus without the letter, so that *H*[74] means codex α 74, which represents the text of recension *H* (i.e., the Egyptian type).

248 See below in part (b).

corrections (3:6; 4:4), as well as a slip into Hellenistic Greek so distinct as in 5:10 (καλοκἀγαθίας instead of κακοπαθείας).

A (δ 4) Alexandrinus; London (5th cent.). The importance of this manuscript is increased if one is not inclined to rely without further ado upon the agreement of B and ℵ. Thus careful consideration must be given those instances where, as in 5:3, A agrees with other witnesses of the "Egyptian" text against B and ℵ (but see also 5:4). More problematic, but at the same time more characteristic for A, are the instances where A agrees with a Latin version.[249]

C (δ 3) Codex Ephraemi rescriptus; Paris (5th cent.). Treatises of Ephraem were later written over the erased text of this manuscript. C contains the text of Jas only up to the expression "you wage war" (πολεμεῖτε) in 4:2. It is a valuable witness of the "Egyptian" text, with traces of the Koine text as well as other peculiarities (cf. 3:17).

0166 Fragment of a parchment majuscule;[250] Heidelberg (5th cent.): Jas 1:11.

0173 *P. Greci e Latini* I, 5;[251] Florence (5th cent.): Jas 1:25–27.

P⁵⁴ *P. Princeton* 15, Pap. L III (1);[252] Princeton (5th cent.): Jas 2:16–18, 22–26; 3:2–4. The text follows B ℵ C for the most part.

P⁷⁴ *P. Bodm.* 17;[253] Geneva (7th cent.): Jas

1:1–6, 8–19, 21–23, 25; 1:27–2:15, 18–22; 2:25–3:1, 5–6, 10–12, 14; 3:17–4:8, 11–14; 5:1–3, 7–9, 12–14, 19–20. The text displays a close kinship to A, although it also contains many special readings.

Ψ (δ 6) Athos (8th/9th cent.)

33 (δ 48) Paris (9th cent.). This is the most valuable of the minuscules,[254] and is related to minuscule 326 (Oxford). Both 33 and Ψ represent in general the "Egyptian" text, with certain deviations in the direction of the "Koine" text.

K ($A^{\pi\rho1}$ and I^1) Moscow (9th cent.): text with catena.[255] This text is of the "Koine"–type.

L (α 5) Rome (9th cent.). L is another representative of the "Koine" text.

P (α 3) Leningrad (9th cent.). This is another palimpsest, i.e., the original text has been erased and the parchment used to copy the commentary of Euthalius on Acts and the Pauline letters. P offers the Koine text very frequently, although it also often follows the Egyptian witnesses (so that von Soden grouped it with the latter).

Other minuscules which will be frequently cited are:

1739 (α 78) Athos (10th cent.). 1739 is of great importance for textual criticism because of the relationship between its Pauline text and that of Origen.[256]

1175 (α 74) Patmos (11th cent.).

249 Cf. Adolf von Harnack, *Beiträge zur Einleitung in das Neue Testament VII: Zur Revision der Prinzipien der neutestamentlichen Textkritik* (Leipzig: Hinrichs, 1916), 125, 128, n. 1.

250 Published in Adolf Deissmann, ed., *Die Septuaginta–Papyri und andere altchristliche Texte*, Veröffentlichungen aus der Heidelberger Papyrus–Sammlung 1 (Heidelberg: Winter, 1905), 85.

251 *Papiri Greci e Latini*, vol. 1, Pubblicazioni della società italiana per la ricerca dei Papiri greci e latini in Egitto (Firenze: Seeber, 1912), no. 5.

252 In Edmund Harris Kase, Jr., ed., *Papyri in the Princeton University Collections*, vol. 2 (Princeton: University Press, 1936), pp. 1–3, no. 15. Cf. Georg Maldfeld and Bruce M. Metzger, "Detailed List of the Greek Papyri of the New Testament," *JBL* 68 (1949): 368 (German version of this list, somewhat

revised, in Georg Maldfeld, "Die griechischen Handschriftenbruchstücke des Neues Testamentes auf Papyrus," *ZNW* 42 [1949]: 228–53).

253 In Rodolphe Kasser, ed., *Papyrus Bodmer XVII: Actes des Apôtres, Epîtres de Jacques, Pierre, Jean et Jude* (Cologny-Genève: Bibliothèque Bodmer, 1961), 211–28.

254 For the minuscules—of which I mention only a few in the commentary, and never those with the Koine text—I use the designations of Caspar René Gregory, *Die griechischen Handschriften des Neuen Testaments* (Leipzig: Hinrichs, 1908).

255 On the catenae and scholia, see the Bibliography at the end of this commentary.

256 Cf. Ed. Freiherr von der Goltz, *Eine textkritische Arbeit des zehnten bzw. sechsten Jahrhunderts, herausgegeben nach einem Kodex des Athosklosters Lawra*, TU

81   (α 162) London (1044 A.D.).[257]
sah   Sahidic or Upper Egyptian version.
boh   Bohairic or Lower Egyptian version.
arm   Armenian version.[258]
aeth   Ethiopic version.

I will designate the Syriac versions with:

sy^vg   The Syriac church Bible (hence the symbol stands for *Syra vulgata*), the so–called Peshitta (beginning of 5th cent.).[259]

sy^hl   The so–called *Syra harclensis*, i.e., the revision of the so–called Philoxenian version (beginning of 6th cent.; now lost to us) by Thomas of Harkel (Heraclea; 7th cent.). It is valuable because it approximates the Greek as closely as possible, and because its preparation involved the comparison of Greek manuscripts of various types (see above, n. 258).

Special interest, and therefore frequent mention in the commentary, is due the Latin versions of Jas. To be sure, because of the late recognition of Jas in the West, these versions are not so ancient as Old Latin versions of other parts of the New Testament, but still they are frequently of value for textual criticism as well as exegesis. Each of the three Old Latin witnesses offers a peculiar text:

ff   Corbeiensis; Leningrad.[260]

s   Bobbiensis; Vienna.[261] This is a palimpsest which is scarcely legible.

m   This sign is used for a work which is preserved in several manuscripts: Pseudo–Augustine, *Liber de divinis scripturis sive speculum*, a collection of biblical proof–texts.[262]

vulg   The mutual relation of the three texts just mentioned, as well as their relationship to the "Vulgate" of Jerome, is a problem which still has not been fully researched.[263] The so–called African text seems to be represented by *m*, while *ff* and *s* seem to offer the European text. As Harnack has shown,[264] vulg essentially offers a revision of the *s*-text. The quotations of Jas found in Priscillian,[265] often agree with *m*. Otherwise, there are only isolated instances where earlier patristic quotations come into consideration for the textual criticism of Jas, which is not

17, 4 (Leipzig: Hinrichs, 1899); cf. there also the most important passages from Jas, on p. 22.

257 On this, cf. Brooke Foss Westcott and Fenton John Anthony Hort, *The New Testament in the Original Greek* (Cambridge and London: MacMillan, 1881), in the "Introduction and Appendix by the Editors," sections 211 and 212.

258 A Latin translation of the Syriac and Armenian versions of the text of Jas is found in Louis Leloir, "Traduction latine des versions syriaques et arméniennes de l'Épître de Jacques," *Le Muséon* 83 (1970): 189–208.

259 That the heading to the Catholic Epistles in the first printed version of sy^vg (Vienna, 1555) designates James, Peter, and John as witnesses to the transfiguration—hence, identifying James as the son of Zebedee—is presumably the contribution of the editors and not the ancient manuscripts; cf. Zahn, *Introduction*, vol. 1, section 5, n. 3.

260 Printed in Mayor and in Johannes Evang. Belser, *Die Epistel des heiligen Jakobus* (Freiburg: Herder, 1909), as well as in Wordsworth, "The Corbey St. James," 113ff (on the thesis of Wordsworth, cf. above in section 5, n. 128). Cf. below in the commentary on 2:18; 3:5; 4:5; 4:14; and 5:2. At the conclusion of the manuscript Jas is called the "son of Zebedee" (filius Zaebedei).

261 The deciphered portions are printed in Henry J. White, ed., *Portions of the Acts of the Apostles, of the Epistle of St. James, and of the First Epistle of St. Peter from the Bobbio Palimpsest (s)*, Old Latin Biblical Texts 4 (Oxford: Clarendon, 1897), and in Josef Bick, ed., *Wiener Palimpseste. Part 1: Cod. Palat. Vindobonensis 16, olim Bobbiensis*, Sitzungsberichte der Kais. Akademie der Wissenschaften in Wien, Philosophisch-Historische Klasse, 159, 7 (Wien, Hölder, 1908), 72ff.

262 Aurelius Augustinus, *Liber qui appellatur speculum et liber de divinis scripturis sive speculum*, ed. Franz Weihrich, Corpus Scriptorum Ecclesiasticorum Latinorum 12 (Vienna: Geroldi, 1887); the passages from Jas are also printed in Mayor.

263 Cf. W. Sanday, "Some Further Remarks on the Corbey St. James (*ff*)," *Studia Biblica* 1 (Oxford: Clarendon, 1885), 233–65; von Soden, *Schriften*, part 1, 1883ff; Harnack, *op. cit.* (above, n. 249), 111ff.

264 Harnack, *op. cit.* (above, n. 249), 111ff.

265 Printed in Mayor.

surprising in view of the history of the letter.[266]

b) Problems

All of the texts which are available to us in manuscripts of the New Testament are texts of the Bible, not copies of the original. Therefore, they do not represent the exact wording of Jas at the time it was published or circulated as an individual document, but rather the text which was in use in the churches after Jas had been accepted into the canon. If one reconstructs the archetype behind a number of manuscripts by observing their points of agreement, this archetype still must not be identified right away with the original text; initially one can identify it only as the Bible text of the church, or of one ecclesiastical province. The manuscripts which represent the same, or a similar, text belong to one group and present the same text–type (or: the same "recension"). In dealing with variants, one must always ask whether what is involved are differences between groups—hence, differences between the texts of individual ecclesisatical provinces—or whether it is a question of peculiarities within individual manuscripts.

The text–critical research of recent decades has taught us to recognize the following groups, although with varying degrees of certainty:

1) The Syrian or Antiochian type, also known as the Lucian recension or the Koine text (= von Soden's recension K). This is the text which was dominant in the 4th century in Syria, and which constituted the basis for both the Byzantine text of the Middle Ages and the so–called *textus receptus* printed in the West (as well as for Luther's translation). It is represented by the bulk of the witnesses (K L; see above regarding P; most of the minuscules; the later church fathers and the later translations). It is the text–type whose value is most limited, and generally its readings are to be rejected when the other groups unanimously agree against it. Since in most cases this type is clearly recognizable, I do not cite the witnesses which represent it, but rather designate the reading simply as *Koine*.

2) The *Egyptian* or Alexandrian text, or Hesychian recension (= von Soden's H), came into existence in Egypt under the influence of Alexandrian textual criticism. For that reason it is very valuable, although Westcott–Hort's[267] optimistic evaluation of its evidence has undergone a certain restriction through the work of von Soden. Prior to von Soden, the inclination was to accept any agreement of the two oldest Egyptian witnesses, B ℵ, as clearly the correct reading. Now the question must be asked: When other Egyptian witnesses deviate from B and ℵ, who represents the Egyptian text? (cf. Jas 2:3, 10; 4:14; 5:3, 11). On the other hand, even if one does not see the Egyptian text–type purely preserved in B ℵ, still the question must be asked whether they have not occasionally preserved the old, authentic reading, which has been corrected in the texts in use among the churches (cf. 4:13; 5:4, 5, and to a certain extent 1:17). In most cases, I cite only the chief representatives of this group: B ℵ A C Ψ 33, and also 1175 and 81.

3) Westcott and Hort have designated the "Western" text as a third type. In the case of Jas, the Western text would essentially have to be reconstructed upon the basis of the Old Latin version, since what are otherwise its best witnesses—the Old Syriac, the earliest church fathers, the "Western" uncials—are out of consideration as far as Jas is concerned. But in place of the "Western" text von Soden sets forth a recension I, which supposedly originated in Jerusalem and Caesarea. This recension is supposed to be reconstructed upon the basis of Greek manuscripts (with a "Western" text, or one related to it), although in none of them would it be preserved in anything even approximating a pure form. Whether this recension I is actually a homogeneous recension, and how the so–called Western text is to be assessed in comparison with the witnesses to I, are questions which must be characterized as still very debatable even today. In the commentary, I have mentioned all the Latin witnesses (see above) in the case of important passages, and occasionally I have pointed out where there is agreement with the witnesses to von Soden's recension I.

Since the very individuality and provenance of this third group is still debated today, it is all the more

---

266 See above in section 9 of the Introduction. For the Old Latin translations, the Vulgate, and the quotations of Jas in the Latin church fathers, cf. now *Vetus Latina: Die Reste der altlateinischen Bibel*, vol. 26, part 1: *Epistolae Catholicae, Apocalypsis*, ed. Walter Thiele (Freiburg: Herder, 1956), 7–64. The manuscripts

necessary to characterize its assessment in relation to the Egyptian text as an unsolved problem of New Testament textual criticism. Yet it is precisely in the textual criticism of Jas that this question is not so much in the foreground, since the Latin text—in accord with the late canonization of Jas in the West—is not so peculiar here as it is in other New Testament writings. On the whole, the text of Jas which has been handed down is relatively homogeneous. Only in a few passages is the sense of a statement dependent upon the choice one makes between different readings which have been preserved (cf. 1:17; 2:20; 3:3, 6, 8; 4:2; 5:7, 11). In view of the history of Jas,[268] this can come as a surprise to no one. Jas was first accepted into the canon at a time when, in a careful concern for the preservation of the texts, the work of comparing, conserving, and revising them had already been begun. So it is that the transmission of the text of Jas does not manifest the colorful multiplicity of variants which we are accustomed to find elsewhere in the New Testament, especially in the Gospels.

Yet one must not rejoice over this picture too quickly. For merely because the textual tradition as we have it shows no evidence of extensive degeneration of the text of Jas, this does not prove that in the history of Jas such a distortion never occurred. The extant variants are evidence only for the Biblical book "Jas"; but the lot of Jas in the relatively long period of its "private existence," before it found general acceptance in the canon, remains unknown to us. It is an intrinsically different matter with the Pauline letters, and especially with the Gospels. They were in use among the churches for a much longer time. Therefore, it may be assumed that the variant readings in them come out of a history which reaches back much further in time, and that the

period of darkness from which we have no evidence is much shorter. Now it is the length of this period which determines the appropriateness of our making conjectural emendations in a text, for every conjecture presupposes that the original wording of a passage has not been preserved at all among the variant readings. The longer that the private existence of Jas lasted, the easier it would have been for the exact wording of a passage to have been lost completely. It would then have been so thoroughly displaced that it would not have been accepted into any of the texts used in the churches. In principle, therefore, greater latitude is due to conjectures in the textual criticism of Jas than is the case with most other books of the New Testament.[269] Yet I have made use of this principle only where the text is considerably improved by the emendation. I have seriously considered conjectures in the following passages: 1:17; 2:1, 18; 3:6, 12; 4:2 (in two places); 4:5; 5:11. But in perhaps half of these cases I have not been able to reach a firm conclusion regarding the acceptance of the conjecture.

In dealing with text–critical questions in the commentary, no mere indexing is intended. In addition to those places where the sense is dependent upon a text–critical judgment, consideration is given in particular to those instances where the text–critical and exegetical tasks point to one another—i.e., where the textual witnesses are used as the oldest commentaries, or where the variants can be explained and grouped genealogically only upon the basis of the exegetical problem. In *these* places, the formulation of the question will be more important for the reader than the conclusion which I provide.

discussed here by Dibelius are designated there as follows: *ff* = 66, *s* (now in Naples) = 53, *m* = (PS-)AU spe.

267 Westcott and Hort, *op. cit.* (above, n. 257).

268 See above in section 9 of the Introduction.

269 Also in the Book of Acts, because of the special history of its text, one must be more open to conjectural emendation than is the case with most other books of the New Testament. For a detailed discussion of this, see Martin Dibelius, "The Text of Acts," in his *Studies in the Acts of the Apostles*, ed. Heinrich Greeven, tr. Mary Ling (London: SCM Press, 1956), 84–92 (first published in *Journal of Religion* 21 [1941]: 421–31).

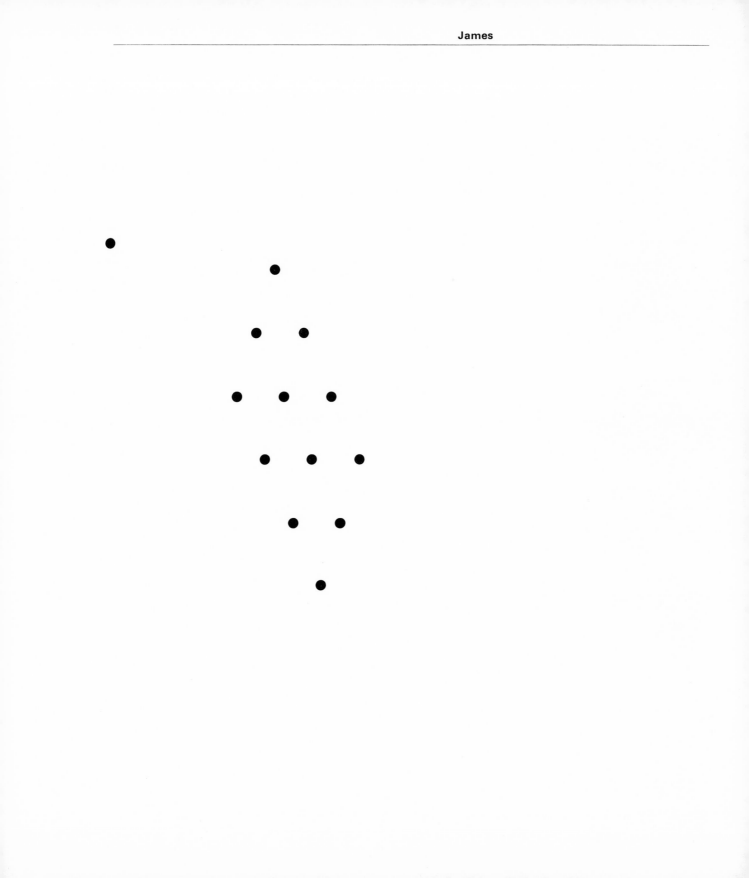

1   Prescript

1   **James, a slave of God and the Lord Jesus
Christ, to the twelve tribes in the Diaspora:
Greeting.**

■ **1:1** In the prescript to the Letter of James the author
mentions both himself and his addressees by name—
that is a part of the pattern for the opening of a letter.
Yet he does not do this in a way which permits us to
identify easily the author himself[1] and to delineate the
circle of his readers. One who believes the document to
be an actual letter of James can utilize this fact in support of his hypothesis: for the exact information about
the addressees and their place of residence did not need
to stand in the prescript, since the messenger would
have read these in the address which would have been
written on the other side of the papyrus but which
would now be lost to us; and as far as the readers were
concerned, they would have known quite well which
James was the sender. But someone who believes the
"Letter" of James not to be an actual letter will evaluate the evidence in a different way: the vagueness of the
address could have been the means by which the author
left the origin and nature of the document surrounded
with intentional ambiguity.[2] Modern readers must
constantly be reminded that such a procedure upon
the part of the author corresponds to the literary customs of the period; hence, it is not misleading and
consequently cannot be labeled as deception.[3]

The expression "slave of God" does not properly
suit Greek sensibility, but no doubt the Oriental could
associate a definite import with this phrase. The desig-
nation of man as "slave" ($\delta o\hat{v}\lambda os$) is the correlate to the
predication of God as "Lord" ($\kappa\acute{v}\rho\iota os$), a predication
which again is of no particular importance upon specifically Greek soil; the significance of the predication

within Hellenism is instead due only to oriental influences.[4] Characteristic are the words which, according to Dio Cassius (63.5.2), the Armenian king
Tiridates speaks to Nero: "I am the descendent of
Arsaces . . . and thy slave. And I have come to thee,
my god, to worship thee as I do Mithras" (᾽Αρσάκου
μὲν ἔγγονός εἰμι . . . σὸς δὲ δοῦλος. καὶ ἦλθον πρὸς σὲ
προσκυνήσων σὲ τὸν ἐμὸν θεὸν ὡς καὶ τὸν Μίθραν). Therefore, the term "slave" expresses a definite relationship
to the God to whose cult a person is committed. In
harmony with this is the fact[5] that also in Hellenistic
mystery religions which come from the Orient the
initiate is considered to be the "slave" of the mystery
divinity, to whom the initiate's entire life henceforth
is to be dedicated.[6]

The only question with regard to our passage is
whether such a relationship to God is ascribed to James
in the same sense as it would refer to Christians in
general,[7] or whether it is meant to characterize James
in some special sense. In the latter case, one could cite
as parallels the passages from the LXX which designate
Moses, David, or the prophets as slaves of God (Mal
4:6; Isa 34:23; Amos 3:7; and frequently).[8] If the
"letter" were genuine, one could think here of a modest
self-designation, with which the author places himself
on the same level with the other Christians. But if one
assumes that it is not a genuine letter, the matter is
different: the actual writer would have prefaced his
document with the name of the brother of the Lord
precisely because he esteemed him as one of the greats
of the classical period. Attaching to him no other predi-

---

1   See above in the Introduction, section 2.

2   See below in the Excursus, "The Twelve Tribes in
the Diaspora."

3   See above in the Introduction, section 2.

4   On what follows, cf. Bousset, *Kyrios Christos*, 138ff;
R. Reitzenstein, *Die Hellenistischen Mysterienreligionen
nach ihren Grundgedanken und Wirkungen* (Leipzig:
Teubner, ³1927; reprint Darmstadt: Wissenschaftliche Buchgesellschaft, 1956), 192f; Hans Lietzmann, *An die Römer*, HNT 8 (Tübingen: Mohr
[Siebeck], ⁴1933), on Rom 1:1.

5   Which we may conclude from Apuleius, *Met.* 11.15:
"servitude to the Goddess" (servitium deae).

6   Apuleius, *Met.* 11.6.

7   Cf. e.g. LXX Isa 42:19; 1 Petr 2:16; and especially
the frequent use of the term "slave of God" ($\delta o\hat{v}\lambda os$
$\tau o\hat{v}$ $\theta\epsilon o\hat{v}$) to mean "Christian" in *Hermas*.

8   Cf. also, perhaps, the reading of a whole group of
minuscules and sy^hl (text) in 2:23: "and he was
called a *slave* of God" ($\kappa\alpha\grave{\iota}$ $\delta o\hat{v}\lambda os$ $\theta\epsilon o\hat{v}$ $\grave{\epsilon}\kappa\lambda\acute{\eta}\theta\eta$), instead of "friend" ($\phi\acute{\iota}\lambda os$)!

cate than this term "slave," he obviously has in mind something special and is comparing James to Israel's men of God rather than to the mass of Christians. Didymus,[9] Oec,[10] and Theoph[11] also understood the designation in this way, as an apostolic title of honor.

In the phrase, "slave of God and of the Lord Jesus Christ," there is nothing to suggest that "God" ($\theta\epsilon\acute{o}\varsigma$) refers to Christ. Spitta[12] deletes the words "and of the Lord Jesus Christ" ($\kappa\alpha\grave{\iota}\ \kappa\upsilon\rho\acute{\iota}o\upsilon\ \mathrm{'I}\eta\sigma o\hat{\upsilon}\ X\rho\iota\sigma\tauo\hat{\upsilon}$) as a Christianizing interpolation; in such a manner, both here and in 2:1, he argues his thesis that the author is to be placed within Judaism.[13] With regard to this passage he can appeal to the fact that of course in the openings of other letters only the one–part formulae "slave of God" ($\delta o\hat{\upsilon}\lambda o\varsigma\ \theta\epsilon o\hat{\upsilon}$), "slave of Jesus Christ" ($\delta o\hat{\upsilon}\lambda o\varsigma\ \mathrm{'I}\eta\sigma o\hat{\upsilon}\ X\rho\iota\sigma\tauo\hat{\upsilon}$) are usually found; yet in the prescripts in Rom 1:1; Tit 1:1; 2 Petr 1:1 and Jude 1 this simplicity is only an illusion, for in these passages there is always another title which follows, either "apostle of Jesus Christ" or something similar (Phil 1:1 is not a parallel because of the plurality of the senders). The full ring which these prescripts maintain by prolonging the text is achieved in Jas through the juxtaposition of God and Christ. Massebieau[14] deletes only the words "Jesus Christ" ($\mathrm{'I}\eta\sigma o\hat{\upsilon}\ X\rho\iota\sigma\tauo\hat{\upsilon}$), but there is no reason for doing this either, since the text which has been transmitted offers not the slightest problem.

The twelve tribes in the Diaspora are named as the addressees. If the author were a Jew, then without further ado we would take this expression in the strict sense of the Jews outside of Palestine.[15] But since the author and the readers are Christians,[16] difficulties arise. These difficulties cannot be solved simply by the favorite speculation that naturally what we have here

are Christian Jews;[17] for nothing is said about their being Christians, and it is precisely in the prescript that one does not as a rule tacitly presuppose such things. Instead, if the readers are Christians then the designation "twelve tribes in the Diaspora" must express just this Christian character. So then, we are forced to a metaphorical interpretation, and there is only one which is possible: namely, to consider the designation as a reference to the true Israel, for whom heaven is home and earth is only a foreign country, i.e., a Diaspora—hence, as a reference to Christendom on earth. But in this case, it seems to me once more that there is no indication that the addressees are of Jewish extraction, since the entire expression must be construed in a completely[18] metaphorical sense.[19]

"The Twelve Tribes of the Diaspora"

One comes nearer to the underlying concept if one calls to mind the significance which the idea of the true Israel held already for Paul and his churches. The Christians are not only heirs of the promises given to Abraham and to his descendents (Rom 4; Gal 4:21–31), they are also the true circumcision (Phil 3:3) as over against the "Israel according to the flesh" (1 Cor 10:18). Yet their home is not the earthly Jerusalem, but rather the Jerusalem which is above (Gal 4:26), i.e., heaven (Phil 3:20). The negative side of the concept—we are foreigners upon the earth—had already been expressed by Philo, probably under Stoic influence,[20] with regard to the entire human race. Commenting upon Lev 25:23 ("You are proselytes and aliens before me" [$\acute{\upsilon}\mu\epsilon\hat{\iota}\varsigma\ \delta\grave{\epsilon}\ \pi\rho o\sigma\acute{\eta}\lambda\upsilon\tau o\iota\ \kappa\alpha\grave{\iota}\ \pi\acute{\alpha}\rho o\iota\kappa o\iota\ \acute{\epsilon}\nu\alpha\nu\tau\acute{\iota}o\nu\ \acute{\epsilon}\mu o\hat{\upsilon}$]), Philo says: "For each of us has come into this world as into a foreign city, in which before our birth we had no part, and in this city he does but

9   Didymus Alexandrinus, *In epistulas catholicas enarratio* (MPG 39, 1749–54), *ad loc.*

10   Oecumenius, *Jacobi Apostoli epistola catholica* (MPG 119, 451–510), *ad loc.*

11   Theophylactus, *Epistola catholica Sancti Jacobi apostoli* (MPG 125, 1131–90), *ad loc.*

12   Spitta, 3–8.

13   See above in the Introduction, section 3.

14   See above in the Introduction, n. 58.

15   The expression "Diaspora" ($\delta\iota\alpha\sigma\pi o\rho\acute{\alpha}$) is a technical expression, and it is not really possible to interpret it as a reference to the situation of the Jewish people in

general. Of course, still less can one think here of those Christians who were "scattered" in the persecution which followed the death of Stephen (so Bede, *Super divi Jacobi epistolam* [MPG 93, 9–42], *ad loc.*).

16   See above, section 3 of the Introduction.

17   So Beyschlag and Belser.

18   Consequently, the interpretation advocated by Hendrik Jan Toxopeus, *Karakter en Herkomst van den Jacobusbrief*, Diss. Amsterdam (Amsterdam: Clausen, 1906), 265ff—that these are the Christian people of God amidst the Gentiles—seems to me to be im-

sojourn" (ἕκαστος γὰρ ἡμῶν ὥσπερ εἰς ξένην πόλιν ἀφῖκται τόνδε τὸν κόσμον, ἧς πρὸ γενέσεως οὐ μετεῖχε, καὶ ἀφικόμενος παροικεῖ Cher. 120).[21] The corresponding designation must have been transferred to the Christian people of God at a relatively early stage, for 1 Petr 1:1; 1:17; 2:11 presuppose that the terms "exiles" (παρεπίδημοι) and "aliens" (πάροικοι) have been reinterpreted to mean the situation of the Christians in the "Diaspora" on earth (cf. Heb 13:14). The same reinterpretation is evidenced by Heb 11:13; 2 Clem. 5.1, 5, and the prescripts of *1 Clement*, the *Epistle of Polycarp*, the *Martyrdom of Polycarp*, and other passages as well. In the first *Similitude* in the *Shepherd of Hermas* and in *Diogn.* 5.5 and 6.8, the concept is found used in a somewhat broader way, reminiscent of that in Philo, but still with the particular application to the Christians. Against the interpretation of our passage from this perspective, Johannes Weiss[22] has raised the objection that the designation of the Christians as "the twelve tribes" is nowhere attested. However, even apart from the ambiguous passage in *Herm. sim.* 9.17, the expression "our twelve tribes" (τὸ δωδεκάφυλον ἡμῶν or something similar: Acts 26:7; *1 Clem.* 55.6; *Protoevangelium of James* 1.3) to mean "the Jews" is still evidence for the possibility that this designation could also be transferred to the "true Israel."

A second objection raised by J. Weiss[23] is a more important one: he argues that such a transferral is nowhere indicated in our passage. In this way, Weiss finds support for his opinion that the prescript is a trimming added by a later collector; the close relation-

ship of v 2 to v 1 argues against this, however.[24] But Weiss' objection is also refuted by the observation that in early Christian literature a type of religious style was developed which used figurative, Biblical-devotional expressions in place of literal ones. We know this sort of thing to be a matter of course in the mysterious style of heavenly letters: in the Book of Revelation, where the heretical doctrine in 2:14 and the heretical woman in 2:20 are designated with Biblical names (Balaam and Jezebel). But similar things are found also in actual letters; the prescripts mentioned above as examples for "to sojourn" (παροικεῖν) demonstrate this, and even more so the designation of a church as "elect lady" and the local church as "her sister" in 2 Jn 1, 13. This style seems even more comprehensible in pseudonymous documents, where the historical situation is sometimes disguised in other ways as well.[25] 1 Peter professes to be written from Rome and speaks in 5:13 of the "fellow–elect in Babylon." But our Jas, whose only epistolary fiction consists of the prescript,[26] does not simply direct itself to Christendom at large, but rather selects a seemingly concrete address[27] and speaks mysteriously of the twelve tribes in the Diaspora. This stylized address, which in fact goes nicely with James the teacher of circumcision, can change nothing as far as the "catholic" character of the document is concerned if the interpretation of the document demonstrates such a character.[28]

The epistolary salutation with the infinitive χαίρειν[29]

---

possible.

19 Pfleiderer, *Primitive Christianity*, vol. 4, p. 298; Windisch, *Katholische Briefe* (1911); but also Friedrich Köster, "Ueber die Leser, an welche der Brief des Jakobus und der erste Brief des Petrus gerichtet ist," *ThStKr* 39 (1831): 581–8.

20 Cf. the evidence which is provided by Wendland, "Philo und die kynisch–stoische Diatribe," 59.

21 Cf. also Philo, *Agric.* 65 (on Gen 47:4): "for in reality a wise man's soul ever finds heaven to be his fatherland and earth a foreign country, and regards as his own the dwelling–place of wisdom, and that of his body as outlandish, and looks on himself as *a stranger and sojourner* in it" (τῷ γὰρ ὄντι πᾶσα ψυχὴ σοφοῦ πατρίδα μὲν οὐρανόν, ξένην δὲ γῆν ἔλαχε, καὶ νομίζει τὸν μὲν σοφίας οἶκον ἴδιον, τὸν δὲ σώματος ὀθνεῖον, ᾧ καὶ παρεπιδημεῖν οἴεται).

22 Weiss, *Primitive Christianity*, vol. 2, p. 743, n. 4.

23 *Ibid.*

24 Cf. above in the Introduction, section 2.

25 Cf. Martin Dibelius and Hans Conzelmann, *The Pastoral Epistles*, tr. Philip Buttolph and Adela Yarbro, ed. Helmut Koester, Hermeneia (Philadelphia: Fortress, 1972), 15f.

26 See above in the Introduction, section 2.

27 Cf. the letter of Baruch to the 9½ tribes who live on the other side of the river Euphrates (*2 Baruch* 78ff).

28 See above in the Introduction.

29 The origin of this infinitive is disputed. Cf. on this G. A. Gerhard, "Untersuchungen zur Geschichte des griechischen Briefes," *Philologus* 64 (1905): 27–65, who supplies "says" (λέγει).

("Greeting") is found elsewhere in the New Testament only in Acts 15:23 and 23:26. But this rarity of the expression is only apparent, for it is χαίρειν which is the usual greeting employed by the writer of a Greek letter,[30] not one of the fuller formulae used elsewhere in the New Testament.[31] That the Christians adopted this form of greeting—but developed along with it more specifically Christian formulae—is probable *a priori*, and is also corroborated by the greetings in the letters of Ignatius, which are largely variations of the simple χαίρειν: = πλεῖστα χαίρειν ("abundant greeting") and similar formulations.

For our author, the simple χαίρειν obviously serves to attach v 2 to v 1, for the similarity in sound between χαίρειν and χαράν ("joy") is intentional. A counterpart to this is found in a pseudo–Platonic letter (*Ep.* 8, 352B): "Plato to the relatives and companions of Dion wishes well–doing. The policy which would best serve to secure your real 'well–doing' is that which I shall now endeavour as best I can to describe to you" (Πλάτων τοῖς Δίωνος οἰκείοις τε καὶ ἑταίροις εὖ πράττειν. ἃ δ' ἂν διανοηθέντες μάλιστα εὖ πράττοιτε, ὄντως πειράσομαι ταῦθ' ὑμῖν κατὰ δύναμιν διεξελθεῖν). To be sure,

the common epistolary greeting, measured against the stylized greetings of the Pauline letters, could evoke the impression that here we have a simple, non–literary letter. But this use of χαίρειν in order to effect a continuity in the text is convincing evidence to the contrary: one who makes the common epistolary greeting an integral part of the letter[32] is restoring to the greeting the significance which formulary usage had taken away from it. Therefore the author is using it as a literary device; and hence, precisely this paronomastic use of the epistolary greeting marks the author as a man who is able to write in literary style. Certainly this is not proof that the writing is pseudonymous; but—if we think of the person of James the "Just," whose environment was the environment of Jesus—it is surely not support for authenticity, either.[33]

30 One should compare epistolary greetings found in the papyri; cf. also Ferdinand Ziemann, *De epistolarum Graecarum formulis sollemnibus quaestiones selectae*, Dissertationes philologicae Halenses 18, 4 (Halle: Niemeyer, 1911), 253ff.

31 Cf. the survey in Wendland, *Hellenistische Kultur*, 411ff.

32 Cf. Pseudo-Plato, *Ep.* 3, 315A, B: "'Plato to Dionysius wishes Joy!' If I wrote thus, should I be hitting on the best mode of address? Or rather, by writing, according to my custom, 'Wishes well–doing,' this being my usual mode of address, in my letters to my friends?" (Πλάτων Διονυσίῳ χαίρειν ἐπιστείλας ἆρ' ὀρθῶς ἂν τυγχάνοιμι τῆς βελτίστης προσρήσεως, ἢ μᾶλλον κατὰ τὴν ἐμὴν συνήθειαν γράφων εὖ πράττειν, ὥσπερ εἴωθα ἐν ταῖς ἐπιστολαῖς τοὺς φίλους προσαγορεύειν).

33 Cf. in the Introduction, section 2.

1 A Series of Sayings Concerning Temptations

2 Regard it with sheer joy, my brothers and sisters, when you encounter various trials, 3/ for you know that this means of testing your faith produces endurance. 4/ Let this endurance effect a perfect product, so that *you* might be perfect and complete, lacking in nothing.

5 But if someone among you lacks wisdom, let him ask from God—who gives to all without hesitation and without grumbling—, and so it will be given to him. 6/ But let him ask in faith, not doubting in any way; for the doubter is like the surging sea driven and tossed by the wind. 7, 8/ But let such a person, a double-minded man who is vacillatory in all his conduct, certainly not expect to receive anything from the Lord.

9 Let the lowly brother boast in his exaltation, 10/ but let the rich man "boast" in his humiliation, because like the flower of the grass he will pass away. 11/ For the sun rises with its scorching heat and withers the grass, and its flower falls, and its beauty perishes: just that quickly will the rich man wither in the midst of his conduct.

12 Blessed is the person who endures trial, for since he is approved he will receive the crown of life which (God) has promised to those who love him.

13 Let no one who is tempted say, "I am tempted by God"; for God is unable to be tempted by evil and he himself tempts no one. 14/ Instead, each person is tempted when he is lured and enticed by his own desire. 15/ Then, when desire has conceived it gives birth to sin, and when sin has become complete it brings forth death.

16 Do not be deceived, my beloved brothers and sisters. Every good gift and every perfect gift comes down from above from the Father of lights, who himself is without change and knows neither turning nor eclipse. 18/ In accordance with his will, he brought us forth by the word of truth in order that we might be a kind of first-fruits among (all) his creatures.

Analysis[1]

That we have here a section which in a definite respect forms a complete unit is shown—in spite of the new beginning in 1:9—by the visible effort in 1:2–8 and 1:12–15 to establish a connection (if only a superficial one) between one saying and another, and furthermore by the obviously not accidental resumption in 1:12ff of the term "trial/temptation" ($\pi\epsilon\iota\rho\alpha\sigma\mu\acute{o}s$) from 1:2. That this unity is nevertheless only superficial is demonstrated particularly by the break in thought which occurs before v 9, but even more by the use of the term "trial" just mentioned. If one looks at 1:2 without any preconceptions one thinks possibly of persecutions of Christians or similar tests of "endurance" ($\dot{\upsilon}\pi o\mu ov\acute{\eta}$);

---

1 Certain results from the detailed exegesis are already employed in the sections of Analysis; in these cases, I indicate this simply with the note "see below."

if one also reads 1:13ff without any preconceptions one thinks of temptation to sin, where "desire lures and entices." An exegesis which in spite of this observation attempts to bring both sayings together under one common denominator is proceeding from the presupposition that what is involved here is a diatribe or some other kind of short treatise, such as can be found for that period both in longer didactic writings (Philo) as well as in actual letters. The correctness of this presupposition must be categorically denied, since the investigation of the individual sayings yields a different result.

The verses 1:2–4 form the first saying[2] of the series. At the conclusion of this saying are the words "lacking in nothing" (ἐν μηδενὶ λειπόμενοι), and the beginning of v 5 supposes a person who "lacks wisdom" (λείπεσθαι σοφίας). But in doing so, v 5 does not introduce an exception to the perfection portrayed in v 4. For v 5 has no connection at all with the content of 1:2–4, but rather it deals with a case of a totally different nature. The verbal reminiscence "lacking—lacks" is therefore only an external connective device: we encounter here for the first time in Jas the connection by means of

catchwords which is so characteristic of paraenesis.[3] The saying in 1:5–8 deals with prayer—not just prayer for wisdom in particular (cf. "anything" [τι] in v 7); but neither is this a saying about doubt, for, as is shown by v 7, the subject in both v 6b and v 8 is not the doubter in general but rather the doubter who is praying.

A saying about the downfall of the rich man follows in 1:9–11.[4] There appears to be no connection at all between v 8 and v 9, for the doubter is to be identified neither with the "rich man" (πλούσιος) nor with the "lowly man" (ταπεινός). Actually one would have to suppose a connection which went all the way back to 1:2–4, equating the lowly man with the person proved by means of trials[5]—certainly a surmise to which the author of the letter would not object, but still no more than a surmise, and one which is not supported by the text and therefore probably not intended by the author.[6] Yet not even a clearly perceptible *external* connection can be observed between the saying about the rich man and what precedes. Someone who does not wish to imagine here a mere attachment without any connection at all might possibly find a sort of connective

---

2   On the content, that trials eventually lead to perfection, see below.

3   This is more carefully examined above in the Introduction, section 1. That the connection is external is demonstrated by the futile attempts to establish some internal connection in thought. One such attempt is to interpret the term "wisdom" in direct connection with 1:2–4: "he says that wisdom is the source of 'the perfect work'" (τὸ αἴτιον τοῦ τελείου ἔργου τὴν σοφίαν λέγει, in the catenae and scholia); "If someone among you is not able to understand the usefulness of temptation . . ., let him ask of God that perception be given to him" (si quis vestrum non potest intelligere utilitatem tentationem . . ., postulet a Deo tribui sibi sensum; so Bede; cf. Mayor) [Trans.]. Or, the attempt has been made to interpret "wisdom" as related in a more general way to the situation in 1:2–4: Wisdom is especially necessary in times of testing (Beyschlag, Windisch, *Katholische Briefe* (1911), and similarly already by de Wette and Gebser). Haupt, review of Spitta, *Der Brief des Jakobus*, 751, thinks of the wisdom of socially oppressed Christians in dealings with their masters. Grafe, *Stellung und Bedeutung*, 11, Belser, and Ropes recognize the break in thought; Spitta wants to derive it from a reminiscence of Wisd 9:6 (cf. below in the Interpretation on 1:5). If, on the other hand,

one even separates 1:5 from 1:6–8 (so Rudolf Bultmann, in a letter of April 21, 1921: v 5 would be dealing with prayer for wisdom, vv 6–8—attached to the word "ask" [αἰτεῖν] in v 5—would concern petition and doubt as to its fulfillment), then v 6 is left as a clause without a subject. One would then have to supply something like "he who asks" (ὁ αἰτῶν) as the subject of a supposed original form of the saying. But with that, one has already observed a transition from pure catchword connection to organic adaptation.

4   The "lowly person" mentioned first is only a foil (see below).

5   So Ropes.

6   Other combinations are even more implausible: The idea that both the poor man as well as the rich man would each be "double-minded" (δίψυχος) if they were guilty of the wrong kind of boasting (J. Chr. K. Hofmann, *Der Brief Jakobi*, in his *Die heilige Schrift neuen Testaments* 7, 3 [Nördlingen: Beck, 1875–76], *ad loc.*; Karl Burger and G. Chr. Luthardt, *Die katholischen Briefe*, Kurzgefasster Kommentar zu den heiligen Schriften Alten und Neuen Testaments sowie zu den Apokryphen, eds. Hermann Strack and Otto Zöckler, part B, vol. 4 [Nördlingen: Beck, 1888], *ad loc.*) is no more to be found in the text than is the idea that proper boasting is supposed to take

device in the superficial kinship between the conclusions: "unstable in all his *ways*" (ταῖς ὁδοῖς αὐτοῦ v 8)—"will perish in the midst of his *conduct*" (ταῖς πορείαις αὐτοῦ v 11). But it can hardly be proven that this kinship is intentional.

1:12 is an isolated saying separated from what precedes it. For the pious man proved by trial is not the rich man who is to perish.[7] And there is not one syllable which intimates that he is to be identified with the lowly man; rather, this has been inferred by interpreters upon the basis of the sequence of the whole series of sayings—but in Jas one cannot rely upon this sort of argument. Nevertheless, the reason that this saying was attached is quite evident: the saying is akin to 1:2ff. Precisely this kinship makes the contrast between 1:12 and the following saying in 1:13–15 all the stronger. For the temptations whose origins are discussed in 1:13–15 are not the "trials" in 1:2 over which one is supposed to rejoice; while these must be dangers from without, 1:13–15 deals with dangers of the inner life. Hence, the latter saying is connected with v 12 only by means of a catchword: πειραζόμενος ("tempted")—πειρασμός ("trial"). Its content is: "Temptations, i.e., dangers to the soul, do not come from God"—and as proof of this it could then have been said: "for only good things come from God." Instead, the saying in vv 16–18 says, "all good comes from God." Hence this saying, or at least v 17, is no doubt really independent; but of course it is added here as evidence for the idea that evil cannot come from God. It must be left undecided whether one has to see in addition to this connection in thought a further connective device in the verbal reminiscence "brings forth" (ἀποκυεῖ 1:15)—"he brought forth" (ἀπεκύησεν 1:18).

Interpretation

■ **1:2–4:** *Concerning persecutions.*

■ **2** Rejoice over trials (πειρασμοί)—that is the first thought presented in the document. The reader, especially if he is not thinking of 1:13, will not be able to interpret "trials" here in any other way than as the persecutions which befall the entire group of "brethren" who are here addressed.[8] That affliction is the lot of the pious could be deduced from a reading of Sir 2:1.[9] Sirach also already substantiates this notion with the heroic motif that it is precisely gold which is tested in fire (Sir 2:5—cf. "means of testing" [δοκίμιον] in our passage), and in this way Sirach arrives at a merely pedagogical view of suffering, somewhat like that in the speech of Elihu of Job 36:8ff or that in Prov 3:11f. In the Maccabaean period the Jewish community had also learned to apply such heroic concepts to the sufferings of the nation—cf. Judith 8:25: "Let us give thanks to the Lord our God, who is putting us to the test as he did our forefathers" (εὐχαριστήσωμεν Κυρίῳ τῷ θεῷ ἡμῶν, ὃς πειράζει ἡμᾶς καθὰ καὶ τοὺς πατέρας ἡμῶν). In the soil of Hellenistic Judaism this concept gained new strength amidst Stoic influences, and at the same time it received through those influences a special emphasis. The best evidence for this is *4 Maccabees*, which, as a "highly philosophical inquiry" (λόγος φιλοσοφώτατος 1.1), formulates its theme as follows: "whether reason is master over the passions" (εἰ αὐτοκράτωρ ἐστὶν τῶν παθῶν ὁ λογισμός 1.13); yet it goes about proving this theme by telling the story of Jewish heroism during the Maccabaean period, and it has the heroine admonish her sons, "You are obliged to endure all things for the sake of God" (ὀφείλετε πάντα πόνον ὑπομένειν διὰ τὸν θεόν 16.19) [Trans.]. Jas nowhere indicates that he is writing during a similarly stirring period of perse-

---

7   place in prayer (H. Ewald, *Das Sendschreiben an die Hebräer und Jakobus' Rundschreiben* [Göttingen: Dieterich, 1870], *ad loc.*). Beyschlag's interpretation of v 9 as comfort for those afflicted in v 2 contradicts the main idea of the saying, which is not intended as "comfort" at all. Spitta's reference to the parallelism of ταπεινός and ἀκατάστατος in Isa 54:11 is not in harmony with the meaning of ἀκατάστατος ("vacillating") in v 8 (see below).

7   See below in the Interpretation.

8   περιπίπτειν with the dative and with a figurative meaning is found already in classical Greek.

9   On the question whether the "trials" here are to be conceived of on an individual level, cf. Alfred Bertholet and Bernhard Stade, *Biblische Theologie des Alten Testaments*, vol. 2 (Tübingen: Mohr [Siebeck], 1911), 170. Already the catenae and scholia cite Sir 2:1 as well as Jn 16:33 with regard to this passage.

cution.[10] But he wants to revive again the heroic sentiment of that epoch in the midst of the present "various trials," whose nature he does not reveal: These trials are supposed to be "sheer joy."[11]

■ **3, 4** Early Christianity was capable of arguing for the necessity of suffering by referring to eschatological (Mk 13:7ff; *Herm. vis.* 4.2.5; 4.3.4) or mystical (Col 1:24)[12] conceptions. Neither is mentioned here; instead, an ethical concept serves as evidence: Affliction teaches endurance. And this concept is not set forth with the fervor of one who is the first to discover it, nor is it substantiated and defended with the dialectics of one involved in a debate; rather, it seems as though the author presupposes the following line of thought to be a familiar one. Then γινώσκειν here will mean "to be aware," as in 5:20.[13]

What follows deserves consideration primarily because of its form. What is involved is a progressive heightening of the thought: From persecution proceeds endurance (ὑπομονή), and endurance makes possible an even higher goal: "that you may be perfect and complete" (ἵνα ἦτε τέλειοι καὶ ὁλόκληροι). The connection between the individual stages in this crescendo is fundamentally schematic: "it produces" (κατεργάζεται), "let it have" (ἐχέτω)—just how this is to take place is as little spelled out here as in Rom 5:3f.[14] In both texts we are dealing with a *concatenation*, a stringing together of abstracts in crescendoing succession in order to describe rhetorically what is usually a psychological process.[15] Here in our passage the schema is varied in various ways. This is seen right away in the first concept: one would expect v 3 to have, "since you are aware that *this trial*, etc." (ὅτι ὁ πειρασμὸς κτλ.); but instead the text reads, "since you are aware that the *means of testing* your faith, etc." (ὅτι τὸ δοκίμιον ὑμῶν τῆς πίστεως).[16]

The meaning "test"[17] cannot be established for δοκίμιον. Instead, there are two meanings of the word which come under consideration: (1) As a substantivized neuter of the adjective δοκίμιος it can mean "genuineness, test–worthiness,"[18] and obviously δοκίμιον has this sense in the parallel passage in 1 Petr 1:7;[19] (2) but also the meaning "means of testing" is found. In LXX Prov 27:21 it is said that "firing is the means of testing silver and gold" (δοκίμιον ἀργύρῳ καὶ χρυσῷ πύρωσις), and the verse continues, "but a man *is tested* by means of the mouths of those who praise him" (ἀνὴρ δὲ δοκιμάζεται διὰ στόματος ἐγκωμιαζόντων αὐτόν) [Trans.]; it is clear enough here that this meaning for δοκίμιον is picked up again by the verb. The word is found corresponding to πειράζεσθαι ("to be tested") in Plutarch, *Apophth. Lac.* 230B: "Namertes . . . asked if this man had any sure means by which the man of many friends might be tested; and when the other

---

10 Cf. to the contrary, above in the Introduction, sections 1 and 7, and cf. below on 2:6f.

11 This use of πᾶς without the article before abstracts to mean "supreme" or "sheer" is probably not to be considered a solecism nor to be attributed to the obliteration of the distinction between πᾶς and πᾶς ὁ. It is the result of a quite understandable development from "every" or "every kind of" to "in every respect": e.g., Acts 4:29; 23:1; 2 Cor 12:12; 1 Tim 2:2; Phil 2:29: "with all joy" (μετὰ πάσης χαρᾶς). Cf. the familiar use of πᾶς with an abstract (also in Tit 3:2; 2 Petr 1:5; Jude 3): "exercising every precaution" (πᾶσαν πρόνοιαν ποιούμενος Ditt. *Or.* II, 669.3), and similar expressions. Ropes provides further examples. Here in Jas 1:2, πᾶσα is used also for the sake of alliteration (see above in the Introduction, section 5).

12 Dibelius later severely limited his evaluation of Col 1:24 as "mystical"; see **Martin Dibelius** and Heinrich Greeven, *An die Kolosser, Epheser, an Philemon,* HNT 12 (Tübingen: Mohr [Siebeck], ³1953), *ad loc.*

13 See also "knowing" (εἰδότες) in Rom 5:3; cf. Theo

dor Nägeli, *Der Wortschatz des Apostels Paulus* (Göttingen: Vandenhoeck & Ruprecht, 1905), 40.

14 On the relation between the two passages, see below in the Excursus on 1:2–4.

15 Cf. the Excursus on 1:15.

16 The omission of "of faith" (τῆς πίστεως) by B^c *ff*, as well as the omission of the whole phrase "of your faith" (ὑμῶν τῆς πίστεως) in sy^{hl}, is too isolated to justify branding the words in question as an interpolation modeled after 1 Petr 1:7. If δοκίμιον is understood to mean the same as δοκιμή ("test by which something is approved"), then the occasional simplification (*ff*: "your proving" [probatio vestrum]) is understandable.

17 So *ff* vulg, also Ropes.

18 On δοκίμιος and δοκίμιον, cf. Adolf Deissmann, *Bible Studies,* tr. A. Grieve (Edinburgh: Clark, 1901), 259–62. In LXX Ps 11:7, δοκίμιον is also the neuter of the adjective: "Silver is tested by fire in the earth, purified seven times" (ἀργύριον πεπυρωμένον, δοκίμιον τῇ γῇ, κεκαθαρισμένον ἑπταπλασίως).

19 Cf. Knopf, *Briefe Petri und Judä, ad loc.*; on the rela

desired to learn, Namertes said, 'By means of misfortune'" (Ναμέρτης . . . ἠρώτησεν, εἰ δοκίμιον ἔχει, τίνι τρόπῳ πειράζεται ὁ πολύφιλος· ἐπιζητοῦντος δὲ θατέρου μαθεῖν ἀτυχίᾳ εἶπεν) [Loeb modified]; cf. also Origen, *Exhortatio ad martyrium* 6: "Therefore we must consider the present trial to be a means of testing and examining our love for God" (δοκίμιον οὖν καὶ ἐξεταστήριον τῆς πρὸς τὸ θεῖον ἀγάπης νομιστέον ἡμῖν γεγονέναι τὸν ἐστηκότα πειρασμόν) [Trans.].[20] In our passage, Belser prefers the first meaning: "what is genuine with regard to your faith," and this is certainly also the opinion of Oec: "δοκίμιον means that which is approved, that which is tested, that which is pure" (δοκίμιον τὸ κεκριμένον λέγει, τὸ δεδοκιμασμένον, τὸ καθαρόν) [Trans.]. But this interpretation results in problems in both directions: In order to have a connection with what precedes one needs a substitute term for "trial" (πειρασμός); that speaks in favor of the translation, "(this) means of testing your faith," and against the other translation, "the genuineness of your faith"—which would have to be supplemented parenthetically with: "which manifests itself amidst the trials." But the connection with what follows is also difficult if we read "the genuineness of your faith produces endurance (ὑπομονή)," for one could just as well have said that through endurance faith is proven to be genuine. By contrast, the other interpretation results in a simpler and clearer thought: The trials as a means of testing your faith produce endurance.

The term "endurance" (ὑπομονή) has a much more active sense in such a context than is usually assumed. Not only is the meaning of this word shown in the reference to Job in Jas 5:11, but also in the story in *4 Maccabees* of the mother of the heros and her sons: "their courage and endurance" (ἐπὶ τῇ ἀνδρίᾳ καὶ τῇ ὑπομονῇ *4 Macc.* 1.11; see also 9.30; 17.12; in no other book of the Greek Old Testament does ὑπομονή occur as often as in this one); one can see that there is more heroism in this word than the translation "patience" would suggest. Paul, also, has this heroic endurance in mind in Rom 5:3 and 2 Cor 12:12.

However, the statement "suffering produces endurance" is not intended merely to stir on to heroism

in the midst of afflictions; it also is intended to instruct. The question of the meaning of suffering was discussed in the Wisdom literature; but contributions toward the solution of the problem were also required from the historical books; for if one wished not merely to surmise the purpose of suffering but also to demonstrate it, he needed demonstrative examples. Abraham and Joseph were favorite examples in which one could see how God educated his own through afflictions. It merely corresponds to the technique of Jewish theology if this education is eventually verified by narrating the trials: "This is the tenth trial wherewith Abraham was tried, and he was found faithful, *patient in spirit*," reads *Jubilees* 19.8, following the account of the death of Sarah [trans. Charles, *APOT*]; in *Test. Jos.* 2.7, Joseph is extolled in similar terms: "He showed me approved by ten *trials*, and I was patient in all of them; for patience is a strong medicine and *endurance* gives many good things" (ἐν δέκα πειρασμοῖς δόκιμον ἀπέδειξέ με καὶ ἐν πᾶσιν αὐτοῖς ἐμακροθύμησα. Ὅτι μέγα φάρμακόν ἐστιν ἡ μακροθυμία καὶ πολλὰ ἀγαθὰ δίδωσιν ἡ ὑπομονή) [Trans.]. Our author is far removed from such theological mathematics; but just as he takes over from Judaism Abraham (2:21) and Job (5:11), so he is also familiar—obviously from the same theology—with the notion that without affliction there is no proof of endurance. Here, therefore, he does not need to offer evidence, but rather he can simply make the assertion: Affliction produces endurance.

As the next and final member of the concatenation, a thought is expressed whose sense we conclude primarily from the final clause: "in order that you might be perfect and complete" (ἵνα ἦτε τέλειοι καὶ ὁλόκληροι). Endurance is said to help human beings toward perfection. But this final clause is dependent upon the clause, "Let endurance effect a perfect work" (ἡ δὲ ὑπομονὴ ἔργον τέλειον ἐχέτω), and besides the imperative in this clause, the much-debated expression "perfect work" (ἔργον τέλειον) is especially striking. Some interpret this in a quite general way to mean the complete outcome of endurance.[21] But the expression sounds strangely specific for this rather bland idea. Therefore, others have taken the words to mean the

---

tion between this passage in 1 Peter to our passage in Jas, see below in the Excursus on 1:2–4.

20 Further examples: Plato, *Tim.* 65C; Dion. Hal.,

Art. rhet. 11, p. 122.22ff Usener; Herodian, *Hist.* 2.10.12.

21 Hofmann, Beyschlag, Belser.

moral manifestation of endurance.[22] But then it is again surprising that there is no mention at all of the "fruits" of endurance—in a "concatenation" one would expect this. Yet precisely the reference to this stylistic schema and its automatic quality can in this case, as so often, point the way out of the exegetical difficulties. The words "let it effect a perfect work" are a continuation of the concatenation; there is no doubt, therefore, that "to effect . . . work" (ἔργον ἔχειν) corresponds to the term "produce" (κατεργάζεσθαι) in the preceding member of the catena; the thought, "Let endurance effect a perfect work," finds its completion in the final clause: "*You* are that perfect work,"[23] Only this interpretation is justified both by the correspondence between "perfect" (τέλειοι v 4b) and "perfect work" (ἔργον τέλειον v 4a) and by the schema of the concatenation; furthermore, it creates no linguistic difficulties.[24]

Hence, it is the perfection of the Christians which Jas expresses with the term "perfect work."[25] But the obscurity of the expression is probably explained by the intention of the author to let the concatenation end, not with a declarative statement, but rather with an admonition; for such is in accord with the paraenetic character of his writing. Therefore he does not say, "Endurance makes you perfect," but rather, "Let it make you perfect"; he then divides this thought still

further into an indicatory demand and an amplificatory final clause, which formally is dependent upon the imperative but in thought is parallel to it: "Let what endurance produces be perfected, and thus you will be perfected."

"Perfect and complete" (τέλειοι καὶ ὁλόκληροι)—Here both words designate moral integrity, as is shown by the conclusion of the verse.[26] In this, Jas is as little worried about the relativity of all human perfection as is didactic Wisdom literature in similar contexts (cf. Sir 44:17; Wisd 9:6; Matt 5:48), and so he uses the term "perfect" here, as also in 3:2, in a completely innocent way. The Greek word used here for "complete" properly designates the external intactness of the physical body, or some other similar concrete notion. But its frequent combination with "perfect" (τέλειος),[27] as well as its use with abstract terms,[28] may have contributed to its having received the ethical sense of "blameless" in which here it is quite obviously used; cf. Philo, *Abr.* 47: "the perfect man (Noah) is complete from the first" (ὁ μὲν γὰρ τέλειος ὁλόκληρος ἐξ ἀρχῆς; contrasted with "half–complete" [ἡμίεργος] and "defective" [ἐλλιπής]).

The Literary Relationships of Jas 1:2–4

The problem of literary dependence is especially difficult in the investigation of the Catholic Epistles. For

22 De Wette, von Soden, Ropes.
23 Similarly, Windisch, *Katholische Briefe* (1911).
24 Epictetus, *Diss.* 1.4.3: "Now if it is virtue that holds out the promise thus to create happiness and calm and serenity, then assuredly progress toward virtue is progress toward each of these states of mind" (εἰ δ' ἡ ἀρετὴ ταύτην ἔχει τὴν ἐπαγγελίαν εὐδαιμονίαν ποιῆσαι καὶ ἀπάθειαν καὶ εὔροιαν, πάντως καὶ ἡ προκοπὴ ἡ πρὸς αὐτὴν πρὸς ἕκαστον τούτων ἐστὶ προκοπή). The idea in the conditional sentence— virtue effects happiness, etc.—is again introduced in *Diss.* 1.4.5 with the words, "What is the work of virtue? Serenity" (τί ἔργον ἀρετῆς; εὔροια).
25 A formal parallel to the correspondence here between "perfection" and "perfect work" is found in Clem. Alex., *Strom.* 4.14.3: "For example, we call martyrdom 'perfection' (τελείωσις), not because the man comes to the end (τέλος) of his life, like other people do; rather, it is because he has displayed the perfect work (τέλειον ἔργον) of love" (Trans.).
26 "Lacking in nothing" (ἐν μηδενὶ λειπόμενοι) corresponds to the Stoic statement in Stobaeus, *Ecl.*

2.7.11 (p. 98 Wachsmuth): "They say that every good and noble man is perfect, since he lacks no virtue" (πάντα δὲ τὸν καλὸν καὶ ἀγαθὸν ἄνδρα τέλειον εἶναι λέγουσι διὰ τὸ μηδεμιᾶς ἀπολείπεσθαι ἀρετῆς cf. also *Ecl.* 2.7.5., p. 65 Wachsmuth) [Trans.]. The positive counterpart is found in Philo, *Abr.* 34: "He says, too, that Noah became 'perfect,' thereby showing that he acquired not one virtue but all, and having acquired them continued to exercise each as opportunities allowed" (φησὶ δ' αὐτὸν καὶ τέλειον γεγονέναι διὰ τούτου παριστάς, ὡς οὐ μίαν ἀρετὴν ἀλλὰ πάσας ἐκτήσατο καὶ κτησάμενος ἑκάστη κατὰ τὸ ἐπιβάλλον χρώμενος διετέλεσεν).
27 Plut., *Comm. not.* 1069f; *Quaest. conv.* 2.636f; Philo, *Migr. Abr.* 33; Dio Chrys., *Or.* 12.34; Iambl., *Myst.* 5.21 (with regard to the coming of the gods and spirits): "properly fulfilling the perfect and complete reception of the divine company" (τέλεον καὶ ὁλόκληρον τὴν ὑποδοχὴν τοῦ θείου χοροῦ καλῶς ἀποπληρώσας) [Trans.].
28 With "righteousness" (δικαιοσύνη) in Wisd 15:3; "piety" (εὐσέβεια) in *4 Macc.* 15:17; "faith" (πίστις)

they do not contain for the most part—and this particularly applies to our Jas—original material. That being the case, the historical significance of their authors consists precisely in the fact that they became spokesmen for the many and passed on ideas and concepts which had already been formulated. Therefore, in this literature kinship in wording and thought is even less a sign of literary dependence than elsewhere. Instead, extensive skepticism vis-à-vis hypotheses of literary dependence is called for here, such as that expressed by Windisch.[29] The investigation cannot be limited to isolating passages for consideration in the form of some sort of synoptic survey, but rather it must be argued on *form–critical* and *religio–historical* grounds. In other words, the investigation must take note of whether the occurrence of similar concepts in the passages being compared is the result of a certain form which is employed, so that the two passages are similar in their wording merely because they make use of a common rhetorical device; and further, the investigation must note whether these concepts were a part of the common intellectual store of contemporaries, or at least of specific groups and orientations.

Our passage displays striking kinship with the Letter to the Romans and with the Epistle of 1 Peter:

Rom 5:3–5	Jas 1:2–4
More than that, we boast in our sufferings, knowing that suffering *produces endurance, and endurance produces confirmation* (δοκιμήν), and confirmation produces hope, and hope does not disappoint us . . .	Regard it with sheer joy . . ., when you encounter various trials, for you know that this *means of testing* (δοκίμιον) *your faith produces endurance*. Let endurance effect a perfect work, so that you might be perfect and complete . . .

οὐ μόνον δέ, ἀλλὰ καὶ καυχώμεθα ἐν ταῖς θλίψεσιν, εἰδότες, ὅτι ἡ θλῖψις ὑπομονὴν κατεργάζεται, ἡ δὲ ὑπομονὴ δοκιμήν, ἡ δὲ δοκιμὴ ἐλπίδα, ἡ δὲ ἐλπὶς οὐ καταισχύνει . . .

πᾶσαν χαρὰν ἡγήσασθε . . ., ὅταν πειρασμοῖς περιπέσητε ποικίλοις, γινώσκοντες ὅτι τὸ δοκίμιον ὑμῶν τῆς πίστεως κατεργάζεται ὑπομονήν. ἡ δὲ ὑπομονὴ ἔργον τέλειον ἐχέτω, ἵνα ἦτε τέλειοι καὶ ὁλόκληροι . . .

Both passages express their thoughts in the form of a concatenation. As can be seen from the Excursus on 1:15, this form is one of the widespread literary devices of the period, and therefore literary dependence cannot be inferred from this external similarity. The concatenation is achieved through linkages of a verbal or prepositional nature; here the members are linked by the verb "to produce" (κατεργάζεσθαι) in a very simple manner, and one which is quite natural in a crescendo; therefore, it ought not to be surprising that both Rom 5 and Jas 1 use this verb (which Jas then alternates with "to effect" [ἔργον ἔχειν]).

However, the agreement in the use of the word "endurance" (ὑπομονή) and the root δοκιμ(-η, -ιον) is no doubt striking at first glance. Obviously it is dependent upon the kinship in thought between the two passages. Now in Jas the leading idea—carried in a beautiful crescendo from afflictions as the means of testing, through endurance, to perfection—is clear right away. In Paul, that the third member continues the crescendo is not so convincing. Paul starts from "suffering" (θλῖψις = πειρασμοί = δοκίμιον in Jas), moves as does Jas to "endurance" (ὑπομονή), but then has "confirmation" (δοκιμή) proceed from "endurance," and "hope" (ἐλπίς) from "confirmation." It could be asked why it is not the other way around, with confirmation proceeding from hope. Obviously Paul places less importance on the compositional layout of

in *Herm. mand.* 5.2.3; "virtues" (ἀρεταί) in Philo, *Sacr. AC.* 43; cf. Philo, *Deus imm.* 4: "complete virtues" (αἱ ὁλόκληροι ἀρεταί) in contrast to "discordant vices" (αἱ ἀνάρμοστοι κακίαι). Perhaps also the ethical significance of cultic "spotlessness" has had an influence in the shift in meaning; cf. Philo, *Spec. leg.* 1.283: "So he who intends to sacrifice must consider not whether the victim is unblemished but whether his own mind is complete and sound" (δεῖ δὲ τὸν μέλλοντα θύειν σκέπτεσθαι, μὴ εἰ τὸ ἱερεῖον ἄμωμον, ἀλλ' εἰ ἡ διάνοια ὁλόκληρος αὐτῷ καὶ παντελὴς καθέστηκε); *Spec. leg.* 1.196, where the whole–burnt–

offering is said to be an expression of the undivided efforts of a person toward God: "complete and whole in itself as it [i.e., the whole–burnt–offering] is, it fits in well with the same qualities in the motive which carries with it no element of mortal self–interest" (ὁλοκλήρῳ καὶ παντελεῖ μηδὲν ἐπιφερομένῃ τῆς θνητῆς φιλαυτίας ὁλόκληρον καὶ παντελῆ) [Loeb modified].

29   See the Preface to Windisch, *Katholische Briefe* (1911). Cf. also the discussion above in the Introduction, section 4.

the thought than on the enumeration of the series: suffering—endurance—confirmation—hope. And with the exception of the last, these concepts recur also in Jas; for at the beginning he already hints at the "confirmation" when he characterizes the "trials" (πειρασμοί) as a δοκίμιον," a means of testing" or "confirming." Therefore, though they do not share the same sequence, these two passages do have in common the grouping together of these concepts.

And that is not surprising. If one calls to mind not only our text and perhaps Jas 1:12 and 5:11, but also *Jubilees* 19.8 (cf. also 17.18) and *Test. Jos.* 2.7, which were cited above with regard to the term "endurance" (ὑπομονή), then one can see how closely the words for affliction, endurance or patience, and confirmation must be linked in Jewish–Christian sentiment. And if one further notices how Judaism repeatedly points to the sufferings or trials of its heros—"what great things endurance produces" (πόσα κατεργάζεται ἡ ὑπομονή *Test. Jos.* 10.1)—then it becomes evident how common must have been the ideas which found expression in our two passages. Nevertheless, the point which is made with them varies from time to time: Jas admonishes the reader to rejoice over afflictions, since these aid the pious toward perfection; Paul says that Christians are to boast in their suffering, since it is precisely through suffering that their hope of heavenly glory is assured. Therefore, the agreement in thought is ultimately based upon the principle that suffering produces endurance. Already the pious Jew had learned, in the school of life and in the school of theology, to think of suffering in this way. Hence, if two texts neither of which stands far removed from Jewish paraenesis express these ideas in similar terms and in the same literary form, this does not prove that there was a direct literary connection between them.

1 Petr 1:6, 7	Jas 1:2, 3
In this [i.e., the call to a heavenly inheritance] you rejoice, though now for a little while you may have to suffer *various trials*, so that the *genuineness of your faith*, more precious than gold which though perishable is tested by fire, may redound...	Regard it with sheer joy ..., when you encounter *various trials*, for you know that this *means of testing your faith* produces endurance.

ἐν ᾧ ἀγαλλιᾶσθε, ὀλίγον ἄρτι εἰ δέον ἐστὶ (another reading omits ἐστί) λυπηθέντες ἐν ποικίλοις πειρασμοῖς, ἵνα τὸ δοκίμιον ὑμῶν τῆς πίστεως πολυτιμότερον χρυσίου τοῦ ἀπολλυμένου, διὰ πυρὸς δὲ δοκιμαζομένου, εὑρεθῇ ...

πᾶσαν χαρὰν ἡγήσασθε ..., ὅταν πειρασμοῖς περιπέσητε ποικίλοις, γινώσκοντες ὅτι τὸ δοκίμιον ὑμῶν τῆς πίστεως κατεργάζεται ὑπομονήν.

The relation of the passages to the larger contexts of their respective documents is not the same in each case. That Christians must suffer in innocence is a leading theme in the whole of 1 Peter, whereas the corresponding words in Jas do not have such a general significance. But to assign right away a secondary character to the Jas passage because of this would leave out of account the literary style of Jas. In some sections (and it is true of this one), Jas strings together admonition after admonition, and it would be erroneous to expect to find for each of these individual sayings moorings which anchor it to the whole of the document.

But the nature of the train of thought does not necessitate the hypothesis of direct dependence at all. Both passages deal with the meaning of afflictions. But according to 1 Peter, this meaning is to be found in the fact that the genuineness of one's faith is proven; according to Jas, it is to be found in the fact that Christians become perfect. As was shown above in the interpretation, the conception which underlies both notions was widespread within Judaism. Obviously both passages are dependent upon this Jewish "Wisdom" and paraenesis. This also explains their lexical similarities, better than the assumption of direct influence of one of the texts upon the other. For the term δοκίμιον is used with a different meaning in the two passages;[30] indeed, the word as it occurs in 1 Petr 1:7 (with the meaning "genuineness") stands in close association with the metaphor of the assaying of gold, which is also well–known as a traditional motif (cf. Sir 2:5; also Prov 17:3; 27:21). Instead of this, Jas has only the idea of confirmation or verification, without any further illustration; and as was shown, δοκίμιον in this context signifies a "means of testing."

If one wished to reduce to a simple formula the relationship of the passage in 1 Petr 1:6f, which is more elaborate and part of a larger context, to the single saying in Jas 1:2–4, one would have to see in Jas the simple paraenesis and in 1 Peter the expanded paraenesis. Then it becomes quite clear that both passages are indeed dependent upon Jewish paraenesis, but not upon one another. Nor can the initially striking appearance of the same expression "various trials" (ποικίλοι πειρασμοί) in both passages change this conclusion in any way. For the term "various" (ποικίλος) is very frequent,[31] and it is a favorite word used in portraying the "variety" of torments, tortures, and persecutions.[32]

■ **1:5–8** *A saying about praying in faith.*
■ **5** The connection with what precedes is superficial, for the concept (lack of wisdom) which is employed for the transition is not carried through the entire saying.[33] The author wants to move from the words "lacking in nothing" (ἐν μηδενὶ λειπόμενοι v 4) to the subject of prayer, and he accomplishes this by means of a catchword link.[34] And indeed, the bridge is not so rickety. For if already some sort of lack was to be mentioned, following precisely the utterance of the word "perfect" (τέλειος), then certainly it would be most appropriate to speak of a lack of wisdom, which indeed was felt to be a divine gift—for naturally this is not the "wisdom of this age" (σοφία τοῦ αἰῶνος τούτου) mentioned in 1 Cor 2:6—, although this gift of wisdom is not to an unlimited degree an inevitable part of faith. One should recall what Paul says in 1 Cor 1:26–2:5 about the superfluity of that divine wisdom in certain situations in the community, and also the solace which he bestows in Phil 3:15 upon those members of

the community who might still be dissenting: "God will reveal that also to you" (καὶ τοῦτο ὁ θεὸς ὑμῖν ἀποκαλύψει).

This is also the view of our author, and consequently he can demand that even those who through afflictions are maturing toward moral perfection pray for wisdom. It is possible that the development discussed in connection with 4:3[35] is also making itself felt here and that disappointments of the confidence that prayers would receive an answer have occasioned this type of restriction of the request to something which is inward.

However, the passage in Wisd 9:6 which Spitta thinks is responsible for the transition in Jas 1:4–5 is not in agreement with the thought in the Jas passage. For first of all, in Wisd 9:6 ("for even if one is perfect among human beings, yet without the wisdom that comes from thee he will be regarded as nothing" [κἂν γάρ τις ᾖ τέλειος ἐν υἱοῖς ἀνθρώπων, τῆς ἀπὸ σοῦ σοφίας ἀπούσης εἰς οὐδὲν λογισθήσεται]) the term τέλειος means a "perfection" in human matters and not one earned through afflictions. Secondly, if our author's thoughts were moving in the direction of the "Solomonic" prayer, he would have dwelled longer on the theme of "wisdom." But as it is, he attaches to the conditional sentence merely a saying about prayer. The portrayal of God and his giving is intended to substantiate the hope that prayer is answered.[36]

The Term ἁπλῶς

The terms ἁπλοῦς and ἁπλότης have a wide range of meanings in Koine Greek. Accordingly, the statement

---

30 Cf. above on 1:3.
31 To be sure, in the New Testament itself it is not frequent; but it certainly is in the LXX and in *Hermas*.
32 *3 Macc.* 2.6: "With various and numerous punishments, you tested . . ." (ποικίλαις καὶ πολλαῖς δοκιμάσας τιμωρίαις); *4 Macc.* 7.4: "No besieged city ever withstood so numerous and various devices" (οὐχ οὕτως πόλις πολλοῖς καὶ ποικίλοις μηχανήμασιν ἀντέσχεν ποτὲ πολιορκουμένη the comparison is with the torments of Eleazar); 17.7: "the mother of the seven sons enduring for the sake of piety various tortures even unto death" (μητέρα ἑπτὰ τέκνων δι᾽ εὐσέβειαν ποικίλας βασάνους μέχρι θανάτου ὑπομείνασαν); 18.21: "killed them by means of various tortures" (βασάνοις ποικίλοις ἀπέκτεινεν) [Trans.]; *Herm. sim.* 6.3.3: "punishes them . . . with various terrible punishments" (τιμωρεῖ αὐτοὺς . . . δειναῖς

καὶ ποικίλαις τιμωρίαις); 6.3.4: "these various punishments . . . the various tortures and punishments" (τὰς ποικίλας ταύτας τιμωρίας . . . τὰς ποικίλας βασάνους καὶ τιμωρίας . . . ἀσθενείαις ποικίλαις); 7.4: "with various afflictions" (ἐν πάσαις θλίψεσι ποικίλαις).
33 Cf. the Analysis.
34 See above in the Introduction, section 1.
35 See below on 4:3.
36 Grammatically, it is noteworthy that here and in 2:15 the genitive is used with λείπεσθαι ("to lack"), but that 1:4 has ἐν μηδενὶ λειπόμενοι ("lacking in nothing"). This is evidence for the linguistic development which curtails the use of the genitive in favor of prepositional combinations yet without completely dropping it. The genitive in this instance is the genitive of separation; cf. Blass–Debrunner, § 180.4. The placing of the adverb at the end of the

in Jas which describes God's giving with the adverb ἁπλῶς has been interpreted in different ways, with ἁπλῶς meaning either "with pure thoughts, without ulterior motives,"[37] or "graciously, generously."[38] Both meanings are attested in the milieu to which our saying belongs.

1) The variation of the original meaning "purity" to the meaning "open-heartedness" or "kindness" can best be observed in the *Testament of Issachar*. The ἁπλότης, of which the speaker represents himself as the model, is the antithesis to being "meddlesome" (περίεργος), "jealous" (φθονερός), "envious" (βάσκανος see *Test. Iss.* 3.3), and to lusting after gold or luxury (4.2; 6.1); therefore, the term here means "uprightness, moderation." Yet along with this stands 3.8, where the meaning "open-heartedness" or "kindness" is found: "For from my earthly goods I provided everything for the poor and the oppressed out of the *kindness* of my heart" (πάντα γὰρ πένησι καὶ θλιβομένοις παρεῖχον ἐκ τῶν ἀγαθῶν τῆς γῆς ἐν ἁπλότητι καρδίας μου) [Trans.]. Here also belongs the passage in Josephus, *Ant.* 7.332: Ornàn the Jebusite desires to give over his threshing-floor to David without charge for the erection of an altar: "The king then said that he admired him for his *generosity* and magnanimity" (ὁ δὲ βασιλεὺς ἀγαπᾶν μὲν αὐτὸν τῆς ἁπλότητος καὶ τῆς μεγαλοψυχίας ἔλεγε). Paul, for whom ἁπλότης means "purity" in 2 Cor 11:3 and Col 3:22 (Eph 6:5), uses the word in connection with giving in 2 Cor 8:2; 9:11, 13, and perhaps also Rom 12:8. The reference in the 2 Cor 8 and 9 passages, at any rate, is to the size of the gift, and the word there means "generosity." However, the passage in Lucian, *Tim.* 56, which Theodor Nägeli[39] introduces as evidence for the meaning "generosity" in our passage, proves nothing; for in the words, "toward a man so simple and ready to share his possessions as you" (πρὸς ἄνδρα οἷον σὲ ἁπλοϊκὸν καὶ τῶν ὄντων κοινωνικόν), the term "simple" (ἁπλοϊκός) is not a synonym for the second adjective, but rather is intended to express

Timon's good-natured simplicity (= εὐήθεια in *Tim.* 8).

2) On the other hand, the original meaning "pure" has also acquired the special nuances "direct," "without mental reservations," "unreservedly." Marcus Aurelius clearly demonstrates this. In a section (11.15) directed against artificial sincerity (ἐπιτήδευσις ἁπλότητος), the word is found still with its fundamental meaning; and the adjectival form of the word occurring in the same paragraph must be understood in the corresponding sense: "the good, *sincere*, and well-disposed man" (ὁ ἀγαθὸς καὶ ἁπλοῦς καὶ εὐμενής 11.15.6).[40] Yet the adverb ἁπλῶς, especially when it is used with "freely" (ἐλευθέρως), is found in Marcus Aurelius with the meaning "unreservedly" or "without mental reservation"; cf. 3.6.6, where "choose the better *unreservedly* and openly" (ἁπλῶς καὶ ἐλευθέρως ἑλοῦ τὸ κρεῖττον) corresponds to the words in 3.6.3: "allow room for nothing else" (μηδενὶ χώραν δίδου ἑτέρῳ) [Trans.]; 5.7.2, where it is said with reference to the prayer of the Athenians, "Either do not pray at all, or pray in this *frank* and open manner" (ἤτοι οὐ δεῖ εὔχεσθαι ἢ οὕτως, ἁπλῶς καὶ ἐλευθέρως) [Trans.]; and 10.8.5: "depart from life not in anger, but *unreservedly*, freely, and with modesty" (ἔξιθι τοῦ βίου μὴ ὀργιζόμενος, ἀλλὰ ἁπλῶς καὶ ἐλευθέρως καὶ αἰδημόνως, cf. also Epict., *Diss.* 2.2.13). A similar narrowing of the meaning is displayed in the *Shepherd of Hermas* in combinations of ἁπλῶς with verbs of giving. Admittedly, in *Herm. mand.* 2.1 and 2.7 the phrase "have simplicity" (ἁπλότητα ἔχε) is found as the equivalent of "be innocent" (ἄκακος γίνου); yet in the same *Mandate* (2.4) it is unambiguously stated, "give *unreservedly* to all who are in need, not considering to whom you should give and to whom you should not give" (πᾶσιν ὑστερουμένοις δίδου ἁπλῶς, μὴ διστάζων τίνι δῷς ἢ τίνι μὴ δῷς) [Trans.]; and similarly, in *Herm. mand.* 2.6, the word ἁπλῶς is explained as "not debating to whom he should give and to whom he should not give" (μηθὲν διακρίνων τίνι δῷ ἢ μὴ δῷ) [Trans.]. *Herm. sim.* 9.24.2f

---

expression "from him who gives to all without hesitation" (παρὰ τοῦ διδόντος πᾶσιν ἁπλῶς) is not unusual in Koine; cf. Radermacher, *Grammatik*, 174; Blass–Debrunner, § 474.5.

37 So most modern commentators; also *ff*: "openly" (simpliciter).

38 F. J. A. Hort, *The Epistle of St. James* (London: MacMillan, 1909), *ad loc.*; see the Appendix in Mayor,

p. 25; Ludwig Gaugusch, *Der Lehrgehalt der Jakobusepistel*, Freiburger Theologische Studien 16, eds. G. Hoberg and G. Pfeilschifter (Freiburg: Herder, 1914); also sy^vg and vulg: "richly" (affluenter).

39 Nägeli, *Wortschatz*, 52.

40 Bonhöffer, *Epiktet und das NT*, 108, because of the parallelism, wants to take ἁπλοῦς here to mean "gracious"; yet the sense of the section as a whole

also obviously belongs here; in that passage it is said of the faithful, who are described as being ἁπλοῖ, that "from their labors they provided for everyone, *without reproaching or hesitating*; the Lord, therefore, seeing their *lack of reservation* and total child–likeness . . ." (ἐκ τῶν κόπων αὐτῶν παντὶ ἀνθρώπῳ ἐχορήγησαν ἀνονειδίστως καὶ ἀδιστάκτως. [ὁ οὖν] κύριος ἰδὼν τὴν ἁπλότητα αὐτῶν καὶ πᾶσαν νηπιότητα) [Trans.];[41] cf. also *Herm. sim.* 2.7: "provide for the poor man without hesitation" (ἀδιστάκτως παρέχει τῷ πένητι) [Trans.].

Judging by these last–mentioned parallels, and by the phrase "without reproaching" (μὴ ὀνειδίζων) which follows ἁπλῶς in our passage, the special sense mentioned in 2) is to be preferred and the word ought to be translated "without hesitation."[42]

The admonition not to allow vacillation and hesitation to hinder giving is found also in Prov 3:28, and in Pseudo–Phocylides 22: "Give to the poor man right away, and do not say, 'Come back tomorrow'" (πτωχῷ εὐθὺ δίδου, μηδ' αὔριον ἔλθεμεν εἴπῃς) [Trans.]. And Jas (as well as *Hermas*) alludes to still another abuse with regard to giving in this verse, viz., grumbling—rudely and with reproach holding up to the recipient the size of the gift, "upbraiding" him with it, as Luther translates it. This admonition seems to belong to the

common store of Greek as well as Jewish moral Wisdom.[43] From there it has been adopted by Christianity, as is shown by—in addition to our verse—the saying in the "Two Ways" in *Did.* 4.7 = *Barn.* 19.11: "Do not hesitate to give nor grumble in your giving" (οὐ διστάσεις δοῦναι οὐδὲ διδοὺς γογγύσεις) [Trans.].[44] God does not operate like that sort of human benefactor. Whoever finds this thought impossible on the grounds that the comparison is improper should read *Ps. Sol.* 5.13–15, or Philo, *Cher.* 122f, where human and divine gifts are compared.

God gives without hesitation and without grumbling: Therefore, whoever asks from him will receive: "and so it will be given to him" (καὶ δοθήσεται αὐτῷ).[45] It is not necessary to hypothesize a literary relationship between our saying and the dominical saying in Matt 7:7. The formulation in each case is self–explanatory (cf. "Ask from me and I will give to you the nations" [αἴτησαι παρ' ἐμοῦ καὶ δώσω σοι ἔθνη κτλ.] in Ps 2:8), and the concept is a frequent commonplace of Jewish–Christian didactic Wisdom. It is found once more in Jas (5:16) and twice in Sirach (7:10; 32:21); it is transmitted as a saying of Jesus in various passages and in various forms (Mk 11:23f = Matt 21:21f; Lk 17:5f; Matt 17:20; cf. also 1 Cor 13:2); but the most extensive treatment of it is provided by *Herm. mand.* 9.

■ **6** At the same time, this passage in *Herm. mand.* 9

---

speaks against this.

41 A later example of this meaning is found in Himerius (4th cent. A.D.), *Ecloga* 5.19, p. 18 Dübner: "If it is not reasonable to receive when someone gives *openly*, how much less when he does not provide the gift freely" (εἰ δὲ ἁπλῶς διδόντος λαβεῖν οὐκ εὔλογον, πῶς οὐ πλέον, ὅτε μηδὲ προῖκα [παρέχει] τὴν δωρεάν) [Trans.]. As the antithesis shows, "to give openly" (ἁπλῶς διδόναι) here means to give without expecting anything in return.

42 Harald Riesenfeld, "ἉΠΛΩΣ: Zu Jak. 1, 5," *Con Neot* 9 (1944): 33–41, cites abundant evidence where the term ἁπλῶς means "without exception," especially in combination with πᾶς ("all, every"). But considering the very close material connection with "to give" (διδόναι) which the word has in Jas 1:5, and which is also found in *Herm. mand.* 2, Riesenfeld wants to relate ἁπλῶς to the verb in the Jas passage and to translate it "without reservation." Cf. also Dibelius, *Der Hirt des Hermas*, on *Herm. mand.* 2.1.4.

43 Plut., *Adulat.* 64A: "Every favour which is made into a reproach is offensive and unpleasant and in-

tolerable" (πᾶσα μὲν γὰρ ὀνειδιζομένη χάρις ἐπαχθὴς καὶ ἄχαρις καὶ οὐκ ἀνεκτή) [Trans.]; further examples are given by Mayor. Among the Jewish texts, cf. especially Sir 18:15ff; 20:14ff; 41:22(28): "After giving, do not then reproach" (μετὰ τὸ δοῦναι μὴ ὀνείδιζε); the source of the "Two Ways" (see above); *Aboth de R. Nathan* 13, where the statement in *Pirke Aboth* 1.13, "Receive all men with cheerful countenance," is explained as follows: Even if a man gives his friend the most valuable gift, and yet he does not do it cheerfully, then that is as good as if he had given him nothing.

44 In Christian literature, the idea occurs also in 1 Petr 4:9; *Sibyl.* 2.91, 273; Macarius Magnes, *Apocriticus* 3.43, p. 149.10 Blondel; Cf. Hans Windisch, *Der Barnabasbrief*, HNT Ergänzungsband, part 3 (Tübingen: Mohr [Siebeck], 1920), on *Barn.* 19.11.

45 We can resolve the coordinating καί here as well as in Matt 7:7 and Jas 4:7f with "and then" or "and so." This parataxis is found elsewhere, not only in translation Greek (e.g. LXX Isa 55:6; Matt 7:7), but also in original Greek: Epict., *Diss.* 1.28.20:

provides the best commentary on our v 6, especially on the synonymous phrases "in faith" (ἐν πίστει) and "with no doubting" (μηδὲν διακρινόμενος).[46] In his warning against "uncertainty" or "double–mindedness" (διψυχία Herm. mand. 9.1), Hermas writes that one who is praying should not say to himself: "How can I ask anything from the Lord and receive it after having sinned so greatly against him?" (πῶς δύναμαι αἰτήσασθαί τι παρὰ τοῦ κυρίου καὶ λαβεῖν, ἡμαρτηκὼς τοσαῦτα εἰς αὐτόν). This admonition is then beautifully and profoundly supported in 9.3ff: Whoever does not rid himself of that anxious question when praying degrades God, for he thinks that God bears grudges with regard to evil in the same way that humans do. But whoever purifies his heart from all the vanities of this world, turns himself to God with undivided heart, and without any doubting places his hope in the granting of the petition, such a one will receive. In the explicit admonition (9.4): "purify your heart from all the vanities of this world" (καθάρισόν σου τὴν καρδίαν ἀπὸ πάντων τῶν ματαιωμάτων τοῦ αἰῶνος τούτου), there is no doubt a warning against expressing in prayer desires which are all too human. Then we might associate this warning with the occasional disappointment of confidence placed in prayer.[47] But even for Hermas the important thing with regard to prayer is firm faith in its fulfillment: "But they who are perfect in faith ask for all things, 'trusting in the Lord,' and they receive them, because they ask without doubting, and are *in no way uncertain*. For every *double–minded man*, unless he repent, shall with difficulty be saved" (οἱ δὲ ὁλοτελεῖς ὄντες ἐν τῇ πίστει πάντα αἰτοῦνται πεποιθότες ἐπὶ τὸν κύριον καὶ λαμβάνουσιν, ὅτι ἀδιστάκτως αἰτοῦνται μηδὲν διψυχοῦντες. πᾶς γὰρ δίψυχος ἀνήρ, ἐὰν μὴ μετανοήσῃ, δυσκόλως σωθήσεται Herm. mand. 9.6) [Loeb modified]; ". . . but put on faith, because it is mighty, and *believe God, that you shall obtain all your requests which you make*" (ἔνδυσαι δὲ τὴν πίστιν, ὅτι ἰσχυρά ἐστι, καὶ πίστευε τῷ θεῷ, ὅτι πάντα τὰ αἰτήματά σου ἃ αἰτεῖς λήψῃ 9.7). It can be

seen that Hermas has here quite unambiguously connected faith and doubt with the granting of petitions made in prayer.

That this is the faith which is intended in our passage was already declared in ancient exegesis of the text; cf. the Catena, under the lemma "Cyril": "For if you have not believed that He fulfills your request, do not approach Him at all, lest unwittingly having uncertainties you be found accusing Him who is in every way powerful" (εἰ γὰρ μὴ πεπίστευκας, ὅτι τὴν σὴν αἴτησιν ἀποπεραίνει, μηδὲ προσῆλθες ὅλως ἵνα μὴ κατήγορος εὑρεθῇς τοῦ πάντα ἰσχύοντος, διψυχήσας ἀβουλήτως).[48]

However, the majority of modern commentators[49] want to take "faith" (πίστις) here in a broader sense. In support of this, they call upon both an exegetical argument and a theological argument. First of all, they refer to v 7: according to this verse, they say, the person who is said to be a doubter nevertheless hopes to receive something from the Lord. Yet in this verse Jas does not at all say, "Such a man is deluded in his hope"; instead, he means only that "a man who doubts when praying will receive nothing," and he expresses this idea in a purely rhetorical paraphrase thusly: "But let him not suppose that. . . ." However, in this he is not saying that the doubter actually has such hopes. Secondly, they make use of a theological argument: the concept of faith discussed in 2:14–26 must underlie this passage as well, and consequently faith and doubt need not be restricted to the granting of petitions made in prayer. But such an argument is not sound when it comes to a paraenetic text such as Jas. For in a paraenesis too many diverse elements are combined to allow one to draw inferences from one passage to another, as can be done in the Pauline letters; there is no "theology" of Jas.[50]

Therefore, if the arguments which have been mentioned are not proof that "faith" and "doubt" are to be construed in a more general sense, then the most natural interpretation seems after all to be to connect

---

"Seek and (then) you will find that he differs in some other respect" (ζήτει καὶ εὑρήσεις ὅτι ἄλλῳ διαφέρει); 2.20.4: "Believe me, and (then) it will be to your advantage" (πίστευσόν μοι καὶ ὠφεληθήσῃ). Therefore, even if one is going to say that the style of our verse is akin in form to a Semitic saying, nevertheless the syntactical phenomenon of this parataxis need not be called "Semitic"; cf. Blass-

Debrunner, § 442.2.

46 μηδέν is the accusative neuter singular used adverbially; cf. Radermacher, *Grammatik*, 54 and n. 8; Franz Völker, *Papyrorum Graecarum syntaxis specimen*, Diss. Bonn (Bonn: Caroli Georgi Univ., 1900), 9.

47 Cf. below, and see also *Herm. mand.* 9.7.

48 The same interpretation is found without the name Cyril in the Scholion (= Christian Friedrich Mat-

them with the granting of petitions made in prayer. *Hermas*, above all, provides positive evidence for this, even if one cannot be convinced (as I cannot) of a relationship of direct literary dependence between that writing and Jas.[51] Nevertheless, precisely because there seems to be no literary dependence between the two, the fact that they reflect a common atmosphere becomes so clear (cf. the designation of the doubter as the "double–minded man" [ἀνὴρ δίψυχος] in Jas 1:8 and *Herm. mand.* 9.6) that the same interpretation of the two texts seems imperative.

Within early Christianity, Jas and *Hermas* by no means stand alone in their connection of faith with the granting of prayer requests. It is demanded in the saying of Jesus about faith which moves mountains (Mk 11:23f = Matt 21:21f).[52] It is also that which is demanded in the Synoptic Gospel miracle stories in Mk 2:5; 4:40; 5:34, 36; 9:23f; Matt 8:10; 9:28. And as inappropriate as it would be to drag in here what Paul otherwise calls faith,[53] nevertheless the "faith" which he mentions among the "gifts of the Spirit" is certainly this faith that a request will be granted, that the miracle will happen (1 Cor 12:9; 13:2; 2 Cor 8:7; Gal 5:22). No doubt the same thing is intended in the "Two Ways" passage in *Barn.* 19.5 = *Did.* 4.4: "Do not be uncertain about whether it will be or not" (οὐ μὴ διψυχήσῃς πότερον ἔσται ἢ οὔ) [Trans.].[54]

Therefore, it is the certainty that the request will be granted which Jas calls "faith." In this, he certainly does not intend—this must be inferred from the attitude otherwise displayed in his writing—to promote a

pneumatic, ecstatic effort to force heaven down to earth. Instead, he is thinking as a teacher (see 3:1) of the example of the heroes of prayer, and he would like to provoke emulation of their faith; this is confirmed by 5:15–18. But he is probably also familiar with disappointments which such confidence has encountered, and therefore in 1:5 he urges his readers to pray for wisdom, in 4:3, to pray correctly, and in 5:16, to confess sins before prayer.[55] His faith in the granting of the prayer requests is not diminished because of this.

In harmony with this is the metaphor of the sea; the point of the comparison is emphasized by means of the two participles;[56] their meanings are rather similar and their identical endings are no doubt intentional, for Jas is fond of such artistic devices.[57] Sea metaphors are used frequently in diatribe and in Philo, so that a comparison of this sort is quite comprehensible in an author such as Jas, who makes use of metaphorical language from this literature in other places as well.[58] But the application of the metaphor here is very simple and natural, and therefore its use at least need not have been transmitted through literary channels. Moreover, the Greek and Jewish parallels which have thus far been adduced[59] generally prove nothing more than the popularity of this group of metaphors. When one also compares the passages in Philo, *Sacr. AC.* 90 and *Gig.*

---

thaei, *SS. Apostolorum Septem Epistolae Catholicae* [Riga, 1782], *ad loc.*) and Theoph; so also Hofmann.

49 E.g., Spitta, Beyschlag, Ropes.

50 Cf. above in the Introduction, sections 3 and 8.

51 Cf. above in the Introduction, section 4, and on our passage, n. 103.

52 See above on 1:5.

53 Cf. the second Excursus on 2:26.

54 Both Rudolph Knopf, *Die Lehre der Zwölf Apostel, Die zwei Clemensbriefe*, HNT Ergänzungsband, part 1 (Tübingen: Mohr [Siebeck], 1920), on *Did.* 4.4, and Windisch, *Barnabasbrief*, on *Barn.* 19.5, want to take the statement as a reference to an eschatological hope, corresponding to the apocryphon from *1 Clem.* 23.3 and *2 Clem.* 11.2 quoted below in n. 65.

55 Cf. above on 1:5, and below on 4:3 and 5:16.

56 ἀνεμίζειν ("to drive with the wind") and ῥιπίζειν ("to toss") occur only here in the New Testament.

The extent to which this is merely an accident can be seen from the use of ῥιπίζειν in LXX Dan 2:35; *Arist.* 70; Philo, *Aet. mund.* 125; Epict., Frag. F 2, p. 487 Schenkl; Dio Chrys., *Or.* 32.23; ἀναρριπίζεσθαι in Philo, *Gig.* 51 (the last three passages are quoted below in n. 59). All these examples use ῥιπίζειν of the wind just as in Jas! Accordingly, one must consider as methodologically unacceptable the assumption of Mayor that the verb ἀνεμίζειν, for which we otherwise have only late attestation, is a creation of our author.

57 See above in the Introduction, section 5.

58 Cf. below on 3:3ff.

59 The image is not distinct in Isa 57:20 and Eph 4:14; Jude 13 does not belong in this context at all. Philo, *Sacr. AC.* 90 resembles our passage only in the expression: "not to be carried hither and thither, ever passive amid the surge and eddy and swirl"

51,[60] then it becomes likely that κλύδων here does not mean "wave," but rather "billowing, surging." Therefore the doubter is not compared with the wave, but with the restless sea stirred up by the wind.

■ **7** The main point of this verse has already been explained. μὴ γάρ means "but (let him) certainly not."[61] The "Lord" (κύριος) here is God, and the same meaning can be assumed with confidence in at least 3:9; 4:10, 15; 5:4, 10, 11.[62] The expression "that person" (ὁ ἄνθρωπος ἐκεῖνος) constitutes a Semitism, as does also the pleonastic use of ἀνήρ in ἀνὴρ δίψυχος ("double-minded man") in v 8. Similar expressions are found in *Hermas*, which is linguistically as well as literarily closely related to our writing: *Herm. mand.* 5.2.7; 11.12.14; *Herm. sim.* 9.6.3.

■ **8** The use of ἀνήρ (strictly, an adult male) to mean the same thing as ἄνθρωπος (a person) is frequent within the LXX in the Psalms and in the Wisdom literature; compare Ps 1:1 (where it translates איש, which usually = "man, husband, etc.") with LXX Ps 31:2 (where it translates אדם, which = "human being").[63]

Luther, Hofmann, and de Wette have understood v 8 as a separate sentence: "A doubter is unstable."[64] Yet since it has still not been said why the doubter receives nothing, this verse must be construed appositionally; the absence of the article cannot be used as a counter-argument to this, since the subject "that person" (ὁ ἄνθρωπος ἐκεῖνος) designates a type and not an individual. Appositional elements are appended in a similar fashion in 3:2, 8 and 4:12.

The meaning of this description is best explained with the words of Hermas, who in the passage already cited from *Herm. mand.* 9.2 demands that one who prays "turn to the Lord with all your heart," and says in 9.5: "For those who have doubts towards God, these are the double-minded, and they shall not in any wise obtain any of their petitions" (οἱ γὰρ διστάζοντες εἰς τὸν θεόν, οὗτοί εἰσιν οἱ δίψυχοι καὶ οὐδὲν ὅλως ἐπιτυγχάνουσι τῶν αἰτημάτων αὐτῶν). Also in harmony with this are the other passages from early Christian literature which equate "the person who is uncertain, the double-minded person" (δίψυχος) with "the person who doubts" (διστάζων), and "uncertainty, double-mindedness" (διψυχία) with "unbelief" (ἀπιστία). In other words, this διψυχ- word group is not at all so peculiar

---

(οὐχ ἵνα σάλον καὶ τροπὴν καὶ κλύδωνα ὧδε κἀκεῖσε φορούμενος ἀστάτως ὑπομένῃς). The simile of the ship and sea, only alluded to in Sir 36(33):2, displays in other texts a kinship with our passage which is worthy of note: Epict., *Frag. F* 2, p. 487 Schenkl: "like a ship without a pilot amidst stormy *billows*, or *tossed* in darkness by contrary winds" (δίκην ἀκυβερνήτου νεὼς ἐν χειμερίῳ κλύδωνι ἢ ὑπ' ἀντιπάλων ῥιπιζομένης ἀνέμων ζόφῳ) [Trans.]. And Philo compares the doubter to a stormed-tossed ship (*Migr. Abr.* 148): "for some men are *irresolute, facers both ways*, inclining to either side like a boat tossed by winds from opposite quarters" (εἰσὶ γάρ τινες ἐνδοιασταὶ καὶ ἐπαμφοτερισταί, πρὸς ἑκάτερον τοῖχον ὥσπερ σκάφος ὑπ' ἐναντίων πνευμάτων διαφερόμενον ἀποκλίνοντες). More akin as far as subject matter is concerned are comparisons of the populace with waves and sea: Demosthenes, *De falsa legatione* 136: "That the populace is the most unstable and capricious thing in the world, like a *restless wave of the sea* ruffled by the breeze" (ὡς ὁ μὲν δῆμός ἐστιν ἀσταθμητότατον πρᾶγμα τῶν πάντων καὶ ἀσυνθετώτατον, ὥσπερ ἐν θαλάττῃ κῦμ' ἀκατάστατον ὡς ἂν τύχῃ κινούμενον) [Loeb modified]; Dio Chrys., *Or.* 32.23 cites both Homer, *Il.* 2.144ff: "Then stirred was the assembly, as the *sea sends forth long billows*" (κινήθη δ' ἀγορὴ ὡς κύματα μακρὰ θαλάσσης), and also the following fragment:

"Unstable and evil is the populace, and just like the *sea* it is *tossed by the wind*" (δῆμος ἄστατον κακὸν καὶ θαλάττῃ πάνθ' ὅμοιον ὑπ' ἀνέμων ῥιπίζεται) [Loeb modified]. Philo also comes close to the metaphor in our passage when he compares the struggle within man to the storm-tossed sea: "For indeed one who sees the perpetual war-in-peace of humans . . . and still more in each individual man—the fierce mysterious storm in the soul, *whipped into fury* by the wild blast of life and its cares—can well wonder that another should find fair weather in the storm, or calm amid the waves of the tempestuous sea" (ἰδὼν γάρ τις τὸν ἐν εἰρήνῃ συνεχῆ πόλεμον ἀνθρώπων . . . μᾶλλον δὲ καὶ καθ' ἕνα ἄνδρα ἕκαστον, καὶ τὸν ἐν ταῖς ψυχαῖς ἄλεκτον καὶ βαρὺν χειμῶνα, ὃς ὑπὸ βιαιοτάτης φορᾶς τῶν κατὰ τὸν βίον πραγμάτων ἀναρριπίζεται, τεθαύμακεν εἰκότως, εἴ τις ἐν χειμῶνι εὐδίαν ἢ ἐν κλύδωνι κυμαινούσης θαλάττης γαλήνην ἄγειν δύναται *Gig.* 51) [Loeb modified].

60 Quoted in the preceding footnote.

61 On γάρ meaning "to be sure," cf. Blass-Debrunner, § 452.2.

62 Cf. below on 5:14, n. 67.

63 On the question of Semitisms, see above in the Introduction, section 5.

64 Cf. also the variant ἀνὴρ γάρ in 88 326 1837, and the reading in vulg: *inconstans est.*

within early Christianity as would appear from the New Testament, which has this root only in Jas 1:8 and 4:8.[65] And we have no right to designate the word "double-minded" (δίψυχος) as an early Christian formation merely because it is not attested earlier; for many of the Christian witnesses point to an earlier period,[66] and the early Christian use of the word no longer exhibits any trace of the graphic character which obviously belonged to the word as it was originally coined.[67]

Therefore, in the interpretation of our passage one must forgo all the examples of a metaphysical dualism such as are usually adduced—perhaps wrongly there also—in the interpretation of Doctor Faustus' saying about the "two souls."[68] The dualism which is mentioned in our passage can in any event be only a practical dualism; what is involved is vacillation between certainty and uncertainty with regard to whether prayer will be answered. And Jewish paraenesis also seems to have warned against precisely this practice. For certainly prayer is what is intended in the second half of the saying in Sirach 1:28: "Do not disobey the fear of the Lord; do not approach him with a divided mind" (μὴ ἀπειθήσῃς φόβῳ κυρίου καὶ μὴ προσέλθῃς αὐτῷ ἐν καρδίᾳ δισσῇ). And a late echo of this admonition is found in the *Midrash Tanhuma* (on Deut 26:16);[69] there it is said with regard to the time when the Israelites pray that "they should not have two hearts."

Since the concluding words of the verse obviously offer a parallel characteristic of the "double-minded man," and not a prophecy of his fate, then ἀκατάστατος κτλ. cannot mean "driven about restlessly,"[70] but rather "vacillating in all his activity and conduct." The expression "in all his ways" (ἐν πάσαις ταῖς ὁδοῖς) has already in the LXX become a fixed expression with this meaning.[71] Thus the admonition of the saying is broadened at the conclusion: The person who in prayer lacks certainty with regard to God is also in his conduct lacking in inner stability—an impressive example of the ethos of our author!

■ **1:9–11** The saying about the downfall of the rich man introduces a new antithesis which is not combined by the author in any way with the preceding antithesis (faith and doubt). The hopelessness of establishing any connection in thought, and the dubiousness of

---

65 *1 Clem.* 23.2: "Therefore, let us not be double-minded" (διὸ μὴ διψυχῶμεν); 23.3: "Let this Scripture be far from us in which he says, 'Wretched are the double-minded, who doubt in their soul . . .'" (πόρρω γενέσθω ἀφ' ἡμῶν ἡ γραφὴ αὕτη, ὅπου λέγει· ταλαίπωροί εἰσιν οἱ δίψυχοι, οἱ διστάζοντες τῇ ψυχῇ); this quotation possibly comes from an (Jewish or early–Christian?) apocalyptic writing; it characterizes the doubters as those who scoff at the non-fulfillment of prophecy. It is also quoted in *2 Clem.* 11.2 as the "prophetic word" (προφητικὸς λόγος). In addition, cf. *1 Clem.* 11.2: With regard to Lot's wife, we are to learn "that those who are double-minded, and have doubts concerning the power of God, incur judgment and become a warning to all generations" (ὅτι οἱ δίψυχοι καὶ οἱ διστάζοντες περὶ τῆς τοῦ θεοῦ δυνάμεως εἰς κρίμα καὶ εἰς σημείωσιν πάσαις ταῖς γενεαῖς γίνονται); *2 Clem.* 19.2: "because of the double-mindedness and unbelief which is in our breasts" (διὰ τὴν διψυχίαν καὶ ἀπιστίαν τὴν ἐνοῦσαν ἐν τοῖς στήθεσιν ἡμῶν cf. 11.5); the passage from the "Two Ways" in *Barn.* 19.5 = *Did.* 4.4: "Do not doubt whether it will be or not" (οὐ μὴ διψυχήσῃς [*Did.* has οὐ διψυχήσεις] πότερον ἔσται ἢ οὔ). To that can be added more than 50 passages in *Hermas* where "to be double-minded" (διψυχεῖν), "double-mindedness" (διψυχία), or "double-minded" (δίψυχος)

are found. And in spite of this abundance of evidence, among which the saying from the "Two Ways" and the quotation in *1 and 2 Clem.* probably go back into the pre–Christian period, Mayor writes regarding this term that it was "seemingly introduced by St. James"! Cf. also above in the Introduction, n. 102.

66 See the preceding footnote.

67 Such a graphic character is found in Ps 12:3: "they speak with a double heart" (lit.: "they speak with a heart and with a heart" בְּלֵב וָלֵב יְדַבֵּרוּ; LXX: ἐν καρδίᾳ καὶ ἐν καρδίᾳ ἐλάλησαν); *1 Enoch* 91.4: "And draw not nigh to uprightness with a double heart, and associate not with those of a double heart" (trans. Charles, *APOT*). Cf. also the parallels from the *Test. XII* which are cited below on 4:8.

68 See Goethe, *Faust*, part 1, line 1112.

69 Salomon Buber, ed., מדרש תנחומא (Wilna: Wittwe & Gebrüder Romm, 1885), p. 46, lines 12f.

70 So Spitta, who appeals to Tob 1:15: "his ways [or 'roads'] were unstable" (αἱ ὁδοὶ αὐτοῦ ἠκατάστησαν). But this passage, which has a completely different construction, does not provide a parallel.

71 On "vacillating" (ἀκατάστατος), cf. *Passow's Wörterbuch der griechischen Sprache*, reedited by Wilhelm Crönert, fascicle 1 (Göttingen: Vandenhoeck & Ruprecht, 1912), *s.v.*

finding any external link, have been portrayed in the Analysis.[72] That part of the antithesis which is really important for the saying is first introduced in v 10: "but the rich man" (ὁ δὲ πλούσιος). And it is on this side of the antithesis that Jas dwells at length, while he speaks of "the lowly person" (ταπεινός) only in passing. This is decisive for the understanding of the saying: it is dealing with the rich man and his downfall.

■ **9** This verse provides only the foil for this theme, and must be interpreted accordingly. Therefore, ὕψος is to be construed as the opposite of "humiliation" (ταπείνωσις) and to be translated "exaltation"; cf. 1 Macc 10:24: "I also will write them words of encouragement and promise them exaltation and gifts" (γράψω κἀγὼ αὐτοῖς λόγους παρακλήσεως καὶ ὕψους καὶ δομάτων) [RSV modified]. And the "lowly person" (ταπεινός) is the counterpart to the "rich man" (πλούσιος), and is therefore the "pious Poor" as portrayed in the Introduction.[73] With a correct feeling for the ταπεινοί in our passage, Dionysius Bar Ṣalibi calls them the "poor in spirit" (pauperes spiritu).[74]

As the continuation shows, the words "let him boast, etc." (καυχάσθω κτλ.) do not contain an actual demand, but rather constitute a form of speech which is also used elsewhere when reality is being distinguished from appearance:[75] That of which a person may boast is that which is held as a sure and eternal possession;

perishable goods are no grounds for boasting. Possibly Jas has been influenced here by Jer 9:23f in particular, for judging by *1 Clem.* 13.1 early Christian paraenesis seems to have made use of this passage. But this literary relationship still does not explain the thought of the saying in Jas.

In vv 9–11, Jas voices the expectation of an imminent reversal of circumstances, which will bring deliverance to the poor man and humiliation to the rich man. That "exaltation" and "humiliation" have an eschatological significance, and not some ethical one, necessarily follows from the history of the consciousness of the pious Poor, as this history is outlined in the Introduction.[76]

■ **10** What must be examined here—before any further consideration of the person of the rich man—is the way in which this idea is worked out in v 10. Even if the author has taken over the thought, he still had the choice of whether to give to the saying a *heroic* or an *ironic* point. He could use the expression "let him boast" (καυχάσθω)—which is to be supplied in v 10 in either case[77]—in a completely serious way to say: "Boast over the coming cosmic transformation, because for that we are destined!" In this case, he would be presupposing the rich man to possess in full measure the heroism of eschatological religion, a heroism which joyfully faces the loss of all earthly goods since for this

---

72 Consequently, one must avoid pushing for some sort of logical significance of the introductory δέ ("but").

73 See above in the Introduction, section 6.

74 Dionysius Bar Ṣalibi, *In Apocalypsim, Actus et epistulas catholicas*, ed. and tr. (Latin) I. Sedlacek, CSCO, Scriptores Syri, series 2, vol. 101 (Rome: Karolus de Luigi, 1909), *ad loc.* ταπεινός occurs now and then in the LXX plainly as a translation for עני ("poor," "without possessions"): LXX Ps 17:28; 81:3; LXX Prov 24:37; Isa 14:32; 49:13; Jer 22:16. In general, it expresses a position midway between "poor" (πένης) and "beggarly" (πτωχός) on the one side, and "meek" (πραΰς) on the other; cf. Th. Häring, "Die עֲנִיִּים und עֲנָוִים im Alten Testament," *Theologische Studien aus Württemberg* 5 (1884): 160, and for the Psalms, the summary in Alfred Rahlfs, עָנִי und עָנָו *in den Psalmen* (Leipzig: Dieterich, 1892), 55ff, which is refuted by Edwin Hatch, *Essays in Biblical Greek* (Oxford: Clarendon, 1889), 74f. Therefore, ταπεινός must be evaluated in each instance according to its context, i.e., in this case, according to 1:10, and not 4:6, where it (in the quotation)

has an ethical significance.

75 LXX Jer 9:23f; 1 Kings 2:10; cf. also 1 Cor 1:31 and Philo, *Spec. leg.* 1.311. That this way of speaking is not only Jewish follows from the totally non-Jewish argument which Philo, in the passage just cited, attaches to his warning that one ought not to base one's pride and boasting upon wealth, honor, might, beauty, power, and similar things: None of these have in them anything of the nature of the Good, and they are subject to sudden change and—now a quite Jewish argument again—they wither away before they have fully bloomed.

76 See above in the Introduction, section 6.

77 There is not the slightest justification in the text for supplying any of the other words which have been suggested from time to time: "let him be ashamed" (αἰσχυνέσθω so Oec); "let him be humble" (ταπεινούσθω); "let him fear" (φοβείσθω); or "he boasts" (καυχᾶται). Herder, p. 546, is quite right in saying of the conjecture "let him fear," that then "all the beauty of the oriental gnome is gone."

78 Moreover, this sort of argument can be used to sup-

price something is gained which surpasses all goods: the coming of the Rule of God. The other possibility is that Jas is indeed completely serious about the poor man "boasting," but that with regard to the rich man he is only speaking ironically: "The rich man has had his day; all he can expect from the future is humiliation; that is the only thing left for him to 'boast about.'" This would then be some "boast"! There is no doubt that according to this second alternative "let him boast" would be said of the rich man in a consciously paradoxical way.

Which interpretation does our saying demand? Arguments based upon other portions of Jas are to be ruled out on methodological grounds;[78] the saying must be interpreted as an isolated saying, although naturally after it has been understood it may be compared with those sections which are related to it in content. Nor does the specific way in which the saying is formulated provide a useful argument; for even if one refers to the fact that it is the rich man himself who perishes, not just his wealth, that therefore the saying is aimed at the rich man,[79] this still is not evidence against the possibility of a heroic interpretation.

It seems to me that only the conclusion of the saying provides a decisive argument with regard to this question: the coming fate of the rich man is depicted with great elaboration, and not without satisfaction; and in fact it is *only* his downfall which is depicted! Nothing is mentioned which would compensate for this loss, no coming of the Kingdom is portrayed. Without any consolation for the rich man, the saying ends with "he will wither" ($\mu\alpha\rho\alpha\nu\theta\dot{\eta}\sigma\epsilon\tau\alpha\iota$). Downfall is the final prospect which Jas holds up to the rich man, and therefore he can only be speaking to him ironically when he refers to "boasting."[80] Hence, from v 10 on the saying is

intended ironically, and Bede is correct in his interpretation: "[The saying] is certainly spoken in derision, which in Greek is called 'irony'" (quod per irrisionem, quae Graece ironia vocatur, dictum esse constat). If, for the most part,[81] commentators have been unwilling to have anything to do with this interpretation, this has usually been due to the fact that their interpretation has been based upon an understanding of "rich man" to mean a rich Christian. But the question "Christian or non–Christian?" is imposed upon this verse from the outside; Jas himself does not have it in mind. Consequently, this problem, which cannot be quickly resolved, can be postponed until the conclusion, and the meaning of the saying need not be made dependent upon its resolution. But furthermore, it has frequently been left out of account in the interpretation of this passage that the antithesis between poor and rich had a history already within Judaism,[82] and that this history does not allow the interpretation of "humiliation" ($\tau\alpha\pi\epsilon\dot{\iota}\nu\omega\sigma\iota\varsigma$) to mean some inner condition, such as the lowly status of being a Christian. Here the fate of the rich man at the great cosmic transformation is spoken of without any sentimentality, and it is precisely such harsh words about and against the rich to which we are accustomed in the "literature of the Poor" in Judaism.

The rich man's fate is portrayed with the image of the grass: "just so" ($o\ddot{\upsilon}\tau\omega\varsigma$ v 11b)—that is to say, the rich man will perish "just this quickly." Grass and vegetation were favorite images in Jewish literature for transitoriness (Job 14:2; Ps 37:2; 90:5f; 103:15; Isa 40:6ff; 51:12; *2 Bar.* 82.7). It is with Isa 40:6ff that our passage has the clearest connection. Probably conscious that he is using words from the Bible, our author makes use of some expressions from the Isaiah

---

port two mutually exclusive viewpoints. For example, one could point out that elsewhere Jas shows himself to be embittered toward the rich, and consequently one must assume that here also there is bitter irony (Windisch, *Katholische Briefe* [1911]); but at the same time, one could infer from 4:13–16 that there were rich people among Jas' readers, and that therefore he could not speak of these people with such irony (Mayor). Still others have made use of the ideas in 1:2–4 for their arguments (Ropes). But none of these arguments are in harmony with the literary character of paraenesis, which lacks the sort

79 of connection which these arguments presuppose.
    So Huther and Beyschlag.

80 Schmidt, *Lehrgehalt*, 51, cites the paradox with which Paul in 2 Cor 11:30 boasts in his weakness; but that is something different, for Paul knows that "power is made perfect in weakness" ($\dot{\eta}\ \gamma\dot{\alpha}\rho\ \delta\dot{\upsilon}\nu\alpha\mu\iota\varsigma\ \dot{\epsilon}\nu\ \dot{\alpha}\sigma\theta\epsilon\nu\epsilon\dot{\iota}\alpha\ \tau\epsilon\lambda\epsilon\hat{\iota}\tau\alpha\iota$ 2 Cor 12:9).

81 Exceptions are Huther, Beyschlag, B. Weiss, Belser, Windisch, *Katholische Briefe* (1911)—cf. Hans Windisch, *Die katholischen Briefe*, 3rd edition by Herbert Preisker (Tübingen: Mohr [Siebeck], ³1951).

82 See above in the Introduction, section 6.

passage (but not from 1 Petr 1:24, where both the way in which the Isaiah passage is quoted and the point which is made with it are different) and he also follows its structure: introduction of the simile, its depiction, and the conclusion. But since he is not aiming toward an antithesis as is the prophet, he arrives at his conclusion by returning to the object of the simile.[83] Since at the end he needs to focus upon the rich man, he has inserted a clause ("and its beauty perishes" [ἡ εὐπρέπεια κτλ.]) to which he attaches the conclusion, "just so shall the rich man, etc." (οὕτως καὶ ὁ πλούσιος); to accommodate this inserted clause, he has—perhaps instinctively—rearranged the parallelism:

LXX Isa 40:6–8	Jas 1:10–11
All flesh is grass and all the glory of man is like the flower of the grass;	because like the flower of the grass he will pass away. For the sun rises with its scorching heat
the grass withers and the flower falls, but the word of our God abides for ever.	and withers the grass, and its flower falls, and its beauty perishes.
πᾶσα σὰρξ χόρτος καὶ πᾶσα δόξα ἀνθρώπου ὡς ἄνθος χόρτου	ὅτι ὡς ἄνθος χόρτου παρελεύσεται
ἐξηράνθη ὁ χόρτος καὶ τὸ ἄνθος ἐξέπεσεν τὸ δὲ ῥῆμα τοῦ θεοῦ ἡμῶν μένει εἰς τὸν αἰῶνα.	ἀνέτειλεν γὰρ ὁ ἥλιος σὺν τῷ καύσωνι καὶ ἐξήρανεν τὸν χόρτον καὶ τὸ ἄνθος αὐτοῦ ἐξέπεσεν καὶ ἡ εὐπρέπεια τοῦ προσώπου αὐτοῦ ἀπώλετο.

Because of the inserted "its" (αὐτοῦ, omitted in sy^hl and some minuscules under the influence of the LXX), the words "the flower falls" (τὸ ἄνθος ἐξέπεσεν) become an independent member in the Jas version. Since we are not certain whether Jas had Isa 40:6ff in mind, we cannot decide the question of whether he has merely rendered the Biblical expressions rather freely or whether he has consciously combined several texts, perhaps even some passages which are unknown to us.[84]

The word used here for "scorching heat" (καύσων) is used numerous times in the LXX to mean the hot east wind; but perhaps in Isa 49:10, and certainly in Matt 20:12 and Lk 12:55, it refers simply to heat. Because of the "with" (σύν), the word here has the second meaning, since the sun does bring with it heat—in Syria,[85] the temperature variations in a given day are far greater than in our country[86]—but not necessarily the hot wind.

The conclusion which Jas wants to draw could not be attached to "falls" (ἐξέπεσεν); accordingly, there follows still another clause, which brings into particular prominence the end of the flower which has fallen. The expression which Jas uses here for "its beauty" means literally "the beauty of its countenance." This use of πρόσωπον ("face, countenance") is also found in LXX Ps 103:30 and Lk 12:56 (see Matt 16:3); as is shown by precisely this passage in Jas, this usage is not an oddity which derives from an extremely slavish translation of a text from the Old Testament, but rather it is a peculiarity of the Greek spoken by Jews and no doubt it is to be traced back to the usage of the Hebrew word for "face, countenance" (פנים): it is therefore a so–called "usual" Semitism.[87]

πορεία means "journey," and it is frequently interpreted by commentators[88] to mean the business trips of the rich man (see 4:13). But like ὁδός (v 8), it can also refer to one's way of life or conduct; this is prob-

---

83   The metaphor is portrayed in the aorist, just as in the LXX, and in both places it is to be considered a gnomic aorist; cf. above in the Introduction, section 5. Herder translates the words in the past tense; but in the first written copy (see Suphan's edition, vol. 7, p. 494 n. 4) he has: "The sun *rises*, etc."

84   Spitta calls particular attention to Job 15:30, where the parching wind is mentioned; but there the word in the LXX is not καύσων, and furthermore, καύσων ("scorching heat") here in Jas 1:11 does not refer to the wind at all (see the discussion above in the text).

85   Given the saying's dependence on the Old Testament, we are justified in bringing up the question of conditions in Syria. But one must refrain from immediately assigning the letter as a whole to some local; cf. above in the Introduction, section 7.

86   Karl Bädeker, *Palestine and Syria: Handbook for Travellers* (New York: Scribner, ⁵1912), p. l.

87   On the distinction between "usual" and "occasional" Semitisms, see Deissmann, *Urgeschichte*, 5f. Naturally, all usual Semitisms were at one time occasional.

88   Cf. Herder, Belser, Mayor, Spitta, Windisch–

ably the meaning in LXX Prov 2:7, and surely the meaning in *1 Clem.* 48.4: "directing their conduct in holiness and righteousness" (καὶ κατευθύνοντες τὴν πορείαν αὐτῶν ἐν ὁσιότητι καὶ δικαιοσύνῃ) [Trans.], and *Herm. sim.* 5.6.6: "for the conduct of this flesh pleased him [i.e. God]" (ἤρεσε γὰρ ἡ πορεία τῆς σαρκὸς ταύτης). If one disregards 4:13—and in a document such as Jas there is no necessity to call upon that passage—, then an allusion to details from the life of the rich man is not to be inferred. Finally, if one is inclined to establish a certain kinship between the conclusion of this saying and the conclusion of the preceding saying,[89] then πορεία will be construed in parallel with "way" (ὁδός) in v 8 and be taken as a reference to the rich man's whole "way of life."[90, 91]

Admittedly, one thing is odd: the Christian who wrote this was thinking of the parousia and the cosmic transformation connected with it, and yet there is no eschatological passion glowing in his words. For comparison, one should call to mind the solemn fervor of 2 Thess 1:6f, or the seriousness of the warning in 1 Petr 4:17–19. Our passage gives no indication that an eschatological secret is being proclaimed: the conclusion which merely repeats the intitial thesis, the common imagery for human transience, the style of the simile using the gnomic aorist—all these point to the teacher, who in a calm tone is setting forth familiar themes. This tone can be explained upon the basis of the Jewish tradition from which both the imagery and the idea derive. The Jewish teachers who formulated them did not—or at least, not always—have in mind the eschatological cosmic transformation, but rather the power of their God, who even in earthly matters "can now exalt, now bring to ruin." What we read here are ideas from Jewish Wisdom which were originally

attuned to a mood of consolation: "The time to come will change much and will bring everyone to his appointed end." The Christian who wrote Jas took over these ideas and probably also reworked their form to suit his own needs, but without altering the traditional style and without introducing a new nuance. Even without this, he and his readers knew what they could hope for from the "time to come": the glorious future of the Rule of God.

Only from this viewpoint can we approach the much discussed question of whether the rich man is a Christian or a non–Christian. It can scarcely be solved by an exegetical route, for here one argument stands opposed to another: reading the passage without any preconceptions, one at first thinks that "brother" (ἀδελφός) must be supplied,[92] but no trace of any allusion to a brotherly relationship can be found in the harsh words of vv 10f.[93] Therefore, it is by no means clear from the outset whether Jas has in mind a rich Christian or non–Christian. The history of the concepts poor and rich in Judaism[94] indicates the reason for this lack of clarity: that portion of the people who called themselves "the Poor" viewed the powerful rich man as the lawless "transgressor." It made no difference whether this transgressor belonged to the Jewish faith externally or not—in any case, he no longer belonged to it inwardly. Jas has taken over this model, and consequently he has said nothing about whether his "rich man" is to be sought within Christianity or not. Whom does he have in mind? In any event, it must be people who are spiritually alien to the pious community, for otherwise the conclusion of the saying could not read as it does. Therefore, he may have had in mind primarily non–Christians; but if he was thinking here of Christians as well, then these are people whom he con-

---

Preisker.

89 See the Analysis.

90 This is probably the understanding of Theoph when he renders πορεία with "the events of this present life" (τὰς κατὰ τὸν παρόντα βίον διεξόδους); the same interpretation in *ff*: "in his conduct" (*in actu suo*; but *s* and vulg have "in his travels" [*in itineribus suis*]), as well as Dionysius Bar Ṣalibi, and among modern commentators, Gebser, Beyschlag, and Ropes.

91 πορίαις is simply another spelling of πορείαις, but it led Luther to the translation "possessions." For many, the conclusion of the saying was too colorless,

and this accounts for the (quite scattered) variations among the manuscripts at this point: "in his prosperity" (εὐπορίαις); "in his wickedness" (πονηρίαις), etc.

92 Gebser, Ewald, Hofmann, Burger, von Soden, Mayor, Ropes.

93 Beyschlag; B. Weiss, *Jakobusbrief*; Belser.

94 See above in the Introduction, section 6.

siders no longer to be included in a proper sense within Christendom.[95]

■ 12 This is an isolated saying which is connected neither with what follows[96] nor with what precedes. For the harsh judgment which vv 9–11 render with regard to the rich man excludes the possibility that here he is praised as "blessed."[97] The saying obviously belongs to the theme touched upon in 1:2–4; therefore, "to endure trial" ($\dot{\upsilon}\pi o\mu\acute{\epsilon}\nu\epsilon\iota\nu\ \pi\epsilon\iota\rho\alpha\sigma\mu\acute{o}\nu$) is to be understood in the same sense as "trials" ($\pi\epsilon\iota\rho\alpha\sigma\mu o\acute{\iota}$) and "endurance" ($\dot{\upsilon}\pi o\mu o\nu\acute{\eta}$) in 1:2 and 1:3. There is only one difference: the "trials" which are presupposed in the earlier verses are troubles involving the community addressed collectively as "brothers"; here, where it is the individual person who is being discussed, we may imagine the misfortune of the individual.

The form of the saying is that of a macarism (beatitude), a form which is frequent in Hebrew didactic poetry. The beginning, "Blessed is the person" ($\mu\alpha\kappa\acute{\alpha}\rho\iota o\varsigma\ \dot{\alpha}\nu\acute{\eta}\rho$),[98] is found very frequently in the LXX.[99]

The expression "approved, tested" ($\delta\acute{o}\kappa\iota\mu o\varsigma$) is comprehensible without any reference to a metaphor—some have thought of the testing of the athlete or the refining of metal. $\delta\acute{o}\kappa\iota\mu o\varsigma\ \gamma\epsilon\nu\acute{o}\mu\epsilon\nu o\varsigma$ naturally is not to be construed as a condition ("*if* he stands the test"), but rather must be translated "*after*" or "*since* he is approved"; no doubt can surface with regard to his confirmation, for here the subject is strictly "he who endures" ($\dot{\upsilon}\pi o\mu\acute{\epsilon}\nu\omega\nu$).

Our author has as little intention of alluding to a concrete metaphor with the expression "crown of life" ($\sigma\tau\acute{\epsilon}\phi\alpha\nu o\varsigma\ \tau\mathring{\eta}\varsigma\ \zeta\omega\mathring{\eta}\varsigma$) as he had with the term "approved, tested." Nevertheless, the genitive "of life," which is not immediately explicable, gives some indication that the expression has a history, and it requires religio-historical orientation. One could think of the garland which is awarded to the contestant in the stadium;[100] in that case, the genitive "of life" would be contrasting the eternal crown with that perishable one. Or one could refer to the practice of bestowing a crown in the mysteries; in that case, "life" would perhaps refer to the life-giving, divinizing power of the crown. But this practice in the mysteries points back to the myth: the initiate is clothed with the apparel of his god; one who is to be like a sun-god receives a radiant diadem; cf. Apuleius, *Met.* 11.24: "a beautiful garland was wound around my head, with bright palm leaves shooting out like rays of light; thus adorned to resemble the sun . . ." (caput: decore corona cinxerat palmae candidae foliis in modum radiorum prosistentibus. sic ad instar Solis exornato me . . .) [Trans.]. It is from the myth that the concept has passed over into eschatology: just as heavenly persons wear crowns of an imperishable sort, so a crown also awaits the believer some day.[101] Passages from the Revelation to John reveal the connection of the two ideas (compare 6:2; 9:7; 12:1; and 14:14, with 3:11; 4:4, 10; and especially 2:10, where "crown of life" [$\sigma\tau\acute{\epsilon}\phi\alpha\nu o\varsigma\ \tau\mathring{\eta}\varsigma\ \zeta\omega\mathring{\eta}\varsigma$] occurs as in our passage). This concept—along with others having to do with heavenly clothing[102]—became extraordinarily popular through the medium of apocalyptic. According to *Test. Levi* 8.2, 9, Levi has a vision in which he is given

95 Cf. above in the Introduction, section 7, as well as the comments below on 4:16.

96 See the Analysis.

97 Spitta wants to see in the "one who endures" a reference to the rich man, and he appeals to the blessing of the blameless rich man in Sir 34:8–11. But the passage in Sirach is directly opposed to the viewpoint in Jas 1:9–11.

98 On $\dot{\alpha}\nu\acute{\eta}\rho$ used for the more generic $\mathring{\alpha}\nu\theta\rho\omega\pi o\varsigma$, see above on 1:8. In 1:12, A and Ψ have $\mathring{\alpha}\nu\theta\rho\omega\pi o\varsigma$.

99 LXX Ps 1:1; 32:2; 33:9; 39:5; 83:6; 111:1; LXX Prov 8:34; 28:14; Sir 14:1, 20; Isa 56:2.

100 This very widespread comparison, found both in Jewish and early Christian texts, was quite understandably applied to our passage by patristic exegesis; cf. the interpretation, traced to Chrysostom, which appears in the Catena (= Scholion, p. 184; it

appears also in Didymus).

101 See Albrecht Dieterich, *Nekyia: Beiträge zur Erklärung der neuentdeckten Petrusapokalypse* (Leipzig and Berlin; Teubner, ²1913), 39ff; Hugo Gressman, *Der Ursprung der israelitisch-jüdischen Eschatologie*, FRLANT 6 (Göttingen: Vandenhoeck & Ruprecht, 1905), 110n; Wilhelm Bousset, *Die Offenbarung Johannis*, KEK 16 (Göttingen: Vandenhoeck & Ruprecht, ⁶1906; reprint 1966), on Rev 2:10; Paul Volz, *Die Eschatologie der jüdischen Gemeinde im neutestamentlichen Zeitalter* (Tübingen: Mohr [Siebeck], 1934; reprint 1966), 381. On the apotheosizing heavenly crown in a tradition about Nimrod–Zoroaster, see the reconstruction by Wilhelm Bousset, *Hauptprobleme der Gnosis*, FRLANT 10 (Göttingen: Vandenhoeck & Ruprecht, 1907), 147.

102 Cf. Wilhelm Bousset, *Die Religion des Judentums im*

the crown of righteousness by men in white apparel. *Test. Ben.* 4.1 admonishes toward the conduct which will earn "crowns of glory" (στέφανοι δόξης); in 2 Tim 4:8, Paul expects to receive "on that Day" the crown of righteousness; *Asc. Isa.* 9.7ff, 9.24ff, and 11.40 mention the crowns of glory which are stored up in the seven heavens for the righteous; according to *Herm. sim.* 8.2.1 and 8.3.6, those who have given up their sticks with buds and fruit will be crowned.

This popular usage could easily lead to the use of the concept as a mere byword,[103] a use in which the concrete prospect no longer stood in the background, i.e., a use in which the boundaries between metaphor and object were obliterated, and a use in which also there was no longer any reflection about genitives such as "of righteousness" (τῆς δικαιοσύνης) or "of life" (τῆς ζωῆς). Since such a usage best suits the literary character of our letter, it is the usage which we must assume in the saying in 1:12,[104] a saying which is isolated and not surrounded by any explanatory context: the crown of life designates the salvation of the final consummation; but whether "of life" is a genitive of quality, or a genitive of content, or an appositive genitive cannot be decided in the case of such a usage.

It is God who has promised this salvation. Probably in the original manuscript the solemn style of this relative clause made no specific mention of God at all;[105] yet that it is God who has made the promise is self–evident to both readers and author, just as in 2:5. Consequently, to explain the wording one need appeal neither to some lost dominical saying,[106] nor to an Old Testament quotation (Zech 6:14),[107] nor to Rev 2:10.[108] But the expression "he has promised to those who love him" (ἐπηγγείλατο τοῖς ἀγαπῶσιν αὐτόν) does call to mind the religious formulary language of early Christianity, and from this source the author could have acquired the thought. As evidence for this assumption one could adduce, in addition to Jas 2:5, especially the quotation in 1 Cor 2:9, which is also employed in *1 Clem.* 34.8 (although with "to those who endure" [ὑπομένουσιν] instead of "to those who love") and which possibly derives from a hymn.[109]

In any case, the formula "those who love him (God, the Lord)" is older and obviously was already a self–designation of the pious among the Jews; cf. in addition to the countless LXX passages,[110] *Ps. Sol.* 4.29; 6.9; 10.4; 14.1; *Test. Sim.* 3.6; *1 En.* 108.8; *Test. Abr.* (Rec. A) 3.[111] Early Christianity took over this formula, as it did so many others; cf. in addition to the passages mentioned, Rom 8:28; Eph 6:24 (in the benediction and, hence, in a formula); *1 Clem.* 59.3 (in a prayer). Therefore, the title "those who love" (οἱ ἀγαπῶντες) is "fixed," so that love for God cannot be termed the condition of salvation. Rather, one can say that as far as the pious are concerned—they are "those who love him"—endurance to the end is assumed as self–evident.

The saying as a whole is obviously intended to admonish endurance to the end by means of the beatitude of "he who endures" (ὑπομένων); such macarisms are frequently intended paraenetically; cf. Dan 12:12 (Theodotion): "Blessed is he who endures" (μακάριος ὁ ὑπομένων); *Shemoth Rabbah* 31 on Ex 32:25: "Happy

---

späthellenistischen Zeitalter, ed. Hugo Gressmann (Tübingen: Mohr [Siebeck], ³1966), 277f.

103 It is possible that in this development the hackneyed use of the metaphor of the crown in the Psalms and Wisdom literature also played a part, or that that use is itself a result of such a development: see Ps 21:3; Prov 4:9; 12:4; 14:24; 16:31; 17:6; Sir 1:11; 1:18; 6:31; 15:6; 25:6; Wisd 5:16.

104 Similarly, also in 1 Thess 2:19; Phil 4:1; 1 Petr 5:4.

105 That is the reading in P²³ P⁷⁴ᵛⁱᵈ B ℵ A Ψ 81 *ff* arm; most witnesses have (ὁ) κύριος ("the Lord"); a few have (ὁ) θεός ("God" 1175 boh s vulg syᵛᵍ *et al.*). Von Soden prefers (ὁ) κύριος, probably because he assumes that the influence of Jas 2:5 has resulted in the omission of (ὁ) κύριος in our passage. Yet precisely the textual tradition of 2:5 and Gal 1:15 bear witness to the inclination to fill out such solemn and

pregnant sayings.

106 Alfred Resch, *Agrapha: Aussercanonische Schriftfragmente,* TU 30, 2 (Leipzig: Hinrichs, 1906; reprint Darmstadt: Wissenschaftliche Buchgesellschaft, 1967), 34.

107 So Windisch–Preisker.

108 E. Zeller, "Ueber Jak. 1, 12," *ZWTh* 6 (1863): 93–6.

109 Cf. Martin Dibelius, *Die Geisterwelt im Glauben des Paulus* (Göttingen: Vandenhoeck & Ruprecht, 1909), 91 n. 1.

110 Cf. Ex 20:6; Deut 5:10; 7:9; Judg 5:31; 2 Ezra 11:5 (= Neh 1:5); Tob 13:14; 14:7; LXX Ps 96:10; 121:6; 144:20; Sir 1:10; 2:15, 16; 31(34):19; Dan 9:4; Bel 38; 1 Macc 4:33.

111 For text and English translation, see *The Testament of Abraham: The Greek Recensions,* tr. Michael E.

is the man who can withstand the test, for there is none whom God does not prove" (trans. Freedman–Simon);[112] *Herm. vis.* 2.2.7: "Blessed are you, as many as endure the great persecution which is coming" (μακάριοι ὑμεῖς ὅσοι ὑπομένετε τὴν θλῖψιν τὴν ἐρχομένην τὴν μεγάλην). The reward for such endurance is mentioned in our saying, but not as though desire for reward were supposed to be the reason for endurance. Jas is writing to the devout, to people "who love God"; he does not need to tell them why they are to bear up under the affliction. This also conforms to the overall attitude of our letter, which was noted with regard to 1:2ff. In this attitude, heroism is not something which characterizes the lives of only a few isolated individuals, but rather it is the self–evident consequence of faith: One who is a Christian must also be able to suffer.[113]

■ **1:13–18** *The source of temptations.* As was demonstrated in the Analysis, these verses contain two sayings which actually differ in the thoughts they present. They are combined here in order to answer the question of the source of temptations. And they are attached to what precedes only by means of a catchword:[114] "is tempted" (πειράζεσθαι)—"trial" (πειρασμός). This attachment is purely external, for the seduction by lusts in vv 13–15 has nothing whatsoever to do with the afflictions in v 12. Therefore, our saying can neither be combined with what precedes,[115] nor be interpreted

in accordance with it;[116] instead, a distinction must be made between the "trial" in v 12 and the "temptation" in vv 13–15.[117]

■ **13** The assertion which is opposed is worded as a direct quotation: "I am tempted by God" (ἀπὸ θεοῦ πειράζομαι). The subtlety stressed by most scholars, that with ἀπό (usually, "from") God is introduced only as a more remote cause, can scarcely be deduced from the text: to begin with, those who originally altered the text to read ὑπό ("by") saw no such subtlety;[118] the replacement of ὑπό with ἀπό in connection with the passive, a substitution which is complete in modern Greek, was frequent in Koine Greek and also in the New Testament.[119]

The problem which the saying raises was much discussed within Judaism.[120] In view of the Hellenistic doctrine of fate, it was important to devout Jews that the notion of God be protected from connection with evil. God could not be the author of sin, for then human responsibility, which in a religion of the law was indispensible, could not be maintained. Those passages where the old tradition seemed not to be unequivocal in this connection were corrected: It was not Yahweh who lured David into numbering the people, but Satan (1 Chron 21:1 against 2 Sam 24:1); not God who tempted Abraham, but Mastema the supreme devil (*Jubilees* 17.16 against Gen 22:1). In the literature

Stone, Texts and Translations 2, Pseudepigrapha Series 2 (Society of Biblical Literature, 1972). The text used there is reprinted from Montague Rhodes James, ed. *The Testament of Abraham*, TS 2, 2 (Cambridge: U. Press, 1892).

112 Strikingly, there is then mention of the testing of rich and poor; yet this similarity with Jas 1:9–11 is accidental, for the train of thought in the midrash is conditioned by the underlying Biblical passage, Ex 32:24.

113 The same idea recurs in the *Gospel of Thomas* (logion 58), and the kinship of its form there with Jas 1:12 is worthy of note: "Blessed is the man who has suffered; he has found the life" (trans. Hennecke–Schneemelcher).

114 See above in the Introduction, section 1.

115 Beyschlag: In v 12, the victor with his crown; in v 13, the defeated combatant whose end is death.

116 According to Hofmann, "I am tempted" (πειράζομαι) is not an excuse but a complaint against God; von Soden wants to translate ἀπείραστος κακῶν "not capable of being tempted by *misfortune*."

117 Spitta attempts to explain the transition from 1:12 to 1:13 on the basis of a literary reminiscence—viz., that the parallel passage in Sir 15:11f follows a mention in 15:6 of a "crown of rejoicing" (στέφανος ἀγαλλιάματος). Yet between those two passages in Sirach there occurs an entirely different sort of saying about the hymn of praise on the lips of a sinner (Sir 15:9f).

118 This reading, found in ℵ and some minuscules, need not be considered the result of assimilation to ὑπὸ τῆς ἐπιθυμίας ("by desire") in 1:14; rather, it corresponds to the uncertainty within the textual tradition with regard to ἀπό = ὑπό, which can be observed elsewhere as well (cf. Mk 8:31; Lk 6:18; 8:43; Acts 4:36; 15:4).

119 See Blass–Debrunner, § 210.2.

120 Cf. W. Lütgert, *Das Problem der Willensfreiheit in der vorchristlichen Synagoge*, BFTh 10, 2 (Gütersloh: Bertelsmann, 1906), 2. To be sure, Lütgert interprets even paraenetic texts such as Jas as polemic against specific theories.

121 In addition to *Leg. all.* 2.78, cf. also the clear polemic

we find echoes of Jewish debates over fate and responsibility, as when Josephus inserts in *Ant.* 16.395ff a discussion about the guilt of Herod and his sons, or when Philo (*Rer. div. her.* 300) polemicizes against the exposition of Gen 15:16 by the "weaker minds" who deduce from the passage that Moses advocated the doctrine of fate (εἱμαρμένη). Certainly with particular force, and apparently with reference to specific opponents, Philo directs his argument against the error in doctrine and conduct which is also opposed by our saying.[121]

However, it is not necessary because of all this to read into our saying a polemic against specific concepts of fate, God and sin.[122] Not a single word of the saying would indicate this, and the saying is not alone in this non–theoretical stance. The quintessence of that debate

regarding fate, the insistence that only good comes from God, at an early stage passed over into the Wisdom literature and paraenesis; and naturally in such a context it did not serve as a theoretical argument, but rather as practical ammunition against the excuse of those who had fallen under temptation. This is the point of Sir 15:11f: "Do not say, 'Because of the Lord I left the right way'; for he will not do what he hates. Do not say, 'It was he who led me astray'; for he has no need of a sinful man" (μὴ εἴπῃς ὅτι διὰ κύριον ἀπέστην· ἃ γὰρ ἐμίσησεν, οὐ ποιήσει.[123] μὴ εἴπῃς ὅτι αὐτός με ἐπλάνησεν· οὐ γὰρ χρείαν ἔχει ἀνδρὸς ἁμαρτωλοῦ); and also of *1 En.* 98.4: "as a mountain has not become a slave, and a hill does not become the handmaid of a woman, even so sin has not been sent upon the earth,

---

in *Det. pot. ins.* 122: "For Moses does not, as some impious people do, say that God is the author of ills. No, he says that 'our own hands' cause them, figuratively describing in this way our own undertakings, and the spontaneous movement of our minds to what is wrong" (οὐ γὰρ, ὡς ἔνιοι τῶν ἀσεβῶν, τὸν θεὸν αἴτιον κακῶν φησι Μωυσῆς, ἀλλὰ τὰς ἡμετέρας χεῖρας, συμβολικῶς τὰ ἡμέτερα παριστὰς ἐγχειρήματα καὶ τὰς ἑκουσίους τῆς διανοίας πρὸς τὸ χεῖρον τροπάς). A controversy among exegetical schools may lie behind the fact that Philo presents this idea twice with regard to the same verse, Ex 21:14, where it is said that unlike the case of the man who commits manslaughter (i.e., he kills because God so arranged it!), he who has killed intentionally is to be carried away even from the altar of God and put to death. On this, Philo says in *Fug.* 79f: "Accordingly it is not right to say that any wrongs committed with secret hostility and with guile and as the result of premeditation are done as God ordains; they are done as we ordain. For as I have said, the treasuries of evil things are in ourselves; with God are those of good things only. Whosoever, therefore, takes refuge, that is, whosoever blames not himself but God for his sins, let him be punished" (οὐδὲν οὖν τῶν ὑπούλως καὶ δολερῶς καὶ ἐκ προνοίας πραττομένων ἀδικημάτων ἄξιον λέγειν γίνεσθαι κατὰ θεόν, ἀλλὰ καθ' ἡμᾶς αὐτούς. ἐν ἡμῖν γὰρ αὐτοῖς, ὡς ἔφην, οἱ τῶν κακῶν εἰσι θησαυροί, παρὰ θεῷ δὲ οἱ μόνων ἀγαθῶν. ὃς ἂν οὖν καταφύγῃ, τὸ δ' ἐστὶν ὃς ἂν τῶν ἁμαρτημάτων μὴ ἑαυτὸν ἀλλὰ θεὸν αἰτιᾶται, κολαζέσθω); on the same Biblical text, Philo says in *Conf. ling.* 161: "For the words 'flee to refuge' lead us to the reflexion that there are many who, wishing to shirk all charges to which they are liable and claiming to escape the penalties of their misdeeds, ascribe the guilty responsibility, which

really belongs to themselves, to God who is the cause of nothing evil, but of all that is good" (τὸ γὰρ καταφύγῃ τοιοῦτον ὑποβάλλει νοῦν, διότι πολλοὶ τὰ καθ' ἑαυτῶν ἀποδιδράσκειν ἐθέλοντες ἐγκλήματα καὶ ῥύεσθαι τῶν ἐφ' οἷς ἠδίκησαν ἀξιοῦντες ἑαυτοὺς τιμωριῶν τὸ οἰκεῖον ἄγος τῷ κακοῦ μὲν μηδενὸς ἀγαθῶν δ' ἁπάντων αἰτίῳ προσβάλλουσι θεῷ). In a similar conceptual context belongs the passage in *Ps. Clem. Hom.* 3.55.2, which is an enumeration of sayings of Jesus adds this one: "And to those who think that God 'tempts,' as the scriptures say, He said, 'The tempter is the Evil One,' who tempted even Him" (τοῖς δὲ οἰομένοις, ὅτι ὁ θεὸς "πειράζει" (ὡς αἱ γραφαὶ λέγουσιν) ἔφη· "'Ο πονηρός ἐστιν ὁ πειράζων," ὁ καὶ αὐτὸν πειράσας) [Trans.]; a tradition is being transmitted here (as also with the other Jesus sayings in the context of that passage in *Ps. Clem. Hom.*), but this is not a quotation from Jas.

122 One could call to mind the familiar (but questionable) assertions of Josephus about the positions of the Pharisees, Sadducees, and Essenes with regard to the doctrine of fate (*Ant.* 18.12–22; *Bell.* 2.162ff); or one might think of Gnosticism; cf. Eus., *Hist. eccl.* 5.20.1, where the letter of Irenaeus to Florinus entitled "That God is not the Author of Evil" (περὶ τοῦ μὴ εἶναι τὸν θεὸν ποιητὴν κακῶν) combats this Gnostic teaching (Pfleiderer, *Primitive Christianity*, vol. 4, pp. 302f).

123 Most LXX manuscripts read ποιήσεις.

but man of himself has created it, and under a great curse shall they fall who commit it" (trans. Charles, *APOT*). Here also belongs *Arist.* 231: "For it is the gift of God to be able to do good actions and not the contrary" (θεοῦ δὲ δῶρον ἀγαθῶν ἐργάτην εἶναι καὶ μὴ τῶν ἐναντίων) [trans. Charles, *APOT*]. Obviously our saying has a similarly practical tendency—against empty excuses. And it is intelligible even without hypothesizing a reference to the corresponding petition in the Lord's Prayer.

The second half of the verse opposes that invalid excuse by making a two–part affirmation about God. The "and" (δέ) in the second part[124] points to the correct understanding of the first part: God is unable to be tempted to do evil, and he himself tempts no one. Thus the context yields the meaning of ἀπείραστος which is also the most natural one: as a passive verbal adjective, such as in the agraphon, "A man who is not tempted is unproven" (ἀνὴρ ἀδόκιμος ἀπείραστος),[125]

except that in our context the meaning naturally demands "*unable to be* tempted."[126] Precisely the contrast between "unable to be tempted" (ἀπείραστος) and "to tempt" (πειράζειν) became a favorite; *Acts of John* 57 (Bonnet, p. 179): "Blessed is he who has not tempted God in you, for he who tempts you tempts him who is unable to be tempted" (μακάριος ὅστις οὐκ ἐπείρασεν ἐν σοὶ τὸν θεόν· ὁ γὰρ σὲ πειράζων τὸν ἀπείραστον πειράζει) [Trans.]; Pseudo-Ignatius, *Ad Philippenses* 11 (to the Devil); "How can you tempt him who is unable to be tempted?" (πῶς πειράζεις τὸν ἀπείραστον;).[127]

"By evil" (κακῶν) represents a type of the genitive of separation, such as in "insatiable for sin" (ἀκαταπαύστους ἁμαρτίας) in 2 Petr 2:14.[128] The term here is to be translated "evil" in accordance with the context of the saying, and not "misfortune" in accordance with v 12.

■ **14** This verse names the true source of temptations: not God, but desire! The phrase "by his own desire"

---

124 The omission of the δέ in, for example, *ff* sah can be at least partially explained from the interpretation of ἀπείραστος in an active sense: "does not tempt"; cf. *ff*: "But God is not one who tempts with evils: he himself tempts no one" (deus autem malorum temptator non est: temptat ipse neminem).

125 Preuschen, *Antilegomena*, 29, no. 21.

126 On ἀπείραστος, cf. the example in Philodemus (1st cent. B. C.), *Volumina Rhetorica* (ed. S. Sudhaus) 1.45: "untested skill" (τέχνη ἀπείραστος); Henry George Liddell and Robert Scott, *A Greek–English Lexicon*, revised by Henry Stuart Jones (Oxford: Clarendon, ⁹1940; reprint 1968), s.v.; Walter Bauer, *A Greek–English Lexicon of the New Testament and Other Early Christian Literature*, tr. and ed. William F. Arndt and F. Wilbur Gingrich (Chicago: University of Chicago Press, 1957), s.v.

127 This wordplay approximates in form those others which show the negative attributes of God; cf. *Corp. Herm.* 5.10: "He is invisible, he is most visible" (οὗτος ὁ ἀφανής, οὗτος ὁ φανερώτατος); in the *Kerygma Petrou* (Clem. Alex., *Strom.* 6.39.3): "The Invisible One, who sees all things, etc." (ὁ ἀόρατος, ὃς τὰ πάντα ὁρᾷ κτλ,). This latter passage displays the contrast between passive and active which is also found in our text, although here the active ("who sees") is a positive affirmation, while in the Jas saying ("he tempts no one") it is negated. Nevertheless, I have no doubt that the expression "unable to be tempted by evil" (ἀπείραστος κακῶν) is also materially rooted in that Hellenistic theology which de-

scribes God's essense by means of circumlocution with negatives; cf. M. Ant. 6.1.1: "it has no wickedness, nor does evil to anything, nor is anything harmed by it" (κακίαν γὰρ οὐκ ἔχει οὐδέ τι κακῶς ποιεῖ οὐδὲ βλάπτεταί τι ὑπ' ἐκείνου); Philo, *Spec. leg.* 2.53: "exempt from all evil, filled with the perfect forms of good" (πάντος μὲν ἀμέτοχος κακοῦ, πλήρης δ' ἀγαθῶν τελείων); *Cher.* 86: "He is without grief or fear or share of ill" (ἄλυπός ἐστι καὶ ἄφοβος καὶ ἀκοινώνητος κακῶν); *Abr.* 202: "without grief or fear and wholly exempt from passion of any kind" (ἄλυπος δὲ καὶ ἄφοβος καὶ παντὸς πάθους ἀμέτοχος). With correct intuition for the sense of the Jas passage, Oec (and Theoph) quotes Epicurus: "in accordance with the one who said (even if he is an outsider to us), 'The divine and blessed being has no trouble himself and brings no trouble to others'" (κατὰ τὸν εἰρηκότα κἂν τῶν θύραθέν ἐστιν ἡμῖν· τὸ θεῖόν τε καὶ μακάριον οὔτε αὐτὸ πράγματα ἔχει οὔτε ἑτέροις παρέχει) [Trans.]; cf. the saying of Epicurus in Diog. Laert., 10.139: "A blessed and eternal being has no trouble himself and brings no trouble upon any other being; hence he is exempt from movements of anger and partiality" (τὸ μακάριον καὶ ἄφθαρτον οὔτ' αὐτὸ πράγματ' ἔχει οὔτ' ἄλλῳ παρέχει, ὥστ' οὔτ' ὀργαῖς οὔτε χάρισι συνέχεται); Cicero, *Nat. deor.* 1.45; Lactantius, *De ira dei* 4.

128 Blass–Debrunner, § 182. Examples from the papyri are in Moulton, *Prolegomena*, 235f (additional note to p. 74)—therefore this is not a Hebraism!

($\dot{\upsilon}\pi\dot{o}$ $\tau\hat{\eta}s$ $\dot{\iota}\delta\dot{\iota}as$ $\dot{\epsilon}\pi\iota\theta\upsilon\mu\dot{\iota}as$) must be connected with the two participles, "lured and enticed" ($\dot{\epsilon}\xi\epsilon\lambda\kappa\dot{o}\mu\epsilon\nu os$ $\kappa\alpha\dot{\iota}$ $\delta\epsilon\lambda\epsilon\alpha\zeta\dot{o}\mu\epsilon\nu os$);[129] this would be required on formal grounds to begin with, but also because the two participles need some supplementary element. Spitta, who links the phrase with the main verb ("is tempted"), wants to see in this verse already an anticipation of the metaphor in the following verse: it is the devil who according to v 14 lures and entices men, it is he who according to v 15 conceives desire. But however consistent Spitta's connection of thoughts is, vv 14 and 15, as they appear one after the other, do not allow this sort of consistency at all; for "desire" ($\dot{\epsilon}\pi\iota\theta\upsilon\mu\dot{\iota}a$) is portrayed as active in v 14, as passive in v 15.

"Desire" is used here in that sense which belongs to an anthropological pessimism. In Jewish literature, this meaning of the word is stressed above all in Sirach, Wisdom, and the *Test. XII*; in early Christian literature, it is emphasized especially by Paul. Therefore, what is meant by the word is desire to do evil, not desire as an emotion in general, as it is condemned in writings influenced by Stoicism (see Philo, *Spec. leg.* 4.79ff). However, our passage does not have in view a specific theory of evil, whether it be demonological as in the *Test. XII* or anthropological as in Paul. The brevity of the saying and its purely practical tendency clearly indicate what is really important to the author: he wants to repudiate, by pointing to human desire, the invalid appeal to God's authorship of temptation.

"His *own*" ($\dot{\iota}\delta\iota os$) is undoubtedly emphatic here and not merely a substitute for the simple personal pronoun ($\dot{\epsilon}\alpha\upsilon\tau o\hat{\upsilon}$). It is from this emphasis upon human authorship of temptation, and not from a mythological concept such as appears from time to time in Paul's statements about "Sin" ($\dot{\alpha}\mu\alpha\rho\tau\dot{\iota}a$), that we are to explain the fact that "desire" appears here almost as a person: it lures and entices.

"To entice" ($\delta\epsilon\lambda\epsilon\dot{\alpha}\zeta\epsilon\iota\nu$), found elsewhere in the New Testament only in 2 Petr 2:14, 18, is frequently used by Philo precisely in connection with desire; moreover, both Philo and others are fond of bringing the word into association with cognates of "to lure" ($\dot{\epsilon}\xi\dot{\epsilon}\lambda\kappa\epsilon\sigma\theta\alpha\iota$).[130]

■ **15** In this verse, "desire" is likewise portrayed as a person, but in a totally different context: Desire conceives and gives birth to sin, and sin brings forth death. It could appear as if this were an allusion to a myth, and accordingly Spitta has drawn attention to the impregnation of the "mind" ($\delta\iota\dot{\alpha}\nu o\iota a$; but not "desire" [$\dot{\epsilon}\pi\iota\theta\upsilon\mu\dot{\iota}a$] as in our verse) by Beliar in *Test. Ben.* 7, and the sexual union of the "spirits" ($\pi\nu\epsilon\dot{\upsilon}\mu\alpha\tau a$) in *Test. Reu.* 2f. If one considers these examples and also the marriage of the satanic Destroyer with Error in *Odes of Sol.* 38.9,[131] one will not reject *a priori* as impossible the view that "desire" ($\dot{\epsilon}\pi\iota\theta\upsilon\mu\dot{\iota}a$), "sin" ($\dot{\alpha}\mu\alpha\rho\tau\dot{\iota}a$), and "death" ($\theta\dot{\alpha}\nu\alpha\tau os$) are depicted here as a family of spirits on the basis of a myth.

However, there are serious objections to this view: In the first place, the most important part in such a genealogy is missing, viz., the declaration of who is the ancestral father. There is no mention at all of the male principle which unites with "desire," nor of that which unites with "sin"—for not a single word hints that it is the human being who with desire begets sin. Secondly, in such mythical genealogies one usually finds all the importance placed precisely on the first part, where the first ancestor of the family is named (cf. Jn 8:44). But our author obviously places most importance upon the mention of the last member, "death."

From this it follows that the tendency of the saying is a practical one: its intention is not to depict mythical events, but rather to exhibit a combination of concepts in the form of a catena, or "chain," and to warn against the first member of the chain by pointing to the last member: Beware of desire, for it ultimately leads to death! Therefore, the actual concern of our passage is to establish the series "desire"—"sin"—"death" (Rom 7:5: "to bear fruit for death" [$\epsilon\dot{\iota}s$ $\tau\dot{o}$

---

129 The rhyme is intentional; see above in the Introduction, section 5.

130 See the examples cited in Mayor, *ad loc.*

131 In *Dial.* 100, Justin says of Eve, "Conceiving the word from the serpent, she gave birth to disobedience and death" ($\tau\dot{o}\nu$ $\lambda\dot{o}\gamma o\nu$ $\tau\dot{o}\nu$ $\dot{\alpha}\pi\dot{o}$ $\tau o\hat{\upsilon}$ $\dot{o}\phi\epsilon\omega s$ $\sigma\upsilon\lambda$-$\lambda\alpha\beta o\hat{\upsilon}\sigma a$, $\pi\alpha\rho\alpha\kappa o\dot{\eta}\nu$ $\kappa\alpha\dot{\iota}$ $\theta\dot{\alpha}\nu\alpha\tau o\nu$ $\dot{\epsilon}\tau\epsilon\kappa\epsilon$) [Trans.]. But this passage belongs among others which show the Eve–Mary parallel to have been a favourite motif. That is already one reason which rules out the positing of a relationship between this text and that in Jas.

καρποφορῆσαι τῷ θανάτῳ]; cf. also *Herm. mand.* 4.1.2). Thus, the way in which the combination is effected recedes into the background, and we can assume that in the expressions "when it has conceived" (συλλαβοῦσα) and "gives birth" (τίκτει) the author is not alluding to a myth, but rather wants to use a metaphor—one which is frequently found in precisely such contexts[132]—to tie together the concepts.

The expression "when it has become complete" (ἀποτελεσθεῖσα) is undoubtedly the rhetorical parallel to "when it has conceived"; but it need not be taken because of that as the conceptual parallel as well, and be interpreted as a reference to the sexual maturity of sin.[133] On the other hand, the indubitable personification of "sin" prohibits interpreting the expression

as a reference to sin which has been "accomplished."[134] The term, which obviously has been added merely for the sake of the formal correspondence just mentioned, designates the effect of sin upon the whole person; cf. Luther's translation: "when it is complete."[135]

Only the conclusion of the concatenation again introduces a metaphorical term: "brings forth (in birth)."[136] But for Jas the important thing here is not the image but the object, not the depiction of the "birth" but the depiction of the fertile connection between desire, sin, and death.

The Concatenation as a Rhetorical Form

The rhetorical form of the concatenation, by means of which the words desire—sin—death are tied to-

---

132 So Philo, *Sacr. AC.* 102 (in the interpretation of Ex 13:12): "she has set in the soul for the generation of things a power by which the understanding conceives and travails and is the mother of many children" (πρὸς γένεσιν πραγμάτων ὥρισεν ἐν ψυχῇ δύναμιν, δι' ἧς κυοφορεῖ καὶ ὠδίνει καὶ ἀποτίκτει πολλὰ διάνοια); and *Leg. all.* 3.181: the birth of "noble things" (καλαὶ πράξεις) from virtue. When in *Cher.* 54ff Philo interprets the words "Adam knew his wife Eve" (ἔγνω Ἀδὰμ Εὔαν τὴν γυναῖκα αὐτοῦ) allegorically as a reference to "Mind" (νοῦς) and "sense–perception" (αἴσθησις), his use of the metaphor of birth is self–explanatory. An entire "progression" is the result, from "desire" to "pleasure" to "wrongs": "And this *desire* [for sexual intercourse] begat likewise bodily *pleasure*, that pleasure which is the beginning of *wrongs* and violation of law" (πόθος οὗτος καὶ τὴν τῶν σωμάτων ἡδονὴν ἐγέννησεν, ἥτις ἐστὶν ἀδικημάτων καὶ παρανομημάτων ἀρχή *Op. mund.* 152). The demon "having entered covertly sows the seed of his own activity, and the mind brings forth that which was sown: adulteries, murders, cruelties to parents, acts of sacrilege, impieties, hangings, jumpings off cliffs, and all other such works of demons" (ὅστις ὑπεισελθὼν ἔσπειρε τῆς ἰδίας ἐνεργείας τὸ σπέρμα, καὶ ἐκύησεν ὁ νοῦς τὸ σπαρέν, μοιχείας, φόνους, πατροτυπίας, ἱεροσυλίας, ἀσεβείας, ἀγχόνας, κατὰ κρημνῶν καταφοράς, καὶ ἄλλα πάντα ὅσα δαιμόνων ἔργα *Corp. Herm.* 9.3) [Trans.].
133 So von Soden, Windisch–Preisker.
134 So de Wette, Ewald, Hofmann, Burger.
135 Cf. the use of ἀποτέλεσμα ("finished product") in parallel with ἐνέργεια ("activity") in Philo, *Leg. all.* 2.40; ἐκτελεῖσθαι in *Corp. Herm.* 1.22: "Even more, I, Mind, will not permit the activities of the body, which assail them [i.e., the pious], to *take their full*

effect" (μᾶλλον δὲ οὐκ ἐάσω αὐτὸς ὁ Νοῦς τὰ προσπίπτοντα ἐνεργήματα τοῦ σώματος ἐκτελεσθῆναι) [Trans.]. Cf. Aristot., *Pol.* 1.1.8, p. 1252b: "since that which each thing is when its growth is completed we speak of as being the nature of each thing" (οἷον γὰρ ἕκαστόν ἐστι τῆς γενέσεως τελεσθείσης, ταύτην φαμὲν τὴν φύσιν εἶναι ἑκάστου).
136 Accented either ἀποκυεῖ (as a contract verb) or ἀποκύει. The contract verb form is more usual, as well as older; the later form is found in LXX Isa 59:13: ἐκύομεν. Since Jas 1:18 has the aorist of the older form, perhaps this is also the form to be preferred in 1:15; see Georg Benedict Winer, *Grammatik des neutestamentlichen Sprachidioms*, 8th edition by Paul Wilh. Schmiedel (Göttingen: Vandenhoeck & Ruprecht, ⁸1894), section 15, under κυέω.
137 Cf. on what follows Gustav Gerber, *Die Sprache als Kunst*, vol. 2 (Berlin: Gaertner, ²1885), 205ff; Richard M. Meyer, *Deutsche Stilistik*, Handbuch des deutschen Unterrichts an höheren Schulen 3, 1, ed. Adolf Matthias (München: Beck, ²1913), section 143; Karl Groos, *The Play of Man*, tr. Elizabeth L. Baldwin (New York: Appleton, 1901), 35ff. I am indebted to my colleagues Eugen Fehrle, Otto Weinreich and Ernst Lohmeyer for several observations.
138 Ancient theorists usually speak of climax or *gradatio*; cf. *Rhetorica ad Herennium* 4.25.34; Quintilian, *Inst. orat.* 9.3.54ff. But *catena* and ἐποικοδόμησις (piling up of expressions) are also mentioned; cf. Gerber, *op. cit.* (above, n. 137), 205ff. Christian Gottlob Wilke, *Die neutestamentliche Rhetorik* (Dresden and Leipzig: Arnold, 1843), section 124gg, treats under the category of *gradatio* even instances where a crescendo involves no catena but does contain terms such as "not only—but" (οὐ μόνον δὲ—ἀλλά), etc. Blass–

gether, demands some special consideration, particularly since the form is found also in Jas 1:2–4.[137] It is best designated "concatenation" because the catena, i.e., the repetition of one word from the preceding member of a series in the member which follows it, is the formal characteristic of the figure. Moreover, the customary designation "climax" refers to the *conceptual* content and is not always typical for the catena: on the one hand, crescendos in thought can be expressed in another form, and on the other hand, schematic concatenations (see 2 Petr 1:5 below) contain no crescendo.[138]

The ultimate sources for this rhetorical device are the age–old and widespread formal impulses to *pile up* and *string together* motifs. A particular favorite in games,

fairy tales, and nursery rhymes[139] is the stringing together of motifs in which the series is increased by one with each repetition: "Here is the door of the house of the little wooden man, here is the lock of the door of the house . . ." This sort of series is also found in the form of a catena—both in narrative form, when the object of one clause becomes the subject of the following clause,[140] and in the form of the lyrical game, when the rhyme or even the thought of the following verse is yanked from the preceding so that the whole sometimes makes sense and sometimes does not: to this category belong both the popular chain–verse as well as many literary poems with lyric structure.[141] Literature employs the same technique to continue the

---

Debrunner, §493 classifies early Christian concatenations under the category of climax.

139 [One of the most well–known examples in English is the nursery verse "The House that Jack Built":

This is the house that Jack built.
This is the malt
That lay in the house that Jack built.
This is the rat,
That ate the malt
That lay in the house that Jack built.
This is the cat, etc.

Among the lyric examples of the same phenomenon, one might mention the song "The Twelve Days of Christmas"—Trans.]

140 Cf. "The House that Jack Built," cited in the preceding footnote, and the verse "For Want of a Nail":

For want of a nail,
The shoe was lost;
For want of a shoe,
The horse was lost;
For want of a horse,
The rider was lost;
For want of a rider,
The battle was lost, etc.

Dibelius cites familiar examples from German folksongs, found in Karl Simrock, *Die deutschen Volksbücher*, vol. 9 (Frankfurt a. M.: Brönner, 1856), such as "Der Herr, der schickt den Jockel aus" (pp. 341ff), or "Vom Tode des Hühnchens";

Sollst mir klare Seide geben,
Seide soll ich Brunnen bringen,
Brunnen soll mir Wasser geben (pp. 320f),

or "Vom Zicklein" (pp. 338ff), or "Ist alles verloren" (pp. 330ff). The stanzas to the English children's song "Farmer in the Dell" are linked by means of the same device:

The farmer takes a wife,
The wife takes a child,
The child takes a nurse,
The nurse takes a dog,
The dog takes a cat, etc.

As an example of the poetic adaptation of this device, Dibelius cites "Eine wilde Jagd" ("A Wild Chase"), from Ernst Kreidolf, *Blumen-märchen* (Köln: Schaffstein, 1922), which is another case of the man–chasing–dog–chasing–cat–chasing–mouse motif:

Und es rennet und läuft
der alte Schäfer,
Der Hund und die Katz
und die Maus und der Käfer.
Die Maus frisst den Käfer,
die Katz frisst die Maus,
Der Hund wird gezüchtigt,
und die Jagd ist aus.

An artistic refinement of this style is found in "Ein Kindergedicht" by Christian Morgenstern (*Melancholia*, in his *Sämtliche Dichtungen* 1, 7 [Basel: Zbinden, 1972], 51):

Spann' dein kleines Schirmchen auf,
Denn es möchte regnen drauf.
Denn es möchte regnen drauf.
Halt nur fest den Schirmchen-Knauf, etc.

141 Cf. the 14th century chain-rhyme (I.V. Zingerle, *Das deutsche Kinderspiel im Mittelalter* [Innsbruck: Wagner, 2 1873], 62):

Es reit ein hêrre,
Sîn schilt was ein gêre,
Ein gêre was sîn schilt.

As an English example of the chain-rhyme device to which Dibelius is referring, compare the following approximation of a German chain–rhyme which he cites from Groos, *op. cit.* (above, n. 137), 36:

thought,[142] and rhetoric finds here an effective device for depicting processes which follow one upon the other.

And with that we find ourselves at a use of concatenation which involves concepts, a use which is usually called "climax." This can be a matter of external processes, as, for instance, in the famous example in Demosthenes, *De corona* 179: "I did not speak thusly without proposing a decree, I did not propose a decree without serving as ambassador, I did not serve as ambassador without persuading the Thebans" (οὐκ εἶπον μὲν ταῦτ᾽, οὐκ ἔγραψα δέ, οὐδ᾽ ἔγραψα μέν, οὐκ ἐπρέσβευσα δέ, οὐδ᾽ ἐπρέσβευσα μέν, οὐκ ἔπεισα δὲ Θηβαίους) [Trans.]; or in Cicero, *Mil.* 61: "He entrusted himself not merely to the people, but also to the Senate; not merely to the Senate, but to the public guards and armies; and not merely to these, but to the discretion of the man . . ." (neque vero se populo solum, sed etiam senatui commisit, neque senatui modo, sed etiam publicis praesidiis et armis, neque his tantum, verum etiam eius potestati); cf. also the poetic examples in Homer, *Il.* 2.102ff, and Epicharmus, Frag. 148.[143]

But here we are even more interested in the use of the concatenation to *depict the regularity of internal processes*.[144] External and internal seemed to be combined in the anticlimax which Paul in Rom 10:13–15 employs in the form of a catena to depict the mission: according to Joel 3:5, only he who calls upon the name of the Lord will be saved; but this calling requires faith; faith presupposes hearing; hearing presupposes preaching; and preaching presupposes the sending of missionaries. The typical example of the concatenating of abstracts is offered by Cicero, *Pro Roscio Amerino* 75: "Extravagance is created in the city, from extravagance avarice inevitably emerges, from avarice insolence breaks forth, from whence all crimes and evil deeds are produced" (in urbe luxuries creatur, ex luxurie exsistat avaritia necesse est, ex avaritia erumpat audacia, inde omnia scelera ac maleficia gignuntur) [Trans.]. Wisd 6:17ff is also characteristic: "The beginning of wisdom is the most sincere desire for instruction, and concern for instruction is love of her, and love of her is the keeping of her laws, and giving heed to her laws is assurance of immortality, and immortality brings one near to God" (ἀρχὴ γὰρ αὐτῆς ἡ ἀληθεστάτη παιδείας ἐπιθυμία, φροντὶς δὲ παιδείας ἀγάπη, ἀγάπη δὲ τήρησις

One, two, three,
You are not me,
I am not you,
Old is not new,
New is not old,
Warm is not cold, etc.

The same sort of pattern is found in a further German example in Groos (p. 36):

Reben trägt der Weinstock,
Hörner hat der Ziegenbock,
Der Ziegenbock hat Hörner, etc.,

in another example from *Mein Heimatland* (1918): 65 (a folklore publication of the country of Baden in Germany):

Drips drips drill,
Der Bauer hat ein Füll,
Ein Füll hat der Bauer,

in the German chain-rhyme about the beautiful pear tree (in Guido Höller and Emil Weber, *Fünf Englein haben gesungen* [Braunschweig: Westermann, 1921], 70), and in the Low German verse (from Höller and Weber, p. 54):

Jochen, Pochen lat mi leben,
Besten Vagel will ik di geben,
Vagel schall mi Stroh geben. . . ."

One might also mention in this connection the Malayan song in Groos, *op. cit.* (above, n. 137), 36,

which uses the second line of one strophe as the first line of the following strophe. The same phenomenon is found polished to artistic perfection in Goethe's "Nachtgesang": "O gib vom weichen Pfühle," where the third line of one strophe becomes the first line of the following.

Cf. also the Manichaean poem from Turfan in Mark Lidzbarski, "Ein manichäisches Gedicht," *NGG* (1918):502:

A thankful disciple am I,
   And from the land of Babel have I arisen;
I have arisen from the land of Babel,
   And before the portal of Truth have I stood.

With regard to this passage, Lidzbarski calls attention to Mandaean liturgies in which the second half of one verse, with its word order reversed, is repeated as the first half of the following verse. A further example is found in the *Left Ginza* 111,23–112,2 (Mark Lidzbarski, ed. and tr., *Ginza: Der Schatz, oder das grosse Buch der Mandäer* [Göttingen: Vandenhoeck & Ruprecht, 1925], 557, lines 25–34), also printed in R. Reitzenstein, *Das iranische Erlösungsmysterium* (Bonn a. Rh.: Marcus & Weber, 1921), 49f.

142 Cf. Falstaff's monologue after Percy's death (Shakespeare, *King Henry IV*, part 1, act 5, scene 4). A similar chain–like continuation is found in Lessing's *Nathan*, act 3, scene 8, lines 2121f, 2145ff, in the

νόμων αὐτῆς, προσοχὴ δὲ νόμων βεβαίωσις ἀφθαρσίας, ἀφθαρσία δὲ ἐγγὺς εἶναι ποιεῖ θεοῦ). The outcome of this entire progression is expressed in 6:20: "so the desire for wisdom leads to a kingdom" (ἐπιθυμία ἄρα σοφίας ἀνάγει ἐπὶ βασιλείαν). "A kingdom" is thereby equated with being "near to God," and therefore is a reference to the Kingdom of God. Now when we find following this (in 6:21) an admonition directed to the monarchs over the people to "rule" (βασιλεύειν) correctly, this is obviously only externally connected with what precedes it, and the "kingdom" (βασιλεία) in 6:20 cannot be interpreted in accordance with this "ruling" in 6:21. Instead, what we have is simply another saying which has been attached to the catena by means of a catchword.[145] Something similar is found in Jas 1:2–4: the climax, which is presented in the form of a catena, properly reads "trials"—"endurance"—"perfection" (πειρασμοί—ὑπομονή—τελειότης). The only thing that is striking is that the final member is paraphrased several times. To the last paraphrase—"lacking in nothing" (ἐν μηδενὶ λειπόμενοι)—there is then attached a new saying by means of a catchword.[146] The passage in Jas 1:14, 15, which we took as our point of departure, offers a purer form of the catena. What is presented in catenated form here are the steps in the crescendo "desire"—"sin"—"death" (ἐπιθυμία—ἁμαρτία—θάνατος). Likewise, the concatenation in Satan's speech

in Klopstock's *Messias*[147] descends into the realm of evil: "You who are tormented by the eternal night of the abyss, and in that night by punitive fire, and in that fire by despair, and in that despair by me!" *Corp. Herm.* 14.3 contains soteriological statements which crescendo in the form of a catena: "It is fitting for one to think thusly, and having thought to marvel, and having marveled to count oneself blessed, having recognized one's true father" (οὕτως ἄξιόν ἐστι νοῆσαι καὶ νοήσαντα θαυμάσαι καὶ θαυμάσαντα ἑαυτὸν μακαρίσαι, τὸν γνήσιον πατέρα γνωρίσαντα) [Trans.]. An outgrowth of this mysticism is offered by the apocryphal dominical saying which according to Clem. Alex., *Strom.* 2.45.5 was found in the *Gospel of the Hebrews*; Clement gives a fuller version of the saying in *Strom.* 5.96.3 which reads as follows: "He that seeks will not rest until he finds; and he that has found shall marvel; and he that has marvelled shall reign; and he that has reigned shall rest" (οὐ παύσεται ὁ ζητῶν, ἕως ἂν εὕρῃ, εὑρὼν δὲ θαμβηθήσεται, θαμβηθεὶς δὲ βασιλεύσει. βασιλεύσας δὲ ἐπαναπαήσεται) [trans. Hennecke–Schneemelcher 1, p. 164].[148] How common such catenae are in the depiction of mystical soteriological revelations is shown also by the "Hermetic" writing *Kore Kosmou*, where it is said of Hermes: "who also saw the Totality, and having seen it understood, and having understood was able to explain it and manifest it" (ὃς καὶ εἶδε τὰ σύμπαντα καὶ

---

monologue of the Knight Templar (Gotthold Ephraim Lessing, *Nathan the Wise*, tr. Patrick Maxwell [New York: Bloch, ³1939], 257f). Cf. further, Friedrich Gundolf, *Shakespeare und der deutsche Geist* (Berlin: Bondi, ⁵1920), 147ff. Paul has structured the proem of 2 Corinthians in accordance with the principle of a chain–like development.

143 Text in Georg Kaibel, ed., *Comicorum Graecorum fragmenta*, Poetarum Graecarum fragmenta 6, 1 (Berlin: Weidmann, 1899), 118. Further examples are found in the passages cited above in n. 132. Cf. also Shakespeare, *Much Ado About Nothing*, act 5, scene 2: "Foul words is but foul wind, and foul wind is but foul breath, and foul breath is noisome." Another example is in *Pirke Aboth* 4.12: "Let the honour of thy disciple be as dear to thee as thine own and as the honour of thy companion, and the honour of thy companion as the fear of thy teacher, and the fear of thy teacher as the fear of Heaven" (trans. Danby).

144 Abstract content, but without universal applicability, is found in the figure in *Rhetorica ad Herennium* 4.25.34: "Diligence brought Africanus excellence,

and excellence fame, and fame imitators" (Africano virtutem industria, virtus gloriam, gloria aemulos conparavit) [Trans.], and that in Shakespeare, *As You Like It*, act 5, scene 2: "for your brother, and my sister, no sooner met but they looked; no sooner looked but they loved; no sooner loved but they sighed; no sooner sighed but they asked one another the reason; no sooner knew the reason but they sought the remedy."

145 See above in the Introduction, section 1.

146 Cf. above on 1:2–4.

147 The translation given here is modified from that in Friedrich Gottlieb Klopstock, *The Messiah*, tr. Joseph Collyer, vol. 1 (Boston: West, 1811), 73.

148 A somewhat fragmentary version which roughly corresponds to this is found in *P. Oxy.* IV, 654 (= *Gospel of Thomas*, logion 2); see Hennecke–Schneemelcher 1, p. 100.

ἰδὼν κατενόησε καὶ κατανοήσας ἴσχυσε δηλῶσαί τε καὶ δεῖξαι *Corp. Herm.* Frag. 23.5, vol. 4, p. 2 Nock–Festugière) [Trans.]. Also relevant is the saying which Aelius Aristides quotes in the fourth Sacred Oration and which he says was revealed to him: "He said that it was necessary for the mind to be moved away from the established order, and having been moved, to associate with God, and having associated, to transcend the human condition" (ἔφη χρῆναι κινηθῆναι τὸν νοῦν ἀπὸ τοῦ καθεστηκότος, κινηθέντα δὲ συγγενέσθαι θεῷ, συγγενόμενον δὲ ὑπερέχειν ἤδη τῆς ἀνθρωπίνης ἕξεως *Or.* 50.52 Keil; cf. also *Or.* 28.116) [Trans.]. Obviously this form of speech was a favorite in Hellenistic theology for portraying man's approach to the divine. This is seen also in Porphyry's statement about the four "principles" (στοιχεῖα), "faith" (πίστις), "truth" (ἀλήθεια), "love" (ἔρως), and "hope" (ἐλπίς): "For one must believe that the only salvation is to turn toward God; and having found faith, to be as eager as possible to know the truth about him; and having known, to love him who is known; and having loved him, to nourish ones's soul during life with good hopes; for it is by good hopes that good people excel above wicked people" (πιστεῦσαι γὰρ δεῖ ὅτι μόνη σωτηρία ἡ πρὸς τὸν θεὸν ἐπιστροφή. καὶ πιστεύσαντα ὡς ἕνι μάλιστα σπουδάσαι τἀληθῆ γνῶναι περὶ αὐτοῦ, καὶ γνόντα ἐρασθῆναι τοῦ γνωσθέντος, ἐρασθέντα δὲ ἐλπίσιν ἀγαθαῖς τρέφειν τὴν ψυχὴν διὰ τοῦ βίου. ἐλπίσι γὰρ ἀγαθαῖς οἱ ἀγαθοὶ τῶν φαύλων ὑπερέχουσι *Ad Marcellam* 24) [Trans.].

In all the examples which have been mentioned thusfar, the content of the concatenation consists of a crescendo which is actually constant and even. In Paul's depiction of the *ordo salutis* in Rom 8:29f, one can recognize this sort of crescendo, which moves from "foreknow" (προγινώσκειν) to "glorify" (δοξάζειν) by means of a catena–like linkage. Nevertheless, the distinction here between "foreknow" (προγινώσκειν) and "predestine" (προορίζειν) is not occasioned exclusively by the matter at hand, but also by Paul's desire to make the series somewhat fuller and to add to it some variety. This can be said even more of *Herm. mand.* 5.2.4, where "silliness" (ἀφροσύνη), "bitterness" (πικρία), "wrath" (θυμός), "rage" (ὀργή), and "fury" (μῆνις) are concatenated. In the Excursus on Jas 1:4 I have already discussed the concatenation in Rom 5:3–5, in which the derivation of "hope" (ἐλπίς) from "confirmation" (δοκιμή) is not compelling, and hence it is not absolutely clear that that member of the series continues the crescendo.[149] Approaching still closer the mere *form* of a catena is *Herm. vis.* 3.8.7, where the seven women who support the tower are interpreted as seven virtues and are arranged together in a mother–daughter relationship: "From Faith is born Continence, from Continence Simplicity, from Simplicity Innocence, from Innocence Reverence, from Reverence Knowledge, from Knowledge Love" (ἐκ τῆς Πίστεως γεννᾶται Ἐγκράτεια, ἐκ τῆς Ἐγκρατείας Ἁπλότης, ἐκ τῆς Ἁπλότητος Ἀκακία, ἐκ τῆς Ἀκακίας Σεμνότης, ἐκ τῆς Σεμνότητος Ἐπιστήμη, ἐκ τῆς Ἐπιστήμης Ἀγάπη). And finally, the passage in 2 Petr 1:5–7 contains a mere list of virtues in catena form; the members of the catena— "faith, virtue, knowledge, self–control, endurance, godliness, brotherly affection, love" (πίστις, ἀρετή, γνῶσις, ἐγκράτεια, ὑπομονή, εὐσέβεια, φιλαδελφία, ἀγάπη)—do not in any way provide a crescendo; indeed, they do not even stand in a clearly perceptible relationship to one another.[150]

Undoubtedly what is involved here is simply the effort to arrange in some way a series which is presented for paraenetic purposes. *Paraenetic objectives* are also

---

149 A similar judgment might apply to the poem of Cäsar Flaischlen, "Den Kopf hoch" (Cäsar Flaischlen, *Zwischenklänge Altes und Neues* [Berlin: Fleischel, 1909], 29), in which we find: "To rely on oneself is power, and power is joy and joy is life and life is creation and creation is victory! And victory is again joy and life and creation and victory."

150 Paul also employs a type of catena in 1 Cor 11:29–32, where v 30 is a parenthetical remark. Hence, the members in the chain are "judging" (διακρίνων RSV: "discerning"), "we judged" (διεκρίνομεν), "we should (not) be judged" (ἐκρινόμεθα), "when

we are judged" (κρινόμενοι). A catena–like connection is found in Jas 4:2f: "You do not have because you do not ask; you ask and you do not receive because you ask wrongly" (οὐκ ἔχετε διὰ τὸ μὴ αἰτεῖσθαι ὑμᾶς· αἰτεῖτε καὶ οὐ λαμβάνετε, διότι κακῶς αἰτεῖσθε); this is a crescendo in the form of a catena, but in the paradoxical style in which the second member affirms what the first member has denied. Quite similar are the words of the Princess in Goethe's *Torquato Tasso*, act 3, lines 1912f:
Fortune is there, but we fail to see it;
We see it, but know not how to esteem it.

clear right away in the case of many of the other examples which actually contain crescendos: the intention in the very first step toward warning or motivating is to point immediately to the end of the whole path: Desire leads to death, strive after wisdom into the Kingdom of God. Other of these series are directed more (or at least also) to the service of *knowledge*: they seek to describe the process of salvation (Rom 8:29f) or, as was obviously popular, to set forth the steps of the mystical union with God. Our passage has a practical intention, as does the document as a whole. A theoretical interest plays a part only insofar as false assertions about temptation which a sinner might use to make excuses for himself are replaced by correct statements.

■ **16–18** If one reads over the saying in vv 16–18, one can easily infer what our author's main interest is here: God gives only good things and not evil things (and therefore not temptation). Nevertheless, the explicit negation which would be particularly important after vv 13ff remains strangely unexpressed.[151] Because of this, it can be assumed that the saying in vv 17f, or at least its beginning, originally existed separately or in another context.[152] It is quite evident how Jas has gone about tacking together the idea in vv 13–15 and the idea in v 17: the formula in v 16 serves this purpose and no other.

■ **16** Here also we find the negation whose absence we felt above: "Do not be deceived, my beloved brethren,"

i.e., do not fall into the error of thinking that God could ever give us anything bad,[153] rather, etc. In other places, also, the author uses an address to the readers for the purpose of transition.[154] The formula "do not be deceived" ($\mu\grave{\eta}\ \pi\lambda\alpha\nu\hat{\alpha}\sigma\theta\epsilon$) probably comes from diatribe:[155] Epictetus cites it in direct speech in *Diss.* 4.6.23: "Shall I go about and make proclamation, and say, 'Men, be not deceived, it is well with me . . .'?" ($\pi\epsilon\rho\iota\epsilon\rho\chi\acute{o}\mu\epsilon\nu\sigma\varsigma\ \kappa\eta\rho\acute{\upsilon}\sigma\sigma\omega\ \kappa\alpha\grave{\iota}\ \lambda\acute{\epsilon}\gamma\omega\cdot\ \mu\grave{\eta}\ \pi\lambda\alpha\nu\hat{\alpha}\sigma\theta\epsilon,\ \mathring{\alpha}\nu\delta\rho\epsilon\varsigma,\ \mathring{\epsilon}\mu\sigma\grave{\iota}\ \kappa\alpha\lambda\hat{\omega}\varsigma\ \mathring{\epsilon}\sigma\tau\iota\nu$); the related expression "do not be led astray" ($\mu\grave{\eta}\ \mathring{\epsilon}\xi\alpha\pi\alpha\tau\hat{\alpha}\sigma\theta\epsilon$) is also found in Epictetus. Paul seems to use the phrase "do not be deceived" ($\mu\grave{\eta}\ \pi\lambda\alpha\nu\hat{\alpha}\sigma\theta\epsilon$) as a fixed expression in 1 Cor 6:9; 15:33 and Gal 6:7; and Ignatius employs the words twice in a manner very similar to that in Paul (Ign. *Eph.* 16.1; *Phld.* 3.3).

■ **17a** That this formula is used in 1 Cor 15:33 to introduce the quotation of a maxim is significant for Jas 1:17, for the beginning of this verse is a hexameter; the hexameter is defective because of the tribrach in the second foot, but that defect could be removed by the addition of merely one Greek letter—viz., by writing $\delta\acute{o}\sigma\iota\varsigma\ \tau'$ instead of $\delta\acute{o}\sigma\iota\varsigma$. That Jas or his predecessor is quoting here, or has used a familiar verse without being aware of its origin, may be considered a possibility and would also correspond to the style of such paraenesis.[156] Other observations which have been made about the author's cultural milieu are also

---

151 To compensate for this lack, many commentators interpret $\pi\hat{\alpha}\varsigma$ ("every") in v 17 by supplying the negation: "*only* good gifts," or "*nothing but* good gifts," etc. (see v 2). Beyschlag argues that it is only in this way that the thought achieves "the force to counter effectively the perverse statement in v 13." But since "good gift" ($\delta\acute{o}\sigma\iota\varsigma\ \mathring{\alpha}\gamma\alpha\theta\acute{\eta}$) and "perfect gift" ($\delta\acute{\omega}\rho\eta\mu\alpha\ \tau\acute{\epsilon}\lambda\epsilon\iota\sigma\nu$) are concrete nouns and not abstracts, as was the case with "sheer joy" ($\pi\hat{\alpha}\sigma\alpha\ \chi\alpha\rho\acute{\alpha}$) in 1:2, there is no justification for this interpretation. Herder also, in his first written copy (see Suphan's edition, vol. 7, p. 494, n. 8), translates: "Only every pure gift."

152 See above in the Analysis.

153 Cf. Bede: "obviously (James means): 'by the judgment that temptations to commit offenses originate from God'" (videlicet aestimando, quod tentamenta

vitiorum, a Deo sumant originem) [Trans.].

154 See above in the Introduction, n. 132.

155 In the LXX, it occurs only in Isa 44:8 (manuscript B): $\mu\eta\delta\grave{\epsilon}\ \pi\lambda\alpha\nu\hat{\alpha}\sigma\theta\epsilon$.

156 That the hexameter by itself does not express a complete thought does not argue against this being a quotation. It is also possible that we have here a collimated saying in which the copula is lacking: Every gift *is* good, etc.; i.e., don't look a gift horse in the mouth; see H. Fischer, "Ein Spruchvers im Jacobusbrief," *Philologus* 50 (1891): 377–9. In this case, Jas would have been employing the saying very freely. Cf. also Teles p. 40, 1 Hense (2nd edition), where a trimeter has been perceived in the statement: "lest he come away having added boastfulness as one of his qualities" ($\epsilon\mathring{\iota}\ \delta\grave{\epsilon}\ \mu\acute{\eta},\ \mathring{\alpha}\lambda\alpha\zeta\sigma\nu\epsilon\acute{\iota}\alpha\nu\ \pi\rho\sigma\sigma\lambda\alpha\beta\grave{\omega}\nu\ \mathring{\alpha}\pi\epsilon\lambda\epsilon\acute{\upsilon}\sigma\epsilon\tau\alpha\iota$). Whether the author him-

in harmony with such a conjecture.[157]

As far as any difference between "good gift" (δόσις ἀγαθή) and "perfect gift" (δώρημα τέλειον) is concerned, at least no importance should be placed upon it. It may be that no distinction at all was made between δόσις (sometimes means "giving") used in this passive sense and δώρημα.

The periphrasis ἄνωθέν ἐστι καταβαῖνον ("comes down from above") is essentially equal to the formulation ἄνωθεν καταβαίνει. Whether the fervor of the saying prompted the author to use this participial periphrasis, or whether without any particular intention in mind he employs it simply because it is a part of his pattern of speech, and finally, whether this pattern of speech must be explained as the influence of Aramaic or whether instead it is a purely Greek development—all this is disputed, and this uncertainty corresponds to the present status of the Semitism question in general.[158] Examples for precisely this periphrasis of the present indicative with the participle are found in 2 Cor 9:12; Gal 4:24; Col 2:23; Herm. vis. 1.2.4. When one compares with our verse Jas 3:15; Herm. mand. 9.11 and 11.5, one is prone to consider the combination "(is) from above" (ἄνωθέν ἐστι) almost as a formula; in the case of Jas 1:17, then, it would be strengthened by the participle.[159]

"Father of lights" (πατὴρ τῶν φώτων) as a title of God naturally refers to the stars, which are called "lights" (φῶτα) in LXX Jer 4:23 and LXX Ps 135:7. Therefore, "Father" (πατήρ) is used here in the cosmological sense which is found particularly in literature which reflects Hellenistic influence.[160] In the so-called Damascus Document, we find "Prince of Lights" as a title of God:[161] "Already in ancient times Moses and Aaron stood on the side of the Prince of Lights" (CD V, 17f).[162] From the continuation of Jas 1:17, we can see that the expression "Father of lights" is not an empty formula, but rather that Jas has heavenly bodies in mind.

■ **17b** The problem with the statement about God as it stands[163] in v 17 is the striking combination within it of technical and non-technical terms. The word παραλλαγή means "change" and was not a technical term associated with astronomy.[164] Even where it is used in connection with astral processes, as in Epict., Diss. 1.14,[165] the word remains non-technical. On the other hand, the term τροπή is used already in the classical period with the meaning "solstice"; therefore it is a technical term, although it was by no means used only by specialists (cf. Deut 33:14; Wisd 7:18).[166] The juxtaposition of φῶτα ("lights" = stars), τροπή, and ἀποσκίασμα ("shadow" = eclipse?) suggests that τροπή is to be given this astral significance here also; otherwise the word would mean "change," and hence be synony-

self was conscious of a trimeter cannot be determined. The same idea as in Jas 1:17 appears in a briefer formulation in the hymn in *P. Oxy.* XV, 1786.5 (second half of the 3rd cent. A.D.): "to Him who alone gives all good things" (δοτῆρι μόνῳ πάντων ἀγαθῶν). On the question of whether the hexameter in Jas 1:17 existed independently, cf. Heinrich Greeven, "Jede Gabe ist gut, Jak. 1, 17," *ThZ* 14 (1958): 1–13.

157 See above in the Introduction, section 3.

158 See above in the Introduction, section 5.

159 On the periphrasis, cf. Blass–Debrunner, § 353; Moulton, *Prolegomena*, 225ff.

160 Philo frequently has "Father of the universe" (πατὴρ τῶν ὅλων); cf. also *Apc. Mos.* 36: "before the Light of the universe, the Father of lights" (ἐνώπιον τοῦ φωτὸς τῶν ὅλων, τοῦ πατρὸς τῶν φώτων); likewise in *Apc. Mos.* 38 (D arm): "Father of lights"; text in *Monumenta sacra et profana*, ed. Antonio Maria Ceriani, vol. 5, part 1 (Milan: Bibliotheca Ambrosiana, 1868), 19–24.

161 Cf. S. Schechter, *Documents of Jewish Sectaries*, vol. 1

(Cambridge: U. Press, 1910).

162 So the literal translation by F. M. Th. Böhl, "Neugefundene Urkunden einer messianischen Sekte im syrisch–palästinischen Judentum," *ThT* 46 (1912): 10 (see also the note on p. 30); Eduard Meyer, *Die Gemeinde des neuen Bundes im Lande Damaskus: Eine jüdische Schrift aus der Seleukidenzeit*, Abhandlungen der preussischen Akademie der Wissenschaften, Philosophisch–historische Klasse (Berlin: de Gruyter, 1919), no. 9, p. 36, translates the phrase, "through the hand of the Prince of Lights," and he takes the expression as a reference to the archangel. Yet the contrast with Belial (in the continuation of the passage) suggests that the reference is to God. Cf. also Philo, *Leg. all.* 3.104: "that sublime reason which is pregnant with divine lights and to which he has given the title 'heaven'" (τὸν μετάρσιον καὶ ἐγκύμονα θείων φώτων λόγον, ὃν δὴ κέκληκεν οὐρανόν) [Loeb modified].

163 On ἔνι = ἐστίν, see Blass–Debrunner, § 98.

164 It is a different matter with the term παράλλαξις; cf. Franz Boll, "Finsternisse," in Pauly–Wissowa, *Real-*

mous with παραλλαγή, and the genitive along with ἀποσκίασμα would be incomprehensible. ἀποσκίασμα is thus far attested only in Christian texts[167] and apparently means the shadow which is cast. The technical term for eclipse is ἔκλειψις, not σκίασμα or one of its compounds. Yet it would be difficult to say what kind of "shadow" is meant here if this is not a matter of an eclipse of sun or moon. And the meaning advocated by Oec and Theoph and some modern commentators:[168] "not a shadow—i.e., not a *trace*—of change," is too weak and furthermore is not attested for this term. However, this approach of the ancient interpreters points to the difficulty of the passage. The problem—both text-critically and in terms of the subject matter involved—concerns the combination of τροπή with ἀποσκίασμα. There are three principal variant readings which come under consideration, although the last two probably represent one and the same text:[169]

1) τροπῆς ἀποσκίασμα So the great majority of the witnesses, including most of the Egyptian witnesses; vulg: *vicissitudinis obumbratio* ("shadow of change"); the translation offered by Augustine could be understood as a rendering of this reading: *momenti obumbratio* ("shadow of movement"), but it might also represent an original ῥοπῆς ἀποσκίασμα.[170]

2a) τροπῆς ἀποσκιάσματος B ℵ P²³

2b) τροπὴ ἀποσκιάσματος 614 *et al.*; apparently boh;

ff also seems to represent this reading: *modicum obumbrationis* ("slight amount of shadow" or "trace of shadow"), and evidently interprets the expression in a manner similar to that of Oec.

If a solution to the problem is to be attempted, one must decide between reading 1 and reading 2. For considering the attestation of 2a and b it will not do to write off reading 2 as simply a scribal error—e.g., to explain ἀποσκιάσματος as resulting from the accidental telescoping of ἀποσκίασμα (in reading 1) with the αὐτός which in some manuscripts (1898 181) is inserted as the first Greek word of the following verse (v 18). To consider reading 2a to be a mistaken transcription of 2b is precarious, perhaps in view of the strong attestation (B ℵ P²³) of 2a to begin with, but certainly because of the poor sense of 2b. For "the solstice of the shadowing" makes no real sense; and if instead τροπή is taken in a non-technical way, i.e., as a synonym of παραλλαγή ("variation"), then it is odd that only τροπή and not παραλλαγή should have received a supplement which makes it more specific. It is much easier to understand how reading 2b could be an attempt to smooth out the difficult text of 2a. It is only a question of whether any sense at all can be made out of reading 2a.

Thus, in order to decide between the variants, one must investigate the possible interpretations of both reading 1: τροπῆς ἀποσκίασμα, and reading 2a: τροπῆ ς

---

encyclopädie der klassischen Altertumswissenschaften, vol. 6 (Stuttgart: Metzler, 1909), 2326–64. I gratefully acknowledge the advice of Franz Boll in the evaluation of this passage.

165 Epict., *Diss.* 1.14.4: "And how else comes it that at the waxing and waning of the moon and at the approach and recession of the sun we see among the things that are on earth so great an *alteration* and change to the opposite?" (πόθεν δὲ πρὸς τὴν αὔξησιν καὶ μείωσιν τῆς σελήνης καὶ τὴν τοῦ ἡλίου πρόσοδον καὶ ἄφοδον τοσαύτη παραλλαγὴ καὶ ἐπὶ τὰ ἐναντία μεταβολὴ τῶν ἐπιγείων θεωρεῖται).

166 Cf. Plut., *Def. Orac.* 4, p. 410F: "[the sun's] course in passing from solstice to solstice" (ἀπὸ τροπῶν ἐπὶ τροπὰς πάροδος); likewise, cf. "summer solstice" (τροπαὶ θεριναί) in 411A.

167 [The occurrence of this term in a work by the non-Christian doxographer Aëtius (1st or 2nd century A.D.) was not noted in Bauer's *Lexicon* until the 4th German edition (1952). The passage in question occurs in an enumeration of the opinions of various philosophers about the outward appearance of the

moon: "Democritus (says) that there is a sort of *shadow* (cast by) the elevated areas which are on it, for it has hollows and glens" (Δημόκριτος ἀποσκίασμά τι τῶν ὑψηλῶν ἐν αὐτῇ μερῶν· ἄγκη γὰρ αὐτὴν ἔχειν καὶ νάπας Aëtius, *De placitis philosophorum* 2.30.3; preserved in Stobaeus, *Ecl.* 1.26.4, p. 222 Wachsmuth; see *Doxographi Graeci*, ed. Hermann Diels [Berlin and Leipzig: de Gruyter, ²1929], p. 361, col. b, line 21)—Trans.]

168 So, among others, Ewald.

169 The reading "variation nor turning nor shadow of turning nor even the slightest suspicion of some shadow" (παραλλαγὴ ἢ τροπῆς ἢ τροπῆς ἀποσκίασμα οὐδὲ μέχρι ὑπονοίας τινὸς ὑπομονὴ [instead of ὑποβολὴ] ἀποσκιάσματος 2138) offers more a survey of all the possibilities than a solution to the problem.

170 So Wordsworth, "The Corbey St. James," 138.

ἀποσκιάσματος. Reading 1 first of all suggests "the shadow" or "the shadowing which is associated with the solstice." But since the shortening of the days following the solstice is not called "shadowing" (ἀποσκίασμα), this interpretation is impossible. Therefore reading 1 is tolerable only if τροπῆς is translated non-technically as an adjective: "*varying* shadowing," or if one assumes that Jas (or popular usage) had linked together half–understood terms with an astral reference without taking into consideration their specific meaning.

Reading 2a is untranslatable in the form παραλλαγὴ ἢ τροπῆς ἀποσκιάσματος. Its supporters, such as Ropes, must read η as an article instead of as the particle ἤ ("or"): παραλλαγὴ ἡ τροπῆς ἀποσκιάσματος; this is a stylistic improvement, but it still does not provide a suitable meaning since "the variation of the turning of the shadow" makes no real sense. Thus, the only possibility left for understanding 2a is conjectural emendation; and, in fact, help can be gained from the same approach by which Könnecke[171] emends reading 1—viz., either changing the position of ἤ, or inserting an additional ἤ before ἀποσκιάσματος. Hence, either παραλλαγὴ τροπῆς ἢ ἀποσκιάσματος, or παραλλαγὴ ἢ τροπῆς ἢ ἀποσκιάσματος—but in either case: "who is without change and knows neither turning nor eclipse." If one wants to take τροπή in its technical sense ("turning" of heavenly bodies), and if one does not wish to have Jas piling up words here which he does not understand, then it seems to me that this emendation is the best solution to the difficulty and at the same time the best explanation for the origin of reading 2a.

Now in this interpretation (but also in the others, which take τροπή non–technically as a synonym of παραλλαγή ["change"]) the main idea does not seem to be an assertion that the essence of God is light. To be sure, many commentators[172] take this to be the most important element in the clause, and then join it with the whole verse thusly: From this shining God nothing evil can come. But they overlook the fact that the discussion is not of the Father of lights, but of the lights themselves, i.e., the heavenly bodies, and also that "shadowing" (ἀποσκίασμα) is mentioned here only as a special instance of "change." According to the construction which is presumed above, the controlling term is "change" (παραλλαγή), and even in other constructions it is still the foremost term and the clearest. It is from this term that the main idea must be inferred: God is without change.[173] From this main idea one is obviously supposed to conclude that God, the giver of good things, is not capable of sending evil as well, for such change is contrary to his nature. And from there, the title "Father of lights" (πατὴρ τῶν φώτων) also becomes understandable. The heavenly bodies do not come into view here as givers of light, but rather as the heralds of eternal change. But their creator and governor is exalted above all change.

With regard to the heavenly bodies, it was above all else the regularity of their changes which Hellenistic reflection[174]—but also Jewish thinking,[175] likewise under the influence of the Orient—observed with inquisitive interest; but in this it was always stressed that the Mover himself was unmoved, the Author of every change was without change.[176] It corresponds to Hellenistic theology, which shies far away from all anthropomorphisms, that Philo writes in *Deus imm.* 22: "For what greater impiety could there be than to suppose that the Unchangeable changes?" (τί γὰρ ἂν ἀσέβημα μεῖζον γένοιτο τοῦ ὑπολαμβάνειν τὸν ἄτρεπτον τρέπεσθαι), and that he makes this the leading motif in

---

171 C. Könnecke, *Emendationen zu Stellen des Neuen Testaments*, BFTh 12, 1 (Gütersloh: Bertelsmann, 1908), 12f, taking his cue from Wisd 7:18 ("the alternations of the solstices" [τροπῶν ἀλλαγάς]), reads παραλλαγὴ τροπῆς ἢ ἀποσκίασμα. But since παραλλαγή has a quite general meaning and is not used in a technical sense in Wisdom of Solomon, it is more correct in terms of the subject matter here to have ἀποσκίασμα also dependent upon παραλλαγή (as in reading 2a).

172 E.g., Ewald, Huther, Beyschlag, Windisch–Preisker, Belser.

173 This is stressed by Bede and Dionysius, and, among modern commentators, by Mayor and Ropes.

174 Cf. on this Bousset, *Kyrios Christos*, 247ff.

175 See Wisd 7:17ff; *1 En.* 41 and 72. Spitta is right in pointing to these passages as examples of reflection upon the astral processes within Judaism, but he is wrong in using them as evidence for the specific meaning of the terms in Jas 1:17.

176 Cf. *Corp. Herm.* 5.5: "to contemplate in a single moment all these things, the immovable being moved and the invisible being made visible" (ὑπὸ μίαν ῥοπὴν πάντα ταῦτα θεάσασθαι, τὸν ἀκίνητον δια-

the entire treatise in *Deus imm.* 20–32, in which he deals with God's apparent change of mind in Gen 6:5–7. And this is contrasted with the changeable character of all created things in *Leg. all.* 2.33: "Now every created thing must necessarily undergo change, for this is its property, even as unchangeableness is the property of God" (πᾶν μὲν οὖν τὸ γενητὸν ἀναγκαῖον τρέπεσθαι, ἴδιον γάρ ἐστι τοῦτο αὐτοῦ, ὥσπερ θεοῦ τὸ ἄτρεπτον εἶναι). This motif seems occasionally to have received almost symbolic significance.[177] In addition, the heavenly bodies are sometimes specifically singled out and compared with the God who "turns not and changes not" (ἄτρεπτος καὶ ἀμετάβλητος Philo, *Cher.* 88–90).

That in such a context τροπή is used in the more general sense of "change" could make the non–technical meaning of the word seem possible also in our passage (with reading 1: τροπῆς ἀποσκίασμα). Nevertheless, one ought to be careful of the assumption that our saying is directly dependent upon Hellenistic diatribe. For, as we have seen, what Jas offers is a mosaic: the saying, which portrays God as the giver of good things, is supposed to confirm the idea that temptations do not come from God; the stressing of his unchangeableness is obviously intended to exclude the possibility that sometimes good comes from God and sometimes evil. If Jas were to have followed the popular philosophers here, he would have stated directly the thought that no evil can come from God and then he would have demonstrated it. There was plenty of material—already in Plato—which could be used for this purpose.[178] That Jas did not use it indicates that either he was not able to employ it or else he did not desire to do so; perhaps it was the saying–form for one thing—perhaps also an ignorance of the other material he might have used—which led Jas to use this aphoristic line of argument. As it stands, when Jas portrays in saying–form the unchangeableness of God, and in doing so makes some use of terms which have been picked up, only a faint echo remains of the philosophical train of thought which was mentioned above.

■ 18 Here the divine will to provide salvation is stressed; this can be seen from the position of "having willed" (βουληθείς). This participle does lack a complementary infinitive, but the further specification of what this will is is added later with the clause "that we should be, etc." (εἰς τὸ εἶναι κτλ.). Therefore, the participle is to be translated "in accordance with his will." Now there must be a connection with v 17 if v 18 is to make any sense: The will of the eternal, unchangeable God (v 17b) is good and brings salvation (and therefore God is the giver of good things—v 17a).

It is also upon the basis of this connection that we must examine the question of whether v 18 is intended

---

κινούμενον, καὶ τὸν ἀφανῆ φαινόμενον) [Trans.]. Variations ("emotions" [πάθη] and "changes" [μεταβολαί]) are characteristics of the demons, who exist "on the boundary between gods and men" (ἐν μεθορίῳ θεῶν καὶ ἀνθρώπων Plut., *Def. orac.* 12, p. 416C); but Plutarch says something rather different in *Def. orac.* 30, p. 426D: "the Deity is not averse to changes, but has a very great joy therein" (οὐ γὰρ ἀπεχθάνεται μεταβολαῖς ἀλλὰ καὶ πάνυ χαίρει τὸ θεῖον). A text from Qumran also speaks of the unchangeableness of God (1 QS III, 15–17): "From the God of Knowledge comes all that is and shall be. Before ever they existed He established their whole design, and when, as ordained for them, they come into being, it is in accord with His glorious design that they accomplish their task without change. The laws of all things are in His hand and He provides them with all their needs" (מאל הדעות כול הווה
ונהייה ולפני היותם הכין כול מחשבתם ובהיותם
לתעודותם כמחשבת כבודו ומלאו פעולותם ואין
להשנות בידו משפטי כול והואה יכלכלם בכול
חפציהם)

[trans. G. Vermes, *The Dead Sea Scrolls in English* (Baltimore, Md.: Penguin, ³1968), 75].

177   Cf. *Corp. Herm.* Frag. 11.2.48, vol. 3, p. 57 Nock-Festugière: "What is God? an unchangeable good. What is the human being? a changeable evil" (τί θεός; ἄτρεπτον ἀγαθόν. τί ἄνθρωπος; τρεπτὸν κακόν) [Trans.]; and Philo, *Leg. all.* 2.89: "How should one come to believe God? By learning that all other things change but He is unchangeable" (πῶς ἄν τις πιστεύσαι θεῷ; ἐὰν μάθῃ ὅτι πάντα τὰ ἄλλα τρέπεται, μόνος δὲ αὐτὸς ἄτρεπτός ἐστι). God is also contrasted with the sun in this same sort of comparison (so Epict., *Diss.* 1.14.10). Similar motifs are found in Jewish writings (Job 25:5; Sir 17:31), and cf. especially the interpolated passage in Philo, *Spec. leg.* 1.300.

178   Cf. on this Ernst Schröder, *Plotins Abhandlung Πόθεν τὰ κακά (Enn. I,8)*, Diss. Rostock (Borna and Leipzig: Noske, 1916), where numerous passages are adduced: p. 8 (Democritus), pp. 22f (Plato), pp. 60f (Maximus of Tyre).

cosmologically or soteriologically. If cosmologically, then "he brought forth" ($\dot{\alpha}\pi\epsilon\kappa\acute{\upsilon}\eta\sigma\epsilon\nu$)[179] would refer to the creation, "word of truth" ($\lambda\acute{o}\gamma os \, \dot{\alpha}\lambda\eta\theta\epsilon\acute{\iota}as$) would refer to the creating word, and "first–fruits" ($\dot{\alpha}\pi\alpha\rho\chi\acute{\eta}$) would mean the paradisaical condition of humans.[180] If soteriologically, then what is being discussed is the rebirth, and "first–fruits" refers to the position of the reborn, i.e., the Christians.[181] Now the cosmological idea does not at all suit the conclusion of v 17; for if God's good will is supposed to be depicted by a reference to the creation of human beings, then this argu-

ment has an extremely weak effect, and the fervor with which this allusion is made to something which is self–evident remains incomprehensible. The concept which is really important here is the stressing of the divine will to provide salvation, and already upon the basis of this general argument the soteriological meaning is to be preferred. Moreover, Spitta's arguments for the cosmological interpretation completely break down in the explanation of the term "first–fruits" (see below).

If the soteriological interpretation is correct, then "he brought forth" ($\dot{\alpha}\pi\epsilon\kappa\acute{\upsilon}\eta\sigma\epsilon\nu$) refers to the rebirth.

---

179 From the use of the verb "to bring forth" ($\dot{\alpha}\pi o\kappa\upsilon\epsilon\hat{\iota}\nu$ or $\dot{\alpha}\pi o\kappa\acute{\upsilon}\epsilon\iota\nu$) here, Carl–Martin Edsman, "Schöpferwille und Geburt Jac 1, 18: Eine Studie zur altchristlichen Kosmologie," *ZNW* 38 (1939): 11–44, comes to the conclusion that Jas 1:18 is unique in its use of this verb with a masculine subject. Edsman stresses that only in Clem. Alex., *Paed.* 6.42 do we find the concept of Christ giving birth to those who are his, and that passage seems to be dependent upon Jas 1:18. Otherwise, especially in the earlier period, the technical, literal use of the verb is so dominant, according to Edsman, that one can scarcely talk about a figurative use (p. 23). But Edsman underrates the importance of the extensive occurrence of the term in "abstract" contexts (cf. also on Jas 1:15): when there is a grammatically feminine subject the "natural–literal" meaning of the word is always confirmed; yet the "single exception" (Iren., *Adv. haer.* 1.15.1 = Epiph., *Haer.* 34.84) is treated by Edsman as a trifling exception. But his whole treatment provides a distorted picture, since the figurative use of the close cognate $\kappa\upsilon\epsilon\hat{\iota}\nu$ (1 ."to be pregnant"; 2. "to bring forth") is evident, even though this word likewise requires a feminine subject (yet the aorist $\acute{\epsilon}\kappa\upsilon\sigma a$ of the synonym $\kappa\acute{\upsilon}\omega$ is used also of a man: "to make pregnant"; see Liddell–Scott, *s.v.* $\kappa\acute{\upsilon}\omega$). Cf. *Corp. Herm.* 9.3 (quoted above in n. 132), where "Mind" (masculine in Greek) is characterized as "giving birth" to all designs ($\nu o\acute{\eta}\mu\alpha\tau a$), which are good or bad depending upon whether he has received the "seeds" ($\sigma\pi\acute{\epsilon}\rho\mu\alpha\tau a$) from God or the demons. Given all of this, it must appear questionable whether behind the term "he brought us forth" there must lie the Gnostic concept of a male–female primordial deity (Edsman, *op. cit.*, 28, 44; similarly, Hermann Schammberger, *Die Einheitlichkeit des Jacobusbriefes im antignostischen Kampf* [Gotha: Klotz, 1936], 59). In any event, one cannot deny the fact that there was a metaphorical use of this word which would fit in naturally with a soteriological train of thought.

Edsman has significantly modified his thesis in "Schöpfung und Wiedergeburt: Nochmals Jac. 1:18," *Spiritus et Veritas* [Festschrift Karl Kundzin] (Eutin: Ozolin, 1953), 43–55. Unfortunately, this article escaped not only my notice until now, but apparently also that of L. E. Elliott–Binns, "James I.18: Creation or Redemption?" *NTS* 3 (1957): 148–61, who prefers to interpret the passage within the framework of the Old Testament creation faith. In the same volume see also the article by O. Betz, "Die Geburt der Gemeinde durch den Lehrer: Bemerkungen zum Qumranpsalm 1 QH III, 1ff," *NTS* 3 (1957): 314–26: "The metaphor of spiritual birth . . . is found already in pre–Christian Judaism" (p. 322; see also p. 323).

180 So Spitta, who appeals here again to the analogy of Jewish texts: Sir 15:11ff; Wisd 1:13ff; 2:23f. Yet the two latter passages are not parallels at all, and Sir 15:14 focuses the problem on the free will given to man in creation, and therefore it has an orientation which diverges completely from that in our passage.

Significantly, patristic exegesis also follows this interpretation: On "first–fruits" ($\dot{\alpha}\pi\alpha\rho\chi\acute{\eta}$), Dionysius Bar Ṣalibi remarks: "He is not indicating that God made humans first, but rather he is pointing to the honor and dominion which were given to the human being"; likewise in the Catena and Scholion (p. 186): "By 'creatures' he means the visible creation, of which he shows the most valuable member to be the human being ($\kappa\tau\acute{\iota}\sigma\mu\alpha\tau a \, \delta\grave{\epsilon} \, \tau\grave{\eta}\nu \, \dot{o}\rho\omega\mu\acute{\epsilon}\nu\eta\nu \, \kappa\tau\acute{\iota}\sigma\iota\nu \, \phi\eta\sigma\acute{\iota}\nu, \, \mathring{\eta}s \, \tau\iota\mu\iota\acute{\omega}\tau\epsilon\rho o\nu \, \tau\grave{o}\nu \, \acute{\alpha}\nu\theta\rho\omega\pi o\nu \, \acute{\epsilon}\delta\epsilon\iota\xi\epsilon\nu$) [Trans.]. Oec and Theoph also seem to have the same view when they take "first–fruits" as a reference to the position of honor, and "having willed" ($\beta o\upsilon\lambda\eta\theta\epsilon\acute{\iota}s$) as a reference to the divine authorship in creation.

181 This is the opinion of most interpreters.

That is not to say that Jas has in mind some external process such as baptism.[182] It is not at all clear *a priori* whether he employs the concept with the full range of its mystical significance[183]—divine re-creation following the death of the old person—or merely in its popularized form, so that rebirth is only another expression for conversion to Christianity.

Consequently, one can also vacillate in the interpretation of the phrase "word of truth" ($\lambda \acute{o} \gamma o s \ \dot{a} \lambda \eta \theta \epsilon \acute{\iota} a s$). In a "mystical" context the meaning would be the divine principle through whose indwelling within human beings the rebirth is brought about; hence, this would be what early Christian texts call "Spirit" ($\pi \nu \epsilon \hat{v} \mu a$) and Hermetic texts, which expressly evidence the mystical conception just mentioned, call "Mind" ($\nu o \hat{v} s$).[184] "Truth" ($\dot{a} \lambda \acute{\eta} \theta \epsilon \iota a$) would then be the divine dominion from which this "word" comes. But even then the term "word" ($\lambda \acute{o} \gamma o s$) could still retain some ambivalence and designate the divine principle which

nevertheless is ultimately the spoken word of revelation that operates in humans.[185] But above all, we find no hint in these words that Jas has in mind the mystical associations mentioned above. Rather, the conclusion of the verse clearly shows that what matters to him is not the miraculous character of the new existence, but the position of the reborn among the other members of creation. From this we can conclude that the "mystical" understanding of rebirth is not important to him, but rather the more common meaning: "rebirth" is "conversion." In this case, "word of truth" ($\lambda \acute{o} \gamma o s \ \dot{a} \lambda \eta \theta \epsilon \acute{\iota} a s$)[186] doubtlessly refers to the gospel.[187]

The goal of the rebirth is stated in the clause "that we should be, etc." ($\epsilon \grave{\iota} s \ \tau \grave{o} \ \epsilon \hat{\iota} \nu a \iota \ \dot{\eta} \mu \hat{a} s \ \kappa \tau \lambda.$); this construction must surely indicate purpose here, for the expression "in accordance with his will" ($\beta o \nu \lambda \eta \theta \epsilon \acute{\iota} s$) which is placed at the beginning of the sentence puts all the emphasis upon the divine will, not upon its actual effect. "A kind of" ($\tau \iota s$) which is added to

182 So Bede and Belser.

183 Cf. on this the Excursus on Tit 3:5 in Dibelius–Conzelmann, *The Pastoral Epistles*; Reitzenstein, *Mysterienreligionen* (see in his Index under "Wiedergeburt"); Richard Perdelwitz, *Die Mysterienreligion und das Problem des I. Petrusbriefes*, RVV 11, 3 (Giessen: Töpelmann [Ricker], 1911), 37ff.

184 In *Corp. Herm.* 13.2, Tat asks, "Who is it, Father, that impregnates?" ($T \acute{\iota} \nu o s \ \sigma \pi \epsilon \acute{\iota} \rho a \nu \tau o s, \ \hat{\omega} \ \pi \acute{a} \tau \epsilon \rho;$), to which Hermes answers, "The will of God, my son" ($\tau o \hat{v} \ \theta \epsilon \lambda \acute{\eta} \mu a \tau o s \ \tau o \hat{v} \ \theta \epsilon o \hat{v}, \ \hat{\omega} \ \tau \acute{\epsilon} \kappa \nu o \nu$). The miracle of the new birth is described by Hermes in 13.3: "and I am no longer who I was before; rather, I have been begotten by Mind" ($\kappa a \acute{\iota} \ \epsilon \grave{\iota} \mu \iota \ \nu \hat{v} \nu \ o \dot{v} \chi \ \dot{o} \ \pi \rho \acute{\iota} \nu,$ $\dot{a} \lambda \lambda' \ \dot{\epsilon} \gamma \epsilon \nu \nu \acute{\eta} \theta \eta \nu \ \dot{\epsilon} \nu \ \nu \hat{\omega}$); cf. *Corp. Herm.* 1.9: "The Mind, who is God . . . brought forth by a word another Mind, the demiurge" ($\dot{o} \ \delta \grave{\epsilon} \ N o \hat{v} s, \ \dot{o} \ \theta \epsilon \acute{o} s, \ldots$ $\dot{a} \pi \epsilon \kappa \acute{\upsilon} \eta \sigma \epsilon \ \lambda \acute{o} \gamma \omega \ \acute{\epsilon} \tau \epsilon \rho o \nu \ N o \hat{v} \nu \ \delta \eta \mu \iota o \nu \rho \gamma \acute{o} \nu$) [Trans.]; R. Reitzenstein, *Poimandres* (Leipzig: Teubner, 1904; reprint Darmstadt: Wissenschaftliche Buchgesellschaft, 1966), 330, deleted the term $\lambda \acute{o} \gamma \omega$ ("by a word"), arguing that it does not fit, and he referred to *Corp. Herm.* 1.12, where a similar formula occurs but without this term; however, Reitzenstein retracted this conjecture in a review of Walter Scott, ed. *Hermetica*, vol. 2, in *Gnomon* 3 (1927): 276; cf. *Corpus Hermeticum*, ed. A. D. Nock, tr. A.–J. Festugière, vol 1 (Paris: Société d'édition "Les Belles Lettres," ²1960), *ad. loc.* C. H. Dodd, *The Bible and the Greeks* (London: Hodder and Stoughton, 1935), 133, n. 1, conjectured that the first passage cited above (*Corp. Herm.* 13.2) has been influenced by

Jas 1:18.

185 1 Petr 1:23, in particular, is an instance of this sort of ambivalent meaning. In that passage, rebirth undoubtedly has a deeper and more mystical significance than in Jas 1:18 (a literary connection does not exist between these two texts, which, moreover, employ quite different terminology); cf. Perdelwitz, *op. cit.* (above, n. 183), 60f. But then this mystical $\lambda \acute{o} \gamma o s$ ("word") of 1 Petr 1:23 is called in 1:25 the "message which was preached unto you" ($\tau \grave{o} \ \dot{\rho} \hat{\eta} \mu a$ $\tau \grave{o} \ \epsilon \dot{v} a \gamma \gamma \epsilon \lambda \iota \sigma \theta \grave{\epsilon} \nu \ \epsilon \grave{\iota} s \ \dot{v} \mu \hat{a} s$). One might also compare the ambivalent meaning of "word" in *Odes of Solomon* 12. In 12.1–3, the poet is depicted as filled with "the words of Truth"; but 12.3b already has a mystical ring: "Because the mouth of the Lord is the true Word and the door of His light." Then in 12.4–8 the cosmic effect of the Word is portrayed. Finally, it is said at the conclusion of the ode in 12.11: "For the dwelling-place of the Word is man, and his truth is love" (trans. Rendel Harris and Alphonse Mingana, ed. and tr., *The Odes and Psalms of Solomon*, vol. 2 [Manchester: University Press, 1920], 272f).

186 This Christian term originates from Judaism; see Ps 119:43; *Test. Gad* 3.1; cf. also *Odes of Solomon* 8.8: "Hear the word of truth, and receive the knowledge of the Most High" (trans. Harris–Mingana, *op. cit.* [above, n. 185], vol. 2, p. 254).

187 No importance need be placed upon the absence of the article. The expression occurs also in 2 Cor 6:7 with the same meaning, and again without the article.

"first–fruits" serves to tone down the metaphorical expression.[188]

The meaning of the metaphor itself is disputed. Those who would interpret the whole verse cosmologically (see above), of course, cannot appeal in support of their view to the point in time at which the first humans were created. The sequence of the acts of creation puts them, not as the "*first*–fruits," but as the *last* (see also Philo, *Op. mund.* 77). Spitta cites *j. Shab.* 2.3: "the first man . . . in his relation to the world was as a pure cake–offering"; but there all the emphasis lies upon the purity. The ancient advocates of the cosmological interpretation evidently had in mind the pre–eminence of the humans among created things; in that case, one would have to be thinking of the Old Testament cultic term "first, best" (רֵאשִׁית = ἀπαρχή): the best is presented to God as "first–fruits" (Ex 23:19, cf. also *Did.* 13.3ff), thus according to Philo, *Spec. leg.* 4.180, the people of Israel are set apart "as a kind of first–fruits to the Maker and Father" (οἷά τις ἀπαρχὴ τῷ ποιητῇ καὶ πατρί); according to Rev 14:4, the "followers of the Lamb" are redeemed from humankind as first–fruits for God. Yet the notion of sacrifice, the offering brought to God, is far from the thought in our passage. Furthermore, what is involved in Jas 1:18 is obviously not first–fruits as a ransom paid in substitution for the whole, but rather first–fruits as a temporary down–payment to be followed by the remaining members of the species. Otherwise, the words would not really have been appropriate to express the will of God which is directed toward the good, and thus to serve as support for the idea in 1:17. Therefore, the arguments of the cosmological interpretation break down when it comes to explaining the meaning of "first–fruits" (ἀπαρχή). For it is not a matter here of honor which one has beyond others, but rather of the salvation which is to be shared by all.

On the other hand, the expression "first–fruits of his creatures" (ἀπαρχὴ τῶν αὐτοῦ κτισμάτων) can be explained quite well in a soteriological context. We find ἀπαρχή used numerous times in this sense, and in such cases the term is always conceived as a first deposit or down–payment of the whole: in the context of the image of the dough in Rom 11:16; as a missionary term, to designate the first converts (Rom 16:5; 1 Cor 16:15; *1 Clem.* 42.4; perhaps also 2 Thess 2:13); and finally in eschatological contexts in 1 Cor 15:20, 23 and *1 Clem.* 24.1, which portray Christ as the first–fruits of those who have fallen asleep.

This is the view in our passage as well: the Christians are the first–fruits whom the other "creatures" (κτίσματα) soon will follow. But "creatures" is not a reference to the reborn,[189] for the metaphor of birth has already been superceded by the mention of "first–fruits." Nor is it a matter here of the elevation of Jewish–Christians from among human kind or from among others Christians,[190] for all those who are now Christians have experienced this rebirth. Jas calls them all first–fruits, and in doing so he expresses the hope that the others also will yet come to salvation, namely, all other people and—since he obviously uses the expression κτίσματα deliberately—all God's creatures in general.[191] The idea expressed in Rom 8:21 is at least intimated here.

The conceptual milieu of Jewish didactic Wisdom, in which our author has moved almost exclusively up to this point, seems to be left behind here in a characteristic way. And as a matter of fact, the verse can be understood only in terms of the milieu of a Christian faith and life. For the cosmological interpretation is not feasible, and hence there remains only the interpretation of the verse as a reference to rebirth. To be sure, given the wide dissemination of this concept, it might be conceivable that also Jews could have depicted their deep religious experiences as a new, miraculous birth. But Jas 1:18 cannot be understood as testimony of a mystic; instead, it speaks of and to an entire group of people who are conscious of the fact they were "reborn," who seem to be quite familiar with this notion, and who seem not to require any further explanation of the concept. And what is more: these people conceive of their rebirth as the prelude to the new creation of the whole world; they are only the "first–fruits" of the great cosmic renewal. These ideas are possible only in the context of a religion which places personal religious experience in direct relationship to the end

---

188 See above in the Introduction, section 5, and Blass–Debrunner, § 301.

189 So von Soden (the first–fruits are those reborn, those "new creatures" [cf. 2 Cor 5:17], who have endured persecutions) and Belser.

190 So Beyschlag and Belser.

of the world.[192] Thus, both the popularization of the concept of rebirth and the eschatological optimism constitute evidence against the Jewish provenance of Jas as a whole and against the hypothesis of Spitta and Massebieau.[193]

Yet the Christian character of this passage should not be overestimated either. Precisely the common and general form of the concept must restrain the interpreter from doing so. With not one word does Jas hint that he is conscious of the entire range of the concept of rebirth. Evidently he has taken over this concept from the language of the community, as perhaps he has also taken over the other notion of the "first–fruits," which receives just as little elaboration; and he has in no way deepened the concept or expanded it. Because of this, one ought not to overburden the words theologically.[194] They are a witness to the Christianity of the author, but they are not proof of the conceptual originality of the whole writing.

---

191 Hofmann, Mayor, Windisch–Preisker.
192 One ought to note the difference between this and the passage from Philo, *Spec. leg.* 4.180, which is cited above. Philo sees in the Jewish people's position as first–fruits the compensation for their isolation among human kind. But he does not say that their position is also a surety for the conversion of all people. The case is similar with *Ass. Mos.* 1.12f: "For he has created the world on behalf of His people. But He was not pleased to manifest this *purpose* [or 'beginning'] *of creation* from the foundation of the world" (creavit enim orbem terrarum propter plebem suam et non coepit eam inceptionem creaturae et ab initio orbis terrarum palam facere) [trans. Charles, *APOT*].
193 See above in the Introduction, section 3.
194 See above in the Introduction, section 8.

1 A Series of Sayings About Hearing and Doing

19 Know this, my beloved brothers and sisters:
Now let every one be quick to hear, slow to
speak, slow to anger; 20/ for human anger
does not produce divine righteousness (in a
person). 21/ Therefore, put away all filth and
all that profuse wickedness and be meek,
when you receive the implanted word which
is able to save your souls. 22/ Be doers of the
word, not merely hearers, deceiving yourselves. 23/ Because if someone is (only) a
hearer of the word and not a doer, he is like
the person who looks at his natural
appearance in a mirror; 24/ for he looks at
himself and goes away, and immediately he
forgets what he looked like. 25/ But someone
who looks into the perfect law of freedom
and perseveres, and is not a forgetful hearer
but an obedient doer, such a person will be
blessed in his doing.

26 If someone thinks he is religious, although he
does not (even) bridle his tongue but rather
deceives himself, then his religion is worthless. 27/ Pure and undefiled religion before
God the Father is this: to look after orphans
and widows in their distress, and to keep
oneself unstained from the world.

Analysis

The section 1:19–27 is far more unified than was the
first section. The fundamental tone is set by the *three–
part saying* in 1:19b which, together with the introductory admonition, opens this portion. 1:20 seems
to be an appendix to the last part of the saying in 1:19b,
just as 1:26 is evidently connected with the second
part of this "triplet." What comes in between, 1:21–25,
is an elaboration about hearing and doing, and therefore is a supplement to the first part of 1:19b: "be quick
to hear" ($\tau\alpha\chi\grave{\upsilon}\varsigma$ $\epsilon\grave{\iota}\varsigma$ $\tau\grave{o}$ $\grave{\alpha}\kappa o\hat{\upsilon}\sigma\alpha\iota$); this thought seems to
be the primary interest of the author here. This is con-
firmed also by 1:27, which externally represents a
supplement attached to 1:26 by means of a catchword
("religion"—"religious" [$\theta\rho\eta\sigma\kappa\epsilon\acute{\iota}\alpha$—$\theta\rho\eta\sigma\kappa\acute{o}\varsigma$]), but

which in its content signifies a return to the author's
chief interest which I have just mentioned.

Therefore, since we can say with relative certainty
what the author's primary concern is, the question
arises as to his reason for incorporating still other
admonitions: the warning against sins of the tongue
in 1:19, 26, and the warning against anger in 1:19, 20.
This is a question to which we must give all the more
serious consideration at just this point, since these very
themes are treated in more detail later on in Jas: the
sins of the tongue in 3:1ff, and anger (at least by im-
plication) in the admonition to "meekness" ($\pi\rho\alpha\ddot{\upsilon}\tau\eta\varsigma$)
in 3:13ff.[1] We may assume[2] that Jas has taken over
the saying in 1:19b, which perhaps was already connected to 1:20. He uses the saying here because of the

---

1 Cladder, "Die Anlage des Jakobusbriefes," 37ff (see
also his article, "Der formale Aufbau des Jakobusbriefes," *ZKTh* 28 [1904]: 295f), uses this observation—i.e., that motifs alluded to in 1:19ff reappear
with a more extensive treatment—as a basis for his
attempt to demonstrate an arrangement of the material within Jas. According to Cladder, the concepts which are introduced in 1:19ff—sins of the

tongue, acts of charity, remaining unstained from
the world—are repeated in 3:17:
"peaceable" ($\epsilon\grave{\iota}\rho\eta\nu\iota\kappa\acute{\eta}$) is supposed to allude to
sins of the tongue (!),
"full of mercy," ($\mu\epsilon\sigma\tau\grave{\eta}$ $\grave{\epsilon}\lambda\acute{\epsilon}o\upsilon\varsigma$ $\kappa\tau\lambda$.) to acts of
charity,
"harmonious, sincere" ($\grave{\alpha}\delta\iota\acute{\alpha}\kappa\rho\iota\tau o\varsigma$, $\grave{\alpha}\nu\upsilon\pi\acute{o}\kappa\rho\iota\tau o\varsigma$)
to renunciation of the world.

admonition "be quick to hear." To that he added his elaboration about hearing and doing which he attached to the warning against anger by means of the admonition to "meekness" ($\pi\rho\alpha\ddot{\upsilon}\tau\eta\varsigma$ 1:21). In order that justice might also be done to the admonition "be slow to speak" ($\beta\rho\alpha\delta\grave{\upsilon}\varsigma$ $\epsilon\grave{\iota}\varsigma$ $\tau\grave{o}$ $\lambda\alpha\lambda\hat{\eta}\sigma\alpha\iota$ 1:19b), he threw in a warning against sins of the tongue in 1:26, but then returned immediately, in 1:27,[3] to his real subject, doing.

Interpretation

■ **19a** The witnesses of the so-called Koine text, as well as P and Ψ, begin this verse with "therefore" ($\ddot{\omega}\sigma\tau\epsilon$), while most other witnesses have "know this" ($\breve{\iota}\sigma\tau\epsilon$). The first reading attempts to connect 1:19 with 1:18, as do many translations, and therefore this reading must be regarded as an emendation.

There can be no doubt about the role of the introductory formula if one observes how Jas effects his transitions elsewhere, and how fond he is of utilizing in his writing just such dialogic motifs from diatribe style.[4] Only someone who demands that such a formula contain some meaningful intrinsic reference will see the words as referring to v 18 and then translate them in the indicative ("You know this").[5] But such a connection is not necessary, given the character of this chapter. The formula does not separate, but neither does it combine the two sections by establishing some coherence (as the reading "therefore" [$\ddot{\omega}\sigma\tau\epsilon$] would do); it simply stands at the head of the next series of sayings.

■ **19b** The beginning of the *three–part saying* is not entirely certain text–critically. While the reading $\kappa\alpha\grave{\iota}$ $\ddot{\epsilon}\sigma\tau\omega$ ("and let him be" A 33 81) really need not be considered, a respectable branch of the tradition (including $\aleph$ B C 33 P* 1739 *ff s m* vulg) has the particle $\delta\acute{\epsilon}$ ("but, now, and") after "let him be" ($\ddot{\epsilon}\sigma\tau\omega$). It is easy to conceive of a reason why this particle might later have been omitted—it disrupts the continuity. Therefore, we may at least take into account the possibility that $\delta\acute{\epsilon}$ is the genuine reading. Many interpreters explain away the difficulty which the particle offers by construing v 19a with what precedes. But that is hardly necessary; for if the saying in v 19b is older than Jas—which is likely anyway—then the $\delta\acute{\epsilon}$ could have functioned in the earlier context and could simply have been kept with the saying when Jas adopted it;[6] cf. 1 Tim 6:7, where the $\ddot{o}\tau\iota$ ("*as* we can take nothing with us . . .") is much stranger still, and perhaps is to be explained in the same way. Given the understanding of 1:19a set forth above, we need not require an inner connection between 1:19b and what precedes it. Consequently, there is also no need to establish such a connection on the basis of Old Testament passages.[7]

In the interpretation of the three abrupt admonitions, one again must refer especially to ideas from Jewish didactic Wisdom since, as will be shown, v 19b is a wisdom saying both in form and in content. The parallels show that already in the first part, "be quick to hear" ($\tau\alpha\chi\grave{\upsilon}\varsigma$ $\epsilon\grave{\iota}\varsigma$ $\tau\grave{o}$ $\dot{\alpha}\kappa\hat{o}\hat{\upsilon}\sigma\alpha\iota$), one is by no means to think only of the hearing of the word of God. When the admonition to be quick to hear occurs in Sirach—"Be

---

Then in 2:1–3:12, the same concepts are supposed to be utilized in a different sequence:

    2:1–13 against respect for worldly values,
    2:14–26 on charity (yet the point of this section is something else entirely!),
    3:1–12 on sins of the tongue.

But this arrangement does violence to the text and also fails to recognize the literary character of the document; the same applies to the arrangement suggested by Ernst Pfeiffer, "Der Zusammenhang des Jakobusbriefes," *ThStKr* 23 (1850): 167, which is structured in accordance with the triad in 1:19; see above in the Introduction, n. 22.

2   See also below on 1:19b, 20.

3   The minuscules 2138 and 614 try to eliminate the isolation of the saying by reading "keep yourselves unstained" ($\dot{\alpha}\sigma\pi\acute{\iota}\lambda o\upsilon\varsigma$ $\dot{\epsilon}\alpha\upsilon\tau o\grave{\upsilon}\varsigma$ $\tau\eta\rho\epsilon\hat{\iota}\tau\epsilon$), thereby

transposing the statement from the tone of a saying into the style of an admonition (see 1:19); cf. the similar phenomenon noted below on 1:26.

4   See above in the Introduction, section 5.

5   So vulg, Hofmann, Beyschlag, Belser; on the most important argument for this interpretation, viz., the $\delta\acute{\epsilon}$ after $\ddot{\epsilon}\sigma\tau\omega$ ("let him be"), see below.

6   In this case, there is no need to suppose that a thought which belonged between v 19a and v 19b has been omitted (so Windisch–Preisker), nor that the $\delta\acute{\epsilon}$ derived from Matt 5:37.

7   Spitta argues for a connection upon the basis of Eccl 4:17 and 5:1: Jas 1:13ff deals with frivolous speech against God, while 1:19 deals with the hearing of God's word and with speaking about divine matters. However, Jas 1:19 is not referring at all to cultic hearing and speaking, and consequently the passage

quick to hear, and be deliberate in answering" (γίνου
ταχὺς ἐν ἀκροάσει σου καὶ ἐν μακροθυμίᾳ φθέγγου ἀπό-
κρισιν Sir 5:11)—what this hearing and answering
refers to is the instruction of the teachers of wisdom.
This instruction included not only the "narrative of
divine matters," but also "wise proverbs"; cf. Sir 6:35:
"Be ready to listen to every narrative of divine matters,
and do not let wise proverbs escape you" (πᾶσαν διήγ-
ησιν θείαν θέλε ἀκούειν, καὶ παροιμίαι συνέσεως μὴ ἐκφευ-
γέτωσάν σε) [RSV modified]; the same sense is to be
found in Sir 6:33(34): "If you love to listen you will
gain knowledge, and if you incline your ear you will
become wise" (ἐὰν ἀγαπήσῃς ἀκούειν, ἐκδέξῃ, καὶ ἐὰν
κλίνῃς τὸ οὖς σου, σοφὸς ἔσῃ); cf. Sir 21:15: "When a
man of understanding hears a wise saying . . ." (λόγον
σοφὸν ἐὰν ἀκούσῃ ἐπιστήμων . . .); likewise, *Pirke Aboth*
5.12, where first of all there is mention of him who is
quick to hear and quick to forget: his gain is cancelled
by his loss; the converse is true of him who is slow to
hear and slow to forget; and then the text says: whoever
is quick to hear and slow to forget is a wise man; slow
to hear and quick to forget—that is an evil lot.

Even less can one say that the second admonition,
"be slow to speak" (βραδὺς εἰς τὸ λαλῆσαι), is limited
to the word of God. What is involved here is one of
those frequent warnings, in both Jewish and extra–
Jewish Wisdom teaching, directed toward all those who
are all too ready with something to say. There is more
hope for a fool, says Prov 29:20, than for a man who is
too hasty with his words. Sir 4:29 warns against being
"rough (τραχύς; variants "quick" [ταχύς], "rash"
[θρασύς]) in speech"; *Pirke Aboth* 1.15 cites the saying
of Shammai: "Say little, do much." In the same way,
our saying is self–explanatory and need not, because of
some alleged connection, be restricted to the hearing
of the word of God[8] or to the hearing of instruction.[9]

There is just as little intention in the third part of
the saying to speak of anger against God.[10] The admonition "be slow to anger" (βραδὺς εἰς ὀργήν) could

be conceived as an intensifying appendix to the second
admonition: Whoever is not able to become master of
his tongue also does not know how to bridle his anger.
But such an inner connection is not necessary.[11] Warnings against anger are frequent in gnomic literature;
cf. Eccl 7:9; LXX Prov 15:1: "Anger destroys even
the prudent" (ὀργὴ ἀπόλλυσιν καὶ φρονίμους); *Pirke
Aboth* 2.10: "Be not quick to anger"; Col 3:8; Eph
4:26, 31; *Did.* 3.2: "Do not be quick–tempered, for
anger leads to murder" (μὴ γίνου ὀργίλος, ὁδηγεῖ γὰρ ἡ
ὀργὴ πρὸς τὸν φόνον) [Trans.]. In this *Didache* passage,
just as in Sir 1:22, attention is called to the result of
anger.

■ **20** And evidently a similar goal is in mind in Jas
1:20. Perhaps already the authors of the variant κατεργάζεται ("to produce" C* Ψ 0246 33 P Koine) have
understood the verse in this way. Still this variant could
be explained by the occurrence of the word in 1:3 and
by the inclination to use compounds, and therefore,
ἐργάζεται must be read.

Many interpreters, from Luther to Ropes, have
taken this verb as a synonym for ποιεῖν ("to do"; the
antithesis would be "to commit sin" [ἁμαρτίαν ἐργάζε
σθαι 2:9]); they cite the expression "to do righteousness" (ποιεῖν τὴν δικαιοσύνην in LXX and New Testament), and they are probably also influenced by the
equation of "righteousness" (δικαιοσύνη) with "righteous or just act" (τὸ δίκαιον). But that expression which
they cite proves nothing for our passage; in fact, the
result would be a triviality: The angry person does not
do the right thing (before God).[12] Since we can rightly
expect to hear in this verse about the effect of wrath,
there is nothing to prevent us from taking "righteousness of God" (δικαιοσύνη θεοῦ) as a human attribute,
and to translate ἐργάζεσθαι as "produce"—as in 2 Cor
7:10, where this word alternates with κατεργάζεσθαι
("to produce"). Man is to attain to the "righteousness
of God"; if he gives way to anger, he never attains to
it; therefore anger blocks the way to his goal.

---

in Ecclesiastes, with its cultic regulations, is not a
     suitable parallel.
8   Gebser, Spitta, Belser.
9   Bede, de Wette.
10   Gebser, Spitta.
11   Cf. below on the form of the three–part saying.
12   Beyschlag reduces the triviality by assuming that
     there is an anti-Jewish polemic: the Jews considered

even anger to be a thing which sometimes was pleasing to God. But the character of the saying points to
Wisdom teaching, not to Christian polemic against
the Jews. Von Soden's claim that the genitive θεοῦ
("of God") is to be taken as a subjective genitive
because it is parallel to ἀνδρός ("of man") is not
justified, for it is possible to have rhetorical parallelism in case and at the same time a syntactical dif-

With the expression "of God" ($\theta\epsilon o\hat{v}$) there surfaces a controversy familiar from the Pauline literature—viz., whether what is meant is God's juridical righteousness, or righteousness from God, or righteousness before God. There can be no general resolution of this question in the case of Jas, who, apart from the quotation in 2:23, uses the term "righteousness" ($\delta\iota\kappa\alpha\iota\sigma\sigma\acute{v}\nu\eta$) elsewhere only in 3:18. Yet one can say, if what is involved is in fact a human attribute, that the first of the three meanings mentioned is hardly to be considered here. However, the other two meanings could not in any case signify in our passage what Paul understands by the "righteousness of God": a miraculous, not a human righteousness, the gift of the grace of God. For Jas what is involved is something which comes about precisely through the action of human beings. Nevertheless, it is conceivable that Paul's formulation, turned completely upside down in meaning and deprived of its depth, reappears here as a common Christian watchword for a life which is "righteous" in the true sense. In this case, a religious language influenced ultimately by Judaism would have brought about this recoloration.

Now a comment about *the form of the three-part saying in 1:19b*: Such threefold groupings are found frequently in Jewish literature[13]—both with and without the three parts being related to each other in content. Explicit reference to groupings by three is made in *Pirke Aboth* 1.2 and 2.10ff. Without doubt, the mnemonic assistance which such numerical data provides plays a role in this sort of reference; cf. the importance of numbers in the sayings of Agur in Prov 30:7, 15, 18, 21, 24, 29.[14] But mnemonics alone do not provide a full explanation for the origin of such three-fold groupings. Rather, one must refer to the age-old and widespread human preference for that smallest odd number greater than one: all good things come in threes. To the Jewish custom which is based upon that preference our saying also owes its three-fold grouping.

Originally, this saying was probably located within a group of other, similarly constructed sayings and not, as it is here, at the head of a section which interpreted the three parts very unequally.[15] Therefore, the saying probably has been taken over by Jas from the tradition. The fact that equal treatment has not been given to all three parts also points to this; Jas does not want to talk about "speaking" at all, but rather about "hearing and doing."[16] Why would he write at all, "Be slow to speak" ($\beta\rho\alpha\delta\grave{v}\varsigma\ \epsilon\grave{\iota}\varsigma\ \tau\grave{o}\ \lambda\alpha\lambda\hat{\eta}\sigma\alpha\iota$), unless these words were handed down to him in the tradition?

Only one thing more needs to be borne in mind: we are dealing here with the transmission of what is perhaps a Jewish idea, but still it was handed down in Greek. For the epigrammatic quality of the saying, at least in its present form, has its real charm only in Greek: $\dot{\alpha}\kappa o\hat{v}\sigma\alpha\iota$—$\lambda\alpha\lambda\hat{\eta}\sigma\alpha\iota$ ("to hear"—"to speak"), $\tau\alpha\chi\acute{v}\varsigma$—$\beta\rho\alpha\delta\acute{v}\varsigma$—$\beta\rho\alpha\delta\acute{v}\varsigma$ ("quick"—"slow"—"slow"). Furthermore, the rhetorical antithesis between "quick" and "slow" is not uncommon in Greek literature.[17] In cases such as that in our saying, the antithesis is then usually underlined by using the particles $\mu\acute{\epsilon}\nu$ ("on the one hand") and $\delta\acute{\epsilon}$ ("on the other hand"); yet these particles are lacking here. Whether this is due to negli-

---

ference (see the datives in Rom 12:10ff). The word-play in Sir 1:21: "unjust anger"—"be justified" ($\theta\nu\mu\grave{o}\varsigma\ \ddot{\alpha}\delta\iota\kappa o\varsigma$—$\delta\iota\kappa\alpha\iota\omega\theta\hat{\eta}\nu\alpha\iota$), is, of course, a different matter.

13 *Pirke Aboth* 1.1f, 4–7, 10, 15, 18; 2.10, 12f; 3.1, 12; Pseudo-Menander, Frag. 47 (in Anton Baumstark, "Lucubrationes Syro-Graecae," *Jahrbuch für classische Philologie*, Supplementband 21 [1894], 480).

14 Cf. also the 4th chapter of *Pirke Aboth*; similarly, in an Arabic version of the *Story of Aḥiḳar*: "There are four things in which neither the king nor his army can be secure, etc." (trans. Charles, *APOT* 2, p. 738); cf. Aug. Wünsche, "Die Zahlensprüche in Talmud und Midrasch," *Zeitschrift der Deutschen Morgenländischen Gesellschaft* 65 (1911): 57–100 (on groupings by 2 and 3), 395–421 (on groupings by 4 and 5), and *ibid.* 66 (1912): 414–59 (groupings by 6 or more).

15 See above in the Analysis.

16 See above in the Analysis.

17 Theognis, *Eleg.* 1.329 (ed. Douglas Young, *Theognis* [Leipzig: Teubner, 1961], 22): "A pursuer who is slow but prudent overtakes a quick man" ($\kappa\alpha\grave{\iota}\ \beta\rho\alpha\delta\grave{v}\varsigma\ \epsilon\ddot{v}\beta o\nu\lambda o\varsigma\ \epsilon\grave{\iota}\lambda\epsilon\nu\ \tau\alpha\chi\grave{v}\nu\ \ddot{\alpha}\nu\delta\rho\alpha\ \delta\iota\acute{\omega}\kappa\omega\nu$) [Trans.]; Pseudo-Isocrates, *Ad Demonicum* 34: "Be slow in deliberation, but be quick to carry out your resolves" ($\beta o\nu\lambda\epsilon\acute{v}o\nu\ \mu\grave{\epsilon}\nu\ \beta\rho\alpha\delta\acute{\epsilon}\omega\varsigma,\ \dot{\epsilon}\pi\iota\tau\acute{\epsilon}\lambda\epsilon\iota\ \delta\grave{\epsilon}\ \tau\grave{\alpha}\ \delta\acute{o}\xi\alpha\nu\tau\alpha\ \tau\alpha\chi\acute{\epsilon}\omega\varsigma$) [Loeb modified]; Aristot., *Eth. Nic.* 6.9.2, p. 1142b: "They say that one should be quick in carrying out decisions but should be slow in deliberation" ($\kappa\alpha\grave{\iota}\ \phi\alpha\sigma\grave{\iota}\ \pi\rho\acute{\alpha}\tau\tau\epsilon\iota\nu\ \mu\grave{\epsilon}\nu\ \delta\epsilon\hat{\iota}\nu\ \tau\alpha\chi\grave{v}\ \tau\grave{\alpha}\ \beta o\nu\lambda\epsilon\nu-\theta\acute{\epsilon}\nu\tau\alpha,\ \beta o\nu\lambda\epsilon\acute{v}\epsilon\sigma\theta\alpha\iota\ \delta\grave{\epsilon}\ \beta\rho\alpha\delta\acute{\epsilon}\omega\varsigma$) [Trans.]; Philo, *Conf. ling.* 48: "slow to help, quick to harm" ($\beta\rho\alpha\delta\grave{v}\varsigma\ \dot{\omega}\phi\epsilon\lambda\hat{\eta}\sigma\alpha\iota,\ \tau\alpha\chi\grave{v}\varsigma\ \beta\lambda\acute{\alpha}\psi\alpha\iota$). There is also a wordplay

gence, or precisely to some refinement in style, cannot be decided since we know nothing about the provenance of the saying.

Considering all of this, the three–part saying—with or without the supplement in 1:20—finds its place in the category of the wisdom saying. And a look at its content confirms this: the saying is not concerned with Jews in the fulfillment of their cultic duties, nor with Christians in their position with respect to God or to Judaism; all these specific interpretations fail. The admonition of the saying directs itself to people in general, although Jas certainly is shouting it to his own fellow–Christians. And even though a slogan of Paul's which is no longer understood is perhaps what is used in 1:20, it still lacks any real Christian motivation. And even though our saying may have a Jewish provenance, as is rendered likely by the parallels which have been adduced, the idea is nevertheless international, as are so many ideas in Jewish Wisdom literature. Thus, we encounter in Greek literature not only parallels to this or that part of our saying,[18] but even a combination of the three ideas into one whole: in *Demon.* 51, Lucian passes on, along with other sayings of his hero, also this answer which is given to a high official in response to the question, ". . . what is the best way to exercise authority. 'Don't lose your temper!' said he: 'Do little talking and much listening!'" (πῶς ἄριστα ἄρξει, ἀόργητος ἔφη καὶ ὀλίγα μὲν λαλῶν, πολλὰ δὲ ἀκούων).

■ **1:21–25** These verses constitute the main part of the whole section. That this is highly probable could be demonstrated on literary grounds;[19] but it is also in accord with the religious character of our document[20] that Jas is primarily interested here in the theme of hearing and doing.

■ **21** This verse represents the transition to that theme. This is best made clear in the words "being meek, receive the implanted word" (ἐν πραΰτητι δέξασθε τὸν ἔμφυτον λόγον). Of course, a common interpretation of these words[21] wants to see in them a reference to the meek, modest manner in which the addressees are supposed to receive the word. This explanation seems to me first of all to be too vague, for a word received with anger or insolence would not be an "implanted word" (λόγος ἔμφυτος) and would not be "received" at all in the sense of our verse. Furthermore, this doubtful interpretation neglects the parallelism with "putting away" (ἀποθέμενοι) and, above all, the contrast with "anger" (ὀργή). As has been mentioned, "anger" here does not mean anger against God but rather anger in general. "Meekness" (πραΰτης) is no doubt an emphatic antithesis to "anger," and therefore what the passage is talking about is a meek, or good–tempered life in general and not a meek reception of the word. Then the preposition ἐν ("*in* meekness") here refers to an accompanying circumstance. Jas wants to say: "Consequently—since anger blocks the way to righteousness—put away, etc., and be meek." But since he is aiming toward the idea of "doing the word," he writes: "Be meek, when you receive the word."[22] This manner of expression reminds one of 2:1, where the chief admonition is likewise expressed with ἐν προσωπολημψίαις (lit: "*in* partiality"); and a still better parallel is Sir 3:17, where "perform your tasks in meekness" (ἐν πραΰτητι τὰ ἔργα σου διέξαγε) means nothing more than "be meek in your conduct." The interpretation of Jas 1:21 which is advocated here offers the advantage of doing justice both to the contrast with "anger" and the significance of the participle "putting away" (ἀποθέμενοι).

Jas has admonished against anger, and it is only in keeping with paraenetic custom (attested in the so–called catalogues of vices, among other places) that he moves from one sin to others: Put them all away. The expression "to put away" (ἀποτίθεσθαι) is common in this context of early Christian paraenesis: Rom 13:12; Eph 4:22, 25; Col 3:8; Heb 12:1; 1 Petr 2:1; *1 Clem.* 13.1; *2 Clem.* 1.6. Therefore, the term here need no longer be alluding to the original concept of the putting

with ταχύς and βραδύς in Dio Chrys., *Or.* 32.2.

18 Such as have been collected by Johann Jakob Wettstein, *Novum Testamentum Graecum etc.*, vol. 2 (Amsterdam: Ex Officina Dommeriana, 1752), *ad loc.*, and Heinrich Heisen, *Novae hypotheses interpretandae felicius epistulae Iacobi apostoli* (Bremen: Rump, 1739), *ad loc.*

19 See above in the Analysis.

20 See above in the Introduction, section 8.

21 Gebser, Beyschlag.

22 Similarly, Belser.

23 Cf. Adolf Deissmann, *Light from the Ancient East: The New Testament Illustrated by Recently Discovered Texts of the Graeco–Roman World*, tr. and ed. Lionel R. M. Strachen (New York: Doran, 1927), 84.

off of a garment. Instead of a specific enumeration of sins, our passage mentions simply "filth" (ῥυπαρία) and "abundance of wickedness" (περισσεία κακίας). Also in the case of "filth" the original metaphor is no longer vivid; the word and its cognates occur elsewhere with a moral sense, but with a very generalized meaning, sometimes with a specific reference (of greediness, like our word "sordid": Plut., *Adulat.* 60E; Teles, pp. 33, 4 and 37, 5 Hense [2nd edition]), sometimes with a general one: Epict., *Diss.* 2.18.25, used of an "impression" (φαντασία); Philo, *Deus imm.* 7 and *Mut. nom.* 49 and 124: "to wash away things that defile" (ἐκνί-ψασθαι τὰ καταρρυπαίνοντα); Ign., *Eph.* 16.2, of the heretic: "He who has become defiled like this shall depart into the unquenchable fire" (ὁ τοιοῦτος ῥυπαρὸς γενόμενος εἰς τὸ πῦρ τὸ ἄσβεστον χωρήσει) [Trans.]. περισσεία can mean "abundance" as well as "surplus,"[23] but this still does not provide us with certainty about the meaning of the word in our passage. There is no indication here of any metaphorical reference, such as to growths which are to be cut away,[24] "scum" which is to be scraped off the soul,[25] or ornamentation which is to be taken off.[26] And to interpret the word as a reference to the "residue" of paganism which still clings to the readers[27] presupposes that both the term "filth" (ῥυπαρία) *and* the term περισσεία go with the genitive "of wickedness" (κακίας)—and in view of the ethical meaning of "filth," this is not likely.[28] It is best, then, to presume that περισσεία has a rather watered-down sense, and that in its import here it resembles an adjective, such as "abundant"; we then

have something like "all that profuse wickedness."

"Implanted word" (ἔμφυτος λόγος)—if ἔμφυτος were to mean "innate, natural" here (as in Plato; Wisd 12:10; Pseudo–Phocylides 128; Justin, *Apol.* 2.8.1; Clem. Alex., *Strom.* 3.3.3), then in accordance with Stoic concepts[29] one would have to think of that portion of the cosmic Reason which is innate in every human being. In fact, Oec, Theoph and Dionysius Bar Ṣalibi have interpreted it in just this way. Yet it would hardly be said of reason that it is able to save souls—an expression which here quite clearly must be understood eschatologically. In addition, the transition, discussed in the Analysis, to the theme "hearing and doing" precludes a reference to reason and demands a reference to the word, indeed, the "saving" word—hence, the gospel.[30] Since in this case the meaning "innate" is not applicable, and since the translation "undistorted"[31] is untenable, then ἔμφυτος here must mean "implanted, deep–rooted."[32]

Here Jas is probably following an already existing Christian usage, for such a usage is indicated in *Barn.* 9.9 (in a formula!): "He knows this who placed the implanted gift of his teaching in our hearts" (οἶδεν ὁ τὴν ἔμφυτον δωρεὰν τῆς διδαχῆς αὐτοῦ θέμενος ἐν ἡμῖν) [Loeb modified]; cf. *Barn.* 1.2: "you have received the implanted grace of the spiritual gift" (ἔμφυτον τῆς πνευματικῆς δωρεᾶς χάριν εἰλήφατε) [Trans.]; and in Pseudo–Ignatius, *Eph.* 17.2, the translation "implanted" is unavoidable: "having received as implanted from Christ our standard concerning God" (ἔμφυτον τὸ περὶ θεοῦ παρὰ Χριστοῦ λαβόντες κριτήριον) [Trans.].

---

24 So Ropes.
25 So Beyschlag.
26 So Spitta, who refers to Ex 28:11–19.
27 Gebser, Belser.
28 Against the interpretation in the Scholion, p. 187 (and in the Catena): "He speaks of sin, which makes a person filthy and which is like a superfluous excess in us" (τὴν ἁμαρτίαν τὴν ῥυπαίνουσαν τὸν ἄνθρωπόν φησι, τὴν ὡς περιττὴν οὖσαν ἐν ἡμῖν) [Trans.]; but also against the translation of Windisch–Preisker: "the whole filthy mass of wickedness."
29 Cf. Bonhöffer, *Epiktet und das NT*, 97.
30 So also already the Catena and Scholion. I disregard the very popular argument based upon the language in 1:18. Given the literary character of Jas, one cannot rely upon such evidence from other sayings. Moreover, the concept in 1:18 is completely

different; and the term "implanted word" in 1:21 seems to be a fixed expression.
31 So Ewald.
32 This is the interpretation accepted by most modern scholars (although most do not give evidence for a terminology that is already fixed); the passage was also understood in this way by boh and sy^vg. The Latin translations (ff: *genitum*; s vulg: *insitum*) are not clear. Friedrich Preisigke, *Wörterbuch der griechischen Papyrusurkunden*, vol. 1 (Berlin: Selbstverlag der Erben, 1925), adduces under ἔμφυτος *P. Masp.* 6.3 (6th cent. A.D.): τοῦτο τὸ ἔμφυτον ἔχω, and he translates the expression: "This has become second nature to me."

But at the same time, one can ask whether this usage employed by Jas is not somewhat influenced by philosophical concepts regarding "seminal reason" (λόγος σπερματικός).[33]

After what has been said above about "in meekness" (ἐν πραΰτητι), no particularly incisive significance can be assigned to the admonition "receive the word" (δέξασθε τὸν λόγον). And again, the term "implanted" (ἔμφυτος) prevents us from thinking here of the reception of the word at conversion, for a prolepsis—"receive it, so that it may grow in you"[34]—would require at least a predicate position for ἔμφυτος. From Deut 30:1: "you will receive into your heart" (δέξῃ εἰς τὴν καρδίαν σου) it can be inferred that also in Jas 1:21 there is justification for the translation "take to heart," or something similar; but perhaps even this solution to the difficulty (already felt by Bede) is a bit too clever. For if "receive the implanted word" constitutes the less important part of the clause, the important part being "in meekness," then perhaps the expression "to receive the word" is intended simply as a periphrasis for the Christian life: Be meek, you who hear the word (which, after all, happened again and again). The adoption of fixed expressions such as the "implanted word" (ἔμφυτος λόγος), and perhaps also "receive the word" (δέχεσθαι τὸν λόγον 1 Thess 1:6; 2:13; Lk 8:13; Acts 8:14; 11:1)[35] offers a much simpler explanation for the passage than the hypothesis of complex trains of thought.

■ **22** This verse brings the principal admonition: Be doers of the word![36] This is how it is to be translated, since γίνεσθαι (usually, "to become") occurs here as a substitute for εἶναι ("to be"), a usage which is frequent elsewhere as well. "Doer of the word" (ποιητὴς λόγου) is considered a Semitism, just as "doer of the Law" (ποιητὴς τοῦ νόμου) in 1 Macc 2:67, and there is justification for this; for to a Greek the first expression would mean someone who is an orator, while the second would be someone who is a legislator. Evidently, a deviation from the standard usage influenced by the Hebrew term for "do, make, etc." (עשה)[37] has been adopted by first the Jewish, then the Christian communities. This does not necessarily prove that our author was a Jew by birth.

The antithesis "hearing—doing" functions quite naturally in instances where ethical instruction is communicated by means of oral proclamation; in the history of the Jewish–Christian religion such cases would be the prophets (Ezek 33:32), the Law (Deut 30:8ff), Wisdom teaching (Prov 6:3; Sir 3:1—with references to salvation in both passages), Jesus (Matt 7:24ff; Lk 6:47ff; because of the context, Jn 13:17 could also come under consideration as a dominical saying), Paul (Rom 2:13), and the Rabbis.[38] Merely hearing is equivalent to self–deception so long as one believes that even then the word can still "save." The participle παραλογιζόμενοι[39] goes with the subject ("you") of the imperative "be" (γίνεσθε) and not with "hearers" (ἀκροαταί), and hence it means "deceiving *yourselves*," not "who deceive *them*selves"; for otherwise we would expect a participle also with "doers" (ποιηταί).

33 So Carl Clemen, *Primitive Christianity and its Non–Jewish Sources*, tr. Robert G. Nisbet (Edinburgh: Clark, 1912), 54.

34 So John Calvin, *Commentaries on the Catholic Epistles*, tr. John Owen (Edinburgh: Calvin Translation Society, 1855), *ad loc.*, and de Wette.

35 An investigation of such terms has been undertaken by Grete Gillet, *Evangelium: Studien zur urchristlichen Missionssprache*, Unpub. Diss. (Heidelberg, 1924).

36 The reading "of the law" (νόμου) instead of "of the word" (λόγου), found in C^c *et al.* (and also in v 23 in some of the witnesses), can be explained from the influence of v 25 (cf. also 4:11).

37 Cf. "to observe the Law" (עשה תורה) in Joshua 22:5; Neh 9:34; *Pirke Aboth* 2.8a; *Siphra* on Lev 20:16 (fol. 92d Weiss); "fulfillment of the Law" (ποίησις νόμου) in Sir 19:20.

38 In *Pirke Aboth* 5.14, there is a description of four types who frequent the House of Study: He who goes but (after hearing) does not practice is rewarded for going; he who practices is rewarded for doing; he who goes and practices is a pious man; he who does neither is an ungodly man. Cf. *Pirke Aboth* 1.17: The important thing is not the exposition, but the doing; cf. 3.9, 18 on wisdom and doing; and 4.5 on learning, teaching, doing. Philo is obviously following Jewish paraenesis in *Praem. poen.* 79: "If, he says, you keep the divine commandment in obedience to his ordinances and accept his precepts, not merely to hear them but to carry them out by your life and conduct, the first boon you will have is victory over your enemies" (ἐὰν, φησί, τὰς θείας ἐντολὰς φυλάττητε καταπειθεῖς γινόμενοι τοῖς προστάγμασι καὶ τὰ διαγορευόμενα μὴ μέχρις ἀκοῆς καταδέχησθε,

■ **23, 24** Here the admonition to action is illustrated with a comparison which has been heavily burdened by the commentators. As a matter of fact, the beginning of v 25 does indeed suggest the interpretation of the "mirror" as a reference to the "law" (νόμος) or to the "word" (λόγος); from that one then moves to the further question of what is the object which is reflected in this mirror; finally one makes observations about the manner of the seeing, and thus the subtilizations go on forever. Over against all that it must be stressed that v 25 only takes its starting–point from the simile, that the simile itself, however, is completely contained within vv 23, 24, and that in *these* verses nothing is said about a comparison of the "word" with the mirror.[40]

The salient point is made clear in v 24: If a person does not conduct himself in accordance with the "word," then what he has heard sticks with him about as much as the mirror image sticks with a person who has observed himself in a mirror: he forgets it. At the same time, one must take care to note the participial introduction of the simile; evidently, the words "he is like the person who looks at his natural appearance in a mirror" are supposed to have said everything, and v 24 is intended only to underscore the comparison. Hence, the "forgetting" must correspond to the popular ideas about mirrors, and in any case it is the ordinary look into the metal mirror which is meant here, not a particularly hasty glance. Accordingly, the aorists in v 24 are portraying the way things usually happen, and thus we must consider them as gnomic aorists and translate them in the present tense.[41] The metaphor of the mirror played a significant role in the literature of antiquity, and precisely in religious literature.[42] However, the way the metaphor is used in our passage has no points of contact with the known examples.[43] As a rule, Jas usually has borrowed such metaphors,

---

ἀλλὰ διὰ τῶν τοῦ βίου πράξεων ἐπιτελῆτε, πρώτην δωρεὰν ἕξητε νίκην κατ᾽ ἐχθρῶν).

39 παραλογίζεσθαι here means "to deceive," as in the LXX; Col 2:4; Ign., *Mg.* 3.2; cf. also Epicurus, Frag. 523 Usener, quoted in Epict., *Diss.* 2.20.7 (where the term is used in parallel with ἐξαπατᾶν ["to deceive"]). This is also how vulg understands our passage, while underlying the translation in *ff*: "showing different judgment" (aliter consiliantes), seems to be a misunderstanding similar to that in the Scholion, p. 187: "reasoning on your own" (λογι-ζόμενοι καθ᾽ ἑαυτούς).

40 This is stressed only by Hofmann, among modern interpreters.

41 Cf. 1:11, and above in the Introduction, section 5. I question whether the perfect tense ἀπελήλυθεν is used here with its special sense ("he *has gone* away"). It may be that it is employed here simply because of its similarity in sound to ἐπελάθετο ("forgets"), and that it is used in the same sense as a gnomic aorist.

42 Cf. the references collected by Johannes Weiss, *Der erste Korintherbrief*, KEK 5 (Göttingen: Vandenhoeck & Ruprecht, 1910), on 1 Cor 13:12, by Mayor in his commentary on our passage, and by Richard Reitzenstein, *Historia Monachorum und Historia Lausiaca*, FRLANT 24 (Göttingen: Vandenhoeck & Ruprecht, 1916), 244ff. Cf. also Hans Conzelmann, *First Corinthians*, tr. James Leitch, ed. George W. MacRae, Hermeneia (Philadelphia: Fortress, 1975), on 1 Cor 13:12. From the circle of literature which is most closely related, cf. Sir 12:11; Wisd 7:26; 1 Cor 13:12; *1 Clem.* 36.2; Theophilus, *Ad Autol.* 1.2;

Odes of Solomon 13.1; and numerous passages in Philo.

43 To be sure, Reitzenstein, *Historia*, 248f, thinks that the metaphor of the "spirit" (πνεῦμα) as a mirror is presupposed by Jas, and that consequently in 1:25 Jas could immediately introduce the thing which is being compared to a mirror, viz., the "perfect law" (νόμος τέλειος), which Reitzenstein takes as a designation for the spirit within us. However, (1) Jas 1:25 is no longer a part of the actual simile at all (see above), and (2) the "perfect law" is not a designation for the spirit within us. Nevertheless, I call attention to the parallel which Reitzenstein adduces from the Syriac work of Zosimus, the *Circle of the Priests* (Reitzenstein, *Historia*, 247f, following M. Berthelot, *Histoire des sciences: La chimie au moyen âge*, vol. 2 [Paris: Imprimerie Nationale, 1893]), where it is said of a *magical mirror*: "The mirror was not provided in order that a person might use it to gaze upon his physical body, *for as soon as he leaves the mirror he instantly forgets his own image.*" However, this is no evidence that Jas had in mind a magical mirror and presupposed that his readers were also familiar with the concept. Rather, it may be that Zosimus, an author from the late 3rd and early 4th century A.D., has restricted a popular notion about forgetting one's mirror image to a magical mirror, since perhaps the notion no longer seemed to him to be suitable in the case of ordinary mirrors. Cf. Martin Dibelius, review of Richard Reitzenstein, *Historia Monachorum und Historia Lausiaca*, in *Wochenschrift für klassische Philologie* 33 (1916): 1037–42.

but in this case there is as yet still no proof of any dependency.[44]

That τὸ πρόσωπον τῆς γενέσεως αὐτοῦ is said instead of simply τὸ πρόσωπον αὐτοῦ ("his face") is best understood if the term γένεσις adds something essential. Thus, πρόσωπον is to be taken to mean "appearance" here as in Jas, 1:11 and γένεσις to mean "life, existence" or "nature" ("his natural appearance")[45] and not "birth" (as in many of the older commentators).

■ **25** That the simile in vv 23, 24 is quite simple and refers merely to the worthlessness of hearing without doing must be maintained even in the face of v 25; to be sure, this verse continues the use of the imagery of seeing which is employed in the simile, but only to drop it as soon as possible with "perseveres" (παραμείνας), and then altogether with "hearer" (ἀκροατής!). This is the oriental method of exploiting a simile, which is so very contrary to Western logic; for every reader of the New Testament, the method is familiar from the metaphorical discourses on the shepherd in John 10. One ought to take warning from this insight and should not press the allegory pedantically. The author only toys with it. There is no reason for us to interpret the "law" (νόμος) as the mirror and to read this identification back into the actual simile in vv 23, 24. The expression "who looks into the perfect law" (παρακύψας εἰς νόμον τέλειον) instead provides merely the connecting link; in the further development of the thought, the simile no longer has any significance.

The expression "perfect law of freedom" (νόμος τέλειος ὁ τῆς ἐλευθερίας) is completely explained, as far as its content is concerned, by the context. For the words "But he who looks, etc." (ὁ δὲ παρακύψας κτλ.) are supposed to be connected with 1:22, as "hearer" (ἀκροατής) in v 25b indicates: the person "who looks" (παρακύψας) is the hearer of the word, hence the "law" (νόμος) is the "implanted word" (ἔμφυτος λόγος v 21). And the commandments which our author considers to be the content of this "law" are shown by 1:27 as

well as by the comments in 2:1–13. The interpretation of these passages will reveal how "law" is to be understood here: as the norm of Christian piety.

The Perfect Law of Freedom

Yet the formulation "the perfect law of freedom" (νόμος τέλειος ὁ τῆς ἐλευθερίας) points to certain concepts whose origins are pre–Christian. It almost goes without saying that the Jew could characterize his Law as "perfect" in contrast to the laws of the Gentiles, and in fact did characterize it with expressions which were at least similar; cf. Ps 19:7; *Arist.* 31: "since the law which they contain, inasmuch as it is of divine origin, is full of wisdom and free from all blemish" (διὰ τὸ καὶ φιλοσοφωτέραν εἶναι καὶ ἀκέραιον τὴν νομοθεσίαν ταύτην ὡς ἂν οὖσαν θείαν) [trans. Charles, *APOT*]. However, the concept of the law of freedom is first encountered in a Greek context.

It is especially the Stoics who have stressed the idea of the freedom of the wise man; cf. the statement of Zeno in Diogenes Laertius 7.121 that only the wise man is free, while bad men are slaves. Properly speaking, the Stoics use the word "freedom" to characterize that condition the knowledge of which they extol as "the truth concerning happiness" (ἀλήθεια περὶ εὐδαιμονίας Epict., *Diss.* 1.4.32); in this connection, one should read Epictetus' diatribe in *Diss.* 4.1 ("He is free who lives as he wills, who is subject neither to compulsion, nor hindrance, nor force, whose choices are unhampered, whose desires attain their end, whose aversions do not fall into what they would avoid" [ἐλεύθερός ἐστιν ὁ ζῶν ὡς βούλεται, ὃν οὔτ' ἀναγκάσαι ἔστιν οὔτε κωλῦσαι οὔτε βιάσασθαι, οὗ αἱ ὁρμαὶ ἀνεμπόδιστοι. αἱ ὀρέξεις ἐπιτευκτικαί, αἱ ἐκκλίσεις ἀπερίπτωτοι *Diss.* 4.1.1]).

But insofar as the true wisdom consists in obedience to that cosmic Reason which governs all and the neglect of which can only lead men into foolish and destructive conflicts, the ethical preaching of Stoicism (especially

---

44   Cf. the preceding footnote.

45   For the translation "life, existence" (so most interpreters), appeal is made to Wisd 7:5: "For no king has had a different beginning of existence" (οὐδεὶς γὰρ βασιλεὺς ἑτέραν ἔσχεν γενέσεως ἀρχήν), and to Jdth 12:18; one might also refer to Pseudo–Aristides, Ἀπελλᾷ γενεθλιακός 30.27 Keil: "the years of your life which have already gone by" (οἱ παρελ-

θόντες ἤδη σοι τῆς γενέσεως ἐνιαυτοί) [Trans.]. For "nature" (Ropes) or "creature," Philo's usage of the term could be cited, e.g., in *Poster. C.* 29: "quiescence and abiding are characteristic of God, but change of place and all movement that makes for such change is characteristic of *creation*" (θεοῦ μὲν ἴδιον ἠρεμία καὶ στάσις, γενέσεως δὲ μετάβασίς τε καὶ μεταβατικὴ πᾶσα κίνησις).

popular Stoicism) indeed demands an obedience which brings with it the state of utmost inner freedom; cf. Seneca, *De vita beata* 15.7: "to obey God is freedom" (deo parere libertas est). As an example of such freedom, Epictetus mentions Diogenes, who was free in every respect " 'because I do not regard my paltry body as my own; because I need nothing; because *the law*, and nothing else, is everything to me.' This is that which allowed him to be a free man" (ὅτι τὸ σωμάτιον ἐμὸν οὐχ ἡγοῦμαι, ὅτι οὐδενὸς δέομαι. ὅτι ὁ νόμος μοι πάντα ἐστὶ καὶ ἄλλο οὐδέν. ταῦτα ἦν τὰ ἐλεύθερον ἐκεῖνον ἐάσαντα Epict., *Diss.* 4.1.158; cf. also 4.1.159, on Socrates). Thus, in everything that is decreed for him the wise man asks: " 'Who was it that sent the order?' Our Prince, or our General, the State, or *the law* of the State [= the world]? 'Give it to me, then, for I must always obey the law in every particular' " (τίς δ' αὐτὸ καὶ ἐπιπέπομφεν; ὁ ἡγεμὼν ἢ ὁ στρατηγός, ἡ πόλις, ὁ τῆς πόλεως νόμος. δὸς οὖν αὐτό· δεῖ γάρ με ἀεὶ τῷ νόμῳ πείθεσθαι ἐν παντί Epict., *Diss.* 3.24.107). With a proper understanding of this cosmic law he is to "guard that which is his own, not to lay claim to what is not his own, but to make use of what is given to him, and not to yearn for what has not been given" (τὰ ἴδια τηρεῖν, τῶν ἀλλοτρίων μὴ ἀντιποιεῖσθαι, ἀλλὰ διδομένοις μὲν χρῆσθαι, μὴ διδόμενα δὲ μὴ ποθεῖν *Diss.* 2.16.28); he is to "do what nature demands" (τὸ ἀκόλουθον τῇ φύσει πράττειν *Diss.* 1.26.1). The "one law" (νόμος εἷς) which governs the world is the "one Reason common to all intelligent creatures" (λόγος κοινὸς πάντων τῶν νοερῶν ζῴων M. Ant. 7.9.2). And to live in accordance with this law means "to act in accordance with one's own nature" (κατὰ τὴν ἰδίαν φύσιν ἐνεργεῖν) and is to the wise man "what indulgence is to the sensual" (οἷόν ἐστι τοῖς ἡδυπαθοῦσιν ἡ τρυφή M. Ant. 10.33.2).

But Philo is evidence that the concept of such a cosmic law, the observance of which brings inner freedom, could also exist in a Jewish context. Admittedly, the distance between Stoicism and Judaism seems at first glance to be enormous: the former displaying a monistic way of thinking, the latter that dichotomy between world history and the history of salvation which is a part of revealed religion. Philo was not able to argue this distinction away, but he at least built a bridge between his Jewish faith and his philosophical convictions. Since he is a believing Jew, the Law is for him the highest authority; but what the Law offers is as reasonable as the philosophically educated man could want (one should note the expression "reasonably" [εἰκότως] used in Philo's paraphrases of the Law, e.g., in *Decal.* 13). Thus Philo not only manages to depict the Patriarchs as representatives of "the unwritten laws" (νόμοι ἄγραφοι *Decal.* 1),[46] but also to assert that the man who is faithful to the Law leads his life in harmony with "nature" (φύσις, in the Stoic sense); hence, he is fulfilling the Stoic demand: ". . . that the world is in harmony with the Law, and the Law with the world, and that the man who observes the Law is constituted thereby a loyal citizen of the world, regulating his doings by the purpose and will of Nature" (ὡς καὶ τοῦ κόσμου τῷ νόμῳ καὶ τοῦ νόμου τῷ κόσμῳ συνᾴδοντος καὶ τοῦ νομίμου ἀνδρὸς εὐθὺς ὄντος κοσμοπολίτου πρὸς τὸ βούλημα τῆς φύσεως τὰς πράξεις ἀπευθύνοντος *Op. mund.* 3); or, "he who would observe the [Mosaic] laws will accept gladly the duty of following nature [in the Stoic sense] and live in accordance with the ordering of the universe, so that his deeds are attuned to harmony with his words and his words with his deeds" (τὸν χρησόμενον τοῖς νόμοις ἀκολουθίαν φύσεως ἀσπασόμενον καὶ βιωσόμενον κατὰ τὴν τοῦ ὅλου διάταξιν ἁρμονίᾳ καὶ συμφωνίᾳ πρὸς ἔργα λόγων καὶ πρὸς λόγους ἔργων *Vit. Mos.* 2.48); and further, "whoever will carefully examine the nature of the particular elements [the "special laws" of the Mosaic legislation] will find that they seek to attain to the harmony of the universe and are in agreement with the principles of eternal Nature [= the Stoic cosmic Reason] (τῶν γοῦν ἐν μέρει διατεταγμένων τὰς δυνάμεις εἴ τις ἀκριβῶς ἐξετάζειν ἐθελήσειεν εὑρήσει τῆς τοῦ παντὸς ἁρμονίας ἐφιεμένας καὶ τῷ λόγῳ τῆς ἀιδίου φύσεως συνᾳδούσας *Vit. Mos.* 2.52). In this context Philo also explains that Moses did not treat human beings as slaves, as other legislators do, but "he suggests and admonishes rather than demands" (ὑποτίθεται καὶ παρηγορεῖ τὸ πλέον ἢ κελεύει), and that his intention is "to exhort rather than to enforce" (προτρέψασθαι . . . μᾶλλον ἢ βιάσασθαι *Vit. Mos.* 2.51).

---

46   On this concept, cf. Rudolf Hirzel, ΑΓΡΑΦΟΣ ΝΟΜΟΣ. Abhandlungen der Königlich sächsischen Gesellschaft der Wissenschaften, Philologisch–hi-storische Klasse 20, 1 (Leipzig: Teubner, 1903).

He demonstrates this also with regard to the affairs of city-states; those who have laws for their protection are free, and it is the same with people: "all whose life is regulated by law are free" (ὅσοι μετὰ νόμου ζῶσιν, ἐλεύθεροι *Omn. prob. lib.* 45).

It may be open to question how far Philo's thoughts are echoed within the Judaism of his time. Yet that the fundamentally Stoic concept of the harmony of the Mosaic Law with the universe was possible for a contemporary Jew, even if he had a different orientation, is proven by Josephus;[47] for he deduces the notion that there should be but one temple (i.e., a prescription of the Law) from the relation of God to the world (i.e., upon the basis of a cosmological argument), and he further supports this derivation with a Greek maxim:[48] "We have but one temple for the one God (for like is always the friend of like), common to all as God is common to all" (εἶς ναὸς ἑνὸς θεοῦ—φίλον γὰρ ἀεὶ παντὶ τὸ ὅμοιον—κοινὸς ἁπάντων κοινοῦ θεοῦ ἁπάντων *Ap.* 2.193).[49] And just how the concept of the freedom of the wise man took on its Jewish stamp (apart from Philo) is shown by *4 Macc.* 14.2, where the reasoning minds of the seven martyred for the sake of the Law are extolled as "the freest of the free" (ἐλευθέρων ἐλευθερώτατοι).

At first glance there seems to be no room for this type of thinking within early Christianity. The preaching of Jesus presupposes the Jewish religion and consequently needs no apology for the Law. And the battle which Paul wages for freedom from the Law is conditioned precisely by the view that the Law has held men in bondage (Gal 4:1ff). Since according to Paul this Law is not kept, nor *can* be kept, one can find no trace in the writings of the Apostle of anything about a harmony between cosmic order and Law; the Law was given only for a limited period of time to this one people, it only "slipped in, in addition" (Rom 5:20; see also Gal 3:19ff). Only brief mention ought to be made of the fact that in addition to this line of thought there is that other line in Paul which in fact must be claimed as a reflection of Stoic influence: the performance of the works of the Law by the Gentiles who do not have the Law (Rom 2:14ff); this idea is touched upon, at least in the letters of the Apostle, only occasionally and in the context of the polemic against the Jews.

Yet, only too easily do we fall into the error—which, to be sure, is fostered by the character of the materials preserved from the early Christian period—of thinking that Paul had influenced every branch of early Christianity. This is in fact an error, for prior to, contemporary with, and subsequent to Paul there were churches who did not trust their salvation to faith alone with that overwhelming energy of Paul's, an energy which most people were quite unable to imitate. And con-

---

47   One might refer here to the saying attributed to R. Joshua, son of Levi (beginning of 3rd cent.), that the only person who is free is he who occupies himself with the Torah (*Pirke Aboth* 6.2); cf. also *Pirke Aboth* 3.5: "He that takes upon himself the yoke of the Law, from him shall be taken away the yoke of the kingdom [i.e., governmental duties] and the yoke of worldly care" (trans. Danby). Of course, the spontaneous formulation of these ideas is also quite possible.

48   Homer, *Od.* 17.218; cf. Aristot., *Eth. Nic.* 9.3.3; 8.1.6.

49   Cf. also Philo, *Spec. leg.* 1.67. That this concept and its formulation are Stoic is shown by the parallel in M. Ant. 7.9.2: "For there is both one Universe, made up of all things, and one God immanent in all things, and one Substance, and one Law, one Reason common to all intelligent creatures, and one Truth, if indeed there is also one perfecting of living creatures that have the same origin and share the same reason" (κόσμος τε γὰρ εἶς ἐξ ἁπάντων καὶ θεὸς εἶς διὰ πάντων καὶ οὐσία μία καὶ νόμος εἶς, λόγος κοινὸς πάντων τῶν νοερῶν ζῴων, καὶ ἀλήθεια μία, εἴγε καὶ τελειότης μία τῶν ὁμογενῶν καὶ τοῦ αὐτοῦ λόγου μετεχόντων ζῴων). That these ideas have had an influence within Christianity has been argued with regard to Eph 4:5f by Martin Dibelius, "Die Christianisierung einer hellenistischen Formel," in *idem, Botschaft und Geschichte,* vol. 2 (Tübingen: Mohr [Siebeck], 1956), cf. 14–29; cf. Dibelius–Greeven, *Kolosser, Epheser, Philemon,* on Eph 4:5f.

       Ethelbert Stauffer, "Das 'Gesetz der Freiheit' in der Ordensregel von Jericho," *ThLZ* 77 (1952): 527–32, argues that חוק חרות in 1 QS X, 6, 8, 11 is to be translated "law of freedom"; this is disputed by Wolfgang Nauck, "*Lex insculpta* (חוק חרות) in der Sektenschrift," *ZNW* 46 (1955): 138–40, who argues that the meaning is "engraved law" (similarly, Dupont–Sommer, *Essene Writings*). Cf. further, F. Nötscher, " 'Gesetz der Freiheit' im NT und in der Mönchsgemeinde am Toten Meer," *Biblica* 34 (1953): 193f.

sequently, they did not banish with Paul's almost inconceivable consistency every confidence in works from the realm of their piety. These were especially those communities where the break with Judaism was not accomplished in the radical fashion with which we are familiar from the Pauline letters. One has only to recall that the churches in Antioch and Rome, and probably also in Tarsus and Alexandria, grew out of the circles of Diaspora Judaism. The polemic against pagan gods, the faith in the one invisible, spiritual God who is creator of all that is, the requirement of a morally pure life—these things united these Christians with these Jews. What differentiated them from the Jews is clear: the Christians were no longer bound to the letter of the Old Testament; they did not need, as did Philo, to explain away the ritualism of the Law by means of allegorical reinterpretation. In Jesus they had found the Messiah; his authority supplemented, outshone, and eventually displaced that of the Torah. It was therefore precisely in these circles that Jesus' words as well as the ethics which developed from or were contained in his words could be conceived as a "new law."[50]

One fact best proves that this kind of thinking existed among the churches in question: the sayings of Jesus were collected in order to serve as a rule of conduct;[51] for example, this is what accounts for the origin of the collection of Jesus' sayings which Matthew has set into the frame of the Sermon on the Mount (Matt 5–7) and Luke into the frame of the Sermon on the Plain (Lk 6:20ff). The sayings of the Lord did not resist this use to which the churches put them; on the contrary, they lent themselves to it. Jesus himself had occasionally spoken of a summary of the Law in his own words (Matt 7:12; Mk 12:28–31 = Matt 22:34–40). Also, the programmatic statements placed at the beginning of the exposition of the Law in the Sermon on the Mount (Matt 5:17–20), statements whose authenticity as well as whose proper interpretation if they *do* in

fact come from the mouth of Jesus has—as is well known—been variously evaluated, nevertheless provide at least the viewpoint of the *collector* regarding the sayings which follow. This enterprise of collecting was by no means carried on under the influence of Paul; indeed, we can take 2 Cor 5:16 as an indication of Paul's fundamentally different orientation. Yet 1 Cor 7:10, 25 seems to give evidence that already at the time of Paul dominical sayings were employed in the sense indicated above, even though they are used seldom enough in the Pauline letters. The situation is totally different in the churches which have grown out of Diaspora Judaism. Already, Hellenistic Judaism had given way in its propaganda to the tendency toward simplifying and concentrating the requirements of the Law. The Christian communities could travel much further down this road since they no longer had to bear the burden of ritualism. That they took in this their point of departure from Judaism is shown by the Christian use and revision of the Jewish moral precepts of the Two Ways in *Did.* 1ff and *Barn.* 18ff. Not without justification has this Christiantiy been called a liberated Diaspora Judaism.[52]

Our document, the Letter of James, has also originated on this soil. The layout of at least individual parts of the document corresponds to the typical features of a Jewish book of sayings, and also with regard to its content there is much that is based upon conscious or unconscious adoption of Jewish Wisdom tradition. This type of literature (cf. also the *Mandates* in the *Shepherd of Hermas*) is possible only if in these circles Christianity is understood as a new law; cf. *Barn.* 2.6: "the new law of our Lord Jesus Christ, which is without the yoke of necessity" (ὁ καινὸς νόμος τοῦ κυρίου ἡμῶν Ἰησοῦ Χριστοῦ, ἄνευ ζυγοῦ ἀνάγκης ὤν), and Irenaeus, *Adv. haer.* 4.34.4, where "law of freedom" (libertatis lex) characterizes the gospel. On the other hand, that Jas completely ignores the question of the Law—it is not even dealt with in 2:14ff—, that he pays no atten-

---

50   One ought not to confuse with this the expression used by Paul in Rom 8:2: "the law of the Spirit of life" (ὁ νόμος τοῦ πνεύματος τῆς ζωῆς), which was coined by Paul because of the need for a rhetorical antithesis to "the law of sin and death" (ὁ νόμος τῆς ἁμαρτίας καὶ τοῦ θανάτου); a similar judgment applies to the phrase "under the law of Christ" (ἔννομος Χριστοῦ) in 1 Cor 9:21. On the other hand,

in the paraenetic sections—precisely where he is less original (see above in the Introduction, section 1)—Paul occasionally follows the terminology of the churches and speaks of the possibility of fulfilling the Law: Gal 6:2; cf. also Gal 5:14, 23.

51   Cf. Dibelius, *From Tradition to Gospel*, 233ff.

52   Bousset, *Kyrios Christos*, 367ff; cf. above in the Introduction, section 6.

tion to even the possibility of ritual commandments, can be explained only if this law is actually perceived as the perfect moral law; in other words—to use Stoic terms—, if it is perceived as a law of those who are truly free, or—to use the expression of our letter—as a "perfect law of freedom" ($\nu\acute{o}\mu os$ $\tau\acute{e}\lambda\epsilon\iota os$ $\tau\hat{\eta}s$ $\grave{e}\lambda\epsilon\upsilon\theta\epsilon\rho\acute{\iota}as$).[53]

Stoic concepts such as those sketched above could easily have influenced this formulation—especially by way of Diaspora Judaism, whose missionary terminology, just like any missionary terminology, made every effort to accommodate the needs of those to whom its mission was directed. But such a hypothesis does not exclude the other possibility that in adopting the expression Jas is looking back already to Paul's struggle over freedom from the Law. Now, since misunderstandings of the Jewish Law are no longer a threat, Jas ventures to call the Christian norm "law" again, albeit "perfect law" and "law of *freedom*"—somewhat in the sense of Gal 5:13. Jas cannot be dated with certainty upon the basis of the passage in 1:25.[54] Yet it can be argued that the expression could have been coined only where there was certainty that it would not be misinterpreted by Judaizers; this certainty may have existed either because Judaizing influences were not active at all in the communities in question or because Judaizers no longer constituted a danger.

The similarity between the compounds $\pi\alpha\rho\alpha\kappa\acute{\upsilon}\psi as$—$\pi\alpha\rho\alpha\mu\epsilon\acute{\iota}\nu as$ ("who looks"—"who perseveres") is perhaps no accident. The meaning of "to persevere" ($\pi\alpha\rho\alpha\mu\acute{e}\nu\epsilon\iota\nu$) becomes even clearer through the participial clause adjoined to the subject:[55] "and is ($\gamma\epsilon\nu\acute{o}\mu\epsilon\nu os$) not a forgetful hearer but an obedient doer." The antithesis between the two genitival expressions must

be rendered into English in some such manner. The first genitive (lit.: "hearer *of forgetfulness* [$\grave{a}\kappa\rho o\alpha\tau\grave{\eta}s$ $\grave{e}\pi\iota\lambda\eta\sigma\mu o\nu\hat{\eta}s$]) substitutes for an adjective; here once again the Hebraism question surfaces.[56] The second genitival expression (lit.: "doer *of deed*" [$\pi o\iota\eta\tau\grave{\eta}s$ $\acute{e}\rho\gamma o\upsilon$]) does not belong to classical Greek either.[57] Evidently it occurs here because of the rhetorical compulsion to form the antithesis with "forgetful hearer" ($\grave{a}\kappa\rho o\alpha\tau\grave{\eta}s$ $\grave{e}\pi\iota\lambda\eta\sigma\mu o\nu\hat{\eta}s$); the pattern of the first genitive in the clause made the second genitive construction necessary. Syntactically, this second genitive is an objective genitive (unlike the first, which is a genitive of quality), yet rhetorically it is nevertheless a parallel to the first genitival expression. Therefore, one must translate the expression into English with an appropriate adjective.[58]

■ 26 The variant readings seems to indicate that efforts were made to supply a connection [59] between this verse and what precedes: the $\delta\acute{e}$ ("but") which follows the $\epsilon\grave{\iota}$ ("if") in some manuscripts[60] is an attempt to bring this saying into better contrast with the preceding, while the $\grave{e}\nu$ $\acute{\upsilon}\mu\hat{\iota}\nu$ ("among you") after $\epsilon\hat{\iota}\nu\alpha\iota$ ("to be") in other manuscripts[61] tries to effect a better adaptation of the saying to the tone of a letter.

The saying is sustained by a fervor which is frequently observed in Jas,[62] a fervor against every piety which does not lead to moral purity, which tolerates gross moral defects and consequently is not genuine. This may not be used as grounds for sketching an overly pessimistic image of the "second generation,"[63] for such polemic was probably not inappropriate at any period. And yet it will be admitted that a differentiation between the "pious" and "others" such as is indicated by the use of the term "religious" ($\theta\rho\eta\sigma\kappa\acute{o}s$) would not be presumed in the period of the missionary effort, but rather in the context of churches which have already

---

53 Cf. also "law of freedom" ($\nu\acute{o}\mu os$ $\grave{e}\lambda\epsilon\upsilon\theta\epsilon\rho\acute{\iota}as$) in 2:12; and see below on 2:8.

54 Cf. above in the Introduction, section 7.

55 Evidently, the Koine witnesses desired to alter this participial construction, since they add a $o\hat{\upsilon}\tau os$ ("this one") before $o\grave{\upsilon}\kappa$ $\grave{a}\kappa\rho o\alpha\tau\acute{\eta}s$ ("not a hearer").

56 Cf. above in the Introduction, section 5, and Blass-Debrunner, § 165.

57 See above on 1:22.

58 Luther has not done this, but instead leaves a gap in the rhythm of the saying: "and is not a forgetful hearer, but a doer." Herder translates it: "not

a hearer inclined to forgetfulness, but a doer in action."

59 On the lack of a connection between this verse and the preceding, see above in the Analysis.

60 C P **0173** 33 1175 1739 *ff s* vulg boh.

61 The Koine witnesses and Ψ.

62 Cf. above in the Introduction, section 8.

63 See the Introduction.

been consolidated.

The term θρησκός ("religious"), attested only in this text, can nevertheless be understood by comparison with the noun form θρησκεία ("religion"): what is involved here is the pious person, in quotation marks, who is distinguished not by a pious attitude in general, but by the fulfillment of the religious (in the thought of antiquity, this means "cultic") obligations—this is the sense of "religion" (θρησκεία). The question of what obligations are involved depends upon each interpreter's overall evaluation of the letter.[64]

The metaphorical force of the word "to bridle" (χαλιναγωγεῖν)[65] is perhaps no longer felt very strongly at all. The topic here is self–deception, in a sense similar to that in 1:22; the person in question is deceiving himself because he fancies himself to be "pious," although he cannot even bridle his tongue. For the first ("not bridling"), and hence also the second participle ("deceiving") must be resolved in this way, with "although";[66] this is true despite the fact that "deceiving" (ἀπατῶν), since it states the judgment, belongs materially in the final clause. That the construction here is inexact is explained by the attempt to introduce a double antithesis: "religious"—"not bridling" (θρησκός—μὴ χαλιναγωγῶν) and "thinks"—"deceiving" (δοκεῖ—ἀπατῶν).

■ **27** The problem with this verse is that its interpretation is dependent upon the way one understands the entire letter—as Windisch in particular has pointed out. If one isolates the verse, then it can be interpreted very easily in Jewish terms: the designation "God

(and) the Father" is Jewish,[67] concern for widows and orphans is already demanded by the prophets,[68] the use of the term "world" (κόσμος) in the sense of "the wicked, evil world" seems quite possible in light of *1 En.* 48.7, and "unstained" (ἄσπιλος) can be interpreted ritualistically. In the mouth of a Jew it would mean: to keep the Jewish laws of ritual purity; in the mouth of a strict Jewish–Christian: to observe them precisely in dealings with Gentile–Christians. In this latter case, one can cite *Ps. Clem. Hom.* 13.4.3 and 5, where Peter portrays "the conduct of our religion" (τῆς ἡμετέρας θρησκείας τὴν πολιτείαν). Following the command to honor God (and parents), it says, "In addition, since we do not conduct our lives indiscriminately, we do not hold table–fellowship with Gentiles, inasmuch as we cannot eat with them because their way of life is impure . . . for especially in religion do we practice this" (πρὸς τούτοις δὲ ἀδιαφόρως μὴ βιοῦντες τραπέζης ἐθνῶν οὐκ ἀπολαύομεν, ἅτε δὴ οὐδὲ συνεστιᾶσθαι αὐτοῖς δυνάμενοι, διὰ τὸ ἀκαθάρτως αὐτοὺς βιοῦν . . . θρησκείᾳ γὰρ διαφερόντως τοῦτο ποιοῦμεν) [Trans.].

Yet a decisive objection can be made against this Jewish or Jewish–Christian interpretation. The observance of the laws of purity is an essential part of Jewish piety; moreover, for Jewish–Christians the question of purity is a problem of the first order. If the author were a Jew,[69] we would expect that the requirement which is only alluded to here would be made more specific, either in this passage or in the example from the "assembly" (συναγωγή) in 2:2ff or somewhere among the individual admonitions in chapters 4 and 5. This makes

---

64 Cf. below on 1:27.

65 Cf. *Herm. mand.* 12.1.1; on this metaphor, see below on 3:2.

66 Hofmann resolves it with "in that"; according to this interpretation, the delusion would consist in the fact that one makes piety into empty talk. But the text does not say that, and one should avoid all such specialized conceptions of the "bridling of the tongue."

67 1 Chron 29:10; Wisd 2:16; *3 Macc.* 5.7; Philo, *Leg. all.* 2.67; for Josephus, cf. Adolf Schlatter, *Wie sprach Josephus von Gott?* BFTh 14, 1 (Gütersloh: Bertelsmann, 1910), 14.

68 Cf. Isa 1:17; Jer 5:28; Ezek 22:7; Zech 7:10. The protection of (strangers,) widows and orphans plays an important role in other books of the Old Testament as well: Deut 10:18; 14:28; 16:11, 14; 24:17–

21; 26:12, 13; 27:19; Ps 10:14, 18; 68:5; 94:6; 146:9; Prov 23:10; Sir 4:10; 32(35):17; cf. also Philo, *Spec. leg.* 1.308, 310; 4.176. It has also been taken over in Christian paraenesis: Ign., *Sm.* 6.2; *Herm. vis.* 2.4.3; *Barn.* 20.2 (on this passage see Windisch, *Barnabasbrief*); Aristid., *Apol.* 15.7; cf. also Adolf Harnack, *The Mission and Expansion of Christianity in the First Three Centuries*, tr. and ed. James Moffatt (London: Williams & Norgate, 1908; reprint New York: Harper, 1961), 159ff. The command to support widows and orphans was so universally in force that already it could give rise to unfair claims (see 1 Tim 5:8; cf. Harnack, *Expansion of Christianity*, 161, n. 1).

69 See above in the Introduction, section 3.

it all the more impossible to assign our passage to a Jewish–Christian who strictly observes these laws. For the question of purity would stand in the forefront of his concern; he would not be able to think of "keeping oneself unstained from the world" (ἄσπιλον ἑαυτὸν τηρεῖν ἀπὸ τοῦ κόσμου) without the complete seriousness of the problem of the Gentile coming to his mind—unless he had written before the beginning of any Gentile mission.[70] And neither our passage nor any other passage in the whole of Jas breathes a word about this problem of dealings with Gentiles. Consequently, "unstained" must be completely restricted here to its ethical sense. This also raises a serious objection to the authenticity of the document, for included in what little evidence we have about James the Just is Gal 2:12: the stance taken by the brother of the Lord against table–fellowship with Gentiles.[71]

So we have to understand the saying in the context of a Christianity which has already become free from the Jewish Law. In this case, it provides a valuable commentary on "the perfect law of freedom" in v 25. Even if the saying in 1:27 seems at first to be only superficially connected with 1:25,[72] nevertheless there can be no doubt that in terms of the point it is making, v 27 is leading back to the fundamental idea of the section: Be doers of the word! This practical orientation of the verse (and of Jas in general) gives evidence for a Christianity which sees the confirmation of its faith in a daily life of brotherly love and moral purity—as Paul would say: in the fruit of the Spirit (Gal 5:22). That Jas is not alone here is shown by other passages with a similar tendency ("unstained" [ἄσπιλος] in *Herm. vis.* 4.3.5; widows and orphans in *Herm. mand.* 8.10 and *sim.* 1.8; Pol., *Phil.* 6.1; *Barn.* 20.2), in which Christian paraenesis evidently continues the non–ritualistic

ethical preaching of the prophets.[73] Christians of such orientation now dare to use quite unreservedly terms which were hotly debated by Paul and his churches; this is done with the consciousness that for those who are a new people, i.e., for the Christians, these terms are filled with a new content: it is in such a sense that one speaks of "law" (νόμος), "work, deed" (ἔργον), and "religion" (θρησκεία).

Everyone can recognize how intrinsically close the general attitude evidenced in our passage is to the gospel of Jesus; but it seems to me that the kinship is occasioned by two things: 1) First of all, there is a kinship in intuition: one is not led to God through the discussion of difficult problems (in Jesus, the problem of the Law; in Jas, questions such as those rejected in 2:14ff), but rather by the simplest thing in the world: a life which is well–pleasing to God. As long as Christianity is alive upon the earth, this intuited truth will exert its influence precisely in critical periods. And as long as these salutary simplifications are not wanting, Christianity will be capable of moving the hearts of the broadest masses.

Our author, by the way, and those who shared his general convictions were not alone in the world of their time. It was precisely the practical bent of the philosophical propaganda in popular philosophy which strove to permeate everyday life with the spirit of moral sincerity and integrity; and it even achieved a certain intuitively based kinship in conduct (not in motivation!) with the life–style demanded in the gospel.[74] And even the spiritualization of the mysticism, as it is represented for us in Poseidonius, Philo, and in the Hermetic literature, was occasionally capable of lending support to this trend of the period toward providing verification through the conduct of one's life;[75] so it is

---

70 But this hypothesis is not feasible; see above in the Introduction, sections 2 and 3.

71 Cf. above in the Introduction, section 2.

72 See above in the Analysis.

73 See above in footnote 68.

74 For purposes of characterization, I quote the somewhat overstated comment about Epictetus made by U. v. Wilamowitz–Moellendorff, *Die griechische und lateinische Literatur und Sprache*, Kultur der Gegenwart 1, 8 (Berlin: Teubner, ³1924), 169: "There is hardly a Christian in the ancient church who would come as close to the actual teaching of Jesus preserved in

the Synoptics as does this Phrygian." One should also compare the saying of the emperor Marcus Aurelius, which in its formulation is akin to our passage: "And service of it [i.e., the divine 'daimon' in one's bosom] is to keep it pure from passion and aimlessness and discontent with anything that proceeds from Gods or human beings" (θεραπεία δὲ αὐτοῦ καθαρὸν πάθους διατηρεῖν καὶ εἰκαιότητος καὶ δυσαρεστήσεως τῆς πρὸς τὰ ἐκ θεῶν καὶ ἀνθρώπων γινόμενα M. Ant. 2.13.2). Of course, the content of the demand here is fundamentally Stoic. But cf. also Isocrates, *Ad Nicoclem* 20.

that we indeed find the best parallel to Jas 1:27 in *Corp. Herm.* 12.23: "In the All, there is nothing which is not [God] . . ., for He is All; and the All penetrates all things and surrounds all things. Worship this Word, my child, and offer to it religious service; for the religion offered to God is one thing only: not to be evil" (ἐν δὲ τῷ παντὶ οὐδέν ἐστιν ὃ μὴ ἔστιν [sc. ὁ θεός] . . . πᾶν γάρ ἐστι. τὸ δὲ πᾶν διὰ πάντων καὶ περὶ πάντα. τοῦτον τὸν λόγον, ὦ τέκνον, προσκύνει καὶ θρήσκευε· θρησκεία δὲ τοῦ θεοῦ μία ἐστί, μὴ εἶναι κακόν) [Trans.]. Here the demand follows from the pantheistic concept of God, just as the Stoic proclamation of the law follows from monism.[76] We are hardly able to say whether Jas had caught wind of these spiritual movements of popular philosophy or Platonizing Stoicism.[77] Judging by his overall diction and also by the content of his writing, he seems to be particularly close to the literary heritage of Judaism. And in addition he may also have been strongly influenced by sayings of Jesus transmitted

within the church—a hint of this possibility is found in at least one passage in the letter (5:12).

2) That is the second reason for the kinship between the thought of our passage and the gospel: "Jas" has come into close contact with Jesus not only by means of intuition, he has also become acquainted with him through the tradition.[78]

And so precisely upon the basis of this unpretentious saying in 1:27 can one delineate the characteristics of the peculiar position of Jas within the history of religions: his words breath the spirit of the gospel as well as of Jewish didactic Wisdom. They betray nothing of the break with Judaism, and nevertheless they stand so far outside of Jewish ritualism that in terms of content they are in accord with practical slogans such as those which the popular philosophy of the period was able to coin.

---

75 One might recall the "Dream of Scipio" (Cicero, *Rep.* 6); this treatise, which reflects the influence of Poseidonius, recommends excellence in the service of one's country.

76 See the Excursus on 1:25.

77 But see the Introduction, section 3.

78 See above in the Introduction, section 4.

2

A Treatise on Partiality

1 My brothers and sisters, do not hold your faith in our glorious Lord Jesus Christ and at the same time show partiality. 2/ For if a man with gold rings and fine clothing comes into your assembly, and a poor man in filthy clothing also comes in, 3/ and you pay attention to the one who wears the fine clothing and say, "Have a seat here, please," while you say to the poor man, "Stand there," or, "Sit here near me on the floor," 4/ then have you not made distinctions among yourselves and become judges with wicked motives?

5 Listen, my beloved brothers and sisters: Has God not chosen those who are poor before the world to be rich in (the sphere of) faith and heirs of the kingdom which he has promised to those who love him? 6/ But you dishonor your poor. Is it not the rich who oppress you? Is it not they who drag you into court? 7/ Is it not they who blaspheme the honorable name which was named over you? 8/ If you really fulfill the royal law in accordance with the scriptural passage, "You shall love your neighbour as yourself," you do well; 9/ but if you show partiality, you commit sin and are convicted by the law as transgressors. 10/ For whoever keeps the whole law but fails in one (commandment) has sinned against all (the commandments). 11/ For he who said, "Do not commit adultery," said also, "Do not murder." If you do not commit adultery but do murder, you have become transgressors of the law. 12/ So speak and so act as those who are to be judged by the law of freedom.

13 For judgment is without mercy to him who has shown no mercy; (but) mercy boasts against judgment.

Analysis

Each of the three sections 2:1ff, 2:14ff, and 3:1ff is introduced by an admonition or (in 2:14) a rhetorical question which contains an admonition. In all three cases, this admonition states the leading interest in that section. Hence, 2:1ff is directed against unjust favoritism. 2:9 shows that this idea in fact permeates all the remarks in this section.

After each of the thematic admonitions there follows a longer discussion on the theme of that section. It is easy to see what distinguishes these elaborations from chapter 1. In chapter 1 the predominating form was that of the saying, the connection was loose, the thought wandered from one thing to another. But here the ideas are grouped together, they are more closely connected, centered around one theme, so that each of the three sections 2:1ff, 2:14ff, and 3:1ff displays a certain consistency. Therefore, in these elaborations a completely different style from that in chapter 1 is dominant. It is essentially the style of the diatribe, and accordingly, these three sections may be characterized

---

1 On this, cf. above in the Introduction, section 5.

2 Cf. Epict., *Diss.* 1.6.23: "But you travel to Olympia to behold the work of Pheidias, etc." (ἀλλ' εἰς Ὀλυμ- πίαν μὲν ἀποδημεῖτε, ἵν' ἴδητε τὸ ἔργον τοῦ Φειδίου κτλ.); 1.16.1: "Marvel not that to the other living creatures has been furnished, ready prepared by

as "treatises."[1] Today this is generally acknowledged with regard to the second of the sections in question (2:14ff); but it can also be demonstrated in the case of the less agitated comments in 3:3ff.

Only 2:1ff, which in its second part addresses the brethren in a monitory and reproving tone, from 2:5 on seems to be less of a diatribe and more of a sermon. Yet even in popular philosophical propaganda a clear distinction between these two styles cannot be drawn. Epictetus' discourse does not move merely in discussions with the (mute) partner, whose objections are read from the look on his face; sometimes it also directs itself to a numberless public, not in order to debate with it, but in order to reprove it and admonish it.[2] And precisely the religious fervor which pervades Epictetus' words makes him often seem less a teacher than a prophet who, with the persuasive power which stems from a genuine missionary consciousness, apostrophizes all of mankind.[3]

After the introductory admonition in 2:1, our section begins like a diatribe with an example narrated in vivid and graphic fashion (2:2–4). For what we have here is in fact an example, and not a special case which has motivated the introductory admonition; and this example is narrated without any concern for its reality, and hence, without any consideration of the question of the community in which, or the circumstances under which, this or even something similar could have taken place. The Excursus on 2:2ff will lay out the reasons for this judgment. Its importance for the interpretation of the section is not to be underestimated.

In the verses which follow upon the example we find sermonic statements, especially in the rhetorical questions in vv 5–7 where the rich are branded as opponents of the Christians. At the end of these questions there should have been the thought (parallel to v 6a): "But you show favor to the rich!"[4] This thought remains unexpressed, but it is presupposed by the discussion which then follows and which returns to a more didactic tone. This discussion seeks to prove that a sin against the commandment of love, such as is represented by the sin of "partiality" ($\pi\rho\sigma\omega\pi\omicron\lambda\eta\mu\psi\iota\alpha$), is a sin against the "whole law." The remarks conclude in v 12 with a renewed admonition.

The following v 13 is an independent, but very appropriate and very pregnant, saying about "judgment" ($\kappa\rho\iota\sigma\iota\varsigma$) and "mercy" ($\epsilon\lambda\epsilon\sigma\varsigma$). There is no material connection between v 13 and what precedes;[5] this verse is fastened on to the term "to be judged" ($\kappa\rho\iota\nu\epsilon\sigma\theta\alpha\iota$) in v 12. Thus, the same technique of connection by means of catchwords is displayed which has been employed in the construction of chapter 1.[6] Therefore the author has anchored the brief treatise in 2:1–12 into his writing by a procedure that is in no way different

---

nature, what pertains to their bodily needs, etc." ($\mu\eta\ \theta\alpha\upsilon\mu\alpha\zeta\epsilon\tau\epsilon\ \epsilon\iota\ \tau\omicron\iota\varsigma\ \mu\epsilon\nu\ \alpha\lambda\lambda\omicron\iota\varsigma\ \zeta\omega\omicron\iota\varsigma\ \tau\alpha\ \pi\rho\omicron\varsigma\ \tau\omicron\ \sigma\omega\mu\alpha\ \epsilon\tau\omicron\iota\mu\alpha\ \gamma\epsilon\gamma\omicron\nu\epsilon\nu\ \kappa\tau\lambda.$) [Trans.].

3 Epict., *Diss.* 3.22.26: "He [the Cynic] must, accordingly, be able, if it so chance, to lift up his voice, and, mounting the tragic stage, to speak like Socrates [see Plato, *Clit.* 407A–B]: 'Alas! people, where are you rushing? What are you doing, O wretched people? Like blind men you go tottering all around. You have left the true path and are going off upon another; you are looking for serenity and happiness in the wrong place, where it does not exist, and you do not believe when another points them out to you'" ($\delta\epsilon\iota\ \omicron\upsilon\nu\ \alpha\upsilon\tau\omicron\nu\ \delta\upsilon\nu\alpha\sigma\theta\alpha\iota\ \alpha\nu\alpha\tau\epsilon\iota\nu\alpha\mu\epsilon\nu\omicron\nu,\ \alpha\nu\ \omicron\upsilon\tau\omega\ \tau\upsilon\chi\eta,\ \kappa\alpha\iota\ \epsilon\pi\iota\ \sigma\kappa\eta\nu\eta\nu\ \tau\rho\alpha\gamma\iota\kappa\eta\nu\ \alpha\nu\epsilon\rho\chi\omicron\mu\epsilon\nu\omicron\nu\ \lambda\epsilon\gamma\epsilon\iota\nu\ \tau\omicron\ \tau\omicron\upsilon\ \Sigma\omega\kappa\rho\alpha\tau\omicron\upsilon\varsigma\ \iota\omega\ \alpha\nu\theta\rho\omega\pi\omicron\iota,\ \pi\omicron\iota\ \phi\epsilon\rho\epsilon\sigma\theta\epsilon;\ \tau\iota\ \pi\omicron\iota\epsilon\iota\tau\epsilon,\ \omega\ \tau\alpha\lambda\alpha\iota\pi\omega\rho\omicron\iota\cdot\ \omega\varsigma\ \tau\upsilon\phi\lambda\omicron\iota\ \alpha\nu\omega\ \kappa\alpha\iota\ \kappa\alpha\tau\omega\ \kappa\upsilon\lambda\iota\epsilon\sigma\theta\epsilon\cdot\ \alpha\lambda\lambda\eta\nu\ \omicron\delta\omicron\nu\ \alpha\pi\epsilon\rho\chi\epsilon\sigma\theta\epsilon\ \tau\eta\nu\ \omicron\upsilon\sigma\alpha\nu\ \alpha\pi\omicron\lambda\epsilon\lambda\omicron\iota\pi\omicron\tau\epsilon\varsigma,\ \alpha\lambda\lambda\alpha\chi\omicron\upsilon\ \zeta\eta\tau\epsilon\iota\tau\epsilon\ \tau\omicron\ \epsilon\upsilon\rho\omicron\upsilon\nu\ \kappa\alpha\iota\ \tau\omicron\ \epsilon\upsilon\delta\alpha\iota\mu\omicron\nu\iota\kappa\omicron\nu\ \omicron\pi\omicron\upsilon\ \omicron\upsilon\kappa\ \epsilon\sigma\tau\iota\nu,\ \omicron\upsilon\delta'\ \alpha\lambda\lambda\omicron\upsilon\ \delta\epsilon\iota\kappa\nu\upsilon\omicron\nu\tau\epsilon\varsigma\ \pi\iota\sigma\tau\epsilon\upsilon\epsilon\tau\epsilon$); for the missionary consciousness, cf. also 3.22.23: "he must know that he has been sent by Zeus to men, partly as a messenger, in order to show them that in questions of good and evil they have gone astray, etc." ($\epsilon\iota\delta\epsilon\nu\alpha\iota\ \delta\epsilon\iota,\ \omicron\tau\iota\ \alpha\gamma\gamma\epsilon\lambda\omicron\varsigma,\ \alpha\pi\omicron\ \tau\omicron\upsilon\ \Delta\iota\omicron\varsigma\ \alpha\pi\epsilon\sigma\tau\alpha\lambda\tau\alpha\iota\ \kappa\alpha\iota\ \pi\rho\omicron\varsigma\ \tau\omicron\upsilon\varsigma\ \alpha\nu\theta\rho\omega\pi\omicron\upsilon\varsigma\ \pi\epsilon\rho\iota\ \alpha\gamma\alpha\theta\omega\nu\ \kappa\alpha\iota\ \kappa\alpha\kappa\omega\nu\ \upsilon\pi\omicron\delta\epsilon\iota\xi\omega\nu\ \alpha\upsilon\tau\omicron\iota\varsigma,\ \omicron\tau\iota\ \pi\epsilon\pi\lambda\alpha\nu\eta\nu\tau\alpha\iota\ \kappa\tau\lambda.$).

4 See below in the Interpretation.

5 See below in the Interpretation.

6 Cf. above in the Introduction, section 1. Individual witnesses have attempted to link together halves of sayings, or to connect sayings with what precedes them, by inserting $\delta\epsilon$ or $\kappa\alpha\iota$; this is probably also the intention of the readings $\kappa\alpha\tau\alpha\kappa\alpha\upsilon\chi\alpha\sigma\theta\epsilon$ C^c 1739* and $\kappa\alpha\tau\alpha\kappa\alpha\upsilon\chi\alpha\sigma\theta\omega$ A 33 1175 81 1739^c *et al.* and $\kappa\alpha\tau\alpha\kappa\alpha\upsilon\chi\alpha\sigma[..]$ P^{74} (see below on 2:13).

from the technique employed to connect the sayings and groups of sayings in chapter 1.

Interpretation

■ **1** The introductory admonition warns against combining the faith with "partiality" (προσωπολημψία):[7] Do not hold[8] your faith with[9] partiality, i.e., do not be Christians who are partial in showing consideration. If the term προσωπολημψία, which is modeled on the Hebraizing πρόσωπον λαμβάνειν ("show partiality"; lit.: "receive face"), was actually coined by Paul,[10] then it would be proven that Jas was written sometime after Paul. The word προσωπολημψία and its cognates occur elsewhere, in Rom 2:11; Col 3:25; Eph 6:9; Pol., *Phil.* 6.1; Acts 10:34; 1 Petr 1:17; *1 Clem.* 1.3; *Barn.* 4.12.[11] Of these passages, those in Colossians and Ephesians (and perhaps that in Polycarp) are particularly important; for there the word occurs in the *Haustafeln* (rules for the household) sections, i.e., in a

paraenetic tradition which possibly is older than Paul.[12] Accordingly, that Paul is the father of this word group does not seem credible to me, and therefore any literary–historical conclusion which is based upon that position seems to me to be untenable.

The real problem of the verse is the use of the odd phrase "faith of our Lord Jesus Christ of glory" (πίστιν τοῦ κυρίου ἡμῶν Ἰησοῦ Χριστοῦ τῆς δόξης) to designate the Christian faith. This strange manner of expression prompted Spitta to excise the words "our" and "Jesus Christ" (ἡμῶν and Ἰησοῦ Χρισοῦ)[13] as a later interpolation, and Massebieau to excise only the name "Jesus Christ" (Ἰησοῦ Χριστοῦ); and in so doing they also eradicated in this passage the indisputable evidence that Jas is Christian.[14] Speaking in favor of this hypothesis is the observation that there are also other places in the New Testament where the personal name is tacked on to "Lord" (κύριος).[15] In fact, one would have to assume that a textual corruption has occurred here,

---

7　On μ before ψ, cf. Winer–Schmiedel, section 5.30, p. 64.

8　μὴ ἔχετε ("do not hold") is imperative; cf. 3:1, and the attachment of v 2 with "for" (γάρ); against Gebser; G. Schwarz, "Jak. 2, 14–26," *ThStKr* 64 (1891): 721; Cladder, "Die Anlage des Jakobusbriefes," 47.

9　ἔχετε πίστιν ("to hold the faith") belongs together as a single expression, and therefore the ἐν before προσωπολημψία is not to be explained after the analogy of ἔχειν ἐν ἐπιγνώσει ("to have in recognition" = "to acknowledge") in Rom 1:28, but rather as a designation of an accompanying circumstance (see 1:21).

10　So Hans Lietzmann, *An die Römer*, HNT 8 (Tübingen: Mohr [Siebeck], ⁴1933), on Rom 2:11.

11　[And, as is noted by Ward, *Communal Concern*, 26, this word group is also found in the *Testament of Job*: "And I will return you to your possessions again and they will be restored to you twofold, in order that you might know that [God] is *without partiality*, rewarding with good things everyone who is obedient" (καὶ πάλιν ἀνακάμψω σε ἐπὶ τὰ ὑπάρχοντά σου, καὶ ἀποδοθήσεταί σοι διπλάσιον, ἵνα γνῷς ὅτι ἀπροσωπόληπτός ἐστιν, ἀποδιδοὺς ἑκάστῳ τῷ ὑπακούοντι ἀγαθά 4.7, 8); "The Lord is just, his judgments are true; with him there is no *partiality*, he judges us all alike" (δίκαιός ἐστιν κύριος, ἀληθινὰ αὐτοῦ τὰ κρίματα· παρ' ᾧ οὐκ ἔστιν προσωπολημψία· κρινεῖ ἡμᾶς ὁμοθυμαδόν 43.13); text edited by S. P. Brock, *Testamentum Iobi*, Pseudepigrapha Veteris Testamenti Graece, ed. A. M. Denis and M. de Jonge, vol. 2 (Leiden:

Brill, 1967). Montague Rhodes James, *Apocrypha anecodota* II, TS 5, 1 (Cambridge: University Press, 1897), xciii, argues that the *Testament of Job* is Christian and that the "author's mind is saturated with New Testament language." On the other hand, K. Kohler, "The Testament of Job: An Essene Midrash on the Book of Job reëdited and translated with introductory and exegetical notes," in *Semitic Studies in Memory of Rev. Dr. Alexander Kohut*, ed. George Alexander Kohut (Berlin: Calvary, 1897), 264–338, believes that the work is a production of the pre-Christian period—Trans.]

12　Cf. Dibelius–Greeven, *Kolosser, Epheser, Philemon*, Excursus on Col 4:1. [Cf. also Eduard Lohse, *Colossians and Philemon*, tr. William R. Poehlmann and Robert J. Karris, ed. Helmut Koester, Hermeneia (Philadelphia: Fortress, 1971), Excursus on Col. 3:18—Trans.]

13　Meyer, *Rätsel*, 118–21, also views the words "our" and "Jesus Christ" as an interpolation.

14　See above in the Introduction, section 3.

15　Spitta, p. 5; cf. also the designation of God as "Lord of glory" (κύριος τῆς δόξης) in *1 En.* 22.14; 25.3, 7; 27.3, 5; 40.3; 63.2; 81.3 (Spitta, pp. iv and 4).

16　The omission of τῆς δόξης ("of glory") in 33 429 sah is an emendation which is easily understandable. The placing of τῆς δόξης before τοῦ κυρίου ("of the Lord") in some witnesses is evidently based upon the interpretation "faith in the glory of our Lord Jesus Christ" (discussed below).

much as in Acts 4:25, through the piling up of genitives, *if* the present wording of the text could not be understood. But if the text *can* be understood as it stands, there is no necessity for the hypothesis of an interpolation which finds no support in the textual tradition,[16] especially not if that hypothesis is then to be burdened with the weighty assertion that the entire document is of Jewish origin. But Spitta's thesis seems questionable even apart from this methodological consideration. The interpolator who is supposed to have Christianized the letter by inserting "our" and "Jesus Christ" would at the very least not have been displaying much adeptness, since he would have created an expression which appears strange to the reader because of its peculiarity. One might ask why the interpolator would not have alleviated this "piling up" effect by omitting the phrase "of glory" ($\tau\hat{\eta}\varsigma$ $\delta\acute{o}\xi\eta\varsigma$).

However, the interpreter of the passage by no means finds himself in a tight spot out of which he can only be helped by the hypothesis of an interpolation. Leaving aside those solutions which are linguistically improbable or impossible,[17] three ways in which the expression can be understood present themselves:

1) "Faith in the glory of our Lord Jesus Christ": Here the phrase "of glory" ($\tau\hat{\eta}\varsigma$ $\delta\acute{o}\xi\eta\varsigma$) is directly modifying "faith" ($\pi\acute{\iota}\sigma\tau\iota\varsigma$),[18] and the possibility of the unusual word order could be demonstrated by analogy with Jas 3:3 or Acts 4:33: "the apostles gave their testimony to the resurrection of the Lord Jesus" ($\mathring{\alpha}\pi\epsilon$-$\delta\acute{\iota}\delta o\upsilon\nu$ $\tau\grave{o}$ $\mu\alpha\rho\tau\acute{\upsilon}\rho\iota o\nu$ $o\acute{\iota}$ $\mathring{\alpha}\pi\acute{o}\sigma\tau o\lambda o\iota$ $\tau o\hat{\upsilon}$ $\kappa\upsilon\rho\acute{\iota}o\upsilon$ $\mathring{I}\eta\sigma o\hat{\upsilon}$ $\tau\hat{\eta}\varsigma$ $\mathring{\alpha}\nu\alpha\sigma\tau\acute{\alpha}\sigma\epsilon\omega\varsigma$ in B). The meaning of the expression would receive an even more specific emphasis from the context: Faith in the glory of Jesus Christ excludes any regard for human glory. Yet since no special attention is drawn to this antithesis, it may be doubted whether the antithesis is intended. There is no intention in v 1 to define more specifically the Christian faith—such as in the expression "gospel of the glory of Christ" ($\epsilon\mathring{\upsilon}\alpha\gamma$-$\gamma\acute{\epsilon}\lambda\iota o\nu$ $\tau\hat{\eta}\varsigma$ $\delta\acute{o}\xi\eta\varsigma$ $\tau o\hat{\upsilon}$ $X\rho\iota\sigma\tau o\hat{\upsilon}$) in 2 Cor 4:4, where this is preceded by the term "light" ($\phi\omega\tau\iota\sigma\mu\acute{o}\varsigma$)—, but rather to stress quite simply that faith in Christ[19] is not consistent with favoritism. Consequently, it is advisable to connect "faith" ($\pi\acute{\iota}\sigma\tau\iota\varsigma$) directly with "our Lord Jesus Christ" ($\tau o\hat{\upsilon}$ $\kappa\upsilon\rho\acute{\iota}o\upsilon$ $\mathring{\eta}\mu\hat{\omega}\nu$ $\mathring{I}\eta\sigma o\hat{\upsilon}$ $X\rho\iota\sigma\tau o\hat{\upsilon}$), and this is also the most obvious way of construing the words.

2) "Faith in our Lord of glory (1 Cor 2:8; *Barn.* 21.9), Jesus Christ":[20] This interpretation would want to make both "of glory" ($\tau\hat{\eta}\varsigma$ $\delta\acute{o}\xi\eta\varsigma$) as well as "our" ($\mathring{\eta}\mu\hat{\omega}\nu$) modifiers of "the Lord" ($\tau o\hat{\upsilon}$ $\kappa\upsilon\rho\acute{\iota}o\upsilon$); but if our author had wanted to say this, is it not more likely that he would have used either the word order $\tau\grave{\eta}\nu$ $\pi\acute{\iota}\sigma\tau\iota\nu$ $\tau o\hat{\upsilon}$ $\kappa\upsilon\rho\acute{\iota}o\upsilon$ $\mathring{\eta}\mu\hat{\omega}\nu$ $\tau\hat{\eta}\varsigma$ $\delta\acute{o}\xi\eta\varsigma$ $\mathring{I}\eta\sigma o\hat{\upsilon}$ $X\rho\iota\sigma\tau o\hat{\upsilon}$, or $\tau\grave{\eta}\nu$ $\pi\acute{\iota}\sigma\tau\iota\nu$ $\mathring{I}\eta\sigma o\hat{\upsilon}$ $X\rho\iota\sigma\tau o\hat{\upsilon}$, $\tau o\hat{\upsilon}$ $\kappa\upsilon\rho\acute{\iota}o\upsilon$ $\mathring{\eta}\mu\hat{\omega}\nu$ $\tau\hat{\eta}\varsigma$ $\delta\acute{o}\xi\eta\varsigma$? For this reason, it seems to me that the third interpretation has

---

17 Among the impossible solutions, I include the translation "faith in our Lord Jesus as Christ of glory" (August Klostermann, review of Wolfgang Friedrich Gess, *Christi Person und Werk nach Christi Selbstzeugnis und den Zeugnissen der Apostel*, part 2, in *Evangelische Kirchen-Zeitung* [1880]: 283); among the improbable ones belongs the combination of the phrase $\tau\hat{\eta}\varsigma$ $\delta\acute{o}\xi\eta\varsigma$ with the term $\pi\rho o\sigma\omega\pi o\lambda\eta\mu\psi\acute{\iota}\alpha$ ("partiality"), no matter whether $\delta\acute{o}\xi\alpha$ is understood to mean "opinion" (Calvin: *opum vel bonorum opinio*), or "honor" (Heinrich Heisen, *Novae hypotheses interpretandae felicius epistulae Iacobi apostoli* [Bremen: Rump, 1739], *ad loc.*, who takes $\pi\rho o\sigma\omega\pi o\lambda\eta\mu\psi\acute{\iota}\alpha$ $\tau\hat{\eta}\varsigma$ $\delta\acute{o}\xi\eta\varsigma$ as an equivalent for $\pi\rho o\sigma\omega\pi o\lambda\eta\mu\psi\acute{\iota}\alpha$ $\tau\hat{\eta}\varsigma$ $\delta\acute{o}\xi\eta\varsigma$ $\mathring{\epsilon}\nu\epsilon\kappa\alpha$ ["partiality because of honor"]).

18 As already in sy[vg]; so also Hofmann, Burger, Zahn, *Introduction*, vol. 1, section 8, n. 7, and Belser.

19 On the interpretation "Jesus' faith," see below in the second Excursus on 2:26, n. 134. It might be mentioned as a curiosity that S. Wiersma, "Enige opmerkingen over de betekenis van de woorden *diakrinesthai* en *pistis* in de brief van Jacobus," *GThT*

56 (1956): 177–9, translates the expression in Jas 2:1 "the trust of our Lord Jesus in honor (i.e., in someone who holds a prominent position)." Wiersma interprets this as a "mild rebuke" by the brother of the Lord, who would be referring to the special trust which Jesus placed in John, a "friend of the High Priest." This—as well as the meanings of $\pi\acute{\iota}\sigma\tau\iota\varsigma$ and $\delta\iota\alpha\kappa\rho\acute{\iota}\nu\epsilon\sigma\theta\alpha\iota$ which Wiersma finds to be so divergent from those in Paul—is supposed to be evidence of the early date and authenticity of the letter. Of course, Wiersma himself must suffer a severe rebuke from J. A. Schep, "Een onaanvaardbare exegese van Jacobus 2:1," *GThT* 58 (1958): 54–6, who maintains among other things that Wiersma impugns either the sinlessness of Jesus or the inspiration of Jas.

20 So de Wette, Windisch–Preisker (with some hesitation); similarly, Herder and von Soden, but with the translation "faith *of* our Lord." The modification of a noun (here, "Lord") with two postpositive genitives ($\mathring{\eta}\mu\hat{\omega}\nu$ ["our"] and $\tau\hat{\eta}\varsigma$ $\delta\acute{o}\xi\eta\varsigma$ ["of glory"]) is crude in Greek but very frequent in Aramaic, as

more to commend itself:

3) "Faith in our glorious Lord Jesus Christ": Here the genitive "of glory" (τῆς δόξης) is viewed as a genitive of quality.[21] This creates no linguistic difficulties, for in other places as well our author uses this (possibly Hebraizing) genitive as a substitute for an adjective.[22] Thus, τῆς δόξης modifies the proper name as an adjective; Eph 6:24 is materially akin to our passage: "our Lord Jesus Christ in his immortality" (τὸν κύριον ἡμῶν Ἰησοῦν Χριστὸν ἐν ἀφθαρσίᾳ), and the expression in Jas 2:1 could be paraphrased: "in our Lord Jesus Christ in his glory." The expression, quite innocent in its content and striking only because of its form, could have originated when Jas[23]—following the ever present need of cultic language for more elaborate forms—added to the common expression "the faith in our Lord Jesus Christ" (τὴν πίστιν τοῦ κυρίου ἡμῶν Ἰησοῦ Χριστοῦ) a further reference to his heavenly glory. One would have to imagine the same sort of origin for the term "of glory" even if it belongs only with "Jesus Christ," and not with the whole expression,[24] or if the words stand in apposition: "in our Lord Jesus Christ, who is the glory."[25] This latter interpretation is possible in view of the use of the genitive in other passages in Jas, but it is surely less probable.

In any case, there are possible ways of interpreting the traditional text. But even if, because of the undeniable difficulty of the passage, one preferred Spitta's hypothesis of an interpolation, one still may not use that without further ado as a foundation upon which to build the hypothesis of the Jewish origin of Jas. Such an interpolation, just as the insertion of the phrase "of glory,"[26] could be comprehended also in terms of other presuppositions.[27] However, the hypothesis of an interpolation is not at all absolutely necessary in this passage.

The Examples in the Letter of James

We begin with a consideration of the text of another passage in Jas. The exposition in 3:1ff is written in order to deter from the calling of teacher the pressing crowd of those who are all too eager for that position. Consider, says the text, the responsibility which lies upon you who occupy yourselves with speaking, or rather with the instrument of speaking: the tongue! And then follows the famous depiction of the danger of the sins of the tongue. In this depiction the colors are applied with increasing intensity until finally there is the assertion: "From the same mouth come blessing and cursing" (3:10). What does the author have in mind when he makes that statement? Surely he is not thinking of the teachers in the church, and perhaps just as surely he does not have in mind those whose rush for the teaching profession he wants to avert; even if one were to suppose that Jas knew these people personally, it cannot seriously be supposed that he means to charge them with such sins of the tongue! But there is also justification for doubting that Jas knows sins of the tongue to be a particular fault of the readers whom he is addressing, for even if he does have in mind a specific circle as his addressees, nevertheless he does not at all portray any individual human beings. The conduct of his readers has not provided the model for his depiction, but rather the universal human experience of the dangerous quality of the tongue. Teachers in the Christian community are more exposed to this danger. Hence, because some of them *could* possibly succumb to it (but not because they *already* had succumbed to it) Jas substantiates the admonition in 3:1 with the treatise on the tongue. Alongside the warning he sets the typical

---

is pointed out by J. Brinktrine, "Zu Jak. 2,1," *Biblica* 35 (1954): 40–42 (cf. also τὸ αἷμά μου τῆς διαθήκης ["my blood of the covenant"] in Mk 14:24; Matt 26:28). To be sure, the apposition Ἰησοῦ Χριστοῦ ("Jesus Christ") is still grammatically troublesome, so that the counter–questions which Dibelius raises above must also be put to Brinktrine.

21 Beyschlag; Feine, *Jakobusbrief*, 34; B. Weiss, *Jakobusbrief*, 22; Ropes.

22 See above in the Introduction, section 5.

23 Or was this done only later by an interpolator? In any event, an interpolation hypothesis which con-

siders only the words "of glory" (τῆς δόξης) to be a later insertion seems to me to be no more difficult than Spitta's hypothesis. To be sure, in supporting such a hypothesis, no appeal could be made to the few witnesses which omit the phrase τῆς δόξης.

24 Ewald: "The faith of our Lord, Jesus Christ of glory."

25 Mayor; Reinhold Seeberg, *Der Ursprung des Christusglaubens* (Leipzig: Deichert, 1914), 19.

26 See above, n. 23.

27 Cf. above in the Introduction, section 3.

28 See below on 2:19.

example, typically depicted. As with modern poster design, the brilliance of the colors is more important here than the agreement of every brushstroke with reality: such an example may be described as *stylized*.

This realization must now be applied also to other passages where Jas tries to strengthen his point by means of a flagrant individual case. Such an individual case is found in 2:19; the faith which is portrayed there is not Jas' "concept of faith," but rather a faith which is fabricated within the polemic and with which the opponent is saddled.[28] The matter is somewhat different in 2:15f, where the individual case is not related as an example but rather for the purpose of comparison; but even here it is necessary to warn against a misunderstanding of the stylized character of the passage and against any consequent generalization. Strictly speaking, the example in 4:13 does not belong here since that passage does not relate a *flagrant* instance and there is no preceding admonition; yet there also one must guard against an excessively realistic interpretation.[29]

But above all, our section in 2:1ff must be evaluated upon the basis of the realization of the stylized character of such examples. "Partiality" ($\pi\rho\sigma\sigma\omega\pi\sigma\lambda\eta\mu\psi\iota\alpha$) surely existed in those churches which had grown larger in Jas' day—just as it will always exist so long as poor and rich live beside one another and have dealings with one another. And naturally when the Christians entered their community assembly, where poor and rich encountered one another, they did not leave this fault outside. But that such unsociable conduct as is portrayed in 2:2ff would have been the order of the day in these assemblies[30] cannot be asserted upon the basis of Jas 2:2ff.[31] Jas simply wants to use an example in support of his argument and for this purpose he selects not a petty but rather a flagrant demonstration of partiality; moreover, in 2:3 he depicts this example in quite unrealistic terms.[32] Therefore, this example, which is related for a paraenetic purpose, cannot be

used as a historical source for actual circumstances within the Christian communities.[33] This statement is made, not because we have some motive for exculpating the Christians of that period, but rather because such a use of Jas 2:2ff is based upon a method of interpretation which is not appropriate given the literary character of Jas.

The method of inferring from early Christian letters the circumstances of the addressees has been used with complete justification in the case of the Pauline letters. It is well-known how much we owe to this methodology for our knowledge of the Corinthian church. Yet already in the exegesis of the Letter to the Romans this method of interpretation cannot be applied without limitation; for we do not know the degree to which Paul is informed about the Roman church, nor the degree to which this letter (which is an actual letter) can be understood as correspondence, i.e., as a reply to reports which have come to Paul from Rome.

Our Jas shows absolutely nothing of the character of correspondence.[34] The author nowhere implies that he has been prompted to write because of reports about one or more Christian churches. Therefore, we cannot with any certainty infer some crisis in the Christian churches from an admonition in Jas.[35] And this is all the more true with respect to examples which he uses. We can state that the author wants the depiction of flagrant examples to have a deterrent effect, but we are not able to say how much he is relating and criticizing actual events in the life of the church. Hence, there is a fundamental difference between the method of interpretation which must be used in Jas 2:1ff and that which must be applied in the case of 1 Cor 5:1ff.

The view which is suggested here is confirmed also by observations which can be made with respect to the diatribes of Epictetus. Epictetus reports numerous individual cases (sometimes with, sometimes without names) of human wisdom and folly which he has personally witnessed. But in addition to these he adduces

29 Cf. below on 4:16.
30 Huther: "something which often occurred."
31 Also, no definite conclusions about whether this was an actual occurrence or only a potentiality can be drawn from the use of $\dot{\epsilon}\acute{\alpha}\nu$ as opposed to $\epsilon\dot{\iota}$, for the distinction between these two was no longer precise in Koine; cf. Blass–Debrunner, § 371.
32 See below on 2:3.

33 The passage is usually used in this way by interpreters; an exception is Hilgenfeld, "Jakobus," 12f, who rejects the notion that the passage refers to actual circumstances because he finds a different community situation presupposed in 2:5ff.
34 See above in the Introduction, section 1.
35 See above in the Introduction, section 7.

examples which are intended to point out the consequences of false conduct; it does not matter how much of this is factual, so long as the example is graphic and clear. For instance, Epictetus ridicules the fact that as soon as the useless slave Phelikon became Caesar's cobbler he was treated respectfully by everyone, even by his former master. But at the beginning of this section, the philosopher, exaggerating the factual situation, asks ironically: "And yet how can the man suddenly become wise when Caesar puts him in charge of his chamberpot?" (πῶς δὲ καὶ φρόνιμος γίνεται ἐξαίφνης ὁ ἄνθρωπος, ὅταν Καῖσαρ αὐτὸν ἐπὶ τοῦ λασάνου ποιήσῃ Epict., *Diss.* 1.19.17)—the statement does not provide certain evidence for such a practice in the imperial court. The instances which are found often in Epictetus where something to be proven is portrayed drastically are part of the technique of diatribe: such as the arrest of the philosopher in *Diss.* 1.29.22; a similar event in *Diss.* 1.18.17; the caricatured speech in *Diss.* 2.19.5ff of the person who knows only the opinions of the philosophers but cannot himself philosophize.

Incidentally, attention might be drawn to the parables of Jesus which also contain stylizing elements similar to those which we surmise in Jas. One should call to mind the unrealistic, but beautifully clear self–characterization of the unjust judge in Lk 18:4f, and then compare with this the equally clear, but also equally unrealistic description in Jas 2:3.

Obviously the understanding set forth here of the examples in Jas also has an influence upon the overall evaluation of the letter. Someone who interprets the passages in question as historical sources and always concludes that an admonition must refer to an actual crisis will receive a very unfavorable impression of the situation within the church.[36] It is a different matter

if one takes into account that the author, with a paraenetic intention, exaggerates and generalizes (cf. the second person plural address) individual cases which occur occasionally or which are merely possibilities, and that he does so in order to show the possible or even necessary consequences of these faults—faults which may very well be present among his readers, since they are universal human shortcomings. One comes about as close to the author's intention and the actual situation of the Christians as the nature of such a purely paraenetic document allows if before such examples as that related in 2:2ff one inserts something like: "Eventually it will one day probably happen that among you . . . (etc.)."[37]

■ **2, 3** These verses form the protasis of the condition ("If a man with gold rings and in fine clothing comes in . . ."), while v 4 forms the apodosis ("have you not then made distinctions among yourselves?"). Other explanations have been attempted, as, for example:

a) The apodosis is v 5 ("If a man . . . then listen, my beloved . . ."), while v 4 is only a parenthetical clause.[38]

b) The apodosis was left out, and v 4 is the last part of the protasis—despite the fact that the indicative is used in v 4, and not the subjunctive ("If a man . . . enters . . . and you look at . . . and you say . . . *and* you do not weigh the matter carefully . . .").[39]

c) The apodosis is v 4, but it is adversative ("If a man [who is a stranger] . . . *and yet* among yourselves you make no such distinctions . . .").[40]

But on the whole, such renderings are possible only if

36   Cf. especially Grafe, *Stellung und Bedeutung*, 2ff.
37   Jacques Marty, *L'epître de Jacques: Étude critique* (Paris: Alcan, 1935), 71, would like to infer from the ardent and picturesque language which Jas uses that this passage reflects information which had been communicated orally and which must have concerned events actually observed. In the case of the more generally applicable and less coherent portions of the letter (chapter 1, and 3:13–5:20), Marty suggests as a hypothesis that these might be viewed as sermon notes which the author adapted or expanded, as the case might be, so that he might

ultimately bequeath them to his hearers as a kind of compendium of Christian instruction.
38   So Ewald.
39   So Herder.
40   So Hofmann.
41   The Koine witnesses (but also ℵ A 33 sah boh sy^vg s vulg) have the conjunction καί also before ἐπι-βλέψητε ("you pay attention to"), while P^74vid B C Ψ P 1175 ff have ἐπιβλέψητε δέ. The latter is no doubt correct, for this variant might also be explained from the proliferation of καί in this verse, which is a difficult verse to begin with and therefore has been

one accepts the reading καί ("and") before οὐ διεκρίθητε ("have you not made distinctions"); yet this reading is probably to be explained from the influence of the preceding or following καί.[41] There is also some textual difficulty in the last sentence in v 3:

στῆθι ἐκεῖ ἢ κάθου ὧδε ὑπό κτλ.[42]

P[74vid] ℵ C[c] Koine "stand there or sit here below etc."

στῆθι ἢ κάθου ἐκεῖ ὑπό κτλ.

B 1175 1739 *ff* "stand or sit there below etc."

στῆθι ἐκεῖ ἢ κάθου ὑπό κτλ.

A C 33 104 81 429 *s* vulg sy[hl] "stand there or sit below etc."

The first reading can quite certainly be traced back to the unwarranted insertion of ὧδε ("here") by analogy with the preceding words spoken in v 3 to the rich man. Yet this reading is based upon the correct recognition that the place "below my footstool" (ὑπὸ τὸ ὑποπόδιόν μου) is thought of as being nearer to the person speaking than is the place where the poor man is told to stand. But this recognition is missing in the second reading; consequently, if one is not as convinced as Ropes is of

the superiority of the text form in B *ff*, then the third reading listed above will be the preferred one.

Now to the example itself: The distinguished person, as later on also the poor man, is portrayed briefly and characteristically.[43] The rich man has gold rings on his fingers—a "white-haired old man with many a gold ring on his fingers" (γέρων πολιὸς χρυσοῦς δακτυλίους ἔχων πολλούς) also plays an unfavorable role in Epict., *Diss.* 1.22.18. His "fine" clothing is contrasted with the "filthy" clothing of the poor man—the same contrast is found in Philo, *Jos.* 105: "Then they put on him a fine and clean raiment instead of his filthy prison clothes" (καὶ ἀντὶ ῥυπώσης λαμπρὰν ἐσθῆτα ἀντιδόντες) [Loeb modified].

Now the principles developed in the preceding Excursus must be taken seriously, and the wording here must not be interpreted too specifically and realistically. What is said to both men is stylized. It is possible that the words to the rich man could actually have been spoken, though in real life they would probably have been phrased somewhat differently,[44] perhaps something like, "If you please, sir, here is a good place." But at least the poor man would scarcely have been

---

emended repeatedly. Characteristic of the confusion caused by the numerous occurrences of καί in the passage is the following: In the comments on the καί before ἐγένεσθε, we find in Oec a discussion of the superfluousness of καί in the apodosis; Theoph offers almost the same explanation—and probably more correctly—in commenting upon καί before οὐ διεκρίθητε (in the Koine text).

In v 4, B* *ff et al.* omit the οὐ before διεκρίθητε. This is probably an emendation based upon some specific understanding of the text and not merely a scribal error (a jump of the eye from the preceding μου ["my"] to ου); yet it ought to warn us against placing too much weight upon readings in the B *ff* text (see above).

42   In the first reading, C[c] has καί ("and") instead of ἤ ("or"), and the same is true in the text of C in the third reading.

43   L. Rost, "Archäologische Bemerkungen zu einer Stelle des Jakobusbriefes (Jak. 2, 2f.)," *Palästina-jahrbuch* 29 (1933): 53–66, would like to perceive in the procedures described in Jas 2:2, 3 data about worship in the synagogue structure of a specific and earlier type which is to be assigned predominantly to Palestine. According to Rost, the cultic center in our passage evidently is located in direct proximity with the entrance, and therefore the distinguished

person is immediately provided with a seat "here," while the poor man must either also take his place near the sanctuary or else be satisfied with a place to stand over "there" in that part of the building which is further from the entrance and the cultic center. Rost argues that this fits exactly with the synagogue type just mentioned, where the entrance is on the narrow side facing Jerusalem, directly beside the Torah shrine which was located there. However, the question remains whether this interpretation does not place too much weight upon the terms "here" (ὧδε) and "there" (ἐκεῖ); for these words may say nothing more than that in one case the guest is lead to a comfortable seat, while the other guest is given merely some lazy gesture: "Over there is a place." In addition, if one is thinking of the assembly of a Christian community, it must be shown why it would be probable that there also one would find a "cultic center" according to which the quality of seats would be rated. Yet one finds nothing of this in the New Testament, nor for a long time thereafter.

44   Obviously Ewald has felt this, when he writes regarding the expression "please" (καλῶς): "It goes without saying that the word is included here more because it makes clear the attitude of the usher than because he would really have always said this."

invited to stand, but would rather have been simply motioned away from the seats with some sort of gesture. And if these words are stylized, one need not rack one's brain about the other place which is specified for the poor man. Naturally, he is not supposed to crawl under the footstool;[45] but the correct translation, "below (i.e., at the base of) my footstool," may not be visualized realistically either. For the thought does not suggest a long bench upon which several people can sit, with a footrest running along in front of it. Instead, both the term "footstool" ($\dot{v}\pi o\pi\acute{o}\delta\iota o\nu$) as well as "my" ($\mu o v$) suggest an individual seat.[46] However, that such individual chairs would have been used in a community gathering is hardly plausible. Therefore, we probably have here a figure of speech[47] which means nothing more than "on the floor": "Sit here near me on the floor."

The term $\sigma\upsilon\nu\alpha\gamma\omega\gamma\acute{\eta}$ ("synagogue, assembly") presents another problem.[48] It is clear that Spitta can make use of the term along the lines of his thesis of the Jewish provenance of Jas,[49] yet it is just as clear that this term contributes nothing in the way of evidence in support of his thesis. The word here has been taken as a reference to a Jewish synagogue by other interpreters as well, such as B. Weiss, who dates the letter in the earliest period, when the Christians still had membership rights in the Jewish synagogues. Yet the phrase "into your $\sigma\upsilon\nu\alpha\gamma\omega\gamma\acute{\eta}$" and the statements which follow it point not only to membership rights, but to domestic authority; the Christians are the ones who determine where people will sit, and therefore we are dealing here with a Christian $\sigma\upsilon\nu\alpha\gamma\omega\gamma\acute{\eta}$.

The Term $\sigma\upsilon\nu\alpha\gamma\omega\gamma\acute{\eta}$

That the word $\sigma\upsilon\nu\alpha\gamma\omega\gamma\acute{\eta}$ could be employed in Christian usage follows already from the history of the term. The LXX uses it frequently to translate עדה ("assembly, meeting"), but also קהל ("convocation, congrega-

---

45 The reading "upon" ($\dot{\epsilon}\pi\acute{\iota}$) instead of "under" ($\dot{v}\pi\acute{o}$) in B^c P Ψ 33 sah 429 614 1739 sy^{h1} et al. is an emendation made because "under" seemed strange in this context. The reading which inserts "for (my) feet" ($\tau\hat{\omega}\nu\ \pi o\delta\hat{\omega}\nu$) after "footstool" ($\dot{v}\pi o\pi\acute{o}\delta\iota o\nu$) can be explained as an instinctive reminiscence of the frequently quoted LXX Ps 109:1.

46 The LXX uses $\dot{v}\pi o\pi\acute{o}\delta\iota o\nu$ to translate הדם, the designation for the footstool before the throne, as is depicted in many ancient pictorial works of various provenances; in Lucian, *Historia quomodo conscr. sit* 27, the "footstool" ($\dot{v}\pi o\pi\acute{o}\delta\iota o\nu$) of the Olympian Zeus is mentioned. From tombs and other monuments we also know of the domestic use of the footstool; cf. also *CPR* I, 22.8, where in a dowry there is specific mention of a "chair with footstool" ($\kappa\alpha\theta\acute{\epsilon}\delta\rho\alpha\ \sigma\dot{v}\nu\ \dot{v}\pi o\pi o\delta\acute{\iota}\omega$); likewise, *CPR* I, 27.11; also *P. Tebt.* I, 45.38.

47 Christian Hülsen has called my attention to the passage in Cicero, *Ad Atticum* 2.24.3: "Caesar, the man who as praetor some years ago had bidden Q. Catulus speak from the lower place" (Caesar is qui olim, praetor cum esset, Q. Catulum ex inferiore loco jusserat dicere) [Loeb modified]; cf. Theodor Mommsen, *Römisches Staatsrecht*, vol. 3, part 1, Handbuch der römischen Alterthümer 3, 1 (reprint of 3rd edition; Graz: Akademische Druck- u. Verlagsanstalt, ³1952), 383f and also p. xii, n. 1. This "lower place" (locus inferior) is either a special platform or the ground-level area in the forum. The one referred to as on the "lower place" stood with his head at about the level of the "footstool" of the presiding magistrate. The expression "below the footstool" could have derived from these sorts of circumstances, which also existed elsewhere. The Jewish synagogue in Capernaum (Tell–Hum), which admittedly dates from a later period (2nd or 3rd cent.), contains two stone benches running one above the other along each side wall (cf. Heinrich Kohl and Carl Watzinger, *Antike Synagogen in Galiläa*, Wissenschaftliche Veröffentlichung der deutschen Orient–Gesellschaft 29 [Leipzig: Hinrichs, 1916], illustration 40 and plate IV). Here also the head of a person seated on the floor would have been at the level of the feet of the person sitting on the upper bench.

48 On $\sigma\upsilon\nu\alpha\gamma\omega\gamma\acute{\eta}$ in Christian usage, cf. further Marty, *op. cit.* (above, n. 37), on Jas 2:2; Otto Michel, *Das Zeugnis des Neuen Testaments von der Gemeinde*, FRLANT, N.F. 39 (Göttingen: Vandenhoeck & Ruprecht, 1941), 12, n. 7; W. G. Kümmel, *Kirchenbegriff und Geschichtsbewusstsein in der Urgemeinde und bei Jesus*, Symbolae Bibilicae Upsalienses 1 (Zürich: Niehams, 1943), 23; Wolfgang Schrage, "$\sigma\upsilon\nu\alpha\gamma\omega\gamma\acute{\eta}$," *TDNT* 7, pp. 798–852.

49 See above in the Introduction, section 3.

50 See Schürer, *Jewish People*, Division 2, vol. 2, p. 58, n. 48.

51 E.g., honorary inscriptions with the formula "the synagogue honored . . ." ($\dot{\eta}\ \sigma\upsilon\nu\alpha\gamma\omega\gamma\dot{\eta}\ \dot{\epsilon}\tau\epsilon\acute{\iota}\mu\eta\sigma\epsilon\nu$); cf. Emil Schürer, *Geschichte des jüdischen Volkes im Zeitalter Jesu Christi*, vol. 2 (Leipzig: Hinrichs, ²1907), 504, n. 11, who cites an inscription from Phocaea (Salomon Reinach, "Une nouvelle syna-

tion"), and in the LXX it designates both the meeting and the community assembly as well as the community in general, the religious fellowship. In later Judaism, the term ἐκκλησία is used frequently for the ideal community, while the word συναγωγή more often denotes the empirical community.[50] We can see the word used in this sense not only in Acts 6:9 and 9:2, and probably Rev 2:9 and 3:9, but also in a number of inscriptions.[51] Every reader of the Gospels is aware that συναγωγή can also denote the place of assembly—i.e., the Jewish house of teaching. But the term also occurs outside Christianity as a technical designation, and in fact as a designation for periodic assemblies[52] as well as for corporations.[53]

Therefore, it is not surprising to find συναγωγή used in the early stages of Christianity in a variety of ways.[54] Of interest to us here are those cases where the word is used in a technical sense, for all those examples in which the choice of the term συναγωγή is dependent

upon the context or upon some other special consideration naturally cannot be called upon for the interpretation of our passage.[55] Without doubt early Christian assemblies were called συναγωγαί, a designation which can be explained quite naturally from the terminological usage of the surrounding "world": Ign., *Pol.* 4.2: "Let the meetings be more numerous" (πυκνότερον συναγωγαὶ γινέσθωσαν); in a passage which is very similar to our text in Jas, Hermas writes of the cultic assembly: "Therefore, when a person who has the Divine Spirit comes into a meeting of righteous men" (ὅταν οὖν ἔλθῃ ὁ ἄνθρωπος ὁ ἔχων τὸ πνεῦμα τὸ θεῖον εἰς συναγωγὴν ἀνδρῶν δικαίων *Herm. mand.* 11.9; similarly 11.14; cf. also 11.13); and Dionysius of Alexandria (Eus., *Hist. eccl.* 7.9.2; 7.11.11, 12, 17) calls someone who takes part in the Christian assemblies τῆς συναγωγῆς μετασχών, and he calls the assemblies themselves συναγωγαί. Also, mention should be made here of Justin, who in *Dial.* 63.5 speaks of "those who believe on

---

gogue grecque, à Phocée," *REJ* 12 [1886]: 236–43), and an inscription from Acmonia (W. M. Ramsay, *The Cities and Bishoprics of Phrygia*, vol. 1, part 2 [Oxford: Clarendon, 1897], 649f).

52 The most well–known examples are the Testament of Epicteta, from around 200 B.C.: "so that there might be a three-day assembly in the Museion" (ὥστε γενέσθαι τὰν συναγωγὰν ἐπ᾿ ἀμέρας τρεῖς ἐν τῷ μουσείῳ *IG* XII, 3, no. 330.118f), and the inscription of Antiochus I of Commagene, 1st cent. B.C.: "for the purpose of assemblies and festival gatherings" (εἰς συναγωγὰς καὶ πανηγύρεις Ditt., *Or.* I, 383.94; see also I, 383.151; cf. II, 556.3; II, 737.1; II, 748.15; Athenaeus, *Deipnosophistae* 5.19, p. 192B; 8.64, p. 362E).

53 Ditt., *Or.* I, 326.11f: "our group and society" (τὴν ἡμετέραν αἵρεσιν καὶ συναγωγήν), with reference to the club of the Attalistai (κοινὸν τῶν Ἀτταλιστῶν 2nd cent. B.C.). A 1st cent. A.D. inscription refers to a barbers' union as a συναγωγὴ τῶν κουρέων (Ernst Kalinka, "Antike Inscriften in Constantinopel und Umgebung," *Archaeologisch–epigraphische Mittheilungen aus Oesterreich–Ungarn* 19 [1896]: 67). "Young men's clubs" (συναγωγαὶ [τῶν] νέων) are frequently attested: F. Hiller, "Inschriften unsicherer Herkunft," *Mitteilungen des kaiserlich deutschen archäologischen Instituts: Athenische Abteilung* 33 (1908): 162; Philippe Le Bas and W. H. Waddington, eds., *Voyage archéologique en Grèce et Asie mineure*, vol. 2 (Paris: Didot, 1872), 282, no. 1188.20; also the disputed inscription in P. Foucart, *Des associations religieuses chez les Grecs: Thiases, éranes, orgéons* (Paris:

Klincksieck, 1873), 238, no. 65, with its mention of a "society of Zeus" (τοῦ Διὸς συναγωγή), may belong here; cf. M. Perdrizet, "Reliefs Mysiens," *Bulletin de correspondance Hellénique* 23 (1899): 592ff; Deissmann, *Urgeschichte*, 36, n. 3.

54 Cf. in general Adolf Harnack, "Beiträge zur Geschichte der marcionitischen Kirchen," *ZWTh* 19 (1876): 102ff; *idem, Expansion of Christianity*, 408; *idem*, "Die älteste griechische Kircheninschrift," *SAB* (1915): 754ff; Oscar Gebhardt and Adolf Harnack, eds., *Hermae pastor Graece*, Patrum Apostolicorum Opera, ed. Oscar Gebhardt, Adolf Harnack, Theodor Zahn, vol. 3 (Leipzig: Hinrichs, 1877), on *Herm. mand.* 11.9; Franz Xaver Funk, ed. *Patres apostolici*, vol. 1 (Tübingen: Laupp, ²1901), on *Herm. mand.* 11.9; Zahn, *Forschungen*, vol. 2, p. 164; *idem, Introduction*, vol. 1, section 4, n. 1; Schürer, *Jewish People*, Division 2, vol. 2, p. 58, n. 11; Deissmann, *Urgeschichte*, 35f.

55 For example, the use of the term in Irenaeus is occasioned by Old Testament references: in *Adv. haer.* 3.6.1 by LXX Ps 81:1, and in *Adv. haer.* 4.31.1, 2 by the story of Lot's daughters in Gen 19. The use of συναγωγή in Theophilus, *Ad Autol.* 2.14 is occasioned by the metaphor of the sea. That in the Christian redaction of *Test. Ben.* 11.2, 3 there is mention of the "synagogue of the Gentiles" (συναγωγὴ τῶν ἐθνῶν) is perhaps part of the redactor's Jewish camouflage. Also, when in Epiphan., *Haer.* 30.18 the Ebionites are designated, not as a "church" (ἐκκλησία), but rather as a "synagogue" (συναγωγή), that is probably to be considered a lingering influence of Juda-

Him, who are of one soul and one assembly and one church" ($\tau o \hat{\imath} s \, \epsilon \hat{\imath} s \, a \hat{\upsilon} \tau \grave{o} \nu \, \pi \iota \sigma \tau \epsilon \acute{\upsilon} o \upsilon \sigma \iota \nu, \, \dot{\omega} s \, o \hat{\vartheta} \sigma \iota \, \mu \iota \hat{q} \, \psi \upsilon \chi \hat{\eta} \, \kappa a \grave{\iota} \, \mu \iota \hat{q} \, \sigma \upsilon \nu a \gamma \omega \gamma \hat{\eta} \, \kappa a \grave{\iota} \, \mu \iota \hat{q} \, \dot{\epsilon} \kappa \kappa \lambda \eta \sigma \acute{\iota} q$) [Trans.]; and also the compound $\dot{\epsilon} \pi \iota \sigma \upsilon \nu a \gamma \omega \gamma \acute{\eta}$ ("assembling") in Heb 10:25.[56]

At least in isolated circles the word $\sigma \upsilon \nu a \gamma \omega \gamma \acute{\eta}$ was probably also used to designate the community in general. Evidently, this term soon fell into disfavor as a designation for the Christian church, since with this word the Christians had been accustomed to think of Judaism.[57] Consequently, $\sigma \upsilon \nu a \gamma \omega \gamma \acute{\eta}$ used in this sense has only isolated and late attestation: in the fifth century, it is used for colonies of Shenoute's Coptic monks.[58] One may at least ask whether the earliest ecclesiastical inscription in Greek: "the synagogue of the Marcionites in the village of Lebaba" ($\sigma \upsilon \nu a \gamma \omega \gamma \grave{\eta} \, M a \rho \kappa \iota \omega \nu \iota \sigma \tau \hat{\omega} \nu \, \kappa \acute{\omega} \mu \eta s \, \Lambda \epsilon \beta \acute{a} \beta \omega \nu \, \kappa \tau \lambda$. Ditt., *Or.* II, 608.1), which is dated in the year 318/19, might be intended as a designation for the community of Marcionites and not—as is usually thought—the building where they meet.[59] At any rate, one can see from this Marcionite inscription that it was not only Jewish–Christians—some of the material in n. 55 could be considered here—who used the term $\sigma \upsilon \nu a \gamma \omega \gamma \acute{\eta}$ in a technical–cultic sense.

The material above shows how precarious it is to conclude from the use of $\sigma \upsilon \nu a \gamma \omega \gamma \acute{\eta}$ anything about the time and place of the incident in Jas 2:1ff. Zahn makes an attempt to infer at least that here we find ourselves "in a Jewish context, or in close proximity to the same." For, argues Zahn, Jas by no means avoids using the term $\dot{\epsilon} \kappa \kappa \lambda \eta \sigma \acute{\iota} a$ ("assembly, church"; see 5:14).[60] Yet given the tendency of Jas to make use now and then of traditional sayings or expressions, Zahn's inference is not justified.

Another issue is whether in Jas 2:2 the assembly or the assembly–*room* is intended by the term $\sigma \upsilon \nu a \gamma \omega \gamma \acute{\eta}$. The mention of seats can hardly be called upon in favor of the second possibility.[61] But in favor of the first explanation, one can cite the Latin translation in s and vulg (*conventus*) and the parallels in *Herm. mand.* 11.9. It is not necessary to suppose any dependence between Jas and *Hermas*, for what is involved is only an agreement in external form.[62]

Finally, we must discuss the frequently treated question of whether the visitors mentioned in the example are Christians or non–Christians. Behind this question lurks the problem which I have treated in section 6 of the Introduction. I argued there that for Jas the Christians are essentially still the Poor, that is, "poor" in the semi–religious sense which the word had acquired in the course of history. It was further shown that as a result of this Jas has taken over the concept of the evil Rich, which had become traditional in Judaism, but that on the other hand various passages in his writing indicates that rich people occasionally sought to associate with the Christians and that our author seems to have some objections to these relationships. Just how many rich people had actually become Christians cannot be estimated.

---

ism rather than evidence of a Christian terminology.

56 The "assembly of the congregation" ($\sigma \upsilon \nu a \gamma \omega \gamma \grave{\eta} \, \tau \hat{\eta} s \, \dot{\epsilon} \kappa \kappa \lambda \eta \sigma \acute{\iota} a s$) at Sinai is mentioned in Clem. Alex., *Strom.* 6.34.3, but that is probably not a technical usage. In the *Acts of Peter* 9 (*Actus Vercellenses*), p. 56, 23 Lipsius, the phrase *exiliens de synagoga* could mean either "hurrying out of the synagogue" or simply "hurrying out of the assembly."

57 Characteristic of this antipathy is that while the Latin version *ff* does have *synagogam vestram* in Jas 2:2, vulg has *conventu vestro* ("your gathering"). In *Hermas*, the Latin translations offer *ecclesia* ("congregation, assembly"), *turba* ("crowd, multitude"), *concilium* ("meeting, assembly"), and *coetus* ("meeting, assembly").

58 Johannes Leipoldt, *Schenute von Atripe und die Entstehung des national ägyptischen Christentums*, TU 25, 1

(Leipzig: Hinrichs, 1903), 96f.

59 But even then the designation is peculiar. Adolf von Harnack, "Die älteste griechische Kircheninschrift," *SAB*(1915): 756, offers the hypothesis that a confusion of $\sigma \upsilon \nu a \gamma \omega \gamma \acute{\eta}$ and $\dot{\epsilon} \kappa \kappa \lambda \eta \sigma \acute{\iota} a$ took place by way of Palestinian Aramaic: $\dot{\epsilon} \kappa \kappa \lambda \eta \sigma \acute{\iota} a$ = כנישתא = $\sigma \upsilon \nu a \gamma \omega \gamma \acute{\eta}$.

60 Zahn, *Introduction*, vol. 1, p. 95.

61 Cf. the remarks above on the term "footstool" ($\dot{\upsilon} \pi o - \pi \acute{o} \delta \iota o \nu$).

62 It might also be noted that this example which Jas has offered in a somewhat incidental manner has motivated an ecclesiastical regulation; cf. G. Horner, *The Statutes of the Apostles* (London: Williams & Norgate, 1904), 195f; *Didasc.* 12, p. 69f Achelis; *Const. ap.* 2.58. The development which makes out of paraenesis a fixed regulation of ecclesiastical order

All of this is confirmed by Jas 2:2f. The example would be meaningless if for the author and his readers it were out of the question that a rich person would visit the Christian assembly. On the other hand, it has been correctly pointed out that in our example neither the rich man nor the poor man seem to belong to the community, since they are shown where to sit.[63] But nothing further can be squeezed out of these considerations, and once again I would warn against the confusion of a paraenetic example with a historical account.[64] After all, is there any point in the discussion of this passage by exegetes? Even supposing that Jas is writing to a specific church, does he really say that the incident actually occurred? Does he really remind them of something with which they are familiar? Does he

disclose his knowledge of the details? And if the document is directed toward all of Christendom, is it really possible that an isolated instance unknown to most readers would be discussed? Even if our author is supposed to have heard about such a thing—which we do not know by any means—, then all we could say is that Jas has stripped the event of its special details; in other words, he has stylized it.

But perhaps he has merely contrived the event, and in any case, he is interested only in setting forth a flagrant example of the attitude which he is opposing. Perhaps he himself had in mind only the antithesis "rich and poor," and was not at all interested in the antithesis "believer and non-believer." And even if he had some definite ideas about this latter distinction,[65]

---

is typical and is illustrated particularly by the Pastoral Epistles, which stand midway between paraenesis and ecclesiastical ordinance; cf. the Introduction to Dibelius–Conzelmann, *The Pastoral Epistles*, pp. 5–8.

63 Many older commentators argued that the rich person as well as the poor man were Christians. More recently, this position was taken by Grafe, *Stellung und Bedeutung*, 4, who sought to mitigate the objections to the contrary by assuming that the rich were unfamiliar with the way the church conducted its affairs and with the place of assembly, or that the people involved here are guests from abroad. B. Weiss, *Jakobusbrief*, 5, appealing to 2:5, sees the poor man as a Christian, the rich man as a Jew. Following the lead of many predecessors, Beyschlag, von Soden, Feine (*Jakobusbrief*, 84), Belser, Windisch–Preisker, and Ropes all hold to the view that both the rich man and the poor man are non-Christians; and they would be correct in this if a historical incident were supposed to underlie Jas 2:2f. However, the argument based upon 2:6 which is employed by some of these interpreters is not valid: for from the fact that in 2:6 unbelieving rich people serve as examples it does not follow that the rich man in 2:2 is likewise an unbeliever (cf. E. Schürer, review of Grafe, *Stellung und Bedeutung*, in *ThLZ* 29 [1904]: 168f; and cf. especially below in n. 64). However, since Jas has both the rich man and the poor man being shown to their places, and since nothing is said about them being out-of-town guests at the assembly, then in fact it is most natural to assume they are unbelievers. Nevertheless, cf. the discussion above in the text. Aland, "Der Herrenbruder," 102, also thinks that the passage presupposes rich people to be members of the community—

and in Aland's opinion this diminishes the distance between Jas and the *Shepherd of Hermas*. But cf. below on 4:16 and 5:6.

64 Cf. the Excursus on 2:1. [Roy Bowen Ward: "Partiality in the Assembly," *HTR* 62 (1969): 87–97, accepts Dibelius' overall evaluation of Jas 2:2f as a paraenetic example and not a historical incident to which Jas is addressing himself. Nevertheless, Ward offers a quite different interpretation of the situation depicted: The rich man and the poor man are not strangers to the community. The instructions about sitting and standing can be explained instead in terms of rabbinic judicial procedure where allowing one litigant to sit while another must stand is a sign of unjust judging and partiality. Ward cites further rabbinic texts where it is also forbidden for one litigant to be dressed expensively while another wears rags—i.e., the same type of situation as is depicted in Jas 2:2f. Ward concludes that the "assembly" in Jas 2:2f is therefore a judicial assembly. Finally, he notes that in 2:2f we find the following parallelism:

2:2 *man with golden rings* enters,
 poor man enters;
2:3 you pay attention to the *man with fine clothing*,
 you say to the *poor man*.

But it is only in 2:6, 7 that the explicit contrast "rich—poor" ($\pi\lambda o\acute{u}\sigma\iota o\varsigma$—$\pi\tau\omega\chi\acute{o}\varsigma$) is found. Ward argues that the "rich" in 2:6, 7 are outsiders, but that Jas may have intentionally avoided using the term "rich man" ($\pi\lambda o\acute{u}\sigma\iota o\varsigma$) in 2:2f, since there he was speaking not of outsiders but of members of the community. Cf. also on this passage, and on the whole of Jas 2:1–13, Ward, *Communal Concern*—Trans.]

65 See the possibilities noted above in n. 63 and n. 64.

he has not brought them forward here. He warns against a cringing servility toward the rich person, no matter what his faith or general convictions might be. The spiritual welfare of the rich man remains totally outside the consideration.[66]

■ **4** As was already mentioned, this verse contains the apodosis, and its interpretation is dependent upon the sense of the two verbs, but especially upon that of the much–debated διεκρίθητε. Right away we can consider as improbable those interpretations which construe this verse as a declarative statement in which the first verb is negated and the second verb is positive.[67] For the following considerations speak against this: The expression "you have become judges with evil motives" (ἐγένεσθε κριταὶ διαλογισμῶν πονηρῶν) is a statement which is unfavorable toward those addressed; since it is joined to οὐ διεκρίθητε by the conjunction "and" (καί) and not by some adversative particle, then διεκρίθητε (without negation) will also have to be read as an unfavorable statement. In fact, there is probably a conscious play on words here (as in Rom 14:23 and 1 Cor 11:31); those addressed are reproached on two counts: the first involves the verb διακρίνεσθαι and the second implies the verb κρίνειν. But then the negative particle οὐ is an interrogative particle here[68] and applies to both verbs in the verse ("Then have you not . . . and have you not become . . . ?"). Now if this verse is read as an apodosis in the form of a question, there are still various possibilities for the translation of διακρίνεσθαι:[69]

The translation "to doubt" has won wide acceptance, especially among disciples of the "New Testament language" as a special idiom. Among other New Testament passages, Jas 1:6 is cited as evidence for this meaning. But in no case is this argument compelling— note how in the short Letter of Jude this term is used to

mean "to contend" in v 9 but "to doubt" in v 22—and in Jas it is not convincing at all. For chapter 1 is composed of sayings, which in part are possibly older than Jas. Therefore, the translation "to doubt" in 1:6, which is assured by the antithesis "in faith" (ἐν πίστει), in no way binds an interpreter of 2:4 (where that antithesis is lacking) to the same translation. But against the translation "to doubt" in 2:4 there is also an objection related to the content of the passage. On Jas 1:6, Beyschlag stresses that faith in Jas is the undivided devotion of a person, and that accordingly doubt means a heart divided between God and world. Yet this verdict, that doubt arises from love of the world, is not expressed in 2:4; in this passage the author has no interest at all in rejecting the love of the world, but rather his interest is in condemning partiality.[70] Finally, the parallel expression "you have become judges" would not fit with the translation "to doubt."

Instead, the expression "you have become judges" suggests the meaning "to separate, make distinctions" for the verb διακρίνειν. The form διεκρίθην could be considered an aorist middle, by analogy with ἀπεκρίθην and similar forms; but the active meaning is also possible. The passive would fit poorly here, since some activity of those addressed is involved, as "you have become judges" shows. But in any case, the phrase ἐν ἑαυτοῖς seems to be equivalent here to ἐν ἀλλήλοις ("among one another, among yourselves"), because against the meaning of "division within one's own heart"[71] the same objection is valid which was just made against the translation "to doubt." Hence, the actual sense here is no longer a problem, and it is fundamentally only a matter of the precise nuance—either active: "Then have you not accepted distinctions?" or possibly better, since it is more striking, middle: "Then

---

66   Cf. above in the Introduction, section 8.

67   In this category belong Oec and Theoph, who interpret οὐ διεκρίθητε to mean "you have lost your critical abilities" (τὸ διακριτικὸν ὑμῶν διεφθείρατε); and also the Scholion, which explains the term διεκρίθητε to mean "giving consideration to the fact that in Christ there is no poor man and rich man" (λογιζόμενοι δηλαδή, ὅτι οὐκ ἔστι πένης καὶ πλούσιος ἐν Χριστῷ).

68   B and ff omit the negative particle οὐ, possibly because of a scribal confusion of μου ("my"; immediately preceding in the Greek text) and ου.

69   On the translation "consider, reflect," see n. 67, and above in the text. The translation "to have scruples" is too weak and does not provide the desired parallel with "you have become judges" (ἐγένεσθε κριταί).

70   This difficulty is evidently felt by Bernard Weiss, *Das Neue Testament, Handausgabe*, vol. 3 (Leipzig: Hinrichs, ²1902), 271, who therefore attempts to justify the translation "to doubt" by assuming that the poor man is a Christian: "But since the faith itself offered no judgment about the value of being rich or poor, this necessarily presupposes that the poor man was a believing brother, and that those

have you not made distinctions among yourselves?''[72] As in Jn 15:6 and Epict., *Diss.* 4.1.39, the aorist expresses here the direct consequence and therefore it need not be designated a gnomic aorist.

The unusual character of this expression, which Ropes felt and used to argue against the interpretation which I have just advocated, must be admitted right away. Nevertheless, that is no reason to give up this interpretation in favor of another, or to alter the text by conjectural emendation.[73] Jas uses the unusual expression because here as elsewhere[74] he intends to employ a paronomasia, or play on words: You have made *distinctions* ($\delta\iota\alpha\kappa\rho\acute{\iota}\nu\epsilon\sigma\theta\alpha\iota$) and you have become *distinguishers* ($\kappa\rho\iota\tau\alpha\acute{\iota}$ "judges") with evil motives. The genitive (lit. "judges *of* evil motives") is used here as a substitute for the adjective; Lk 18:6 offers a further New Testament example for this usage with "judge" ($\kappa\rho\iota\tau\acute{\eta}s$). Therefore, the expression is probably to be explained as a Semitism, just as "forgetful hearer" ($\mathring{\alpha}\kappa\rho\circ\alpha\tau\mathring{\eta}s\ \mathring{\epsilon}\pi\iota\lambda\eta\sigma\mu\circ\nu\mathring{\eta}s$ 1:25) and "glorious Lord Jesus Christ" ($\mathring{\prime}I\eta\sigma\circ\mathring{\upsilon}\ X\rho\iota\sigma\tau\circ\mathring{\upsilon}\ \tau\mathring{\eta}s\ \delta\acute{o}\xi\eta s$ 2:1).[75] For the other interpretation, "Judges over (your own) wicked thoughts," is far–fetched and does not provide a parallel to "you have made distinctions."

■ **5** The new address[76] leads into a further development of the theme mentioned in 2:1. The author brings two factors to bear against the degradation of the poor and the favoritism shown the rich: (a) The poor are chosen by God as heirs of the Kingdom of God, (b) but the rich have frequently proven themselves to be the enemies of Christianity. And indeed it is a matter here of the poor and the rich in general, not specifically those people in the example in vv 2–4. That example is out of the picture now; vv 5ff do not warn against partiality in the distribution of seats, but rather against partiality of any sort. At most, the opening words of v 6 might be reminiscent of the individual case in vv 2–4, but even in v 6 the words can be interpreted in a generalizing sense (see below).

The ideas which the author expresses here are examined within a broader context in section 6 of the Introduction. There it was shown how the idea that the poor person is the true pious person is connected with a religious nuance which has been given to the concept "poor," and which in the gospel of Jesus as well as in Jas is simply presupposed as self-evident. Because of this, the question which often is particularly stressed by interpreters of this section in Jas: "Is the text talking about poor Christians or poor non–Christians?" is a question which must recede into the background. If these poor are Christians, then they can expect to inherit the Kingdom; if they are not Christians, then the Christian is supposed to view them as at least candidates for this priviledged position. Precisely because of this connection with the anticipation of the End, we may affirm that the pride of the Poor which surfaces in 2:5 is not to be understood upon the basis of proletarian motives, but rather upon the basis of pietistic and eschatological motives.[77]

The antithesis in our verse demands special consideration. The reading "the poor *of* the world" ($\tau\circ\mathring{\upsilon}s\ \pi\tau\omega\chi\circ\mathring{\upsilon}s\ \tau\circ\mathring{\upsilon}\ \kappa\acute{o}\sigma\mu\circ\upsilon$) is found in the Koine witnesses and in other texts which are probably influenced by the Koine; this reading may have arisen because of 1 Cor 1:27f. The reading "*in* the world" ($\mathring{\epsilon}\nu\ \tau\mathring{\omega}\ \kappa\acute{o}\sigma\mu\mathring{\omega}$), which is found only occasionally, is quite certainly to be considered an emendational smoothing of the text. Therefore, we must read $\pi\tau\omega\chi\circ\mathring{\upsilon}s\ \tau\mathring{\omega}\ \kappa\acute{o}\sigma\mu\mathring{\omega}$ and translate the dative either as a type of dative of advantage (*dativus commodi*): "those who are poor before the

---

who treated him contemptuously had become uncertain as to the value of their own faith." Cf. further Friedrich Büchsel, in *TDNT* 3, pp. 946–9; Wilfred L. Knox, *The Sources of the Synoptic Gospels*, ed. H. Chadwick, vol. 2 (Cambridge: University Press, 1957), 104, n. 1.

71 So Mayor.

72 Similarly, von Soden.

73 Könnecke, *Emendationen*, 14, conjectures that "judges" ($\kappa\rho\iota\tau\alpha\acute{\iota}$) should be deleted: "and are you not of evil thoughts, i.e., do you not act with evil intentions?" But in doing so he overlooks the fact

that the connection of $\kappa\rho\iota\tau\alpha\acute{\iota}$ ("judges") to $\delta\iota\epsilon\kappa\rho\acute{\iota}\theta\eta\tau\epsilon$ ("you have made distinctions") is a rhetorical device of the type of which Jas is quite certainly capable (see above in the Introduction, section 5).

74 See above in the Introduction, section 5.

75 See section 5 of the Introduction. [Cf. Mayor's attempt to show the adjectival force of this genitive: "wrong–considering judges"—Trans.].

76 See above in the Introduction, n. 132.

77 See above in the Introduction, section 6.

world" (cf. 2 Cor 10:4: "mighty before God" [δυνατὰ τῷ θεῷ]; Acts 7:20: "beautiful before God" [ἀστεῖος τῷ θεῷ]),[78] or as a dative of respect: "those poor in worldly goods." Now evidently πλουσίους ἐν πίστει does not mean "rich with regard to faith," for then faith would be conceived as some sort of compensation for earthly poverty, whereas this compensation actually consists in the claim to the heavenly inheritance.[79] Rather, the poor are rich within that sphere which is called here "faith" (πίστις), and consequently, πτωχοὺς τῷ κόσμῳ is also to be understood accordingly: Poor before the world (dative of advantage). "In faith" (ἐν πίστει) forms the antithesis to "before the world" (τῷ κόσμῳ); Paul would probably have written "in Christ" (ἐν Χριστῷ). Therefore, one may not reconstruct Jas' "concept of faith" upon the basis of this passage.[80]

The significance and provenance of the formula "those who love him" (οἱ ἀγαπῶντες αὐτόν) has already been examined in the interpretation of 1:12. It has the same sense here as it did there: that God has promised a glorious inheritance to those who love him is something which both the Christian and the Jew know without it having to be demonstrated to them by means of Biblical quotations.

It is possible that the first beatitude in Lk 6:20 underlies our whole saying, with its focus upon the poor. Yet even without this connection the saying is understandable within the context of the thought world which I have examined in section 6 of the Introduction.

■ 6a This position of honor accorded to the poor man is contrasted with the way in which he is dishonored (ἀτιμάζειν) in the church (cf. Prov 14:21; Sir 10:23). That the statement refers to the example in 2:2f is not clear right away, for the aorist "you have dishonored"

(ἠτιμάσατε) could be interpreted in several ways. In any event, the aorist is not purely historical, for if in v 1 it were simply a matter of the censure of a single case, then the generalization of the admonition and the accusation in v 6 would have been inappropriate. Nowhere else does Jas indicate that he is thinking of only one church. Instead, he always seems to have in mind Christendom—represented, of course, by churches which Jas knew. Partiality is present among the Christians (see v 1), but perhaps nowhere in the flagrant form which is depicted in the example in 2:2f, not *everywhere* in that form, in any event.[81] Thus, it would have made no sense to say to the readers, "You once treated that poor man badly" (for that would apply only, if at all, to a limited group); but Jas can reprove the general inclination toward partiality among his readers as a whole: "You are in the habit of treating your poor[82] badly, your thinking is no better than that of the people in the situation just described." Thus, the reproach is oriented toward an actual or supposed case—consequently the aorist is used in the Greek; but the reproach refers to the *general* inclination toward partiality—consequently we may translate using the English present: "You dishonor the poor."[83]

■ 6b, 7 These verses support the reproach against partiality with three indictments against the rich. The problem of the passage consists in the lack of a clear distinction between anti–poor and anti–Christian motives for the behaviour of the rich. The first of the three indictments: "Is it not the rich who oppress you?" brings to mind social oppression: as poor people, the members of the Christian community are dependent upon the rich non-Christians[84] and in that position they must endure hardship. Is this because of the fact that they are Christians? At least the third one of the

78   A. T. Robertson, *A Short Grammar of the Greek New Testament* (New York: Hodder & Stoughton, [4]1916), 113, says that the expression in this case "may be" a Hebraism. But to demonstrate this one may not appeal to other Semitisms in Jas, since the same dative also occurs elsewhere.

79   In order to get around this difficulty, some interpreters have construed "rich" (πλουσίους) and "heirs" (κληρονόμους) appositionally ("he has chosen the poor, those rich in faith and heirs of, etc."), and left "has chosen" (ἐξελέξατο) without any further modification or explanation (so Luther, Gebser).

But this produces a tautology, for quite obviously people who are "heirs" would also be "chosen."

80   Cf. below in the second Excursus on 2:26.

81   See above in the Excursus on 2:2.

82   The singular τὸν πτωχόν is used here collectively, as in 5:6.

83   Cf. the present tense in *ff*: "but you disappoint the poor man" (vos autem frustratis pauperem), and in Herder: "and do you scorn the poor man?" The aorist here cannot actually be called "gnomic," but merely "timeless"; yet it approximates the character of the gnomic aorist, since the latter also is properly

parallel questions: "Is it not they who blaspheme[85] the glorious name which was named over you?" expresses a religious antithesis: they experience misfortune not only because they are poor, but also because they are Christians. The second question: "Is it not they who drag you into court?" could refer to court action against poor (in general) as well as against Christians. It is impossible to make a decision upon the basis of exegetical arguments. Instead, the interpretation must cover a wider horizon of texts and problems.

At the time when Jas is writing, the churches which he has in mind are not having to suffer under a massive persecution instigated by the rich.[86] For what Jas is opposing here is not an antagonism or anxiety with regard to the rich, but rather a cringing servility. It is not the churches to whom he is writing who are advocating the pietistic attitude of the devout "Poor"; rather, it is the author himself who first reminds them of these ideas. Instances such as that in 2:2f cannot be considered something which happened everywhere in just that way, but on the other hand it must be admitted that in our author's opinion friendship between rich and poor could be more dangerous to the churches than enmity. Therefore, "the Rich" cannot have taken a public stand as enemies of the Christians.

A comparison with 1 Peter is also very instructive for the interpretation of our passage. Also with regard to 1 Peter there is the well-known issue of whether that writing has in mind merely an occasional enmity or whether it already presupposes an organized persecution.[87] But compared with Jas, the words in 1 Peter about persecution sound so much more specific! The problem seems so much more urgent! The crisis of the hour weighs so much more heavily upon the mind of the author, who in the list of "household rules" has

enlarged the duties of servants to include a passage about suffering (2:20ff), and has written the words of consolation in 4:12ff! Our Jas writes of "trials" ($\pi\epsilon\iota\rho\alpha\sigma$-$\mu o\acute{\iota}$), not because he is worried about persecuted churches, but rather because he knows that the Christians are the heirs of the "poor and needy" of the Old Testament, and that genuine Christianity without suffering is inconceivable.

In our passage, also, he obviously does not have in mind specific, sensational events. If such things had actually taken place, then the anti–Christian character of the rich would have been clear enough, and Jas would not have needed to expose this publicly. What he is calling attention to must be the ordinary experiences of the Christians in their contacts with the rich. They are so common that his readers no longer feel them to be extraordinary; so common that they have all but forgotten to see in the rich the enemies of their cause; in fact, so common that they have even stooped to disgraceful servility before the rich. To these readers, who are so far removed from that "pride of the Poor," Jas shouts, "Think a moment! Who is it that have always shown themselves to be your enemies? Is it not the rich?"

The three questions in 2:6, 7 are to be interpreted in accordance with the preceding observations. Therefore, the words "they drag you into court" ($\emph{ἕλκουσιν ὑμᾶς εἰς κριτήρια}$) need not refer to an actual "Christian persecution" at all. If the same expression does occur in the apocryphon *P. Oxy.* IV, 654,[88] then there it refers to action taken by Jews. One might call to mind the role which the Jews play in Acts 13ff: it is generally the Christians who disturb the synagogue circles, it is generally therefore the Jews who are the informers to the Roman authorities. But in our passage, there is no

---

a product of the abstraction of an individual case; cf. Moulton, *Prolegomena*, 134f. For the most part, interpreters do not pay enough attention to the grammatical question in this passage, since for them the issue which stands in the foreground is whether the characters in the passage are Christians or non-Christians.

84 With this plural Jas surely has in mind non-Christians; see the reproof in v 7 and the phrase "over you" ($\emph{ἐφ' ὑμᾶς}$). Cf. in addition above on pp. 134f.

85 On this expression, see below.

86 Cf. above in the Introduction, p. 2 and section 7.

87 Cf. Knopf, *Briefe Petri und Judä*, 22f, 179f, 195.

88 As Deissmann, *LAE*, 427, restores the text. The text is also found in Preuschen, *Antilegomena*, 23f, and in Erich Klostermann, ed., *Apokrypha*, vol. 2, Kleine Texte für Vorlesungen und Übingen 8, ed. Hans Lietzmann (Berlin: de Gruyter, ³1929), 18. Deissman's reconstruction would read: "How can those who drag us into court say that the Kingdom is in heaven? Can the birds of the air know what is under the earth? . . . and yet the Kingdom is surely within you, etc." ([$\pi\tilde{\omega}\varsigma$ $\lambda\acute{\epsilon}\gamma ουσιν$] οἱ ἕλκοντες ἡμᾶς [εἰς τὰ κριτήρια, ὅτι] ἡ βασιλεία ἐν οὐρα[νῷ ἐστιν; μήτι

reason to limit the expression to Jews.

In a manner quite similar to that of the Jews according to Acts, Gentile rich in other locales may have felt threatened by the advances of Christianity. In the case of the owners of the slave girl (Acts 16:19), in the story of the silversmiths in Ephesus (Acts 19:24), the Book of Acts adduces examples which illustrate that sometimes the Christian mission could lead to damage done precisely to the economic interests of the rich. It is not difficult to imagine similar instances, and these would have caused the rich whom Jas has in mind to instigate official interrogations, arrests, and convictions of Christians—in short, to "drag them into court." Nor, when they had opportunity, would they have missed a chance to harm and oppress the Christians in private life; in 1 Petr 2:20 it is servants, in Jas 5:4 it is laborers: this is probably the sort of thing to which the term "oppress" ($\kappa\alpha\tau\alpha\delta\nu\nu\alpha\sigma\tau\epsilon\acute{\nu}\epsilon\iota\nu$) in the first question in our passage refers.

There may also have been other reasons, in addition to the economic ones, which occasioned the rich to harm the Christian "little people": Christian propaganda among the members of his household may have annoyed many a master. One might call to mind examples from the apocryphal Acts: In the *Acts of Paul* 26f (p. 254 Lipsius), the influential Alexander brings Thecla before the court of the proconsul; in the *Acts of Peter* 33 (p. 84 Lipsius), the renunciation of sexual intercourse by Agrippa's concubines arouses the animosity of the prefect toward the Christians. Along with hatred for the disquieting preaching of repentence, the

rich possibly also felt dislike for the Christians' "sheer obstinacy" ($\psi\iota\lambda\grave{\eta}$ $\pi\alpha\rho\acute{\alpha}\tau\alpha\xi\iota\varsigma$ M. Ant. 11.3.2), contempt for the "pernicious superstition" (exitiabilis superstitio; Tacitus, *Annales* 15.44), and possibly even a disgust for the Jewish origins of Christianity.[89] All of this, but especially the feelings mentioned first, provided the rich with sufficient cause to blaspheme the Christian name. What is meant here is that they abuse and revile it, not that they "bring dishonor upon it" (see Rom 2:23f); for then the passage would have in mind Christian rich people, and it would not have said "over *you*" ($\dot{\epsilon}\phi'$ $\acute{\nu}\mu\hat{\alpha}\varsigma$). One must assume direct blasphemy (see 1 Cor 12:3), but also all the reproaches which popular gossip had brought against the Christians.[90]

But what is meant by the circumlocution "the honorable name which was named over you" ($\tau\grave{o}$ $\kappa\alpha\lambda\grave{o}\nu$ $\ddot{o}\nu o\mu\alpha$ $\tau\grave{o}$ $\dot{\epsilon}\pi\iota\kappa\lambda\eta\theta\grave{\epsilon}\nu$ $\dot{\epsilon}\phi'$ $\acute{\nu}\mu\hat{\alpha}\varsigma$)? It is a Christian formula which is modeled after a very similar Jewish formula. If one wants to say that the people of Israel belong to God, one says that the name of Yahweh was named over them.[91] The expression is not only used in connection with the people, or with persons (as with the prophet in Jer 15:16), but also the ark and the temple are designated as God's possessions in the same way.[92] This custom either goes back to an ancient practice of laying claim to possessions, which is otherwise unattested (in this case, there would have been a time when the name of the human owner used to be invoked over his property), or the custom was always limited to holy names, in which case it would originally have been conceived of as an "apotropaic" rite (the holy name wards off the

---

$\delta\acute{\nu}\nu\alpha(\nu)\tau\alpha\iota]$ $\tau\grave{\alpha}$ $\pi\epsilon\tau\epsilon\iota\nu\grave{\alpha}$ $\tau o\hat{\nu}$ $o\dot{\nu}\rho[\alpha\nu o\hat{\nu}$ $\dot{\epsilon}\pi\iota\gamma\iota\nu\acute{\omega}\sigma\kappa\epsilon\iota\nu,]$ $\tau\acute{\iota}$ $\dot{\nu}\pi\grave{o}$ $\tau\grave{\eta}\nu$ $\gamma\hat{\eta}\nu$ $\dot{\epsilon}\sigma\tau[\iota\nu;]$ ... $\kappa\alpha\grave{\iota}$ $\dot{\eta}$ $\beta\alpha\sigma[\iota\lambda\epsilon\acute{\iota}\alpha$ $\ddot{o}\mu\omega\varsigma$ $\mu\acute{\epsilon}\nu$-$\tau o\iota]$ $\dot{\epsilon}\nu\tau\grave{o}\varsigma$ $\acute{\nu}\mu\hat{\omega}\nu$ $[\dot{\epsilon}]\sigma\tau\iota[\nu]$ $\kappa\tau\lambda.$) [Trans.]. If this restoration is correct, then I would consider the saying to be an elaboration of Lk 17:21 which is now directed to a different audience. In Lk 17:21 it was directed to the Pharisees, but here to the disciples as representatives of Christendom. But in that case, "those who drag" ($\ddot{\epsilon}\lambda\kappa o\nu\tau\epsilon\varsigma$), who think that the "Kingdom is (still?) in heaven," would obviously be the Jews.

However, the Coptic *Gospel of Thomas*, discovered in 1945 and of which *P. Oxy.* IV, 654 is a Greek fragment, has not confirmed Deissmann's restoration. Instead, $o\acute{\iota}$ $\ddot{\epsilon}\lambda\kappa o\nu\tau\epsilon\varsigma$ $\dot{\eta}\mu\hat{\alpha}\varsigma$ are Christian ("catholic") seducers ("who *draw* us"), and the saying of Jesus in Lk 17:21 is used by the Gnosticizing group to oppose the efforts of these teachers. See the *Gospel*

of Thomas, logion 3 (and Hennecke–Schneemelcher 1, p. 101).

89 Cf. the judgments of antiquity regarding the Jews discussed in the appendices to Martin Dibelius, *An die Thessalonicher I, II, an die Philipper*, HNT 11 (Tübingen: Mohr [Siebeck]: [3]1937). On the motives for hatred of Christians, cf. Knopf, *Briefe Petri und Judä*, 99ff.

90 The extent to which Christians were plagued with such ill–favored gossip can be seen in the warnings against giving any occasion for such blasphemy, e.g., in 1 Peter (see also Ign., *Tr.* 8.2).

91 Deut 28:10 (Amos 9:12); Jer 14:9; Isa 43:7; 2 Chron 7:14; 2 Macc 8:15; *Ps. Sol.* 9.18(9), *et al.* See also *4 Ezra* 4.25.

92 2 Sam 6:2 (1 Chron 13:6?); 1 Kings 8:43; cf. Wilhelm Heitmüller, *"Im Namen Jesu": Eine sprach– und*

unholy spirits). The use of the name in blessings might point to this latter alternative (Num 6:27).

But whatever the origin of the formula was, its use in early Christian literature is clear; the name of Jesus has replaced the name of Yahweh, and when it is said that the Christians bear the name, or that it is named over them, this is more than just a metaphor. For in baptism the name of Jesus is named over the one who is baptized as a sign that he is the possession of Jesus.[93] And this use of the name of Jesus is so self-evident that occasionally one can speak simply of "the name."[94] This explains the designation of Christians as "those who are called by the name of the Lord" (οἱ κεκλημένοι τῷ ὀνόματι κυρίου Herm. sim. 8.1.1), and the use of Old Testament expressions for Christians: "the name of the Lord which was named over them" (τὸ ὄνομα κυρίου τὸ ἐπικληθὲν ἐπ' αὐτούς Herm. sim. 8.6.4); "those who call upon his name" (οἱ ἐπικαλούμενοι τῷ ὀνόματι αὐτοῦ, if this is the reading in Herm. sim. 9.14.3). It is in this sense that one can use a phrase such as "to take the name of the son of God" (λαμβάνειν τὸ ὄνομα τοῦ υἱοῦ τοῦ θεοῦ Herm. sim. 9.12.4, 8; 9.13.7), or "to bear the name" (φορεῖν or βαστάζειν τὸ ὄνομα Herm. sim. 8.10.3; 9.13.2f; 9.15.2; 9.16.3; 9.28.5); and in Ign., Eph. 7.1 we find: "For there are some who make a practice of carrying about the Name with wicked guile" (εἰώθασιν γάρ τινες δόλῳ πονηρῷ τὸ ὄνομα περιφέρειν).

This is the way in which we are also to understand our passage: the name and the one who bears it belong together; whoever abuses the bearer also abuses the "honorable name."[95] That it actually is the name of Jesus which is intended here follows from the phrase "over you" (ἐφ' ὑμᾶς). Obviously a distinction is made between those who bear the name and their rich opponents, to whom the "honorable name" does not belong. Yet the Jewish literature of the Poor makes no such distinction.[96] Instead, it finds its rich opponents among its own people. But the poor in our passage do not see the rich to be bearers of the same name which is named over the poor. Therefore, this cannot be the name of the God of Israel, but rather must be a name which belongs exclusively to the poor, the name of Jesus. Thus, these words provide evidence that Jas originated in Christian circles.

■ 8 Upon first reading, it is not clear how this verse is connected with what precedes. Yet the connection must have been clear to the author, for the conjunction μέντοι does not simply mark a continuation,[97] but rather points to a specific connection with what precedes. Both ancient as well as modern commentators[98] have given the word a concessive force. According to such an interpretation, the readers might have appealed in support of their behavior toward the rich to the commandment to love one's neighbour, and to this Jas

---

religionsgeschichtliche Untersuchung zum Neuen Testament speziell zur altchristlichen Taufe, FRLANT 1, 2 (Göttingen: Vandenhoeck & Ruprecht, 1903), 171ff; and Martin Dibelius, *Die Lade Jahves*, FRLANT 7 (Göttingen: Vandenhoeck & Ruprecht, 1906), 20ff.

93 Cf. Heitmüller, *"Im Namen Jesu,"* 88ff, 115ff; *idem*, "Namenglauben im N. T.," RGG[1] 4, 661–6; *idem*, "ΣΦΡΑΓΙΣ," in *Neutestamentliche Studien* (Festschrift Georg Heinrici), UNT 6 (Leipzig: Hinrichs, 1914), 56ff; Bousset, *Kyrios Christos*, 295ff.

94 Cf. Acts 5:41; 3 John 7; *Herm. sim.* 9.28.5; also Ign., *Eph.* 7.1 probably is to be interpreted in accordance with these other passages, and is not to be understood to refer to the name "Christians"; for the mysterious expression "to carry around the name" (τὸ ὄνομα περιφέρειν) points to the holy name. Cf. the characteristic expression for baptism in the *Acts of Peter* 2 (*Actus Vercellenses*), p. 50 Lipsius (which admittedly refers to the name of God, since the trinitarian baptismal formula is mentioned in what precedes): "because God had accounted Theon worthy of his name" (quod dignum habuisset deus

Theonem nomine suo) [trans. Hennecke-Schneemelcher]. With regard to the absolute use of "name" (ὄνομα), Walter Bauer, *Die Briefe des Ignatius von Antiochia und der Polykarpbrief*, HNT Ergänzungsband, part 2 (Tübingen: Mohr [Siebeck], 1920), on Ign., *Eph.* 3.1, rightly mentions in addition to this passage also Ign., *Phld.* 10.1; *2 Clem.* 13.1, 4; *Herm. sim.* 8.10.3; 9.13.2 (first in importance, as far as our present discussion is concerned); 9.28.3; Tertullian, *Apolog.* 2: "confession of the name" (confessio nominis). On the other hand, the term is used in the context of *1 Clem.* 43.2 in reference to the priesthood in Israel, and in 44.1 to the office of bishop.

95 Deissmann, *LAE*, 277, compares with the expression "honorable name" (καλὸν ὄνομα) a phrase in a graffito from Pompeii, where the lover declares what is the numerical equivalent of the "honorable name" (τοῦ καλοῦ ὀνόματος) of his beloved "lady" (κυρία).

96 See above in the Introduction, section 6.

97 See Gebser.

98 Cf. Beyschlag; von Soden; Haupt, review of Spitta, *Der Brief des Jakobus*, 774; B. Weiss, *NT Handausgabe*,

would be responding: Admittedly (μέντοι), the fulfillment of this commandment is good, but if you show partiality, etc.[99] But in the first place, this appeal to the command to love one's neighbour which Beyschlag assumes the readers to be making would be a very pitiful apology for the practice of partiality, and secondly, the counter–argument which this theory supposes Jas to be making, and which would not be a natural argument at all, is simply not in the text.

If something must be supplied, as μέντοι does in fact demand, then one ought to look to v 6a. After the first question (v 5) follows the indictment: But you dishonor the poor! And we are capturing the meaning of the questions in vv 6, 7 if we then add: But you show favoritism toward the rich! Now that is a sin against the commandment of love, and the much–debated μέντοι ("really") refers to this antithesis between the conduct of the readers and the commandment of love, an antithesis which is more felt than explicitly stated.

In what follows (vv 8–11) it is explained that a sin against one commandment is a transgression of the whole law. Therefore, it is only this one commandment which is under discussion here, the commandment of love from Lev 19:18 (LXX)—and not, as is the opinion of Spitta, the commandment a few verses earlier in Lev 19:15: "You shall not be partial to the poor nor show favoritism to the mighty" (οὐ λήμψη πρόσωπον πτωχοῦ οὐδὲ θαυμάσεις πρόσωπον δυνάστου).[100] However, this section from the Old Testament might explain what interest our author has here in the commandment of love. Jas might be dependent upon a Jewish paraenesis which dealt with partiality in the context of its treatment of the commandment of love on the basis of Lev 19. That such paraeneses on the basis of sections from the Law did exist is demonstrated, for example, by the poem of Pseudo–Phocylides, which draws very heavily precisely upon Lev 19.

One thing can be established, at any rate: The commandment of love is not considered in our passage to be the chief commandment, in the sense of the famous saying of Jesus (Mk 12:31 par); instead, it is one commandment alongside others, for otherwise the argument in vv 10f would make no sense. Therefore, the dominical saying just mentioned does not seem to be on the author's mind at all, and if that is true, then there is no reason to take "royal law" (νόμος βασιλικός) as a reference to the commandment of love. Instead, the expression refers to *the* law,[101] of which the commandment in question is only a part. And naturally the expression "royal law" is also not to be derived from "Christ the King," but at best could be interpreted as the "law of the Kingdom of God" = "Christian law"; cf. how Clem. Alex., *Strom.* 6.164.2, instead of "you will not enter into the Kingdom of heaven" (οὐ μὴ εἰσέλθητε εἰς τὴν βασιλείαν τῶν οὐρανῶν Matt 5:20), says, "You will not be royal" (οὐκ ἔσεσθε βασιλικοί). However, probably even this is not what Jas is intending. Rather, what he wants to do is to represent the law as important and unconditionally binding. Many interpreters of this expression have construed it in a similar way,[102] but they have usually referred to the saying of Jesus and then interpreted "royal law" to mean the command-

ad loc.; Mayor; Ropes.

99   Objections against this exegesis of the passage are also found in Belser, Hofmann, and Windisch, *Katholische Briefe* (1911). The latter two make use of the meaning "actually" (*wirklich*) for μέντοι. The point of Belser's (and Ewald's) interpretation resembles that of the interpretation proposed above.

100   The relationship between v 8 and v 9, especially, speaks against Spitta's view (not to mention the all too literary technique which he presupposes Jas to be employing here, and throughout the writing); for v 9 does not mean, "You sin against a minor commandment which stands near this one," but rather, "You sin against this major commandment."

101   The article is lacking here, just as in 2:11, 12; 4:11 and with "the word" (λόγος) in 1:22, 23; but see 1:25: εἰς νόμον τέλειον τὸν τῆς ἐλευθερίας ("into the perfect law, the law of freedom"). Therefore, the interpretation of the term here cannot be made dependent upon the presence or absence of the article any more than in the case of its use in Paul.

102   Gebser, Beyschlag, von Soden.

103   Cf. Pseudo-Plato, *Ep.* 8, p. 354c: "since Law became with them supreme king over people instead of people being despots over the laws" (νόμος ἐπειδὴ κύριος ἐγένετο βασιλεὺς τῶν ἀνθρώπων, ἀλλ' οὐκ ἄνθρωποι τύραννοι νόμων) [Loeb modified].

104   On Philo, cf. Joseph Pascher, *Η ΒΑΣΙΛΙΚΗ ΟΔΟΣ: Der Königsweg zu Wiedergeburt und Vergottung bei Philon von Alexandreia*, Studien zur Geschichte und Kultur des Altertums 17,3–4 (Paderborn: Schöningh, 1931; reprint New York: Johnson, 1968).

ment which includes all the others within itself.

It would be better to refer to passages where βασιλεύς ("king") and its cognates are used to express the surpassing significance of abstract concepts, especially of laws and ideas. Philo not only calls astronomy the "queen of the sciences" (βασιλὶς τῶν ἐπιστημῶν *Congr.* 50) and piety the "queen of the virtues" (βασιλὶς τῶν ἀρετῶν *Spec. leg.* 4.147), but he also writes, "so that it follows at once that the king is a living law, and the law a just king" (ὡς εὐθὺς εἶναι τὸν μὲν βασιλέα νόμον ἔμψυχον, τὸν δὲ νόμον βασιλέα δίκαιον *Vit. Mos.* 2.4).[103] In *4 Macc.* 14.2, the Reason of the seven martyrs is adressed thusly: "O reasoning minds, more royal than a king, freer than free men" (ὦ βασιλέως λογισμοὶ βασιλικώτεροι καὶ ἐλευθέρων ἐλευθερώτεροι) [Trans.]; Justin, *Apol.* 1.12.7, speaks of the Logos, "than whom we know no prince more royal and just, except for the God who begat him" (οὗ βασιλικώτατον καὶ δικαιότατον ἄρχοντα μετὰ τὸν γεννήσαντα θεὸν οὐδένα οἴδαμεν ὄντα) [Trans.]. Hence, this usage involves a comparison with the king's position of authority.

But other possibilities are opened up by Philo's[104] treatment of the passage in Num 20:17, where the King's Highway, the "royal road" (βασιλικὴ ὁδός) is mentioned. Philo derives this expression from the fact that "God is the first and sole King of the universe" (πρῶτος καὶ μόνος τῶν ὅλων βασιλεὺς ὁ θεός *Poster. C.* 101; similarly, *Gig.* 64). But in *Spec. leg.* 4.168, he brings this together with the duty of the king to abide by the golden mean, "beause in a set of three the midmost holds the leading place" (τὸ μέσον ἐν τριάδι τὴν ἡγεμο-

νίδα τάξιν εἴληχεν).[105] "Royal road" means "worthy of a king" also in Clem. Alex., *Strom.* 7.73.5: "So when someone is righteous, not from compulsion or fright or fear, but by deliberate choice, this road is called 'royal'; it is the one which the royal nation travels" (ὅταν οὖν μὴ κατὰ ἀνάγκην ἢ φόβον ἢ ἐλπίδα δίκαιός τις ᾖ, ἀλλ' ἐκ προαιρέσεως, αὕτη ἡ ὁδὸς λέγεται βασιλική, ἣν τὸ βασιλικὸν ὁδεύει γένος) [Trans.].[106]

It follows from these examples that βασιλικὸς νόμος can mean "the law with royal authority" as well as "the law which is set for kings." In either case, Jas—by decorating the law with this predicate—wants to applaud obedience to the law. Since he neither explains this predicate nor reveals a motivation for its formulation, we may assume that he has not created this expression.

It is significant that the same attributes, "free" and "royal," with with Jas extols the law (1:25; 2:8) are combined in *4 Macc.* 14.2 in order to glorify unflinching Reason. That Reason is a true king who leads to true freedom is the Stoic concept which underlies both expressions. The universal human possession to which the concept refers was found by Hellenistic Jews to be embodied in the Law. Thereby they claimed for the Law universal authority instead of particular validity for the Jews alone. But the Christians transferred these predicates to a new Christian law whose core was the ethical teaching of the old Jewish Law. Of course, this transferral was possible only in those places where the conflict in which Paul was engaged with regard to the Law had either died out, or had never been heard of

---

105 I call attention also to Epict., *Diss.* 3.21.19, where the offices of various philosophers are mentioned and Diogenes is cited as an example of the "office of rebuking people in a kingly manner" (βασιλικὴ καὶ ἐπιπληκτικὴ χώρα). In a manuscript now located in Berlin, there is mention of a "royal" (i.e., intended for the king?) book of revelation, which comes to shore in a shipwrecked vessel rescued by a god: "from the royal book found cast up in the area of Trapezus (?), lying in the vessel saved by a god" (ἀπὸ τοῦ εὑρεθέντος βασιλικοῦ βιβλίου πάλιν τοῦ ἐν τῷ θεοσώστῳ στόλῳ ἐγκειμένου παρεκβληθέντος ἐν τῇ τραπεζητικῇ [τραπηζουνιτῇ?] *Catalogus codicum astrologorum graecorum*, ed. Franz Boll, vol. 7 [Brussels: Lamertin, 1908], 59). That "royal law" (βασιλικὸς νόμος) occurs twice in the Platonic literature is merely accidental: the term "royal" (βασιλικός) has

a very precise meaning in *Min.* 317c: "that which is right is the *royal law*" (τὸ μὲν ὀρθὸν νόμος ἐστὶ βασιλικός), and in Pseudo-Plato, *Ep.* 8, p. 354c: "to become subject to *royal* laws" (δουλεῦσαι νόμοις βασιλικοῖς).

106 That Clement is referring to Jas is as out of the question here as also in the passage in *Strom.* 6.164.2 cited above; it is more likely that *Strom.* 7.73.5 could be shown to be dependent upon Philo.

at all.[107]

Now it is clear why the term νόμος ("law") is found here, and not ἐντολή ("commandment"). The predicate "royal" befits the whole law. But it is a Christian law,[108] and consequently it is not obeyed by being ever so careful in tiny matters, but rather by fulfilling the great commandment of love (κατὰ τὴν γραφήν "in accordance with the scriptural passage").

■ **9** Of course, at the same time the consequence which is categorically stated in v 9 also holds good: Partiality is a sin, and indeed (this is the force of the participle) it is a sin against the whole law, not merely against a single commandment. Therefore, παραβάτης here is the "transgressor" of the whole law. The word is found with a similar meaning in Rom 2:25, 27 and Gal 2:18 and in the apocryphal story which is found in manuscript D after Lk 6:4: "You are cursed and a transgressor of the Law" (ἐπικατάρατος καὶ παραβάτης εἶ τοῦ νόμου). Symmachus uses it in Jer 6:28 to translate סוררים ("rebellious"; Aquila has ἐκκλίνοντες) and in Ps 138(139):19 to translate רשע ("wicked"; LXX: ἁμαρτωλούς; Aquila: ἀσεβῆ). Naturally, the phrase "by the law" (ὑπὸ τοῦ νόμου) also means the whole law.

■ **10**[109] This verse is supposed to prove the thesis that whoever sins against the one commandment of love stands as a sinner before the forum of the whole law. And in fact the proof here is one which comes from the synagogue. For the principle "whoever fails in one [commandment] has sinned against all [the commandments]" (ὃς πταίσει ἐν ἑνί, γέγονεν πάντων ἔνοχος)[110] is of demonstrably Jewish origin.

"Whoever is Guilty of One is Guilty of All"

The principle in Jas 2:10 is found in similar wording in *b. Hor.* 8b, and in fact it is apparently used there as a kind of canon of interpretation by means of which Ulla b. Ishmael expands guilt with regard to *one* commandment into general guilt: "Whoever is liable for one is liable for all" (then the principle is applied to one who is "not liable"). A tradition in *Midrash Bemidbar Rabbah*[111] presupposes the same rule. But that the principle is substantially older is shown by Gal 5:3 and *Ps. Clem. Hom.* 13.14.3, where evidently an allusion is made to it.[112]

The concept which it contains seems to have been applied especially in the common Jewish distinction

---

107 Cf. the Excursus on 1:25 and the second Excursus on 2:26.

108 In saying this, I am conscious of the fact that a similarly grandiose conception could also have been attained by a Hellenistic Jew. Yet from Jas' point of view, the predicate "royal" belongs to *his* law, i.e., to that which he as a Christian calls "the law."

109 The manuscript tradition for this verse is not unified. Of course, the variants which have only scattered attestation can be eliminated from consideration precisely because they are so isolated: τελέσει ("will complete"), πληρώσει ("will fulfill"), πληρώσας τηρήσει ("having fulfilled . . . will keep"), ποιήσει ("will perform"). It is more difficult to decide between the subjunctives τηρήσῃ and πταίσῃ ("would keep" and "would fail"; attested, for example, in ℵ B C 1175) on the one hand, and their corresponding future indicatives on the other. The subjunctive seems to be an emendational smoothing of the text. Yet those who are inclined to follow the earliest uncials, as was the case with most modern commentators prior to von Soden's *Schriften des Neuen Testaments*, naturally prefer the subjunctive.

110 The term ἔνοχος ("liable, guilty, has sinned against") is used here with the genitive of the authority against which one has transgressed, as in 1 Cor 11:27. The word "sinner" (ἁμαρτωλός) is used in a similar way

in inscriptions (e.g., Ditt. *Or.*, I, 55.31f: "sinner *against* all the gods" [ἁμαρτωλὸς θεῶν πάντων]); cf. Deissmann, *LAE*, 114f.

111 In *Midrash Bemidbar Rabbah* 9.12 on Num 5:14, it is related that the disciples of Rabbi Huna, father of Rabbi Aḥa, said: "You have taught us, Master, that the adulterer and adultress transgress the Ten Commandments" (trans. Freedman–Simon). They then demonstrate how it is that in fact nine of the ten commandments would be broken by the adulterer; but regarding one commandment, the sabbath commandment, they are unable to say anything, and Rabbi Huna then provides them with the information they desire.

112 On Gal 5:3, see below. *Ps. Clem. Hom.* 13.14.3: "For the prophet said that even though she does all that is good, she must be punished for a single sin of adultery" (καὶ γὰρ εἰ διαπράξαιτό τις, μιᾷ τῇ πρὸς τὸ μοιχήσασθαι ἁμαρτίᾳ κολασθῆναι δεῖ, ⟨ὡς⟩ ὁ προφήτης ἔφη) [Trans.].

113 *4 Macc.* 5.20: "for the transgression of the Law, be it in small things or in great, is equally heinous" (τὸ γὰρ ἐν μικροῖς καὶ ἐν μεγάλοις παρανομεῖν ἰσοδύναμόν ἐστιν) [trans. Charles, *APOT*]; Philo, *Leg. all.* 3.241: "But he that exercises perfect self–control must shun all sins, both the greater and the lesser, and be found implicated in none whatever" (τὸν δὲ

144

between lesser and greater commandments.[113] No doubt one can see here a dangerous consequence of any nomistic religion: one loses the ability to see the difference in the value of individual commandments, ritual commandments become equal in value to ethical ones, lesser commandments equal in value to greater ones. And psychologically it is understandable that the lesser is what receives attention, that, as the saying in Matt 23:24 put it, one strains at the gnat and swallows the camel. At the same time, one ought not to miss the fact that the axiom in question has both spiritual power and value: behind individual actions which are contrary to law one recognizes a general attitude which is contrary to law, and which must always be condemned no matter in what commandment it expresses its transgression.

It is significant that we find a counterpart to the statement in Jas 2:10 in the Stoic notion of the solidarity of the virtues (and vices): whoever has one, has all of them.[114] Augustine, *Epistula 167 ad Hieronymum* 4, has combined our passage with this Stoic notion: "whoever has one virtue has all of them, and whoever does not have a particular one has none. If this is true then the statement [in Jas] is confirmed" (at enim, qui unam virtutem habet, omnes habet, et qui unam non habet, nullam habet. hoc si verum est, confirmatur ista sententia) [Trans.]. Evidently, Augustine[115] feels very strongly the contradiction between his Christianity, which presupposes universal sinfulness, and both the Stoic notion as well as that in Jas.[116] And he is quite

---

τελείως ἐγκρατῆ δεῖ πάντα φεύγειν τὰ ἁμαρτήματα καὶ τὸ μεῖζω καὶ τὸ ἐλάττω καὶ ἐν μηδενὶ ἐξετάζεσθαι τὸ παράπαν). In *Pirke Aboth* 2.1 there is found a saying of Rabbi Judah the Patriarch which employs a characteristic argument: Be just as careful about a minor precept as about a major one, for you do not know which precepts will bring great reward when obeyed and which will bring less. *Pirke Aboth* 4.2: Be just as much in a hurry to fulfill a minor precept. One might also recall *Test. Asher* 2, where various instances of fulfilling certain commandments while transgressing others are depicted, and the verdict which is rendered is: "there are two aspects to the situation, but the whole is evil" (καὶ τοῦτο διπρόσωπόν ἐστιν, τὸ δὲ ὅλον κακόν ἐστιν 2.8).

114 On this notion, cf. the question posed already in Plato, *Prot.* 329e: "if you get one, must you have them all?" (ἢ ἀνάγκη ἐάνπερ τις ἓν λάβῃ, ἅπαντ' ἔχειν); Diog. Laert., 7.125 (Zeno): "the possessor of one [virtue] is the possessor of all" (τὸν μίαν ἔχοντα πάσας ἔχειν); Stobaeus, *Ecl.* 2.7.5b5, p. 63 Wachsmuth: "for the possessor of one is the possessor of all" (τὸν γὰρ μίαν ἔχοντα πάσας ἔχειν); Cicero, *Off.* 2.10.35: "for it is agreed . . . that he who has one virtue has them all" (cum . . . constet . . . qui unam haberet, omnes habere virtutes); Philo, *Vit. Mos.* 2.7: "And of them [i.e., the Graces] it may justly be said, what is often said of the virtues, that the possessor of one is the possessor of all" (ἐφ' ὧν δεόντως εἴποι τις ἄν, ὃ καὶ ἐπὶ τῶν ἀρετῶν εἴωθε λέγεσθαι, ὅτι ὁ μίαν ἔχων καὶ πάσας ἔχει) [Loeb modified]. Hence, Philo knows this doctrine in the form of a well-known axiom (cf. also *Virt.* 216).

115 Christian Fürchtegott Gellert (died 1769), in the moral with which he prefaces his narrative poem "Herodes und Herodias," also brings together both

of these views; for he derives his wisdom from "Scripture and Reason":

> He who loves one vice, friend, loves them all.
> Whoever fails in only one virtue
> Violates through this single case
> The others as well, in his heart.
> O, you say, what a strange moral philosophy
> The spirit of melancholy inspires within you!
> Supposing I were a slave of lust;
> Does that make bloodthirst also my master?
> I trust, my friend, you will pardon me;
> Scripture and Reason indeed teach this.

And then a few lines later:

> Intentionally violate only one duty:
> Already you have the frightening capacity
> By which your heart shirks all the others.

Here Gellert expresses the generous understanding of the principle which applies it to one's general attitude, and consequently this understanding is not narrowed even by the reservations mentioned by Gellert himself (for the text of "Herodes und Herodias," see Chr. F. Gellert, *Sämtliche Fabeln und Erzählungen, Geistliche Oden und Lieder* [München: Winkler, 1965], 120–4).

116 One can interpret in this same way the attempts to restrict the application of the principle, e.g., by taking the words "in one" (ἐν ἑνί) as a reference to the commandment of love; cf. Oec and Theoph.

145

right in paralleling the Stoic concept with that of Jas 2:10, despite the fact that originally they had nothing to do with one another. For if one reads Philo's formulation in *Leg. all.* 3.241,[117] one can hardly distinguish any longer between the principle of Jewish legal praxis and the Stoic doctrine. It is also probable from the outset that Hellenistic Jews had clothed ideas from the Law in the dress of the Stoic doctrine which was familiar to them.[118] For Hellenistic Judaism was fond of equating its national Law with the law of Nature. That Jas 2:10 has been influenced by Judaism is apparent; but one may still find it questionable whether also the Stoic form was determinative for Jas. In any event, both the Stoic as well as the Jewish concept would have been important for him only as a demand regarding a general attitude. Consequently, he did not know the difficulties which Augustine felt.

Also instructive is a comparison with Paul. He presupposes the Jewish notion—and *only* the Jewish—in Gal 5:3 when he demands that everyone who has been circumcised keep the whole Law. One could formulate the principle as Paul understood it thusly: Whoever accepts the Law in one point must obey it in all points. Whoever gives nomism a finger must give it the whole hand. When applied in this way, especially with regard to the ritual prescriptions of the Law, there is in fact something alarming about this Jewish principle. Indeed, Paul intends to alarm his readers with it and to deter them from any pact with the Law.

But as we have already seen in 1:25, when Jas thinks of "law" he no longer thinks about ritual prescriptions at all. Consequently, he can confidently repeat the old Jewish principle: Whoever violates so much as one point of this law (which Jas calls the "law of freedom") is actually a "transgressor" of the whole law, for this law cannot be broken up into individual prescriptions. *Jas seems to have no concern at all about his statements being interpreted in the Jewish sense,* for he uses the terms "law" (νόμος), "works" (ἔργα), and "unstained from the

world" (ἄσπιλος ἀπὸ τοῦ κόσμου) just as innocently as he uses the rule in 2:10.

The re–interpretations which these expressions have undergone are surely not to be characterized as his own doing, for if they were he would have been more concerned about their being properly understood. Obviously the way had already been prepared for him by Diaspora Judaism, for in its propaganda this Judaism was forced to simplify its nomism and to minimize ritualism. At the same time, by assuming a Hellenistic spirit it was brought to a rational interpretation of its own laws which frequently—and not only in Philo— may have been far removed from Pharisaic theory and praxis.[119] Within this framework belongs the interpretation of the rule in Philo's formulation mentioned above.

To be sure, it was the Christians who first came to a fundamental and innocent freedom vis–à–vis ritualism —yet not Christians such as Paul, who were always reminded by words such as "law" and "works" of heated conflicts and difficult problems. Rather, it was Christians of another stamp, whose Christianity had developed in the context of Hellenistic Judaism without any real break. This is how we are to understand the fact that, compared with Paul's discussions on the theme "law," passages such as Jas 2:10f make such an innocent and non–theological impression.[120]

■ **11** That in fact Jas does conceive of the Jewish principle, "Whoever violates one commandment, violates all," in terms of an ethic involving a general disposition is proven by v 11. That principle is valid because God stands behind every commandment, i.e., sin against any particular commandment means rebellion against God.[121] It is possible that Jas intends to introduce the commandments which he mentions here in the order in which he finds them in the Decalogue. If so, then our passage constitutes a witness for an order—attested

117 See above, n. 113.
118 See Philo, *Vit. Mos.* 2.7 (above in n. 114).
119 See the Excursus on 1:25.
120 Here one might raise the question whether precisely this innocence of Jas does not prove that he had not *yet* experienced the struggles in which Paul was engaged, and that therefore Jas wrote *before* Paul. But in my opinion the section 2:14ff is a decisive argu-

ment against this view, as is also the way in which "unstained" (ἄσπιλος) is conceived of in 1:27 (cf. above on 1:27). Also Kittel, "Der geschichtliche Ort," 94–102, argues that Jas was written prior to the full eruption of Paul's struggles over the question of ritual. According to Kittel, the peculiar polemic of Jas (2:14ff) belongs to an early stage of this problem, before the principles had been clearly defined

elsewhere as well—in which the fifth and sixth commandments in our Bible are reversed.[122]

Again, what the reader is supposed to infer from the second statement in our verse[123] is left unsaid. Obviously we are to supply: "If you keep other commandments but transgress the commandment of love through your partiality, then you also are transgressors of the law" ($\pi\alpha\rho\alpha\beta\acute{\alpha}\tau\alpha\iota$ $\nu\acute{o}\mu o\nu$)—which was what the author wanted to demonstrate (see v 9).

■ **12** Here follows a concluding admonition to this treatise which combines the reference to the "law of freedom" with the prospect of judgment: You will one day be judged by the law—and indeed by the "law of freedom." This latter expression is used here in the same sense as in 1:25. And if one considers the use which Jas has just made of that Jewish legal principle, one can scarcely avoid thinking that here he wants to justify the application of that principle to Christians. The principle holds good for Christians as well, for they also must stand before the law, but precisely the "law of freedom"! The mention of "speaking" ($\lambda\alpha\lambda\epsilon\hat{\iota}\nu$) and "doing" ($\pi o\iota\epsilon\hat{\iota}\nu$) may be dependent upon catechetical custom: So act in word and deed!

■ **13** This verse is an isolated saying, for there is a difference between "to show mercy" ($\pi o\iota\epsilon\hat{\iota}\nu$ $\acute{\epsilon}\lambda\epsilon o\varsigma$) and "to treat the poor justly." In the LXX, the phrase "to show mercy" is usually used of God, but also about the acts of human beings, e.g., Sir 29:1: "The person who shows mercy will lend to his neighbour" ($\acute{o}$ $\pi o\iota\hat{\omega}\nu$ $\acute{\epsilon}\lambda\epsilon o\varsigma$ $\delta\alpha\nu\iota\epsilon\hat{\iota}$ $\tau\hat{\omega}$ $\pi\lambda\eta\sigma\acute{\iota}o\nu$), and especially in *Test. Zeb.* 5.1. If the topic in the preceding verses was love of neighbour, then v 13 speaks about a particular manifestation of love of neighbour—and in no way the same as that which is called for in 2:1ff. Therefore, the connections which most interpreters see between this verse and what precedes are in actuality merely read into the text.[124] The only connection between 2:12 and 2:13 is the similarity between "to be judged" ($\kappa\rho\acute{\iota}\nu\epsilon\sigma\theta\alpha\iota$) in v 12 and "judgment" ($\kappa\rho\acute{\iota}\sigma\iota\varsigma$) in v 13. This kinship also effects the content: the statement about judgment can be used as support (note the $\gamma\acute{\alpha}\rho$: "for") for the reference to judgment in v 12. But the actual point of v 13 provides no special support for the leading themes of the preceding section.

That v 13 is an independent saying is also shown by its compact form: it moves from judgment to mercy and

---

(see above in the Introduction, n. 162).

121 One who misunderstands the intention of the examples in Jas (cf. the Excursus on 2:1) and wants to draw inferences from them about historical situations within the community will think it strange to find murder included among the transgressions of the law which are mentioned here. Hence, Kittel, "Der geschichtliche Ort," 87f, postulates that both this passage and Jas 4:2 reflect a familiarity with the dominical saying in Matt 5:21f, and Kittel paraphrases our text: "if you do that which the Lord has called 'murder.'" But nowhere else in early Christianity do we find simply the expression "to murder" ($\phi o\nu\epsilon\acute{u}\epsilon\iota\nu$) used as a metaphor for conduct not governed by love, i.e., as a technical term which could have been understood without any additional explanation.

122 This is the reading in the manuscript B (among others) of LXX Deut 5:17, 18; it is also the reading in a few minuscules in LXX Ex 20:13ff, while B in this passage has the prohibition of killing only after that of stealing. This transposition of murder and adultery is also found in the Hebrew papyrus published by F. C. Burkitt, "The Hebrew Papyrus of the Ten Commandments," *Jewish Quarterly Review* 15 (1903): 392–408. It is also presupposed by Philo in *Decal.* 51, 121, 168, and 170; *Spec. leg.* 3.8; Mk

10:19 in one part of the manuscript tradition; Lk 18:20 (against Matt 19:18); Rom 13:9. Finally, cf. Theophilus, *Ad Autol.* 2.34; 3.9; Clem. Alex., *Strom.* 6.146.3; 6.147.2 (and in *Quis div. salv.* 4, in the account of the story of the rich man); perhaps also in the lists in *Barn.* 20.1 and Justin, *Dial.* 93. In our passage, some witnesses (such as C) have corrected the order to correspond to that in the Masoretic text.

123 On the construction $\epsilon\acute{\iota}\ldots o\grave{u}$ ("if...not"), normal in Koine, see Blass-Debrunner, § 428.

124 Gebser: "Certainly, the concept of heartfelt sympathy—love, which is opposed to partiality—is present here in the term 'mercy' ($\acute{\epsilon}\lambda\epsilon o\varsigma$)"; Beyschlag: "The Christian . . . still needs mercy at the Judgment, for he has not complied absolutely with the 'law of freedom' ($\nu\acute{o}\mu o\varsigma$ $\acute{\epsilon}\lambda\epsilon u\theta\epsilon\rho\acute{\iota}\alpha\varsigma$)"; Windisch-Preisker: "In the 'law of freedom' the duty to love has a preeminent place; only if this duty is shirked does judgment remain without mercy."

from mercy back to judgment again; particles combining the two halves of the statement are lacking. There is a slight shift in nuance: ἀνέλεος ("without mercy")[125] is speaking of the mercy of God, ἔλεος ("mercy") is speaking of human mercy.

The first statement is intended to apply the familiar prophetic as well as rabbinic principle: the punishment fits the sin. We are familiar with the application of this principle from Matt 18:21ff; 25:34ff (see also 5:7). But it is also applied in Jewish texts; cf. *Test. Zeb.* 5.3: "Therefore, have compassion in your hearts, for what someone does to his neighbour, that the Lord will also do with him" (ἔχετε οὖν ἔλεος ἐν σπλάγχνοις ὑμῶν, ὅτι εἴ τι ἂν ποιήσῃ τῷ πλησίον αὐτοῦ, οὕτω Κύριος ποιήσει μετʼ αὐτοῦ cf. also 8.1–3) [Trans.]; cf. the story of heavenly judgment on a sinful women in *Test. Abr.* [Rec. B] 10; and the discussion of the subject in *b. Shab.* 151b.

The textual tradition for the second statement in Jas 2:13 reveals that the sense in which it is to be taken has long been a puzzle: For the term "mercy," the Koine witnesses have ἔλεον. Instead of the third person indicative of the verb, some texts have "let it boast against" (κατακαυχάσθω), others, "(you pl.) boast against!" (κατακαυχᾶσθε).[126] The correct sense of the statement has already been captured in the Scholion: "For mercy rescues from punishment those who in purity practice mercy, since at the time of judgment it stands by the royal throne" (ἡ γὰρ ἐλεημοσύνη τοὺς καθαρῶς αὐτὴν ἐργαζομένους ἐξαρπάζει τῆς κολάσεως, ἐν καιρῷ τῆς κρίσεως παρὰ τῷ θρόνῳ ἑστῶσα τῷ βασιλικῷ) [Trans.]. This is the same idea which is expressed also in the paraenetic section in Tobit: "For mercy delivers from death . . . and for all who practice it mercy is an excellent offering in the presence of the Most High" (ἐλεημοσύνη ἐκ θανάτου ῥύεται . . . δῶρον γὰρ ἀγαθὸν ἐστιν ἐλεημοσύνη πᾶσι τοῖς ποιοῦσιν αὐτὴν ἐνώπιον τοῦ ὑψίστου Tob 4:10f); cf. further, Sir 3:30; Dan 4:24. Because of the compact formulation of the saying, the thought in our passage has found a particularly forceful expression.

---

125   This is the spelling which should be read, and not ἀνίλεως or ἀνίλεος, as is found in a number of manuscript witnesses.

126   In the expression "to boast against someone" (κατακαυχᾶσθαί τινος), the genitive τινος is governed by the verbal prefix κατα– which in this case and in 3:14 means "against"; so the verb here and in Rom 11:18 is to be considered analogous to the verbs καταγελᾶν ("to laugh at"), καταψεύδεσθαι ("to lie against"), καταλαλεῖν ("to speak against, slander"; Jas 4:11); see Blass-Debrunner, § 181.

2

14   My brothers and sisters, of what use is it if
someone should claim to have faith and yet
does not have works? Can faith save that one?
15/ If a brother or sister has nothing to wear
and is in lack of daily food, 16/ and one of you
says to them, "May things go well for you;
clothe yourselves warmly and eat your fill,"
without giving them the bodily necessities, of
what use is that? 17/ So also faith alone, if it
does not have works, is barren. 18/ But someone will say, "You have faith and I have
works." Show me your faith-apart-from-
works, and I will show you faith by my works.
19/ You believe that God is one; you do well.
Even the demons believe, and shudder!

20   Do you want to be shown, you braggart, that
faith apart from works is useless? 21/ Was our
father Abraham not justified by works, when
he offered his son Isaac upon the altar?
22/ You (sing.) see that faith assisted his
works, and works perfected his faith. 23/ And
the scripture was fulfilled which says,
"Abraham believed God and it was recorded in
his account as righteousness," and he was
called the "friend of God." 24/ You (pl.) see
that a person is justified by works (also), and
not by faith alone. 25/ And in the same way was
not also Rahab the harlot justified by works
when she received the messengers and sent
them out another way? 26/ For just as the
body without the soul is dead, so also faith
without works is dead.

Analysis

A connection between this treatise and the preceding
one cannot be established. To construe a connection
between the example in 2:15f and the statement in
2:13 is to overlook the fact that 2:13 is isolated to begin
with and that the example in 2:15f is only an illustrative instance and in no way represents the main point of
the section. Instead, the point of the section is expressed
in the introductory rhetorical question in v 14: the
section deals with faith and works and the relationship
between the two. What was said in the Analysis of the
preceding section regarding the thematic significance
of the introductory statements is corroborated here.
Furthermore, just as in the previous treatise, also here
the depiction of an individual case (vv 15, 16) follows

the introduction. The "stylized" character of this
depiction excludes the question of when and where
these things took place. There is even less doubt about
this character here than in 2:2–4. Yet there is also a
difference between these two passages: Jas does not
introduce here as he did there an example of the attitude which he is reproving. Instead he refers to another
type of specific instance for comparison.[1] In v 17, the
conclusion is drawn from this comparison and thus the
first train of thought in this section is rounded off.

If anywhere, it is in the second train of thought which
commences in v 18 that the stylistic consideration must
be the first thing to come to the fore. For here Jas employs the form of fictitious discussion which is common
in diatribe. He himself introduces the interlocutor, he

---

1   Cf. below in the Interpretation and also above in the
Excursus on 2:2.

himself answers him. Characteristic of the difficulty of the passage is the fact that the point at which the objection of the opponent ends and the answer of the author begins can be disputed. Obviously, arguments which result from the analysis of the content must provide the final decision. But first of all the boundaries within which this final decision is to be made must be determined upon stylistic grounds. In this case, the result is the following:

1. The phrase "But someone will say" (ἀλλ' ἐρεῖ τις) is a formula which conforms to the dialogic style of diatribe,[2] and it serves to introduce the "mute mask" (κωφὸν πρόσωπον)[3] of an unnamed opponent. That Jas himself is concealed behind this "someone"[4] is ruled out on stylistic grounds, since a fictitious introduction of the author himself would be suitable only in a more elaborate scene. But stylistic considerations also prohibit the other hypothesis, viz., that the opponent introduced in v 18 is only opposing the other "someone" in v 14; the person in v 18 would in this case be an ally of Jas, either a Christian ally[5] or a non–Christian, who would be in agreement with him.[6] Yet no reader could have supposed that someone other than an opponent of Jas is introduced by the formula "but someone will say." Moreover, the ally hypothesis, with its reference to v 14, totally fails to recognize the fact that the "someone" in v 14 is introduced without himself saying anything. Therefore he is not animated nearly enough for the other "someone" in v 18 to be introduced in order to oppose him. What is involved is not a dramatic, lively scene at all, but rather a stylistic schema which has long ago lost its original, dramatic power of illusion. We must at least try out *the* understanding of this schema which would be evident as a matter-of-course to every reader of that time (as can easily be demonstrated from Epictetus)—i.e., that the formula "but someone will say"[7] introduces the objection of an opponent.

2. The interlocutor can champion the watchword of a specific faction, he can represent the common point of view, or finally he can dish up an objection which is not particularly weighty but serves only to provide an opportunity for the author to corroborate further his own idea. The latter would be the case if the author is not very interested in a realistic scene which also does justice to his opponent, but interested only in an objection contrived in opposition to the correct view in order that the latter might shine all the more brilliantly.[8] Now the scene in James 2:18ff is not played out vividly and realistically at all. (Proof of this is the uncertainty upon the part of exegetes as to the identity and intention of the interlocutor). Therefore, we must deal with at least the possibility that even *the objection in v 18 constitutes only the sophism of an imaginary opponent*, and not an

2 Cf. Rom 9:19; 11:19; 1 Cor 15:35; Norden, *Kunstprosa*, vol. 1, pp. 129ff; vol. 2, pp. 556f; Hirzel, *Dialog*, 369ff (Hirzel speaks of the "exhaustion" and "death throes of the dialogic spirit"); Bultmann, *Stil*, 10ff. I mention with gratitude that on this section I was able to obtain the counsel of Eduard Norden, who provided substantial assistance for my interpretation although it did not agree with his own.

3 Cf. Philo, *Flacc.* 20: "as a mute mask upon a stage" (κωφὸν ὡς ἐπὶ σκηνῆς προσωπεῖον); Plut., *An resp. ger. sit* 15: "whereas the former, like a mute guardsman on the stage, was the mere name and figure of a king, exposed to the wanton insults of those who happened to have the real power" (ὁ δ' ὥσπερ ἐπὶ σκηνῆς δορυφόρημα κωφὸν ἦν ὄνομα βασιλέως καὶ πρόσωπον ὑπὸ τῶν ἀεὶ κρατούντων παροινούμενον). I am indebted to Hermann Diels for the reference to these passages.

4 Schwarz, "Jak. 2, 14–26," 715; G. Karo, "Versuch über Jac. 2, 18," *PrM* 4 (1900): 159f; Albert Köhler, *Glaube und Werke im Jakobusbrief*, Beilage zum Jahres-berichte des Gymnasiums zu Zittau, Easter 1913 (Zittau: Menzel, 1913), 7.

5 This is the most frequent interpretation, which is advocated (with certain variations) by Gebser, Ewald, Burger, Beyschlag, Mayor, Belser, and by Grafe, *Stellung und Bedeutung*, 34n; J. Böhmer, "Der Glaube im Jakobusbriefe," *NKZ* 9 (1898): 251–6.

6 Zahn, *Introduction*, section 4, n. 4, considers the interlocutor to be a Jew (similarly, Hofmann, *ad loc.*); Erich Haupt, review of David Erdmann, *Der Brief des Jakobus*, and of W. Beyschlag, *Kritisch-exegetisches Handbuch über den Brief des Jakobus*, in *ThStKr* 56 (1883): 187, considers him to be a moralist; Wilhelm Weiffenbach, *Exegetisch–theologische Studie über Jak 2, 14-26* (Giessen: Ricker, 1871), 15ff, takes this to be the appearance of a third person, but one who is a mediator, and he takes "you" (σύ) as a reference to some second person who is the opponent of Jas.

7 The formula "but someone will say" (ἀλλ' ἐρεῖ τις) is found also in 1 Cor 15:35. It is most natural to read Jas 2:18 in the same way. To be sure, the punctuation preferred by Gebser and others cannot be

objection to be taken seriously.

3. Epictetus delivered his diatribes in lectures. He could indicate by inflection and gesture where the speech of the opponent ended and where his own statements commenced once again. Jas could use neither this aid nor the modern device of quotation marks. We would expect that he might indicate in some other way which were his own words, and in fact he does so quite clearly in v 20: the person who is addressed there is characterized by the invective which is used against him[9]—he is therefore the interlocutor. *Hence his speech, which commences in v 18, must end somewhere before v 20.* Nothing more can be proven upon stylistic grounds. Thus the response by the author to the objection begins either in v 18b or v 19 or not until v 20.

To this is added the Abraham example in vv 21–23. And in v 24 the author drops the dialogue with the "mute mask." The address is no longer "you (sing.) see," but rather "you (pl.) see."[10] The addresses to whom the outcome of the discussion of the Abraham example is presented are again the readers. Then the example of Rahab is brought before them in v 25. To this is added in v 26 the result of the entire discussion. But the Abraham and Rahab examples are doubtlessly understood as parallel (see "likewise" [ὁμοίως] in 2:25). Nevertheless, as far as form is concerned, the first example is addressed to the "braggart" (ἄνθρωπος

κενός) and the second to the readers, who had already become the addressees again in v 24.

So we see clearly how little the author cares about the realistic animation of the dialogue scene. The introduction of the interlocutor is much more a matter of rhetorical art than dramatic art—hence, the possibility which was mentioned above under 2. is confirmed. As was just shown, what is involved here is a well–worn technique which had already become routine, and whose devices must have been familiar to the readers. But then there is no justification for seeing in the "someone" in v 18 anyone other than the person into whose mouth such interlocutions were ordinarily placed—an opponent. Thus the hypothesis which was proposed under 1. is also confirmed.

Interpretation

■ **14** The rhetorical question, reminiscent of similar formulae in the diatribes of Epictetus,[11] states the theme.[12] The following brief treatise is directed against those people who say that they have faith but who in their conduct perform no works. From the next sentence we can add, "no works which would be able to save them." Jas does not say what is intended by the word "faith." Hence, he cannot possibly be concerned about a theologically refined concept of faith. There is no special doctrine presupposed here, but rather the com-

---

ruled out entirely: " 'But,' someone will say, 'you have faith.' "

8   Cf. Epict., *Diss.* 1.4.13f: It is not a realistic depiction but rather a conscious contrivance when Epictetus introduces an athlete who answers the request, "Show me your shoulders" (δεῖξόν μοι τοὺς ὤμους), by saying, "Look at my jumping–weights" (ἴδε μου τοὺς ἁλτῆρας). And it is also a contrivance that the bad philosopher responds to the request, "Show me your progress" (δεῖξόν σου τὴν προκοπήν), by saying, "Take the treatise *Upon Choice* [lit. *Upon 'Onward Movement'*] and see how I have mastered it" (λάβε τὴν περὶ ὁρμῆς σύνταξιν καὶ γνῶθι πῶς αὐτὴν ἀνέγνωκα). But the goal of this contrivance is to expose the pitiful excuses given by people who merely read philosophical books and do not live according to them, and to impress upon them the demand of Epictetus, "It is not that [i.e., the reading] I am looking into, you slave, but how you act in your choices and refusals, your desires and aversions . . ." (ἀνδράποδον, οὐ τοῦτο ζητῶ, ἀλλὰ πῶς ὁρμᾷς καὶ ἀφορμᾷς, πῶς ὀρέγῃ καὶ ἐκκλίνεις . . .).

9   On the invective, cf. Bultmann, *Stil*, 14, 60f, and 1 Cor 15:36. The peculiar use of "do you want" ([οὐ] θέλεις) also appears to be a part of the style; cf. Epict., *Diss.* 4.6.18, and the index in the edition by Heinrich Schenkl, *Epicteti dissertationes ab Arriano digestae* (Leipzig: Teubner, 1916), *s.v.* (B).

10 For this reason it is impossible that the speech of the interlocutor comes to an end only with v 23 (Gebser) for then there would be no response from the author at all.

11 The reading τί ὄφελος in B C* in Jas 2:14, 16 could have originated by a jump from τι to το. On the other hand, this could be the original text and the τό could be an emendation.

12 See above, the Analysis of 2:1–13.

mon meaning of the word "faith." It is the same meaning of the word as in 2:1, viz., the Christian faith to which every baptized convert belongs. This sense is also indicated by the much discussed "should claim" ($\lambda\acute{\epsilon}\gamma\eta$) in v 14. For it is not without significance that Jas writes, "if someone should *claim* to have faith," and not, "if someone *has* faith" ($\dot{\epsilon}\grave{\alpha}\nu$ $\pi\acute{\iota}\sigma\tau\iota\nu$ $\tau\iota\varsigma$ $\check{\epsilon}\chi\eta$). A person whose faith is not expressed in deeds can show it only through words. For this reason the author probably avoided the expression "if someone has faith." On the other hand, one cannot read into the words "should claim" what was inferred by earlier commentators from the lack of the article before "faith" ($\pi\acute{\iota}\sigma\tau\iota\nu$)— viz., that what is meant here is a false faith, one which is only alleged. Jas certainly never sets the correct faith over against such an alleged faith. How *serious* Jas presupposes this faith to be—i.e., whether with "should claim" he has in mind only profession in the course of conversation, or whether he is thinking of worship and prayer—is an idle question. Here again one must not confuse paraenetic example with historical testimony! In any event, for Jas what counts is that faith which does not declare itself in works cannot save anyone. This is the sense of the second question, in v 14b. Here Jas uses the article before "faith" ($\acute{\eta}$ $\pi\acute{\iota}\sigma\tau\iota\varsigma$), but this is not to be read "*this* faith," as many interpreters from Bede to Mayor have argued. Jas is not speaking of any particular brand of faith (see above). The only attributive which is expressed in $\acute{\eta}$ $\pi\acute{\iota}\sigma\tau\iota\varsigma$ is this: faith, which "has" no works.[13] But this is still the Christian faith and not an "alleged, false faith."

And just as in the word "faith," so also in the term "save" one must forget all theological determinations and leave aside all the various answers to the questions "From what?" and "By what means?" That Christian faith saves[14] is the common Christian conviction, and since early Christianity is an eschatological religion this conviction relates chiefly to the final judgment. Hence, this is the obvious meaning here also, since "is able" ($\delta\acute{\upsilon}\nu\alpha\tau\alpha\iota$) points to the future rather than to the past: Is faith able to save him, once that time comes? The thought is certainly that faith alone is *not* able to save him. Yet this does not say that works alone can save him. The verse speaks only of works which those who have faith perform, for "and yet he does not have works" ($\check{\epsilon}\rho\gamma\alpha$ $\delta\grave{\epsilon}$ $\mu\grave{\eta}$ $\check{\epsilon}\chi\eta$) is said explicitly of the Christian who is reproved here. Therefore, the author considers it to be only natural that a man who professes (Christian) faith also "has works."

■ **15, 16** Here a particular case is described. The description begins so abruptly[15] that at first one might think that this is a simple example of faith without works. But this notion would be incorrect.[16] For in addition to the fact that the wish "go in peace" is not an expression of faith but rather of a certain friendly attitude, v 17 also clearly demonstrates what Jas means: he does not wish to portray faith without works, but rather to compare faith without works to an example of goodwill without works. The common point to which both relate is "barrenness": Just as well–wishing without active aid is in vain, so faith without works is in vain. To be sure, it is probably no accident that in this "little parable"[17] an instance of the neglect of the poor is related—i.e., an instance from the area in which Jas would especially like to see "works" done by Christians. Nevertheless, this individual case is not an example but a comparison.

Already with an example[18] it is true that the intention is not to testify to something which has actually happened but only to cite a possibility. How much more

13   *ff*: "can *faith alone* save him?" (numquid potest fides eum sola salvare).

14   On the verb "to save" ($\sigma\acute{\omega}\zeta\epsilon\iota\nu$), cf. Wilhelm Wagner, "Über $\sigma\acute{\omega}\zeta\epsilon\iota\nu$ und seine Derivata im Neuen Testament," *ZNW* 6 (1905): 205–35, and, on the other hand, the Excursus on 2 Tim 1:10 in Dibelius–Conzelmann, *The Pastoral Epistles*.

15   This opinion would still hold good even if one were to read "now if" ($\dot{\epsilon}\acute{\alpha}\nu$ $\delta\acute{\epsilon}$) as in A C and the Koine witnesses. "Now" ($\delta\acute{\epsilon}$) would still be only a very loose connective, not an introduction of the polemic against an imaginary opponent—who does not ap-

pear on the battlefield until v 18. But, this $\delta\acute{\epsilon}$ is probably to be viewed as the attempt (of a later redactor) to connect v 15 to v 14.

16   It is advocated by Robert Kübel, *Über das Verhältnis von Glauben und Werken bei Jakobus* (Tübingen: Fues, 1880), 36; cf. against this, Schwarz, "Jak. 2, 14–26," 709.

17   As it is characterized by Ropes.

18   Cf. the Excursus on 2:2!

19   This is the sense of "naked" ($\gamma\upsilon\mu\nu\acute{o}\varsigma$) here. For the common occurrence of this meaning in the vernacular, cf. *P. Magd.* 6.7; *P. Fay.* 12.20; *BGU* 111,

is this the case with a comparison! Admittedly, that such a thing might actually happen is not impossible, but we can observe that the author by no means upbraids the offenders angrily. Therefore, such a case has hardly been reported to him as having actually happened, much less as having been a common occurrence. No interpreter is justified in characterizing the community which Jas addresses as corrupt merely because the author contrives here a case of the lack of a readiness to give help.

That this is in fact a contrived instance is shown also by an examination of the details. "A brother or sister" (therefore, no specific instance is referred to) has nothing to wear[19] and nothing to eat. The two great concerns of life (see Matt 6:25ff)[20] afflict them. Everything is as typical as possible, even the expression "lacking food for the day."[21] What the well-meaning, but unhelpful well-wisher says is also typical: "Go in peace" (ὑπάγετε ἐν εἰρήνῃ). This is a Jewish word of farewell[22] which means something like "may it go well with you." The following words clearly reveal themselves to be stylized. Spoken in a real situation they would be mockery; but with the stylized phrases Jas is able to

show precisely how useless a merely friendly attitude is in such a circumstance if there is no action.[23] θερμαίνειν is a reference to clothing (as in Hag 1:6 and Job 31:20) and so the two verbs would mean, "clothe yourself warmly and eat your fill." In spite of the fact that it occurs only here in the New Testament, the word "necessary" (ἐπιτήδειος) is also a common term for designating bodily nourishment and bodily necessities.[24]

■ **17** This verse has already been discussed with regard to its significance for the preceding verses. It completes the comparison; in this verse the point of the metaphor, to be applied to the theme faith without works, is expressed by the term "barren, unfruitful" (νεκρά).[25] The only thing which is ambiguous is the expression καθ᾽ ἑαυτήν. It can be translated "by itself, alone,"[26] or "in itself, in reference to itself, inwardly."[27] The first translation could be rejected on the grounds that it is tautological and the second on the grounds that it is superfluous. The parallels in the LXX (Gen 30:40; 43:32; 2 Macc 13:13) where καθ᾽ ἑαυτόν means "apart, separate" tend to support the first meaning (as does also Acts 28:16 [and Rom 14:22?]), but without

---

846.9; perhaps also *P. Oxy.* IV, 839.

20   The third great vital concern of the present—the concern for shelter—is absent both in the words of Jesus and here in Jas. In the Gospel this can be explained from the economic circumstances of Galilee. But no inference regarding the environment of Jas can be drawn from our passage, since Jas certainly does not intend to enumerate every kind of necessity.

21   Cf. Dion. Hal., *Ant. Roma.* 8.41.5: "He went out of the house alone, oh women, without a servant, without means, and without even taking from his stores (wretched man) food for the day" (ἀπῆλθεν ἐκ τῆς οἰκίας μόνος, ὦ γυναῖκες, ἄδουλος, ἄπορος, οὐδὲ τὴν ἐφήμερον ὁ δύστηνος ἐκ τῶν ἑαυτοῦ χρημάτων τροφὴν ἐπαγόμενος) [Loeb modified]; Heliodorus, *Aethiopica* 6.10: "In this way we will less likely fall victim to the plots of those whom we encounter . . . and we will more easily have plenty of the necessary daily food" (οὕτω γὰρ ἧττόν τε ἐπιβουλευσόμεθα πρὸς τῶν ἐντυγχανόντων . . . τῆς τε καθ᾽ ἡμέραν ἀναγκαίου τροφῆς ῥᾷον εὐπορήσομεν) [Trans.]; Ael. Arist., *De paraphthegmate* (*Or.* 28) 139: "begging and in lack of food for the day" (ἂν δ᾽ αὐτὸς προσαιτῶν καὶ τῆς ἐφημέρου τροφῆς ἀπορῶν) [Trans.].

22   See Judg. 18:6; 1 Sam 1:17; 20:42; 29:7; 2 Sam 15:9; Jdth 8:35; *Jub.* 18.16; Mk 5:34; Acts 16:36.

23   So it makes no difference in this regard whether the

imperatives here are understood as passive or as middle.

24   Cf., e.g., the indices in Wilhelm Dittenberger, *Sylloge inscriptionum Graecarum* (Hildesheim: Olms, ⁴1960) and *idem, Orientis Graeci inscriptiones selectae* (Hildesheim: Olms, reprint 1960). Characteristic is Ditt., *Or.* 1, 200.23f (4th cent. A.D., but non–Christian): "providing them with all the necessities and clothing them" (δωρησάμενοι αὐτοῖς πάντα τὰ ἐπιτήδ[ε]ια κ[αὶ] ἀμφιάσαντες αὐτούς) [Trans.]. Cf. also *P. Hibeh* I, 110.10: "To Philocles, for the necessities" (Φιλοκλεῖ εἰς τὰ ἐπιτήδ[ε]ια, likewise, *P. Lille* I, 25.35) [Trans.]; 1 Macc 14:34: "whatever was necessary for their restoration" (καὶ ὅσα ἐπιτήδεια πρὸς τῇ τούτων ἐπανορθώσει); *P. Fay.* 22.24: "providing the necessities" (τὰ ἐπιτήδεια παρέχων see also 22.27) [Trans.].

25   νεκρός also occurs in Epict., *Diss.* 3.16.7 and 3.23.28 with the meaning "unfruitful."

26   So *ff*: "so also faith, if it does not have works, is dead *by itself*" (sic et fides, si non habeat opera, mortua est sola) [Trans.]; Gebser; Ernst Kühl, *Die Stellung des Jakobusbriefes zum alttestamentlichen Gesetz und zur Paulinischen Rechtfertigungslehre* (Königsberg i. Pr.: Koch, 1905), 28; Köhler, *Glaube und Werke*, 11.

27   Vulg: "in itself" (in semetipsa); Beyschlag; von Soden; Mayor; Belser; Ropes.

allowing complete certainty on this point.

■ **18** I will now attempt an interpretation of the problematic v 18, one of the most difficult New Testament passages in general. The literary Analysis of this whole section has already prepared us with stylistic arguments. I have shown in the Analysis that the words "but someone will say" (ἀλλ' ἐρεῖ τις) introduce in any event the objection of an opponent, and that the first investigation incumbent upon the interpreter is to determine how far the opponent's objection extends and where the author's words begin again. Stylistic criteria can prove only that Jas is obviously speaking again in v 20, since the "braggart" (κενὸς ἄνθρωπος) is the interlocutor.[28]

From this point of certainty we work backwards. In v 20, the assumption that faith without works can accomplish something, or (as v 14 expresses it) can "save," is contested. But obviously it is this belief which v 19 wishes to carry out *ad absurdum*. If Christianity is to be nothing more than what the demons also have, this faith is in bad shape. Thus the author must already be speaking again in v 19; he wants to show how unchristian "faith without works" appears. Accordingly,

it could be conjectured that v 19 is the answer to the demand in v 18b, "Show me your faith without works," and in this case v 18b would be the demand of the opponent. However, as is shown by the continuation of the passage, this demand is probably intended ironically: You will not be able to show faith without works; at least, you will not be able to show that it is of any value. And v 19 is conveyed with the same attitude— i.e., it is an ironic demonstration of faith without works, with the conclusion that this faith is worthless. *Thus the same person is speaking in v 18b as in v 19*, namely (as has been demonstrated already from v 19), the author. It is he who states the ironic demand, "show me your faith without works." And then, in the certainty that the person whom he is addressing will not be able to comply with the demand, it is the author himself who undertakes the demonstration in v 19.[29]

Therefore, only v 18a remains as an objection made by the interlocutor. In other words, if one accepts the common punctuation which is suggested by the style and sentence structure, the words which are spoken by the interlocutor are, "You have faith and I have works" (σὺ πίστιν ἔχεις κἀγὼ ἔργα ἔχω).[30] It is at this point that

---

28 Cf. above in the Analysis.

29 There are also examples of this kind of ironic demand in the diatribes of Epictetus. In *Diss.* 1.27.9 he desires to show that death cannot be escaped, and he says, "And where can I go to escape death? Show me the country, show me the people to whom I may go, upon whom death does not come; show me a magic charm against it. If I have none [Thus, nothing like this can be found], what do you wish me to do?" (καὶ ποῦ φύγω τὸν θάνατον; μηνύσατέ μοι τὴν χώραν, μηνύσατε ἀνθρώπους, εἰς οὓς ἀπέλθω, εἰς οὓς οὐ παραβάλλει, μηνύσατε ἐπαοιδήν· εἰ μὴ ἔχω, τί με θέλετε ποιεῖν;). In *Diss.* 2.11.12, Epictetus refers to the fact that everyone is of the opinion that his own preconceptions fit the data, and Epictetus asks, "Can you, then, show me anything higher than your own opinion which will make it possible for us to apply our preconceptions better?" (ἔχεις οὖν δεῖξαί τι ἡμῖν πρὸς τὸ αὐτὰς ἐφαρμόζειν ἄμεινον ἀνωτέρω τοῦ δοκεῖν σοι). But then without break he continues this questioning with an argument *ad absurdum*: The madman also *thinks* that what he does is correct. *Diss.* 3.22.99 is still clearer. There Epictetus asks the person who gives an impertinent admonition (when he himself does not live in accordance with it), "Why, who are you? Are you the bull of the herd, or the queen bee of the hive? Show me the tokens of your leadership"

(τίς γὰρ εἶ; ὁ ταῦρος εἶ ἢ ἡ βασιλίσσα τῶν μελισσῶν; δεῖξόν μοι τὰ σύμβολα τῆς ἡγεμονίας). Naturally the addressee cannot do so. Epictetus continues, "But if you are a drone" (εἰ δὲ κηφὴν εἶ)—i.e., this person *is* in fact only a drone. The case is somewhat different with *Diss.* 3.26.18. Here Epictetus again makes an ironic demand that an opponent show him what makes men happy. But this time the opponent does manage to get out an answer, "See, I do show you" (ἰδοὺ δεικνύω), although his demonstration is, to be sure, quite pitiful: "I will analyze syllogisms for you" (ἀναλύσω σοι συλλογισμούς)—i.e., the truth is, he cannot show it. Cf. also the example above in n. 8.

Irony is used in another way by the Christian apologist Theophilus, *Ad Autol.* 1.2: "But if you say, 'Show me your God,' I might respond to you, 'Show me your Human Being and I will show you my God'" (ἀλλὰ καὶ ἐὰν φῇς, δεῖξόν μοι τὸν θεόν σου, κἀγώ σοι εἴποιμι ἄν, δεῖξόν μοι τὸν ἄνθρωπόν σου κἀγώ σοι δείξω τὸν θεόν μου) [Trans.]. Naturally, the passage is not evidence for the dependence of Theophilus upon Jas, but only for the former's use of the diatribe style. A further example is in Epict., *Diss.* 1.11.5: The partner in the conversation thinks that his desperate flight from the sick bed of his daughter was done "in accordance with nature" (φυσικῶς). Epictetus: "'But really, you must first convince me of

we encounter the actual difficulty of the passage: *This protest, in which the speaker ascribes works to himself and faith to another, does not seem to come at all from one who is an opponent of our author.* Indeed, the speaker seems to appeal precisely to his works! This difficulty is the point of departure for the "ally hypothesis." But since this hypothesis seems unacceptable on stylistic grounds, as shown in the Analysis, we must seek other solutions to the puzzle. Three possible solutions present themselves: 1) One could try to make sense out of the wording while operating under the presuppositions which have already been stated; 2) one could try another punctuation; 3) one could assume that there has been a corruption of the text, and could seek to restore the original text.

1) What evokes surprise in the present wording is that after "You have faith, etc." the answer is, "Show me your faith." This can only be understood if one reads further into the address and rejoinder. The opponent says, "You have faith and I have works"; therefore, the first part obviously implies, "You have faith *without* works." To this the author answers, "First of all show me this 'faith without works' which you assert to be a possibility."[31] In this context the expression "your (σου) faith" can only be understood in this way, as the assertion of ("this faith of yours"), not the possession of, faith without works. Obviously the meaning is that one cannot easily demonstrate the existence of such

a faith at all.[32] That fits with the implication of the words "if he should *claim* (λέγῃ) in v 14 (see above). Next the author says, "I will show you faith from my works." Only in this way can faith be manifested; thus the opponent must have contested that very point. Therefore—to conclude from what can be seen in v 18b—, the main point of the opponent in v 18a is not the *distribution* of faith and works to "you" and "me," but rather the *total separation* of faith and works in general.

Perhaps a stylistic argument can lend even more probability to this interpretation. The contrast in v 18b is not between "your faith" and "my faith" at all, but between "your (faith) without works" and "my works." The former contrast might be expected if the text were supposed to say that the one has the correct faith and the other has a false faith, but this is not the intended meaning. Jas is not making a distinction between concepts of faith at all;[33] what he contests is the total separation of faith and works. For this reason, the pronoun in v 18b stands with "faith" (πίστις) the first time and with "works" (ἔργα) the second time, and

---

this, that you *were* acting naturally,' said he, 'and then I will convince you that whatever is done in accordance with nature is rightly done'" (ἀλλὰ μὴν τοῦτό με πεῖσον, ἔφη, σύ, διότι φυσικῶς, καὶ ἐγώ σε πείσω, ὅτι πᾶν τὸ κατὰ φύσιν γινόμενον ὀρθῶς γίνεται); the demand is repeated in *Diss.* 1.11.8: "*show me, therefore, how your conduct is in accordance with nature*" (δεῖξον οὖν μοι σύ, πῶς κατὰ φύσιν ἐστίν). Here it is especially interesting that after the demand to produce evidence which, in fact, cannot be produced, there follows immediately the announcement of the thing which the speaker (Epictetus) himself intends to prove, just as in Jas 2:18b. And this is done even though the partner then begins to speak again in order to justify his actions, an opportunity which is not granted the opponent by the author in Jas 2:19. On the ironic imperative, cf. also Bultmann, *Stil*, 32f.

30   On the other renderings of this objection which involve different punctuation, see below.

31   The Koine reading "*from* works" (ἐκ τῶν ἔργων) could only be more ironic than the reading "apart

from, without" (χωρίς). But the correctional emendations in the Koine text which are discussed below in n. 34 probably demonstrate that this also is a correctional emendation (or an assimilation to ἐκ τῶν ἔργων in the following clause).

32   See below on v 19.

33   See above on v 14.

what results is a stylistically attractive criss–cross pattern:[34]

your faith	apart from works
from *my* works	faith
τὴν πίστιν σου	χωρὶς τῶν ἔργων
ἐκ τῶν ἔργων μου	τὴν πίστιν

The distribution to "you" and "me" is an incidental matter.[35] Jas treats the interlocutor as if he had said, "The one has faith, the other has works."[36] "Quite wrong," replies Jas, "for works cannot be inferred from faith, but faith can be inferred from works."

But whom must Jas have in mind when he introduces so sophistic an opponent? It has been shown in the Analysis[37] that in the case of such an objection introduced for a literary purpose it frequently is not a matter of an allusion to an actual opponent at all, but a mere contrivance. The possibility that this is the case here becomes a probability if one considers what opinion or what party could possibly be represented by an inter-

locutor who says to Jas, "You have faith and I have works." This is not supposed to be a quotation of party slogans, for to ascribe the slogan "faith" (πίστις) to our author would be absurd. The sentence, "You have faith, etc.," must be merely a hypothetical statement, and indeed, one which is contrary to fact.

Therefore, what the interlocution is supposed to represent is neither Judaism, nor moralism,[38] nor any other known historical viewpoint. Instead it is simply a *sophistic separation of faith and works.* Nor does the author combat this because it is being advocated as a doctrine in his community, but *because he wants to develop his own opinion in contrast to this.* It is for this reason that the objection in v 18a is delivered in such a brief, subtle, and as a result, enigmatic manner. It is also for this reason that there is so little debate with the interlocutor.[39]

2) The second of the possibilities which were mentioned involves a different distribution of the address

---

34 The Koine readings which have σου between ἔργων and κἀγώ (also C Ψ 1175), and μου after πίστιν (also P⁷⁴ A Ψ) destroy this criss-cross pattern. These readings obviously originate from the notion that the passage is dealing chiefly with the distribution of faith and works to "me" and "you".

35 Ropes draws attention to a passage in Teles, pp. 5f Hense (2nd edition), in which "you" and "I" are contrasted in a similar way. Teles, quoting a teaching of Bion, urges that everyone must play the role which Fate has assigned to him: "If you are the second speaker, do not be envious of the role of the protagonist, lest by doing so you commit some blunder" (μὴ βούλου δευτερολόγος ὢν τὸ πρωτολόγου πρόσωπον. εἰ δὲ μή, ἀναρμοστόν τι ποιήσεις). Hence, the "second speaker" is addressed here. But Teles then continues with "you" and "I," and now "I" seems to be the second-ranking person who was just admonished: " 'You are a ruler, I am a subject,' he [Bion] says. 'You rule over many, while I, as a tutor, am in charge of only this one; and you grow wealthy and give generously, while I receive from you with confidence and courage, without fawning or degrading myself or complaining' " (σὺ μὲν ἄρχεις καλῶς, ἐγὼ δὲ ἄρχομαι, φησί, καὶ σὺ μὲν πολλῶν ἐγὼ δὲ ἑνὸς τουτουΐ παιδαγωγὸς γενόμενος, καὶ σὺ μὲν εὔπορος γενόμενος δίδως ἐλευθερίως, ἐγὼ δὲ λαμβάνω εὐθαρσῶς παρὰ σοῦ οὐχ ὑποπίπτων οὐδὲ ἀγεννίζων οὐδὲ μεμψιμοιρῶν) [Trans.]. This distribution of "you" and "I" is not the one which is expected from what precedes, yet—precisely as in Jas—it must be inferred from the content. The explanation for this is similar

to the explanation for what appears in Jas, viz., that the author is not concerned about exact identification of the "you" and "I."

36 The beginnings of this interpretation are to be seen in Erasmus, *ad loc.* He argues that there are two interlocutors who one-sidedly champion their slogans: one, "faith," the other, "works." Jas combats both. Also Alb. Klöpper, "Die Erörterung des Verhältnisses von Glauben und Werken im Jakobusbriefe (cap. 2, 14–26)," *ZWTh* 28 (1885): 291ff, attempts to deal with the traditional text under the assumption that the interlocutor is an opponent. But in his approach, the opposition of "you" and "I" plays too large a role (much the same is true with regard to the article of Paul Mehlhorn, "Noch ein Erklärungsversuch zu Jac. 2, 18," *PrM* 4 [1900]: 192–4).

My interpretation is most closely in agreement with those of David Julius Pott, in J. B. Koppe, *Novum Testamentum Graece perpetua annotatione illustratum* 9, 1: *Epistula Jacobi* (Göttingen: Dieterich, ³1816); Hermann Boumann, *Commentarius perpetuus in Jacobi epistulam* (Utrecht: Kemink, 1865); and James Hardy Ropes, " 'Thou Hast Faith and I Have Works' (James ii.18)," *Expositor*, ser. 7, vol. 5 (1908): 547–56. They also assume that "James uses 'you and I' (συ καγω) to mean 'the one and the other' (αλλος και αλλος)" [Pott]. But I would prefer not to see in the two speakers "two representatives of different types of religion" (Ropes, in his commentary, *ad loc.*). Instead, I would rather view v 18a as merely a sophistic objection which Jas contrives in order to develop his own argument.

and rejoinder. For example, the address of the opponent could be limited to the words σὺ πίστιν ἔχεις and construed as a question: "Do you have faith?" Having been asked this, the author might first of all have added, parenthetically as it were, "*And* I have works," in order to reply then with, "Show me your faith, etc."[40] But if the meaning "Do you have any faith?" for the formulation σὺ πίστιν ἔχεις (without μή used as an interrogative particle) is strange to begin with, then the introduction of the author's response with "and I" (κἀγώ) certainly becomes very improbable.[41] One can expect a clearer indication of where the opponent ceases and Jas begins again.[42] However, according to the view set forth here, the first occurrence of the expression "and I" (κἀγώ) in v 18 would introduce the rejoinder of the author and the second "and I" would continue it. At least this one dissimilarity would be eliminated if "and I" were interpreted both times as an introduction to the author's answer: "Someone will say, 'Do you have faith?' and I (answer), 'I have works.' (He): 'Show me, etc.' And I (answer again) 'I will show you faith from my works.'" Yet the principal objection to this interpretation is the style of the sentence. The mere "and I" does not express the contrast which this interpretation assumes, and above all, "Show me, etc." is not the beginning of the second speech of the opponent.

But the interpretations which have just been mentioned also pose a difficulty with respect to the content. After the words of the author in vv 14–17, is the opponent supposed to have nothing more to say to him than, "Do you have faith?"[43] And above all, is the opponent supposed to demand that the author, who just spoke of the invalidity of mere faith, display this "mere" faith "apart from works" (χωρὶς τῶν ἔργων)? On the other hand, the expressions of the opponent according to this second interpretation would not be sophistic enough for a sophism such as that which could be assumed under number 1).

Remaining to be mentioned is the interpretation advocated by Bernhard Weiss,[44] who thinks that although the clause, "You have faith and I have works," is structured as a direct address, it is intended as an indirect address: "But, someone might say, you (the opponent of Jas) have faith and I (Jas) have (only) works." Yet this peculiar mixture of direct and indirect address is much too improbable. The question of whether in this interpretation the content of the verse would fit the context will be discussed under number 3).

3) The possibility of a textual corruption in such an unusually obscure passage as this demands substantially more serious consideration than would otherwise be the case. Because of the relatively meager textual tradition, there is always the possibility that readings have been totally lost and that the difficulty of the traditional text here simply demands an emendation, as with Jas 3:6.

The simplest emendation is that proposed again around the turn of the century by Otto Pfleiderer.[45] Pfleiderer reverses the position of the words "faith" (πίστιν) and "works" (ἔργα) in the objection in v 18a. This form of the statement is presupposed also in *ff*: "you have works, I have faith" (tu operam [opera]

---

37   See above in the Analysis, under number 2.

38   Cf. above, n. 6.

39   Cf. above in the Analysis.

40   So von Soden; similarly, Eugène Ménégoz, "Étude comparative de l'enseignement de saint Paul et de saint Jacques sur la justification par la foi," *Études de théologie et d'histoire* (Paris: Fischbacher, 1901), 126, n. 1.

41   Neither can it be said that "and I have works" (κἀγὼ ἔργα ἔχω) is only a continuation, as it were, of the sentence, "But someone will say" (ἀλλ' ἐρεῖ τις), and that the two are separated by the intervening quotation. The words "but someone will say" are not the author's speech in the same sense as the words "and I have works" are supposed to be according to the view mentioned under number 2). "But someone will say" is instead a literary formula;

it can only be an introduction and it cannot be continued.

42   Cf. what is said under number 3. in the Analysis.

43   Otto Kuttner, "Einzelne Bemerkungen über das Verhältnis von Jac. ii zu Röm. xii–xiv," *ZWTh* 31 (1888): 36–40, wishes to meet this objection with the hypothesis that Jas has taken over these words from Rom 14:22. But in order to construe this hypothesis he must make an emendation in the Pauline passage as well.

44   B. Weiss, *NT Handausgabe, ad loc;* similarly, Kühl, *Stellung,* 29ff, although Kühl allows the introduction of an impartial third person.

45   Pfleiderer, *Primitive Christianity,* vol. 4, p. 304, n. 1.

habes, ego fidem habeo). Then the reply of the author has the appearance of a defense against an opinion which is held in earnest and is to be taken seriously. This is the principal difference between this solution and the one first mentioned.[46] The only question is whether this sincerely held opinion in its present form would suit the context here. After the categorical statement of the author, "Faith, if it does not have works, is barren, etc.," could the opponent actually boast of his faith (κἀγὼ πίστιν ἔχω as Pfleiderer reads it), without saying anything about his works? This difficulty is taken into account by the proposal of Spitta,[47] who conjectures that the actual objection which originally followed "but someone will say" has been omitted. What we now read at this point ("You have faith and I have works") is already the reply of the author, who is taking up the objection of the opponent. Then this objection must have read something like this: "You have only works, but I have faith. Where is your faith?" *If one rejects the solution which was mentioned first,[48] one would probably do best to adopt this hypothesis.* Objections can be raised against it, first of all by way of a fundamental skepticism (no doubt justified) with regard to the facile assumption of such lacunae. But then doubt might also be raised with respect to the thought in the passage: Is the objection which is postulated in Spitta's hypothesis really one which would be obvious to a *serious* opponent. Would he not first have to say a word about faith and its true nature? Would he not have to defend that view before he attacked that of Jas?

Obviously, the solutions attempted by B. Weiss,[49] Pfleiderer, and Spitta all have the same goal. They want to reconstruct the objection of the opponent from the answer of Jas—indeed, the objection of a serious opponent who is taken seriously by Jas because he

expects such a reply from within his audience. The question is whether this approach does not grant too much respect to the opponent, i.e., whether a sincere objection in opposition to Jas is actually expressed here. Stylistic considerations suggest that what is involved is merely an opponent contrived by Jas in order to provide a sharper statement of his thoughts. If these kinds of considerations are to be followed, then the first solution is preferable. Otherwise, the third solution, especially in the form in which Spitta presents it, commends itself.

The understanding of the *second sentence* in v 18 follows from what was said in the interpretation of the first: The opponent is to show the "faith without works" which is presupposed in his objection. Jas for his part promises to demonstrate faith from works. The opponent cannot fulfill the demand, since such faith simply is not capable of "being shown." Thus the author himself undertakes the examination which he is demanding.

■ **19** In this verse he attempts to state in one sentence— obviously certain of agreement from his partner—the content of the "faith without works" which is in question: "That God is one" (ὅτι εἷς ἐστιν ὁ θεός).[50] He does so in order then to strap it to the whipping post: Some faith! Even the demons believe that! The irony is unmistakable. But just as clear is the fact that precisely the unique content of the Christian faith is not represented here.

The result is twofold. First of all, what was already concluded from other observations is corroborated here—viz., that the author does not intend to represent some contemporary in the form of an opponent. If he had in mind a current allusion, then a specifically Christian statement of faith would have to appear here,

46   See above under number 1).
47   Also, Windisch–Preisker, and Georg Hollmann and Wilhelm Bousset, *Der Jakobusbrief*, SchrNT 3 (Göttingen: Vandenhoeck and Ruprecht, ³1917), *ad loc.*
48   See above under number 1).
49   See above under number 2).
50   In the evaluation of the readings for this text the religio–historical considerations employed above must be kept in mind insofar as the reading εἷς θεός ἐστιν (B *et al.*, and *ff*: *quia unus deus*) is suspect of being an accommodation to the Christian kerygma (1 Cor 8:6; Eph 4:6; 1 Tim 2:5), since all the other read-

ings support the inclusion of the article before "God" (θεός). The Koine reading ὁ θεὸς εἷς ἐστιν is suspect on the basis of external attestation. Therefore, apart from patent emendations such as the omission of the "one" (εἷς), there remain: 1) the reading of C minuscules sy^hl εἷς ὁ θεός ἐστιν (Priscillian: *unus deus est*); and 2) the reading in P⁷⁴ ℵ A sah boh 1739 εἷς ἐστιν ὁ θεός (*s* vulg: *unus est deus*). As compared with this latter reading, reading 1) could be understood as an approximation to the Christian kerygma, and the reading in B would have carried this approximation even further. Thus the reading in P⁷⁴ ℵ A is to be

such as "you believe that the Lord was really raised" (πιστεύεις ὅτι ὄντως ἠγέρθη ὁ κύριος), or something similar.[51] The author has not characterized the opponent in accordance with any specific model. The opponent is not even thought of as a type. Therefore one should be wary of drawing inferences from this verse about the faith of the Christian community at the time of Jas. The second thing, however, which can be seen from such an illustration of "faith without works" is that the author is in active touch with the spiritual heritage of Judaism. It is most natural for him to employ here those formulations of the monotheistic faith which were familiar to Judaism from Deut 6:4–9—and doubly familiar, since this passage formed the beginning of the Jewish creedal prayer, the Shema. And the custom of reciting the Shema in the morning and the evening had already originated even in the first century A.D.[52] Since this is the provenance of the statement in Jas 2:19, we must translate it accordingly: The words of Deut 6:4 did not mean to the Jew who was praying what interpreters of the Old Testament have (rightly) understood them to mean: "Hear, O Israel, Yahweh is our God, Yahweh alone," but rather, " 'The Lord' is our God, 'The Lord' is one."

Of course, in spite of the relationship of this formula to Jewish texts one should not forget the extent to which the thought and even its formulation accomodates the philosophical theology of the Greeks. "There is one God" (εἷς θεός) is the avowal of enlightened, pious minds among the Greeks from Xenophanes to Marcus Aurelius.[53] In turn, Jewish propaganda took advantage of this agreement just as the Christian Apologists did later. In *Conf. ling.* 170, Philo applies the Homeric "let there be one God" (εἷς κοίρανος ἔστω)[54] to monotheism. Athenagoras employed to a similar purpose a spurious Sophoclean fragment which had been produced in Jewish circles.[55] Precisely this give and take shows how difficult it is to separate Jewish and Greek elements here.[56] However, *the formulation* of our passage undoubtedly points to a Jewish heritage. It must only be added that the enlightened Greek must also have understood the idea, and indeed have been sympathetic with it.

Everyone who claims that his sympathies are with this confession, and yet has nothing else to exhibit (i.e., works), now falls under the verdict of Jas: Even the

---

preferred, since it is presupposed by the other variants.

51 This was also felt by the ancient exegetes; by Bede, when to the words, "For the demons also do this" (hoc enim et daemones faciunt) he adds, "They believe not only in God the Father but also in the Son" (nec solum Deum patrem sed et filium credunt); by Oec, when he writes, "Wherefore we learned that even the demons believe that he is the Son of God" (καθὸ καὶ τοὺς δαίμονας ἔγνωμεν πιστεύειν ὅτι θεοῦ υἱός; Theoph has "believe in Christ" [εἰς Χριστόν]).

52 Cf. the evidence given by Oscar Holtzmann in *Die Mischna: Text, Übersetzung und ausführliche Erklärung*, ed. G. Beer and O. Holtzmann, vol. 1, part 1: *Berakot* (Giessen: Töpelmann [Ricker], 1912), 6–10. See also below on Jas 5:7.

53 Xenophanes, Fragment 23 in Hermann Diels, *Die Fragmente der Vorsokratiker*, 7th edition by Walther Kranz (Berlin: Weidmann, ⁷1954): "There is one God who is greatest among gods and men" (εἷς θεός, ἔν τε θεοῖσι καὶ ἀνθρώποισι μέγιστος) [Trans.]; M. Ant. 7.9: "For there is both one Universe, made up of all things, and one God immanent in all things" (κόσμος τε γὰρ εἷς ἐξ ἁπάντων καὶ θεὸς εἷς διὰ πάντων). Cf. also Erik Peterson, εἷς θεός: *Epigraphische, formgeschichtliche und religionsgeschichtliche Unter-*

suchungen, Diss. Göttingen (Göttingen: Hubert, 1920). Peterson's dissertation appeared, greatly expanded, as a book with the same title in the series FRLANT, N.F. 24 (Göttingen: Vandenhoeck & Ruprecht, 1926). On pp. 295–9 of the book he includes Jas 2:19 in the larger context of the widespread epigraphical formula "there is one God" (εἷς θεός), and he finds confirmation of its apotropaic function in the reference to the trembling of the demons. According to Peterson, the formula is connected with the Aion theology. He does not consider the reading in B (see above, n. 50) to be suspect of accommodation, but rather he thinks that it deserves serious consideration because of its agreement with the formula which is epigraphically well attested.

54 Hom., *Il.* 2.204f.

55 Athenag., *Suppl.* 5.2.

56 Cf. Martin Dibelius, "Die Christianisierung einer hellenistischen Formel," in his *Botschaft und Geschichte*, vol. 2 (Tübingen: Mohr [Siebeck], 1956), 14–29.

demons have this kind of faith. He is alluding here to an idea which occurs elsewhere in Jewish and syncretistic literature as well, viz., that the demons shudder before God.[57] The best examples are in the *Leiden Magical Papyrus J 384*, lines 239–40:[58] "Lord, whose secret name is ineffable, and at the sound of which the demons are terrified" (κύριε, οὗ ἔστιν τὸ κρυπτὸν ὄνομα ἄρρητον, ὃ οἱ δαίμονες ἀκούσαντες πτοοῦνται) [Trans.], and the *Great Paris Magical Papyrus*, lines 3017f (referring to an apotropaic tin tablet to be fastened around the neck of the sick person): "a frightening thing for every demon, a thing which he fears" (παντὸς δαίμονος φρικτόν, ὃ φοβεῖται) [Trans.].[59] That an older expression is preserved here is demonstrated by other passages, especially Justin, *Dial.* 49.8: "You can perceive that God's hidden power was in the crucified Christ, before whom the demons as well as all the principalities and powers of the earth shudder" (νοῆσαι δύνασθε, ὅτι κρυφία δύναμις τοῦ θεοῦ γέγονε τῷ σταυρωθέντι Χριστῷ, ὃν καὶ τὰ δαιμόνια φρίσσει καὶ πᾶσαι ἁπλῶς αἱ ἀρχαὶ καὶ ἐξουσίαι τῆς γῆς) [Trans.]. What is said here of Christ appears elsewhere as a predication of the Godhead; cf. the *Acts of Philip* 132 (p. 63 Bonnet): "O God, before whom all the aeons shudder . . . principalities and powers of the heavenly places tremble before you" (θεὲ ὃν φρίττουσιν οἱ πάντες αἰῶνες . . . σὲ τρέμουσιν ἀρχαὶ καὶ ἐξουσίαι τῶν ἐπουρανίων) [Trans.]; the oracle in Lactantius, *De ira dei* 23.12: "Before whom both earth and heaven, the sea and the innermost parts of the Tartarean regions tremble and the demons shudder" (ὃν τρομέει καὶ γαῖα καὶ οὐρανὸς ἠδὲ θάλασσα ταρτάρεοί τε μυχοί, καὶ δαίμονες ἐρρίγασιν) [Trans.]; an Orphic fragment in Clem. Alex., *Strom.* 5.125.1: "Before whom the demons shudder and the multitude of the gods are afraid" (δαίμονες ὃν φρίσσουσι[ν], θεῶν δὲ δέδοικεν ὅμιλος) [Trans.]. That

similar beliefs were expressed in Jewish literature is shown by the Prayer of Manasseh 4: "at whom all things shudder and tremble before thy power" (ὃν πάντα φρίττει καὶ τρέμει ἀπὸ προσώπου δυνάμεώς σου); and especially Josephus, *Bell.* 5.438: "the frightening name of God" (τὸ φρικτὸν ὄνομα τοῦ θεοῦ); cf. also the Jewish-Christian or Christian *Test. Abr.* [Rec. A] 9 (TS 2, 2, p. 86): "Since, therefore, all things obey your command and shudder and tremble before your power" (ἐπειδὴ οὖν τῇ σῇ προστάξει πάντα ὑπείκει καὶ φρίττει καὶ τρέμει ἀπὸ προσώπου δυνάμεώς σου) [Trans.]; in *Test. Abr.* [Rec. A] 16, "Death" (θάνατος) appears before God "shuddering, groaning and trembling" (φρίττων, στένων καὶ τρέμων).

However, this picture of the shuddering demons is not really the important thing in Jas 2:19. For the reader of Jas, what matters is that he sees how Jas leads his opponent from one admission to another. Whoever acknowledges that the content of his faith is "that God is one" (ὅτι εἷς ἐστιν ὁ θεός) must also admit that he shares this faith with the demons.[60] Therefore, since the demons will be destroyed at the End, this faith is not a faith which "can save."

■ **20–24** The example of Abraham in these verses does not introduce a new train of thought, for what is involved is still the demonstration which was announced in v 18b. But whoever expects to find the second statement in that announcement ("I will show you faith from my works") fulfilled here will be surprised. For the author speaks here not as a defender of his slogan "works," but still chiefly as a critic of the slogan "faith without works." How this hangs together is shown by a glance at v 24: It is no longer the "braggart" who is addressed but rather the readers,[61] and so the author moves imperceptibly out of the dialogue form, which

57   Kittel, review of Dibelius, *Der Brief des Jakobus*, 4, in commenting upon Jas 2:19, refers to the reactions of the demons at their encounter with Jesus (Mk 1:24; 5:7; *et al.*). According to Kittel, the idea of the shuddering of the demons is therefore "not theoretical speculation, but a part of the concepts of early Christianity formed in the observation of the story of Jesus."

58   Karl Preisendanz, ed., *Papyri Graecae Magicae: Die griechischen Zauberpapyri*, vol. 2 (Leipzig and Berlin: Teubner, 1931), 74.

59   Preisendanz, *op. cit.* (above, n. 58), vol. 1, p. 170.

60   It is almost a matter of a feeling for the correct idiom whether one expresses a contrast in the translation of καὶ φρίσσουσιν—"*and yet* they tremble" (cf. "and yet he feeds them" [καὶ τρέφει] in Matt 6:26)—, or whether one suppresses it in order to stress just how little such a trembling faith is really a Christian faith. The latter is probably the intention of the parataxis. In any event, the coordination of the two verbs is more striking in this type of Greek than is a participial construction. Moreover, it is in line with the development of the Hellenistic vernacular. Cf. Blass-Debrunner, § 442.

was only an episode. Thus, he obviously is not concerned with refuting this opponent to the very last.
Instead, he is interested in using the (merely initiated)
refutation of the inerlocutor as a basis for developing
for his readers his own ideas. Therefore, as severe as the
words "you braggart!" (ὦ ἄνθρωπε κενέ) sound, they
have little to do with an actual opponent. The address,
"You braggart!"[62] corresponds to the invective which
is customary in diatribe.[63] The juxtaposition of ἔργων
and ἀργή is also an artistic device:[64] "Without *works*
faith does not *work.*"[65]

■ **21–23** Now comes the example of Abraham, "our
father"—as he is called not only by Jews (*Pirke Aboth*
5.19) and Jewish–Christians such as Paul (Rom 4:1,
12; even to the Gentile–Christians; cf. 1 Cor 10:1;
Rom 4:16f; Gal 3:7, 29), but also by Gentile–Christians (see *1 Clem.* 31.2). Therefore, no inferences about
the author's past can be drawn from this characterization of Abraham.

The understanding of the Abraham example is
dependent upon the evaluation of the scriptural quotation in v 23. It could be, and has been, thought[66] that
the argument is completed in v 22 and that v 23 is
added as supplementary scriptural evidence. What
speaks against this thesis is v 22, with its mention of
Abraham's faith. In v 21, only "justification" by
"works" is mentioned. But then v 22 continues: Hence

you see—i.e., from this demonstrated justification—
that the faith of Abraham has only the significance of a
coadjutant factor. Yet, so far nothing at all had been
said about this faith. Thus v 22 presupposes that at the
mention of Abraham the opponent (or the readers)
would immediately think of Abraham's faith. Indeed,
v 22 presupposes that against the thesis of v 21 the
opponent would already be prepared with an objection:
"But everyone knows that Abraham was justified by
faith." If at the mention of the patriarch the addressee(s)
would in this way immediately think of "faith" (πίστις),
or even of "to be justified by faith" (δικαιοῦσθαι ἐκ
πίστεως), this could be motivated only by the familiar
Biblical passage, Gen 15:6, or by a specific interpretation of this passage. This is precisely the passage which
Jas promptly quotes. Therefore, we are on the right
track if we suppose that Jas and his opponent had this
locus classicus in mind from the outset. Then v 23 is not
an extra which could be omitted, but rather the main
point. The goal of vv 21–24 is the proper understanding
of this "faith" passage, and the preceding verses are to
be understood in light of this realization.

■ **21** In Jewish tradition Abraham is the man who is
proven by means of many trials, and whose constancy
and faith is rewarded by God. Illustrations of this are
presented in the Excursus which follows (see below).
For v 21 it is only necessary to demonstrate what is

61   See above in the Analysis.
62   κενός means "he who boasts foolishly" in Epict.,
Diss. 2.19.8 and in Justin, *Dial.* 64.2. If the word is
rendered in this way in Jas 2:20, then all the reflections about emptiness of faith (Oec) or "want of true
intrinsic worth" (Huther, Beyschlag) become superfluous. It is also futile to draw attention to Matt
5:22; to be sure, the invective "you fool!" (רֵיקָא)
in that verse is perhaps intended as an equivalent to
κενός, but even if that is true there is no direct connection between Matt 5:22 and Jas 2:20.
63   Cf. above in the Analysis.
64   Admittedly, by far the greater number of witnesses
have "dead, barren" (νεκρά). "Idle, inactive" (ἀργή)
is the reading in B C* sah 1739 and some other minuscules, s (*otiosa,* following *o homo inanis*), part of
the vulg texts, and arm. "Empty, vain," etc. (κενή)
is supported by P74 *ff* (*vacua,* following *o homo vacue*).
Because of this "remarkably weak" attestation, von
Soden (*Schriften,* part 1, p. 1891) prefers to avoid a
definite conclusion (regarding the *I-H-K* text). But
the suspicion that the reading νεκρά in 2:20 derives

from 2:26 speaks very much in favour of the reading
ἀργή. Then, too, νεκρά is the more common form,
and it can hardly be conjectured that a corrector
would have replaced it with ἀργή in order to bright-
en up the passage with a play on words. On the other
hand, this paronomasia could have been penned by
the author, who is fond of such formal devices (see
above, section 5 in the Introduction).
65   Besides "inactive," ἀργός also frequently has the
meanings "unused," "unprofitable": Josephus,
Ant. 12.378; Philo, *Spec. leg.* 2.86,88; *P. Amherst*
97.9f; Ditt., *Syll.* 533.23f.
66   So Gebser, Belser.

intended in this context by the expression "was justified" (ἐδικαιώθη). There is no need to consider the exegetical controversy about whether one is merely pronounced righteous or is actually made righteous,[67] for both the Pauline term and concept "as a gift" (δωρεάν) are totally lacking in our text.

Instead, one must appeal to the thoroughly clear understanding of the "righteousness" (δικαιοσύνη) of Abraham in Jewish exegesis. As will be shown, this understanding has either directly or indirectly influenced Jas: Abraham is not considered a "justified" sinner, but a righteous man who is recognized and rewarded by God. This understanding is also of help with respect to other questions which are dealt with by interpreters. It cannot be doubted that the expression "was justified" (ἐδικαιώθη) must actually mean approval by God,[68] and that Abraham received this approval not merely at the final judgment;[69] according to Jas, the patriach is granted approval by God already during his lifetime. From the material treated in the Excursus (see below), I will single out here only one passage which clearly and succinctly expresses the viewpoint which was current within Judaism: 1 Macc 2:52. There the dying Mattathias presents to his sons the model of the patriarchs who achieved fame and immortality through their deeds. In each case he mentions two things—the deed and its reward. For example, Joseph kept the commandment of God and became lord of Egypt; Joshua became a judge of Israel because he fulfilled the command. At the top of the list he places Abraham: "was he not found faithful when tested, and righteousness was reckoned to him?" (οὐκ ἐν πειρασμῷ εὑρέθη πιστὸς καὶ ἐλογίσθη αὐτῷ δικαιοσύνη; a variant reading has "and it was reckoned to him as righteousness" [εἰς δικαιοσύνην], as in Gen 15:6). In other words, God found him faithful and (as a reward) "attributed righteousness" to him. The content of the first clause is also found in Jas 2:21: God found Abraham righteous.

With regard to the plural "by works" (ἐξ ἔργων), it is striking that immediately afterwards only *one* work is mentioned. Perhaps this is due to ἐξ ἔργων being used simply as a formula for "by his conduct." Perhaps also it is caused by the recollection of the customary Jewish enumeration of ten trials,[70] but under no circumstances should one assume because of this enumeration, as Spitta does, that the offering of Isaac is mentioned here merely in order to fix the point in time when the justification of Abraham took place. For then the author's thesis would be left without evidence—and that is precisely what he must avoid in this passage where (without expressly stating it) he is already combating a misunderstanding of the Biblical passage quoted in v 23. Also decisive against Spitta's view is the analogy of v 25, where the participle "having received" (ὑποδεξαμένη) certainly provides the *grounds* for justification, not merely the point in time at which it took place. Moreover, in the tradition in general, even in the enumeration of the ten trials, the offering of Isaac appears as the greatest and most significant. "*Now* I know that you fear God," says God in *Jub.* 18.11. The thought of Jas in 2:21 is that since Abraham "offered" his son upon the altar he was approved by God as a

---

67   Cf. especially the discussions by Beyschlag and Belser. For the first interpretation (the "forensic" view), cf. among others Schmidt, *Lehrgehalt*, and Weiffenbach, *Jak 2, 14-26*, 27. For the second view, see P. Schanz, "Jakobus und Paulus," *ThQ* 62 (1880): 259ff, and Bernhard Bartmann, *St. Paulus und St. Jacobus über die Rechtfertigung*, BSF 2, 1, (Freiburg: Herder, 1897), 135ff. Characteristically, advocates of both views claim that the Jas passage agrees with Paul.

68   See below on v 23. Against the interpretation of δικαιοῦσθαι to mean "to show oneself to be righteous" there is 1) the traditional Jewish view of the example of Abraham, 2) the evidence of v 23 (see below), and finally 3) the context: the main point is that Abraham received approval *from God* (and became "a friend of God")—otherwise his example would

be of little help for the Christian. The intention is precisely to show that faith alone before God is not sufficient.

69   The expression in v 23, "he was called a friend of God" (φίλος θεοῦ ἐκλήθη) shows that the approval is already given in the present. With respect to Beyschlag's thesis that the reference in this section is to the final judgment, it is true that such approval does become effective at that time (*Jub.*19.9: "he was recorded on the heavenly tablets as the friend of God" [trans. Charles, *APOT*]). On the other hand, the parallelism referred to by Beyschlag between "to save" (σῴζειν) in 2:14 and "to justify" (δικαιοῦν) in 2:21ff is not proof in support of his thesis, since in the case of Abraham what is involved is not an eschatological religion at all, and hence, not principally "salvation" at the final judgment.

righteous man by virtue of his deeds.

■ **22** I have already explained why v 22 presupposes the faith of Abraham without any further introduction: Jas counts on the fact that his opponent or his readers would adduce in opposition to the statement in v 21 the famous faith of Abraham, and thus Jas begins by presupposing this faith.

It seems to me that the understanding of the verse is dependent upon the recognition of the fact that the two halves of the verse correspond stylistically. "The faith of Abraham assisted[71] his works and his works perfected his faith." We know (and will notice again in the formulation of v 24) that the two factors are not of equal importance for Jas. But here he is obviously interested in juxtaposing the two things, for he wants to express that they work together. For this reason, one cannot read into the verb "was perfected" ($\dot{\epsilon}\tau\epsilon\lambda\epsilon\iota\dot{\omega}\theta\eta$) that it is only through works that faith really becomes faith. Jas does know of a faith without works. Therefore, in referring to the "perfection" of Abraham's faith he clearly has in mind something higher, the goal toward which both factors, faith and works, aim—viz., the righteousness of Abraham. But then the stylistic correspondence between the two halves of the verse must be taken seriously and the verb "assisted" ($\sigma\upsilon\nu\dot{\eta}\rho\gamma\epsilon\iota$) must mean assisting toward the common goal, and not assisting in the production of works:[72] You see[73] that

the famous faith of Abraham was only an assistance in the attainment of this goal: namely, that Abraham was approved by God as righteous.

To be sure, after what was said in vv 14–20 and in light of what is said later in v 24, it is surprising that faith apparently is placed here on equal rank with works, to which it is considerably subordinated as far as its effectiveness is concerned.[74] But we will make the same observation in v 23 and will recognize there also the reason for this apparent self-contradiction: Jas intends to justify his opinion before the forum of Gen 15:6, and therefore he endeavours to put the faith of Abraham which is stressed in that passage into its proper place. This explains the correspondence between the two clauses in v 22, which must not be diminished for the sake of logical–exegetical considerations. In addition, one must avoid the mistake of closely connecting the expression "and it was fulfilled" ($\kappa\alpha\dot{\iota}\ \dot{\epsilon}\pi\lambda\eta\rho\dot{\omega}\theta\eta$) in v 23 with "was perfected" ($\dot{\epsilon}\tau\epsilon\lambda\epsilon\iota\dot{\omega}\theta\eta$) in v 22, for v 23 constitutes a new beginning and the two corresponding clauses in v 22 round off that verse by itself:[75] faith assists works—works perfect faith.

■ **23** The introduction of the Gen 15:6[76] passage by the verb "it was fulfilled" ($\dot{\epsilon}\pi\lambda\eta\rho\dot{\omega}\theta\eta$) creates problems. According to normal usage, the first thing which comes to mind is the fulfillment of a prophecy,[77] which in this case would be the words "it was reckoned to him as

---

70   See below in the first Excursus on 2:26.

71   On $\sigma\upsilon\nu\epsilon\rho\gamma\epsilon\hat{\iota}\nu$ in this sense, cf. also Mk 16:20. $\aleph^*$ A *ff* have the present tense, "assists" ($\sigma\upsilon\nu\epsilon\rho\gamma\epsilon\hat{\iota}$), instead of "assisted" ($\sigma\upsilon\nu\dot{\eta}\rho\gamma\epsilon\iota$). However, the "is confirmed" (*confirmatur*, in contrast with the Greek texts, which unanimously read the past tense, "was perfected" [$\dot{\epsilon}\tau\epsilon\lambda\epsilon\iota\dot{\omega}\theta\eta$]) for the following verb in this verse in *ff* demonstrates the existence of a tendency to transform the statement into the present tense. The reading $\sigma\upsilon\nu\epsilon\rho\gamma\epsilon\hat{\iota}$ can also be explained as a result of this tendency.

72   So, e.g., von Soden, and Holtzmann, *Theologie*, vol. 2, p. 375. For the interpretation which is advocated above, cf. especially Kühl, *Stellung*, 35ff, who, however, fails to note the stylistic evidence.

73   There is no reason to render $\beta\lambda\dot{\epsilon}\pi\epsilon\iota\varsigma$ as a question ("Do you see?"). To the contrary, one would think that in a reproachful question the author would again specifically address his partner.

74   At this point Dibelius noted from his seminar a suggested explanation for the surprising way in which works and faith are placed on equal rank in 2:22:

In order to be able to foist "works" upon "he believed" ($\dot{\epsilon}\pi\dot{\iota}\sigma\tau\epsilon\upsilon\sigma\epsilon\nu$) in v 23, Jas in v 22b suddenly raises the position of faith, now a higher sort of faith, to be sure, which is characterized by works.

75   Therefore, Hofmann's combinations, "by his works (the scripture) was fulfilled" ($\dot{\epsilon}\kappa\ \tau\hat{\omega}\nu\ \dot{\epsilon}\rho\gamma\omega\nu\ \dot{\epsilon}\pi\lambda\eta\rho\dot{\omega}\theta\eta$) and "because of his works he was called" ($\dot{\epsilon}\kappa\ \tau\hat{\omega}\nu\ \dot{\epsilon}\rho\gamma\omega\nu\ \dot{\epsilon}\kappa\lambda\dot{\eta}\theta\eta$), as well as von Soden's assertion that the verbs "was perfected" ($\dot{\epsilon}\tau\epsilon\lambda\epsilon\iota\dot{\omega}\theta\eta$), "was fulfilled" ($\dot{\epsilon}\pi\lambda\eta\rho\dot{\omega}\theta\eta$), and "was called" ($\dot{\epsilon}\kappa\lambda\dot{\eta}\theta\eta$) are coordinated, are to be rejected upon stylistic grounds.

76   The LXX probably has $\kappa\alpha\dot{\iota}\ \dot{\epsilon}\pi\dot{\iota}\sigma\tau\epsilon\upsilon\sigma\epsilon\nu$. Jas has $\dot{\epsilon}\pi\dot{\iota}\sigma\tau\epsilon\upsilon\sigma\epsilon\nu\ \delta\dot{\epsilon}$, as in Philo, *Mut. nom.* 177; Rom 4:3, *1 Clem.* 10.6; Justin, *Dial.* 92.

77   Beyschlag, Belser, Mayor, Ropes.

righteousness" (ἐλογίσθη αὐτῷ εἰς δικαιοσύνην). The mere reckoning of faith as righteousness of Gen 15:6 would have to point to the real righteousness which Abraham would earn in Gen 22, and the offering of Isaac would be the "fulfillment" of that saying which speaks of reckoning. Perhaps against this interpretation is already the fact that in Judaism (cf. 1 Macc 2:52 above) the clause "it was reckoned, etc." was taken as a reference to Abraham's reward and not as a temporary promissory note for the future. But the chief objection is that the clause "he was called a friend of God" (φίλος θεοῦ ἐκλήθη) is even more certainly a reference to the reward, the goal which Abraham achieved. If this clause is supposed to go with what precedes (to be understood as promise), then "was fulfilled" no longer is valid, for in the statement about the "friend of God" there is nothing more to be "fulfilled" in the sense suggested above. However, if the clause is separated from what precedes it, then it is isolated and meaningless.[78]

Therefore, the difficulty must be eliminated in some other way. Above all it must be made clear that the author does not think of the passage historically, but supra–historically. He does not take it as a statement about the religious position of Abraham at some specific period—the period narrated in Gen 15—, but as a divine saying or oracle which applies to the whole of Abraham's life. The proof of this is provided by the words "and he was called a friend of God" (καὶ φίλος θεοῦ ἐκλήθη), which, to be sure, cannot be found in Gen 15:6 but which undoubtedly belong with that passage as it appears here in Jas 2:23—otherwise they would be totally unconnected and stylistically problematic.[79] If this is the case, then the author does not have the exact wording of the Biblical passage in mind (much less before his eyes), but rather the form which the devotional paraphrase of that text had probably already taken long before. What he brings in here is not actually a quotation, but rather it is the sort of "automatic" statement which is often made in devotional language. The hypothesis that the "friend of God" saying was already attached to the Biblical passage in the tradition will find further confirmation in the discussions in the first Excursus on 2:26. That the words could be construed as a divine oracle about Abraham, and not as an item from the story of Abraham, is shown also by Philo. In *Abr.* 262, Philo tells of the "praise" of Abraham which is attested by a divine oracle (χρησμοί) coming from Moses, and then Philo cites the words "he believed God." Philo continues, "Now that is a little thing if measured in words, but a very great thing if made good by action" (ὅπερ λεχθῆναι μὲν βραχύτατόν ἐστιν, ἔργῳ δὲ βεβαιωθῆναι μέγιστον). If one understands our passage as this sort of divine oracle, there is no doubt about the meaning of the expression "it was fulfilled" (ἐπληρώθη). What God said about Abraham (and what the writings of Moses transmitted to men) was "fulfilled" by Abraham through his action.

A further difficulty arises when the passage explained in this way is incorporated into the context of this section in Jas. The thesis of the author is that Abraham was approved by God as righteous as a result of his action, and that therefore the famous faith of Abraham had to be considered as only one factor along with works. This must be what he is demonstrating in v 23, and thus v 23 must be speaking about both faith and works. Whoever comes to Jas after a look at Paul (Rom 4) must completely forget Paul's interpretation of Gen 15:6 (faith reckoned as righteousness). According to Jas, this divine oracle knows how to praise both faith and works. This realization is reflected in Hofmann's thesis, that the phrase "by works" (ἐξ ἔργων) is to be combined with both "was fulfilled" (ἐπληρώθη) and "was called" (ἐκλήθη); but his interpretation has already been rejected.[80] The same requirement is taken into account by Windisch, who thinks that he perceives in the second part of the "saying" a kind of addition: faith is added on to righteousness (already procured by works).[81] Yet that meaning cannot be extracted without difficulty, and above all, the thesis of the author would be only indirectly proven in this way.

However, these efforts upon the part of the interpreters clearly reveal one thing: in the second part of the passage, specifically in the term "it was reckoned" (ἐλογίσθη), there *must be an allusion to works*. Only then

78 Sensing this, Ewald argued that this clause must have been included in Gen 15:6 in the Bible used by Jas.

79 "Was called" (ἐκλήθη) parallel to "was fulfilled" (ἐπληρώθη), with a change in subject?

80 See above, n. 75.

is the author justified in appealing to this text. Only then does the third part of the saying follow naturally: Abraham owes his position of honor as friend of God to his faith and his works.

Now just this understanding of "it was reckoned, etc." as a reference to justification by works (i.e., mainly, by the offering of Isaac) was the common Jewish interpretation of Gen 15:6. *This agreement between the synagogue exegesis and the interpretation to which we are plainly forced by our text provides the conclusive evidence for the dependence of this section in Jas upon Jewish Biblical interpretation.* This evidence is further corroborated by the title "friend of God" which is used by our author as well as by the Jews.[82] This interpretation of "it was reckoned" seems to have originated from the fact that Jewish exegetes quite universally saw the main evidence of Abraham's faith in his offering up of his son, i.e., they were tying together Gen 15 with Gen 22 in their interpretation; cf. 1 Macc 2:52.[83] Jas did not follow the exact wording found in the 1 Maccabees passage: "righteousness was reckoned to him."[84] Nevertheless, he still reads a reference to works in the wording "it was reckoned as righteousness" ($\epsilon\lambda o\gamma i\sigma\theta\eta$ ϵis $\delta\iota\kappa\alpha\iota o\sigma\nu\nu\eta\nu$).[85] For in the word "righteousness" ($\delta\iota\kappa\alpha\iota o\sigma\nu\nu\eta$) he, like the Jews, understood an actual righteousness based upon works,[86] and in the expression "it was reckoned" ($\epsilon\lambda o\gamma i\sigma\theta\eta$) he, like the *Book of Jubilees*,[87]

thought of a kind of heavenly book–keeping. Thus he was able to associate the clauses within the Gen 15:6 passage with the two factors, faith and works: "he believed" ($\epsilon\pi i\sigma\tau\epsilon\nu\sigma\epsilon\nu$)—therefore, *faith* (referring not only to the point of time in Gen 15:6, but to the whole of Abraham's life); "it was reckoned" ($\epsilon\lambda o\gamma i\sigma\theta\eta$), i.e., counted or entered in the books as "righteousness"—therefore, *works*.[88]

Jas differs from Paul in his assumption (already expressed in v 21) of a righteousness by works, while Paul interprets Gen 15:6 as a reference to a faith accepted by grace in lieu of the righteousness which is lacking. But Judaism understood faith to be a work or a pattern of living which included works. Therefore, Jas differs from the synagogue in his ability to think of faith and works as separate factors.[89] Jas wants to demonstrate both of them with Gen 15:6, and that might seem ambiguous as over against the consistency of Paul or of Judaism. In commenting upon v 22, I have already stressed that by taking into account two quantities (faith and works) Jas does damage to his own line of thought, and already I have attempted to interpret v 22 by considering the relationship of the whole to Gen 15:6. But the approach of Jas is fully comprehended only if one assumes that faith and works were stamped as exclusive opposites by someone prior to Jas. That is the subject of the second Excursus on 2:26. For

---

81 Windisch, *Katholische Briefe* (1911).

82 See below in the first Excursus on 2:26.

83 Adolf Schlatter, *Der Glaube im Neuen Testament* (Stuttgart: Calwer Vereinsbuchhandlung, [5]1963), 18.

84 Jas writes ϵis $\delta\iota\kappa\alpha\iota o\sigma\nu\nu\eta\nu$, not $\delta\iota\kappa\alpha\iota o\sigma\nu\nu\eta$. But Dibelius stands here on Swete's edition of the LXX, which reads $\delta\iota\kappa\alpha\iota o\sigma\nu\nu\eta$ in 1 Macc 2:52 with A and one minuscule. On the other hand, Rahlfs and also Werner Kappler (*Maccabaeorum liber I*, Septuaginta Auctoritate Societatis Litterarum Gottingensis, vol. 9, 1 [Göttingen: Vandenhoeck & Ruprecht, 1936]) have ϵis $\delta\iota\kappa\alpha\iota o\sigma\nu\nu\eta\nu$, which is supported by the other witnesses, above all by א. [In subsequent sections of this edition of the commentary, the reading of the more recent editions will be used in quotes of 1 Macc 2:52.—Trans.]

85 Cf. also the first Excursus on 2:26.

86 See above on v 22. Ménégoz, "Justification par la foi," 122f, interprets righteousness in Jas to mean absolution, forgiveness of sins. In doing so, he appeals to Jas 2:12f. However, given the literary char-

acter of Jas, such arguments are suspect from the beginning. Moreover, the lack of any appropriate indication of this within Jas 2:14–26 itself speaks against this interpretation and the conclusions which are drawn from it, as does also the history of the Abraham example (cf. the Excursus below).

87 Cf. the first Excursus on 2:26.

88 On $\lambda o\gamma i\zeta\epsilon\sigma\theta\alpha\iota$, cf. Hans-Wolfgang Heidland, *Die Anrechnung des Glaubens zur Gerechtigkeit: Untersuchungen zur Begriffsbestimmung von חשׁב und $\lambda o\gamma i\zeta\epsilon\sigma\theta\alpha\iota$*, BWANT 4, 18 (Stuttgart: Kohlhammer, 1936); *idem*, *TDNT* 4, pp. 284–92; Gerhard von Rad, "Die Anrechnung des Glaubens zur Gerechtigkeit," *ThLZ* 76 (1951): 129–32.

89 Cf. the survey in the second Excursus on 2:26.

Jas *this* antithesis does not exist, and for him the name "friend of God" characterizes precisely the model of faith as well as of works. For that reason, too, the last words of the verse cannot be separated from the divine "saying."

■ **24** In this verse[90] Jas returns in his utilization of the Abraham example to the emphasis upon works. Faith is mentioned only in the negative; yet faith itself is not rejected, only its absolute power: "not by faith alone" (οὐκ ἐκ πίστεως μόνον). Therefore the slogan "faith, not works" must have been formulated already by Jas' time. With the term "you (pl.) see" (ὁρᾶτε), the verse directs itself once again to the readers. Conclusions have been drawn in the Analysis (see above) regarding this transition from dialogue to epistolary style.

■ **25** The second example, that of Rahab, is introduced as a parallel to the Abraham example. In fact, Jas intends to prove the same thing here—namely, that there is no justification without works. The expression "was justified" (ἐδικαιώθη) means the same thing here as in v 21. The two most important moments in the work of Rahab on behalf of the spies[91]—"having received" (ὑποδεξαμένη) and "having sent on" (ἐκβαλοῦσα)—are cited as evidence. But the brevity with which this instance is treated is not only striking in comparison with that of Abraham, but also leaves open some legitimate questions.

The woman is a prostitute and a pagan. We might expect that a reference to "righteousness" in a case such as this would be treated somewhat more carefully than would be necessary in the case of Abraham, the model of piety. In the Christian (and Jewish) tradition these reservations were eliminated, it seems, by the fact that Rahab has been made a heroine of faith in view of her confession of the God of Israel as reported in the account in Josh 2:11. At least this is the case in Heb 11:31 and *1 Clem.* 12, sections which no doubt are dependent upon Jewish lists.[92] Also, the interpretation of the scarlet cord as a reference to the blood of Christ,[93] "by which those who were at one time harlots and unrighteous persons out of all nations are saved" (Justin, *Dial.* 111) shows how one could settle the problem.

The mention of the faith of Rahab would have been quite appropriate in our context, since it involves precisely the cooperation of faith and works and since, given an occasion, an opponent would have been able to appeal to the faith of Rahab as an argument against Jas. That Jas omits any reference to Rahab's faith, although the Old Testament confirms it and (as can be inferred from Hebrews and *1 Clement*) Jewish tradition would also have mentioned it, must be regarded as most remarkable.

Something else is also missing in Jas: the mention of the reward of Rahab, the counterpart to the epithet "friend of God" in v 23. The proof that Rahab had really been approved by God as righteous would be furnished only if Jas had shown how God had not only preserved this woman at the destruction of Jericho, but also had subsequently deemed her worthy of higher honors. For Jewish tradition must have told of such honors. To be sure, we are here again dependent upon inferences which are drawn from later texts, but they are inferences which may be drawn with at least some certainty. Clearly the author of Matt 1:5 has not as a result of his own or another Christian's fabrication introduced a woman of ill repute into the genealogy of Jesus. Rather, Jewish tradition had already made the prostitute from Jericho an ancestress of King David. Admittedly, the tradition which is known to us in the Talmud and Midrash does not relate this fact, but it does tell other praiseworthy things about her.[94] Clearly perceptible throughout is the desire to make Rahab one of the people of Israel and to assign to her a place as a glorious ancestress.

Out of all this tradition Jas presents nothing. One might ask why he mentions Rahab at all. In this connection, the list of pious persons in *1 Clem.* 10–12 might be called to mind once again. There, following the

90   Joined to the preceding in the Koine witnesses with "hence" (τοίνυν).

91   The Greek manuscripts (C L and minuscules) which read "spies" (κατασκόπους) in Jas 2:25 instead of "messengers" (ἀγγέλους) are not sufficient in number and importance to make their reading a competitive alternative, especially since the interpolation of the more specific term in place of the less

specific is understandable. This also applies to translations such as that in *ff*: "scouts, spies" (exploratores).

92   We are familiar with lists of a similar nature from Sir 44–50; 1 Macc 2:51ff; *3 Macc.* 6.4–8.

93   *1 Clem.* 12.7; Justin, *Dial.* 111; Iren., *Adv. haer.* 4.20.12, with an appeal to Matt 21:31.

94   According to Rabbi Ēna, eight prophets descended

brief mention of Enoch and Noah in *1 Clem.* 9, mention is made of three Old Testament examples: Abraham, "because of his faith and hospitality" ($\delta\iota\grave{\alpha}\ \pi\acute{\iota}\sigma\tau\iota\nu\ \kappa\alpha\grave{\iota}\ \phi\iota\lambda o\xi\epsilon\nu\acute{\iota}\alpha\nu$ 10.7), Lot, "because of his hospitality and piety" ($\delta\iota\grave{\alpha}\ \phi\iota\lambda o\xi\epsilon\nu\acute{\iota}\alpha\nu\ \kappa\alpha\grave{\iota}\ \epsilon\mathring{v}\sigma\acute{\epsilon}\beta\epsilon\iota\alpha\nu$), and Rahab, "because of her faith and hospitality" ($\delta\iota\grave{\alpha}\ \pi\acute{\iota}\sigma\tau\iota\nu\ \kappa\alpha\grave{\iota}\ \phi\iota\lambda o\xi\epsilon\nu\acute{\iota}\alpha\nu$). It has long been recognized[95] that these kinds of lists were already well-known within Judaism and obviously already traditional for the authors of Hebrews and *1 Clement.* Thus from *1 Clem.* 10–12 the inference can be drawn that Abraham and Rahab, but not Lot, were famous examples of faith. As such they are mentioned here by Jas, and thus the solution to the problem already proposed earlier is confirmed.[96] It also provides an explanation for the fact that Jas mentions Rahab, but does not treat the Rahab story exegetically. The proof which interests him he has furnished in the Abraham story. He moves from Abraham to Rahab because elsewhere she is frequently mentioned together with

Abraham. So he mentions Rahab and once more states his thesis in connection with this example. But since he obviously considers it superfluous to renew this line of argument, he lets the matter rest with one sentence and adds as a conclusion to the whole section a simile in v 26 which is explicitly added to v 25 as a supporting argument.[97]

■ **26** The main point of this verse, "faith without works is dead," needs no further explanation. The same thing is said in v 17, and in other terms in v 14 and v 20. It is self-evident that the point of the comparison here is only the condition of death. Countless futile attempts at expounding upon this verse[98] demonstrate only the impossibility of matching up all of the details in this simile. Faith is as dead without works as the "body" is without "soul."[99] Here also there is confirmation of the fact that in Jas we cannot speak of a slogan, "by works alone." That one has faith (i.e., that which Jas calls "faith") is presupposed from the outset in this section.

---

from Rahab. According to R. Naḥman, Rahab repented and Joshua married her (both of these statements are in *b. Meg.* 14b). According to *Midrash Ruth Rabbah* 2.1, Rahab was accepted into the tribe of Judah; cf. Theodor Zahn, *Das Evangelium des Matthäus* (Leipzig: Deichert, ⁴1922), on Matt 1:5. Cf. moreover, Ropes, *ad loc.*, and Hans Windisch, "Zur Rahabgeschichte: Zwei Parallelen aus der klassischen Literatur," *ZAW* 37 (1918): 188–98. Parallels to the midrash are in August Wünsche, *Der Midrasch Ruth Rabba*, in his *Bibliotheca Rabbinica* (Leipzig: Schulze, 1883), 61.

95 Carl Ludwig Willibald Grimm, *Kurzgefasstes exegetisches Handbuch zu den Apokryphen des Alten Testamentes*, vol. 3, *Das erste Buch der Maccabäer* (Leipzig: Hirzel, 1853), on 1 Macc 2:51; W. Wrede, *Untersuchungen zum Ersten Klemensbriefe* (Göttingen: Vandenhoeck & Ruprecht, 1891), 70ff; cf. also the conjectures of Wilhelm Bousset, *Jüdisch–christlicher Schulbetrieb in Alexandria und Rom: Literarische Untersuchungen zu Philo und Clemens von Alexandria, Justin und Irenäus* (Göttingen: Vandenhoeck & Ruprecht, 1915), 311f; cf. further Paul Drews, *Untersuchungen über die sogen. clementinische Liturgie im VIII. Buch der apostolischen Konstitutionen*, in his *Studien zur Geschichte des Gottesdienstes und des gottesdienstlichen Lebens*, vol. 2 (Tübingen: Mohr [Siebeck], 1906), 23ff.

96 See above, p. 161. It should be observed that *1 Clem.*10.1 says "Abraham, who was called 'the Friend'" ($^{\prime}A\beta\rho\alpha\acute{\alpha}\mu,\ \acute{o}\ \phi\acute{\iota}\lambda o\varsigma\ \pi\rho o\sigma\alpha\gamma o\rho\epsilon\upsilon\theta\epsilon\acute{\iota}\varsigma$), and in 17.2 we find, "and [Abraham] was called the Friend

of God" ($\kappa\alpha\grave{\iota}\ \phi\acute{\iota}\lambda o\varsigma\ \pi\rho o\sigma\eta\gamma o\rho\epsilon\acute{\upsilon}\theta\eta\ \tau o\widehat{\upsilon}\ \theta\epsilon o\widehat{\upsilon}$). Therefore, *1 Clement* (i.e., the tradition behind it) also traces—as Jas does—this designation back to a passage of scripture ("it was testified" [$\acute{\epsilon}\mu\alpha\rho\tau\upsilon\rho\acute{\eta}\theta\eta$] in 17.2 is parallel to "it is written" [$\gamma\acute{\epsilon}\gamma\rho\alpha\pi\tau\alpha\iota$] in 17.3), or to a divine oracle. Cf. also the following footnote.

97 This particle "for" ($\gamma\acute{\alpha}\rho$) which is used to introduce the supporting argument deserves attention (it is lacking in B 1175 syʸᵍ arm and characteristically it is represented by *autem* in *ff*). The relationship between v 25 and v 26 is this: Rahab was justified by works; she could not have been justified in any other way, for without works faith is dead. *Therefore, the faith of Rahab is presupposed* (Cassiodorus rightly comments: "[Rahab] is known to have been justified not only by faith but also by works" [quae non fide tantum, sed opere justificata cognoscitur]), and again there is confirmation of the conjecture which was proposed above, viz., that Jas knew of Abraham and Rahab as examples of faith.

98 The interpretations which take $\acute{\epsilon}\rho\gamma\alpha$ to mean works performed by the will (Haupt, review of Erdmann, *Der Brief des Jakobus*, 190) and $\pi\nu\epsilon\widehat{\upsilon}\mu\alpha$ to mean breath (Mayor), as well as Spitta's conjectured $\kappa\iota\nu\acute{\eta}\mu\alpha\tau o\varsigma$ instead of $\pi\nu\epsilon\acute{\upsilon}\mu\alpha\tau o\varsigma$, are intended to make possible the equation of "works" ($\acute{\epsilon}\rho\gamma\alpha$) with "breath" ($\pi\nu\epsilon\widehat{\upsilon}\mu\alpha$ or "motion" [$\kappa\acute{\iota}\nu\eta\mu\alpha$]) and "faith" ($\pi\acute{\iota}\sigma\tau\iota\varsigma$) with "body" ($\sigma\widehat{\omega}\mu\alpha$). But this is not necessary at all.

99 We can translate $\pi\nu\epsilon\widehat{\upsilon}\mu\alpha$ in this way, for the popular view of the dichotomy of body and soul or life–spirit is presupposed.

It is only the appeal to faith alone, with the exclusion of works, which our author attacks.

The Abraham Example[100]

An attempt was made in the interpretation above to show that the treatment of the Abraham example by our author cannot be explained from the Old Testament or LXX wording, but that instead it is dependent upon the exegetical tradition of Judaism. One piece of evidence for this dependence is the way in which the honorary title "friend of God" is introduced. Another proof of it is the fact that Jas finds in the statement about the faith of Abraham in Gen 15:6 a reference to righteousness by works.

Our author is not the only teacher within early Christianity who makes use of the Jewish Abraham tradition. Even though Paul interprets Gen 15:6 in a so completely non–Jewish fashion, it goes without saying that he knew of this tradition, as the wording of Rom 4:1 possibly indicates.[101] The lists of examples in Heb 11 and *1 Clem.* 10ff have also been influenced directly or indirectly by Jewish tradition. Jewish influence is particularly clear in *1 Clem.* 10 and 12, where "hospitality" ($\phi\iota\lambda o\xi\epsilon\nu\iota a$) occurs beside "faith" ($\pi\iota\sigma\tau\iota\varsigma$) as one virtue beside another. That would be as easily understood by the Jew as it would be incongruous with what Paul has in mind when he speaks of "faith." That there is influence of Jewish tradition does not at all imply that early Christians must have been familiar with all the stories and notions about Abraham—or even with all of merely the older Haggadah—as these are now gathered for us in the *Midrash Rabbah* on Genesis.[102] However, the dominant conception of the figure of Abraham was dependent upon Jewish tradition. It is this conception which must be dealt with here.

Which benefits the Jews had through Abraham is said with utmost clarity already in Sir 44:19ff (the statement about Abraham in the section "in praise of the fathers" in Sirach): keeping of the Law,[103] circumcision, testing[104]—those are the merits of Abraham for which he received great reward ("the nations would be blessed through his posterity" [$\epsilon\nu\epsilon\nu\lambda o\gamma\eta\theta\hat{\eta}\nu a\iota\ \ddot{\epsilon}\theta\nu\eta\ \dot{\epsilon}\nu\ \tau\hat{\omega}\ \sigma\pi\dot{\epsilon}\rho\mu a\tau\iota\ a\dot{v}\tau o\hat{v}$]). Another enumeration of the fathers of Israel, in 1 Macc 2:52, mentions only the greatest deed: "Was not Abraham found faithful when tested, and it was reckoned to him as righteousness?" He was "perfect in all his deeds with the Lord, and well–pleasing in righteousness all the days of his life"—the author of the *Book of Jubilees* (23.10) describes him with these words in an epilogue. It is obvious that the authors within Hellenistic Judaism knew of similar praises of Abraham (Philo, *Abr.* 271), and that finally in the Talmud there were also such summary statements of the merits of Abraham: He had persisted in righteousness from beginning to end (*b. Meg.* 11a), and the evil inclination had held no power over him (*b. Baba Bathra* 17a).

The offering of Isaac was repeatedly characterized as the greatest of all of Abraham's deeds, as in Philo, *Abr.* 167: "For I might almost say that all the other actions which won the favour of God are surpassed by this" ($\dot{o}\lambda\dot{\iota}\gamma o\upsilon\ \gamma\dot{a}\rho\ \delta\dot{\epsilon}\omega\ \phi\dot{a}\nu a\iota\ \pi\dot{a}\sigma a\varsigma\ \ddot{o}\sigma a\iota\ \theta\epsilon o\phi\iota\lambda\epsilon\hat{\iota}\varsigma\ \dot{v}\pi\epsilon\rho\beta\dot{a}\lambda$-

100 On this cf. B. Beer, *Leben Abrahams nach Auffassung der jüdischen Sage* (Leipzig: Leiner, 1859); P. Billerbeck, "Abrahams Leben und Bedeutung für das Reich Gottes nach Auffassung der älteren Haggada," *Nathanael: Zeitschrift für die Arbeit der evangelischen Kirche an Israel* 15 (1899): 43ff; 16 (1900): 33ff. Cf. further Otto Schmitz, "Abraham im Spätjudentum und im Urchristentum," *Aus Schrift und Geschichte* [Festschrift Adolf Schlatter] (Stuttgart: Calwer Vereinsbuchhandlung, 1922), 99–123; Samuel Sandmel, *Philo's Place in Judaism: A Study of Conceptions of Abraham in Jewish Literature* (Cincinnati: Hebrew Union College, 1956).

101 That is, if the word "gained" ($\epsilon\dot{v}\rho\eta\kappa\dot{\epsilon}\nu a\iota$ lacking in B 1739 *pc*) is to be read and the whole verse is to be understood as one sentence. To be sure, neither the text nor the interpretation of Rom 4:1 are certain.

102 The *Midrash Bereshith Rabbah*, English translation by H. Freedman in *Midrash Rabbah*, vol. 1, ed. H. Freedman and Maurice Simon (London: Soncino, 1939).

103 In Sir 44:20b, the words "and was taken into covenant with him" ($\kappa a\iota\ \dot{\epsilon}\gamma\dot{\epsilon}\nu\epsilon\tau o\ \dot{\epsilon}\nu\ \delta\iota a\theta\dot{\eta}\kappa\eta\ \mu\epsilon\tau'\ a\dot{v}\tau o\hat{v}$) are not enumerating another deed of Abraham but rather are parallel to the first half of the verse: "he kept the Law of the Most High" ($\ddot{o}\varsigma\ \sigma\upsilon\nu\epsilon\tau\dot{\eta}\rho\eta\sigma\epsilon\nu\ \nu\dot{o}\mu o\nu\ \dot{v}\psi\dot{\iota}\sigma\tau o\upsilon$). Cf. Ernest Lohmeyer, *Diatheke: Ein Beitrag zur Erklärung des neutestamentlichen Begriffs*, UNT 2 (Leipzig: Hinrichs, 1913), 109ff.

104 Sir 44:20: "he established the covenant in his flesh and when he was tested he was found faithful" ($\kappa a\iota\ \dot{\epsilon}\nu\ \sigma a\rho\kappa\dot{\iota}\ a\dot{v}\tau o\hat{v}\ \ddot{\epsilon}\sigma\tau\eta\sigma\epsilon\nu\ \delta\iota a\theta\dot{\eta}\kappa\eta\nu\ \kappa a\iota\ \dot{\epsilon}\nu\ \pi\epsilon\iota\rho a\sigma\mu\hat{\omega}\ \epsilon\dot{v}\rho\dot{\epsilon}\theta\eta\ \pi\iota\sigma\tau\dot{o}\varsigma$).

λει). Without doubt, when the texts speak of only one *testing of Abraham*, they always mean this most difficult and important test. This conclusion follows above all from the allusions in *4 Maccabees*. Already the designation of the martyrs as "sons of Abraham" ('Αβραμιαῖοι 9.21; 18.23) presupposes that Abraham had suffered similar tortures at least inwardly.[105] An even clearer reference to the fortunes of Abraham occurs in 16.19f in the speech of the mother to her sons: "therefore you owe it to God to endure all pain for his sake; for whom also our father Abraham made haste to sacrifice his son Isaac, the ancestor of our nation" (καὶ διὰ τοῦτο ὀφείλετε πάντα πόνον ὑπομένειν διὰ τὸν θεόν. δι' ὃν καὶ ὁ πατὴρ ἡμῶν Ἀβραὰμ ἔσπευδεν τὸν ἐθνοπάτορα υἱὸν σφαγιάσαι Ἰσαάκ) [trans. Charles, *APOT*]. The author of the book has in mind the same deed of Abraham when he compares with Abraham the mother of the sons (14.20; 18.20?), her "courage" (καρτερία 15.28), and even her "child-bearing" (παιδοποιία 17.6; the word here means rearing them to be ready to die). The allusion to the testing of Abraham in Jdth 8:26 is also clear.

Just this tradition, that Abraham was tested by God, was then expanded by the Jewish Haggadah. First of all, there was the doctrine of the ten trials of Abraham. This is mentioned briefly, and without an enumeration of the trials, in the numerical sayings in *Pirke Aboth* 5.3. In other writings the ten events are elaborated, but in various ways.[106] The original and understandable situation could have been that the offering of Isaac—the most difficult trial, which outweighed all the rest and without which Abraham would have lost all the

rest (*Midrash Bereshith Rabbah* 56 on Gen 22:15)—was numbered as the last trial. Because of the particularly high esteem of the story of Sarah's burial in Gen 23, this narrative was counted as the tenth trial in *Jubilees*[107] and in some of the later Aboth commentaries.[108] But even in the *Book of Jubilees* (18.15ff) the offering of Isaac is the most difficult test. Indeed, we find here precisely an introduction to the story which is also encountered elsewhere, and which further indicates the esteem in which the trials of Abraham were held in the Haggadah: by analogy with the prologue to the Book of Job, a heavenly court is described at which Mastema causes God to test Abraham. *Midrash Bereshith Rabbah* 55 on Gen 22:1, which likewise contains a similar narrative, reports that in a dispute with Ishmael, Isaac asserted that he wished God to make a sacrifice of his life if need be. Finally, the same midrash and the Talmud (*b. Sanh.* 89b) extend the mandate of God in Gen 22:2 into a dialogue by inserting answers upon the part of Abraham—clearly new versions of the story of the offering of Isaac which point out its significance and increase its glory!

It is in the context of these narratives that one must understand what Jewish tradition says about *the faith of Abraham*. In the expression εὑρέθη πιστός used in Sir 44:19–21 and 1 Macc 2:52, as well as in the corresponding Hebrew, Aramaic, and Ethiopic (*Jub.* 18.16)[109] expressions, one can choose between the translations "believing" and "faithful." For the point of both translations amounts to the same thing. In spite of the testing Abraham remained faithful to his God—

---

105 It does not refer to the incineration of Abraham which according to the Haggadah (*Midrash Bereshith Rabbah* 38) was attempted by Nimrod, for on that occasion Abraham did not suffer at all thanks to the intervention of God.

106 In *Pirke de R. Eliezer* 26, numbers 1 and 2 are two events from the haggadic childhood legends, 3) is the migration, 4) famine, 5) the taking of Sarah by Pharaoh, 6) the war with the kings, 7) the covenant between the pieces (Gen 15:7–21), 8) circumcision, 9) Ishmael's expulsion, and 10) the offering of Isaac. *Aboth de R. Nathan* 33 relates numbers 3–10 of this list in addition to a trial from the childhood legends and the banishment of Hagar. Cf. on this Beer, *Leben Abrahams*, 190ff. The *Book of Jubilees* (17.17) mentions numbers 3, 4, 6, 5 (possibly counted as two trials—see Gen 12:9ff and Gen 20), 8, 9, and Hagar;

add to that *Jubilees* 18 and 19, which relate the offering of Isaac and the burial of Sarah (see above in text and cf. next footnote).

107 It dovetails with the way in which the author of *Jubilees* follows closely the story as found in the Priestly Code (E. Littmann, in E. Kautzsch, *Die Apokryphen und Pseudepigraphen des Alten Testaments*, vol. 2: *Die Pseudepigraphen des Alten Testaments* [Tübingen: Mohr (Siebeck), 1900], 37) that precisely the P narrative of the burial of Sarah receives special attention in *Jubilees* and is numbered as the tenth trial.

108 Cf. Beer, *Leben Abrahams*, 191f.

109 See Littmann, *op. cit.* (above n. 107), *ad loc.*

in that his belief is revealed; and because he trusted God's will, he held out even in the face of the most severe testing—thus his fidelity is explained. The statement of the faith of Abraham in Gen 15:6 also belongs in this context. For Jewish interpretation, the faith of Abraham attested in Gen 15:6 is not something which is to be differentiated from conduct, i.e., from works.[110] Rather, it is itself a work, just as is the act of "being faithful" ($\pi \iota \sigma \tau \grave{o} \nu$ $\epsilon \hat{\iota} \nu \alpha \iota$) in the ten trials. There is something of a trial involved in the divine promise of descendents (see Rom 4:19), and in that instance Abraham's faith consists in the fact that he accepts the promise without argument.

All of this provides an explanation for the fortune of the Gen 15:6 passage in the Haggadah. In the first place, it seems understandable why this passage plays no great role in general. If faith is not the essential function of religion in life, but only one achievement among others, then Gen 15:6 is not a fundamental statement; and it is understandable that the second half of the verse, which one reads as a reference to the reward of Abraham (cf. below), held at least just as much interest. It is also understandable that this verse rarely received any special attention in the context of the story to which it belongs.[111] But also it appears understandable *that Gen 15:6*—separated and isolated from its context in the usual rabbinic manner—*could be applied* to the whole of Abraham's life and *especially to the great principal trial in Gen 22*. Tests of faith were certainly to be found throughout his life and especially in this particular story. This application of Gen. 15:6 to the whole of the life of Abraham is shown by 1 Macc 2:52, which combines the clear allusion to the offering of Isaac with "and it was reckoned to him as righteousness" ($\kappa \alpha \grave{\iota}$ $\epsilon \dot{\upsilon} \lambda o \gamma \acute{\iota} \sigma \theta \eta$ $\alpha \dot{\upsilon} \tau \hat{\omega}$ $\epsilon \dot{\iota} s$ $\delta \iota \kappa \alpha \iota o \sigma \acute{\upsilon} \nu \eta \nu$) from Gen 15:6; by *Jub.* 18.6, which praises the "faithful" (= believing) Abraham; and by texts which have undoubtedly been influenced by Jewish exposition, our passage in Jas 2:21ff as well as Heb 11:17.[112] The list in Hebrews which mentions the deeds of Abraham as works of faith (Heb 11:8, 9, 11, 17) nevertheless reveals at the same time how Gen 15:6 was used as a motto for the whole of Abraham's life. That Christian authors (*1 Clem.* 10; 31.2; *Barn.* 13.7) did this is obvious, but from the examples of faith in *1 Clement* we can probably also infer the existence of similar Jewish lists. In fact, in *Mekilta*, tractate *Beshallaḥ* 7 on Ex 14:31,[113] both this world and the world to come are dedicated to Abraham as a reward for his faith, and with this Gen 15:6 is quoted. In the same midrash, tractate *Beshallaḥ* 4 on Ex 14:15,[114] the miracle at the Red Sea appears as a reward for the faith of Abraham in Gen 15:6. Likewise, this passage is cited in *b. Shab.* 97a, where the concern is to show that the Israelites are "descendents of believers."

To be sure, Philo understands the passage in Gen 15:6 to refer also to the promise of Isaac's birth (*Mut. nom.* 177). He even gives a detailed exposition of it in the context of Gen 15 (*Rer. div. her.* 90–101) and in doing so develops a concept of faith based upon typical Hellenistic presuppositions.[115] However, the use of Gen 15:6 by Philo in the book in which he treats the story of Abraham in the manner of a Hellenistic Jewish exegete (*Abr.* 262) is of a different nature. Admittedly, it is the new, Hellenistic concept of faith (trust in God and mistrust of the "bodily and the external" [$\tau \grave{\alpha}$ $\sigma \omega \mu \alpha \tau \iota \kappa \grave{\alpha}$ $\kappa \alpha \grave{\iota}$ $\tau \grave{\alpha}$ $\dot{\epsilon} \kappa \tau \acute{o} s$ *Abr.* 269]) which is described here also, but this is not achieved by allegorical interpretation of the context of the passage but rather by considering the words "he believed in God" ($\dot{\epsilon} \pi \acute{\iota} \sigma \tau \epsilon \upsilon \sigma \epsilon$ $\tau \hat{\omega}$ $\theta \epsilon \hat{\omega}$) as an isolated divine oracle and by applying it to the whole life of Abraham: "There is another record of praise attested by words from Moses' prophetic lips. In these it is stated that he 'believed in God'" ($\dot{\epsilon} \sigma \tau \iota$ $\delta \grave{\epsilon}$ $\kappa \alpha \grave{\iota}$ $\dot{\alpha} \nu \acute{\alpha} \gamma \rho \alpha \pi \tau o s$ $\dot{\epsilon} \pi \alpha \iota \nu o s$ $\alpha \dot{\upsilon} \tau \hat{\omega}$ $\chi \rho \eta \sigma \mu o \hat{\iota} s$ $\mu \alpha \rho \tau \upsilon \rho \eta \theta \epsilon \acute{\iota} s$. $o \hat{\upsilon} s$ $M \omega \upsilon \sigma \hat{\eta} s$ $\dot{\epsilon} \theta \epsilon \sigma \pi \acute{\iota} \sigma \theta \eta$, $\delta \iota$' $o \hat{\upsilon}$ $\mu \eta \nu \acute{\upsilon} \epsilon \tau \alpha \iota$ $\delta \tau \iota$ $\dot{\epsilon} \pi \acute{\iota} \sigma \tau \epsilon \upsilon \sigma \epsilon$ $\tau \hat{\omega}$ $\theta \epsilon \hat{\omega}$) [Loeb modified]. What can already be perceived here is stated with even more clarity in *Praem. poen.* 27;

---

110 Cf. Schlatter, *Glaube*, 11, and 551–61.

111 In *Jub.* 14.6, the verse is quoted without any further elaborations. In his rendering of Gen 15, Josephus (*Ant.* 1.183f) does not mention the faith of Abraham at all. Likewise, *Midrash Bereshith Rabbah* (44) provides no exposition of this verse in that context. Cf. for the rest the brief discussion of the rabbinic passages in question in Billerbeck, *op. cit.* (above,

n. 100), 44, n. 432.

112 The exception which *1 Clem.* 10.7 makes precisely with respect to the offering of Isaac is noteworthy: "because of *obedience* he offered him as a sacrifice" ($\delta \iota$' $\dot{\upsilon} \pi \alpha \kappa o \hat{\eta} s$ $\pi \rho o \sigma \acute{\eta} \nu \epsilon \gamma \kappa \epsilon \nu$ $\alpha \dot{\upsilon} \tau \grave{o} \nu$ $\theta \upsilon \sigma \acute{\iota} \alpha \nu$)—but perhaps this formulation is connected with the viewpoint of the whole of *1 Clement*: "Learn to be submissive" ($\mu \acute{\alpha} \theta \epsilon \tau \epsilon$ $\dot{\upsilon} \pi o \tau \acute{\alpha} \sigma \sigma \epsilon \sigma \theta \alpha \iota$ 57.2).

Philo sees in the Gen 15:6 passage a recognition which the scripture, i.e., God, bestows upon the patriarch because of his piety. Nothing else is meant when Philo, in the passage just mentioned, says of Abraham that "he received for his reward belief in God" (ἆθλον αἴρεται τὴν πρὸς θεὸν πίστιν—just as Isaac received joy and Jacob the vision of God). Gen 15:6 is applied to the whole of Abraham's life in a similar way (although more as a motto than as a reward) in *Leg. all.* 3.228 and *Virt.* 216. In the latter passage Abraham is the one who is said by the Biblical word to have been the originator of monotheism.

The interpretation of the expression "was fulfilled" (ἐπληρώθη) in Jas 2:23 which was proposed above is corroborated by these passages in Philo which record Gen 15:6 as a divine oracle concerning the life of Abraham. *That is the same way in which Jas speaks of Abraham's conduct fulfilling the holy Word of God, which is conceived of as something beyond Time.* Admittedly, Jas has in mind Abraham's behavior in a specific instance. But we also find this association of the Genesis passage with the offering of Isaac in Philo. In *Deus imm.* 4 he explains the binding together of Isaac's feet (Gen 22:9) as an expression of faith: "it may be that he was taught to see how changeable and inconstant was creation, through his knowledge of the unwavering stedfastness that belongs to the Existent; for in this we are told that he had put his trust" (παρόσον ἀνίδρυτον καὶ ἄστατον κατεῖδε τὴν γένεσιν, ὅτε τὴν περὶ τὸ ὂν ἀνενδοίαστον ἔγνω βεβαιότητα, ᾗ λέγεται πεπιστευκέναι).[116] Therefore, Philo also stands under the influence of the exegetical

tradition which is described in this Excursus and which undoubtedly is employed by Jas.

However, precisely in looking at Philo and even more so in looking at Paul one feature in the Jewish figure of Abraham must especially be emphasized; his faith is not the faith of the sinner, a faith by which the sinner comes to God, but rather the faith of the righteous man whose relationship with God is that of close friendship. Faith here is a work of the pious man, not the salvation of the evil man. Although tradition makes Abraham the son of an idol worshipper and dealer in idols,[117] the older Haggadah has no appreciable interest in the inner development of Abraham, in the way in which he came to believe. The Haggadah has him go through life not as one who is seeking but one who knows, one who is a teacher of the true knowledge of God.[118] Actually, already in the narrative of the Priestly Code in Gen 17 the idea is expressed that Abraham initiated a new knowledge of God. It is understandable that this conception would have to find its own special expression in Hellenistic Judaism. The propaganda of an ethical monotheism could certainly point out in the life of Abraham the living example of all its presuppositions: the possibility of the knowledge of God from the works of nature,[119] the possibility of a life in accordance with the Law without actual possession of the Law.[120] On the other hand, one can understand why rabbinic writings do not express this last idea. For them, it is self-evident that the ancestral father of Israel also shared in Israel's greatest possession, the Law.[121] Thus they make him into the elder of a school who is skilled

113 Text and ET in Jacob Z. Lauterbach, ed. and tr. *Mekilta de-Rabbi Ishmael*, vol. 1 (Philadelphia: Jewish Publication Society of America, 1933), 253.

114 See Lauterbach 1, p. 220.

115 Cf. the following Excursus.

116 This explanation is given by Philo as one of two alternative interpretations.

117 Cf. *Jub.* 12. Here Terah is an involuntary worshipper of idols. A different and more detailed account is in *Midrash Bereshith Rabbah* 38 on Gen 11:28.

118 According to *Jub.* 12.1ff, Abraham tried to convert his father. According to *b. Yoma* 28b, Abraham was an elder. But also in Josephus (see in the text below) a similar thing is the true goal of Abraham's life— *Ant.* 1.155: "Hence he began to have more lofty conceptions of virtue than the rest of mankind, and determined to reform and change the ideas universally current concerning God" (διὰ τοῦτο καὶ φρονεῖν ἐπ' ἀρετῇ μεῖζον τῶν ἄλλων ἠργμένος, καὶ τὴν περὶ τοῦ θεοῦ δόξαν, ἣν ἅπασι συνέβαινεν εἶναι, καινίσαι καὶ μεταβαλεῖν ἔγνω cf. also *Ant.* 1.161).

119 Josephus, *Ant.* 1.156: "This he inferred from the changes to which land and sea are subject" (εἴκαζε δὲ ταῦτα τοῖς τῆς γῆς καὶ θαλάττης παθήμασι κτλ.); cf. Philo, *Abr.* 60.

120 Josephus, *Ant.* 1.256, calls him "a man excelling in every virtue" (ἀνὴρ πᾶσαν ἀρετὴν ἄκρος). The popular theme of "the unwritten law" (ἄγραφος νόμος, cf. Wendland, *Hellenistische Kultur*, 356 n. 4) is applied by Philo to the figure of Abraham in *Abr.* 275f.

121 In *Midrash Bereshith Rabbah*, 56 on Gen 22:19, Abraham confesses that every good thing which has befallen him he owes only to the Torah.

in the Law (*b. Yoma* 28b), and they show him as having at his disposal far more traditions about the interpretation of the Law than are known even to the greats of the synagogue (*b. ʿAbodah Zarah* 14b). He had learned the Torah on his own, for his two kidneys became like two pitchers, brimming over with the Torah (*Midrash Bereshith Rabbah* 95 on Gen 46:28).

If the sense in which the righteousness of Abraham was understood by Jewish tradition is to be understood, one must keep in mind not the forms of expression, which are diverse and are, in part, of late attestation, but rather the fundamental idea of these passages which is stressed with unanimity by both Hellenistic and rabbinic Judaism: Abraham's life is rich in good works. Among the works, faith also had its place. Therefore it is out of the question that Gen 15:6 would have been understood by Jewish tradition in the sense of Rom 4:4—i.e., that Abraham lacks righteousness from works, but his faith is "reckoned" in lieu of such a righteousness. Here Jas agrees with the synagogue. He takes the expression "was reckoned" (ἐλογίσθη) as proof of Abraham's righteousness by works. This is the righteousness which is meant when the Jewish expositors extol Abraham's piety by taking certain Biblical passages as references to this ancestor,[122] or at other times in summary sayings (see above) and honorary titles.[123] But one of these honorary titles turns out to be even more of a favorite than the predicate "righteous" (δίκαιος)—namely, the title which Jas himself mentions: *friend of God*.

This title has its Biblical basis in the expression "my friend" (אהבי) and the corresponding designations for Abraham in Isa 41:8; 51:2; 2 Chron 20:7; Dan 3:35. In the first two passages the LXX has "whom I loved" (ὃν ἠγάπησα), and in the second two, "beloved" (ἠγαπημένος). The text of Genesis, especially in 18:17, seems to have offered the opportunity for the insertion of this title. Cf. Philo, *Sobr.* 56: "Shall I hide anything from Abraham, my Friend?" (μὴ ἐπικαλύψω ἐγὼ ἀπὸ Ἀβραὰμ τοῦ φίλου μου), and the Jerusalem Targum.[124] Thus the title was adopted into the Abraham story and, besides the instances in Philo, it is mentioned in *Jubilees* (see below), in *1 Clem.* 10.1 and 17.2 (obviously dependent upon Jewish tradition), and in Iren., *Adv. haer.* 4.16.2.[125] In the *Testament of Abraham* the account is directly dependent upon the presupposition that even Death must make an exception in the case of the "Friend of God."[126] The understanding which Philo has of this title is shown by *Abr.* 273, where it is said that God "repaid him with faithfulness by confirming with an oath the gifts which He had promised, and here He no longer talked with him as God with man but as a friend with a familiar" (πίστιν ἀντιδίδωσιν αὐτῷ, τὴν δι᾿ ὅρκου βεβαίωσιν ὧν ὑπέσχετο δωρεῶν, οὐκέτι μόνον ὡς ἀνθρώπῳ θεός, ἀλλὰ καὶ ὡς φίλος γνωρίμῳ διαλεγόμενος, Gen 22:16 is then cited). In this, Philo has in mind the familiar concept of the wise man as a friend of God.[127] Another context which is even more significant for Jas is seen in the *Book of Jubilees* 19.9 (after the account of the tenth trial of Abraham): "he was found faithful, and was recorded on the heavenly tablets as the friend of God" (trans. Charles, *APOT*).

---

122 Thus, Isa 33:15 is taken as a reference to Abraham because of Gen 18:19, and Ps 15:1 because of Gen 17:1 (*b. Mak.* 24a).

123 Philo, *Abr.* 270ff.

124 Schlatter, *Glaube*, 437.

125 In the Irenaeus passage, Gen 15:6 occurs in combination with the statement about Abraham being called friend of God (see above in the Introduction, section 4) Nevertheless, it is questionable that one can suppose Irenaeus to be dependent upon Jas here, for this combination was probably already established in Jewish tradition (cf. below and the Introduction, section 4). In the *Damascus Document*, not only are Isaac and Jacob called friends of God (CD III, 3), but also Abraham—if in CD III, 2 the restoration of the lacuna proposed by Louis Ginzberg (*Eine unbekannte jüdische Sekte*, part 1 [New York:

Ginzberg, 1922], 14f), or that proposed by Israël Lévi ("Un écrit sadducéen antérieur à la destruction du temple," *REJ* 61 [1911]: 177 n. 1) is correct.

126 See *Testament of Abraham* (Rec. A) 16 (text in TS 2, 2). Cf. also *Apocalypse of Abraham* 10, where the angel says to Abraham, "Stand up, Abraham, Friend of God who loveth thee" (trans. G. H. Box and J. I. Landsman, *The Apocalypse of Abraham* [London: S.P.C.K., 1919]).

127 Cf. in Philo, *Rer. div. her.* 21; *Omn. prob. lib.* 42; *Vit. Mos.* 1.156; elsewhere, cf. Wisd 7:27; Plato, *Leg.* 4.716d; Xenophon, *Mem.* 2.1.33; Epict., *Diss.* 4.3.9. Philo, *Sobr.* 55, even gives a reason: "For wisdom is rather God's friend than His servant" (φίλον γὰρ τὸ σοφὸν θεῷ μᾶλλον ἢ δοῦλον). The concept of the friend of God is traced through Greek, Biblical, and early Christian literature by Erik Peterson, "Der Gottes-

Here is further evidence for what I have already presented as a probability in the interpretation of Jas 2:23, viz., that Jewish tradition had already associated the predicate "friend of God" with Abraham's faith. But in accordance with the Jewish concept of faith, this means that the title "friend of God" stands in a very close relationship to the merit of the righteous person.[128]

If this concept is to be understood, one must disregard Paul's idea that no man can fulfill the demands of God. Also, the other thesis (Lk 17:7–10), that only one who has done more than his duty may properly claim a reward, does not apply here. According to the Jewish view, there is a reward for every merit, and every fulfillment of a command is merit.[129] Therefore it is not a question of whether Abraham was perfectly sinless. His merits are many, thus his reward is very great.[130]

This reward is credited to the pious man by means of a sort of heavenly book–keeping. "The account–book lies open and the hand writes and everyone that wishes to borrow let him come and borrow; but the collectors [i.e., angelic officials] go their round continually every day and exact payment of men with their consent or without their consent, for they have that on which they can rely" (*Pirke Aboth* 3.17) [trans. Danby]. *Jub.* 30.19f tells of another "friend of God"— Levi: "and so they inscribe as a testimony in his favour on the heavenly tablets blessing and righteousness before the God of all: and we [the angels] remember the righteousness which the man fulfilled during his life, at all periods of the year; until a thousand generations they will record it, and it will come to him and to his descendents after him, and he has been recorded on the heavenly tablets as a friend and a righteous man" (trans. Charles, *APOT*). Therefore, this is also the meaning in *Jub.* 19.9, where it is reported that Abraham has been recorded as a friend of God. Now Jas obviously has taken the Old Testament words "it was reckoned to him as righteousness" (ἐλογίσθη αὐτῷ εἰς δικαιοσύνην) as a reference to this heavenly accounting. In a very similar way, *Jub.* 30.23 says, "and it [i.e., what the sons of Jacob did] was written for a blessing" (trans. Charles, *APOT*). We now understand also why Philo, who in *Rer. div. her.* 94 writes, "his faith was reckoned to him as righteousness" (λογισθῆναι τὴν πίστιν εἰς δικαιοσύνην), can in *Leg. all.* 3.228 paraphrase in this way: "Abraham believed God and was held to be righteous" (Ἀβραάμ γέ τοι ἐπίστευσε τῷ θεῷ καὶ δίκαιος ἐνομίσθη). In point of fact, that Abraham is considered a righteous man means the same thing as that something is recorded in his account "as righteousness." Now it is understandable how the honorary title "friend of God" can appear directly beside "reckoned as righteousness" (λογισθῆναι εἰς δικαιοσύνην), for this title is also written down in Abraham's account in the heavenly books. This is further evidence that Jas was not the first to combine the designation of Abraham as the "friend of God" with the Gen 15:6 passage.[131]

Thus, in his Abraham example Jas reveals a dependence upon the tradition of the synagogue. He is dependent not upon the later form of this tradition, but upon

---

freund: Beiträge zur Geschichte eines religiösen Terminus," *ZKG* 42 (1923): 161–202.

128 Even today Abraham is called in Arabic "the Beloved"; cf. Hans Schmidt and Paul Kahle, *Volkserzählungen aus Palästina*, FRLANT 17 (Göttingen: Vandenhoeck & Ruprecht, 1918), 204; Hermann Rönsch, "Abraham der Freund Gottes," *ZWTh* 16 (1873): 585, n. 1; and in the *Koran* 4.124.

129 In the Mishnah, *Makkoth* 3.15, with reference to the prohibitions in Lev 18 which are obeyed by *not* doing certain things (and in application of the promise of Lev 18:5), it is said that to someone who sits and commits no transgression a reward is given as though he has fulfilled a (positive) command. Also, according to *Midrash Bereshith Rabbah* 39 (on Gen 12:1) and 55 (on Gen 22:2), God did not totally reveal his intention right away in the two trials in Gen 12 and 22, in order that he might reward Abraham for each one of his steps (in the migration) and his words (in the conversation about the offering of Isaac).

130 In *Midrash Bereshith Rabbah* 44 on Gen 15:1, God says to Abraham: "Fear not . . . all that I have done for thee in this world I did for nought; but in the future that is to come, thy reward shall be exceeding great" (trans. Freedman-Simon).

131 See above in the commentary on v 23.

the Haggadah which Philo uses, which the *Book of Jubilees* passes on, the influence of which is traceable in *1 Clement*, and to which also may belong many of the motifs which are preserved for us only in the later rabbinic literature. As for Abraham's merit, Jas is in full agreement with the synagogue: Because of his works, Abraham obtained his place in the heavenly list of righteous people and he is recorded as a friend of God. The connection of faith with the story of the sacrifice of Isaac also derives from the Haggadah. But here there is a noticeable difference: for the Jewish exegetes, the faith of Abraham represents a work or a series of works, but in Jas, the connection of "he believed" ($\dot{\epsilon}\pi\acute{\iota}\sigma\tau\epsilon\nu\sigma\epsilon$) and "it was reckoned" ($\dot{\epsilon}\lambda o\gamma\acute{\iota}\sigma\theta\eta$) is not so clear. Jas does not want to show that faith is a work, but that faith and works work together. Because of this his interpretation of the Gen 15:6 passage is not totally consistent, for one cannot tell whether "he believed" is supposed to refer only to the offering of Isaac in v 21 (so the synagogue), or only to the "faith" ($\pi\acute{\iota}\sigma\tau\iota s$) in v 22, or to both of them at the same time. In the first case, the argument in v 22 would be lost; in the second case, "it was reckoned" would lack a reference to works. Thus we are left with the third possibility, but that would not be a very clear interpretation. The root of the difficulty lies in the fact that Jas has introduced into the Jewish proof of Abraham's righteousness by works his own thesis, first formulated upon the basis of Christian presuppositions, about the intimate connection between faith and works. Why he does this must be shown in the following Excursus.

Faith and Works in Paul and Jas[132]

In a comparison of the views regarding faith and works in Paul and Jas one must observe above all that neither of the two has defined the essence of faith. Instead, both speak only of how much or how little depends upon faith under certain circumstances. And still another thing must be considered: in reality, two incomparable things are being placed beside one another. They are incomparable not only because we possess long letters written by one author and only this short writing by the other, but above all because only one of these authors has proposed an original view of the importance of faith which is grand and audacious and which is presented sometimes in didactic, sometimes in enthusiastic language. On the other hand, the efforts of the other author, Jas, appear to be directed merely toward the goal of rejecting an estimation of faith which seems to him to be harmful. To do this he points out the necessity of works which ought to proceed from this faith. He speaks with the conviction of a teacher who is confident of the assent of every sincere person. Paul speaks with the certainty of one who has an inner calling, whose

---

132 Out of the abundant literature which deals specifically with Jas 2:14–26 I will mention here the following:
Weiffenbach, *Jak 2, 14–26.*
P. Schanz, "Jakobus und Paulus," *ThQ* 62 (1880): 3–46; 247–86.
Alb. Klöpper, "Die Erörterung des Verhältnisses von Glauben und Werken im Jakobusbriefe (cap. 2, 14–26)," *ZWTh* 28 (1885): 280–319.
L. Usteri, "Glaube, Werke und Rechtfertigung im Jakobusbrief," *ThStKr* 62 (1889): 211–56.
Schwarz, "Jak. 2, 14–26."
Th. Tielemann, "Versuch einer neuen Auslegung und Anordnung des Jakobusbriefes," *NKZ* 5 (1894): 580–611.
Bernhard Bartmann, *St. Paulus und St. Jacobus über die Rechtfertigung,* BSF 2, 1 (Freiburg: Herder, 1897).
J. Böhmer, "Der 'Glaube' im Jakobusbriefe," *NKZ* 9 (1898): 251–6.
Ménégoz, "Justification par la foi."
Kühl, *Stellung.*
Köhler, *Glaube und Werke.*
Charles Johnston, "The Controversy between St. Paul and St. James," *Constructive Quarterly* 3 (1915): 603–19.
Georg Eichholz, *Jakobus und Paulus: Ein Beitrag zum Problem des Kanons,* Theologische Existenz heute, N. F. 39, ed. K. G. Steck and Gg. Eichholz (München: Kaiser, 1953).
Joachim Jeremias, "Paul and James," *ET* 66 (1955): 368–71.
Eduard Lohse, "Glaube und Werke: Zur Theologie des Jakobusbriefes," *ZNW* 48 (1957): 1–22.
Georg Eichholz, *Glaube und Werke bei Paulus und Jakobus,* Theologische Existenz heute, N. F. 88 (München: Kaiser, 1961).
Zane C. Hodges, "Light on James Two from Textual Criticism," *Bibliotheca Sacra* 120 (1963): 341–50.
Rolf Walker, "Allein aus Werken: Zur Auslegung von Jakobus 2, 14–26," *ZThK* 61 (1964): 155–92.
Roy Bowen Ward, "The Works of Abraham: James 2:14–26," *HTR* 61 (1968): 283–90.

preaching is considered by the world as foolishness and an irritation, while its divine power has been revealed precisely to him. Our investigation must commence with *Paul's* preaching, as the more original and personal proclamation.

Rom 4 is the section in which Paul testifies most clearly to the essence of the power of his faith. In doing this he also utilizes the Abraham example, obviously with Jewish tradition in mind. His understanding of the Gen 15:6 passage, according to which the term "it was reckoned" (ἐλογίσθη) plainly excludes righteousness by works, is well-known. Thus the saying is interpreted on the basis of its context in such a way that Abraham's faith involves the promise of offspring. And just at that point the supreme significance of faith becomes apparent to Paul: what Abraham believes is the most unbelievable thing in the world. His years and Sarah's age seem to contradict the promise—yet he believes "against all hope" (παρ' ἐλπίδα ἐπ' ἐλπίδι Rom 4:18). This faith of Abraham becomes for Paul a model of the Christian faith. The Christian also must believe against all hope: the improbable idea, that God allowed the Messiah to be killed and then brought him back to life and glory (Rom 4:25), and the most improbable idea of all, that in this way God "justifies the sinner" (Rom 4:5). What is not visible to human eyes, what is impossible according to human standards, that is what faith converts into a certain fact for the believer (Col 2:12). Faith knows what it does not see. *Believing and seeing are opposites* (2 Cor 5:7).

This turning of faith towards a supernatural reality which contradicts all human calculation is intimately connected with the personal experience of Paul. He had experienced the fact that God calls into being that which is not (Rom 4:17) and makes real what is impossible: he had made an apostle out of the persecutor of the church, a missionary to the Gentiles out of a Pharisee. And just as paradoxical as his conversion is the gospel which the converted Paul preaches, the gospel of the death of the Messiah on the cross and of salvation for sinners and Gentiles: everything which had once been precious, sacred and holy to Paul he had been obliged to cast into the dust so that he might be

able to believe this message "against all hope" (Phil 3:7ff). And God's management of the world had been equally paradoxical, since he allowed the people of the Law to go astray and called the Gentiles to salvation. It is, indeed, no accident that in two sections of Romans in which we can see trains of thought which are current in Paul's preaching Paul puts into the mouth of the hearer the question, "Is God not unjust?" (Rom 3:5; 9:14). Thus "faith" becomes the catchword for the acceptance of this marvelous divine decree which justifies the sinner through the death of the Son of God. Whoever says "Yes" to this paradox thereby declares his willingness to renounce the acquisition of righteousness through works ("his own righteousness" [ἰδία δικαιοσύνη] Rom 10:3) and to allow himself to be "justified" by God. This then is called "righteousness by faith" (Gal 2:16; Rom 10:6), and with respect to this idea the religions are separated: the "principle of works" (νόμος ἔργων) here, the "principle of faith" (νόμος πίστεως) there (Rom 3:27; see also Gal 3:23, 25). From this point of view *the opposite of believing* is no longer seeing, but *doing.*

Yet many statements and expressions of Paul testify to another view of faith alongside this one. The most important passage for understanding this other view is Rom 10:9: Faith is the inner process which operates side by side with the external confession with the mouth that Jesus is Lord. How this takes place is described in 10:14, 15: Faith comes into being from hearing the preaching of salvation. Therefore it means first the acceptance of, and then the holding fast to, this message. This is the way in which Paul uses the word in Rom 1:5, 8; 1 Cor 2:5; Phil 1:25; Col 1:4; 1 Thess 1:8. Then "faith" can designate the Christian conviction (2 Cor 1:24; but especially Rom 14:1, 22, 23), and finally Christianity in general (Gal 1:23).[133] In all of these passages "faith" is a catchword for membership in the community of Christians. Its opposite is "*to be unbelieving, i.e., a non-Christian.*"

In Rom 10:9, 14 Paul presupposes that this meaning is a familiar one within the Roman church, which was not founded by him. Therefore he was not the first to coin it. Indeed, one might say that only if this view of

---

133 Passages which are unclear or ambiguous will not be considered here, where we are dealing only with types. Nor will we consider such particularized uses

as the special nuances which "faith" has in the juxtaposition of "faith" and "love." Also, the use of "faith" to mean trust in the miracle worker does not

faith is based upon a common Christian usage does it make any sense at all. There are also other considerations (see below) which make this probable. Finally, one expression which Paul uses repeatedly but never explains becomes intelligible in the multiplicity of its combinations only if the apostle has taken it over as an already fixed term from the stock of religious concepts in early Christianity: the term is "the faith in Jesus Christ" (πίστις Ἰησοῦ Χριστοῦ), or "faith in Jesus" (πίστις Ἰησοῦ), or "faith in Christ" (πίστις Χριστοῦ). If "faith" is a catchword for membership in a religious community, then "faith in Jesus Christ" is the Christianization of this word.[134] Hence, this expression means that someone has the faith which is presupposed among the members of the Christian community. In this way the expression "faith in Jesus Christ" becomes the bracket for the whole variety of meanings which simply the term "faith" can have in Paul.

One can gain an understanding of this co-existence of the several concepts of faith in Paul by looking at the spiritual environment from which Paul comes. Of course, this does not mean that the peculiar Pauline concept of justification by faith (vis-à-vis works) is capable of being directly "traced back" to anything. But we have already come to understand this concept of faith as a specialization of the other concept, which has as its content confidence in a divine world which is inaccessible to the senses. That this idea presupposes the Hellenistic dualism ("visible" [φαινόμενον]—"invisible" [ἀφανές]) should be obvious. But that prior to Paul it had already penetrated the Jewish thought

world, indeed, had already been used for the interpretation of the Abraham example, is shown by Philo's eloquent remarks in *Rer. div. her.* 90ff about the words, "Abraham believed God" (ἐπίστευσε Ἀβραὰμ τῷ θεῷ):[135] "Who would *not* believe in God?" asks a fictitious opponent, in order to reduce the praise accorded the patriarch. Philo answers, "You will clearly understand that to trust in God alone and join no other with him is no easy matter, by reason of our kinship with our yokefellow, mortality, which works upon us to keep out trust placed in riches and repute and office and friends and health and strength and many other things" (σαφῶς γνώσῃ ὅτι μόνῳ θεῷ χωρὶς ἑτέρου προσπαραλήψεως οὐ ῥᾴδιον πιστεῦσαι διὰ τὴν πρὸς τὸ θνητὸν ᾧ συνεζεύγμεθα συγγένειαν· ὅπερ ἡμᾶς καὶ χρήμασι καὶ δόξῃ καὶ ἀρχῇ καὶ φίλοις ὑγείᾳ τε καὶ ῥώμῃ σώματος καὶ ἄλλοις πολλοῖς ἀναπείθει πεπιστευκέναι, cf. *Praem. poen.* 28–30). That is the Hellenistic root from which grew Paul's expression, "beyond all hope" (παρ' ἐλπίδα ἐπ' ἐλπίδι). Just how strongly religious can be the motivation for this advance from appearance to being is shown by *Corp. Herm.* 9.10, where inner or spiritual vision (νοῆσαι) is equated with "to believe" (πιστεῦσαι).[136]

It is also in Hellenism that one can find the basis for the other concept of faith which—as we have seen—presupposes a religious community. As long as the identity of the religious community equaled that of a certain nation there was no need for a special religious designation. Whoever belongs to the people of Israel is also a servant of Yahweh. But in Diaspora Judaism, where proselytes and "god-fearers" (σεβόμενοι) obeyed

---

belong here, although this designation has its significance in the Gospels and is also not foreign to Jas (see 1:6; 5:15).

134 This explanation of the origin of the expression, which is *a priori* the most probable one (cf. "we have believed in Jesus Christ" [εἰς Χριστὸν Ἰησοῦν ἐπιστεύσαμεν] Gal 2:16), would be proven to be impossible only if one accepts Johannes Haussleiter's interpretation of the genitive as a subjective genitive (*Der Glaube Jesu Christi und der christliche Glaube: Ein Beitrag zur Erklärung des Römerbriefes* [Erlangen and Leipzig: Deichert (Böhme), 1891]). That the expression cannot be interpreted directly upon the basis of the other statements by Paul about faith has been stated several times; see Weinel, *Biblische Theologie*, section 49.2; Bousset, *Kyrios Christos*, 200ff.

135 On what follows, cf. Reitzenstein, *Mysterienreligionen*,

234–6; Bousset, *Kyrios Christos*, 200ff.

136 Cf. also *Corp. Herm.* 4.6, where the dualism is described as follows: "For since there are two kinds of beings, corporeal and incorporeal, and since the mortal belongs to one category and the divine to the other, the choice of one or the other is left to him who desires to make that choice" (δύο γὰρ ὄντων τῶν ὄντων, σώματος καὶ ἀσωμάτου, ἐν οἷς τὸ θνητὸν καὶ τὸ θεῖον, ἡ αἵρεσις θατέρου καταλείπεται τῷ ἑλέσθαι βουλομένῳ) [Trans.]. Following that, 4.9 says, "The visible things please us, but the invisible things cause us to doubt. The evil things are more visible, while the Good is invisible to things which are visible, for it has no shape or figure" (τὰ μὲν γὰρ φαινόμενα τέρπει, τὰ δὲ ἀφανῆ δυσπιστεῖν ποιεῖ. φανερώτερα δέ ἐστι τὰ κακά, τὸ δὲ ἀγαθὸν ἀφανὲς τοῖς φανεροῖς· οὐ γὰρ μορφὴ οὔτε τύπος ἐστὶν αὐτῷ) [Trans.].

the message of ethical monotheism, one could have Jewish convictions without being a Jew. Perhaps following the Stoic model, Philo uses "faith" ($\pi\iota\sigma\tau\iota\varsigma$) to designate this conviction.[137] We have already seen how he turns the word to be used with reference to God or the supernatural world; here also he is the predecessor of Paul in the double-sided use of the term. Yet that use of "faith" to mean the religious conviction of the Jew is by that time common knowledge among the Jews.[138] That cannot be considered surprising in a period when the national community no longer existed, or existed only in limited measure.[139]

We are, however, concerned with one problem in particular—the relationship of this concept of faith, which indicates membership in the community of believers, to doing and therefore to "works." The word "faith" includes first of all conviction and confession. But the more importance piety places upon "doing," the more closely associated works become with faith. Thus we can understand that the documents of the religion of the Torah occasionally mention works alongside faith. This is done not to stress the difference between the two things, but precisely in order to emphasize the intimate connection between works and faith: One who confesses the Torah must act in accordance with it! The best examples are found in the book of *4 Ezra*, such as the passage in 3.32: "Has any other nation known thee beside Israel? Or what tribes have so believed thy covenants as those of Jacob?" (in 5.29, the antithesis is the Gentiles, who "have denied thy promises") [trans. Charles, *APOT*]. In 6.5 there is mention of the sealing of those who "gather the treasures of faith." Obviously, these are the pious, as opposed to the "sinners" who were mentioned previously. But in the phrase "treasures of faith" one can think of the spiritual conduct of the pious and all the accomplishments which are connected with it, i.e., once again the works which are commonly mentioned in Jewish literature with the metaphor "treasures."[140]

Thus faith and works belong together, and so they are mentioned together when there is a discussion of him who is "able to escape on account of his works or his faith by which he has believed" (*4 Ezra* 9.7; hence, it is presupposed that this faith is challenged), and when salvation is assured to those who have "fallen into peril," if they "have works and faith toward the Most High and the Mighty One" (13.23) [trans. Charles, *APOT*]. There is scarcely any material difference between a faith such as this which stands the test of persecution and a "work." The parallelism in 7.24 is also instructive: "In his statutes they have put no faith, and have set at naught his works" (trans. Charles, *APOT*).

These passages explain a phenomenon which has already been noticed in the investigation of the Abraham example: On the one hand, "faith" designates a specific conduct, especially in a period of persecution or trial, and therefore it designates an accomplishment, a work; for this reason, the saying about Abraham's faith can be taken as a reference to his conduct in the offering of Isaac. On the other hand, "faith" is used to characterize the inner disposition which underlies all works, and in this context the Gen 15:6 passage is applied to the whole of Abraham's life. This second meaning is stated with particular clarity in *Mekilta*, tractate *Beshallaḥ* 7 on Ex 15:31: "R. Nehemiah says: Whence can you prove that whosoever accepts even one single commandment with true faith is deserving of having the Holy Spirit rest upon him?" And then there follows evidence for this from Ex 14:31 and 15:1, after which we find the statement: "And so also you find that our father Abraham inherited both this world and the world beyond only as a reward for the faith with which he believed . . ." (Trans. Lauterbach 1, pp. 252f); Gen 15:6 is quoted as evidence. Therefore the passage pictures Abraham as a man who takes the commandment upon himself "in faith." Also significant for this concept is the Talmudic passage *b. Makkoth*

---

137 *Virt.* 216: "a firm and unswerving conception" ($\dot{\alpha}\kappa\lambda\iota\nu\dot{\eta}\varsigma$ $\kappa\alpha\dot{\iota}$ $\beta\epsilon\beta\alpha\dot{\iota}\alpha$ $\dot{\upsilon}\pi\dot{o}\lambda\eta\psi\iota\varsigma$); cf. Bousset, *Kyrios Christos*, 200.

138 The few passages in the Old Testament in which faith is mentioned occasioned and promoted this use of the term. But the new religious situation of Judaism gave the terminology a significance which did not belong to it according to the Old Testament.

139 Cf. further Schlatter, *Glaube*, chapters 1 and 2.

139 Cf. the preceding Excursus and especially *4 Macc.* 15.24; 16.22; 17.2.

140 The references are collected in Bertholet, vol. 2, p. 454.

24a, where there is a description of how the original number of precepts in the Law (365 prohibitions plus 248 commands, according to *b. Makkoth* 23b) was constantly reduced by condensation. In conclusion it is said (this conclusion of the thought is ascribed to R. Naḥman b. Isaac [d. 356]): "But it is Habakkuk who came and based them all on one [principle], as it is said, 'But the righteous shall live by his faith'" (trans. Epstein). From all of this it becomes clear that in any event faith stands in a very close relationship to works. *A fundamental contrast between the two is not common in Judaism.*[141]

This survey of the development of the idea of faith was necessary at this point, since Jas never says what he understands by the term "faith." Just for that reason it cannot be said that Jas has introduced a new concept of faith different from those which have been described. Instead, it is only a matter of deciding in which of the groups described above we must place Jas. The best explanation is provided by Jas 2:1. Jas wants to say: "Christians, favoritism is not compatible with your faith," and he says, "Do not hold *the faith* and at the same time show partiality" ($\pi\rho\sigma\omega\pi\sigma\lambda\eta\mu\psi\acute{\iota}\alpha$).[142] Hence, "faith" here clearly has the common meaning of spiritual allegiance to a confession and membership in the community of that confession. The same thing is meant in 1:3, where the testing of faith in persecutions is mentioned. The danger of the persecutions lies in the fact that they can shake the individual's allegiance to the confession. In 2:5 the phrase "rich in faith" ($\pi\lambda\sigma\upsilon\sigma\acute{\iota}\sigma\upsilon\varsigma\ \acute{\epsilon}\nu\ \pi\acute{\iota}\sigma\tau\epsilon\iota$) seems to approximate the other Hellenistic concept of faith (faith in contrast to "sight"). But this statement is governed by the force of the antithesis, and for this reason nothing can be inferred from it with respect to Jas 2:14–26. This last judgment also applies to both of the passages in which the prayer of faith is mentioned—1:6 and 5:15. Here "faith" has the special meaning "trust that the request will be granted," but it is only the combination with "prayer"

which achieves this meaning—therefore, this meaning cannot be generalized and traced throughout all of Jas either. But in all of the instances which have been examined thusfar what is involved is the faith which the Christian has, never the faith of the sinner which first brings him to God.

The results of the examination of 2:14ff agree with these observations. The faith which is mentioned in this section can be presupposed in every Christian. Indeed, as an example of the confession, Jas 2:19 even selects a statement in which not only Christians but also Jews (and enlightened Gentiles) are agreed. But precisely the fact that he does this shows that he is not concerned with a specific concept of faith within Christianity or of any specific Christian group.[143] 2:18 also confirms this. For if the interpretation attempted above is correct, Jas in this imaginary dialogue is not making a distinction between one concept of faith which includes works and another which excludes them, but rather he sees in the separation of faith from works a mere artificiality. Faith which does not display itself in works is an inferior faith! That shows what Jas is driving at. It is not a matter of correcting an opinion about faith. His intention is not dogmatically oriented, but practically oriented: *he wishes to admonish the Christians to practice their faith, i.e., their Christianity, by works.*

That still does not solve the question of the relationship to Paul. But one thing must be recognized to begin with: it is impossible that our author would have combated the Epistle to the Romans in this way if he had really read and understood it. This follows, above all, from Jas' understanding of "works." From Galatians we know well enough which "works" above all are on Paul's mind when he speaks of faith without works. These are the works of the ceremonial law, circumcision, keeping of festivals, rites of purity. Paul sees the enforcement of these among Gentiles Christians as a corruption of the gospel. Jas discusses none of this. His "works" consist in the fulfillment of the simplest ethical

---

141 This conclusion holds true in spite of the fact that in *4 Ezra* 8.32–36 there are found the famous statements about the merciful God which are reminiscent of Paul: "For if to us, who do not have works of righteousness, you desire to show mercy, then you will be called 'the Merciful One' . . . for your righteousness and your goodness, Lord, will be declared in the fact that you have been merciful to those who do not have a wealth of good works" [Trans.]. But the pessimism with regard to sin which is found in *4 Ezra* is an exception on the whole, and then too there is no mention in this passage of a faith which points out to the sinner the possibility of salvation. The meaning of the preceding verses is rather that God shows mercy upon the whole people because of the few who are righteous.

directives, especially those of love and mercy (see 1:27; 2:1–13; but also 3:18; 5:4). The situation is similar with respect to his understanding of faith. The faith which believes the impossible and depends upon it in order to gain access to God is alien to Jas. The salvation which Jas, too, says (2:14) is promised to faith is something which every sincere Christian hopes to find at the great transformation of the world. Here also it is apparent that Jas is speaking of the faith which the Christian has, not that by which the sinner first becomes a Christian.

Now the question arises as to whether one must see in our "letter" evidence of "pre-Pauline" Christianity, i.e., whether Jas originates from the period before Paul's struggle over the Law. Up until now, the answer given by some scholars to this question has been "yes."[144] Nevertheless, I believe that the investigations in this Excursus combined with those of the preceding Excursus suggest another conclusion: the author, indeed, does stand within an early Christian development which does not directly derive from Paul—otherwise he would have understood Paul better or have been more clearly in opposition to him—, *but his remarks in 2:14ff are still inconceivable unless Paul had previously set forth the slogan "faith, not works."*

We have seen how closely combined faith and works are in the Jewish view. An alternative such as "either faith or works" has no place in this sphere of thought. At first Jas appears to be treating the problem in this way, since he demonstrates the absurdity of faith without works. The fact that Jas utilizes the Abraham example (and the Rahab example) could also be well understood upon the basis of these views from the Judaeo-Christian tradition. But not the manner in which he discusses the Abraham example! For Jas does not wish to prove with Gen 15:6 that in the case of Abraham works proceeded from faith—which would be the correct Jewish or "pre-Pauline" Christian view—, but rather that faith and works worked together in the justification of Abraham (see 2:22). Therefore, they are for him two distinct entities! And, as was already shown, he introduces into his interpretation of Gen 15:6 a remarkable ambiguity: on the one hand, he finds in the passage a reference to faith which was recorded "as righteousness," and on the other hand he understands the same words as a reference to righteousness by works.[145] That is intelligible only if this whole "non–Jewish" tearing apart of faith and works had already been expressed, i.e., the alternative had already been posed. This Paul did, and he was the first to do it—at least he was the first as far as the effect upon world history is concerned; if we wished to postulate a predecessor for Paul, then his struggle with respect to the Galatians would be unintelligible. Thus Jas cannot be called an opponent of Paul, but neither can Jas be imagined without the Pauline mission.[146]

The question still remains: Against whom is Jas actually writing? He could have in mind an idle, inactive Christianity which appeals to Paul without justification. But also he could be thinking of people who advocate the genuine ideas of Paul, and whom Jas misunderstands. Yet the existence of such true

---

142 See above on 2:1.

143 See above in the Interpretation.

144 Among modern scholars, I will mention Beyschlag; Zahn, *Introduction*, section 4; Schlatter; B. Weiss, *Jakobusbrief*, 33f; Mayor; Belser; so also G. Kittel, "Der geschichtliche Ort" (see above on 2:10, n. 120).

145 To get a better overview, the views of the Genesis passage which are in question are summarized once more in the form of paraphrases of this passage: Gen 15:6

$$\dot{\epsilon}\pi\dot{\iota}\sigma\tau\epsilon\upsilon\sigma\epsilon\nu \ '\!A\beta\rho\alpha\grave{\alpha}\mu \ \tau\hat{\omega} \ \theta\epsilon\hat{\omega}$$
$$\kappa\alpha\grave{\iota} \ \dot{\epsilon}\lambda\circ\gamma\dot{\iota}\sigma\theta\eta \ \alpha\dot{\upsilon}\tau\hat{\omega} \ \epsilon\dot{\iota}\varsigma \ \delta\iota\kappa\alpha\iota\sigma\sigma\dot{\upsilon}\nu\eta\nu$$

Judaism:
Abraham believed God
and this faith was recorded as a work in his account "as righteousness."

Paul:
Abraham believed God
and this faith, as if it were a work, was reckoned to his account in lieu of works.

James:
Abraham believed God
and both his faith and his works were recorded in his account "as righteousness."

146 Gerhard Barth, in Günther Bornkamm, Gerhard Barth, Heinz Joachim Held, *Tradition and Interpretation in Matthew*, tr. Perry Scott (Philadelphia: Westminster, 1963), 159–64, compares the antinomians with whom Jas is concerned to those against whom Matt 5:17ff; 7:15ff and 24:11ff are directed. The latter "rely on their charismata, their spiritual gifts, but not on their $\pi\dot{\iota}\sigma\tau\iota\varsigma$" (p. 164).

disciples of Paul is very doubtful. In fact, it was Paul's fate to be misunderstood within the church. Nor is the other possibility in any way certain. For we must remind ourselves that our author does not write these "treatises" as a polemicist against existing positions and factions, but as a teacher who recognized possible dangers which were at most only partially a reality at that time. Jas wished to warn the community about these dangers. He sees one such danger in the slogan "faith without works," a danger not for faith but for life. But what he does not see is the original meaning of this slogan and the significance which it can have for a human being who is despairing of all his own actions and is longing for God.

The lot and influence of Jas are limited by this one-sidedness. It must be said of him that he disagreed with a watchword which in its original intention expressed a great, creative experience. And the closer that people of succeeding generations have come to this spiritual experience, the more intolerable they have found the argument of our author. But the criticism which Jas offers does not go against the experience of Paul at all, since the depth of Paul's experience was closed to Jas. And not only to him. The full titanic power of the Pauline slogan "apart from works, through faith" has hardly ever in the course of Christian history been grasped by the masses. For the precondition was lacking, and will always be lacking for the majority of those who are Christians by birth—the experience of catastrophe, which naturally can never be replaced by a vicarious experience of crisis effected through Bible reading. Jas writes as a Christian who obviously has found his God without this shaking of his soul, and he writes for other such Christians. For these people, the slogan "without works," no longer understood in its original sense, is something which is perplexing, for what would piety be without works? Jas has the distinction of having openly expressed this perplexing contradiction. Thereby he became the spokesman for a circle of Christians whose Christianity found its affirmative expression in good conduct which was religiously motivated. Certainly they were not the boldest and greatest minds, yet a religion which wants to conquer the world is not only confronted with great minds. And the Christianity of that majority has become the bearer of a great Christian movement; these people who gradually over the course of the centuries learned to review and to deal with the duties of daily life in a Christian manner have paved the way for the Christianization of a society of good citizenship and of the duties involved therein. Whoever sees our author as a participant in this work, as one among the many, recognizes his significance in history better than one who hoists him up into direct proximity with the greatest apostle.

3   A Treatise on the Tongue

1 Let not many of you be teachers, my brothers and sisters, knowing that we (teachers) will receive harshers penalties; 2/ for we all commit many sins. If someone commits no sins in speaking that one is perfect, able to bridle the whole body also.

3 If we put bits into the mouths of horses that they may obey us, we also guide their whole bodies. 4/ Look at the ships also, though they are so great and are driven by strong winds, they are guided by a very small rudder wherever the will of the pilot directs. 5/ So the tongue is a little member and yet it boasts of great things. Behold how great a forest is set ablaze by a small fire! 6/ And the tongue is a fire, [the tongue presents itself among our members as the evil world,] staining the whole body and setting on fire the cycle of becoming and being set on fire by Gehenna. 7/ For every species of beast and bird, of reptile and sea creature, is tamed and has been tamed by the human species; 8/ but no human being can tame the tongue—a restless evil, full of deadly poison. 9/ With it we bless the Lord and Father, and with it we curse human beings who are made in the likeness of God. 10/ From the same mouth come blessing and cursing. My brethren, this ought not to be so. 11/ Does a spring pour forth from the same opening fresh water and brackish? 12/ Can a fig tree, my brothers and sisters, yield olives? Or a grapevine figs? [—Nor does a salt spring yield fresh water.]

Analysis

There is no indication of a connection between this section and the preceding treatise, nor should one be expected given the literary character of the whole. The attempt to establish a connection in spite of everything inevitably leads to an artificiality in the exegesis. This is seen in the Chrysostom fragment in the Catena: "Since teaching without doing is not only of no profit but also brings great ruin and condemnation to one who is so careless in the management of his life, he [Jas] expels the contentiousness of those who are not willing to practice (what they teach), forbidding teaching upon the part of those who teach without doing, and imposing great judgment upon them" (ἐπειδὴ τὸ διδάσκειν ἄνευ τοῦ ποιεῖν οὐ μόνον κέρδος οὐδέν, ἀλλὰ καὶ ζημίαν πολλὴν καὶ κατάκρισιν φέρει τῷ μετὰ τοσαύτης ἀπροσεξίας διοικοῦντι τὸν βίον τὸν ἑαυτοῦ, τὴν φιλονεικίαν τῶν μὴ βουλομένων ἐργάζεσθαι ἐκκόπτων, τὸ διδάσκειν ἀπεῖπε τοῖς ἄνευ ἔργου διδάσκουσι, κρίμα μέγα ἐπιτιθείς) [Trans.]. But also the agreement which exists between this section and the two admonitions in 1:19, 26, which are related in content, cannot be utilized to construe a literary connection.[1]

The brief treatise in this section describes by means of a series of metaphors the effects of the tongue, specifically its evil effects. At least, there is no doubt about this from v 5b on. However, in v 1 there is a warning against excessive thronging for the profession of "teacher" (διδάσκαλος). This admonition would be totally isolated if it were not elucidated in v 2: Teachers are

---

1   Cf. above in the Analysis of 1:19–27.

exposed more than others to the danger of committing a verbal offense. Hence, v 2 is closely tied to v 1 and constitutes a transitional verse.[2] Yet in spite of this supporting argument added in v 2, the distance between the admonition in v 1 and the following treatise is still recognizable. For it is out of the question that Jas seriously wished to ascribe to the teachers of the community, or to those who wished to become such (even if he were supposed to have known them personally), all of the sins to which he alludes in what follows, and one of which, cursing, he mentions specifically in v 10. A similar tension between the introduction and the subsequent treatise was observed in the Analyses of 2:1ff and 2:14ff. In both of those texts, and in Jas 3:1ff, admonitions to the community which require no specific occasion for their justification are supported by treatises in diatribe style. In accordance with this style, these treatises bring forward flagrant offenses from the area under discussion which are intended as deterrent examples. The interpreter must guard against regarding these examples as actual events and imputing them to the readers.[3] A difference between the treatise in Jas 3:1ff and the preceding ones is to be recognized in the fact that in 3:1ff the introductory admonition involves a special case while the treatise deals with a general theme. In the preceding treatises, imperatives which stress the proper general attitude are illustrated by specific examples of flagrant mistakes; but in Jas 3:1ff, the warning against a possible "committing of sins in speaking" ($\pi\tau\alpha\acute{\iota}\epsilon\iota\nu$ $\acute{\epsilon}\nu$ $\lambda\acute{o}\gamma\omega$) in the special situation of teaching is placed upon a broader basis through a discussion of sins of the tongue in general. Among the commentators, Spitta especially has seen this tension between the admonition and the subsequent discussion. Geffcken[4] accounts for this tension by arguing that 3:3ff is a diatribe of Hellenistic–Jewish origin.

As a matter of fact, it can be maintained despite certain reservations that not only 3:5bff but also 3:3–5a belongs to this diatribe. To begin with, the metaphors in vv 3–5a share a common character and provenance with those which follow. But if vv 3–5a belong with the treatise, then these verses cannot be interpreted one-sidedly in accordance with v 2: The tongue, although

it is a small thing, achieves great things, namely mastery of the whole body.[5] Rather, the phrase "it boasts of great things" ($\mu\epsilon\gamma\acute{a}\lambda\alpha$ $\alpha\mathring{\upsilon}\chi\epsilon\hat{\iota}$) in v 5 must in this context prepare the way for the following judgment (vv 5b–8) of the tongue and its effects, a judgment which is not optimistic at all: The small member has a great effect (images of the horse and the ship), the small tongue does great damage (images of the fire and the beasts). To this are added the metaphors of the spring and the plants in vv 9–12, with the moral, "The tongue ought not to have such divergent effects." But the neat arrangement which is indicated here does not quite obtain in the treatise. Instead, we observe how the ideas bump against or even clash with one another—evidence that the author is transmitting school material. The explanation for this must be provided in the Interpretation.

Interpretation

■ 1 "Let not many of you be teachers." So reads the admonition which precedes the treatise on the tongue. Since "many" ($\pi o\lambda\lambda o\acute{\iota}$) does not stand alone here, it cannot be construed with "to become" ($\gamma\acute{\iota}\nu\epsilon\sigma\theta\alpha\iota$) and be regarded as parallel to the expression "to become numerous" ($\pi o\lambda\lambda o\grave{\iota}$ $\gamma\acute{\iota}\nu\epsilon\sigma\theta\alpha\iota$) in LXX Gen 6:1[6]. The adverbial rendering "to appear (in the role of teacher) frequently"[7] is to be rejected on the same grounds. Moreover, a glance at the concordance demonstrates that $\gamma\acute{\iota}\nu\epsilon\sigma\theta\alpha\iota$ frequently is a substitute for $\epsilon\hat{\iota}\nu\alpha\iota$ ("to be") precisely in paraenetic imperatives.[8] Therefore the meaning here is: "Not many of you are to be teachers." Neither arguments based upon an alleged context nor arguments based upon the content of the admonition itself (such as that the abuse which is reproved is not otherwise in evidence) can be used as evidence against this rendering, since the admonition is totally isolated.[9]

The warning is supported by the argument that "we (teachers) will receive harsher penalties" than others. Another possible translation, both lexically and contextually, is "judgment by more strict criteria."[10] However, in early Christian paraenesis the meaning of $\kappa\rho\acute{\iota}\mu\alpha$ which is particularly adopted is "sentence of

2 See below in the Interpretation.
3 Cf. the Excursus on 2:2.
4 Johannes Geffcken, *Kynika und Verwandtes* (Heidel-

berg: Winter, 1909), 45–53.
5 So Windisch, *Katholische Briefe* (1911).
6 So Gebser.

punishment."[11] This is the context in which the expression in Jas 3:1 "to receive judgment" (κρίμα λαμβάνεσθαι) belongs. It occurs also in Rom 13:2, and in a dominical saying which is even more closely related in wording, Mk 12:40 (= Lk 20:47; Matt 23:14 in the Koine text): "They will receive the greater condemnation" (οὗτοι λήμψονται περισσότερον κρίμα).

■ **2a** The author clearly considers himself among the teachers. 3:1, 2a is thus the only passage in which we learn something about the author himself. He includes himself under the verdict that teachers are threatened by harsher penalties than are those who are taught. Naturally, it is presupposed that this is true only "if they commit sin." However, the following confession, "we all commit many sins," shows that he is not wandering into academic reflections. Not presupposed, however, is any special theory of reward and punishment, sin and grace. In 1 Cor 3:12ff, Paul also holds out the prospect of reward and punishment on the Day of the Lord precisely to missionaries and teachers.

The interpretation of vv 1, 2a has shown that Jas does not have in mind the occasional functioning of Christians as teachers, but rather a certain thronging toward the vocation of teacher. If this epistle is not to be transposed into a Jewish context (as Spitta would have it), then this admonition refers not to the rabbinate[12] but to the position of early Christian teacher,[13] and so the author is recognized as being such a teacher also. It is rather doubtful that this admonition by the author was occasioned by specific problems within specific communities, since he does not occupy himself with this admonition any further. Reason for such warnings was always present in view of the certainly very lively effort to gain new insights from the Scripture and to impart to the community what one had learned in his personal reading. Also, the esteemed position of "Teacher" may have been attractive, while the responsibility involved with it was less valued.[14] Therefore, there is no need to read into this admonition specific historical events such as the displacement of the charismatic calling of teachers by the institutional office, or the appearance of leaders of Gnostic schools. Obviously, our author himself felt the responsibility of the teaching vocation, and Jewish parallels for this are not lacking.[15] On the other hand, the main emphasis does not lie upon this brief personal comment. For the reason for caution

---

7 So Belser.

8 Cf. above on 1:22.

9 Nor is there any reason for conjectural emendations, such as "deceitful teachers" (πλάνοι διδάσκαλοι), or "volunteer teachers" (ἐθελοδιδάσκαλοι Herm. sim. 9.22.2). The reading of L, πολυδιδάσκαλοι, results from one of the common confusions in spelling; the translation in m, "talkative" (multiloqui), is obviously intended to establish the connection between the admonition and the subsequent treatise.

10 So Windisch, Katholische Briefe (1911).

11 See Rom 3:8; 1 Clem. 51.3; cf. also the expression "incur condemnation" (κρίμα ἔχειν 1 Tim 5:12), "become a judgment" (εἰς κρίμα γίνεσθαι 1 Clem. 21.1; Ign., Eph. 11.1), "bear judgment" (βαστάζειν τὸ κρίμα Gal 5:10).

12 The saying of R. Shemaiah in Pirke Aboth 1.10 which Spitta cites is probably not a parallel. For וּשְׂנָא אֶת־הָרַבָּנוּת does not mean "hate the office of rabbi," but rather "hate mastery." As evidence for this, Hermann L. Strack, ed. and tr., Pirqê Aboth: Die Sprüche der Väter (Leipzig: Hinrichs, ⁴1915), 5, points to b. Pesachim 87b, which is a woe against "lordship." R. Travers Herford (in Charles, APOT 2, p. 692) compares b. Sotah 13b: "Josef died before his brethren because he behaved with rabbanuth. (i.e. domineering behaviour)." The same saying is in

Aboth de R. Nathan 11.1, 3.

13 Cf. von Harnack, Expansion of Christianity, 333f, 354–66.

14 Cf. Heb 13:7 and Pirke Aboth 4.12: "Let the fear of thy teacher be as the fear of Heaven" (trans. Charles, APOT), and Baba Metzia 2.11, where it is pointed out that the teacher has priority over one's father, "for his father did but bring him into this world, but his teacher that taught him wisdom brings him into the world to come" (trans. Danby).

15 R. Abtalion, Pirke Aboth 1.11: "You Wise, be careful in your words" (trans. Charles, APOT). The warning against an error in study which results in sin (Pirke Aboth 4.13a) also belongs here, as well as the admonition in b. Baba Metzia 33b to be cautious, "for an error in Talmud ['teaching'] is accounted as intentional" (trans. Epstein).

given in v 2 is not a personal confession of guilt such as in *2 Clem.* 18.2, but rather a commonplace expression:[16] We all commit many sins.[17]

■ **2b** One might expect that the general rule in v 2a would be made more specific in v 2b: But whoever makes a mistake "in word," i.e. in teaching, must expect especially harsh punishment. But, instead, a positive statement is made: One who avoids such sins is "perfect" (τέλειος). The basis for this kind of continuation of the thought is easy to see. Jas wants to find a transition to the treatise. He achieves this by adding to the description "perfect" that such a person is "able also to bridle the whole body." Now suddenly we arrive at the metaphor which Jas[18] had already used of the tongue in 1:26, and which he is about to use here, although in a different sense.

The attempt to establish a connection between the admonition in v 1 and the treatise in vv 3ff, despite the difference between them, is obvious (cf. the twice-used expression "the whole body" [ὅλον τὸ σῶμα] in v 2 and v 3). 3:3ff seem to be a coherent section into which Jas wants to find a transition. Indeed, one is forced already at this point to a conjecture for which evidence will be provided below, namely, that in the following verses Jas *takes over* not just small traditional pieces but *a whole series of examples which were associated previously.* Jas adopts the whole composition, if not also its actual

wording. To be specific, the first of these examples is obviously that of the horses. It is only to this *metaphor,* and not to the actual *thought* in vv 3, 4,[19] that v 2 provides a bridge. Therefore, v 2 is a transitional verse. Its conclusion is conditioned by the first example which follows. Consequently, neither for the author nor for the interpreter is there any reason here to define human perfection, especially since the admission of human weakness is made in the same verse.[20] Nor is it necessary to discuss the concept of the body which might underlie the words of the author and with which the older commentaries on this verse dealt.[21]

■ **3, 4** The beginning of the actual treatise is text–critically uncertain. The two readings which are most probable are εἰ δέ (A B K L) and ἴδε (C P and very many later witnesses [the Koine text, according to von Soden]). The difference between these two readings would be purely orthographical (ει written for ι, or vice versa) if it were not for the fact that the two spellings permit two different meanings, and either meaning could fit here: "if" (εἰ δέ), or "See!" (ἴδε).[22]

A decision should not be made upon the basis of the context.[23] Mayor attempted to do so by presupposing that if v 3 were conditional (with the reading εἰ δέ), then it should be in parallel with the conditional sentence in v 2b. According to Mayor, we would then expect: "If (εἰ δέ) we put the bits into the horses'

16 "All" (ἅπαντες) refers not to the teachers but to all people. The adverbial "many times" (πολλά) is not a reference to teaching only, but to all kinds of occasions. Georg Wandel, "Zur Auslegung der Stelle Jak. 3, 1–8," *ThStKr* 66 (1893): 683ff, who disputes this interpretation, fails to recognize the transitional character of the verse. That a commonplace expression underlies the verse is shown also by parallels such as Sophocles, *Ant.* 1023f; Thuc. 3.45.3; Aristot., *Rhet. Al.* 37, p. 1444a; Seneca, *De clem.* 1.6.3; Epict., *Diss.* 1.11.7; cf. also Philo, *Deus imm.* 75, and Pol., *Phil.* 6.1. But Spitta ought not to have mentioned *4 Ezra* 8.35 as a parallel, since a much more profound perception of the problem of sin is expressed there.

17 In boh *s* vulg ("*you* assume" [sumitis]) and *m* ("*you* will receive" [accipietis]) the author is not included in v 1 at all. But probably the second person in v 1a is responsible for this and not the desire of Jas to exclude himself from responsibility. Is the alliteration with π here intentional?

18 And others—cf. in addition to Plut., *De garrulitate* 3,

19 especially Philo, *Spec. leg.* 1.53; *Det. pot. ins.* 23, 44, 174; *Mut. nom.* 240; *Som.* 2.275.

19 Cf. above in the Analysis.

20 Cf. above, on 1:4. On the term "man" (ἀνήρ), cf. above on 1:8.

21 Wandel, *op. cit.* (above, n. 16), 687ff, takes σῶμα to be a reference to the "body" of the community. This meaning is prohibited already by the fact that with "to bridle" (χαλιναγωγῆσαι) and "the whole body" (ὅλον τὸ σῶμα) Jas wants to establish a transition to the metaphor in v 3.

22 Since the itacistic pronunciation of ει like the long ι has early attestation, we must reckon with two possibilities: (a) that ιδε was written phonetically when actually ειδε was intended; (b) that properly speaking it was customary to write ει only for long ι, but then finally for ι whether long or short. Since the manuscript B frequently uses ει in this latter way, its evidence for the reading εἰ δέ is problematic. On the other hand, special note must be taken of the fact that C has ἴδε here, yet it has, for example, σοφείας in 1:5. I would include the original text of

mouths that they may obey us (protasis) . . . let us also for the same purpose put a bridle on our own lips (apodosis)." Since this apodosis is not what is found in the text, Mayor argues that the conditional reading is to be rejected and "See!" (ἴδε) is to be preferred. However, the parallelism which is presupposed by Mayor between vv 2b and 3 is not to be expected in the first place, since v 2 is a transitional verse[24] and is related to v 3 only so far as the bridling image is concerned.[25] Nor can one point to the beginning of v 4, "*and see* the ships" (ἰδοὺ καὶ τὰ πλοῖα), as evidence that v 3 must also have begun with "*See!*" (ἴδε). The "and" (καί) merely joins the first example in the treatise to the second one. The "see" (ἰδού) in v 4 does not require an original reading of "See!" (ἴδε) in v 3. To the contrary,

the fact that some later manuscripts read "see" in v 3 with the spelling ἰδού evidences the tendency to alter v 3 in accordance with v 4. But then the spelling ἴδε might also be accounted for by this tendency (and by the phonetic spelling), and the original diatribe could have begun with "if" (εἰ δέ).

■ **3** If this verse is to be read as a conditional sentence, as seems probable, then the apodosis begins with the καί ("also"; the apodosis would be: "we also guide their whole bodies"). The assumption of an aposiopesis is unnecessary.[26] But then v 3 and v 4 are making the same point, despite their difference in syntax. In v 4 it is said that we steer a great ship with a small rudder. Accordingly, v 3 would read: A great horse is controlled by a small bit.[27] Admittedly, the small size of the bit is

---

Sinaiticus (ℵ*) among the witnesses for ἴδε, since it has ειδε γαρ (the γαρ was later omitted).

The manuscript evidence can therefore be variously interpreted. Among the ancient translations, sy^vg hl and arm have "See," *ff s* vulg have "for if" (si autem), and *m* also seems to point to a conditional sentence: "In the case of horses, therefore, why are bits put into their mouths unless it is that they might be controlled by us through this means and we might guide the whole body?" (quare ergo equis frena in ore mittuntur, nisi in eo ut suadeantur a nobis et totum corpus circumducamus) [Trans.].

23 Instead of "should not be made" (*Man darf . . .*), Dibelius probably means "*cannot* be made" (*Man kann . . .*), as he tries to demonstrate in what follows, Yet apart from the context, there is no other court to which one can appeal for a decision on this text, for the orthographic leveling of εἰ, long ι, and short ι render a judgment based upon manuscript attestation impossible. The spellings here in the Greek manuscripts are interpretations, just as the translations are. To the translations mentioned by Dibelius would have to be added the Sahidic versions, which also presuppose an ἰδού or ἴδε. In addition to the fragments from the 9th to 11th centuries used by G. Horner (*The Coptic Version of the New Testament in the Southern Dialect*, vol .7 [Oxford: Clarendon, 1924], 212), this Sahidic translation is also attested in a more recently discovered fragment in the Louvain collection (Louis Théophile Lefort, *Les manuscrits coptes de l'Université de Louvain*, vol. 1: *Textes littéraires* [Louvain: Bibliothèques de l'Université, 1940], 96f, no. 23).

24 See above on v 2b.

25 Since v 2 is a transitional verse, the connective δέ in the reading εἰ δέ also should cause no difficulty

(against Mayor).

26 Beyschlag (cf. also Spitta) provides as an argument in favor of assuming an aposiopesis that a conditional sentence here would have to be completed thusly: "so we also ought to do to ourselves" (see v 2!). He also argues that the δέ would be unintelligible without assuming an aposiopesis. But these arguments are based upon an erroneous valuation of the connection with v 2 and have already been rejected above in the text–critical discussion of this verse. However, it seems to me that one makes the same error if parallelism with v 2 is adduced as proof of the construction which I am advocating (so Roland Schütz, *Der parallele Bau der Satzglieder im Neuen Testament, und seine Verwertung für die Textkritik und Exegese*, FRLANT, N.F. 11 [Göttingen: Vandenhoeck & Ruprecht, 1920], 25f.)

27 Since the ancients knew of the bit, χαλινός must be translated in this way. Of course, the case is different in LXX Ps 31:9, where χαλινός and κημός occur together. Cf. Xenophon, *De re equestri* 6.7: "In order to put the bit in properly, first let the groom approach on the near side of the horse. Then let him throw the reins over the head and drop them on the withers, and next lift the headstall with the right hand and offer the bit with the left" (ἵνα δὲ ὁ ἱπποκόμος καὶ τὸν χαλινὸν ὀρθῶς ἐμβάλῃ, πρῶτον μὲν προσίτω κατὰ τὰ ἀριστερὰ τοῦ ἵππου, ἔπειτα τὰς μὲν ἡνίας περιβαλὼν περὶ τὴν κεφαλὴν καταθέτω ἐπὶ τῇ ἀκρωμίᾳ, τὴν δὲ κορυφαίαν τῇ δεξιᾷ αἱρέτω, τὸ δὲ στόμιον τῇ ἀριστερᾷ προσφερέτω cf. also 6.8; 9.9). A characteristic parallel is the famous image in Plato, *Phaedr.* 254 b, c, d: The charioteer pulls the reins (τὰς ἡνίας) so violently that the horse falls on his haunches, and both the bit and the fall cause pain (τῆς ὀδύνης, ἣν ὑπὸ τοῦ χαλινοῦ τε ἔσχεν καὶ τοῦ

not expressly mentioned. However, the phrase "the whole body" in the apodosis shows that the author has in mind the contrast which exists between the smallness of the instrument and the greatness of its effect. Only this antithesis gives to the apodosis a content which goes beyond what would already be self-evident in the preceding words, "in order that they might obey us" ($\epsilon i\varsigma$[28] $\tau\grave{o}\ \pi\epsilon\acute{\iota}\theta\epsilon\sigma\theta\alpha\iota\ \alpha\grave{v}\tauο\grave{v}\varsigma\ \acute{\eta}\mu\hat{\iota}\nu$).

The history of the metaphor also confirms these points. Already in Sophocles' *Antigone*, Kreon, expressing the idea that a proud attitude is easily tripped up, uses a metaphor which expressly emphasizes the paltriness of the means: "I know that spirited horses are broken by the use of a small bit" ($\sigma\mu\iota\kappa\rho\hat{\omega}\ \chi\alpha\lambda\iota\nu\hat{\omega}\ \delta'$ $o\hat{\iota}\delta\alpha\ \tauο\grave{v}\varsigma\ \theta\upsilon\muο\upsilon\mu\acute{\epsilon}\nu\upsilon\varsigma\ \acute{\iota}\pi\pi\upsilon\varsigma\ \kappa\alpha\tau\alpha\rho\tau\upsilon\theta\acute{\epsilon}\nu\tau\alpha\varsigma$ Soph., *Ant.* 477f) [Trans.]. Now since diatribe literature was fond of utilizing classical quotations, sometimes in a totally different sense than in the original,[29] such a parallel is also not without significance for the interpretation of our passage. This is all the more true since not only are there parallels which foreshadow our text, but also there are certain discrepancies between these parallels and our text. These discrepancies clearly demonstrate that *the metaphors which are used here have behind them a history by which the frequently noted difficulties in our text are explained.*

It was shown in the Analysis that already the first two metaphors, the horse and the ship, have in this context a pessimistic meaning; small cause, great effect; so also the small tongue has a great effect, specifically a bad effect. But if one examines the parallels

which have been collected by previous scholars,[30] and which I have augmented in the pages that follow, one will find scarcely a hint of any pessimistic emphasis.[31] Therefore, those interpreters who, by assuming an aposiopesis, interpret v 3 to refer to the mastery of man over his tongue, and in so doing destroy the parallelism with v 4, are led by a correct intuition. This optimistic meaning which they propose cannot have been the one which Jas intended, but perhaps it does restore the original sense of the metaphor, and also that of the ship metaphor in v 4.

For that these two metaphors are akin and attract one another is demonstrated by their history. Admittedly, it is impossible to trace such ideas to their ultimate origins. A passage in Aristotle[32] which is frequently quoted in commentaries with that goal in mind actually proves nothing more than that the relationship between cause and effect was contemplated with respect to rudder and ship. But the real significance of the above–mentioned kinship between the two metaphors is already revealed when the mariner is compared with the equestrian, and vice versa.[33] And it is revealed still more clearly in the philosophical use of the two metaphors, the one of the ship and helmsman, the other of the horse and the one who guides it, frequently the charioteer. Both appear in the series of metaphors used in the teleological argument for the existence of God.[34] Individual metaphors in this series became commonplace expressions in Stoicism.[35] Individually, they are mentioned by various authors;[36] in combination, they constitute almost a title of God, especially in

---

$\pi\tau\acute{\omega}\mu\alpha\tauο\varsigma$); when the horse later bolts, it takes the bit in its teeth ($\acute{\epsilon}\nu\delta\alpha\kappa\grave{\omega}\nu\ \tau\grave{o}\nu\ \chi\alpha\lambda\iota\nu\acute{o}\nu$). Cf. also Philo, *Agric.* 70.

The plural in Jas 3:3 is naturally to be understood to indicate a general statement, just as with "mouths" ($\tau\grave{\alpha}\ \sigma\tau\acute{o}\mu\alpha\tau\alpha$). A portion of the witnesses (among them, P[20] A 33 81 sy) have the singular, "mouth" ($\tau\grave{o}\ \sigma\tau\acute{o}\mu\alpha$).

28 ℵ B C Ψ 1739. The majority of the witnesses have $\pi\rho\acute{o}\varsigma$ (because of $\epsilon i\varsigma\ \tau\grave{\alpha}\ \sigma\tau\acute{o}\mu\alpha\tau\alpha$?).

29 Examples in Wendland, "Philo und die kynisch-stoische Diatribe," 23, 24, n. 1.

30 Especially by Wettstein, *Novum Testamentum Graecum*; Spitta; Mayor; and Geffcken, *Kynika*.

31 Siegfried Herrmann, "Steuerruder, Waage, Herz und Zunge in ägyptischen Bildreden," *Zeitschrift für ägyptische Sprache und Altertumskunde* 79 (1954): 106–

15, shows that these metaphors and their combination have a long history in Egypt and that also in Egypt the judgement about the tongue becomes more pessimistic the later the period.

32 Aristot., *Quaest. mechan.* 5, p. 850b: "Why does the rudder, which is small and at the end of the vessel, have so great power that it is able to move the huge mass of the ship, though it is moved by a smaller tiller and by the strength of but one man, and then without violent exertion?" ($\delta\iota\grave{\alpha}\ \tau\acute{\iota}\ \tau\grave{o}\ \pi\eta\delta\acute{\alpha}\lambda\iotaο\nu\ \mu\iota\kappa\rho\grave{o}\nu$ $\acute{o}\nu\ \kappa\alpha\grave{\iota}\ \acute{\epsilon}\pi'\ \acute{\epsilon}\sigma\chi\acute{\alpha}\tau\omega\ \tau\hat{\omega}\ \pi\lambdaο\acute{\iota}\omega\ \tauο\sigma\alpha\acute{v}\tau\eta\nu\ \delta\acute{v}\nu\alpha\mu\iota\nu\ \acute{\epsilon}\chi\epsilon\iota$ $\acute{\omega}\sigma\tau\epsilon\ \acute{v}\pi\grave{o}\ \mu\iota\kappa\rho\upsilon\hat{\varsigma}\ \upsilon\acute{\iota}\alpha\kappaο\varsigma\ \kappa\alpha\grave{\iota}\ \acute{\epsilon}\nu\grave{o}\varsigma\ \acute{\alpha}\nu\theta\rho\acute{\omega}\pi\upsilon\ \delta\upsilon\nu\acute{\alpha}\mu\epsilon\omega\varsigma$ $\kappa\alpha\grave{\iota}\ \tau\alpha\acute{v}\tau\eta\varsigma\ \acute{\eta}\rho\epsilon\mu\alpha\acute{\iota}\alpha\varsigma\ \mu\epsilon\gamma\acute{\alpha}\lambda\alpha\ \kappa\iota\nu\epsilon\hat{\iota}\sigma\theta\alpha\iota\ \mu\epsilon\gamma\acute{\epsilon}\theta\eta\ \pi\lambdaο\acute{\iota}\omega\nu$).

33 Philo, *Flacc.* 26; *Agric.* 69; cf. *Jos.* 149.

34 Cf. the series in Pseudo-Aristotle, *Mund.* 6, p. 400b: "In a word, then, as the helmsman in his ship, as the charioteer in his chariot, as the leader in a chorus, as

Philo.[37] Now since in this literature an inference is sometimes drawn about God based upon observations regarding the human spirit (Pseudo–Aristotle, *Mund.* 6, p. 399b), and sometimes the direction of the inference is reversed (i.e., from God to the human spirit; Cicero, *Tusc.* 1.70), it is not surprising that we find both metaphors applied also to the supremacy of the spirit within man. This is true whether these metaphors have been transferred from the sphere of ideas involved in the teleological argument for God,[38] or whether this parallel usage has originated spontaneously. Thus Reason (λογισμός) is called the "helmsman,"[39] and the mind (νοῦς) is called charioteer and helmsman, as is God.[40] We are even more within the domain of our diatribe in Jas when it comes to texts which illustrate the mastery of the human being over his body, his affections, and his conduct by using the metaphors of the helmsman and the rider.[41]

It might be argued that a paraenetic author of this period could be led from the one metaphor to the other by simple association. But a few observations are perhaps appropriate in order to shed more light on the

the lawgiver in a city, as the commander in a military camp, so is God in the cosmos" (καθόλου δὲ ὅπερ ἐν νηὶ μὲν κυβερνήτης, ἐν ἅρματι δὲ ἡνίοχος, ἐν χορῷ δὲ κορυφαῖος, ἐν πόλει δὲ νόμος, ἐν στρατοπέδῳ δὲ ἡγεμών, τοῦτο θεὸς ἐν κόσμῳ).

35 Hermann Binder, *Dio Chrysostomus und Posidonius: Quellenuntersuchungen zur Theologie des Dio von Prusa*, Diss. Tübingen (Borna-Leipzig: Noske, 1905), derives the whole series from Poseidonius. Skepticism with regard to the continual search for, and discovery of, reminiscences of Poseidonius is in order. But from Lucian, *Jup. trag.* 50, it follows that the example (παράδειγμα) of the ship belongs among the Stoic commonplaces (τὰ κοινὰ ταῦτα). Cf. Paul Wendland, *Philo's Schrift über die Vorsehung: Ein Beitrag zur Geschichte der nacharistotelischen Philosophie* (Berlin: Gaertner, 1892), 23, n. 4.

36 For the metaphor of the ship, cf. Dio Chrysostom 12.34; Cicero, *Nat. deor.* 2.34.87; Lucian, *Jup. trag.* 47ff; *Bis accus.* 2; Philo, *Cher.* 36; *De prov.* 1.75; cf. also *Spec. leg.* 1.33; *Leg. all.* 3.98 (but in these last two passages, as in *De prov.* 1.72, a shipwright is inferred and not a helmsman). For the metaphor of the charioteer, cf. Dio Chrysostom 36.50; Philo, *Spec. leg.* 1.14; *Decal.* 60.

37 E.g., this designation for God is presupposed in Philo, *Abr.* 70; *Rer. div. her.* 228, 301; *De aetern.* 83; *Op. mund.* 88. Cf. also *Conf. ling.* 115. Does this indicate the influence of Egyptian–Hellenistic terminology? Cf. the address to Horus in the *Great Paris Magical Papyrus*, lines 993f (in Preisendanz, vol. 1, p. 106): "(who) guides and steers the helm [of the ship of the sun]" (ἡνιοχῶν καὶ κυβερνῶν οἴακα).

38 The transfer is clear in Philo, *Op. mund.* 88: "So the Creator made the human being after all things, as a sort of charioteer and helmsman, to drive and steer the things on earth, and charged him with the care of animals and plants, like a governor subordinate to the chief and great King" (ἡνίοχον δή τινα καὶ κυβερνήτην ἐφ' ἅπασιν ὁ ποιητὴς ἐδημιούργει τὸν ἄνθρωπον, ἵνα ἡνιοχῇ καὶ κυβερνᾷ τὰ περίγεια ζώων καὶ φυτῶν λαβὼν τὴν ἐπιμέλειαν οἷά τις ὕπαρχος τοῦ πρώτου καὶ μεγάλου βασιλέως) [Loeb modified].

39 *4 Macc.* 7.1–3. The daimon is called "helmsman" in Aristot., *Eth. Eud.* 8.2.6f: "As for instance a badly built ship often gets through a voyage better, though not owing to itself, but because it has a good man at the helm. But on this showing the fortunate person has the deity as helmsman" (οἷον πλοῖον κακῶς νεναυπηγημένον ἄμεινον πολλάκις δὲ πλεῖ, ἀλλ' οὐ δι' αὑτό, ἀλλ' ὅτι ἔχει κυβερνήτην ἀγαθόν. ἀλλ' οὗτος εὐτυχῶν τὸν δαίμον' ἔχει κυβερνήτην ἀγαθόν) [Loeb modified].

40 Philo, *Migr. Abr.* 67: "The fool's whole course through every moment of his journey depends on this pair, anger and desire; since he has cast away Mind, who is charioteer and monitor. The man of the opposite character has exscinded anger and desire, and chosen as his patron and helmsman the Divine Word" (πορεύεται δὲ ὁ ἄφρων δι' ἀμφοτέρων, θυμοῦ τε καὶ ἐπιθυμίας, ἀεὶ μηδένα διαλείπων χρόνον, τὸν ἡνίοχον καὶ βραβευτὴν νοῦν ἀποβαλών· ὁ δ' ἐναντίος τούτῳ θυμὸν μὲν καὶ ἐπιθυμίαν ἐκτέτμηται, κυβερνήτην δὲ ἐπιγέγραπται λόγον θεῖον) [Loeb modified]; cf. also *Leg. all.* 3.223f, quoted below in n. 45. Cf. in addition, Philo, *Det. pot. ins.* 53: "[perception] is bridled by the mind, which has skill to direct the irrational powers within us like a helmsman or a charioteer" (ἐγχαλινωθῆναι δὲ ὑπὸ νοῦ κυβερνᾶν καὶ ἡνιοχεῖν τὰς ἀλόγους ἐν ἡμῖν δυνάμεις ἐπισταμένου) [Loeb modified], and 23: "[the intellect] holding and curbing the tongue with the reins of conscience, checks . . . its course" (ἐπιστομίζων ταῖς τοῦ συνειδότος ἡνίαις τὸν . . . δρόμον γλώττης ἐπέσχεν).

41 In Lucretius, *De rerum natura* 4.898–904, the movement of the body while walking, which takes place by the mind and will of man but also by the wind pressing upon the body, is illustrated with the following comparision: "Again, there is no need to be surprised that elements so small can sway so large a body and turn about our whole weight. For indeed the wind, which is thin and has a fine substance,

origin of this series of metaphors. In *Op. mund.* 83ff, Philo answers the question, Why was the human being created last of all the creatures? with the thought: It was intended that by his sudden appearance he might strike terror in the other creatures and thus achieve mastery over them. As an example of this mastery Philo mentions the rider, who is able to tame the most spirited of all beasts.[42] But the creation of the human being at the conclusion of the entire series of divine acts of creation does not imply a derogation of the position of humankind, continues Philo, for God has created humans as the charioteers and helmsmen of earthly things. As the latter have their place in the rear of the ship and the former have their place behind the animals which are drawing the chariot, so humans stand at the end of the acts of creation.[43] Now Jas introduces the metaphor of the taming of the beasts in v 7, and we have already discovered that vv 3, 4 actually allow the anticipation of this optimistic sense:[44] As rider and helmsman produce a great effect through the use of a small instrument, we also can control our whole body with our mind. The pessimistic meaning which is

---

drives and pushes a great gallion with mighty momentum, and one hand rules it however fast it may go, and one rudder steers it in any direction" (nec tamen illud in his rebus mirabile constat, / tantula quod tantum corpus corpuscula possunt / contorquere, et onus totum convertere nostrum. / Quippe etenim ventus subtili corpore tenvis, / trudit agens magnam magno molimine navem, / et manus una regit quantovis impete euntem / atque gubernaclum contorquet quolibet unum). Cf. further Stobaeus, *Ecl.* 3.17.17 (p. 493 Hense): "A saying of Aristippus: 'The one in control of pleasure is not he who abstains, but he who partakes and yet is not carried away by it. Just as with both a ship and a horse, it is not the person who does not use them who is in control, but rather the person who guides them wherever he wishes" (Ἀριστίππου· κρατεῖ ἡδονῆς οὐχ ὁ ἀπεχόμενος, ἀλλ' ὁ χρώμενος μέν, μὴ παρεκφερόμενος δέ· ὥσπερ καὶ νεὼς καὶ ἵππου οὐχ ὁ μὴ χρώμενος, ἀλλ' ὁ μετάγων ὅποι βούλεται) [Trans.]; Plut., *Quom. adol. poet. aud. deb.* 33F: "'It is the character of the speaker which persuades, and not his speech.' No, rather it is both character and speech, or character by means of speech, just as a horseman uses a bit, or a helmsman uses a rudder, since virtue has no instrument so human or so akin to itself as speech" (τρόπος ἐσθ' ὁ πείθων τοῦ λέγοντος, οὐ λόγος. καὶ τρόπος μὲν οὖν καὶ λόγος ἢ τρόπος διὰ λόγου καθάπερ ἱππεὺς διὰ χαλινοῦ καὶ διὰ πηδαλίου κυβερνήτης, οὐδὲν οὕτω φιλάνθρωπον οὐδὲ συγγενὲς ἐχούσης τῆς ἀρετῆς ὄργανον ὡς τὸν λόγον) [Loeb modified]; Theophylactus Simocatta (7th cent. A.D.), *Ep.* 70: "We guide horses with reins and whips, and we sail the ship by unfurling the sails and we bring it into harbour by 'bridling' it with anchors. In the same way, Axiochus, it is necessary also to steer the tongue" (ἡνίαις καὶ μάστιγι τοὺς ἵππους ἰθύνομεν καὶ ναυτιλλόμεθα πῆ μὲν τοῖς ἱστίοις τὴν ναῦν ἐκπετάσαντες, πῆ δὲ ταῖς ἀγκύραις χαλινώσαντες καθορμίζομεν· οὕτω κυβερνητέον καὶ τὴν γλῶτταν, Ἀξίοχε) [Trans.]. Hence, in this late witness there is the same optimistic applica-

tion of the image to the mastery over the tongue which one actually would expect in Jas 3 as well. Cf. also the parallel of helmsman, charioteer and physician to the king in Dio Chrys. 4.25. Similarly, in *Leg. all.* 2.104, Philo moves from the rider, the symbol of him who masters his passions, to the helmsman—the metaphor and its development are dependent upon Ex 15:1 in this case. On the praises of the human being as a commonplace, cf. Karl Reinhardt, *Kosmos und Sympathie: Neue Untersuchungen über Poseidonios* (München: Beck, 1926), 142f. On the charioteer, cf. further Robert Eisler, *Orphisch-dionysische Mysterien-Gedanken in der christlichen Antike*, Vorträge der Bibliothek Warburg 2, 2, ed. Fritz Saxl (Leipzig and Berlin: Teubner, 1925), 94, n. 1.

42 Philo, *Op. mund.* 86: "Nay, even the horse, most spirited of all animals, is easily controlled by the bit" (καὶ μὴν τό γε θυμικώτατον ζῷον ἵππος ῥαδίως [ἄγεται] χαλιναγωγηθείς).

43 Philo, *Op. mund.* 88: "Charioteers and helmsmen are evidence of this. The former, though they come after their team and have their appointed place behind them, keep hold of the reins and drive them just as they wish. . . . Helmsmen again, taking their way to the stern, the hindmost place in the ship, are, one may say, superior to all on board, for they hold in their hands the safety of the ship and those on board it" (μάρτυρες δ' ἡνίοχοι καὶ κυβερνῆται· οἱ μὲν γὰρ ὑστερίζοντες τῶν ὑποζυγίων καὶ κατόπιν αὐτῶν ἐξεταζόμενοι ᾗ ἂν ἐθέλωσιν αὐτὰ ἄγουσι τῶν ἡνίων ἐνειλημμένοι . . . οἱ δ' αὖ κυβερνῆται πρὸς τὸ τῆς νεὼς ἔσχατον χωρίον πρύμναν παρελθόντες πάντων ὡς ἔπος εἰπεῖν εἰσιν ἄριστοι τῶν ἐμπλεόντων, ἅτε τῆς νεὼς καὶ τῶν ἐν αὐτῇ τὴν σωτηρίαν ἐν χερσὶ ταῖς αὐτῶν ἔχοντες) [Loeb modified]. For the continuation of this passage, see above, n. 38. Another application of the metaphor of the position of the helmsman at the stern of the ship is found in Philo, *Praem. poen.* 51.

44 Cf. Theophyl. Simocatta, above, n. 41.

45 Philo, *Leg. all.* 3.223ff: "When the charioteer is in command and guides the horses with the reins, the

demanded by the context as it now stands is not expected: Such a mastery by the small over the large is exercised by the tongue within our bodies. Therefore, it may be conjectured that *the metaphors in vv 3, 4, 7 arose originally from an optimistic representation of human dominion.* This hypothesis would explain the formulation of vv 3, 4, which gives no hint of the pessimistic remarks which follow and which has led some commentators to an optimistic interpretation of at least v 3.

Furthermore, I think that I recognize in the Stoic tradition at least the beginnings of the pessimistic twist which our text gives to the metaphors. In *Leg. all.* 3.223f, Philo discusses the fact that the mind controls the life of humans just as a charioteer and helmsman. But when they yield to sensuality, the mind is ignited

and a fire is kindled such as Moses describes in Num 21:30.[45] Plutarch, in his treatise on loquaciousness, explains that once the spoken word has left the harbor (of the mouth) it cannot be stopped with cables and anchors as can a ship. Instead it rushes forth and becomes a source of great danger which, as is said in a passage from Euripides (Nauck, vol. 3, Frag. 415) which Plutarch quotes at this point, can be compared with a fire.[46] Hence, in both authors a pessimistic twist to the metaphor of fire is illustrated, the same metaphor which is used by Jas for the same purpose in vv 5, 6. *Therefore, he seems to be dependent upon tradition here also, and consequently it seems that all of the metaphors which have been mentioned are ones which Jas has borrowed. Indeed, Jas may have also borrowed a fixed associa-*

---

chariot goes the way he wishes, but if the horses have become unruly and got the upper hand, it has often happened that the charioteer has been dragged down. . . . A ship, again, keeps to her straight course when the helmsman grasping the tiller steers accordingly, but capsizes when a contrary wind has sprung up over the sea, and the surge has settled in it. Just so, when Mind, the charioteer or helmsman of the soul, rules the whole living being . . . the life holds a straight course, but when irrational sense gains the chief place, a terrible confusion overtakes it . . . for then, in very deed, the mind is set on fire and is all ablaze, and that fire is kindled by the objects of sense which Sense-perception supplies. Moses, moreover, gives intimations of such a conflagration of the mind as this, occasioned by the senses, when he says: 'And the women kindled yet further a fire in Moab'" (ὥσπερ οὖν ἄρχοντος μὲν ἡνιόχου καὶ ταῖς ἡνίαις τὰ ζῷα ἄγοντος ᾗ βούλεται ἄγεται τὸ ἅρμα, ἀφηνιασάτων δὲ ἐκείνων καὶ κρατησάντων ὅ τε ἡνίοχος κατεσύρη πολλάκις . . . καὶ ναῦς εὐθυδρομεῖ μέν, ἡνίκα τῶν οἰάκων λαβόμενος ὁ κυβερνήτης ἀκολούθως πηδαλιουχεῖ, περιτρέπεται δ' ὅτε πνεύματος ἐναντίου περιπνεύσαντος τῇ θαλάττῃ ὁ κλύδων ἐνῴκησεν, οὕτως ἐπειδὰν μὲν ὁ τῆς ψυχῆς ἡνίοχος ἢ κυβερνήτης ὁ νοῦς ἄρχῃ τοῦ ζῴου ὅλου . . ., εὐθύνεται ὁ βίος, ὅταν δὲ ἡ ἄλογος αἴσθησις φέρηται τὰ πρωτεῖα, σύγχυσις καταλαμβάνει δεινή . . . · τότε γάρ, εἰ δεῖ τἀληθὲς εἰπεῖν, ἐμπίπραται φλεγόμενος ὁ νοῦς, τῶν αἰσθήσεων τὴν φλόγα ἐγειρουσῶν τὰ αἰσθητὰ ὑποβεβλημένων. καὶ Μωυσῆς μέντοι δηλοῖ περὶ τῆς τοιαύτης ἐμπρήσεως, ἣ γίνεται διὰ τῶν αἰσθήσεων, τοῦ νοῦ, ὅταν λέγῃ· καὶ αἱ γυναῖκες ἔτι προσεξέκαυσαν πῦρ ἐν Μωάβ). In *Spec. leg.* 4.79, Philo says: "So if a person does not set bounds to the impulses and bridle them like horses which defy the reins . . . that defiance will

cause that one to be carried away before he knows it like a charioteer borne by his team into ravines or impassable abysses" (εἴ τις οὖν μὴ μέτρα ταῖς ὁρμαῖς ὁρίζει μηδὲ χαλινὸν ὥσπερ τοῖς ἀφηνιασταῖς ἵπποις ἐντίθησι . . . λήσεται διὰ τὸν ἀφηνιασμὸν ἐξενεχθεὶς οἷα ὑπὸ ἁρμάτων ἡνίοχος εἰς φάραγγας ἢ βάραθρα δυσαναπόρευτα) [Loeb modified], and in 4.83 the desires are compared with a fire (see below on 3:5, 6). Similarly, *Decal.* 49 speaks of those who do not obey the Law: "while all who are rebellious will continue to be burnt, aye and burnt to ashes, by their inward lusts" (ὅσοι δ' ἀφηνιασταί, καιόμενοι καὶ κατακαιόμενοι διατελοῦσιν ὑπὸ τῶν ἔνδον ἐπιθυμιῶν). Here again is the juxtaposition of the two metaphors! The reason for their combination is more closely examined below in the exegesis of 3:5, 6.

46 Plut., *De garrulitate* 10: "So when a ship has been caught by a wind, they try to check it, deadening its speed with cables and anchors, but if a story runs out of harbor, so to speak, there is no roadstead or anchorage for it, but, carried away with a great noise and reverberation, it dashes upon the man who uttered it and submerges him in some great and terrible danger. 'With but a little torch one might set fire to Ida's rock; and tell one man a tale, soon all the town will know'" (νεὼς μὲν γὰρ ἁρπαγείσης ὑπὸ πνεύματος ἐπιλαμβάνονται, σπείραις καὶ ἀγκύραις τὸ τάχος ἀμβλύνοντες· τοῦ λόγου δ' ὥσπερ ἐκ λιμένων ἐκδραμόντος οὐδ' ἔστιν ὅρμος οὐδ' ἀγκυροβόλιον, ἀλλὰ ψόφῳ πολλῷ καὶ ἤχῳ φερόμενος προσέρρηξε καὶ κατέδυσεν εἰς μέγαν τινὰ καὶ δεινὸν τὸν φθεγξάμενον κίνδυνον. μικροῦ γὰρ ἐκ λαμπτῆρος Ἰδαῖον λέπας / πρήσειεν ἄν τις· καὶ πρὸς ἄνδρ' εἰπὼν ἕνα, / πύθοιντ' ἂν ἀστοὶ πάντες).

tion of these metaphors. Naturally, the reconstruction of such an association is impossible, but its postulation completely explains certain obscurities and abrupt transitions within our text.

Now in some of the passages mentioned the two metaphors are even developed by means of the same motifs and in terminology which is similar to that which is found in Jas. This corroborates the hypothesis of a previous association of the metaphors,[47] and at times also provides a commentary to the words in our Jas passage. I note the following parallels: The guiding and leading activity of the rider and the helmsman is characterized in Jas by the terms "guide, steer" (μετάγειν) and "guide straight, steer" (εὐθύνειν). Likewise, εὐθύνειν is found in Philo, *Abr.* 70; *Conf. ling.* 115; *Leg. all.* 3.224. Cf. the cognate κατευθύνειν in Dio Chysostom 12.34; Sextus, *Adv. math.* 9.27; Philo, *Decal.* 60; and the cognate ἰθύνειν in Theophylactus Simocatta, *Ep.* 70. κατάγειν is found in the passage cited from Sextus; μετάγειν in Stobaeus, *Ecl.* 3.17.17 (p. 493 Hense); and ἄγειν in Philo, *Op. mund.* 88; *Leg. all.* 4.223. Corresponding to the words "we put bits" (τοὺς χαλινοὺς βάλλομεν) in Jas 3:3 are "he puts in the bit" (χαλινὸν ἐντίθησι) in Philo, *Agric.* 69 and *Spec. leg.* 4.79, and "in order to put in the bit" (χαλινὸν ἐμβάλῃ) in Xenophon, *De re equestri* 6.7. The smallness of the instrument is mentioned with regard to the bit in Sophocles, *Ant.* 477, with regard to the rudder in Aristot., *Quaest. mechan.* 5, and in our passage. Jas mentions the contrary winds in order to express the power of the helmsman; Philo, *Leg. all.* 3.223, mentions them in order to deny the power of the helmsman in such circumstances. But especially characteristic is the free will of the one who is guiding. In Pseudo-Aristotle, *Mund.* 6, p. 400b, it says: "he moves and directs all things as and where he wishes"

(πάντα κινεῖ καὶ περιάγει, ὅπου βούλεται καὶ ὅπως). Philo, *Leg. all.* 3.223, has "the way he wishes" (ᾗ βούλεται), and in *Op. mund.* 88, "just as they wish" (ᾗ ἂν ἐθέλωσιν). Cf. Aristippus in Stobaeus *Ecl.* 3.17.17 (p. 493 Hense): "wherever he wishes" (ὅποι βούλεται), and Lucretius, *De rerum natura* 4.903f: "how fast it may go . . . in any direction" (quantovis impete . . . quolibet). Corresponding to all of these is "wherever the will of the pilot directs" (ὅπου ἡ ὁρμὴ τοῦ εὐθύνοντες βούλεται) in Jas 3:4. The meaning of ὁρμή is established through these parallels. What is meant is the will of the one who is guiding,[48] not the mechanical pressure which he exerts on the helm.

If one glances over these two verses, then the placing of the term "of horses" (ἵππων) at the beginning does not appear strange. The word goes with "mouths" (στόματα)—since this combination is the important thing—and not with "bits" (χαλινούς). The "fierce winds" (v 4) have just been discussed. In contrast to Philo, Jas has stressed them in a thoroughly optimistic sense: In spite of the size of the ship, in spite of the blowing of the wind, the "tiny helm" retains control. Thus up to the end of v 4 we are prepared for an optimistic meaning, and it is not surprising that we read in Oec, "The words 'so also the tongue' signify that the tongue also ought to be guided by right reason and not to do the thing which it actually does" (τὸ γὰρ οὕτω καὶ ἡ γλῶσσα τοῦτο σημαίνει, ὅτι οὕτως ὀφείλει καὶ ἡ γλῶσσα μετάγεσθαι τῷ ὀρθῷ λόγῳ ἀλλ' οὐ τοῦτο ποιεῖν ὃ ποιεῖ) [Trans.].[49] The old optimistic meaning of the metaphors, which was disclosed by a look at their history, can be heard here in Jas, also.

■ **5a** And yet this meaning must be rejected as far as our text is concerned, as is shown by v 5a. *Jas has changed the emphasis of the metaphors: the one who is steering*

---

47   Among the parallels which do not apply to the Jas text, I call attention to the following: That the helmsman directs the ship although he is located in the extreme end of it is stressed by Aristot., *Quaest. mechan.* 5, and Philo, *Op. mund.* 88. The restraining activity of the anchor is a simile used with regard to speech in Plut., *De garrulitate* 10 and Theophylactus Simocatta, *Ep.* 70. In *Agric.* 69, Philo says of the helmsman: "to the ports which he is anxious to reach" (ἐφ' οὓς ἐπείγεται παραπέμπει λιμένας), and in *Op. mund.* 86, of the rider: "to the places where he is anxious to be" (εἰς οὓς ἂν ἐπείγηται γίνεσθαι τόπους

ἐκεῖνος). There are points of contact between the wording in Sextus, *Adv. math.* 9.27: "as soon as he sees in the distance a ship . . . he concludes that there is somebody who directs its course" (ἅμα τῷ θεάσασθαι πόρρωθεν ναῦν . . . συνίησιν ὅτι ἔστι τις ὁ κατευθύνων ταύτην), and the wording in Cicero, *Nat. deor.* 2.87: "When you observe from a distance the course of a ship, you do not doubt that its motion is guided by reason and by skill (cumque procul cursum navigii videris, non dubitare, quin id ratione atque arte moveatur) [Loeb modified].

48   Cf. *ff*: voluntas; *m* vulg: impetus.

is not the human being, not reason, but the tongue. Admittedly, what Jas says about the tongue in v 5a is still neutral: "it boasts of great things."[50] But the following statements give the neutral saying a pessimistic meaning: The things of which the tongue boasts are bad things. The fact that one is not forced to a pessimistic interpretation until after v 5a has occasioned the disagreement among interpreters:

1) It has caused some interpreters to explain v 3 in accordance with v 2 (we must guide the tongue as we do the horse) and to attempt to derive a neutral sense from vv 4, 5a (the small helm accomplishes great things and so does the small member). In this way, justice is done to the intuition that at this point in the text there is still no mention of the bad effect of the tongue. However, I believe that I have shown that this interpretation of v 3 in accordance with v 2 is unreliable and that this intuition is therefore only partly correct.

2) On the other hand, the coherence of our text is correctly recognized by another group of exegetes who *connect all the metaphors to the evil control exercised by the tongue*. But I believe that the fact that this association is not expressed earlier in the text can be explained satisfactorily from the history of the metaphors: *Jas has adopted material from the tradition here, but he has not entirely reworked it to conform to his own intention*.[51]

■ **5b** A third metaphor follows: "A small fire is able to ignite a great forest." Certainly this is the sense, yet there is no need to accept the reading ὀλίγον ("small"),[52] for such an obvious elucidation of the wordplay is unnecessary. The use of ἡλίκος to express the contrast "how small—how great" is rather charming, and in addition it is corroborated by parallels.[53] Therefore, ὕλη must be understood in such a way as to make the contrast as sharp as possible. Hence, it certainly does not mean "fuel," and because of ἡλίκος it cannot be taken to mean "wood," either. Instead, the meaning here is "forest," especially since this meaning

49   Characteristic of the difficulty of this passage is the other interpretation which Oec records in addition to the one quoted above. Someone might ask, he says, "'What trouble is it to steer in this way a small member?' or 'What harm could result from the least member?'" (τίς κόπος μικρὸν οὕτω κυβερνῆσαι μέλος; ἢ τίς ἡ ἀπὸ τοῦ ἐλαχίστου γενησομένη βλάβη) [Trans.], and according to this interpretation Jas would answer with the metaphors of the bit, helm, and sparks. Therefore this interpretation assumes that the three metaphors are parallel. In Theoph and the Catena, only the interpretation which is quoted in the text above is transmitted. Bede also interpreted v 3 according to v 2; yet he allegorized v 4 to refer to the "minds of men" (mentes hominum) and interpreted the expression "boasts of great things" (μεγάλα αὐχεῖ) in v 5 to mean both good *and* bad things, depending upon the kind of leadership which the mind exercises. On the other hand, Cassiodorus vigorously elaborated the pessimistic sense of the first two images: "For just as we guide horses with bridles and ships with helms, and on the other hand ignite great forests with a small fire, so also our tongue is indeed a small member, but becomes enlarged by boasting" (nam sicut frenis equos, naves gubernaculis regimus, magnas autem silvas modico igne succendimus; ita et lingua nostra parvum quidem membrum est, sed magna exultatione dilatatur) [Trans.]; the term "indeed" (quidem) occurs also in *s* vulg in Jas 3:5, but not in *ff m*.

50   I prefer the spelling μεγάλα αὐχεῖ (two separate words, as apposed to μεγαλαυχεῖ) because of the

contrast with "small member" (μικρὸν μέλος).

51   It comes as no surprise that already at an early stage an effort was made to alter what Jas had allowed to stand. Perhaps the spelling μεγαλαυχεῖ (P²⁰ ℵ K L and the majority of the manuscripts) is already an effort to bring out the aspect of reproof. This certainly applies to the translation in Codex Fuldensis of the vulg: *exultat*; and to the translation in *m*: *magniloqua*; on the other hand, *ff* has *gloriatur*. The alliteration μικρὸν μέλος ... μεγάλα in this verse is perhaps intentional; cf. the Introduction, section 5.

52   As do the Koine as well as part of the Egyptian witnesses (A* Ψ). Cf. "tiny fire" (pusillum ignis) in *ff*, and "small fire" (parvus ignis) in *m*; *s* and vulg have "how [small]" (quantus).

53   ἡλίκος meaning "how small" is found in Lucian, *Hermot.* 5 and Epict., *Diss.* 1.12.26. A good example is found also in Philostratus, *Vit. Ap.* 2.11.2, where Damis says in amazement at a thirteen–year–old boy who is able to guide an elephant, "For it seems to me a super-human feat for *such a tiny* mite to manage *so huge* an animal" (τὸ γὰρ θηρίῳ τηλικούτῳ ἐπιτετάχθαι τηλικόνδ' ὄντα ... δαιμόνιον ἔμοιγε δοκεῖ).

would be warranted by the history of the metaphor.[54]

We have already become familiar with the important data of this history:[55] Using the metaphor of the charioteer and the ship, Philo describes the laudable human condition where reason rules. But in order to depict the opposite condition he uses the metaphor of fire. In other passages as well Philo moves from one of these metaphors to the other. The same thing can be established in the case of Plutarch.[56] The significance of the metaphor of fire explains these connections with the other metaphors: *as the helmsman and the charioteer are typical illustrations of the dominance of reason, so fire is a favorite metaphor in diatribe to represent the rule of the passions and desires.* Since it is a matter of the traditional use of this metaphor in a specific sense, I disregard its use with any other sense, and I would prefer not to grant too much significance to the occasional poetic use, either.[57] Again it is Plutarch and Philo who attest to the use of the metaphor in order to characterize passion. Plutarch stresses that the spark is fed or extinguished, depending upon the material.[58] Philo depicts the growth of the flame in the wood.[59] But both want

---

54 L. E. Elliott-Binns, "The Meaning of ὕλη in Jas. iii. 5," *NTS* 2 (1956): 48–50, presents both linguistic as well as material arguments that what is intended here is a thicket or brush rather than a forest in our sense.

55 See above, n. 45.

56 See above, n. 46.

57 Pindar, *Pyth.* 3.36f; Ps 120:3, 4. For further examples, see Rossbroich, 80f.

58 Plut., *Praec. coniug.* 4, p. 138F: "Just as fire catches *readily in chaff, fibre, and hare's fur,* but goes out rather quickly, unless it *gets hold of* some other thing that can retain it and feed it, so the keen love between newly married people that blazes up fiercely as the result of physical attractiveness must not be regarded as enduring or constant, unless by being centred about character and by gaining a hold upon the rational faculties, it attains a state of vitality" (ὥσπερ τὸ πῦρ ἐξάπτεται μὲν εὐχερῶς ἐν ἀχύροις καὶ θρυαλλίδι καὶ θριξὶ λαγῴαις, σβέννυται δὲ τάχιον, ἂν μή τινος ἑτέρου δυναμένου στέγειν ἅμα καὶ τρέφειν ἐπιλάβηται, οὕτω τὸν ἀπὸ σώματος καὶ ὥρας ὀξὺν ἔρωτα τῶν νεογάμων ἀναφλεγόμενον δεῖ μὴ διαρκῆ μηδὲ βέβαιον νομίζειν, ἂν μὴ περὶ τὸ ἦθος ἱδρυθεὶς καὶ τοῦ φρονοῦντος ἁψάμενος ἔμψυχον λάβῃ διάθεσιν). That this relatively optimistic application of the metaphor to marital love has arisen from the pessimistic reference to ignoble passions is shown in *De cohib. ira* 4, p. 454E–F, where quite similar expressions are used, although in a way which conforms to the simile there: "And so, just as it is an *easy matter to check a flame which is being kindled in hare's fur or candlewicks or rubbish,* but if it ever *takes hold of* solid bodies having depth, it quickly destroys and consumes 'with youthful vigour lofty craftsmen's work,' as Aeschylus had it, so the man who at the beginning gives heed to his temper and observes it while it is still smoking and catching flame little by little from some gossip or rubbishy scurrility need have no great concern about it . . . for he who gives no fuel to fire puts it out" (καθάπερ οὖν τὴν φλόγα θριξὶ λαγῴαις ἀναπτομένην καὶ θρυαλ-
λίσι καὶ συρφετῷ ῥᾴδιόν ἐστιν ἐπισχεῖν· ἐὰν ἐπιλάβηται τῶν στερεῶν καὶ βάθος ἐχόντων, ταχὺ διέφθειρε καὶ συνεῖλεν ὑψηλὸν ἡβάσασα τεκτόνων πόνον, ὥς φησιν Αἰσχύλος· οὕτως ὁ τῷ θυμῷ προσέχων ἐν ἀρχῇ καὶ κατὰ μικρὸν ἔκ τινος λαλιᾶς καὶ βωμολοχίας συρφετώδους ὁρῶν καπνίζοντα καὶ διακαόμενον οὐ μεγάλης δεῖται πραγματείας . . . καὶ γὰρ τὸ πῦρ ὁ μὴ παρασχὼν ὕλην ἔσβεσε). Cf. also the comparison of the effect of a word with fire in *De garrulitate* 10, quoted above in n. 46. The comment regarding passion in Pseudo-Lucian, *Amores* 2 also belongs here: "fire is not quenched by fire" (πυρὶ γὰρ οὐ σβέννυται πῦρ), as well as the fragment of the Epicurean Diogenes of Oinoanda (2nd or 3rd cent A.D.) 38.3ff (p. 46 William): "and by an exceedingly tiny spark so great a fire is ignited that it consumes harbors and cities. It is difficult for most people to imagine the superiority of these passions" (καὶ σπιν[θῆρι] μεικρῷ πάνυ τη[λικό]νδε ἐπεξάπτεται [πῦρ, ἡ]λίκον καταφλέ[γει λ]ιμένας καὶ πόλεις. [δυσε]πιλόγιστος δέ ἐσ[τι το]ῖς πολλοῖς ἡ τῶν [ψυχι]κῶν τούτων ὑπερ[οχὴ] παθῶν) [Trans.].

59 Philo, *Spec. leg.* 4.83: "Desire darts through the whole soul and leaves not the smallest bit of it uninjured. In this it imitates *the force of fire working on an abundance of fuel* which it kindles into a blaze and devours until it has utterly consumed it" (ἡ ἐπιθυμία δι' ὅλης ἄττουσα τῆς ψυχῆς οὐδὲν οὐδὲ τὸ βραχύτατον ἀπαθὲς αὐτῆς ἐᾷ, μιμουμένη τὴν ἐν ἀφθόνῳ ὕλῃ πυρὸς δύναμιν· ἐξάπτει γὰρ καὶ ἀναφλέγει, μέχρις ἂν διαφαγοῦσα πᾶσαν αὐτὴν ἐξαναλώσῃ, then a discussion regarding the tongue follows in 4.90!). *Decal.* 49: "while all who are rebellious will continue to be burnt, aye and burnt to ashes, by their inward lusts, which like a flame will ravage the whole life of those in whom they dwell" (ὅσοι δ' ἂν ἀφηνιασταί, καιόμενοι καὶ κατακαιόμενοι διατελοῦσιν ὑπὸ τῶν ἔνδον ἐπιθυμιῶν, αἳ φλογὸς τρόπον πορθήσουσι τὸν συμπάντα τῶν ἐχόντων βίον). *Decal.* 173: "For nothing escapes desire, and as I have said before, *like a flame in the forest,* it spreads abroad and consumes and destroys

to depict the nature and danger of the passions. It can be readily supposed that the effect of the tongue was occasionally compared to a fire, as were other excesses of passion.[60] The passage from Plut., *De garrulitate*, quoted above in n. 46, expresses this thought without specifically mentioning the tongue. The allusion to this application of the metaphor found in a late Jewish witness, the *Midrash Rabbah*,[61] could go back to the model in Sir 28:22,[62] or it could be connected with influences from Jewish diatribe such as those evidenced by Philo.

Therefore, we can assume something like the following to have been the content of the series of metaphors employed by Jas: The mastery of man over the appetites was portrayed with the metaphor of the horse and ship—in their optimistic sense—and perhaps also was paralleled to the mastery of man over beasts (Jas 3:7). Then the metaphor of fire was used to depict the opposite circumstance, in which the mind had lost control and passion (or perhaps already the tongue was explicitly mentioned) had gained mastery. Indeed, we have been able to see with Plutarch and Philo a similar transition from optimistic to pessimistic reflection.[63]

■ **6** To be sure, the understanding of the metaphors still does not guarantee the understanding of v 6, which in its present form is among the most controversial in the New Testament.[64] In interpreting this verse we must disregard all the ancient and modern attempts to understand the expression "the world of unrighteousness" (ὁ κόσμος τῆς ἀδικίας) in any other sense than that

---

60 everything" (διαφεύγει γὰρ οὐδέν, ὡς καὶ πρότερον ἐλέχθη, τὴν ἐπιθυμίαν, ἀλλ' οἷα φλὸξ ἐν ὕλῃ νέμεται δαπανῶσα πάντα καὶ φθείρουσα). Probably what is said in *Som.* 2.93 (in connection with Gen 37:8) about the "champion of vainglory" (προστάτης τῆς κενῆς δόξης) should also be included here: "For they see that he is not yet become strong, that he is not as a flame fully kindled and shining brightly *with abundance of fuel to feed it*, but is still a mere smouldering spark" (οὔπω γὰρ ἰσχυκότα ὁρῶσιν αὐτόν, οὐχ ὡς φλόγα ἡμμένον τε καὶ λάμποντα ἐν ἀφθόνῳ ὕλῃ νεμόμενον, ἀλλ' ἔθ' ὡς σπινθῆρα ἐντυφόμενον). Finally, there is the obviously corrupt passage in *Vit. Mos.* 2.58: The Sodomites kindled the "pleasures" (ἡδοναί) and "desires" (ἐπιθυμίαι) through lavish diversions, "*like a flame when the forest brush* is piled upon it" (ὥσπερ φλόγα λασίῳ ὕλη κεχυμένη). If λασίῳ is to be read (Cohn changes it in his translation to "wild olive" [ἐλαίῳ]), then ὕλη here would refer to the forest or brush, as in Jas. Otherwise, the word would be translated "wood" in this passage. Nevertheless, some connection between the texts which have been adduced here, as well as a connection between them and the text in Jas, cannot be denied. It is also the case in the history of other such expressions that the term remains but its meaning varies. Another passage which is probably dependent upon the commonplace diatribe on desires is the admonition in Pseudo-Phocylides 143f to suppress evil at the very beginning, lest it spread: "Cut off evil at the beginning; heal the wound. From such a small spark an *enormous forest* blazes" (ἀρχόμενον τὸ κακὸν κόπτειν, ἕλκος δ' ἀκέσασθαι· ἐξ ὀλίγου σπινθῆρος ἀθέσφατος αἴθεται ὕλη) [Trans.]. Whatever the various relationships of dependence between these passages may be, these witnesses confirm the judgment that there

---

was also within Jewish moral teaching a firmly established commonplace with this content.

60 Among Jews, this perhaps occurred in connection with Sir 28:22, where it is said of the tongue, "It will not be master over the godly, and they will not be burned in its flame" (οὐ μὴ κρατήσῃ εὐσεβῶν, καὶ ἐν τῇ φλογὶ αὐτῆς οὐ καήσονται).

61 *Midrash Vayyikra Rabbah* 16 on Lev 14:4: "R. Eleazar said in the name of R. Jose b. Zimra: A human being has two hundred and forty-eight body-parts, some upright and some prone; the tongue is [prone, and] set between two cheeks, whilst a water-channel passes beneath it, arranged in numerous folds. Yet see how many conflagrations it has caused! How much more then had it been in an upright position!" (trans. Freedman–Simon). Cf. also *Midrash Debarim Rabbah* 5.10 on Deut 17:14, where the snake answers the question, Why does your poison spread to all the members when you bite only one member? by responding, "why not ask the slanderer, who though he be in Rome slays by his slander someone in Syria" (trans. Freedman–Simon). It seems doubtful that the transfer of the images for passion to the tongue is to be explained by a special mythical symbolism of the tongue. Hans Windisch, "Urchristentum und Hermesmystik," *ThT* 52 (1918): 221, has brought our text together with a Memphitic inscription (Adolf Erman, "Ein Denkmal memphitischer Theologie," *SAB* [1911]: 916–50) according to which heart and tongue were referred to as Thot and Horus. But Windisch himself observes that the tongue simply has the function of the Logos here.

62 See above, n. 60.

63 See above, n. 45 and n. 46.

64 Those variants which obviously are emendations cannot be considered in the establishment of the

which was self-evident to Jews as well as to Christians: the evil world.[65] In *1 En.* 48.7 there is a quite similar expression: "They have hated and despised this world of unrighteousness' (trans. Charles, *APOT*). Cf. the so–called Freer–Logion (Mk 16:14 W): "This age of lawlessness and unbelief is under Satan" (ὁ αἰὼν οὗτος τῆς ἀνομίας καὶ τῆς ἀπιστίας ὑπὸ τὸν σατανᾶν ἐστιν; Jerome, *Contra Pelag.* 2.15 has *saeculum istud iniquitatis et incredulitatis*). 1 Jn 5:19 says that "the whole world is in the power of the evil one" (ὁ κόσμος ὅλος ἐν τῷ πορηρῷ κεῖται), and the Hermetic mystic expresses the same pessimism in *Corp. Herm.* 6.4: "for the world is full of evil" (ὁ γὰρ κόσμος πλήρωμά ἐστι τῆς κακίας). This interpretation disposes of the attempts made already by the ancient commentators to interpret κόσμος in some other way, either as "ornamentation" (in the sense, "the tongue cloaks unrighteousness"), or as "the whole."[66] No reader would have heard either of those two meanings in this expression. As a technical term in

religious language for "the wicked, evil world" it was absolutely unambiguous.

"The evil world" must be connected with the following words, and functions as a predicate nominative which in this case has the article.[67] On the one hand, this phrase would not fit well in apposition to "fire" (πῦρ).[68] On the other hand, the expression "presents itself" (καθίσταται) would be too colorless without an attributive. Therefore, the meaning of the Greek text as it now stands is, "the tongue presents itself among our members as the evil world which stains the whole body. . . ."

Yet this is hardly satisfactory. In fact, there are few verses in the New Testament which suggest the hypothesis of a textual corruption as much as this one does. In general, the interpreters who have emended the text have been bothered by the first half of the verse and have omitted the words from the beginning of the verse through "of unrighteousness" (ἀδικίας).[69] Yet, as

---

text. This is the case with the omission of καί at the beginning of the verse, attested only in א*, and the replacement of the article before "staining" (σπιλοῦσα) with καί, also in א*. In both of these instances Tischendorf prints the א* text! (Constantine Tischendorf, ed., *Novum Testamentum Graece*, vol. 2 [Leipzig: Giesecke & Devrient, 1872], 259). He takes "the tongue" (ἡ γλῶσσα) in v 6a as the postpositive subject of the clause which begins with "Behold!" (ἰδού) in v 5b. But "so small a fire" (ἡλίκον πῦρ) must be the subject of that clause, since only then does the contrast with "so great a forest" (ἡλίκην ὕλην) result. The reading καὶ σπιλοῦσα allows the combination of καθίσταται and σπιλοῦσα, but this also might be a smoothing of the text. I am also unable to avoid the conclusion that οὕτως after ἀδικίας in the Koine witnesses *et al.* (P 33) is an emendation as well. The attempt to lend clarity to the stilted style, in imitation of the beginning of v 5, is too clearly recognizable, especially when we find in L *et al.* an even closer agreement with v 5: "so also the tongue presents itself" (οὕτως καὶ ἡ γλῶσσα καθίσταται). Therefore, the text reads: καὶ ἡ γλῶσσα πῦρ ὁ κόσμος τῆς ἀδικίας ἡ γλῶσσα καθίσταται ἐν τοῖς μέλεσιν ἡμῶν ἡ σπιλοῦσα . . .

65 The genitive is a substitute for the adjective, as in the expressions "unrighteous mammon" in Lk 16:9 = 16:11, and "unrighteous judge" in Lk 18:6. On the question of Hebraisms, see above, section 5 of the Introduction. Cf. Moulton, *Prolegomena*, 73f.

66 Cf. also vulg: *universitas iniquitatis*; Luther: "a world of evil." Isidore of Pelusium, *Epist.* 4.10 (MPG 78,

1057), takes κόσμος to mean "ornament" (ἐγκαλλώπισμα), as do Oec, Theoph, the Catena, and the scholia (the latter two follow the wording of Isidore). Following the ancient commentators in this is Arthur Carr, "The Meaning of Ὁ ΚΟΣΜΟΣ in James iii. 6," *Expositor*, ser. 7, vol. 8 (1909): 318–25. This interpretation is also advocated by Ewald and others. But it presupposes an active meaning of κόσμος (cf. *Corp. Herm.* 9.8) which would be equivalent to a participle (ὁ κοσμῶν). This meaning is improbable in our context. Isidore and the catenae and scholia also offer the interpretation πλῆθος ("crowd, host, throng") for κόσμος, referring to Jn 1:10. The other meaning rejected above (κόσμος = *universitas*, or "the whole") is advocated by Bede, but also by many modern scholars, such as de Wette, Hofmann, Beyschlag, and Belser. But this explanation has against it the use of κόσμος as a technical term, as shown by the parallels quoted above in the text. This verdict is not changed by the passage in LXX Prov 17:6a (itself ambiguous): "The whole world of wealth belongs to the faithful man, while the unfaithful man has not even an obol" (τοῦ πιστοῦ ὅλος ὁ κόσμος τῶν χρημάτων, τοῦ δὲ ἀπίστου οὐδὲ ὀβολός) [Trans.], which is often cited to justify the meaning "whole" or "sum."

67 Blass-Debrunner, § 273.1.

68 As von Soden construes it.

69 Spitta's explanation, that this is a table of contents for 3:1–12 ("the tongue is a fire") and 3:13–4:12 ("the evil world") which has found its way into the text, is a little too subtle. Windisch, *Katholische Briefe*

v 5a provides an explanation to the preceding metaphors, one must expect that v 6 would provide an explanation of the metaphor which is only tersely alluded to in v 5b. Hence, I would prefer to retain the words "and the tongue is a fire" (καὶ ἡ γλῶσσα πῦρ) in v 6a, especially since the participles "setting on fire" (φλογίζουσα) and "being set on fire" (φλογιζομένη) would follow that theme well. The phrase "staining the whole body" (ἡ σπιλοῦσα ὅλον τὸ σῶμα) can also remain uncontested,[70] even though this new metaphor seems quite disruptive at first glance. For in reality this "metaphor" is an already very hackneyed expression which is unable to shatter the continuity of the fire imagery.[71] Hence, the words from ὁ κόσμος through ἡμῶν must constitute a gloss. Either there are two different foreign elements here: "the evil world" as an explanatory gloss on "forest" (ὕλη),[72] and the addition "the tongue presents itself among our members" as an indication of the extent to which the tongue "stains" our whole body;[73] or these two parts belong together, in which case the whole gloss would be an explanation of the term "staining" (σπιλοῦσα). In this second case, "the world" would have to be the subject, while "the tongue" would be an appositive or even a later intrusion into this gloss. The sense of the gloss would in this latter case roughly correspond to the translation in *m*: "and the evil world exists within our members by means of

the tongue" (et mundus iniquitatis per linguam constat in membris nostris) [Trans.]. One of these two solutions, or at any rate the hypothesis of a textual corruption, seems to me to be suggested by the problems involving both form and content which the present wording poses for the exegete.[74]

Undoubtedly the sense of what follows is this: The effect of the tongue (depicted with the hackneyed metaphor "to stain") extends throughout the whole body. Indeed, this effect (depicted with the resumed metaphor of fire) extends even further, throughout the whole of life. This further dominion of the tongue is called the "cycle of becoming" (τροχὸς τῆς γενέσεως). Since it can be shown that this technical term "cycle of becoming" was originally native to a world with which Jas had nothing to do, it is natural to assume that a fixed expression has been adopted in this passage.[75] Thus, "setting on fire" (φλογίζουσα) simply signals the resumption of the fire metaphor, and it is not—through some combination with "cycle" (τροχός)—a new metaphor; thus neither the verb "to stain" (σπιλοῦν) nor the verb "to set on fire" (φλογίζειν) compels the reader to visualize a complete similitude. The feeling of Isidore of Pelusium seems to have been correct when he (perhaps unintentionally) reversed the positions of the two verbs.[76] Bede also had the correct feeling when he interpreted one verb by means of the other.

(1911), comes to the general conclusion that "the whole text is corrupt."

70   Against Spitta.

71   Cf. *Test. Asher* 2.7: "He [i.e., one who defrauds] stains his soul, yet makes his body resplendent" (τὴν ψυχὴν σπιλοῖ [sc. ὁ πλεονεκτῶν] καὶ τὸ σῶμα λαμπρύνει) [Trans.].

72   Cf. sy^vg: "The tongue is a fire and the wicked world is a forest," and *ff*: "and the tongue is the fire of an evil world" (et lingua ignis saeculi iniquitatis).

73   G. A. van den Bergh van Eysinga, "De Tong . . . en Erger! Proeve van Verklarung van Jakobus 3, vs. 6," *NThT* 20 (1931): 303–20, interprets the tongue in this sentence as a designation for the male sex organ. But he is able to produce examples of this metaphor only from other cultural groups (e.g., South Slavic), apart from some combinations from mythological concepts.

74   Cf. the principles mentioned above in the Introduction, section 10, part (b).

75   Kittel, *Probleme*, 141–61, has shown that the image of the wheel of life was used in Palestine from the

second century A.D. on, and he cites Jas as proof that this was already the case even 50–100 years earlier. Admittedly, even Kittel seeks the origin of the image outside Palestine, specifically in Hellenism or—more probably—in India. Cf. Kittel, "Der geschichtliche Ort," 80, and Meyer, *Rätsel*, 289, n. 2. Cf. also the Bhavacakra, the "wheel of existence," which as a spoked wheel belongs to the symbolism of ancient Buddhism—Willibald Kirfel, *Symbolik des Buddhismus*, Symbolik der Religionen 5, ed. Ferdinand Herrmann (Stuttgart: Hiersemann, 1959), 38–41. More recently, the evidence of 1 QH XII, 5–8 renders the early use of the image in Palestine even more probable. In that text, where the petitioner hymns the divinely appointed cycle (תקופה) of day and night and seasons, there appears in addition the concept of the births of Time (מולדי עת).

76   Isidore of Pelusium, *Epist.* 2.158 (MPG 78, 613): "The tongue is set admist our members, setting on fire the whole body and staining the wheel of our life" (ἡ γλῶσσα καθίσταται ἐν τοῖς μέλεσιν ἡμῶν φλογίζουσα ὅλον τὸ σῶμα καὶ σπιλοῦσα τὸν τροχὸν τῆς

"The Cycle of Becoming"

Jas has not concerned himself further with the provenance and original meaning of the term "cycle of becoming" (τροχὸς τῆς γενέσεως).[77] Nevertheless, we must look around for the provenance of the term if we wish to know what it may have meant for Jas. Also, only after such an inquiry can there be a decision regarding the old question of whether the word is "circle, wheel" (with the accent on the ultima, τροχός) or "course" (with the accent on the penult, τρόχος). The pre–history of this expression is not clarified by the metaphors with which death is portrayed in Eccl 12:6, and among which is the expression, "until the wheel runs down to the cistern" (ἕως συντροχάσῃ ὁ τροχὸς ἐπὶ τὸν λάκκον); for one would then have to postulate a development of which there is in fact no trace. But this is not necessary, for it is apparent that the term originates from another sphere.

Commentators have been correct in referring to the Orphic notions of the cycle of becoming and passing away.[78] The soul cannot perish, and so long as it is not sanctified and purified it must repeatedly be born from death to a new earthly existence. Therefore the goal of Orphic sanctification is to bestow salvation from this fate, freedom from the cycle.[79] In the texts which have been preserved, this constantly repeated return is usually called a κύκλος ("circle"), but in one passage the term "wheel" or "cycle of becoming" (τῆς γενέσεως τροχός) is used for it. Admittedly, this does occur in

---

ζωῆς ἡμῶν) [Trans.]. This letter of Isidore's has also supplied the Catena and Scholion.

77 A similar case is found in Paul, who in Rom 8:39 employs the astrological terms "height" (ὕψωμα) and "depth" (βάθος) in order to signify the heavenly realm or rather the spirits which dwell within it.

78 Hilgenfeld, "Jakobus," 19f, and his, *Historisch–kritische Einleitung in das Neue Testament* (Leipzig: Fues [Reisland], 1875), 539, n. 2. Cf. also Grafe, *Stellung und Bedeutung*, 45n.

79 Cf. especially the inscription on the Orphic gold plate from Thurii, *IG* 14, 641 (1.6f): "I flew forth from the grievous and painful circle; with swift feet I have reached the longed–for crown" (κύκλου δ' ἐξέπταν βαρυπένθεος ἀργαλέοιο, ἱμερτοῦ δ' ἐπέβαν στεφάνου ποσὶ καρπαλίμοισι) [Trans.]. Cf. in addition Procl., *In Tim.* (5, 330A) 3, p. 296 Diehl: "This one salvation of the soul is offered by the Demiurge and *it frees the soul from the circle of becoming* and from its continuous wandering and aimless life; it is the ascent to the intellectual form of the soul, the flight from all things which have fastened upon us because of becoming" (μία σωτηρία τῆς ψυχῆς αὕτη παρὰ τοῦ δημιουργοῦ προτείνεται τοῦ κύκλου τῆς γενέσεως ἀπαλλάττουσα καὶ τῆς πολλῆς πλάνης καὶ τῆς ἀνηνύτου ζωῆς, ἡ πρὸς τὸ νοερὸν εἶδος τῆς ψυχῆς ἀναδρομὴ καὶ ἡ φυγὴ πάντων τῶν ἐκ τῆς γενέσεως ἡμῖν προσπεφυκότων) [Trans.]; and 3, p. 297 Diehl: ". . . having laid off its former state which resulted from its relation to becoming in general and to the irrational part which binds the soul to becoming, and mastering by reason the irrational part while supplying intelligence to opinion, leading the whole soul away from its wandering in the realm of becoming into that blessed life which those who with Orpheus are initiates to Dionysus and Kore pray to attain: '*to be delivered from the circle and to rest from suffering*'" (τὴν οὖν πρώτην ἕξιν κατὰ τὴν σχέσιν ἀφεῖσα τὴν πρὸς πᾶσαν τὴν γένεσιν καὶ τὸ ἄλογον τὸ ποιοῦν αὐτὴν γενεσιουργόν, λόγῳ μὲν κρατοῦσα τὸ ἄλογον, νοῦν δὲ χορηγοῦσα τῇ δόξῃ, πᾶσαν δὲ τὴν ψυχὴν εἰς τὴν εὐδαίμονα περιάγουσα ζωὴν ἀπὸ τῆς περὶ τὴν γένεσιν πλάνης, ἧς καὶ οἱ παρ'Ορφεῖ τῷ Διονύσῳ καὶ τῇ Κόρῃ τελούμενοι τυχεῖν εὔχονται, κύκλου τ' ἂν λῆξαι καὶ ἀναπνεῦσαι κακότητος); Procl., *In rem pub.* (p. 116 Schoell) 2, p. 339 Kroll: "And then Orpheus also distinctly taught that there was a passing over of human souls even into other animals when he said, 'Wherefore the souls of men, changing according to the circles of time, transfer from one animal to another'" (ἔπειθ' ὅτι καὶ εἰς τὰ ἄλλα ζῷα μετάβασίς ἐστι τῶν ψυχῶν τῶν ἀνθρωπίνων, καὶ τοῦτο διαρρήδην'Ορφεὺς ἀναδιδάσκει, ὁπηνίκα ἂν διορίζηται· οὕνεκ' ἀμειβομένη ψυχὴ κατὰ κύκλα χρόνοιο ἀνθρώπων ζώοισι μετέρχεται ἄλλοθεν ἄλλοις) [Trans.]; cf. also the index to that edition by Wilhelm Kroll, *Procli Diadochi in Platonis Rem publicam commentarii*, vol. 2 (Leipzig: Teubner, 1901; reprint Amsterdam: Hakkert, 1965), under the word κύκλος; Simplicius (see following footnote); Clem. Alex., *Strom.* 5.45.4f, quotes some Orphic verse in connection with the words of Dionysius Thrax on the Egyptian symbol of the wheel: "but all things move round and round, and to stop in any part is not permitted" (ἀλλὰ κυκλεῖται πάντα πέριξ, στῆναι δὲ καθ' ἓν μέρος οὐ θέμις ἐστίν) [Trans.]. On the whole question, cf. Erwin Rohde, *Psyche: The Cult of Souls and Belief in Immortality Among the Greeks*, tr. W. B. Willis (New York: Harcourt & Bruce, [8]1925), p. 357, n. 48, and p. 345.

The terminology of Empedocles is also relevant here. On his relation with the Orphics, see Otto Kern, "Empedokles und die Orphiker," *Archiv für Geschichte der Philosophie* 1 (1888): 498–508, and es-

connection with the saga of Ixion, who was supposed to be bound to a wheel as punishment for his insolence.[80]

It is possible that more common Greek metaphors of the varying cycle or revolution of life were combined with this Orphic conception.[81] Certainly the corresponding expressions were adopted by Jewish authors.

Probably borrowed from an earlier gnomic poet[82] is the verse in Pseudo-Phocylides 27 (which is almost identical with *Sibyl.* 2.87, p. 31 Geffcken): "Misfortunes are common to all; life is a wheel; happiness is unstable" (κοινὰ πάθη πάντων· ὁ βίος τροχός· ἄστατος ὄλβος) [Trans.]. In *Som.* 2.44, Philo remarks concerning the golden necklace which Joseph received in Gen

---

pecially 505; cf. Empedocles, Frag. 17, 13 (in Hermann Diels, *Die Fragmente der Vorsokratiker*, 7th edition by Walter Kranz [Berlin: Weidmann, ⁷1954]): "unmoved in the circle" (ἀκίνητοι κατὰ κύκλον); 17, 27–29: "For these [Philia, Neikos, and the four element-gods] are all equal and of the same age, though each has a different office and each its own character, and each in its turn controls *revolving Time*" (ταῦτα γὰρ ἰσά τε πάντα καὶ ἥλικα γένναν ἔασι, / τιμῆς δ' ἄλλης ἄλλο μέδει, πάρα δ' ἦθος ἑκάστωι, / ἐν δὲ μέρει κρατέουσι περιπλομένοιο χρόνοιο); 26,1f: "Each in its turn controls the *revolving circle*; they fade away into one another, and then increase, as destiny decrees" (ἐν δὲ μέρει κρατέουσι περιπλομένοιο κύκλοιο / καὶ φθίνει εἰς ἄλληλα καὶ αὔξεται ἐν μέρει αἴσης) [Trans.]. Also compare what Diogenes Laertius 8.14 says of Pythagoras: "He was the first, they say, to declare that the soul, bound now in this creature, now in that, goes on *a circle ordained of necessity*" (πρῶτόν τέ φασι τοῦτον ἀποφῆναι τὴν ψυχὴν κύκλον ἀνάγκης ἀμείβουσαν ἄλλοτ' ἄλλοις ἐνδεῖσθαι ζῴοις cf. the last of the passages quoted from Proclus above) [Loeb modified].

   Virgil, *Aen.* 6.748 provides a rendering of Orphic–Pythagorean thought: "All these, when they have rolled time's wheel through a thousand years . . ." (has omnis, ubi mille rotam volvere per annos); on this cf. Eduard Norden, ed. and tr., *P. Vergilius Maro: Aeneis Buch VI* (Leipzig and Berlin: Teubner, ³1926), 19, n. 1, and in general, Chr. August Lobeck, *Aglaophamus sive de theologiae mysticae Graecorum causis* (Regimontii Prussorum: Borntraeger, 1829), 798ff; on Orphics and Pythagoreans, Albrecht Dieterich, "De hymnis Orphicis," in his *Kleine Schriften*, ed. Richard Wünsch (Leipzig: Teubner, 1911), 91ff; Dieterich, *Nekyia*, 84ff; cf. also Hans Leisegang, *Der Apostel Paulus als Denker* (Leipzig: Hinrichs, 1923), 41; Eisler, 86–92.

   The Orphic texts which have been cited here can be found in the collection of Otto Kern, *Orphicorum fragmenta* (Berlin: Weidmann, 1922), under the numbers 32c (the gold plate), 229 and 224 (Proclus, from whom 205 also is taken), 277 (Clem. Alex.). Also apparently belonging to this context is fragment 132, according to which Rhea pours forth the "revolving birth" (γενεὴ τροχάουσα) on each and

every thing: "For having first received into marvelous wombs the potentialities of all things, she pours forth revolving birth upon everything" (πάντων γὰρ πρώτη δυνάμεις κόλποισιν ἀφράστοις / δεξαμένη γενεὴν ἐπὶ πᾶν προχέει τροχάουσαν; Wilhelm Kroll, *De oraculis Chaldaicis* [reprint Hildesheim: Olms, 1962], 30).

80 Simplicius, *In Aristot. de caelo comm.* 2, 168b (p. 377 Heiberg), first relates, "Learning from Hera what had happened, Zeus fastened Ixion to a wheel so that he might be ceaselessly borne upon it" (γνόντα δὲ τὸν Δία παρὰ τῆς Ἥρας τροχῷ τὸν Ἰξίονα προσδῆσαι, ὥστε ἀπαύστως ἐπ' αὐτῷ φέρεσθαι) [Trans.], and then he explains the meaning of the myth: "Bound to *the wheel of fate and becoming* by the creator god, who apportions to everyone that which he deserves, it is impossible to be set free, according to Orpheus, except by propitiating those gods 'who are under orders' from Zeus '*to grant release and refreshment from the circle* of suffering' to human souls" (ἐνδεθῆναι δὲ ὑπὸ τοῦ τὸ κατ' ἀξίαν πᾶσιν ἀφορίζοντος δημιουργοῦ θεοῦ ἐν τῷ τῆς εἱμαρμένης τε καὶ γενέσεως τροχῷ, οὗπερ ἀδύνατον ἀπαλλαγῆναι κατὰ τὸν Ὀρφέα μὴ τοὺς θεοὺς ἐκείνους ἱλεωσάμενον οἷς ἐπέταξεν ὁ Ζεὺς κύκλου τ' ἀλλῆξαι καὶ ἀμψῦξαι κακότητος τὰς ἀνθρωπίνας ψυχάς) [Trans.]. Rohde, *op. cit.* (see previous footnote), p. 357, n. 48, and following him, Ernst Diehl, in his edition of *Procli Diadochi in Platonis Timaeum commentaria*, vol. 3 (Leipzig: Teubner, 1906; reprint Amsterdam: Hakkert, 1965), 297, read more correctly ἀλλῦσαι and ἀναψῦξαι. The subject of these verbs here is the gods, while in the quotation in Proclus (see previous footnote) the subject is the souls who are praying.

81 Geffcken, *Kynika*, 52n, refers to two passages which depict the swift change of fortune: Herodotus 1.207, and Philostratus, *Vit. Ap.* 8.8. Cf. also Lobeck, *op. cit.* (above, n. 79), 905. Examples of the expression "human existence is a wheel" (τροχὸς τὰ ἀνθρώπινα), and similar formulations, are in Rossbroich, 39. The precise distinction between the use of the wheel image to designate changeableness on the one hand, and its use to designate the recurrence of events or reincarnation on the other hand (Ropes) cannot be made among the texts.

82 Jacob Bernays, "Über das phokylideische Gedicht:

41:42: "In the next place he puts round his neck 'a golden collar,' a conspicuous halter, a circle and wheel of unending necessity" (εἶτα κλοιὸν χρυσοῦν, ἀγχόνην ἐπιφανῆ, κύκλον καὶ τροχὸν ἀνάγκης ἀτελευτήτου περιτίθεται) [Loeb modified]. With that should be compared the quotations from Clement of Alexandria and Simplicius in the footnotes above. Notice how Simplicius explains the wheel of Ixion in accordance with Orphic ideas, and how Clement associates the Egyptian wheel with Orphic concepts. This agreement is not to be considered accidental. To the contrary, one must assume that the "cycle of becoming" (τροχὸς τῆς γενέσεως) had come to be an alternate expression for "circle of becoming" (κύκλος τῆς γενένεως),[83] and that Jewish groups have adopted this expression. Admittedly, they did not adopt the original technical meaning. The expression had probably already lost its Orphic character and had become a familiar expression for the ups and downs of life—much as the expression "struggle for existence," which belongs to Darwinian language, may cause us to think of general social situations rather than specific relationships involving the laws of nature.

Therefore, the term must be accented τροχός and translated "wheel" or "cycle of becoming." But it must be kept in mind that in his use of this term Jas is signifying little more than "life,"[84] perhaps with a pessimistic overtone such as others of the period heard in the words "Necessity" (Ἀνάγκη see Philo) and "Fate" (Εἱμαρμένη see Simplicius).[85] Therefore, the adoption of an originally Orphic expression by an author such as ours can be understood. Moreover, this hypothesis fits with the character of this entire section. Hence, the derivation of this term from more remote religious circles—India or Babylon[86]—may be rejected.

The effect of the tongue on the whole of existence is portrayed with the participle "setting on fire" (φλογίζουσα), and is traced back to Satan. For that is the sense of the last part of the sentence, involving a word-play with the antithesis of active and passive: "being set on fire by Gehenna" (φλογιζομένη ὑπὸ τῆς γεέννης). Still, it cannot be seriously considered that this hell-fire is the fire of punishment such as is inflicted at the judgment of the world. Jas wants to derive the fire from the realm of evil, and therefore he mentions the hell-fire. That Satan dwells there is expressly stated for the first time in the *Apocalypse of Abraham*.[87] Jas 3:6 is therefore evidence of great significance for the history of religions.

■ **7, 8** These verses introduce a new metaphor. That this metaphor belongs in its present context, i.e., that just as the other metaphors it obviously stems from the series of metaphors employed by our author, has al-

---

Ein Beitrag zur hellenistischen Litteratur," *Gesammelte Abhandlungen von Jacob Bernays*, ed. H. Usener, vol. 1 (Berlin: Hertz, 1885), 206n.

83 This is also perhaps corroborated by the meaning which Plut., *Vita Numae* 14.5, gives to the precept of Numa, "turn as you worship" (τὸ προσκυνεῖν περιστρεφομένους): "unless, indeed, this change of posture, like the Egyptian wheels, darkly hints and teaches that there is no stability in human affairs, but that we must accept contentedly whatever twists and turns our lives may receive from the Deity" (εἰ μὴ νὴ Δία τοῖς Αἰγυπτίοις τροχοῖς αἰνίττεταί τι καὶ διδάσκει παραπλήσιον ἡ μεταβολὴ τοῦ σχήματος, ὡς οὐδενὸς ἑστῶτος τῶν ἀνθρωπίνων ἀλλ' ὅπως ἂν στρέφῃ καὶ ἀνελίττῃ τὸν βίον ἡμῶν ὁ θεός, ἀγαπᾶν καὶ δέχεσθαι προσῆκον).

84 Cf. Isidore of Pelusium, *Epist.* 2.158 (MPG 78,613), who refers to the "wheel of our life" (τροχὸν τῆς ζωῆς ἡμῶν). "Becoming, birth" (γένεσις) is equivalent to "necessity" (ἀνάγκη) in *Ps. Clem. Recog.* 8.4 and elsewhere.

85 This change in meaning is not borne in mind by Beyschlag when he comments, in opposition to the idea that the term was derived from Orphism: "As if this (the cycle of the souls) could be 'set on fire' by the evil tongue." This objection would hold good only if there were validity in the method which always seeks original metaphors in Jas. The gloss "our" (ἡμῶν) added to "becoming" (γένεσις) in ℵ vulg sy^vg is of no material significance.

86 The Indian provenance of the expression is defended by Richard Garbe, *India and Christendom: The Historical Connection Between Their Religions*, tr. Lydia Gillingham Robinson (LaSalle, Illinois: Open Court Publishing Co., 1959), 59: "Buddha too compares the sense organs to flaming fire in one of his earliest speeches (*Mahavagga* 1, 21, 2, 3), where 'the tongue stands in flame' corresponds literally to 'the tongue is a fire' in our passage in the Epistle of James." According to Garbe, Albert J. Edmunds, *Buddhist and Christian Gospels*, vol. 2 (Philadelphia: Innes, ⁴1909), 263, following Goblet d'Alviella, has argued for the Babylonian origin of the term. Cf. further,

ready been shown.[88] It is probable that the dominant position of the human being in nature was originally compared with the mastery of man over his desires. For just as the metaphors of the rider and helmsman, this one has actually an optimistic import as well and was used for the glorification of the human race. This is shown by the statements in Cicero[89] and Seneca,[90] which at the same time demonstrate that the control of wild beasts by humans was a favorite Stoic theme. Here also, as with the metaphor of the horse, the influence of Greek tragedy can be established. For the most

famous chorus of Sophocles' *Antigone* portrays the general lordship of humans, including their mastery over the beasts.[91] The reception of this commonplace motif by Hellenistic Judaism can also be demonstrated; Philo alludes to it in *Decal.* 113[92] and *Op. mund.* 148, and elaborates upon it in *Op. mund.* 83–86. He answers the question, Why were humans not created until the end of the creative process?: It was so that they would strike terror within the beings which had already been created, for the humans were destined to become their master. That this is now a fact is proven by observation,

---

Eisler, 91, and Kittel, *Probleme*, 141–68 (see above, n. 75).

87 *Apc. Abr.* 14: "Say to him: 'Be thou the burning coal of the furnace of the earth; go, Azazel, into the inaccessible parts of the earth,'" and 31: "For they shall putrefy in the body of the evil worm Azazel, and be burnt with the fire of Azazel's tongue" (trans. G. H. Box and J. I. Landsmann, *The Apocalypse of Abraham* [London: S.P.C.K., 1919]). Cf. on this G. Nathanael Bonwetsch, *Die Apokalypse Abrahams: Das Testament der vierzig Märtyrer*, Studien zur Geschichte der Theologie und Kirche 1,1, eds. N. Bonwetsch and R. Seeberg (Leipzig: Deichert, 1897), 65ff. That Gehenna was thought to be the dwelling place of Satan is contested by Schlatter, 224; also Werner Foerster, *TDNT* 2, p. 80, n. 49—yet a decision regarding Jas 3:6 must not be made upon the basis of the statements in Revelation mentioned by Foerster. On the pre-existence of Gehenna and its relationship to Hades, cf. Joachim Jeremias, *TDNT* 1, pp. 657f.

88 See above on vv 3, 4 and 5, 6.

89 Cicero, *Nat. deor.* 2.60.151: "We also tame the four-footed animals to carry us on their backs, their swiftness and strength bestowing strength and swiftness upon ourselves. We cause certain beasts to bear our burdens or to carry a yoke, we direct to our service the marvellously acute senses of elephants and the keen scent of hounds" (efficimus etiam domitu nostro quadrupedum vectiones, quorum celeritas atque vis nobis ipsis adfert vim et celeritatem. Nos onera quibusdam bestiis, nos iuga imponimus, nos elephantorum acutissimis sensibus, nos sagacitate canum ad utilitatem nostram abutimur; cf. also 2.63.158f).

90 Seneca, *Ben.* 2.29.4: "Accordingly, whoever you are, you unfair critic of the lot of humankind, consider what great blessings our Father has bestowed upon us, how much more powerful than ourselves are the creatures we have forced to wear the yoke, how much swifter those that we are able to catch,

how nothing that dies has been placed beyond the reach of our weapons" (proinde, quisquis es iniquus aestimator sortis humanae, cogita, quanta nobis tribuerit parens noster, quanto valentiora animalia sub iugum miserimus, quanto velociora consequamur, quam nihil sit mortale non sub ictu nostro positum). But cf. also the appearance of this idea in other contexts, e.g., in the Plutarch fragment from his treatise "Depreciation of Strength" (κατ᾽ ἰσχύος), in Stobaeus *Ecl.* 4.12.14 (p. 344 Hense): Nature has provided the brute animals with strength, "But the proper strength of humans is the mind's power of reason, which has bridled horses and yoked cattle to ploughs, and in the forests captured elephants in traps, and fetched down the birds of the air by fowlers' rods and brought up in nets the denizens of the deep" (ἡ δὲ ἀνθρώπων ἴδιος ἰσχὺς ὁ ψυχῆς ἐστι λογισμός, ᾧ καὶ ἵππους ἐχαλίνωσε καὶ βόας ἀρότροις ὑπέζευξε καὶ ἐλέφαντας ὑπὸ δρυμὸν εἷλε ποδάγραις καὶ τὰ ἐναέρια κατέσπασε καλάμοις καὶ τὰ βύθια δεδυκότα δικτύοις ἀνήγαγε) [Loeb modified].

91 Sophocles, *Ant.* 342ff: "Surrounding them with the meshes of the net, the skillful man catches the class of carefree birds, the groups of animals which inhabit the fields, and the species living in the sea. Using contrivances he masters the mountain–roaming beast of the field; and he will bring under the yoke the shaggy-maned horse and the tireless mountain bull" (κουφονόων τε φῦλον ὀρ/νίθων ἀμφιβαλὼν ἀγρεῖ/καὶ θηρῶν ἀγρίων ἔθνη/πόντου τ᾽ εἰναλίαν φύσιν/σπείραισι δικτυοκλώστοις/περιφραδὴς ἀνήρ·/κρατεῖ δὲ μηχαναῖς ἀγραύλου/θηρὸς ὀρεσσιβάτα, λασιαύχενά θ᾽/ἵππον ὑπάξεται ἀμφίλοφον ζυγόν/οὔρειόν τ᾽ ἀκμῆτα ταῦρον) [Trans.].

92 Philo, *Decal.* 113: "Indeed, I have often known lions and bears and panthers become tame, not only with those who feed them, in gratitude for receiving what they require, but also with everybody else, presumably because of the likeness to those who give them food" (πολλάκις ἔγνων ἡμερωθέντας λέοντας, ἄρκτους, παρδάλεις, οὐ μόνον πρὸς τοὺς τρέφοντας διὰ τὴν ἐπὶ

for all beasts obey the human being, even the most spirited, the horse.[93] As has been already mentioned, Philo compares the human being to a charioteer and helmsman. But the same (optimistic) meaning of these comparisons must be postulated as well for the series of metaphors employed in Jas 3:3, 4. Thus once again there is confirmation of the dependence of our author upon a diatribe which spoke of the mastery of the human beings over their desires by using the metaphors of charioteer and helmsman and illustrated the danger of passion by pointing out the effect of fire.

The recognition of the fact that Jas reproduces a motif which is also used in Hellenistic Judaism provides at the same time the answer to some questions of exegetical detail. The division of the animal Kingdom into land animals, birds, creeping things, and aquatic life is explained. The same division is found in Gen 1:26, 9:2, and Philo, *Spec. leg.* 4.110–116.[94] The "beasts" ($\theta\eta\rho\iota\alpha$) mentioned in Jas 3:7 correspond to what Philo calls "land animals" ($\chi\epsilon\rho\sigma\alpha\hat{\iota}\alpha$), i.e., the land animals with the exception of "reptiles" ($\dot{\epsilon}\rho\pi\epsilon\tau\dot{\alpha}$). What kind of beasts were favorite examples in this commonplace motif of taming is shown by the quotation from Philo above in n. 92. The use of $\phi\acute{\upsilon}\sigma\iota\varsigma$ to mean "kind, sort, species" in this context has its parallel in the section just mentioned from Philo, *Spec. leg.* 4.116, and in the chorus from Sophocles above in n. 91.[95] The double use of the verb, "is tamed and has been tamed" ($\delta\alpha\mu\acute{\alpha}\zeta\epsilon\tau\alpha\iota$ $\kappa\alpha\dot{\iota}$ $\delta\epsilon\delta\acute{\alpha}\mu\alpha\sigma\tau\alpha\iota$), is probably due to a rhetorical formulation rather than a need upon the part of Jas to establish the permanence of the action. Parallels to this

are found in Jn 10:38 and Heb 6:10.

The two expressions in the conclusion of v 8 also have a rhetorical ring to them. These expressions should actually be in apposition to "the tongue" ($\tau\dot{\eta}\nu$ $\gamma\lambda\hat{\omega}\sigma\sigma\alpha\nu$) in v 8a, but they are in the nominative case and consequently must be considered to be relatively independent—as exclamations. Since they also have a rich and poetic sound, Spitta's impression that the whole second half of v 8 derives from "another, poetic context" cannot be rejected out of hand. If this is correct, we have no reason to set aside the reading "unstable, restless" ($\dot{\alpha}\kappa\alpha\tau\dot{\alpha}\sigma\tau\alpha\tau\sigma\nu$) on the basis of content—i.e., because it does not fit the context—in favor of the variant "uncontrollable" ($\dot{\alpha}\kappa\alpha\tau\dot{\alpha}\sigma\chi\epsilon\tau\sigma\nu$) which is likewise well attested.[96] The latter term might be an emendation made to suit the context, and could be taken from an expression regarding the tongue quoted from another place or it could be simply a commonly used epithet of the tongue. There is justification for calling attention to Plut., *De garrulitate* 14: "but none the less there is no checking or chastening a loose tongue" ($\dot{\alpha}\lambda\lambda'$ $\ddot{\omega}\mu\omega\varsigma$ $\sigma\dot{\nu}\kappa$ $\ddot{\epsilon}\sigma\tau\iota$ $\gamma\lambda\dot{\omega}\sigma\sigma\eta\varsigma$ $\dot{\rho}\epsilon\sigma\dot{\upsilon}\sigma\eta\varsigma$ $\dot{\epsilon}\pi\dot{\iota}\sigma\chi\epsilon\sigma\iota\varsigma$ $\sigma\dot{\upsilon}\delta\dot{\epsilon}$ $\kappa\sigma\lambda\alpha\sigma\mu\dot{\sigma}\varsigma$). The fact that in *De garrulitate* 13 garrulity is called "an unconquerable evil" ($\ddot{\alpha}\mu\alpha\chi\dot{\sigma}\nu$ $\tau\iota$ $\kappa\alpha\kappa\dot{\sigma}\nu$), and especially the fact that in *Herm. mand.* 2.3 "slander" ($\kappa\alpha\tau\alpha\lambda\alpha\lambda\dot{\iota}\alpha$) is called a "restless demon" ($\dot{\alpha}\kappa\alpha\tau\dot{\alpha}\sigma\tau\alpha\tau\sigma\nu$ $\delta\alpha\iota\mu\dot{\sigma}\nu\iota\sigma\nu$), demonstrates the currency of such expressions. The term in Jas 3:8 is to be translated "restless" rather than "fickle." With respect to the term "deadly poison," Spitta has referred to a Sibylline fragment[97] where the conclusion of the hexa-

---

τοῖς ἀναγκαίοις χάριν, ἀλλὰ καὶ πρὸς τοὺς ἄλλους, ἕνεκά μοι δοκῶ τῆς πρὸς ἐκείνους ὁμοιότητος).

93   See the quotation from Philo above, n. 42.

94   Another four-group division, in which the aquatic life is omitted, is found in Acts 11:6. A three-fold division is in Acts 10:12 (the reading "and the beasts" [καὶ τὰ θηρία] in C (E) Koine sy^hl is an addition taken from 11:6).

95   Eisler, 86f, takes φύσις as a reference to the temperament of man, which is partly rational (human) and partly irrational (beastly). On the division of the animal kingdom, cf. Eisler, 117 and n. 2. In v 7b, the dative τῇ φύσει used with the passive could be the instrumental dative, or it could be the dative of agent corresponding to ὑπό with the genitive. There are analogies for both possibilities; cf. Blass-Debrunner, § 191.

96   "Uncontrollable" (ἀκατάσχετον) can be considered to be the Koine reading, which is not surprising in light of what was said above. But C Ψ 33 81 *m* also support this reading. On the other hand, the best witnesses in the Egyptian recension (א A B P) have "restless" (ἀκατάστατον cf. *ff*: *inconstans*, and vulg: *inquietum*). Von Soden (*Schriften*, part 2, *ad loc.*) thinks that the second reading resulted from the influence of 1:8, and therefore he decides in favor of "uncontrollable" (ἀκατάσχετον). But an emendation in accordance with the immediately preceding words in 3:7, 8a is more natural than an emendation in accordance with 1:8 (cf. above on ἀκατάστατον in 1:8). On the combination "restless evil" (ἀκατάστατον κακόν), cf. the alternate "unstable evil" (ἄστατον κακόν) in Dio Chrysostom 32.23 (see above on Jas 1:6, footnote 59).

meter indeed seems to have been predestined to become a familiar quotation. But it is probably more important that the poet says of his enemies in LXX Ps 139:4: "They whet their tongue as sharp as that of a snake; the poison of asps is under their lips" (ἠκόνησαν γλῶσσαν αὐτῶν ὡσεὶ ὄφεως, ἰὸς ἀσπίδων ὑπὸ τὰ χείλη αὐτῶν) [Trans.].

The ancient exegetes were offended by the assertion that no person can tame the tongue.[98] In point of fact, even the idea of the mastery of humankind over the beasts—which, if my guess is correct, actually derives from a laudation of humankind—has a pessimistic meaning in Jas. It serves only as a foil for the statement that the mastery of humankind ceases when it comes to the tongue. But one must understand the exaggerated paradox of such statements: precisely in the negation lies the incentive to continue in the effort to tame the tongue.[99] Therefore, there is no need to translate v 8 as a question, as do the catenae and scholia, in order to avoid the paradoxical pessimism.

■ **9, 10** A similar problem troubled the ancient commentators also with regard to these two verses. They recoiled at the positive statement—in the "we" style,

no less!—that blessing and cursing come from the same mouth. Theoph, at least, found help in the same solution which he recommended for v 8: "It is necessary that this, too, be heard as a question" (καὶ τοῦτο κατὰ ἐπαπόρησιν ἀκουστέον) [Trans.]. But here also the style of the sentence explains the form of the statement, especially since the author adds in v 10b an energetic "it ought not to be so!" The limitation of the "we" to teachers[100] is therefore contrary to the style. It would also be wrong either to take this general reference to human sins of the tongue as a genuine indictment of a particular audience,[101] or to stress the author's modesty in that he includes himself. His "we" in this passage is to be understood just as that in v 2. In both instances what is involved is a commonplace expression which affirms human weaknesses and faults (not especially Christian weaknesses, or ones particularly prevalent among the readers).

The Stoics include among their anecdotes some which treat the tongue and its diverse effects—effects which are sometimes good, sometimes bad.[102] But a connection between Jas 3:10 and these stories cannot be demonstrated. More important for our purposes are the

---

97 *Orac. Sib.* 3.32f:
  "There are gods who lead on weak–willed persons by guile,
  from whose very mouth deadly poison is poured"
  (εἰσὶ θεοὶ μερόπων δόλῳ ἡγητῆρες ἀβούλων,
  τῶν δὴ κἀκ στόματος χεῖται θανατηφόρος ἰός)
  [trans. Charles, *APOT*].
  Among the other examples of "poison" (ἰός) and "deadly" (θανατηφόρος) which are cited by Spitta, Mayor, and Windisch-Preisker, *Test. Gad* 5.1 is especially important for our investigation (to begin with, because of the document in which it is found). In this passage it is said of Hatred that "it fills the heart with devilish poison" (καὶ ἰοῦ διαβολικοῦ τὴν καρδίαν ἐκπληροῖ) [Trans.].

98 The Koine text οὐδεὶς δύναται ἀνθρώπων δαμάσαι is probably to be considered an emendation, and one is left with the choice between οὐδεὶς δαμάσαι δύναται ἀνθρώπων (B C 1739 P[20vid]) and οὐδεὶς δύναται δαμάσαι ἀνθρώπων (ℵ A K P et al., von Soden's recension *H*). The alliteration is probably intentional here; see above in the Introduction, section 5.

99 Cf. also the passage quoted above from Plut., *De garrulitate* 14.

100 Gebser, *et al.*

101 See Grafe, *Stellung und Bedeutung*, 5, and the portrayal of the situation by Belser. Cf. also above in the

Analysis.

102 Plut., *De garrulitate* 8: "Therefore Pittacus did not do badly when the king of Egypt sent him a sacrificial animal and bade him cut out the fairest and foulest meat, when he cut out and sent him the tongue, as being the instrument of both the greatest good and the greatest evil" (ὅθεν ὁ Πιττακὸς οὐ κακῶς, τοῦ Αἰγυπτίων βασιλέως πέμψαντος ἱερεῖον αὐτῷ καὶ κελεύσαντος τὸ κάλλιστον καὶ χείριστον ἐξελεῖν κρέας, ἐξέπεμψεν ἐξελὼν τὴν γλῶτταν ὡς ὄργανον μὲν ἀγαθῶν ὄργανον δὲ κακῶν τῶν μεγίστων οὖσαν), and *Aud.* 2: "And Bias of old, on receiving orders to send to Amasis the portion of the sacrificial animal which was at the same time the best and the worst, cut out the tongue and sent it to him, on the ground that speech contains both injuries and benefits in the largest measure" (καὶ Βίας ὁ παλαιὸς Ἀμάσιδι, κελευσθεὶς τὸ χρηστότατον ὁμοῦ καὶ φαυλότατον ἐκπέμψαι κρέας τοῦ ἱερείου, τὴν γλῶτταν ἐξελὼν ἀνέπεμψεν, ὡς καὶ βλάβας καὶ ὠφελείας τοῦ λέγειν ἔχοντος μεγίστας). The same story is told of Pittacus in Plut., *Frag.* 11.41.2, and of Bias in Plut., *Sept. sap. conv.* 2. Cf. also Diog. Laert. 1.105 on Anacharsis: "To the question, 'What among men is both good and bad?' his answer was, 'The tongue'" (ἐρωτηθεὶς τί ἐστι ἐν ἀνθρώποις ἀγαθόν τε καὶ φαῦλον, ἔφη γλῶττα). This story, which already recurs in various forms in Plutarch,

fact that Jewish didactic poetry and paraenesis are able to speak of the two-fold nature of the tongue.[103] In his commentary on the Old Testament prohibition against perjury, Philo says that the one who swears ought to examine himself to see whether his body and soul are pure and his tongue not stained by slander (*Decal.* 93): "for it would be sacrilege to employ the mouth by which one pronounces the holiest of names, to utter any words of shame" (οὐ γὰρ ὅσιον, δι' οὗ στόματος τὸ ἱερώτατον ὄνομα προφέρεταί τις, διὰ τούτου φθέγγεσθαί τι τῶν αἰσχρῶν). That is approximately the same import as in our passage, though adapted to the special occasion of the Philonic instruction on oaths.

Therefore, in Jas 3:10 we are once again dealing with material which has been taken over by Jas. However, it seems that this material consists not of Judaized commonplaces from popular philosophy, but rather of Jewish tradition. At the same time it must be said that these sayings—and, as will be shown, vv 11, 12—do not come from the same context to which I traced vv 3ff., viz., the series of metaphors illustrating the power and weakness of man. But that Jas is in fact adopting traditional material here must be assumed not only

upon the basis of the parallels which were mentioned from Jewish texts, but also upon the basis of more general considerations: The ancient Christian commentators were correct in sensing that the statement about blessing and cursing is non-Christian. "These things ought not[104] to be so" (οὐ χρὴ ταῦτα οὕτως γίνεσθαι) is the Christian emendation of the adopted saying. The formulation of the statement reveals a Jewish character. The designation of God as "Lord and Father" (κύριος καὶ πατήρ) is obviously Jewish. To be sure, it does not otherwise occur anywhere in the literary witnesses of the period, but it can in no way be originally Christian.[105] At any rate, the closest parallels are Jewish,[106] and the lack of literary witnesses is not conclusive with respect to cultic language. The expression "we bless" (εὐλογοῦμεν)[107] also calls to mind Jewish formulary language, and here we have at our disposal a considerable number of examples: The extraordinarily frequent εὐλογεῖν ("to bless") in the LXX to translate ברך ("to bless"), with God as the object, especially in the later books of the Old Testament; the name "the Blessed" (εὐλογητός) for God in Mk 14:61 (cf. also Rom 9:5, if the doxology is addressed

has also come into the Jewish Haggadah, as the following anecdote of Rabbi Simeon ben Gamaliel (hence, around 70 at the earliest) found in *Midrash Vayyikra Rabbah* 33 on Lev 25:1 seems to prove: "R. Simeon b. Gamaliel said to Tabbai his servant: 'Go and buy me good food in the market.' He went and bought him tongue. He said to him: 'Go and buy me bad food in the market.' He went and bought him tongue. Said he to him: 'What is this? When I told you to get good food you bought me tongue, and when I told you to get bad food you also bought me tongue!' He replied: 'Good comes from it and bad comes from it. When the tongue is good there is nothing better, and when it is bad there is nothing worse'" (trans. Freedman-Simon). Gunnar Rudberg, "Einige Platon-Parallelen zu neutestamentlichen Stellen, *ThStKr* 94 (1922): 182, calls attention to an older example in Plato, *Leg.* 2.659A: The judge in a competition ought not, when he knows better, to "give his verdict carelessly through cowardice and lack of spirit, thus swearing falsely out of the same mouth with which he invoked Heaven when he first took his seat as judge" (δι' ἀνανδρίαν καὶ δειλίαν ἐκ ταὐτοῦ στόματος, οὗπερ τοὺς θεοὺς ἐπεκαλέσατο μέλλων κρίνειν, ἐκ τούτου ψευδόμενον ἀποφαίνεσθαι ῥαθύμως τὴν κρίσιν).

103 Sir 5:13: "Glory and dishonour comes from speak-

ing, and a person's tongue is his downfall" (δόξα καὶ ἀτιμία ἐν λαλιᾷ, καὶ γλῶσσα ἀνθρώπου πτῶσις αὐτῷ). Also Sir 28:12 shows how different things can come from the same mouth. It is said in *Test. Ben.* 6.5 in praise of the good mind, "The good mind does not possess two tongues, one which blesses and one which curses" (ἡ ἀγαθὴ διάνοια οὐκ ἔχει δύο γλώσσας εὐλογίας καὶ κατάρας) [Trans.].

104 χρή has receded into the background in Hellenistic Greek in favor of δεῖ. Its occasional use seems to suggest literary style. Thus, the word appears in the whole LXX only once (Prov 25:27), but also once in Pseudo-Aristeas. In early Christianity, it is encountered only here, in Justin and Tatian, and once in Aristides. It has especially receded into the background in Epictetus, but it is relatively frequent in Marcus Aurelius. Cf. Wilhelm Schmid, *Der Attizismus in seinen Hauptvertretern von Dionysius von Halikarnass bis auf den zweiten Philostratus*, vol. 4 (Stuttgart: Kohlhammer, 1896; reprint Hildesheim: Olms, 1964), 592.

105 Cf. Bousset, *Kyrios Christos*, 291, and in general, 287ff. The Koine reading "God" (θεόν also vulg) is a correction in accordance with Christian usage.

106 1 Chron 29:10: "Lord, God of Israel, our Father" (κύριε, ὁ θεὸς Ἰσραήλ, ὁ πατὴρ ἡμῶν); Isa 63:16: "You, Lord, our Father" (σύ, κύριε, πατὴρ ἡμῶν);

to God); the expression "The Holy One, blessed be He" (הַקָּדוֹשׁ בָּרוּךְ הוּא) which is so frequent in the Talmud;[108] and finally the formula "Blessed art Thou" (בָּרוּךְ אַתָּה) encountered frequently in the Eighteen Benedictions.[109] The presupposition that "we" curse other people does not conform with the ethos of the early Christian community, as is shown by both the criticism in Jas and the admonition of Paul in Rom 12:14: "bless and do not curse" (εὐλογεῖτε καὶ μὴ καταρᾶσθε)—not to mention Lk 6:28. But the Old Testament tells stories of cursings without hesitation, has no qualms about mentioning curses, and prohibits only certain types of curses.[110]

The embarrassment of the ancient commentators over this Christian cursing is therefore very well-grounded, for the entire view reflected in vv 9, 10a comes not from the life of the early Christian community, but from the life of the Jewish community. Therefore the criticism in v 10b is at the same time an indirect criticism of Jewish customs, a criticism which could have been made, of course, from within Judaism itself.[111] Naturally, the contradiction with the Old Testament cannot be evaded by arguing that only very

specific curses are forbidden, i.e., that "those who are made in the likeness of God" (τοὺς καθ' ὁμοίωσιν θεοῦ γεγονότας) refers only to a specific group of godlike persons. Precisely the godlikeness of *every* human being is stressed in Jewish literature.[112]

■ 11 The criticism of this misuse of the tongue is supported in vv 11, 12 by two (or three) metaphors. They do not concern the nature of the tongue, as do those in vv 3–8, but instead they portray the incompatibility of "blessing" (εὐλογία) and "cursing" (κατάρα). There is no need for any more far-reaching interpretation, although in the eyes of many interpreters an allegorical reference to the human being in the word "spring" (πηγή)[113] and to the mouth in the word "opening" (ὀπή) has seemed to be a quite natural interpretation. Such an allegorical interpretation is superfluous, since by it the thought is at most made more confusing and is in no way clarified.

The material in these metaphors is obvious to the Oriental. For the first image,[114] one can refer to *4 Ezra* 5.9 where among the apocalyptic signs of the end mention is made of the fact that "salt waters shall be found in the sweet" (trans. Charles, *APOT*), and to

Sir 23:1,4: "Lord, Father and Ruler of my life" (κύριε, πάτερ καὶ δέσποτα τῆς ζωῆς μου) and "Lord, Father and God of my life" (κύριε, πάτερ καὶ θεὲ ζωῆς μου Sir 51:10 is uncertain); Joseph., *Ant.* 5.93: "God, Father and Ruler of the Hebrew race" (ὁ θεός, πατὴρ καὶ δεσπότης τοῦ Ἑβραίων γένους).

107 On the instrumental ἐν used with εὐλογοῦμεν, cf. Blass-Debrunner, § 195.

108 But cf. Gustaf Dalman, *The Words of Jesus Considered in the Light of Post-Biblical Jewish Writings and the Aramaic Language*, tr. D. M. Kay (Edinburgh: Clark, 1902) vol. 1, p. 200.

109 Text in O. Holtzmann, *Berakot*, 10ff.

110 In narrative sections: Gen 9:25; 49:7; Josh 6:26; Judg 9:20(57); 2 Kgs 2:24; Neh 13:25; in Judg 5:23 cursing is even ordered by Yahweh or his angel. No scruples about cursing appear in the several references to it which are found in the Wisdom literature: Prov 11:26; 24:24; 26:2; Eccl 7:21; Sir 4:5; 21:27. Cursing of parents is forbidden in Ex 21:17 *et passim*; of a ruler, in Ex 22:28 (cf. Acts 23:5), of a deaf person, in Lev 19:14.

111 *Midrash Bereshith Rabbah* 24.7 on Gen 5:1: "Hence you must not say, since I have been put to shame, let my neighbor be put to shame. R. Tanḥuma said: If you do so, know whom you put to shame, [for] 'In the likeness of God made He him'" (trans. Freed-

man-Simon).

112 Gen 1:26, where the expression "in the likeness" (καθ' ὁμοίωσιν) is also found; Gen 9:6. In the Wisdom literature, Sir 17:3; Wisd 2:23; cf. also *4 Ezra* 8.44; also relevant here are *Ps. Clem. Hom.* 3.17; *Ps. Clem. Recog.* 5.23.

113 "Brackish and bitter spring" (ἁλμυρὰ καὶ πικρὰ πηγή) is apparently also used by Philo of speech, in *Som.* 2.281. Yet the text of that passage is disputed.

114 The transitive use of βρύειν to mean "pour forth", which occurs only seldom in earlier periods, is found in early Christian literature also in Justin, *Dial.* 114.4; *Ps. Clem. Hom.* 2.45.2.

the Christian *Paralipomena Jeremiae* 9.16, where it is said in the same apocalyptic context that "the sweet waters will become salty in the great light of God's gladness" (τὰ γλυκέα ὕδατα ἁλμυρὰ γενήσονται ἐν τῷ μεγάλῳ φωτὶ τῆς εὐφροσύνης τοῦ θεοῦ) [Trans.].[115]

■ **12a** For the second metaphor, of the fig tree and the grapevine, the saying of Jesus in Matt 7:16 = Lk 6:44 comes first to mind.[116] But the circumstances are peculiar in the case of this metaphor. Much closer to our saying in content and purpose than the saying of Jesus are certain Stoic similes which all belong to a specific context.

What is involved is an optimistic Stoic view of nature which crescendos to a religious fervor: In the realm of nature all things are interrelated and depend upon each other. In this condition of reciprocity every peculiarity has its justification. From this two dictates emerge: (1) One ought not to be amazed when each does only that which is one's proper role according to one's place in nature; (2) each ought to strive to fulfill his role and be satisfied with whatever is allotted him in the great cosmic family. The first thought is so repeatedly explained (especially by Marcus Aurelius) by use of the fig tree and grapevine imagery (the two metaphors used by Jas) that the fixing of this concept by the school tradition is clearly perceived.[117] Epictetus used the metaphor of the grapevine in the same sense.[118] But the second dictate—everyone should do that which is proper to him—is supported by Marcus Aurelius with various images, among which the fig tree metaphor is again encountered.[119] Plutarch used the grapevine, fig tree, and olive tree (i.e., illustrative material which is very similar to that in Jas) to show that the merits of various callings and characters cannot all be united in one person.[120] Seneca used the metaphor of the fig tree and olive tree to characterize incompatible opposites,[121] much as Jas does. Therefore it becomes probable that the thought in Jas 3:12a derives from

---

115 Rhetorical enumerations of things which are contradictory (such as in 2 Cor 6:14ff) might also be considered as parallels—so *Test. Gad* 5.1, with its depiction of Hatred which reverses everything: "it calls what is sweet 'bitter'" (τὸ γλυκὺ πικρὸν λέγει). Hence there is no need to assign to Jas a familiarity with the hot salt springs of Tiberias (Hort).

116 The form of this saying in Matthew also has μήτι for the introduction of the question (Blass-Debrunner, § 440 and § 427.2). Cf. the corresponding Arabic proverbs in Rudolph Bultmann, *History of the Synoptic Tradition*, tr. John Marsh (New York and Evanston: Harper and Row, ²1968), 202, n. 1 (from G. W. Freytag, *Arabum proverbia, vocalibus instruxit, latine vertit, commentario illustravit*, 3 vols. [Bonn: Marcum, 1838–43]).

117 Compare M. Ant. 4.6.1: "Given such people, it was in the nature of the case inevitable that their conduct should be of this kind. To wish otherwise, is to wish that *the fig tree has no acrid juice*" (ταῦτα οὕτως ὑπὸ τῶν τοιούτων πέφυκε γίνεσθαι ἐξ ἀνάγκης· ὁ δὲ τοῦτο μὴ θέλων θέλει τὴν συκῆν ὀπὸν μὴ ἔχειν) with 12.16.2: "Note that whoever would not have the wicked do wrong is as one who would not have the *fig tree secrete acrid juice in its fruit*" (ὅτι ὁ μὴ θέλων τὸν φαῦλον ἁμαρτάνειν ὅμοιος τῷ μὴ θέλοντι τὴν συκῆν ὀπὸν ἐν τοῖς σύκοις φέρειν). Cf. 8.15: "Remember that, as it is monstrous to be surprised at *a fig tree bearing figs*, so also is it to be surprised at the Universe bearing its own particular crop" (μέμνησο, ὅτι, ὥσπερ αἰσχρόν ἐστι ξενίζεσθαι, εἰ ἡ συκῆ σῦκα φέρει, οὕτως, εἰ ὁ κόσμος τάδε τινὰ φέρει, ὧν ἐστι

φόρος); 8.46: "Nothing can befall a human being that is not a natural human contingency; nor befall an ox, that is not natural to oxen, *nor a vine that is not natural to a vine*" (ἀνθρώπῳ οὐδενὶ συμβαίνειν τι δύναται, ὃ οὐκ ἔστιν ἀνθρωπικὸν σύμπτωμα, οὐδὲ βοΐ, ὃ οὐκ ἔστι βοικόν, οὐδὲ ἀμπέλῳ ὃ οὐκ ἔστιν ἀμπελικόν).

118 Epict., *Diss.* 2.20.18f: "Such a powerful and invincible thing is human nature. *For how can a vine be moved to act, not like a vine, but like an olive, or again an olive to act, not like an olive, but like a vine?* It is impossible; inconceivable. Neither, then, is it possible for a human being absolutely to lose the human affections" (οὕτως ἰσχυρόν τι καὶ ἀνίκητόν ἐστιν ἡ φύσις ἡ ἀνθρωπίνη. πῶς γὰρ δύναται ἄμπελος μὴ ἀμπελικῶς κινεῖσθαι, ἀλλ' ἐλαϊκῶς, ἢ ἐλαία πάλιν μὴ ἐλαϊκῶς ἀλλ' ἀμπελικῶς; ἀμήχανον, ἀδιανόητον, οὐ τοίνυν οὐδ' ἄνθρωπον οἷόν τε παντελῶς ἀπολέσαι τὰς κινήσεις τὰς ἀνθρωπικάς). On "to be moved to act" (κινεῖσθαι) and "affection, movement" (κίνησις) in this context, cf. Eduard Norden, *Agnostos Theos: Untersuchungen zur Formengeschichte religiöser Rede* (Leipzig: Teubner, 1913; reprint Darmstadt: Wissenschaftliche Buchgesellschaft, 1956); 19f.

119 M. Ant. 10.8.6: "and that a human being should do a human's work, as *the fig tree does the work of a fig tree*, the dog of a dog, and the bee of a bee" (καὶ εἶναι τὴν μὲν συκῆν τὰ συκῆς ποιοῦσαν, τὸν δὲ κύνα τὰ κυνός, τὴν δὲ μέλισσαν τὰ μελίσσης, τὸν δὲ ἄνθρωπον τὰ ἀνθρώπου).

120 Plut., *Tranq. an.* 13: "But as it is, we do not expect *the vine to bear figs nor the olive grapes*, but, for ourselves, if we have not at one and the same time the advan-

Stoic tradition. We can see from Seneca that the ideas which have been quoted here from Marcus Aurelius are older than this philosophizing Caesar,[122] and it can be demonstrated from Paul that the Stoic dictate: "discover what is befitting from what is the name" (ἀπὸ τῶν ὀνομάτων τὰ καθήκοντα εὑρίσκειν) has passed over into early Christian paraenesis already at an early stage.[123] But there is also confirmation here that the concepts in vv 9–12 have nothing to do with the series of metaphors which must be assumed as the source for vv 3–8. For while there we have a fixed context, here what is involved is a commonly used metaphor[124] which maintains its value in the most diverse of associations.

■ **12b** To these two images is joined yet a third, at least if the text of v 12b reads "nor can a salt spring yield fresh water" (οὔτε ἁλυκὸν γλυκὺ ποιῆσαι ὕδωρ). The text of the Koine witnesses has "so also no one spring can yield both salt water and fresh water" (οὕτως οὐδεμία πηγὴ ἁλυκὸν καὶ γλυκὺ ποιῆσαι ὕδωρ). This is an example of the smoothing out of difficult sayings which is so frequent in the Koine witnesses, and this reading must already be rejected for that reason. But in addition, the declaration in the Koine reading is based upon a misunderstanding; it simply repeats the idea of v 11, but it represents it as the interpretation of v 12a (see οὕτως): *One* spring can no more provide both salt water and fresh than the fig tree can produce olives. But in reality v 11 and v 12 are parallel metaphors for the incompatibility of cursing and blessing.

What is the intention of the shorter text, then? Its abrupt "nor" (οὔτε)—if this is to be read[125]—can be explained: the "neither" which belongs to this "nor" is contained within the preceding rhetorical question, since it presupposes that the answer is "no." ἁλυκόν probably means the "salt spring" not salt water. Otherwise the statement would be too self-evident and insipid.[126] But then the verb ποιῆσαι is a problem. It

---

tages of both the wealthy and the learned, of both commanders and philosophers, of both flatterers (etc.) . . . we slander ourselves and are displeased with ourselves" (νῦν δὲ τὴν ἄμπελον σῦκα φέρειν οὐκ ἀξιοῦμεν οὐδὲ τὴν ἐλαίαν βότρυς· αὐτοὶ δὲ ἑαυτούς, ἐὰν μὴ καὶ τὰ τῶν πλουσίων ἅμα καὶ τὰ τῶν λογίων καὶ τὰ τῶν στρατευομένων καὶ τὰ τῶν φιλοσοφούντων καὶ τὰ τῶν κολακευόντων . . . ἔχωμεν προτερήματα, συκοφαντοῦμεν καὶ ἀχαριστοῦμεν αὐτοῖς).

121 Seneca, on the assertion, "Good does not come from evil" (bonum ex malo non fit), *Ep.* 87.25: "Hence, Good does not spring from evil, any more than figs grow from olive trees" (non nascitur itaque ex malo bonum non magis quam ficus ex olea).

122 Seneca, *De ira* 2.10.6: "The wise person will have no anger toward sinners. Do you ask why? Because he knows that nobody is born wise, but one is only made wise, and he knows that only the fewest in every age turn out wise, because he has fully grasped the conditions of human life, and no sensible person becomes angry with nature. Do you think a sane person would marvel because apples do not hang from the brambles of the woodland? Would he marvel because thorns and briars are not covered with some useful fruit? No one becomes angry with a fault for which nature stands sponsor" (non irascetur sapiens peccantibus. Quare? Quia scit neminem nasci sapientem sed fieri, scit paucissimos omni aevo sapientis evadere, quia condicionem humanae vitae perspectam habet; nemo autem naturae sanus irascitur. Quid enim, si mirari velit non in silvestribus dumis poma pendere? quid, si miretur spineta sen-

tesque non utili aliqua fruge compleri? Nemo irascitur, ubi vitium natura defendit). This is the same thought as in the passages in n. 117 and n. 118 above, and basically even the same imagery, which is used to support rational demands by pointing to rational precedents in nature.

123 Cf. my remarks concerning the rules for the household (*Haustafeln*) in "Ἐπίγνωσις ἀληθείας," 4f.

124 The details vary, cf. the quotation from Seneca above in n. 122. Cf. also the vulg translation: "Can a fig-tree produce grapes?" (numquid potest ficus uvas facere), which should hardly be considered in the determination of the Greek text; *ff* has *olivas*.

125 Besides the shorter text which is assumed above (B A C* arm) and the Koine text, there are intermediate forms with οὕτως at the beginning, or οὐδέ instead of οὔτε, or both. Von Soden (*Schriften*, part 2 *ad loc.*) takes οὕτως οὐδὲ ἁλυκὸν γλυκὺ ποιῆσαι ὕδωρ (ℵ 33) as the reading of his recension *H*, and therefore he prefers it. Yet one cannot avoid the suspicion that in this reading there is contamination from the Koine text, especially since other intermediate forms also occur: οὕτως οὔτε C*c* *ff* vulg; also οὐδέ without οὕτως is found, as well as the Koine text with οὔτε.

126 Moreover, one would expect the article here also, as with "bitter" (πικρόν) in v 11.

must mean, "Nor does a salt spring *yield* fresh water," and this meaning of $\pi o\iota \epsilon \hat{\iota} \nu$ is only justified by v 12a. But this connection between v 12b and v 12a offers the solution to the puzzle about the intention of v 12b. Although the metaphors of the spring and the plants were parallel in purpose, whoever wrote v 12b obviously felt the lack of a parallelism in form: in v 11 it says, "both do not come from the same place," but in v 12a, "one does not bring forth the other." In the shorter version of v 12b, the first metaphor is remodeled after the pattern of the second, so that now it is also said of water that "one does not bring forth the other, i.e., a salt spring does not yield fresh water."

Is this variant to be ascribed to Jas? I hardly think so. He himself could scarcely have felt the dissimilarity between v 11 and v 12a to be bothersome. In v 11 he had formed, out of traditional material, a metaphor which precisely suited the subject matter. To this he had added a familiar metaphor and thus had provided the thought with a more general basis. He did not need to create artfully an agreement in form between the two metaphors. But this could be done by someone else, perhaps the same person whose interpretive activity has found a place in the text in 3:6, also. And if v 12b is a gloss, its abrupt form is also explained.[127]

---

127 E. Klostermann, "Zum Texte des Jakobusbriefes," *Verbum Dei manet in aeternum* (Festschrift O. Schmitz), ed. Werner Foerster (Witten: Luther-Verlag, 1953), 71f, proposes for discussion the following repair of the damage: By homoioteleuton, the present text would be a mutilation of:

"so also neither is a fresh spring able to yield salt water nor is a salt spring able to yield fresh water."

($o\H{\upsilon}\tau\omega\varsigma$ $o\H{\upsilon}\tau\epsilon$ $\gamma\lambda\upsilon\kappa\grave{\upsilon}$ $\nu\hat{\alpha}\mu\alpha$ $\delta\acute{\upsilon}\nu\alpha\tau\alpha\iota$ $\acute{\alpha}\lambda\iota\kappa\acute{o}\nu$, $o\H{\upsilon}\tau\epsilon$ $\acute{\alpha}\lambda\iota\kappa\grave{o}\nu$ $\gamma\lambda\upsilon\kappa\grave{\upsilon}$ $\pi o\iota\hat{\eta}\sigma\alpha\iota$ $\H{\upsilon}\delta\omega\rho$)

Certainly ℵ does not read $o\H{\upsilon}\tau\omega\varsigma$ $o\H{\upsilon}\tau\epsilon$ as Klostermann assumes. On the justification of conjectural criticism in Jas, cf. above in the Introduction, section 10, part (b).

206

3 A Group of Sayings Against Contentiousness

13 Who is wise and understanding among you? By a good life let him show his works in meek wisdom. 14/ But if you bear bitter jealousy and party spirit in your hearts, do not boast with lies in defiance of the truth. 15/ This wisdom is not that which comes down from above; rather it is earthly, psychical, demonic. 16/ For where jealousy and party spirit exist, there will be disorder and every vile practice. 17/ But the wisdom which is from above is first pure, then peaceable, gentle, tractable, full of mercy and good fruits, harmonious, sincere.

18 The fruit of righteousness is sown in peace for those who make peace.

4

1 What causes conflicts, and what causes fightings among you? Is it not your passions that are at war in your members? 2/ You desire, and you do not have; you are jealous and envious, and you do not obtain (what you covet); you fight and strive, and you do not have because you do not ask; 3/ you ask, and you do not receive because you ask with the wrong motive, in order to spend it on your passions.
   4/ Adulteresses! Do you not know that friendship with the world is enmity with God? Therefore whoever wishes to be a friend of the world proves himself to be an enemy of God. 5/ Or do you suppose it is in vain that the scripture says, "He (i.e., God) yearns jealously after the spirit which he has made to dwell within us"? 6/ But he gives all the more grace; therefore it says, "God opposes the proud, but gives grace to the humble."

7 Submit yourselves therefore to God. Resist the Devil and he will flee from you. 8/ Draw near to God and he will draw near to you. Cleanse your hands, you sinners, and purify your hearts, you double-minded! 9/ Be wretched and mourn and weep! Let your laughter be turned to mourning and your joy to sorrow! 10/ Humble yourselves before the Lord and he will exalt you. 11/ Do not slander one another, brothers and sisters. Whoever slanders his brother or judges his brother, slanders the law and judges the law. But if you judge the law you are not a doer of the law but a judge. 12/ There is only one lawgiver and judge, he who is able to save and to destroy. But, you who judge your neighbour, who are you (but a mere human)?

Analysis

There is no indication of a connection with the preceding section, and the Interpretation will reveal that there is no connection in thought either. Perhaps a link through the use of a catchword is intended, so that

"bitter" ($\pi\iota\kappa\rho\acute{o}\nu$) in 3:11 would correspond to "bitter" ($\pi\iota\kappa\rho\acute{o}\nu$) in 3:14, but this is uncertain. It is easy to see that the warning against jealousy and strife in 3:13–4:6 and again in 4:11f are important in this section, but this uniformity in tendency still does not guarantee a unity in the train of thought nor a unity of form.

To begin with, 3:18 turns out upon closer examination to be an isolated saying. Certainly it is to be separated from the admonition in 4:1ff, which begins a new thought. However, that it also does not belong with the preceding group has been correctly perceived by some interpreters, yet they have failed to draw consequences for the literary analysis.[1]

The small section 3:13–17 is completely unified: Whoever wishes to be wise cannot be contentious, for if he is contentious, his is an earthly and not a heavenly wisdom, since heavenly wisdom is peace–loving.[2]

Now as far as its emphasis upon peace is concerned, 3:18 fits with the subject matter which precedes it. Yet it is surprising to find here a reference to the "fruit of righteousness" instead of the "fruit of wisdom," for neither the term "righteousness" ($\delta\iota\kappa\alpha\iota\sigma\sigma\acute{\nu}\nu\eta$) nor the topic occurs anywhere in the context. To think that the "fruit of righteousness" ($\kappa\alpha\rho\pi\grave{\sigma}\varsigma\ \delta\iota\kappa\alpha\iota\sigma\sigma\acute{\nu}\nu\eta\varsigma$) is the antithesis to "every vile practice" ($\pi\hat{\alpha}\nu\ \phi\alpha\hat{\nu}\lambda\sigma\nu\ \pi\rho\hat{\alpha}\gamma\mu\alpha$) in 3:16 is to overlook the fact that 3:16 is only a side comment intended to justify the harsh judgment upon false, contentious wisdom: Wherever strife prevails, in reality, *all* evil is present. The main thought continues directly from 3:15 to 3:17, and therefore 3:18 is not the antithesis to 3:16. It will be seen in the Interpretation that 3:18 possesses an independent wholeness and inclusiveness in form. It demands no more intimate connection with the context, and in fact it has none. A looser kind of connection is achieved through the presence of a common tendency, and perhaps also through the connection by use of a catchword, since the correspondence between "fruits" ($\kappa\alpha\rho\pi\hat{\omega}\nu$) in v 17 and "fruit" ($\kappa\alpha\rho\pi\sigma\varsigma$) in v 18 is hardly accidental.

4:1–6 is an inclusive whole. But the thought has shifted, and above all the mood has changed. Contentiousness constitutes only the point of departure for the discussion. The evil lies deeper than that, in the "passions" ($\dot{\eta}\delta\sigma\nu\alpha\acute{\iota}$), in the worldly disposition against which the author now directs sharper indictments, with stirring language and with the total seriousness of a preacher of repentence.

To this sermon the admonitory imperatives in 4:7ff

stand in clear contrast. The first part of v 7 and also v 10 fit the subject matter of the last words of 4:1–6. However, the remaining admonitions, which are parallel in form, have a totally different content which is in no way uniform, and the preceding sharpness in tone is achieved only in v 9. Obviously we have here a series of admonitions which are alike in form but different in content, as is often encountered in paraenesis (cf. Rom 12:9–13). The author has taken these over and perhaps altered them. They occur in this verse because the subject matter of their first member (v 7a) fits well with what precedes. In spite of certain hesitations, I would like to include vv 11f in this series of admonitions. The imperative here is formally connected with the others; what then follows is a commentary to that admonition and is certainly different in character. However, in the Introduction[3] I have tried to show what role these explanations play in the history of paraenesis: as the need arises, commentaries are attached to some, but by no means all, of the statements in a series of admonitions. As these commentarial accessories grow, an admonition becomes independent. What results is the developed paraenesis such as is found in the *Mandates* of the *Shepherd of Hermas*. We stand here at a moderate, initial stage in this process, and for this reason I do not consider vv 11f to be an isolated saying.

So the whole section breaks down into the two admonitions in 3:13–17 and 4:1–6, between which stands the isolated saying 3:18, and to which is joined the series of imperatives in 4:7–12.

Interpretation

■ **13–17** From the analysis it follows that in these verses our author executes his arguments against contentiousness by using the concept of wisdom. He has in mind the possibility that disputes could be carried on in the name of and for the sake of wisdom, and he wishes to prove the fallacy of using such an excuse for strife. This possibility exists in the most diverse of human situations. Therefore the general basis for this admonition need not be narrowed for the sake of a connection with 3:1–12 so that the admonition is interpreted as a reference to teachers, as the catenae and scholia have done.

1   Belser expresses the feeling that actually the subject must be the fruit of wisdom (instead of the fruit of righteousness). Huther and Beyschlag call the verse

a "sententious expression."
2   Cladder, 37–57, sees in 3:13–18 the center of the epistle. Concerning this and other attempted ar-

Indeed, this is ruled out by the fact that, as we have seen, the paraenesis from 3:3 on no longer has anything to do with teachers. Also, the connection stressed by some interpreters between this false wisdom and the sins of the tongue dealt with previously is nowhere indicated, even though it could have been easily constructed psychologically. However, I believe that I have shown that the literary style of Jas and of paraenesis in general shows no concern for such connections. And finally, once again the construction of a historical occasion for this admonition must be resisted here. Windisch, in the 1911 edition of his commentary, hinted at such a historical occasion: "The excessive interest in the cultivation of wisdom perhaps led to strife and dissension ... perhaps the readers prided themselves on their religious concern." Whether such things were especially upon the author's mind or not, he says what for him appears to be useful and necessary *for all situations*. More important for paraenesis than some actually existing historical situation is that the cultural mentality which the paraenesis presupposes be both likely and *generally* valid.

■ **13** The rhetorical question and the imperative response express in animated fashion what is usually said by means of conditional clauses. Diatribe tends to favour such rhetorical liveliness of the discourse.[4] The LXX offers parallels for this form (e.g., Judg 7:3; Ps 33:13; Isa 50:10), and one might further compare *1 Clem.* 54.1f: "Who then among you is noble, who is compassionate, who is filled with love? Let him cry ..." (τίς οὖν ἐν ὑμῖν γενναῖος, τίς εὔσπλαγχνος, τίς πεπληρο-

φορημένος ἀγάπης; εἰπάτω κτλ). That the adjective "understanding" (ἐπιστήμων) is found only here in the New Testament is purely accidental, for it occurs five times in the Greek version of Sirach and the combination "wise and understanding" (σοφὸς καὶ ἐπιστήμων) occurs in LXX Deut 1:13, 15 and 4:6.

The imperative clause containing the answer to the question sounds somewhat involved because it combines two thoughts. First, the wise person provides factual proof of this wisdom by a good life.[5] Secondly, the wise person shows this wisdom in meekness;[6] the relation to the question is indicated by the genitival combination "meekness of wisdom" (πραΰτης σοφίας), which is a further example of the author's tendency to use this—Semiticizing?—construction.[7] Here the genitive "of wisdom" replaces the adjective, while in English one would reverse the adjective and the noun: "in meek wisdom" (instead of "in wise meekness").

■ **14** The idea of the contentious attitude is paraphrased here with the words "bitter jealousy" (ζῆλος πικρός) and the problematic term ἐριθεία.[8] This word, which originally signified corruption or corruptibility in political struggles, appears, judging by the Jewish–Christian examples, to have been used in these circles to mean "party spirit" and "factiousness." In such a development, the influence of the root-word ἔριθος ("day–labourer," "hired servant") would have been less important than the false assimilation of the word to the totally different term ἔρις ("strife"). This becomes especially probable in light of the possibly already

---

3 See above in the Introduction, p. 3.

4 The poorly attested reading "If someone ..." (εἴ τις ...) offers a quite correct, but prosaic interpretation of our passage. This reading should not be considered original because of the fact that v 14 begins with εἰ, as Roland Schütz argues (*Der parallele Bau der Satzglieder im Neuen Testament, und seine Verwertung für die Textkritik und Exegese*, FRLANT 11 (Göttingen: Vandenhoeck & Ruprecht, 1920), 26). Manuscript K *et al.* have the completely simplified reading, "Let the wise and understanding person among you show ..." (σοφὸς καὶ ἐπιστήμων ἐν ὑμῖν δειξάτω κτλ.).

5 *1 Clem.* 38.2: "Let the wise manifest his wisdom not in words but in good deeds" (ὁ σοφὸς ἐνδεικνύσθω

τὴν σοφίαν αὐτοῦ μὴ ἐν λόγοις ἀλλ' ἐν ἔργοις ἀγαθοῖς). In the formulation in Jas 3:13b the author perhaps follows the Hellenistic preference for paraphrases using ἐκ. Examples are given by Radermacher, *Grammatik*, 21f. On the expression "way of life" (ἀναστροφή) in the ethical sense, cf. Deissmann, *Bible Studies*, 88, 194; Theodor Nägeli, *Der Wortschatz des Apostels Paulus* (Göttingen: Vandenhoeck & Ruprecht, 1905), 34.

6 Sir 3:17: "My son, perform your tasks in meekness" (τέκνον, ἐν πραΰτητι τὰ ἔργα σου διέξαγε).

7 Cf. above in the Introduction, section 5.

8 Cf. the explanation in Hort's commentary, *ad loc.*: "ἐριθεία really means the vice of a leader of a party created for his own pride: it is partly ambition, partly rivalry," Cf. also Hans Lietzmann, *An die Römer*, HNT 8 (Tübingen: Mohr [Siebeck], [4]1933), on

rangements, cf. the Introduction, section 1, especially n. 22.

"fixed" sequence in the paraenetic catalogues in the Pauline letters: Gal 5:20: "enmity, strife, jealousy, anger, party spirit, dissension, schism" (ἔχθραι ἔρις ζῆλος θυμοί ἐριθεῖαι διχοστασίαι αἱρέσεις); 2 Cor 12:20: "strife, jealousy, anger, party spirit, slander, gossip" (ἔρις ζῆλος θυμοί ἐριθεῖαι καταλαλιαί ψιθυρισμοί). In both cases ἐριθεία is a particular kind of strife, a "party spirit," and the other examples confirm this.[9] It is this attitude which is intended in this verse: "If you bear fierce bitterness and a party spirit in your heart, then do not boast with lies in defiance of the truth." The final clause is to be understood in this way, and not as a question.[10] The sentence as a whole is not introducing a new special case, but rather it accuses all wise people who are contentious of being liars. The boast which defies the truth is their claim of wisdom, for true wisdom can not be contentious. This line of thought is immediately picked up in v 15, while every other explanation of v 14 must first construe a special content of the boast implied in the term "boast against" (κατα-καυχᾶσθαι).[11] The formulation suffers from redundancy. Instead of, "Do not boast in defiance of the truth," Jas says, "Do not boast and lie." The phrase "against the truth" (κατὰ τῆς ἀληθείας) is probably connected with both verbs, and in this case κατακαυχᾶσθαι would have the same meaning as in 2:13.[12]

■ 15 "This wisdom" (αὕτη ἡ σοφία) is the subject of the sentence, and the phrase "comes down from above" (ἄνωθεν κατερχομένη), which formally is a periphrastic conjugation with the verb "to be" (εἶναι), is used instead of an adjective.[13] The sense is: "This wisdom is not that which comes from heaven and is divine," and the three predicates which then are applied to this wisdom form a crescendo from "earthly" to "demonic." Therefore, the word ψυχικός ("psychical") which is the middle member in this list must have a decisively negative meaning: not "natural," but "sensual." The author presupposes that the word is a familiar one. Even though fully conclusive examples are as yet lacking, nevertheless, in recent years research has singled out with great probability the sphere from which this word comes: ψυχικός could assume the sense which is demanded here only in the context of a pronounced pneumatic piety, a "gnostic" religiosity, if the word "gnostic" is used in the broadest religio–historical sense.[14]

---

9   Rom 2:8.
    Philo, *Leg. Gaj.* 68: "The only correct government is that which is without strife and party spirit" (ἡγε-μονία δὲ ἀφιλόνεικος καὶ ἀνερίθευτος ὀρθὴ μόνη) [Trans.]. While the meaning of ἐριθεία in Rom 2:8 is quite general, concrete situations which are not clear to us are intended in Phil 1:17. The word is paralleled there with "jealousy" (φθόνος see Phil 1:15). In Phil 2:3 (μηδὲν κατ᾽ ἐριθείαν μηδὲ κατὰ κενοδοξίαν) the meaning is again clearly "contentiousness" which, like excessive ambition, can lead to dissension within the community. The admonition of Ign., *Phld.* 8.2: "Do nothing from a party spirit, but rather according to the teaching of Christ" (μηδὲνκατ᾽ ἐριθείαν πράσσειν, ἀλλὰ κατὰ χριστομαθίαν) [Trans.], is aimed not at disputatiousness, but rather at the practice of staying away from the worship because of a party spirit. The references in *Phld.* 4.1, 7.2 and 8.1 are clear enough, and the theme of doing nothing without the bishop, etc., in the letters of Ignatius always has to do with cultic matters (cf. Bousset, *Kyrios Christos*, 355f).
10   As Belser interprets it.
11   Beyschlag: "As though a heart full of divine thoughts and motives prompts you to speak and teach." Windisch, *Katholische Briefe* (1911): "religious concern."

12   If κατὰ τῆς ἀληθείας ("against the truth") should go only with ψεύδεσθε ("you lie"), as both Mayor and Ropes argue, then κατακαυχᾶσθαι would have a perfective sense such as "do not be presumptuous." As is seen in the textual variants, the ancient editors simply disposed of the whole problem:
    κατακαυχᾶσθε τῆς ἀληθείας καὶ ψεύδεσθε ℵ*
        "boast against the truth and lie"
    κατακαυχᾶσθε κατὰ τῆς ἀληθείας καὶ ψεύδεσθε ℵᶜ syᵛᵍ
        "boast against the truth and lie"
    καυχᾶσθε καὶ ψεύδεσθε κατὰ τῆς ἀληθείας A, and a large number of minuscules
        "boast and lie against the truth"
    And *ff* should probably be added to this list: "Why do you boast, lying against the truth?" (quid alapamini mentientes contra veritatem).
13   The expression "comes down from above" and the terms "earthly" (ἐπίγειος) and "demonic" (δαιμο-νιώδης) are discussed below under v 17.
14   To what follows, cf. Reitzenstein, *Mysterienreligionen*, 70ff, 324ff; *idem*, *Historia*, 141; Bousset, *Kyrios Christos*, 181ff, 258ff. [And more recently, cf. Birger Albert Pearson, *The Pneumatikos-Psychikos Terminology in 1 Corinthians*, Diss. Harvard, SBL Dissertation Series 12 (Society of Biblical Literature, 1973), esp. pp. 7–14—Trans.].

The Term ψυχικός

What is involved here is the notion that the divine "spirit" (πνεῦμα) replaces the human "soul" (ψυχή), a view which is in no way genuinely Christian.[15] For this notion we must refer for want of other witnesses to the introductory prayer in the "Mithras liturgy" edited by Dieterich.[16] There we find in line 26 (= Preisendanz, 523ff.): "while withdrawn from me for a little while is my human psychical power, which I shall receive again undiminished after the present bitter necessity by which I am hard pressed" (ὑπ⟨εξ⟩εστώσης μου πρὸς ὀλίγον τῆς ἀνθρωπίνης μου ψυχικῆς δυνάμεως, ἣν ἐγὼ πάλιν μεταπαραλήμψομαι μετὰ τὴν ἐνεστῶσαν καὶ κατεπείγουσάν με πικρὰν ἀνάγκην ἀχρεοκόπητον) [Trans.]. The "human psychical power," which the petitioner leaves behind during the mysteries in order to receive it again afterwards, is invoked in line 32 (= Preisendanz, 533): "Stand still, perishable human nature" (ἔσταθι, φθαρτὴ βροτῶν φύσι) [Trans.]. From this equation of "soul" (ψυχή) with "nature" (φύσις)[17] one can explain the fact that ψυχικός could acquire the meaning "natural" or "of nature," which Paul presupposes in 1 Cor 15:44, 46 (RSV: "physical"). However, another meaning of ψυχικός is now intelligible: If the initiate must leave behind his "psychical power" (ψυχικὴ δύναμις), "since it is not possible for me as a mortal to ascend with the golden gleams of immortal brilliance" (ἐπεὶ οὐκ ἔστιν μοι ἐφικτὸν θνητὸν γεγῶτα συνα⟨ν⟩ιέναι ταῖς χρυσοειδέσιν μαρμαρυγαῖς τῆς ἀθανάτου λαμπηδόνος "Mithras liturgy," lines 30ff, = Preisendanz, 529ff.)

[Trans.], then during the mysteries he is without "soul." Human beings who do not experience this state are always tied to the "soul" or "psyche" (ψυχή), and therefore they might be called "psychical" (ψυχικοί). This is the meaning which Paul uses in 1 Cor 2:14 (RSV: "unspiritual"), where the psychical person stands in sharp contrast to the pneumatic, or "spiritual" person. The term "spiritual" (πνευματικός) does not refer here to every Christian, but only to the person who beholds the "deep things of God" (1 Cor 2:10) and knows that hidden wisdom of which Paul here with stirring language provides more praise than description. To be sure, these psychical persons are not considered to be "lost," and therefore they could be compared with the middle class of individuals which also bear the name "psychical" in the Valentinian system.[18]

However, an exclusively "pneumatic" religion which does not recognize such intermediate classes must lay out this contrast in a radical fashion: The "psychical" (ψυχικός) person is the unsaved, unspiritual person, the absolute opposite of the "pneumatic" (πνευματικός) being. This is the true Gnostic point of view, which sees in the "soul" (ψυχή) only a fetter.[19] Clearly it is in this sense that the Gnostics opposed by the Letter of Jude called their opponents "psychical" (ψυχικοί), and the author of the letter returns this very invective (Jude 19; RSV: "worldly people") back upon "these who set up divisions" (ἀποδιορίζοντες).

I would not like to call this language "Pauline terminology," as Bousset does,[20] although the Gnostics have cloaked themselves in the words of Paul. Instead, what

---

15 On the pre-Christian history of this view, cf. also L. Troje, *Die Dreizehn und die Zwölf im Traktat Pelliot: (Dogmen in Zahlenformeln) Ein Beitrag zu den Grundlagen des Manichäismus*, VFVRUL, 2nd series, vol. 1 (Leipzig: Pfeiffer, 1925), 72f, n. 1.

16 Albrecht Dieterich, *Eine Mithrasliturgie* (Leipzig: Teubner, [3]1923; reprint Darmstadt: Wissenschaftliche Buchgesellschaft, 1966). [The text used by Dibelius was that in Reitzenstein, *Mysterienreligionen*, 174–6. For a new edition with German translation see Preisendanz, vol. 1, p. 88 line 475 to p. 100, line 834.—Trans.]

17 Cf. also Reitzenstein, *Historia*, 61, n. 5.

18 Iren., *Adv. haer.* 1.6.1f; Clem. Alex., *Exc. ex Theodoto* 54, 57.

19 The Marcosians according to Iren., *Adv. haer.* 1.21.5; cf. the similar statements of the Valentinians in

Clem. Alex., *Exc. ex Theodoto* 64: "The spiritual things having put off their souls" (ἀποθέμενα τὰ πνευματικὰ τὰς ψυχάς) [Trans.], and in Iren., *Adv. haer.* 1.7.1; cf. in the book "Baruch" of Justin the Gnostic, in Hippolytus, *Ref.* 5.26.25: "The soul is arrayed against the spirit and the spirit against the soul" (ἡ ψυχὴ κατὰ τοῦ πνεύματος τέτακται καὶ τὸ πνεῦμα κατὰ τῆς ψυχῆς) [Trans.]. Perhaps the characterization of catholic Christians as "psychical" by the Montanists also belongs in this category (Clem. Alex., *Strom.* 4.93.1; Tertullian, *De jejun.* 1).

20 Bousset, *Kyrios Christos*, 187, n. 87.

appears to me to be characteristic is precisely the fact that Paul snatches up the term $\psi\nu\chi\iota\kappa\acute{o}\varsigma$ only incidentally in two totally distinct contexts, and also the fact that the true Gnostic meaning of $\psi\nu\chi\iota\kappa\acute{o}\varsigma$ in the sense of a radical dualism can not be perceived at all in those two Pauline texts. This meaning is extra-Christian and is at home in the syncretism of a pneumatic or Gnostic piety which distinguishes only between the few spiritual persons on the one hand, and the mass of psychical persons outside grace on the other. Yet it is precisely this meaning which must be presupposed in James 3:15, for only this meaning provides the bridge from the term "earthly" ($\grave{\epsilon}\pi\acute{\iota}\gamma\epsilon\iota o\varsigma$) to the term "demonic" ($\delta\alpha\iota\mu o\nu\iota\acute{\omega}\delta\eta\varsigma$).

However, the Gnostic term $\psi\nu\chi\iota\kappa\acute{o}\varsigma$ does not give us the right to consider Jas a Gnostic work or to suppose that it is opposing Gnostics by employing their own weapons.[21] Nowhere in the whole writing is there found an indisputable reference to Gnostic teaching or praxis, and the literary style of Jas renders a polemic against concrete situations in specific churches improbable.[22] Thus, there is no reason to assume that Jas is related to, or directed against Gnostics. The explanation of the terminology in 3:15 is along the same lines as that for "cycle of becoming" ($\tau\rho o\chi\grave{o}\varsigma\,\tau\hat{\eta}\varsigma\,\gamma\epsilon\nu\acute{\epsilon}\sigma\epsilon\omega\varsigma$) in 3:6: the author has employed a technical expression without adopting the underlying concept.

■ **16** As the Analysis has shown, this verse is an aside intended to justify the unfavourable judgment of the preceding verses: Contentiousness is ultimately the root of all evil. This far–reaching assertion—which is not even always corroborated by the history of Christianity—shows quite clearly where the real interests of the

author lie. As far as he is concerned, all wisdom which leads to disunity is ungodly. He would rather renounce more lively intellectual activity than pay for it with tensions within the community. There is for him no independent rational judgment regarding intellectual controversies.

He is akin in his one-sidedness to *the teachers of Jewish didactic poetry*, to whom he owes so much.[23] The basic practical orientation of this didactic poetry, an orientation towards the life of average people, refuses to acknowledge the investigation and research of the solitary thinker.[24] The best parallels to Jas 3:13–16 are indeed found in Sirach: "But the knowledge of wickedness is not wisdom, nor is there prudence where sinners take counsel" ($\kappa\alpha\grave{\iota}\,o\grave{\nu}\kappa\,\acute{\epsilon}\sigma\tau\iota\nu\,\sigma o\phi\acute{\iota}\alpha\,\pi o\nu\eta\rho\acute{\iota}\alpha\varsigma\,\grave{\epsilon}\pi\iota\sigma\tau\acute{\eta}\mu\eta,\,\kappa\alpha\grave{\iota}\,o\grave{\nu}\kappa\,\acute{\epsilon}\sigma\tau\iota\nu\,\acute{o}\pi o\nu\,\beta o\nu\lambda\grave{\eta}\,\acute{\alpha}\mu\alpha\rho\tau\omega\lambda\hat{\omega}\nu\,\phi\rho\acute{o}\nu\eta\sigma\iota\varsigma$ Sir 19:22), and, "Better is the God-fearing man who lacks intelligence, than the highly prudent man who transgresses the Law" ($\kappa\rho\epsilon\acute{\iota}\tau\tau\omega\nu\,\acute{\eta}\tau\tau\acute{\omega}\mu\epsilon\nu o\varsigma\,\grave{\epsilon}\nu\,\sigma\nu\nu\acute{\epsilon}\sigma\epsilon\iota\,\acute{\epsilon}\mu\phi o\beta o\varsigma\,\grave{\eta}\,\pi\epsilon\rho\iota\sigma\sigma\epsilon\acute{\nu}\omega\nu\,\grave{\epsilon}\nu\,\phi\rho o\nu\acute{\eta}\sigma\epsilon\iota\,\kappa\alpha\grave{\iota}\,\pi\alpha\rho\alpha\beta\alpha\acute{\iota}\nu\omega\nu\,\nu\acute{o}\mu o\nu$ Sir 19:24).

Just as certainly as literature of this sort has influenced the author of Jas, so also it is certain that the one-sidedness which stands out in 3:16 corresponds precisely to the author's own personal ethos: he is distrustful of everything which looks like friendship with the world.[25] It is by this criterion that he also evaluates all striving after wisdom. And certainly the general development of the Christian communities offered occasion for such distrust. Already in Paul the Christianity of pneumatics separated itself from the faith of the community (at least in 1 Cor 2:6–16), in spite of all the emphasis upon unity. In other localities, where the influences of syncretistic Magi and wandering prophets worked as powerful lures, such aristocratic tendencies were able to operate with less restriction, and the Gnostic pneu-

---

21 Schwegler, 442; Pfleiderer, *Primitive Christianity*, vol. 4, pp. 301f, with reference to the relationship of Jas 3:15 to *Herm. mand.* 11.8ff. (On this passage from *Hermas*, see below on Jas 3:17). Weinel also understands this text, and the whole of Jas, as a polemical testimony against a radical Gnostic Paulinism (*Biblische Theologie*, section 91). Cf. also on this the discussion above in the Introduction, pp. 24f.

22 See above in the Introduction, section 7.

23 Cf. Bertholet, vol. 2, section 8; W. Stärk, *Lyrik* (*Psalmen, Hoheslied und Verwandtes*), Die Schriften des Alten Testaments 3, 1, ed. Hugo Gressmann, *et al.*

(Göttingen: Vandenhoeck & Ruprecht, ²1920), 99f, 117f.

24 Characteristic in this regard is the conclusion of the chapter on wisdom in Job. After a description with various metaphors of the unattainability of wisdom which God alone possesses, the concluding sentence (which stems not from the poet, but from a teacher) states: "Behold, the fear of the Lord, that is wisdom; and to depart from evil is understanding" (Job 28:28).

25 See above in the Introduction, p. 48.

matics are only particularly striking examples of this development. Also mention might be made of the spread of scribal activity and rhetoric, the penetration of popular philosophy, and perhaps also the consolidation of the organization of the churches. Each of these phenomena could, in the area where it was active, lead to the singling out of a kind of "first class" Christianity. Each of them could provoke from a Christian such as Jas the ethically motivated distrust which finds expression in these verses. However, precisely because there are so many possibilities before us,[26] and because we see in addition that paraenetic tradition and the inclination of the author himself lead in this direction, it seems to me that it is impossible to explain this admonition in Jas 3:14ff as reflecting the appearance of a specific orientation such as Gnosis.

■ **17** Even v 17 with its literary connections can in no way alter this judgment. The portrayal of the false prophets in *Herm. mand.* 11.8 has frequently and with justification been compared with our verse: "In the first place, he who has the [divine] spirit which is from above, is meek and gentle, and lowly-minded, and refrains from all wickedness and evil desire of this world" ($\pi\rho\hat{\omega}\tau o\nu$ $\mu\grave{\epsilon}\nu$ $\acute{o}$ $\check{\epsilon}\chi\omega\nu$ $\tau\grave{o}$ $\pi\nu\epsilon\hat{\upsilon}\mu\alpha$ [$\tau\grave{o}$ $\theta\epsilon\hat{\imath}o\nu$] $\tau\grave{o}$ $\check{\alpha}\nu\omega\theta\epsilon\nu$ $\pi\rho\alpha\hat{\upsilon}\varsigma$ $\grave{\epsilon}\sigma\tau\iota$ $\kappa\alpha\grave{\iota}$ $\acute{\eta}\sigma\acute{\upsilon}\chi\iota o\varsigma$ $\kappa\alpha\grave{\iota}$ $\tau\alpha\pi\epsilon\iota\nu\acute{o}\phi\rho\omega\nu$ $\kappa\alpha\grave{\iota}$ $\grave{\alpha}\pi\epsilon\chi\acute{o}\mu\epsilon\nu o\varsigma$ $\grave{\alpha}\pi\grave{o}$ $\pi\acute{\alpha}\sigma\eta\varsigma$ $\pi o\nu\eta\rho\acute{\iota}\alpha\varsigma$ $\kappa\alpha\grave{\iota}$ $\grave{\epsilon}\pi\iota\theta\upsilon\mu\acute{\iota}\alpha\varsigma$ $\mu\alpha\tau\alpha\acute{\iota}\alpha\varsigma$ $\tau o\hat{\upsilon}$ $\alpha\grave{\iota}\hat{\omega}\nu o\varsigma$ $\tau o\acute{\upsilon}\tau o\upsilon$). The similarity rests first of all in the use of the same pattern of discourse, viz., an enumeration of adjectives without further clarification (cf. *Herm. mand.* 5.2.3f). Secondly, in both catalogues there is an emphasis upon peaceableness. One would not want,

because of this correspondence, to identify the false wisdom of which Jas speaks with the false prophets whom Hermas combats. Nevertheless, the parallel is perhaps specific enough to throw light upon the style and mode of expression in the text in Jas. "From above" ($\check{\alpha}\nu\omega\theta\epsilon\nu$) and "come down from above" ($\check{\alpha}\nu\omega\theta\epsilon\nu$ $\kappa\alpha\tau\epsilon\rho$-$\chi o\mu\acute{\epsilon}\nu\eta$) by no means appear only as a predicate of wisdom. If one compares *Herm. mand.* 11.5, 8, 9, 21, one finds there descriptions of the spirit which comes "from above" and from these passages it is easy to see that "from above" ($\check{\alpha}\nu\omega\theta\epsilon\nu$) is another way of saying "divine" ($\theta\epsilon\hat{\imath}o\nu$).[27] What is applied to the spirit in these passages is applied to faith in *Herm. mand.* 9.11, and also the antithesis is formulated in both instances in a way quite similar to that in the text in Jas: *Herm. mand.* 9.11: "Double-mindedness is an *earthly* spirit from *the devil*" ($\acute{\eta}$ $\delta\grave{\epsilon}$ $\delta\iota\psi\upsilon\chi\acute{\iota}\alpha$ $\grave{\epsilon}\pi\acute{\iota}\gamma\epsilon\iota o\nu$ $\pi\nu\epsilon\hat{\upsilon}\mu\acute{\alpha}$ $\grave{\epsilon}\sigma\tau\iota$ $\pi\alpha\rho\grave{\alpha}$ $\tau o\hat{\upsilon}$ $\delta\iota\alpha\beta\acute{o}\lambda o\upsilon$); 11.11: "concerning the spirit which is *earthly*" ($\pi\epsilon\rho\grave{\iota}$ $\tau o\hat{\upsilon}$ $\pi\nu\epsilon\acute{\upsilon}\mu\alpha\tau o\varsigma$ $\tau o\hat{\upsilon}$ $\grave{\epsilon}\pi\iota\gamma\epsilon\acute{\iota}o\upsilon$). Jas 3:15, with its terms "earthly" ($\grave{\epsilon}\pi\acute{\iota}\gamma\epsilon\iota o\varsigma$) and "demonic" ($\delta\alpha\iota\mu o\nu\iota\acute{\omega}\delta\eta\varsigma$), also belongs in the framework of this antithesis. However, from such a similarity no literary dependence can be inferred, since only the schema of the statement is the same, not the subject. But consideration can be given to the question of whether v 17 has been formulated for this context in Jas. The priority given to "pure" ($\grave{\alpha}\gamma\nu\acute{o}\varsigma$) does not fit well with the train of thought, for "pure" in this case sounds very general.[28] It is only after this word that the adjectives which emphasize the peaceable character of wisdom appear: peaceable,

---

26 Even the concrete examples which could be pointed out as analogies are diverse in nature: On the one hand are Simon Magus in Acts 8 or people such as Peregrinus in Lucian (*Pergr. mort.* 11) or those who are mentioned in *Did.* 11.7ff; *Herm. mand.* 11. On the other hand are the adherents of "wisdom" of whom Paul speaks in 1 Cor 1–4, or the people whose behaviour *1 Clement* censures.

27 Therefore an allusion to the myth in *1 En.* 42, according to which Wisdom found no place among the sons of men and so returned to heaven, does not underlie Jas 3:15–17. The subject in the latter text is precisely the authority of heavenly wisdom upon earth. Also "demonic" ($\delta\alpha\iota\mu o\nu\iota\acute{\omega}\delta\eta\varsigma$) does not contain, as Spitta thought, a reference to the instruction of men by fallen angels (*1 En.* 8.1ff), but is simply a value-judgment.

28 Eugen Fehrle, *Die kultische Keuschheit im Altertum*, RVV 6 (Giessen: Töpelmann, 1910), 44, assigns to $\grave{\alpha}\gamma\nu\acute{o}\varsigma$ and its cognates the fundamental meaning of "religious awe," corresponding to "that which is indicated by the Polynesian word 'tabu.'" Especially important for Jas 3:17 is the LXX, where beside the much more frequent verbal form $\grave{\alpha}\gamma\nu\acute{\iota}\zeta\epsilon\iota\nu$ (which usually translates קדשׁ) the adjective $\grave{\alpha}\gamma\nu\acute{o}\varsigma$ is strikingly infrequent. In fact, apart from 2 Macc 13:8 (the holy fire and ashes of the altar) and two Psalm passages (LXX Ps 11:7; 18:10) the adjective occurs only in paraenetic literature. Thus $\grave{\alpha}\gamma\nu\acute{o}\varsigma$ is used of the chastity of the maiden in *4 Macc.* 18.7f and of the purity of the souls of the martyrs in *4 Macc.* 5.37 and 18.23. The heart (Prov 20:9), prayers (LXX Prov 19:13), and the fear of God (LXX Ps 18:10) can be called "pure," and "the pure" in general can be

gentle,[29] tractable.[30] The next designations must go together: "Mercy" manifests itself by "fruits"—i.e., good works.[31] The last two members of the series are formally tied together through the similarity in the sound of the two Greek words. There can be no doubt that the second word (ἀνυπόκριτος) means "without hypocrisy" or "sincere."

All the more questionable is the meaning of ἀδιά-κριτος. Since the nature of this document and, moreover, the nature of enumerations such as the one in 3:17 prohibit conclusions based upon the context, one may not conclude upon the basis of 1:6 that the meaning here is "not doubting,"[32] nor upon the basis of 2:4 that the meaning is "impartial."[33] The examples from classical and post-classical Greek for the meanings "indistinguishable" and "uncertain" are out of the question here, as is also the meaning "without hesitation."[34] Within the literature more closely related to Jas, only Ignatius provides useful examples of this word. These examples are all the more important since it follows from them that ἀδιάκριτος could be used in a positive sense. In *Mg.* 15.1 it obviously means "simple" or "of one accord" or "harmonious": "Farewell in

godly concord and may you possess a harmonious spirit, for this is Jesus Christ" (ἔρρωσθε ἐν ὁμονοίᾳ θεοῦ, κεκτη-μένοι ἀδιάκριτον πνεῦμα, ὅς ἐστιν Ἰησοῦς Χριστός) [Loeb modified]. The same is true for *Tr.* 1.1: "I have learned that you possess a mind free from blame and of one accord in endurance" (ἄμωμον διάνοιαν καὶ ἀδιά-κριτον ἐν ὑπομονῇ ἔγνων ὑμᾶς ἔχοντας) [Loeb modified]. The meaning of *Eph.* 3.2, where Christ is called "our harmonious life" (τὸ ἀδιάκριτον ἡμῶν ζῆν), is also to be sought in this direction and is to be understood in the sense of the mysticism of unity in Ignatius.[35] Of course the basis for this meaning is the originally negative sense of the word, "without division," "without party." Significant for the transition to the positive sense is Clem. Alex., *Strom.* 2.87.2, where it is said of love that "it is undivided in all things, harmonious, sharing" (ἀμέριστός ἐστιν ἐν πᾶσιν, ἀδιάκριτος, κοινωνική). The meaning of ἀδιάκριτος in the catalogue of the virtues of wisdom in Jas 3:17 is also along these lines, since here also we have the independent use of the word in an enumeration of terms. Here it means "simple" or "harmonious."

■ **18** This verse is an isolated saying, as has already been

---

contrasted with "the unjust" (Prov 15:26). However, particularly significant for Jas 3:17 is the fact that the works of God are described as pure in contrast to the crooked paths of "the crooked" (σκολιοί) in Prov 21:8, and in the same way the *words of the Lord* can be described as "pure" (ἁγνά), like silver which has been purified seven times (LXX Ps 11:7): therefore, the wisdom from above also has a share in the immaculacy and purity of God's world.

29   In Judaeo–Christian literary circles of this period, as also in other literature, ἐπιεικής and its cognates have the meaning "gentle": A bad neighbor provides exercise for my gentle nature (ἐπιεικές Epict., *Diss.* 3.20.11); the ungodly test the gentleness (ἐπιεί-κεια) of the righteous with insult and torture (Wisd 2:19); after the Shepherd had spoken angrily, he began to speak a second time more gently (ἐπιεικέσ-τερον, *Herm. mand.* 12.4.2). The parallelism with "meekness" (πραΰτης) in 2 Cor 10:1 is also characteristic, as is the juxtaposition of "gentle" (ἐπιεικής) and "not quarrelsome" (ἄμαχος) in 1 Tim 3:3 and Tit 3:2. 1 Petr 2:18 is also one clear example.

30   This meaning of εὐπειθής without the supplementary dative is found in Musonius, p. 83.19 Hense: "He who heeds one who is giving proper advice and follows willingly, such a one is tractable" (ὁ τῷ τὰ προσ-ήκοντα παραινοῦντι κατήκοος ὢν καὶ ἐπόμενος ἑκου-

σίως, οὗτος εὐπειθής) [Trans.]. According to Epict., *Diss.* 2.10.8, deference (παραχώρησις), tractability (εὐπείθεια), and kindly speech (εὐφημία) are the characteristics of brotherly behaviour among men. Philo (*Virt.* 15) says that the Law instructs the tract-able (εὐπειθεῖς) gently and the intractable (ἀπειθεῖς) sternly.

31   As is supplied in the text by C *et al.*

32   So Beyschlag.

33   So Spitta, Windisch-Preisker.

34   See below, n. 35.

35   Given the fluctuating character of the language of Ignatius, it is difficult to nail down each individual expression (cf. Theodor Zahn, *Ignatius von Antiochien* [Gotha: Perthes, 1873], 429, n. 1). In Ign., *Phld.* proem, ἀδιακρίτως apparently means "without hesi-tation," and has to do with faith in the Passion of the Lord which is free from doubt. Similarly, ἀδιά-κριτος can appear as an adjective of "faith" (πίστις) in Clem. Alex., *Paed.* 2.38.3. While the meaning in Ign., *Rom.* proem, cannot be precisely determined, the word obviously means "without hesitation" in *Test. Zeb.* 7.2: "Show compassion and mercy with-out hesitation to all men" (ἀδιακρίτως πάντας σπλαγχνιζόμενοι ἐλεᾶτε) [trans. Charles, *APOT*], for here we have the well-known exhortation to give without making distinctions (cf. above on Jas 1:5).

indicated above in the Analysis. It deals with the "fruit of righteousness" (καρπὸς δικαιοσύνης), an expression which appears to be a rather fixed term in the language of the LXX.[36] In the LXX the use of the term καρπός ("fruit") for the *seed* of the fruit already occurs: "From the fruit (i.e., the fruit seed) of righteousness grows the tree of life" (ἐκ καρποῦ δικαιοσύνης φύεται δένδρον ζωῆς Prov 11:30). Because of the term "is sown" (σπείρεται) in Jas 3:18, this must be the meaning of καρπός here. The special sense which the term and the metaphor have in this verse is connected with the correspondence between "in peace" (ἐν εἰρήνῃ) and "those who make peace" (τοῖς ποιοῦσιν εἰρήνην). Because of the relationship between the two expressions, "in peace" must certainly go with "is sown" (σπείρεται). It is then impossible to take "those who make peace" (τοῖς ποιοῦσιν εἰρήνην) as a dative of agent,[37] for that righteousness is sown in peace, and therefore *by* peaceable people, is already stated by the phrase ἐν εἰρήνῃ. Therefore, our

conclusion—and the one which is now generally accepted—is that this dative is the dative of advantage: "*for* peaceable people."[38] Within the framework of this correspondence: *by* those who are peaceable—*for* those who are peaceable, we grasp the meaning of the metaphor used here: Righteousness is sown and harvested only in peace.[39] At the same time, the conclusion stated in the Analysis is confirmed: The saying possesses its own wholeness and inclusiveness, and it need be connected neither with what precedes nor with what follows.

■ **4:1** The new section of admonition (4:1–6) traces the cause of all strife to the "passions" (ἡδοναί),[40] and the following verses show how far–reaching is the intent of this expression. This idea appears frequently in the philosophical tradition from the time of Plato on, and especially where a dualistic viewpoint influences the ethic.[41] Here in Jas the idea is introduced by means of a question which has a rather clumsy gait. Occasionally

---

P. Oxy. IV, 715.36 is also to be understood in this way, if the entry there must be translated "I have registered [the property] without further examination" (κατακεχώ[ρικα] ἀδιακ[ρίτως]) [with Ulrich Wilcken, in a bibliographical survey in *Archiv für Papyrusforschung und verwandte Gebiete* 4 (1907): 254]. For ἀδιάκριτος in this verse, the Latin manuscript *ff* has "without decision, blameless" (sine dijudicatione irreprehensibilis), while vulg and *s* both have "not passing judgment or deciding" (non judicans).

36 At least in Amos 6:12; Prov 11:30 and 13:2. In the last two passages there is no equivalent expression in the original Hebrew text. Instances of early Christian usage are Phil 1:11 and Heb 12:11. Of course, the metaphor does occur elsewhere, as in Epicurus, Frag. 519 (p. 317 Usener): "The fruit of righteousness is abundant calm" (δικαιοσύνης καρπὸς μέγιστος ἀταραξία = Clem. Alex., *Strom.* 6.2). On this see the comments of G. A. van den Bergh van Eysinga in a review article in *NThT* 10 (1921): 228.

37 I.e., "is sown *by* those who make peace" (de Wette, Ropes).

38 Only if one argues for a close relationship between this verse and 3:1, as Spitta does, can one arrive at the conclusion that "those who make peace" (τοῖς ποιοῦσιν εἰρήνην) refers to the soil in which righteousness is sown—i.e., the people who are to be taught.

39 Heb 12:11 is related to this idea, since there also the expression "fruit of righteousness" (καρπὸς δικαιοσύνης) is used. But in that text, as also in *Herm. sim.* 9.19.2, "fruit" (καρπός) refers to that which is

harvested not that which is sown, and in Heb 12:11 "peaceful" (εἰρηνικόν) is not the main idea as it is in Jas 3:18. Probably the similarity between these two verses is overestimated.

40 That the word ἡδονή, which would normally mean "pleasure" or "enjoyment," is used in this verse to mean "passion" or "desire" and therefore is equivalent here to ἐπιθυμία (against Ropes) can be seen first of all from what follows this verse—i.e., what is to blame for all evil is not that "you enjoy," but rather that "you desire." The examples in the following footnote show that what is said of the ἡδοναί in Jas 4:1 is said elsewhere of the ἐπιθυμίαι. Finally, ἡδονή is described in this sense by Philo in connection with the discussion of the Ten Commandments (Philo, *Decal.* 143): "The presentation to the mind of something which is actually with us and considered to be good, arouses and awakes the soul when at rest and like a light flashing upon the eyes raises it to a state of great elation. This sensation of the soul is called passion" (τοῦ παρόντος καὶ νομισθέντος ἀγαθοῦ φαντασία διεγείρει καὶ διανίστησι τὴν ψυχὴν ἠρεμοῦσαν καὶ σφόδρα μετέωρον ἐξαίρει καθάπερ ὀφθαλμοὺς φῶς ἀναστρέψαν· καλεῖται δὲ τουτὶ τὸ πάθος αὐτῆς ἡδονή).

41 Plato, *Phaed.* 66c: "The body and its desires are the only cause of wars and factions and battles" (καὶ γὰρ πολέμους καὶ στάσεις καὶ μάχας οὐδὲν ἄλλο παρέχει ἢ τὸ σῶμα καὶ αἱ τούτου ἐπιθυμίαι); Cicero, *Fin.* 1.44: "Desires are the source of hatred, quarreling and strife, of sedition and of war" (ex cupiditatibus odia, discidia, discordiae, seditiones, bella nascuntur) [Loeb modified]; Lucian, *Cynicus* 15: "For from

scribes have attempted to lend agility to the syntax here by the omission of the second πόθεν ("whence?" or "what causes?") in the sentence,[42] or by the transposition of the phrase "among you" (ἐν ὑμῖν). "Conflicts" (πόλεμοι, strictly, "wars, battles") and "fightings" (μάχαι) do not refer to political or national conflicts,[43] for these two terms are used in such admonitions as synonyms for strife and quarreling.[44]

In this verse, even more than in others, the consequences of supposing that the complete seriousness of this call to repentence is directed toward a concrete situation within a community are impossible. For if a definite group of Christians provided the model for this description—not by virtue of their general human weaknesses, but by virtue of specific severe wrongdoing in which they were engaged—then the author could not have written to this group as heroically as he did in 1:2ff, or in so consoling a fashion as 5:7ff. Certainly personal experiences of the author are not without significance for this passage, but not experiences with a specific group of addressees. Furthermore, along with the author's experience the influence of the paraenetic tradition has been operative here, as the examples above

in n. 41 reveal.

This tradition must also be taken into account in the interpretation of the words which follow in this passage. The metaphor of the "strife" of the base passions within our bodily members is certainly used with an eye to the "conflicts" and "fightings" just mentioned. However, one is also reminded of Rom 7:23, where within a human being's members the "law of sin" does battle with the "law of the mind." If, upon the basis of Jas 2:14ff, one assumes at least an indirect acquaintance upon the part of this author with Pauline terminology,[45] then the possibility of the influence of the Romans passage (perhaps an indirect influence) cannot be completely ruled out. Jas employs several metaphors and slogans whose native territory is alien to him. Certainly he has not invented the metaphor which he used in this passage.[46] In thinking of the "conflicts" and "fightings" he speaks of the "warring passions"; one can hardly ask against whom the strife is directed. The mention of the "members" localizes the "passions," just as Paul does in Rom 7:23.[47]

■ **2, 3** The Tantalus–like frustration of desires which Philo also had impressively portrayed,[48] appears in

---

the desire for these [i.e., gold and silver] grow up all human ills—civic strife, wars, conspiracies and murders" (πάντα γὰρ τὰ κακὰ τοῖς ἀνθρώποις ἐκ τῆς τούτων ἐπιθυμίας φύονται, καὶ στάσεις καὶ πόλεμοι καὶ ἐπιβουλαὶ καὶ σφαγαί); Philo, *Decal.* 151ff: "Consider the passion whether for money or a woman or glory or anything else that produces pleasure (ἡδονή): are the evils which it causes small or casual? Is it not the cause why kinsmen become estranged and change their natural goodwill to deadly hatred, why great and populous countries are desolated by internal factions . . . ? For all the wars of Greeks and barbarians between themselves or against each other, so familiar to the tragic stage, are sprung from one source, desire (ἐπιθυμία), the desire for money or glory or pleasure. These it is that bring disaster to the human race" (χρημάτων ἔρως ἢ γυναικὸς ἢ δόξης ἤ τινος ἄλλου τῶν ἡδονὴν ἀπεργαζομένων ἆρά γε μικρῶν καὶ τῶν τυχόντων αἴτιος γίνεται κακῶν· οὐ διὰ τοῦτον συγγένειαι μὲν ἀλλοτριοῦνται τὴν φυσικὴν εὔνοιαν μεθαρμοζόμεναι πρὸς ἀνήκεστον ἔχθραν, χῶραι δὲ μεγάλαι καὶ πολυάνθρωποι στάσεσιν ἐμφυλίοις ἐρημοῦνται . . .; οἱ γὰρ Ἑλλήνων καὶ βαρβάρων πρός τε ἑαυτοὺς καὶ πρὸς ἀλλήλους τραγῳδηθέντες πόλεμοι πάντες ἀπὸ μιᾶς πηγῆς ἐρρύησαν, ἐπιθυμίας ἢ χρημάτων ἢ δόξης ἢ ἡδονῆς· περὶ γὰρ ταῦτα κηραίνει τὸ τῶν ἀνθρώπων γένος). Philo also speaks of war caused by

the appetites in *Det. pot. ins.* 174, *Ebr.* 75, and *Jos.* 56. On the other hand, Epictetus, who is optimistic, rational, and not dualistically inclined, assigns all the blame for strife among people to the incorrect use of the concepts (προλήψεις) of good and bad (see Epict., *Diss.* 1.22.1–21).

42 Koine text, *et al.*

43 As was the opinion of Hugo Grotius, *Annotationes in Novum Testamentum*, reedited by Christ. Ern. de Windheim, vol. 2, part 2 (Erlangen and Leipzig: Tetzschner, 1757), *ad loc.*

44 For πόλεμος, cf. Philo, *Gig.* 51; *Test. Sim.* 4.8; *Test. Gad* 5.1; *1 Clem.* 3.2: "From this arose jealousy and envy, strife and sedition, persecution and disorder, war and captivity" (ἐκ τούτου ζῆλος καὶ φθόνος, ἔρις καὶ στάσις, διωγμὸς καὶ ἀκαταστασία, πόλεμος καὶ αἰχμαλωσία). For μάχη, cf. *Test. Jud.* 16.3; *Test. Ben.* 6.4; *2 Tim* 2:23; *Tit* 3:9.

45 See above in the Introduction, section 4.

46 1 Petr 2:11 also speaks of "passions of the flesh that wage war against your soul" (σαρκικαὶ ἐπιθυμίαι αἴτινες στρατεύονται κατὰ τῆς ψυχῆς), and Philo, *Migr. Abr.* 60, speaks of "passions" (ἡδοναί) and "desires" (ἐπιθυμίαι) acting as military commanders (ταξιαρχοῦσι).

47 Philo, too, speaks in many places of the restriction of desire to the body—e.g., *Leg. all.* 3.116: "If, there-

these verses with a somewhat more stunning and effective crescendo. To be sure, this is not fully felt in the text tradition as it now stands.

The verb "you murder" (φονεύετε) especially destroys the effect, although this word is attested by all the manuscripts. "You murder" neither fits well with the following "you are envious" (ζηλοῦτε), which sounds slightly out of place after an accusation of murder, nor does it fit the sense of the section as a whole. Appeal to the terms "conflicts, wars" (πόλεμοι) and "fightings" (μάχαι) in 4:1, or to the general use of strong expressions in Jas,[49] still does not justify the use here of the word "murder," which allows of no weakening in sense.[50] Various explanations have been attempted: (a) The interpretation, "They murder their own souls by these audacious efforts,"[51] is simply contrary to the text; (b) the explanation of this simple and straightforward accusation ought not to be burdened with the notion of the equality of wrath or hatred with murder found in Matt 5:21ff and 1 Jn 3:15;[52] (c) the solution, based upon Jas 3:14, which sees here a Hebraism equivalent to φονεύοντες ζηλοῦτε still does not result in the meaning desired by its advocates[53]—i.e., "You

rival one another to the point of death"; (d) placing a full stop after "you murder"[54] does away with the difficulty of the connection of this verb with "you are envious," but it does not help in finding for the first verb (φονεύετε) a meaning which fits the context; (e) the old conjectured emendation to "you are bloodthirsty" (φονᾶτε) does soften φονεύετε, but again, it does not fit well with "you are envious"; (f) therefore, the emendation, already proposed by Erasmus,[55] of "you murder" (φονεύετε) to "you are jealous" (φθονεῖτε) is really a rather obvious solution. This conjecture can find support in the frequent occurrence of similar textual corruptions,[56] as well as in the probability that the association of πόλεμοι ("wars, conflicts") and μάχαι ("fightings") with outward violence could assist in the triumph of the reading "you murder" (φονεύετε) once it had been introduced into the text tradition. Another consideration in favour of "you are jealous" (φθονεῖτε) as the original reading would be the connection with the following "you are envious" (ζηλοῦτε), since these

---

fore, O mind, you ever attempt to discover what territory pleasure has been allotted, do not consider the place occupied by the head, where the reasoning faculty resides . . . but look for it in the breast and belly, where high spirit and desire are, portions of the irrational" (ἐὰν οὖν ποτε ζητῆς, ὦ διάνοια, τίνα χῶρον ἡδονὴ κεκλήρωται, μὴ σκέπτου τὸν περὶ κεφαλὴν τόπον, ὅπου τὸ λογιστικόν, . . . ζήτει δ' ἐν στήθει καὶ κοιλίᾳ, ὅπου ὁ θυμὸς καὶ ἡ ἐπιθυμία, μέρη τοῦ ἀλόγου) [Loeb modified]. Of course, Philo can appeal to the tradition originating from Plato, for which especially Plato's *Phaedo* was decisive, e.g., cf. Plato, *Phaed.* 81b: "But, I think, if when it [i.e., the soul] departs from the body it is defiled and impure, because it was always with the body and cared for it and loved it and was fascinated by it and its desires and pleasures . . ." (ἐὰν δέ γε οἶμαι μεμιασμένη καὶ ἀκάθαρτος τοῦ σώματος ἀπαλλάτηται, ἅτε τῷ σώματι ἀεὶ συνοῦσα καὶ τοῦτο θεραπεύουσα καὶ ἐρῶσα καὶ γοητευομένη ὑπ' αὐτοῦ ὑπό τε τῶν ἐπιθυμιῶν καὶ ἡδονῶν κτλ.). Eduard Schweizer, "Die hellenistische Komponente im neutestamentlichen σάρξ-Begriff," *ZNW* 48 (1957): 251f, considers Jas 4:1 to be an example of the influence of the Hellenistic notion of "flesh" (σάρξ).

48 In the same selection from which the quotations in n. 40 and n. 41 are drawn, *Decal.* 149: "As he [Tan-

talus] missed everything that he wished for just when he was about to touch it, so the person who is mastered by desire, ever thirsting for what is absent remains unsatisfied, fumbling around his baffled appetite" (ἐκεῖνός τε γὰρ ὧν ὀρεχθείη πάντων ὁπότε μέλλοι ψαύσειν, ἀπετύγχανεν, ὅ τε κρατηθεὶς ἐπιθυμίᾳ, διψῶν ἀεὶ τῶν ἀπόντων, οὐδέποτε πληροῦται περὶ κενὴν ἰλυσπώμενος τὴν ὄρεξιν).

49 Haupt, review of Erdmann, *Der Brief des Jakobus*, 181.

50 A weakened sense of the verb is not even required in Jas 5:6.

51 τοὺς τὴν ἑαυτῶν ψυχὴν ἀποκτιννύντας ταῖς τολμηραῖς ταύταις ἐπιχειρήσεσι (Oec).

52 See de Wette and Beyschlag; so also Kittel, "Der geschichtliche Ort," 87f (cf. above on Jas 2:11, n. 121).

53 E.g., Gebser.

54 So Hofmann, Ropes.

55 This conjecture has also been taken up by many modern scholars, e.g., Spitta, Mayor, Belser, and Windisch-Preisker, and H. J. Vogels, *Handbuch der Textkritik des Neuen Testaments* (Bonn: Hanstein, ²1955), 220.

56 In *Test. Ben.* 7.2, Charles (*APOT* 2, p. 357) reads φόνος for φθόνος. In 1 Petr 2:1, B and 1175 read φόνους instead of φθόνους. If φόνοι is genuine in Gal

two Greek roots for "jealousy" appear together frequently in related texts.[57]

Once the textual corruption had been introduced, it possibly had an influence upon the words which follow in the text. The interpretations of the reading "you murder" (φονεύετε) have frequently appealed to the succeeding "you fight and wage war" (μάχεσθε καὶ πολεμεῖτε). It would not be surprising, then, for these two latter verbs to have been understood as referring to acts of outward violence because of the reading "you murder" which preceded them. However, once the clause "you fight and wage war" was understood in this way, a close connection between it and the following clause, "You do not have because you do not ask" (οὐκ ἔχετε διὰ τὸ μὴ αἰτεῖσθαι ὑμᾶς) became impossible. For someone who is well on the road to violence would not be reproved by Jas merely for the neglect of prayers.

It is my opinion that these two clauses were not separated in the original text, but that there was a connective "and" (καί) between them.[58] The later omission of this "and" could have resulted from a misunderstanding of the clause μάχεσθε καὶ πολεμεῖτε ("you fight and strive"), which originally referred not to physical violence but to quarreling and strife.[59] To be sure, the text without the connective has better attestation, but in it the abrupt stop after "you fight and strive" leaves us hanging.[60] On the other hand, if we

leave in the connective "and", vv 2, 3 fall into the pattern a b b a, the b–members having two verbs in the initial clause and the a–members having only one. It seems to me that this schema best justifies the inclusion of the "and" (καί):[61]

a$_1$	"You desire — *and you do not* have;
b$_1$	you are jealous and envious — *and you do not* obtain (what you covet);
b$_2$	you fight and strive — *and you do not* have because you do not ask;
a$_2$	you ask — *and you do not* receive because you ask with the wrong motive . . ."
a$_1$	ἐπιθυμεῖτε — καὶ οὐκ ἔχετε
b$_1$	φθονεῖτε καὶ ζηλοῦτε — καὶ οὐ δύνασθε ἐπιτυχεῖν
a$_2$	μάχεσθε καὶ πολεμεῖτε — καὶ οὐκ ἔχετε διὰ τὸ μὴ αἰτεῖσθαι ὑμᾶς
a$_2$	αἰτεῖτε — καὶ οὐ λαμβάνετε, διότι κακῶς αἰτεῖσθε κτλ.

Members a$_1$ and b$_1$ are parallel in content, since they both assert that "your desires profit you nothing." Members b$_2$ and a$_2$ are also parallel, at least in so far as both trace the "not having"[62] somehow back to prayer, either omitted prayer or prayer with base

---

5:21, then its omission would be explained by a similar confusion.

57 1 Macc 8:16; *Test. Sim.* 4.5; it is also instructive to observe that *Test. Sim.* 2.7 speaks of the "spirit of envy" (πνεῦμα τοῦ ζήλου), while 4.7 also speaks of this spirit but uses the other Greek work for "envy" (πνεῦμα τοῦ φθόνου), so that the textual variant τοῦ ζήλου in 4.7 is quite understandable. ζῆλος and φθόνοι also occur in the catalogue of vices in Gal 5:20f. Cf. especially *1 Clem.* 3.2; 4.7; 4.13; 5.2.

58 This is the reading offered by what are, after all, rather respectable witnesses: ℵ Ψ P 1175 *et al.* boh sy ff s vulg (not Codex Fuldensis).

59 See above on v 1, esp. n. 44.

60 In this case, one would be forced to conjectures. For example, Windisch considers the possibility of the omission of an original final clause after "you fight and strive" (μάχεσθε καὶ πολεμεῖτε), corresponding to the final clause "and you are not able to obtain" (καὶ οὐ δύνασθε ἐπιτυχεῖν) in the preceding sentence. This final clause for which Windisch looks I find in "and you do not have" (καὶ οὐκ ἔχετε). Another

possible conjecture would be to omit μάχεσθε καὶ πολεμεῖτε upon the assumption that these verbs had been interpolated because of the influence of the corrupt reading "you murder" (φονεύετε) and the corresponding nouns in v 1, πόλεμοι καὶ μάχαι.

61 A misunderstanding of this schema could have led to the attempt to connect the clauses which were contrasted with one another. Therefore, I would prefer to regard the reading αἰτεῖτε δέ (in P^{74vid} P Ψ 33 1175 *et al.*) in 4:3 as an attempted smoothing (von Soden, *Schriften*, part 1, p. 1891, treats this as an uncertain case). To the style of Jas 4:2, 3, cf. the reprimand of the soldiers by Scipio before Carthage (Appian, *Rom. Hist.* 8.548):

"You plunder like robbers, rather than make war;
and you run away, you do not take up your positions;
and your greed makes you seem to be enjoying a festival, not laying siege"
(λῃσεύετε μᾶλλον ἢ πολεμεῖτε,
καὶ διαδιδράσκετε, οὐ στρατοπεδεύετε·

intentions.[63]

The apparent contradiction between "you do not ask" in b₂ and "you ask and you do not receive" in a₂ increasingly occupied the ancient commentators the more the statement in a₂ appeared to stand in contradiction to the words of Jesus in Matt 7:7 = Lk 11:9. The solution of the problem which one finds in Didymus (in Latin translation) and in the other catenae and scholia (in the Greek version, which is to some extent much clearer) involves a comparison with the example of a "grammar teacher" ($\delta\iota\delta\acute{a}\sigma\kappa\alpha\lambda\sigma\varsigma\ \gamma\rho\alpha\mu\mu\alpha\tau\iota\kappa\acute{\sigma}\varsigma$) who promises all his pupils that he will teach them "the knowledge of grammar" ($\tau\grave{\eta}\nu\ \tau\hat{\omega}\nu\ \gamma\rho\alpha\mu\mu\alpha\tau\iota\kappa\hat{\omega}\nu\ \acute{\epsilon}\pi\iota\sigma\tau\acute{\eta}\mu\eta\nu$). If this turns out not to be true for a poor pupil because of his own inability, then the teacher cannot be accused of having lied. In the same way, answer to prayer was understood as tied to the manner in which one prays. One who asks for gnosis or the gift of the Spirit and does not receive it, obviously must have prayed with frivolous motives.

However, *pace* this dogmatic and ethical interest which the ancient commentaries emphasize, Jas 4:2, 3 possesses a historical significance. No doubt the enthusiastic certainty in the answer to prayer was widespread in the earliest communities due to particular experiences.[64] A highly intensified pneumatic consciousness and the feeling of belonging to the community of the last days, which was the bearer of all the promises, together have produced this certainty. Disappointments were inevitable, and they necessarily led to the qualification of the promise, so that answer to prayer became dependent either upon the disposition of the petitioner or upon the type of the petition. Thus the assurance which in Matt 7:11 applies to prayer for "good things" in general, applies in Lk 11:13 only to the prayer for "the Holy Spirit." The parable of the unjust judge, which evidently was originally a promise of the answer to prayer in general, in its present form in Lk 18:7 speaks only of answer to the prayer of the "elect" who are asking for recompense. A qualification is also implied in 1 Jn 5:14, where answer is assured for a prayer which is according to the will of the Son of God.[65] This also provides an explanation for *Herm. vis.* 3.10.6, where self-humiliation through fasting is required in order for the prayer to be effective, and *Herm. mand.* 9.4, where the requirement is the purification of the heart from all vanity. In this sort of context—indeed, precisely in the neighborhood of the last mentioned passage from Hermas—belongs what Jas says of prayer here.[66] What is meant by "you ask with the wrong motive" ($\kappa\alpha\kappa\hat{\omega}\varsigma\ \alpha\iota\tau\epsilon\hat{\iota}\sigma\theta\alpha\iota$) is explained by the following final clause in 4:3: Jas accuses them of praying only to satisfy their own desires.

■ **4** The expression "adulteresses" ($\mu\sigma\iota\chi\alpha\lambda\acute{\iota}\delta\epsilon\varsigma$) is an

---

καὶ πανηγυρίζουσιν ὑπὸ τῶν κερδῶν, οὐ πολιορκοῦσιν ἐοίκατε) [Trans.]

62 "You do not have" (οὐκ ἔχετε) is certainly parallel to "you do not receive" (οὐ λαμβάνετε), so the meaning of "have" (ἔχειν) here must be determined accordingly. "To have" (ἔχειν) is used in connection with the answer to prayer also in 1 Jn 5:15.

63 The final clauses in b₂ and a₂ are formally connected by the repeated verb "to ask" (αἰτεῖσθαι). The active αἰτεῖν and the middle αἰτεῖσθαι are the same in meaning in this passage, for obviously "you ask" (αἰτεῖτε active) in a₂ takes up the "you (do not) ask" (αἰτεῖσθαι middle) in b₂, and is itself resumed by "you ask" (αἰτεῖσθε middle) in the final clause of a₂. For the synonymous use of αἰτεῖν and αἰτεῖσθαι, cf. also 1 Jn 5:15; Jn 16:24, 26; *Herm. vis.* 3.10.7; *Herm. mand.* 9.7. Cf. further Blass-Debrunner, § 316.2; Moulton, *Prolegomena*, 160f. However, Moulton still agrees with Mayor with regard to a distinction between the two forms in Jas 4:3 (the active implies asking without the spirit of prayer). In this he overlooks the formal connections within

the verse which I have attempted to point out in the schema above. On the chain-like connection, cf. above in the Excursus on 1:15, n. 150.

64 Besides the saying in Matt 7:7 par, the promise offered the trusting petitioner in Mk 11:23f; Matt 17:20 and Lk 17:5f gives evidence for this belief. This promise is alluded to by Paul in 1 Cor 13:2 and is turned into a leading motif in the farewell discourse in Jn 13–17. Also Jas 5:16 must be mentioned here.

65 Cf. 1 Jn 5:16, where answer to prayer is promised in the case of an intercession for a sinner.

66 What is said regarding prayer in 1:5 and 5:16 possibly belongs in this context, also.

address which belongs with what follows, since it is only with what follows that it has any relation in content. The fact that the feminine gender is used here[67] is to be explained from the traditional image of the "sacred marriage" ($\iota\epsilon\rho\grave{o}s$ $\gamma\acute{a}\mu os$) of the land and the people with God. Ever since Hosea had branded Israel as an adulteress (Hos 1–3), this reproach had not disappeared from the prophetic literature.[68]

How this metaphor, characterizing the people and community as a whole, came to be used of individual persons is quite evident. On the one hand, this concept (among others) appears to have been individualized under the influence of an individualized piety. Philo is a good example of this when he interprets the Hellenistic mystery of the "sacred marriage" ($\iota\epsilon\rho\grave{o}s$ $\gamma\acute{a}\mu os$) as an image of God and the soul.[69] On the other hand, the reproach of adultery upon the part of the people as a whole has been transferred to its individual members or to particular groups among the people. This process possibly began when they were called "offspring of the harlot," as in Isa 57:3, and when later the term "adulterous generation" ($\gamma\epsilon\nu\epsilon\grave{a}$ $\mu o\iota\chi\alpha\lambda\acute{\iota}s$) came into use, a name which is found in the Gospels (Mk 8:38; Matt 12:39; 16:4) as a fixed and self-evident expression. It is no big step from this accusation to the address "adulteresses" ($\mu o\iota\chi\alpha\lambda\acute{\iota}\delta\epsilon s$). The more self-evident the notion was, the less was there any need for specific explications

to justify the accusation in Jas 4:4, especially since the following words place the idea on a broader base.

These words deal with the alternative God/world. "World"[70] ($\kappa\acute{o}\sigma\mu os$) is not used here in the sense of a partly eschatological, partly metaphysical dualism, as is found in Paul (e.g., 1 Cor 1:20ff). Instead, it is to be understood from the standpoint of a radical ethical dualism, such as that which finds expression in the farewell discourse in the Gospel of John and in 1 John (esp. 2:15ff)—in Jas 1:27 the word has a slightly different emphasis. In Jas 4:4, relentless determination is demanded. Love for God and love for the world are mutually exclusive. It makes no difference in this understanding to what extent "friend" ($\phi\acute{\iota}\lambda os$) is thought of as active or passive,[71] since in any case the formal correspondence remains: "Friendship" ($\phi\iota\lambda\acute{\iota}a$) is resumed by "friend" ($\phi\acute{\iota}\lambda os$), while "enmity" ($\check{\epsilon}\chi\theta\rho a$) and "enemy" ($\acute{\epsilon}\chi\theta\rho\acute{o}s$) form the exact antithesis to these terms. What appears noteworthy is the resumption itself—i.e., the fact that v 4b practically repeats the thought of v 4a. Spitta thought that v 4a was a quotation which the author employs and then reiterates in v 4b.[72] That is a plausible hypothesis, especially if it is not limited to direct quotation, but rather makes room for the possibility of an allusion to familiar statements from the paraenetic tradition.

■ **5, 6** The interpreter of these two difficult verses faces

---

67   The feminine gender of the address had already been seen as a difficulty by the author of the variant reading "adulterers and adulteresses" ($\mu o\iota\chi o\grave{\iota}$ $\kappa a\grave{\iota}$ $\mu o\iota\chi\alpha\lambda\acute{\iota}\delta\epsilon s$ $\aleph^c$ Ψ Koine witnesses).

68   This is demonstrated by the allusions in Jer 3:1f; Isa 1:21; 57:3; and the allegorical interpretation of history by the prophet in Ezek 16 and 23. Cf. the image used by Paul in 2 Cor 11:2f.

69   Philo, *Cher.* 50: "But when God begins to consort with the soul, He makes what before was a woman into a virgin again, for he takes away the degenerate and emasculate passions by which it was made womanish and plants instead the native growth of unpolluted virtues" ($\check{o}\tau a\nu$ $\delta\grave{\epsilon}$ $\dot{o}\mu\iota\lambda\epsilon\hat{\iota}\nu$ $\check{a}\rho\xi\eta\tau a\iota$ $\psi\nu\chi\hat{\eta}$ $\theta\epsilon\acute{o}s$, $\pi\rho\acute{o}\tau\epsilon\rho o\nu$ $a\dot{\upsilon}\tau\grave{\eta}\nu$ $o\check{\upsilon}\sigma a\nu$ $\gamma\nu\nu a\hat{\iota}\kappa a$ $\pi a\rho\theta\acute{\epsilon}\nu o\nu$ $a\check{\upsilon}\theta\iota s$ $\dot{a}\pi o$-$\delta\epsilon\acute{\iota}\kappa\nu\nu\sigma\iota\nu$, $\dot{\epsilon}\pi\epsilon\iota\delta\grave{\eta}$ $\tau\grave{a}s$ $\dot{a}\gamma\epsilon\nu\nu\epsilon\hat{\iota}s$ $\kappa a\grave{\iota}$ $\dot{a}\nu\acute{a}\nu\delta\rho o\nu s$ $\dot{\epsilon}\pi\iota\theta\nu\mu\acute{\iota}a s$, $a\hat{\iota}s$ $\dot{\epsilon}\theta\eta\lambda\acute{\nu}\nu\epsilon\tau o$, $\dot{\epsilon}\kappa\pi o\delta\grave{\omega}\nu$ $\dot{a}\nu\epsilon\lambda\grave{\omega}\nu$ $\tau\grave{a}s$ $a\dot{\upsilon}\theta\iota\gamma\epsilon\nu\epsilon\hat{\iota}s$ $\kappa a\grave{\iota}$ $\dot{a}\kappa\eta$-$\rho\acute{a}\tau o\nu s$ $\dot{a}\rho\epsilon\tau\grave{a}s$ $\dot{a}\nu\tau\epsilon\iota\sigma\acute{a}\gamma\epsilon\iota$) [Loeb modified]. Rom 7:1–3 contains another such comparison. But see also *Ps. Clem. Hom.* 3.27.3–28.1: "For every human being is a bride when, after the bright word of truth is implanted by the true prophet, the mind is il-

lumined. Therefore it is necessary to heed solely the one prophet of truth, knowing that whoever is implanted with the word of another is charged with adultery and is cast out by the bridegroom from his kingdom" ($\nu\acute{\nu}\mu\phi\eta$ $\gamma\acute{a}\rho$ $\dot{\epsilon}\sigma\tau\iota\nu$ $\dot{o}$ $\pi\hat{a}s$ $\check{a}\nu\theta\rho\omega\pi os$, $\dot{o}\pi\acute{o}\tau'$ $\check{a}\nu$ $\tau o\hat{\nu}$ $\dot{a}\lambda\eta\theta o\hat{\nu}s$ $\pi\rho o\phi\acute{\eta}\tau o\nu$ $\lambda\epsilon\nu\kappa\hat{\omega}$ $\lambda\acute{o}\gamma\omega$ $\dot{a}\lambda\eta\theta\epsilon\acute{\iota}as$ $\sigma\pi\epsilon\iota$-$\rho\acute{o}\mu\epsilon\nu os$ $\phi\omega\tau\acute{\iota}\zeta\eta\tau a\iota$ $\tau\grave{o}\nu$ $\nu o\hat{\nu}\nu$. $\delta\iota'$ $\dot{o}$ $\dot{\epsilon}\nu\grave{o}s$ $\mu\acute{o}\nu o\nu$ $\tau o\hat{\nu}$ $\tau\hat{\eta}s$ $\dot{a}\lambda\eta\theta\epsilon\acute{\iota}as$ $\pi\rho o\phi\acute{\eta}\tau o\nu$ $\dot{a}\kappa o\acute{\nu}\epsilon\iota\nu$ $\delta\epsilon\hat{\iota}$, $\epsilon\dot{\iota}\delta\acute{o}\tau a$ $\check{o}\tau\iota$ $\dot{o}$ $\pi a\rho'$ $\dot{\epsilon}\tau\acute{\epsilon}$-$\rho o\nu$ $\sigma\pi a\rho\epsilon\grave{\iota}s$ $\lambda\acute{o}\gamma\omega$, $\mu o\iota\chi\epsilon\acute{\iota}as$ $\check{\epsilon}\gamma\kappa\lambda\eta\mu a$ $\lambda a\beta\acute{\omega}\nu$, $\dot{\omega}s$ $\dot{\upsilon}\pi\grave{o}$ $\nu\nu\mu\phi\acute{\iota}o\nu$ $\tau\hat{\eta}s$ $\beta a\sigma\iota\lambda\epsilon\acute{\iota}as$ $a\dot{\upsilon}\tau o\hat{\nu}$ $\dot{\epsilon}\kappa\beta\acute{a}\lambda\lambda\epsilon\tau a\iota$) [Trans.]. This removes the objection of Spitta, who denies the presence of the Old Testament image in Jas 4:4 because it is a matter here of individual persons.

70    $\aleph$ s vulg sy^{vg} arm make the comment "*this* world."

71   That "enmity" ($\check{\epsilon}\chi\theta\rho a$) and "enemy" ($\dot{\epsilon}\chi\theta\rho\acute{o}s$) are intended in the active sense must be assumed from the nature of the presupposed religious relationship. There is no need to take $\check{\epsilon}\chi\theta\rho a$ adjectivally and accent it $\dot{\epsilon}\chi\theta\rho\acute{a}$ because of the reading "inimical" (inimica) in *ff* s vulg, though perhaps the text of $\aleph$ ($\epsilon\chi\theta\rho a$ $\epsilon\sigma\tau\iota\nu$ $\tau\omega$ $\theta\epsilon\omega$) may be congruent with the adjectival accentuation (In Tischendorf's edition

first of all the question of whether there are two quotations here or only one. A second question intersects with this first one, namely, Does the expression "jealously" (πρὸς φθόνον) form the end of the question in v 5a, or does it form the beginning of the following statement, whether the latter is a quotation or not? The construction and meaning of the sentence in v 5b ("He yearns . . .") depends upon the answers to these two questions. The most natural reading of this passage would be to expect a quotation after "the scripture says" (ἡ γραφὴ λέγει). If the ancient commentators and many modern interpreters have avoided this understanding of the text, their reason for doing so is based above all upon the impossibility of demonstrating that the following words are a text from "Scripture."[73] However, as will be shown, there is no insuperable difficulty in the way of regarding v 5b as a quotation.

There is some question, however, as to whether the alternative interpretation, which finds no quotation in v 5b, does not create the greater difficulty. For this explanation must always resort to forced interpretations of this passage.[74] If v 5b is not supposed to be a quotation, the introductory clause in v 5a must refer to the quotation in v 6. In this case, v 5b would have to be either a continuation of the introductory clause, or a parenthesis, or a kind of midrash in which the following quotation is embedded.

1) The first possibility is most clearly advocated by Oec, who takes the expression "jealously" (πρὸς φθόνον) with what precedes: "For it is not 'in vain' or idly or 'jealously' that the scripture gives commands which are difficult for us and strain our ability, but rather the scripture 'yearns after' or seeks after the grace which has been made to dwell within us through the exhortation of the scripture itself" (οὐ γὰρ κενῶς ἤτοι ματαίως, ἢ πρὸς φθόνον ἡ γραφὴ τὰ ἀμήχανα ἡμῖν καὶ ἀποτείνοντα τὴν ἡμετέραν δύναμιν παραγγέλματα διαγορεύει, ἀλλ' ἐπιποθοῦσα ἤτοι ἐπιζητοῦσα τὴν διὰ τῆς παρακλήσεως αὐτῆς ἐγκατοικιζομένην ἡμῖν χάριν).

2) Examples for the second interpretation are provided by the various scholia in Matthäi's collection.[75] These scholia sometimes interpret the intermediate clause in v 5b without including the expression "jealously" (πρὸς φθόνον) as a part of it: The divine Spirit within us (p. 32) or the Spirit who causes the scripture to speak (p. 193), longs after our salvation. On the other hand, when "jealously" is included as a part of v 5b, then either the divine "intellectual power" (νοερὰ δύναμις) within us is said to be "envious of" the devilish, antagonistic power (p. 32), or Christ is said to destroy the death which arose from the envy of the Devil (p.

---

this accentuation stands in the text! Cf. above on 3:6.).

72 In this case, καθίσταται would surely mean "he proves to be."

73 For neither the texts having to do with the jealousy of God, such as Ex 20:5; 34:14; Deut 6:15; 32:16, 19ff; Isa 63:8ff; Zech 8:2, nor those which in some way treat the jealousy and desire of humans, such as Ps 37:1; 73:3; 119:20f, nor others, such as Gen 4:7, are the same as Jas 4:5b either in form or even merely in content. On this verse, cf. Eduard Engelhardt, "Bemerkungen zu Jac. 4, v. 5 u. 6," ZLThK 30 (1869) 232–43; Fred. Friedrich Zyro, "Zur Erklärung von Jakob. 4, 5.6," ThStKr 13 (1840): 432–50; idem, "Noch einmal Jakob. 4. 5.6," ThStKr 34 (1861): 765–74; idem, "Ist es mit Jakobus 4, 5 nun im Reinen?" ThStKr 45 (1872): 716–29; Eugen Paret, "Noch ein Wort über Jac. 4, 5 nebst 1 Mos. 4, 7," ThStKr 36 (1863): 113–8; idem, "Nochmals das Zitat in Jak. 4, 5," ThStKr 80 (1907): 234–46; Wilibald Grimm, "Über die Stelle Br. Jakobi IV. v 5 und 6a," ThStKr 27 (1854): 934–56.

74 The suggestion of de Wette is to be separated from the debate at the outset. De Wette thought that the quotation referred to by the phrase "the scripture says" (ἡ γραφὴ λέγει) is Jas 4:4, and he wanted to find in that verse a quotation from the New Testament (Rom 8:7; Matt 6:24; or 1 Jn 2:15). This identification is just as impossible as the identification of v 5b with an Old Testament quotation.

75 See below in the Bibliography in the section "The Ancient Church." On p. 32, Matthäi offers a scholion which is supposed to be by Methodius Pataransis and which contains the two interpretations mentioned here. On p. 193, in the appendix to his work, there is a longer scholion in which the first interpretation (which puts πρὸς φθόνον with the preceding question; see above) corresponds to the first interpretation in the Catena. The second interpretation in this scholion (involving the jealousy of the Devil) corresponds to what in Theoph appears under the name Cyril and is also found in the Catena. (Citations above in the text refer to these pages in Matthäi).

193).[76] These interpretations are impossible because they drag into the clause either an object or subject which is too remote.[77] Moreover, the connection of the expression $\pi\rho\grave{o}\varsigma$ $\phi\theta\acute{o}\nu o\nu$ with the first clause must be considered doubtful for much the same reason, since the text does not read "in vain or jealously" ($\kappa\epsilon\nu\hat{\omega}\varsigma$ $\mathring{\eta}$ $\pi\rho\grave{o}\varsigma$ $\phi\theta\acute{o}\nu o\nu$). If one translates it as Gebser does: "Or do you think that the scripture speaks without reason, jealously," then the expression "jealously" is left flapping at the end in an intolerable way.

3) There still remains the third possibility, viz., that v 5b is a kind of midrash. According to this hypothesis, after the question "Or do you think that the scripture speaks in vain?" there follows an interpretation of the scripture which is still to be quoted (in v 6). In this interpretation, the subject of the verb "strives after" ($\epsilon\pi\iota\pi o\theta\epsilon\hat{\iota}$) is understood to be God in accordance with the implication of the preceding verb, "it[78] says" ($\lambda\acute{\epsilon}\gamma\epsilon\iota$): "He strives jealously after the spirit, but he gives the greater grace," and then the first $\lambda\acute{\epsilon}\gamma\epsilon\iota$ in v 5 is picked up again by "therefore it says" ($\delta\iota\grave{o}$ $\lambda\acute{\epsilon}\gamma\epsilon\iota$) in v 6. But according to this theory, the quotation in v 6 is introduced solely for the sake of the final words in that verse,

which are words of promise; this would be indicated by the midrash–like introduction, since this introduction would relate only to these final words. However, the question in v 5a makes sense only if it is followed by a threat, and only if all the emphasis lies upon this threat. Therefore, any interpretation which wants to get by without a quotation in v 5 runs up against difficulties which are all but insuperable.

Thus one must assume—as almost all modern interpreters do—that v 5 contains a quotation, although it is a quotation with which we are not familiar. It is superfluous to suppose that this is a paraphrase or restatement of the contents of the Old Testament passages about the jealousy of God,[79] for it will be shown that the quoted words possess a unique content of their own. Precisely for that reason one must avoid premature attempts to emend the text, for our knowledge is not sufficient for us to state with certainty that the wording as it now stands is indeed impossible. And for the same reason, the more obvious connection of $\pi\rho\grave{o}\varsigma$ $\phi\theta\acute{o}\nu o\nu$ with the quotation must not be rejected out of hand.[80] Instead, an attempt will be made to understand the text from $\pi\rho\grave{o}\varsigma$ $\phi\theta\acute{o}\nu o\nu$ on as words from an unknown source.

---

76 In this last interpretation, $\pi\rho\grave{o}\varsigma$ $\phi\theta\acute{o}\nu o\nu$ $\epsilon\pi\iota\pi o\theta\epsilon\hat{\iota}$ is obviously translated "he struggles against envy" (cf. Luther's translation: "the Spirit's desire is opposed to hatred").

77 Bede also connected $\pi\rho\grave{o}\varsigma$ $\phi\theta\acute{o}\nu o\nu$ with v 5b and believed that the question in v 5a introduces scriptural passages which warn of fellowship with wicked persons. Yet he said nothing about the relation of the clause in v 5b to the whole text, and as a result he did not reach any final decision on this clause. He left three possibilities open: 1) The clause could be taken as a question, with $\pi\rho\grave{o}\varsigma$ $\phi\theta\acute{o}\nu o\nu$ as the object of the desire: "Does the Spirit of grace long for you to be jealous of one another?" (nunquid spiritus gratiae . . . hoc concupiscit, ut invideatis alterutrum?). 2) $\pi\rho\grave{o}\varsigma$ $\phi\theta\acute{o}\nu o\nu$ could mean "against jealousy": "'Its desires are against jealousy,' that is, it desires that the sickness of jealousy be vanquished and rooted out from your minds" (adversus invidiam concupiscit, hoc est invidiae morbum debellari, atque a vestris mentibus exstirpari desiderat). 3) $\pi\nu\epsilon\hat{\upsilon}\mu\alpha$ could mean the human spirit: "Be unwilling to long after, be unwilling to cling to friendships with this world. For when the spirit of your mind longs after earthly things, it is undoubtedly longing with jealousy; when you long to possess these things yourselves, you are jealous of others

who have them" (nolite concupiscere, nolite mundi huius amicitiis adhaerere, quia spiritus mentis vestrae, dum terrena concupiscit, ad invidiam utique concupiscit, dum ea quae ipsi acquirere concupiscitis, alios invidetis habere).

78 I.e., the Scripture, which is "personified" and "points to God, with whom it is, as it were, identified" (Huther).

79 See above, n. 73.

80 Spitta considers "with regard to jealousy" as a possible meaning for $\pi\rho\grave{o}\varsigma$ $\phi\theta\acute{o}\nu o\nu$, in order to have "jealousy" as the subject of the verb in the quotation. But then the quotation is intolerably obscure (cf. below in n. 82). The authors of the variants $\acute{o}\tau\iota$ $\epsilon\pi\iota\pi o\theta\epsilon\hat{\iota}$ (241) and $\pi\rho\grave{o}\varsigma$ $\phi\theta\acute{o}\nu o\nu$ $\acute{\upsilon}\mu\hat{\omega}\nu$ (489) probably understood the words in much the same way. The text of ff apparently assumes the same division of the clause: "Or do you think that the scripture says with regard to jealousy that the spirit which abides within you grows strong" (aut putatis quoniam dicit scriptura ad invidiam convalescit spiritus qui habitat in vobis) [Trans.]. The expression "grows strong" (convalescit) is striking. Did the text in front of the translator have $\epsilon\pi\iota\pi o\lambda\acute{\alpha}\zeta\epsilon\iota$ ("prevail")? It is more probable that he desired to emend the difficult reading ($\epsilon\pi\iota\pi o\theta\epsilon\hat{\iota}$), or that he simply misread it.

That these words are quoted as "scripture" ($\gamma\rho\alpha\phi\dot\eta$) ought not to evoke surprise. Texts of unknown provenance are solemnly quoted in a similar fashion, and sometimes expressly as "scripture," in several places in early Christian literature.[81] Here in Jas 4:5, also, we have some sort of "prophetic word" ($\pi\rho\circ\phi\eta\tau\iota\kappa\grave{o}\varsigma$ $\lambda\acute{o}\gamma\circ\varsigma$ 2 Clem. 11:2), i.e., an apocryphal book which is considered holy.[82]

The Spirit which Dwells Within

Apart from the context, we have only one point of departure for the understanding of the quotation:[83] The expression "the spirit which he has made to dwell within us" ($\tau\grave{o}$ $\pi\nu\epsilon\hat{\upsilon}\mu\alpha$ $\grave{o}$ $\kappa\alpha\tau\acute{\omega}\kappa\iota\sigma\epsilon\nu$ $\grave{\epsilon}\nu$ $\dot{\eta}\mu\hat{\iota}\nu$)[84] is found almost verbatim in Herm. mand. 3.1: "the spirit which God has made to dwell in this flesh" ($\tau\grave{o}$ $\pi\nu\epsilon\hat{\upsilon}\mu\alpha$ $\grave{o}$ $\grave{o}$ $\theta\epsilon\grave{o}\varsigma$ $\kappa\alpha\tau\acute{\omega}\kappa\iota\sigma\epsilon\nu$ $\grave{\epsilon}\nu$ $\tau\hat{\eta}$ $\sigma\alpha\rho\kappa\grave{\iota}$ $\tau\alpha\acute{\upsilon}\tau\eta$), and the concept is also expressed in Herm. mand. 5.2.5; 10.2.6; 10.3.2. Thus, this notion is found precisely in the paraenetic section of Hermas, the section whose kinship in style to the paraenesis in Jas we had to emphasize repeatedly. However, in all three Mandates, especially in the fifth and tenth, the statements about the spirit dwelling in us are

associated with a view of the Spirit and spirits which—even if it is not expressed in a totally clear manner—is in any case almost unique in early Christian literature. The "Holy Spirit" in these texts is not the divine organ which the pneumatics are confident that they possess. Rather, it is something which is originally pure yet can still be darkened (Herm. mand. 5.1.2); it is received as a "truthful" ($\check{\alpha}\psi\epsilon\upsilon\sigma\tau\circ\nu$) spirit yet often is returned as a "lying" ($\psi\epsilon\upsilon\delta\acute{\epsilon}\varsigma$) spirit (3.2). This happens when an evil spirit chokes out or drives out the good spirit. This notion is presented in Herm. mand. 5.1.2f in such a way that "ill temper" ($\grave{o}\xi\upsilon\chi\circ\lambda\acute{\iota}\alpha$) appears as an evil spirit and "long-suffering" ($\mu\alpha\kappa\rho\circ\theta\upsilon\mu\acute{\iota}\alpha$) as a good spirit. In one the devil dwells, in the other the Lord. However, in 5.2.4–8, there are suddenly more evil spirits mentioned who, living in the same vessel as the Holy Spirit, allow him no room but instead drive him out. In fact, in addition to "ill temper" ($\grave{o}\xi\upsilon\chi\circ\lambda\acute{\iota}\alpha$), there is mention here of "bitterness" ($\pi\iota\kappa\rho\acute{\iota}\alpha$), "wrath" ($\theta\upsilon\mu\acute{o}\varsigma$), "rage" ($\grave{o}\rho\gamma\acute{\eta}$), and "fury" ($\mu\hat{\eta}\nu\iota\varsigma$). This is in harmony with the fact that also in Herm. mand. 10.1.2 it is said of "grief" ($\lambda\acute{\upsilon}\pi\eta$) that it wears out the Holy Spirit and corrupts man more than all the other spirits.[85] Hence, there

---

81 1 Cor 2:9 and 1 Clem. 46.2, where both times the expression "it is written" ($\gamma\acute{\epsilon}\gamma\rho\alpha\pi\tau\alpha\iota$) is used; Eph 5:14; and probably Jn 7:38, with "scripture" ($\gamma\rho\alpha\phi\acute{\eta}$); but especially 1 Clem. 23.3, which has the term "scripture" ($\gamma\rho\alpha\phi\acute{\eta}$), and the text of which occurs with some variations in 2 Clem. 11.2 as the warning of "the prophetic word" ($\pi\rho\circ\phi\eta\tau\iota\kappa\grave{o}\varsigma$ $\lambda\acute{o}\gamma\circ\varsigma$).

82 Spitta wants to derive the text from the Book of Eldad and Modad which is quoted in Herm. vis. 2.3.4. For this he offers the following arguments: 1) In Num 11:29, Moses replies to Joshua's protest regarding Eldad and Modad: "Are you jealous on my account? Would that all the people of the Lord were prophets when the Lord bestows his spirit upon them" ($\mu\grave{\eta}$ $\zeta\eta\lambda\hat{o}\hat{\iota}\varsigma$ $\sigma\grave{\upsilon}$ $\grave{\epsilon}\mu\acute{\epsilon}$; $\kappa\alpha\grave{\iota}$ $\tau\acute{\iota}\varsigma$ $\delta\acute{\omega}\eta$ $\pi\acute{\alpha}\nu\tau\alpha$ $\tau\grave{o}\nu$ $\lambda\alpha\grave{o}\nu$ $K\upsilon\rho\acute{\iota}\circ\upsilon$ $\pi\rho\circ\phi\acute{\eta}\tau\alpha\varsigma$, $\grave{o}\tau\alpha\nu$ $\delta\hat{\omega}$ $K\acute{\upsilon}\rho\iota\circ\varsigma$ $\tau\grave{o}$ $\pi\nu\epsilon\hat{\upsilon}\mu\alpha$ $\alpha\grave{\upsilon}\tau\circ\hat{\upsilon}$ $\grave{\epsilon}\pi$' $\alpha\grave{\upsilon}\tau\circ\acute{\upsilon}\varsigma$). But do we know that this story was included in the book which purported to be the prophecy of Eldad and Modad, and whether, therefore, there was any discussion in this book about jealousy for the possession of the spirit? 2) In Midrash Bemidbar Rabbah, 15.19 on Num 11:16, the great privileges of Eldad and Modad are mentioned, as well as their humility. But that would be related only to Jas 4:6, and it is probable that the quotation ends with v 5. 3) The Shepherd of Hermas, which in some other respects is related to Jas, quoted the Book of Eldad

and Modad. Naturally, none of these three arguments constitutes proof. There is no need to be driven to such questionable identifications because of nervousness about an item which is unknown. Cf. above in the Introduction, n. 102.

83 Cf. also b. Shab. 152b, where the quotation of Eccl 12:7 is introduced with, "Our Rabbis taught" (תנו רבנן), and followed by the comment, "Render it [the spirit (רוח)] back to him in purity (בטהרה) as he gave it to you in purity" (trans. Epstein modified).

84 The Koine reading, "which dwelt" ($\kappa\alpha\tau\acute{\omega}\kappa\eta\sigma\epsilon\nu$), can be dismissed as a variant which smoothes out the text by supplying a subject for the relative clause, and which is easily produced by itacistic pronunciation.

85 The concept in Herm. mand. 10 is positively obscure and in no way unified. According to 10.1.2, "grief" ($\lambda\acute{\upsilon}\pi\eta$) is the worst of the evil spirits, but it effects both destruction and salvation at the same time. According to 10.2.3f, the author understands this salvation to be the "repentance" ($\mu\epsilon\tau\acute{\alpha}\nu\circ\iota\alpha$) which follows upon ill temper. Then, immediately after this, doubt and ill temper are said to be the vices which grieve the Spirit, and to the detriment of the person.

seem to be as many evil spirits as there are vices. Correspondingly, in *Herm. mand.* 5 the Holy Spirit is essentially identical with "long-suffering" ($\mu\alpha\kappa\rho o\theta\nu\mu\iota\alpha$), while in 3.4, where the subject is the praise of truth, it can also be called the "spirit of truth" ($\pi\nu\epsilon\hat{\nu}\mu\alpha$ $\tau\hat{\eta}s$ $\dot{\alpha}\lambda\eta\theta\epsilon\iota\alpha s$). However, there is never any mention of several co-existent holy spirits—so dominant is the Christian concept of the *one* Holy Spirit.

On the other hand, there is no doubt that the doctrine of the Spirit presupposed by *Hermas* does not originally correspond to that early Christian concept, but rather belongs in the context of a demonological ethic based upon dualistic foundations; parallels appear especially in the *Testaments of the Twelve Patriarchs*, and such dualism does not seem to be without examples in the syncretism of the period.[86] The Holy Spirit, which God allows to dwell within a person is the "good identity" of the person,[87] which must assert itself in opposition to an "evil identity." One might call to mind the concept which popular usage attaches to the word "heart": The heart within a child is considered still pure and unspotted, as though coming from the creator's hand.

This meaning of $\pi\nu\epsilon\hat{\nu}\mu\alpha$, "the good spirit within the person which is given by God," is also possible in the

apocryphal text quoted in Jas 4:5. Indeed, it is the probable meaning because of the agreement of the relative clause in Jas with that in *Hermas* (see above). However, this means that the subject of the relative clause is also the subject of the main clause, viz., God. The principal objection which might be raised against understanding God to be the subject of the main clause—namely, that God could not be jealous of his own Spirit, but only of the heart or of the human being[88]—is of no avail. For $\pi\nu\epsilon\hat{\nu}\mu\alpha$ is probably not the Divine Spirit in the Christian sense, but rather is to be equated more with the "heart."

But once that is said, much—indeed, everything—is achieved in the interpretation of the verse. For now there need be no hesitation about including $\pi\rho\dot{o}s$ $\phi\theta\acute{o}\nu o\nu$ in the quotation, naturally with the adverbial sense of "jealously" ($\phi\theta o\nu\epsilon\rho\hat{\omega}s$).[89] The sense of the quotation is that God jealously longs after the human spirit. We must not haggle with the prophet about the fact that God is characterized here by a human affection, for the prophet's style and thought world are unknown to us; and especially we must not haggle with Jas for having introduced the quotation, for the words are very properly adduced after the address "adulteresses" ($\mu o\iota\chi\alpha\lambda\acute{\iota}\delta\epsilon s$) in v 4. The quotation is a threat, just as we should expect after the introductory question.

■ **6** In this verse Jas has appended a saying, Prov

---

86 Cf. Bousset, *Kyrios Christos*, 286, n. 136. *Test. Ben.* 6 especially comes to mind: The Lord dwells within the "good inclination" ($\dot{\alpha}\gamma\alpha\theta\dot{o}\nu$ $\delta\iota\alpha\beta o\acute{\nu}\lambda\iota o\nu$) which is equated with the "good mind" ($\dot{\alpha}\gamma\alpha\theta\dot{\eta}$ $\delta\iota\acute{\alpha}\nu o\iota\alpha$). According to *Test. Ben.* 7, on the other side stands the "malice of Beliar" ($\kappa\alpha\kappa\acute{\iota}\alpha$ $\tau o\hat{\nu}$ $B\epsilon\lambda\acute{\iota}\alpha\rho$), which gives to its followers a sword which is the mother of seven evils. Cf. also the twelve "punishments" ($\tau\iota\mu\omega\rho\acute{\iota}\alpha\iota$) in *Corp. Herm.* 13.7. I propose to go into these relationships in more detail elsewhere; cf. Dibelius, *Der Hirte des Hermas*, in the Excursus on *Herm. mand.* 5.2.7, which discusses the pneumatology of the *Mandates*. A "demonological ethic based upon dualistic foundations" is now found everywhere in the writings from Qumran. "Inclination" (יצר) and "knowledge" (דעת) are the concepts which correspond to the "spirit" ($\pi\nu\epsilon\hat{\nu}\mu\alpha$) in the *Shepherd of Hermas*. Cf. also the article by Wolverton mentioned above in the Introduction, n. 102. On God's "longing after" ($\dot{\epsilon}\pi\iota\pi o\theta\epsilon\hat{\iota}\nu$) in Jas 4:5, J. Jeremias ("Jac. 4, 5: $\dot{\epsilon}\pi\iota\pi o\theta\epsilon\hat{\iota}$," *ZNW* 50 [1959]: 137f), refers to Job 14:15b (Theod.) and the Targum fragment on

Gen 2:2. J. Michl, "Der Spruch Jakobusbrief 4, 5," *Neutestamentliche Aufsätze* (Festschrift Josef Schmid), ed. J. Blinzler, O. Kuss, F. Mussner (Regensburg: Pustet, 1963), 167–74, takes "spirit" as the subject of the main clause and interprets it as the life-spirit of man. He assumes a hexameter (which, however, is defective!) which is supposed to originate from an unknown Jewish–Hellenistic poem.

87 This follows from *Herm. mand.* 5.2.7: When the good spirit leaves the person, he is "empty of the righteous spirit" ($\kappa\epsilon\nu\dot{o}s$ $\dot{\alpha}\pi\dot{o}$ $\tau o\hat{\nu}$ $\pi\nu\epsilon\acute{\nu}\mu\alpha\tau os$ $\tau o\hat{\nu}$ $\delta\iota\kappa\alpha\acute{\iota}ov$), or, as is stated further on, "he is blinded and ceases to have a good intention" ($\dot{\alpha}\pi o\tau\nu\phi\lambda o\hat{\nu}\tau\alpha\iota$ $\dot{\alpha}\pi\dot{o}$ $\tau\hat{\eta}s$ $\delta\iota\alpha$-$\nuo\acute{\iota}\alpha s$ $\tau\hat{\eta}s$ $\dot{\alpha}\gamma\alpha\theta\hat{\eta}s$). Here, therefore, the "Holy Spirit" = the "good mental attitude."

88 So Spitta.

89 This can be concluded right away by analogy with such expressions as $\pi\rho\dot{o}s$ $\dot{o}\rho\gamma\acute{\eta}\nu$ and $\pi\rho\dot{o}s$ $\dot{\alpha}\lambda\acute{\eta}\theta\epsilon\iota\alpha\nu$. Cf., for example, Philo, *Spec. leg.* 3.3: "and ceased not to pull me down violently" ($o\dot{\nu}$ $\pi\rho\acute{o}\tau\epsilon\rho o\nu$ $\dot{\epsilon}\pi\alpha\acute{\nu}$-$\sigma\alpha\tau o$ $\kappa\alpha\theta\acute{\epsilon}\lambda\kappa\omega\nu$ $\pi\rho\dot{o}s$ $\beta\acute{\iota}\alpha\nu$ [$= \beta\iota\alpha\acute{\iota}\omega s$]) [Loeb modified]. Matt 5:28, "every one who looks at a woman

3:34,[90] and he is interested principally in stressing the promise which is contained in it. Yet we are not prepared for such a promise after v 5a, so the author must find some kind of transition to the new mood. It is hardly credible that the first quotation, of unknown origin, just happened to provide this transition. To the contrary, according to v 5a, this first quotation contained only a threat. Therefore we have to see in v 6a a transition which has been created by the author himself, a midrash preparing the way for the next quotation: "If you are true to him, he gives all the more grace to you in exchange." Thus Jas reveals which part of the saying possesses the most significance for him in this context.

The difficult vv 5, 6 therefore appear strange only because of the first quotation, in v 5b. Yet the fact that a saying of unknown provenance does not dovetail right away with concepts which are familiar to us from the classical records of early Christianity really need not be particularly surprising. Therefore, I prefer to disregard all the ancient and modern suggestions for the textual emendation of v 5.[91]

■ **7** Jas 4:7ff now picks up the imperatives, which—as has already been discussed above in the Analysis— exhibit variety in content in spite of formal homogeneity.[92] I also conjectured that the grouping did not originate with Jas. In fact, an author who was writing without the restraints of a prior grouping would probably have placed first the idea which is now in v 10, for the saying in v 6 was quoted for the sake of the promise which it made to the humble. But precisely the fact that the admonition in v 7 is attached to this quotation in v 6 indicates that there must be some further connection.

The same quotation is found in 1 Petr 5:5 in the framework of a traditional paraenesis. Here, however, it has been modified by the author to suit his purpose: the "younger" (νεώτεροι) are instructed to "be subject" (ὑποτάγητε) to the "elders" (πρεσβύτεροι), and all Christians are instructed to be humble. As an authority for this, the "Solomonian" proverb is quoted. However, to this saying is added the admonition that the Christians humble themselves under the mighty hand of God; and following this—in connection with the imperatives, "Be sober, be watchful" (νήψατε γρηγορήσατε)—there is a reference to the "Devil" (διάβολος) whom Christians are to resist (ἀντίστητε). Submission, humility, then the quotation on that subject, and finally the opposition to the Devil—that is also approximately the content of part of the sayings in Jas 4:6–10. The material in 1 Peter is merely more coherent, is contained in greater detail, and is utilized in a more creative way. For example, the motif of submission is applied to the relationship to the "elders," and the devil is portrayed as

---

in order to lust after her" (πᾶς ὁ βλέπων γυναῖκα πρὸς τὸ ἐπιθυμῆσαι αὐτήν), is rendered in Clem. Alex., *Strom.* 7.82.3 thusly: "Do not look at another woman *lustfully*" (μὴ ἐμβλήψῃς πρὸς ἐπιθυμίαν ἀλλοτρίᾳ γυναικί). This adverbial meaning of πρὸς φθόνον in Jas 4:5 is even assumed by Oec, though he interprets the passage in an entirely different way.

90 Here it is the LXX version of Prov 3:34, as over against the original. But both here and in 1 Petr 5:5 "God" (ὁ θεός) is the subject rather than "the Lord" (κύριος), as in the LXX. *1 Clem.* 30.2 also quotes this verse with "God" instead of "the Lord."

91 On the *ff* version, cf. above in n. 80. The omission by P L 81 *et al.* of the words "therefore it says" (διὸ λέγει) and of the second quotation is probably due to an accidental jump from the first "grace" (χάριν) in v 6a to the second in v 6b, rather than to a conjectural emendation. The deletion of v 6a (Jakob Hottinger, *Epistolae d. Iacobi atque Petri I.* [Leipzig: Dyck, 1815], *ad loc.*; Johannes Schulthess, *Epistola Iacobi* [Zürich: Schulthess, 1824], *ad loc.*) does not compensate for the difficulties in v 5. The suggestion

of Lücke (in a letter to Gebser; see the latter's commentary, p. 337n) that originally the words from πρὸς φθόνον to ἡμῖν followed immediately after v 4, then ἢ δοκεῖτε to λέγει, then the quotation in v 6b (with v 6a deleted as a gloss), is dictated merely by the desire to avoid treating v 5b as a quotation. Of the modern scholars, Windisch assumes that there is radical textual corruption in this verse; Peter Corssen (in a review of B. Weiss's commentary) in *GGA* 2 (1893):596f, emends the text to read, "You jealously yearn; the spirit . . . gives the greater grace" (πρὸς φθόνον ἐπιποθεῖτε· τὸ πνεῦμα . . . μείζονα δίδωσιν χάριν); O. Kirn, in "Ein Vorschlag zu Jakobus 4, 5," *ThStKr* 77 (1904):127–33, and in "Noch einmal Jakobus 4, 5," *ThStKr* 77 (1904):593–604, and Könnecke, *Emendationen*, 51 have taken up again the conjecture of Wettstein and read πρὸς (τὸν) θεόν instead of πρὸς φθόνον. One could then point by way of comparison to LXX Ps 41:2 and Eccl 12:7, but in this form the text would not contain the threat which must certainly be expected after v 5a.

92 The problematic character of this unity perhaps

the author of persecution. Already because of these last differences between Jas and 1 Peter any literary dependence is ruled out: no one could have elaborated rules for the mutual relationships among Christians from the context in Jas, which refers only to the relationship to God. Nor is there any dependence in the other direction, since the abrupt text in Jas is not an excerpt from 1 Peter.

Evidently there is an underlying paraenetic schema of loosely connected admonitions which makes use of Prov 3:34. The author of 1 Peter has expanded this schema and employed it with some freedom, while Jas has possibly varied it, but on the whole has remained true to the original style of this series of imperatives. *1 Clem.* 30.2 also probably contains an echo of this schema: a quotation is placed between a catalog of vices and an admonition to humility, i.e., between two traditional pieces of paraenesis, and slander is explicitly mentioned in both pieces (cf. Jas 4:11). Perhaps the admonition to be subordinate to the bishop in Ign., *Eph.* 5.3 (cf. 1 Peter 5:5), where this admonition is connected with the quotation from Proverbs, is also tied in with this schema. At any rate, this survey confirms the hypothesis that there was a grouping which underlies our verses and which was fixed prior to Jas. At the same time it helps us to understand these verses, for the variety of their content despite their kinship in form is no longer a puzzle.

■ **7b, 8a** Points of contact with tradition—specifically, with Jewish tradition—are easy to trace in what follows. 4:7b, 8a contains a twofold saying which in each of its two members consists of an admonition and a promise.[93] The first admonition is already familiar to us as a traditional one. The promise that the Devil will flee is found almost verbatim—and, more importantly,

it is repeated several times—in the *Test. XII* (*Test. Iss.* 7.7; *Test. Dan.* 5.1; *Test. Naph.* 8.4). In *Hermas*, also, there is a promise very similar in wording to that in Jas: "If then you resist him [i.e., the Devil], he will be conquered and flee from you in shame" (ἐὰν οὖν ἀντισταθῆτε αὐτῷ, νικηθεὶς φεύξεται ἀφ' ὑμῶν κατῃσχυμμένος *Herm. mand.* 12.5.2; cf. also 12.4.7). In the *Test. XII* there are also parallels to the admonition in Jas 4:8a— e.g., *Test. Dan* 6.2: "Draw near to God and to the angel who intercedes on your behalf" (ἐγγίσατε τῷ θεῷ καὶ τῷ ἀγγέλῳ τῷ παραιτουμένῳ ὑμᾶς) [Trans.]. The promise is stated reciprocally in our verse;[94] this is also the case in the similar expression with the verb "to return" (ἐπιστρέφεσθαι) in Zech 1:3 and Mal 3:7, but it is in keeping with Hellenistic piety as well.

Perhaps a natural association led the first author of this saying from the idea of the nearness of God and nearness to God to the thought in the following saying.

■ **8b** The beginning of this saying, the demand that the hands be pure, originally had a cultic or ritual reference. The demand appears with cultic associations in both Christian and non-Christian statements about prayer. But wherever this motif appears in early Christianity, it is a favourite practice to apply the cultic metaphors to the conduct of one's life.[95] In our passage this is also suggested by the parallel imperatives: Both hands and heart are to be free from evil. Perhaps Ps 23(24):4 has provided the model for the combination of these two demands: "He who has innocent hands and is pure in heart" (ἀθῷος χερσὶν καὶ καθαρὸς τῇ καρδίᾳ). But the reference in our passage to both deeds and thoughts is still clear enough even if there is no reminiscence of the text from the Psalms.

We have come to know the "double-minded person" (δίψυχος) in Jas 1:8 and *Herm. mand.* 9 as the person

explains some peculiar readings in the following verse. None of these readings, however, has attestation which is convincing enough to be considered in the determination of the text: The omission of δέ after "resist" (ἀντίστητε) in v 7; the omission of καί before "weep" (κλαύσατε) in v 9; the insertion of οὖν after "humble yourselves" (ταπεινώθητε) in v 10 (see 1 Petr 5:6); the insertion of γάρ before "he who slanders" (καταλαλῶν) in v 11.

93   On the consecutive καί, cf. above on 1:5.

94   In Jas 4:8, *B* has (instead of the ἐγγιεῖ in all the other Greek manuscripts) ἐγγίσει because this form

of the future is the usual one in the New Testament, in contrast with the LXX usage. Cf. the survey of corresponding variants in other passages in Blass-Debrunner, § 74.1. The assertion by Tischendorf, *ad loc.*, and Henr. Jos. Vogels, ed., *Novum Testamentum Graece* (Düsseldorf: Schwann, 1920), *ad loc.*, that ἐγγίσει is in A is incorrect. [Vogels corrected this in his 1922 Greek–Latin edition—Trans.]

95   Especially in *1 Clem.* 29.1: "Let us then approach him in holiness of soul, raising pure and undefiled hands to him" (προσέλθωμεν οὖν αὐτῷ ἐν ὁσιότητι ψυχῆς, ἁγνὰς καὶ ἀμιάντους χεῖρας αἴροντες πρὸς

whose prayers are not offered in faith. But the address here is to be understood more generally, in accordance with the parallel "sinners" (ἁμαρτωλοί), and means simply the "unbelieving" who still have a bit of the world within them. *Test. Ben.* 6 speaks of the good mind which does not have double sight or double hearing and does not have two tongues, nor does it desire corruptible things—riches, luxuries, and pleasures. There is a similar admonition in *Test. Asher* 3.1: "Therefore, my children, do not be two–faced like they are, having the face of goodness and the face of wickedness; but rather cling only to goodness" (μὴ γίνεσθε κατ᾽ αὐτοὺς διπρόσ-ωποι, ἀγαθότητος καὶ κακίας, ἀλλὰ τῇ ἀγαθότητι μόνῃ κολλήθητε) [Trans.]. Our saying belongs within the context of this sort of thinking.

■ **9** This verse is even sharper in tone and is more a judgment than an admonition. Consequently, we may also consider this saying to have been originally a small, independent unit. In this context, of course, the saying wants to create readiness for repentence. The emphasis lies not upon reform towards better conduct, as in v 8b, but upon the feeling of remorse, upon lamentation over sins which have been committed. While we can immediately understand the imperatives "mourn and weep" (πενθήσατε καὶ κλαύσατε) in this sense, the expression ταλαιπωρήσατε poses some difficulty. For ταλαιπωρεῖν can only mean "be miserable"—since the

transitive meaning is out of the question here—, yet how the word is used with this sense in the imperative is not entirely clear. An old interpretation[96] of this verse is that it is a call to voluntary asceticism. However, the intransitive ταλαιπωρεῖν has to do with something endured, not something practiced.[97] Therefore, the meaning of this verb must be approximated to that of the following verbs, and must be translated (with most commentators) "feel miserable" or "lament."

There can then be no doubt about the reference of the second sentence in v 9: Instead of the pleasure and joy which they experienced in the time of their sinfulness, the persons addressed are now to let mourning and sorrow come upon them.[98] Nevertheless, I am somewhat dissatisfied with this interpretation. I cannot avoid the feeling that these words originally had another sense, and that instead of a command they constituted a prophetic proclamation of disaster which was worded in the form of a command. In that case, Lk 6:21, 25 would be a good parallel: Those who weep are to laugh and those who laugh are to cry. The woes in *1 En.* 94ff and in Jas 5:1 might be cited as well. Then "be wretch-ed" (ταλαιπωρήσατε) would also fit, for if the prophet is calling into view the time of the End when he says "be wretched," then he means that they will soon be in a state of wretchedness and distress.[99]

But this conjecture applies only to the possible *past*

αὐτόν). This sounds cultic, but actually it is the introduction to a general paraenesis. The mention of praying hands in *1 Clem.* 2.3 also occurs in a context of a more general nature. The admonition to raise holy hands in 1 Tim 2:8 perhaps stems originally from a regulation for men and women which is of the *Haustafel* (rules for the household) type; cf. Dibelius-Conzelmann, *The Pastoral Epistles, ad loc.*

96 Erasmus; Grotius (*op. cit.*, above, n. 43); among modern scholars, Mayor.

97 This applies also to the passage which Mayor cites, LXX Ps 37:7: "I was miserable and utterly overcome. I went about all day with a gloomy countenance" (ἐταλαιπώρησα καὶ κατεκάμφθην ἕως τέλους· ὅλην τὴν ἡμέραν σκυθρωπάζων ἐπορευόμην). Furthermore, in all other LXX passages where ταλαιπωρεῖν is not used in a transitive sense it means to suffer hardship, to be miserable or crushed. The same is true for *Herm. vis.* 3.7.1; *Herm. sim.* 6.2.7 and 6.3.1 (passive, "to be tormented"); *2 Clem.* 19.4; Epict., *Diss.* 1.26.11: "I know a certain man who clung in tears to the knees of Epaphroditus and said

that he was in misery; for he had nothing left but a million and a half sesterces" (ἐγώ τινα οἶδα κλαίοντα Ἐπαφροδίτου τῶν γονάτων ἁπτόμενον καὶ λέγοντα ταλαιπωρεῖν· ἀπολελεῖφθαι γὰρ αὐτῷ μηδέν κτλ.).

98 B P 1739 *et al.* have "let it be turned" (μετατραπήτω) instead of "let it be changed" (μεταστραφήτω). The attestation is not strong enough for this reading to be considered in determining textual recensions. However, there is always the possibility that in those isolated witnesses a poetic term is retained which had to yield in the ecclesiastical texts to the more common μεταστραφήτω.

99 Such imperatives would not be unusual in the prophetic style—cf. Isa 6:9: "Hear and hear, but do not understand"; and especially 32:11f: "Tremble ... shudder ... strip and make yourself bare ... beat upon your breasts"; according to 32:10, what is meant is that "you *will* shudder."

history of the saying. In the present context the words surely refer to repentence, as is immediately made clear by the promise in v 10.

■ **10** With this promise: If you humble yourselves, he will exalt you,[100] Jas has clearly asserted that the ultimate outcome of the present time of repentence and suffering will be glory. Thereby, he has turned again squarely onto the path of the paraenesis of which we picked up traces when comparing this section in Jas with 1 Petr 5:5ff. Here the agreement with 1 Petr 5:6 is obvious. Sir 2:17 should be compared as well: "Those who fear the Lord will prepare their hearts, and will humble themselves before him" (οἱ φοβούμενοι Κύριον ἑτοιμάσουσιν καρδίας αὐτῶν, καὶ ἐνώπιον αὐτοῦ ταπεινώσουσιν τὰς ψυχὰς αὐτῶν).

■ **11, 12** As was indicated above in the Analysis, vv 11, 12 can be included as far as their form is concerned within the series of imperatives in 4:7ff. Yet in terms of subject matter, 4:11 introduces something new, as is indicated also by the change in tone: instead of "sinners" (ἁμαρτωλοί) or "double-minded" (δίψυχοι) the address in v 11 is "brothers and sisters" (ἀδελφοί). The fact that within a series of such general admonitions as those found in vv 7–10 this specific warning in v 11 also occurs is understandable if we notice the importance of this prohibition elsewhere in paraenetic material: Slander is mentioned in a number of early Christian catalogues of vices, but particularly in 1 Petr 2:1 where it has a special place alongside the more or less general terms "wickedness" (κακία), "guile" (δόλος), "insincerity" (ὑποκρίσεις), and "envy" (φθόνοι). In *1 Clem.* 30.1, 3, slander is condemned at the beginning of a paraenesis which cites the same passage (Prov 3:34) as Jas 4:6. In *Herm. mand.* 2, when the general Christian ideal of "simplicity" (ἁπλότης) is to be portrayed— "Have simplicity and be innocent and you shall be as children" (ἁπλότητα ἔχε καὶ ἄκακος γίνου, καὶ ἔσῃ ὡς τὰ νήπια cf. 1 Petr 2:2)—, the prohibition of slander has first place among the specific demands which are made.

Similar examples can be cited already from Jewish texts: In the portrayal of piety in Ps 101:5, slander is denounced as a primary individual sin. In *Test. Iss.* 3.4, slander is mentioned in the portrayal of "simplicity" (ἁπλότης), just as in *Herm. mand.* 2, and it is also mentioned in *Test. Gad.* 3.3 and 5.4 in the depiction of hatred and righteousness. Therefore, in Jewish as well as Christian paraenesis, slander is felt to be an especially grave sin, and one which is particularly characteristic of a life of wickedness.[101] It is an aspect of the "worldly" disposition which is expressed by the sin of slander. Thus in *Herm. sim.* 8.7.2, the slanderers are mentioned together with the "double-minded" (cf. Jas 4:8).

All of these associations seem to me to confirm the fact that the admonition in v 11 belongs with the other imperatives. It differs from them only in that it is elaborated by the addition of a supporting argument.[102] It accords with the significance which paraenetic texts attribute to the prohibition against slander that here the argument which is made for the prohibition is not a rational argument, as in Wisd 1:11, but rather a religious one, and this, indeed, on a very broad basis. Slander is not a transgression of merely one commandment, but a transgression against the authority of the law in general, and therefore against God—this is the thought here. It is expressed by the rhetorical use of the same words in the two halves of the verse: He who speaks against his brother or makes himself his brother's judge[103] speaks against the law and makes himself judge of the law. Hence, the use of these verbs with regard to the law is necessitated by the rhetorical correspondence, but the sense itself is quite simple: "He transgresses the law." In this, the author does not have in mind some specific commandment against slander found in the law—for then the statement would contain simply a truism—, but rather the commandment of love in Lev 19:18 (notice "neighbor" [πλησίον] in v 12 and cf. Jas 2:9ff). The same argument is given in the warning against hatred in the *Testament of Gad.*[104] The

---

100 On καί, cf. Jas 1:5.

101 A noteworthy piece of evidence for this perception in a later period is the saying of R. Asi in *Midrash Debarim Rabbah* 6.14 on Deut 24:9: "The man who slanders finally denies even God" (trans. Freedman-Simon).

102 Cf. above in the Analysis.

103 The verb "judge" (κρίνω) must have the same meaning in both v 11 and v 12. Only by failing to recognize the force of the form which here dominates the passage can one (Spitta) lament a lack of clarity in the contrast "doer—judge" (ποιητής—κριτής) or interpret the verb "judge" (κρίνω) to mean "condemn" (κατακρίνω); this latter error is made by Oec, who is more correct in his second interpretation of κρίνω: "despise" (καταφρονεῖ).

inadmissibility of such behaviour is stressed in Jas 4:11 by the contrast between the "doer of the law" ($\pi o\iota\eta\tau\dot{\eta}s$ cf. 1:22ff) and the "judge of the law" ($\kappa\rho\iota\tau\dot{\eta}s\ \nu\acute{o}\mu o\upsilon$).[105]

■ **12** The gravity of the violation is stressed in v 12 by a reference to him who alone stands above the law and can be called "judge." One who perceives the impact of the rhetorical correspondence here will understand the fact that "judge" now has a somewhat different ring. It is no longer a matter of "judging the law" ($\kappa\rho\acute{\iota}\nu\epsilon\iota\nu\ \tau\dot{o}\nu\ \nu\acute{o}\mu o\nu$), but rather of "judging" in general. Likewise, "lawgiver" ($\nu o\mu o\theta\acute{\epsilon}\tau\eta s$) is not the logical opposite of one of the preceding verbs, but instead a kind of contrasting metaphor: God who is the Lord of the law and the Lord of all the world is, as the conclusion of the verse shows, contrasted with the person who outrageously violates the authority of the law.

The subject "one" ($\epsilon\hat{\iota}s$) belongs with "who is able . . ." ($\dot{o}\ \delta\upsilon\nu\acute{a}\mu\epsilon\nu o s\ \kappa\tau\lambda.$) and therefore has the meaning "*only one, i.e., another one.*" Who this one is indicated by a

divine predication which obviously was familiar; cf. especially *Herm. mand.* 12.6.3: "fear him who has all power, to save and to destroy" ($\phi o\beta\acute{\eta}\theta\eta\tau\epsilon\ \tau\dot{o}\nu\ \pi\acute{a}\nu\tau a\ \delta\upsilon\nu\acute{a}\mu\epsilon\nu o\nu,\ \sigma\hat{\omega}\sigma a\iota\ \kappa a\grave{\iota}\ \dot{a}\pi o\lambda\acute{\epsilon}\sigma a\iota$), and *Herm. sim.* 9.23.4.[106]

Next, just as in the last–mentioned passage from *Hermas*, the weak human creature is impressively contrasted with the judge of the world. A human being's behaviour is characterized here merely with the verb "to judge" ($\kappa\rho\acute{\iota}\nu\epsilon\iota\nu$).[107] Perhaps from that one may infer that the entire phrase which is used here as a supporting argument originally applied only to uncharitable judges, and that later it was joined to the prohibition against slander. That such religious arguments move about in this way would not be surprising, and this would also be a good explanation for the rather striking introduction of the passage with "*or judges*" ($\dot{\eta}\ \kappa\rho\acute{\iota}\nu\omega\nu$ v 11)—as if it were a matter of *two* sins.[108]

---

104 *Test. Gad* 4.1f: "Beware, therefore, my children, of hatred; for it works lawlessness even against the Lord Himself. For it will not hear the words of His commandments concerning the loving of one's neighbour, and it sins against God" ($\phi\upsilon\lambda\acute{a}\xi a\sigma\theta\epsilon\ o\hat{\upsilon}\nu,$ $\tau\acute{\epsilon}\kappa\nu a\ \mu o\upsilon,\ \dot{a}\pi\dot{o}\ \tau o\hat{\upsilon}\ \mu\acute{\iota}\sigma o\upsilon s,\ \ddot{o}\tau\iota\ \kappa a\grave{\iota}\ \epsilon\dot{\iota}s\ a\dot{\upsilon}\tau\dot{o}\nu\ \tau\dot{o}\nu\ K\acute{\upsilon}\rho\iota o\nu$ $\dot{a}\nu o\mu\acute{\iota}a\nu\ \pi o\iota\epsilon\hat{\iota}.\ o\dot{\upsilon}\ \gamma\grave{a}\rho\ \theta\acute{\epsilon}\lambda\epsilon\iota\ \dot{a}\kappa o\acute{\upsilon}\epsilon\iota\nu\ \lambda\acute{o}\gamma\omega\nu\ \dot{\epsilon}\nu\tau o\lambda\hat{\omega}\nu$ $a\dot{\upsilon}\tau o\hat{\upsilon}\ \pi\epsilon\rho\grave{\iota}\ \dot{a}\gamma\acute{a}\pi\eta s\ \tau o\hat{\upsilon}\ \pi\lambda\eta\sigma\acute{\iota}o\nu\ \kappa a\grave{\iota}\ \epsilon\dot{\iota}s\ \Theta\epsilon\dot{o}\nu\ \dot{a}\mu a\rho\tau\acute{a}$-$\nu\epsilon\iota$) [trans. Charles, *APOT*].

105 Here, where it is only the terseness of the expression that matters, there can be no thought of allusions to specific historical situations, such as a Gnostic criticism of the Old Testament law (Pfleiderer, *Primitive Christianity*, vol. 4, p. 303).

106 Cf. also 1 Sam 2:6; Matt 10:28 = Lk 12:5; *Mekilta*, tractate *Amalek* 1 on Ex 17:9: "Is it not God alone that can kill and bring back to life again, as it is said: 'The Lord kills and makes alive' (1 Sam 2:6)?" (trans. Lauterbach 2, p. 141); *1 Clem.* 59.3; *Shemone*

Esre 2 (Babylonian recension): "He who kills and makes alive and causes salvation to spring forth."

107 The Koine witnesses have $\ddot{o}s\ \kappa\rho\acute{\iota}\nu\epsilon\iota s$; von Soden (*Schriften*, part 2, *ad loc.*) accepts this reading and wants to explain the reading offered by the majority of the remaining witnesses ($\dot{o}\ \kappa\rho\acute{\iota}\nu\omega\nu$) from the influence of parallel texts. In fact, dependence of the variants upon Rom 14:4 must at least be taken into consideration.

As a conclusion to v 12 there occur in some witnesses the words "because the steps of man are not directed by man but by God" ($\ddot{o}\tau\iota\ o\dot{\upsilon}\kappa\ \dot{\epsilon}\nu\ \dot{a}\nu\theta\rho\acute{\omega}\pi\omega$ $\dot{a}\lambda\lambda'\ \dot{\epsilon}\nu\ \theta\epsilon\hat{\omega}\ \tau\grave{a}\ \delta\iota a\beta\acute{\eta}\mu a\tau a\ \dot{a}\nu\theta\rho\acute{\omega}\pi o\upsilon\ \kappa a\tau\epsilon\upsilon\theta\acute{\upsilon}\nu\epsilon\tau a\iota$). This is the ancient chapter heading to 4:13ff which later worked its way into the text itself; cf. von Soden, *Schriften*, part 1, p. 458.

108 As one might expect, the Koine witnesses and Ψ emend to "*and judges*" ($\kappa a\grave{\iota}\ \kappa\rho\acute{\iota}\nu\omega\nu$). In v 12 they omit "and judge" ($\kappa a\grave{\iota}\ \kappa\rho\iota\tau\acute{\eta}s$).

4

A Group of Sayings Against Worldy-Minded Merchants and Rich People

13   Come, you who say, "Today or tomorrow we will go into such and such a city and spend a year there and carry on business and make a profit" —14/ you who do not even know what will happen tomorrow. For what is your life, really? For you are a smoke which appears for a little time and then disappears—, 15/ instead of your saying, "If the Lord wills, we shall live and we shall do this or that." 16/ As it is, you boast in your arrogance. All such boasting is evil.

17   Whoever is able to do something good and does not do it, for him it is sin.

5

1   Come, you rich, weep and wail at the miseries which are coming upon you! 2/ Your wealth has rotted and your garments are moth-eaten. 3/ Your gold and silver have rusted, and their rust will testify against you, and the rust will devour your flesh like fire. You have stored up treasure (even) in the Last Days! 4/ Behold, the wages of the workers who mowed your fields, wages which were withheld by you, cry out; and the cries of those who have harvested have gone up to the ears of the Lord of hosts. 5/ You have lived on earth in luxury and pleasure; you have fattened your hearts on a day of slaughter. 6/ You have condemned, you have murdered the righteous person; he offers no resistance.

Analysis

4:13–16 is unquestionably an independent section. It is directed in prophetic style with a vigorous address against persons who are all too clever about making their future plans, and to whom Jas brings home the folly of their thinking. There is no connection between this passage and the preceding series of imperatives.[1] The content of this section, however, fits well with the main idea of 4:1ff, and it is understandable how the author could continue the general warning of people with a wordly mind with a polemic against a specific instance of this worldly disposition. It is more a question here of a similar mood in two adjacent sections than a question of a literary connection, for the two related texts are separated by the series of imperatives in 4:7ff.

The section in 5:1ff also shares in this mood: as a polemic against the rich it deals with a further specific instance of a wordly disposition.[2] Moreover, the author consciously joins these two sections (4:13ff and 5:1ff) containing vigorous harangues, as is shown by the same beginning ("Come now") in both 4:13 and 5:1.

Therefore, what we have here is not a series of sayings in which one saying is loosely appended to the other, but rather a group of sayings which gives the impression of being unified because the beginnings are identical in form and the ideas are parallel. On the other hand, the inner unity of the section in 5:1ff cannot be as readily affirmed as in 4:13ff. In 5:1–6, the announcement of the punishment and the indictment appear to be combined in a peculiar fashion, and not without

1   Bede asserted such a connection: "The person who likes to make plans for the following day, without weighing carefully the frailty of his condition and the uncertainty of temporal existence, displays his foolhardiness" (temeritatem arguit eius, qui proximum delectatur judicare, nec suae statum fragili-

some artificiality. The destruction of riches is described first, and the guilt of rich people is the last thing to be portrayed. The transition is not immediately clear, but must lie in v 3. Here, as is so often the case in Jas, we must take into account that he utilizes traditional paraenesis and by its use has disrupted the continuity.[3]

4:17 requires special consideration. There have been futile attempts at connecting this verse with what precedes it, although most commentators have perceived that the verse is rather general in character.[4] In fact, the verse does not tie in with either what precedes or what follows, for it speaks of sins of omission, whereas the transgressions censured in the context consist of evil deeds and not of the failure to do good. Obviously, 4:17 is as loosely inserted into the context as is the saying in 2:13, and in the case of 4:17 one cannot observe even a superficial link with the context, such as that between "to be judged" ($\kappa\rho\acute{\iota}\nu\epsilon\sigma\theta\alpha\iota$) and "judgment" ($\kappa\rho\acute{\iota}\sigma\iota\varsigma$) in 2:12, 13. It is difficult to say what the author's reason was for inserting the saying here. He might have added it with a view toward the "sin of omission" committed by the rich when they leave their gold and silver lying idle.[5] Of course, that would be only an association, and not an actual connection, between the verse and its context. Or the saying might have been a part of the paraenesis which Jas used for 5:1ff, and in that context it might have constituted the conclusion to an exhortation to do good deeds.[6] Whatever the reason for this saying having been placed here, one thing is certain: it stands isolated between two related texts.

Interpretation

4:13–16 is delivered in the style of a prophetic address. The prophet cries out his words among the masses, unconcerned about whether his accusations reach the ears of those whom he accuses. At the outset, therefore, we must once again be warned against forming an opinion of Jas' audience based upon this reproof.

■ **13** The singular imperative, "Come" ($\check{\alpha}\gamma\epsilon$), has become frozen grammatically as a particle, a fact which is demonstrated by its use here with the following plural, "those who say."[7] The meaning of the word is governed by whatever follows in any given instance. In the lively speech of everyday life both interrogative and imperative sentences are often introduced by "come" ($\check{\alpha}\gamma\epsilon$). The specific force of $\check{\alpha}\gamma\epsilon$ here in Jas 4:13 is not immediately clear. The intention is chiefly to reprove those who are making plans for the future, not to enjoin them to any particular action. Also, v 15 contains no formal command. Therefore, it seems advisable to hear in $\check{\alpha}\gamma\epsilon$ the beginning of a (rhetorical) question, and then to explain the subsequent anacoluthon accordingly. James probably wished to lead whose whom he addressed with $\check{\alpha}\gamma\epsilon$ to reflect upon the question: "What is your life, really?" But the construction is interrupted when he adds to the rather long address the subordinate clause: "you who do not know about tomorrow" ($o\check{\iota}\tau\iota\nu\epsilon\varsigma$ . . .), and then to that he attaches the question: "For what is your life, really . . ." ($\pi o\acute{\iota}\alpha\ \gamma\acute{\alpha}\rho$ . . .).[8] As a result, the $\check{\alpha}\gamma\epsilon$ is left without any continuation.

The words which are put into the mouths of those who are making their plans are naturally intended to ring as animated and as true to everyday life as possible. This must be kept in mind in the interpretation, and especially in evaluating the textual variants. For one must reckon with the possibility that the vernacular style of the original might have been transmuted by the ancient editors of the text into speech more in accord with literary usage. This was certainly the case with the reading "today as well as tomorrow" ($\sigma\acute{\eta}\mu\epsilon\rho o\nu\ \kappa\alpha\grave{\iota}$

---

tatis ac vitae temporalis incertum perpendere curat).

2 Cf. *1 En.* 97.8f: "We have become rich with riches and have possessions; and have acquired everything we have desired. And now let us do what we purposed: For we have gathered silver . . ." [trans. Charles, *APOT*].

3 See below, on 5:1ff.

4 Könnecke, for example, believed this so strongly that he allowed only the option between the deletion of the "therefore" ($o\check{\upsilon}\nu$) or the transposition of the entire verse (Könnecke, *Emendationen*, 16).

5 See below, on 5:3.

6 Cf. the similar saying in *Herm. vis.* 3.9.5, which occurs immediately before the passage whose relationship with Jas 5:4 is discussed below (*ad loc.*).

7 Cf. Blass-Debrunner, § 144.

8 B omits the first $\gamma\acute{\alpha}\rho$ in v 14 (so also ℵ* sy^hl arm, but the majority of the Egyptian witnesses do not). B also does not have $\acute{\eta}$ before $\zeta\omega\acute{\eta}$ and $\tau\acute{o}$ before $\tau\hat{\eta}\varsigma$ $\alpha\check{\upsilon}\rho\iota o\nu$ (other texts read $\tau\acute{\alpha}$). Therefore, in the resulting text $\pi o\acute{\iota}\alpha$ is dependent upon $\dot{\epsilon}\pi\acute{\iota}\sigma\tau\alpha\sigma\theta\epsilon$: "you who do not know what sort of life you will have tomorrow." A person who has not taken an oath of allegiance to the authority of B will have to consider

αὔριον). The ones making plans in Jas 4:13 say "today or tomorrow" (σήμερον ἢ αὔριον).[9] Perhaps the replacement of the future tense of the four verbs with subjunctive expressions also falls into this category, and if the future tense was not original in each of the four verbs, certainly also the assimilation of the four verbs to one another would be a product of this later editorial activity.[10] The expression "a year" (ἐνιαυτόν) without the adjective "one" (ἕνα) is perhaps the vernacular, and therefore original, expression here.[11] Finally, the term "such and such a city" (τήνδε τὴν πόλιν) is also a possible example of vernacular usage in this passage.[12]

■ 14 Now the actual theme of the whole admonition is mentioned in the relative clause which presumably has disturbed the grammatical construction:[13] A person does not know what will happen tomorrow. This is a thought which understandably is expressed in various poetic and paraenetic texts. Because of the possibility of a connection with our text here, the Jewish[14] and the popular philosophical[15] parallels are of interest. Also of interest is the relationship in thought between this passage in Jas and the parable in Lk

---

9   The attestation is in favour of the reading ἤ ("or"). Besides the Koine witnesses, A and P have καί ("and"). The influence of Lk 13:32f, where καί occurs in the same expression, would be possible. It is more probable that the desire was to place into the mouths of the planners as confident a declaration as possible (see below, n. 11). Therefore, καί was written instead of ἤ, though this was at the expense of the animation of the language.

10   Although the confusion of o and ω is admittedly one of the most common of scribal errors. Involved here are the four verbs: (a) "we will go" (πορευσόμεθα); (b) "we will spend" (ποιήσομεν); (c) "we will carry on business" (ἐμπορευσόμεθα); (d) "we will make a profit" (κερδήσομεν). The Koine text, Ψ 81 et al., have the subjunctive instead of the future in all four cases. The future is found in all four verbs in ff (negotiabimur is probably to be read instead of negotiamur) s vulg and certain manuscripts. Von Soden (Schriften, part 2, ad loc.) claims that the future is found in all four places in the text group which he calls recension I, but this is more strongly attested in (c) and (d), and especially in (a), than in (b). From the Egyptian text group, B(P) has the future for all four verbs. Most of the Egyptian witnesses have the future for (c) and (d). 1175 has it for (a). In the case of (b), the defection of the Egyptian witnesses to the subjunctive is so great that von Soden grants that recension H favours the subjunctive, and therefore he takes ποιήσωμεν as the original reading of the text. However, it still must be asked whether πορευσόμεθα καὶ ποιήσωμεν is really a better reading—i.e., in this case, a reading which is more in line with everyday speech. In this passage, the manuscript evidence should not be overrated, since it could be a case of misspelling. If the corresponding variants in v 15 are brought into consideration, it seems obvious that all the subjunctives are due to recension.

11   The reading ἐνιαυτόν without ἕνα is attested to in

B ℵ P et al. sah boh ff vulg. As a result it was accepted as the reading of the text by the modern text critics prior to von Soden, while von Soden (Schriften, part 2, ad loc.) assigned this reading neither to recension H nor to recension I, nor to the original text. However, it could be that the effort of the ancient editors to have the planners make as specific assertions as possible comes into play here also. Then ἕνα would still be a later insertion, but one which would have found its place in the majority of the witnesses.

12   Luther correctly arrived at the meaning "such and such a city" for εἰς τήνδε τὴν πόλιν here, and the parallel "we will do this or that" (ποιήσομεν τοῦτο ἢ ἐκεῖνο) in v 15 makes this meaning probable. Older commentaries shied away from understanding τήνδε as an alternative for the usual Greek expressions for "such and such" (τὴν δεῖνα or τὴν καὶ τήν). They pointed out that there is no other example for this meaning of τήνδε, and that the passage which is usually cited as evidence for it (Plut., Quaest. conv. 1.6.1) could itself be interpreted differently. But if one proceeds from the general presupposition which I have set forth above for the speech of these persons in making plans in Jas, viz., that it must be retained in the vernacular as much as possible, and if one further considers that modern Greek has the usage of ὁ τάδε(ς) to mean ὁ δεῖνα, then the possibility cannot be rejected out of hand that ὅδε is also used in this way here in Jas, and that the source of this usage is the common idiom (Cf. Blass-Debrunner, § 289).

13   See above, on v 13.

14   Prov 27:1 (already adduced in this context by the catenae and scholia): "Do not boast about tomorrow, for you do not know what the coming day will bear" (μὴ καυχῶ τὰ εἰς αὔριον, οὐ γὰρ γινώσκεις τί τέξεται ἡ ἐπιοῦσα); Pseudo-Phocylides 116f: "No one knows what will happen the day after tomorrow, or even an hour from now, for trouble has no regard for mortals and the future is uncertain" (οὐδεὶς, γινώσκει τί μεταύριον ἢ τί μεθ' ὥραν· ἄσκοπός ἐστι βροτῶν κάματος, τὸ δὲ μέλλον ἄδηλον) [Trans.]; Sir

12:16–20, and with the portion of the section of woes in *1 En.* 97:9f, where the rich say, "And now let us do what we proposed," and the apocalyptist answers them, "Your riches shall not abide but speedily ascend from you" [trans. Charles, *APOT*]. However, no dependence at all can be proven between these texts and the one in Jas.

To the question, "What is your life, really?" the answer is given, "For *you* are smoke" (ἀτμὶς γάρ ἐστε), which does not seem to follow very consistently. Yet in reality this is not surprising, at least not if the explanation given above of the construction with ἄγε is correct, so that after the interruption of that construction by the subordinate clause (οἵτινες . . .) and the question (ποία γάρ . . .) there is a return here to the originally intended thought.[16] ἀτμίς could mean "vapour" or "smoke," and is doubtlessly used here in the second of these senses,[17] since the word signifies transitoriness in a way similar to the apocryphal quotation in *1 Clem.* 17.6: "But I am as smoke from a pot" (ἐγὼ δέ εἰμι ἀτμὶς ἀπὸ κύθρας).[18] The transitoriness is further emphasized through the use of the wordplay which was also popular elsewhere: "to appear"—"to disappear" (φαίνεσθαι—

ἀφανίζεσθαι).[19]

■ **15** This verse is another clear example of how loose the construction is in this complex of sentences. The words "instead of your saying" (ἀντὶ τοῦ λέγειν ὑμᾶς) pick up the "Come now you who say" (ἄγε νῦν οἱ λέγοντες) in v 13, but they do so as if they were picking up a statement in the indicative.[20]

Now the author recommends the famous "*conditio Jacobaea*" ("If God wills"), which is named after him but is in reality much older. Minucius Felix (*Octavius* 18.11), in providing various evidences of the agreement of his thesis with the common consensus, characterizes the expression "if God shall grant" (si deus dederit) as "the natural speech of the common people" (vulgi naturalis sermo). Similarly, other literary and epistolary witnesses to this usage can be cited, beginning with Plato.[21] That the customary usage has been adopted in the Christian epistolary style is demonstrated

---

11:18f; cf. the uncertainty of plans emphasized in Philo, *Leg. all.* 3.226f and *1 En.* 97.8 (quoted above in n. 2).

15 Seneca, *Epist.* 101.4: "But how foolish it is to set out one's life when one is not even owner of the morrow!" (quam stultum est aetatem disponere ne crastini quidem dominum). Cf. also Plut., *Cons. ad Apoll.* 11, and the anthology of Stobaeus, *Ecl.* 4.41 (pp. 927–48 Hense), under the title "The Good Fortune of Humans is Unstable" (ὅτι ἀβέβαιος ἡ τῶν ἀνθρώπων εὐπραξία). Cf. further parallels in Rossbroich, 73f.

16 The omission of γάρ ("for"), after ἀτμίς (A 33 s vulg boh) and the readings "it will be" (ἔσται A P Ψ K et al.) and "it is" (ἐστιν L ff s vulg) appear then to be smoothings of the text which are easily understandable.

17 Oec, somewhat too eruditely, takes both meanings into consideration. The translation in *ff*: "For it is an instant" (momentum enim est), is probably a rendering of the Greek word ἄτομος. A parallel to this confusion of ἀτμίς with ἄτομος, which means "incapable of being cut" (hence, a moment as the smallest unit of time), would be found in Sir 24:15, where "as the smoke of incense" (ὡς λιβάνου ἀτμίς) is translated in a Latin version as "incense which is not cut up/off (?)" (libanus non incisus).

18 On smoke as an image for transitoriness, cf. Hos 13:3; Ps 37:20 (?); 68:2; 102:3 (?); Isa 51:6; Wisd 5:14 (15), and 1 QM XV, 10: "their power shall be as vanishing smoke" (נגבורתם כעשן נמלח) [trans. Dupont-Sommer, *Essene Writings*, p. 192].

19 Cf. Pseudo-Aristot., *Mund.* 6, p. 399a; and Aristot., *Hist. an.* 6.7.11.

20 Cf. below, on v 16.

21 The most characteristic example is Plato, *Alc.* 1.135d: "If you wish, Socrates."—"That is not well said, Alcibiades."—"Well, what should I say?"— "If God wills." (ἐὰν βούλῃ σύ, ὦ Σώκρατες.—οὐ καλῶς λέγεις, ὦ Ἀλκιβιάδη.—ἀλλὰ πῶς χρὴ λέγειν;— ὅτι ἐὰν θεὸς ἐθέλῃ) [Loeb modified]. Cf. the expression "if God wills" (ἐὰν θεὸς ἐθέλῃ) and similar ones in Plato, *Phaed.* 80d; *Theaet.* 151d; *La.* 201c; *Hi. maior* 286c; "to say with God's help" (σὺν θεῷ εἰπεῖν), in Plato, *Theaet.* 151b; Aristoph., *Pl.* 114 (see also 347, 405, 1188); in a more solemn context and with greater emphasis, the expression is found in *Corp. Herm.* Frag. II A, 1–2, vol. 3, pp. 4f Nock-Festugière. For epistolary examples, cf. *BGU* II, 423.18: "if the gods will" (τῶν θεῶν θελόντων), and the same expression in *BGU* II, 615.4f; "if the gods will" (θεῶν δὲ βουλομένων) in *BGU* I, 248.11f and 249.13; "if the gods permit" (θεῶν ἐπιτρεπόντων) in *BGU* II, 451.10f; "as God has willed" (ὡς ὁ θεὸς ἤθελεν) *BGU*

by early Christian examples.[22]

These parallels already provide reason enough to assume that the formula which Jas uses here is "if God wills," and not "if God wills *and we live.*" But furthermore, the mention of a second proviso along with the will of God would be strange from a religious perspective. On the other hand, the phrase "we shall both live and . . ." ($\kappa\alpha\grave{\iota}\ \zeta\acute{\eta}\sigma o\mu\epsilon\nu$) fits excellently with the beginning of the final clause, since through the conjunctives "both—and" ($\kappa\alpha\acute{\iota}—\kappa\alpha\acute{\iota}$) the enumeration of the plans in v 13 is recalled.[23]

■ **16** The construction is put right again in this verse. The indicative statement presupposed in v 15 but not actually present is now added here. This verse adds nothing materially new to v 13. By the expression "arrogance" ($\grave{\alpha}\lambda\alpha\zeta o\nu\epsilon\acute{\iota}\alpha$)[24] the plans expressed in v 13 are meant. Parallels to this use of the term $\grave{\alpha}\lambda\alpha\zeta o\nu\epsilon\acute{\iota}\alpha$ are found in *Test. Jos.* 17.8: "And I exalted not myself among them *in arrogance* because of my worldly glory, but I was among them as one of the least" ($\kappa\alpha\grave{\iota}\ o\grave{\upsilon}\chi$ $\ddot{\upsilon}\psi\omega\sigma\alpha\ \grave{\epsilon}\mu\alpha\upsilon\tau\grave{o}\nu\ \grave{\epsilon}\nu\ \alpha\grave{\upsilon}\tau o\hat{\iota}\varsigma\ \grave{\epsilon}\nu\ \grave{\alpha}\lambda\alpha\zeta o\nu\epsilon\acute{\iota}\alpha\ \delta\iota\grave{\alpha}\ \tau\grave{\eta}\nu\ \kappa o\sigma\mu\iota\kappa\acute{\eta}\nu$ $\mu o\upsilon\ \delta\acute{o}\xi\alpha\nu,\ \grave{\alpha}\lambda\lambda'\ \ddot{\eta}\mu\eta\nu\ \grave{\epsilon}\nu\ \alpha\grave{\upsilon}\tau o\hat{\iota}\varsigma\ \grave{\omega}\varsigma\ \epsilon\hat{\iota}\varsigma\ \tau\hat{\omega}\nu\ \grave{\epsilon}\lambda\alpha\chi\acute{\iota}\sigma\tau\omega\nu$) [trans. Charles, *APOT*], and *1 Clem.* 21.5: "Let us offend foolish and thoughtless people, who are exalted and *boast in the arrogance* of their words, rather than God" ($\mu\hat{\alpha}\lambda\lambda o\nu\ \grave{\alpha}\nu\theta\rho\acute{\omega}\pi o\iota\varsigma\ \check{\alpha}\phi\rho o\sigma\iota\ \kappa\alpha\grave{\iota}\ \grave{\alpha}\nu o\acute{\eta}\tau o\iota\varsigma\ \kappa\alpha\grave{\iota}\ \grave{\epsilon}\pi\alpha\iota\rho o\mu\acute{\epsilon}\nu o\iota\varsigma$ $\kappa\alpha\grave{\iota}\ \grave{\epsilon}\gamma\kappa\alpha\upsilon\chi\omega\mu\acute{\epsilon}\nu o\iota\varsigma\ \grave{\epsilon}\nu\ \grave{\alpha}\lambda\alpha\zeta o\nu\epsilon\acute{\iota}\alpha\ \tau o\hat{\upsilon}\ \lambda\acute{o}\gamma o\upsilon\ \alpha\grave{\upsilon}\tau\hat{\omega}\nu\ \pi\rho o\sigma$-$\kappa\acute{o}\psi\omega\mu\epsilon\nu\ \ddot{\eta}\ \tau\hat{\omega}\ \theta\epsilon\hat{\omega}$) [Loeb modified].

Now we can turn to the question of what circumstances 4:13–16 presupposes. In doing this, we again encounter the problem which has been dealt with

frequently in this commentary[25]—viz., whether Jas ever alludes to specific historical situations. However, in this case a special answer is called for. It is certain that the author of 4:13ff knows people who devise such plans and that his religious sensitivity is offended by such presumptuous thoughtlessness. The possibility that, being guided by the tradition, he is simply taking up a traditional admonition in his paraenesis is out of the question here. He makes too little use of the traditional expressions of proverbial wisdom, and the situation before his eyes here is too animated. But also the other hypothesis which I suggested with regard to 2:1ff is of no help in this case—viz., that Jas has contrived the case as a deterrent example. For this example is not flagrant at all! And even if the saying "if God wills" is the "natural speech of the common people," still the making of plans without serious thoughts about human transitoriness is all the more natural, and, then as now, a rather widespread phenomenon. Yet precisely for this reason we need not assume that Jas is attacking a specific instance of this sort of behaviour among his addressees. The matter is related vividly, but not at all in detail.

Therefore, nothing more need be presupposed than that Jas feared a danger for the Christians which was associated with business plans and intentions. He could have feared that as soon as Christians involved in trade had become a typical phenomenon within the community. What he wishes to warn against and condemn is this bad habit seeping in from the world—regardless of whether this is still just a possibility or already a

---

I, 27.11. "If fortune permits" ($\tau\hat{\eta}\varsigma\ \tau\acute{\upsilon}\chi\eta\varsigma\ \grave{\epsilon}\pi\iota\tau\rho\epsilon$-$\pi o\acute{\upsilon}\sigma\eta\varsigma$) in *BGU* I, 248.15f has a more secular ring, and finally, cf. Seneca, *De tranquill.* 13.2: "unless something happens" (nisi si quid inciderit). A Jewish tale in the *Alfabetum Siracidis* 9b is intended to prove that in all their undertakings people must say, "If the Name (God) decrees" (אם יגזור השם), or, "If it is pleasing (to God)" (אם ירצה) [quoted by A. Marmorstein, "Legendenmotive in der rabbinischen Literatur," *Archiv für Religionswissenschaft* 16 (1913), 175]. A further example is found in Friedrich Bilabel, ed., *Veröffentlichungen aus den badischen Papyrussammlungen*, vol. 2 (Heidelberg: Winter, 1923), 61 (No. 39. 2.8f): "if the gods are willing" ($\check{\alpha}\nu\ \theta\epsilon o\grave{\iota}$ $\beta o\acute{\upsilon}\lambda\omega[\nu]\tau[\alpha\iota]$, in a letter copy–book, 100–150 A.D.). Cf. Deissmann, *LAE*, 235f.

22 1 Cor 4:19 and 16:7, where "Lord" ($\kappa\acute{\upsilon}\rho\iota o\varsigma$) is used

both times; 1 Cor 16:12 (?); Heb 6:3 (cf. also Acts 18:21); Ign., *Eph.* 20.1: "If it be the will . . ." ($\grave{\epsilon}\grave{\alpha}\nu$ $. . .\ \theta\acute{\epsilon}\lambda\eta\mu\alpha\ \mathring{\eta}$).

23 Text-critical considerations also agree with this conclusion. The indicative "we shall both live and do" ($\kappa\alpha\grave{\iota}\ \zeta\acute{\eta}\sigma o\mu\epsilon\nu\ \kappa\alpha\grave{\iota}\ \pi o\iota\acute{\eta}\sigma o\mu\epsilon\nu$) must be read, and not the subjunctive. The Koine reading with the subjunctives ($\zeta\acute{\eta}\sigma\omega\mu\epsilon\nu\ \pi o\iota\acute{\eta}\sigma\omega\mu\epsilon\nu$) may be viewed as an emendation similar to that in v 13, although great caution must be taken here because of the frequent interchange of o and ω. The omission of $\kappa\alpha\acute{\iota}$ before $\pi o\iota\acute{\eta}\sigma o\mu\epsilon\nu$ is naturally dependent upon the interpretation "if God wills and we live" (minuscules, s vulg sy[vg] sah boh arm). B P 81 *et al.* have $\theta\acute{\epsilon}\lambda\eta$ instead of $\theta\epsilon\lambda\acute{\eta}\sigma\eta$.

24 On the spelling, see Winer-Schmiedel, 5.13c.

25 Cf. above in the Introduction, section 7, and the

reality. The direct address is a prophetic apostrophe directed to anyone to whom this might apply.[26]

Therefore, while this passage is evidence of the fact that we no longer stand at a beginning stage of the Christian community, there is also no reason to conclude from this passage that a radical secularization has already made its entrance. We do not know whether among the Christians there were already many people such as the Roman Hermas, who is entangled in shady business dealings (*Herm. vis.* 2.3.1), speaks untruthfully with everyone (*Herm. mand.* 3.3), and knows of restless schemers among the Christians (*Herm. sim.* 6.3.5). The comparison with the *Shepherd of Hermas* is instructive, however, since *Hermas* is a witness for the completion of the development feared by Jas, and since we recognize the difference between the paraenetic utilization of specific personal experiences in *Hermas* and the more general paraenesis in Jas.

17 If the saying in v 17 is read as a thought unconnected with what precedes or follows, as was argued in the Analysis, then it is a general precept concerning sins of omission. This precept is quite certainly of Jewish origin, even if we cannot show specific evidence for it. The expression "for him it is sin" (ἁμαρτία αὐτῷ ἐστιν) is reminiscent of "sin will be in you" (ἔσται ἐν σοὶ ἁμαρτία) and other such expressions (Deut 23:21f; 24:15).[27] The content corresponds to the typically Jewish search after hidden guilt, in which every sin of omission is important. Thus Job, when examining himself for transgressions, expressly mentions sins of omission (31:16–18), and Zophar had already (11:6) hinted at

the possibility of secret guilt.[28]

5:1–6 As the Analysis has shown, 5:1–6 is externally parallel to 4:13–16. However, there are essential differences to be observed between the two sections as far as their internal homogeneity and the provenance of their content is concerned. By contrast with 4:13ff, 5:1ff has strong connections with the tradition. The theme, the accusation of the rich, is also treated in *1 En.* 94ff, and is important in Wisd 2 and *Herm. vis.* 3.9.3–6. The language is prophetic; the call to "wail" or "cry out" (ὀλολύζειν) is especially frequent in Isaiah.[29]

1 This call in v 1, therefore, is not to be understood as a kind of admonition to repent, but rather as a proclamation: In the future affliction, it will come to pass that you will weep and wail.[30] The thought world of this section is also traditional and we are familiar with it already from the introductory examination of the topic of the poor and the rich.[31] It is the rich people above all others who must be afraid in the face of the coming day of judgment, for they are—and this is assumed as a matter of course—the unrighteous, and therefore from the imminent transformation of the world they must expect nothing but disaster. This is the ancient verdict of the "pious" regarding the rich, a verdict known to us from the Psalms. Also seen here is the ardor of the pride of the Poor as it has lived on in the Wisdom literature, substantially heightened by the strength of the eschatological expectation, which assures the poor people of the imminence of their salvation; for the "last days" have already dawned (end of v 3).

    Excursus on 2:1.

26 That it is precisely the Christians who especially cultivate this bad practice is not said; if this were the case, it would have been stated and in no uncertain terms. Jas is not singling out Christians as the offenders, as Grafe, *Stellung und Bedeutung*, 3, believes: "In chapters 4 and 5, there is little doubt that the author has Christians in mind in the direct address in 4:13ff and 5:1." However, cf. how in the section of woes in *1 Enoch* the address changes: In *1 En.* 94.1, Enoch speaks to his "sons," but then 94.8 reads, "Woe to you rich," and this "you"-style continues. But in 95.3 and 96.1–3, the righteous and the suffering are addressed, and also in 97.1. Yet the address is to the sinful rich in 95.1, 2, 4–7; 96.4–8 and 97.2–10.

27 The pleonastic αὐτῷ is explained here by the formal-

ized style of the sentence (cf. further, Blass-Debrunner, § 466.4).

28 On the other hand, Philo censures Flaccus all the more severely since the latter sinned not "through ignorance" (ἐξ ἀγνοίας) but "with knowledge" (ἐξ ἐπιστήμης *In Flacc.* 7).

29 E.g., LXX Isa 10:10; 13:6; 14:31, *et passim*.

30 I have already considered this rhetorical use of the imperative in 4:9 for the verb "be wretched" (ταλαιπωρήσατε), but in that instance this applied only to the original form of the saying (see above, on 4:9).

31 See above in the Introduction, section 6.

■ **2, 3a** Here the announcement of disaster in v 1 is spelled out by means of three assertions. The perfect tense is used, but it contradicts the mood here if this tense is interpreted logically—i.e., since this has already happened, then soon still more disaster will overtake you. Instead, the perfect tense expresses here the prophetic anticipation of things to come, and therefore a future meaning results: Your wealth will be of no more use to you at that time, for it will be gone.

1) In the first assertion the expression "has rotted" (σέσηπεν) has occasioned a great number of interpreters to take "wealth" (πλοῦτος) as a specific reference to perishable goods, perhaps something such as grain. The accusations of *1 En.* 97.9 against those who have filled their granaries would provide a good parallel. However, the verb also admits of a metaphorical, or at least an expanded, meaning,[32] and in the noun πλοῦτος no such specific reference to perishable goods must be perceived. Therefore, it probably simply means that "your wealth has wasted away." 2) The second assertion involves the old motif of the "moth-eaten garments."[33] 3) Finally, the third assertion, in v 3a, is most naturally understood by the reader as simply a parallel to the other two: Your gold and silver are also gone. That Jas speaks of rust here, although precious metals do not rust, is striking and has been variously explained.[34] If one is hesitant to assume merely a generalized or metaphorical

use here of "to rust" (κατιοῦσθαι), as with the verb "to rot" (σήπεσθαι) earlier, then it is best here also to call to mind the tradition. As will be seen below,[35] the tradition does speak in a specific context of the rusting of money (= ἀργύριον) : in the popular speech, the rich could be warned that their treasures (Matt 6:20, after mention of the "moth"!), i.e., "gold and silver" would rust.

■ **3b** That we are standing here on traditional ground is seen in this verse. For something more is now said about rust: It will testify against the rich.[36] The movement in thought is shown also by the shift to the future tense. What is intended by the idea of rust giving testimony is suggested by Sir 29:10: "Lose your silver for the sake of a brother or a friend, and do not let it rust under a stone and be lost" (ἀπόλεσον ἀργύριον δι' ἀδελφὸν καὶ φίλον, καὶ μὴ ἰωθήτω ὑπὸ τὸν λίθον εἰς ἀπώλειαν). The rust bears witness that the money remains lying around and that therefore the rich man has neglected his duty to give alms. This is an ancient accusation against the rich.[37] But in the context of Jas 5:3b it expresses a new thought: the question is now no longer one of punishment, as in vv 2, 3a, but rather of guilt. Oec sought to achieve homogeneity in this whole passage by subsuming (contrary to the text) vv 2, 3a under the thought of v 3b: Decay, damage done by moths, and rust would all testify against the rich. On

---

32 Cf. the passage in Sir 14:19, which deals with the products of human activity in general : "Every product decays and ceases to exist, and the one who made it will pass away with it" (πᾶν ἔργον σηπόμενον ἐκλείπει, καὶ ὁ ἐργαζόμενος αὐτὸ μετ' αὐτοῦ ἀπελεύσεται). Cf. also Curt Lindhagen, "Die Wurzel ΣΑΠ im NT und AT," *Uppsala Universitats Årsskrift* (Leipzig : Harrassowitz; Uppsala: Lundequistska, 1950, no. 5), 27–33.

33 Cf. Isa 51:8; Sir 42:13. The term "moth-eaten" (σητόβρωτος) occurs in Job 13:28 and *Sibyl. Frag.* 3.26 (Theoph., *ad Autol.* 2.36). The Latin *ff* has "your things" (res vestrae) for "your garments" (τὰ ἱμάτια ὑμῶν). Wordsworth, "The Corbey St. James," 143f, derives this reading in *ff* from the Syriac *mân*, which could refer to clothes as well as to other provisions, and upon the basis of this and other observations he proposes the hypothesis that there was a primitive Aramaic version of Jas (see above in the Introduction, n. 128). However, this derivation of the *ff* reading is not necessary. J. B. Mayor, in a brief note in *Classical Review* 5 (1891) : 69, has rightly

stated in opposition to Wordsworth that a fragment from Hegesippus regarding the martyrdom of James in Eus., *Hist. eccl.* 2.23.18 : "the club with which he used to beat out *clothes*" (τὸ ξύλον ἐν ᾧ ἀποπιέζει τὰ ἱμάτια), is translated by Rufinus as "the fuller seized the club with which *things* are usually pressed out" (fullo arrepto fuste in quo res exprimere solent) [Trans.]. Mayor concludes that there was a use of the term *res* to mean "clothes," and he has drawn attention to the similar idiom in English: "things" = "clothes" (cf. the German word *Sachen*).

34 Mayor refers to Epistle of Jeremiah 11, where it is said of silver, golden, and wooden gods that they "cannot save themselves from rust and moths" (οὐ διασώζονται ἀπὸ ἰοῦ καὶ βρωμάτων) [trans. Charles, *APOT*]; cf. also Epistle of Jeremiah 23, where the "rust" of gold is mentioned. Here the term ἰός is probably used in a broader sense.—Windisch concludes that Jas must be from a lower social class since he appears not to be well acquainted with gold and silver and their properties.

35 See below on v 3b.

the other hand, some[38] have taken the opposite approach and have interpreted v 3b in accordance with vv 2, 3a: Rust is for the rich a witness that they themselves are perishing. Yet in both cases the simple meaning of the statement, which is also indicated by the tradition, is sacrificed for the dubious advantage of establishing homogeneity in the whole passage.

■ **3c** That it is the homogeneity which must be sacrificed, however, is shown by what follows. Still a third motif for rust is introduced. Now rust is no longer a sign of perishableness nor a testimony against the rich and their lack of mercy, but rather a threat: Rust will eat your own flesh—i.e., you yourself will perish just as your riches.

"Flesh" ($\sigma\acute{a}\rho\kappa\epsilon s$) is used here as in Jdth 16:17: "fire and worms he will give to their flesh" ($\delta o\hat{v}\nu a\iota$ $\pi\hat{v}\rho$ $\kappa a\grave{\iota}$ $\sigma\kappa\acute{\omega}\lambda\eta\kappa a s$ $\epsilon\grave{\iota}s$ $\sigma\acute{a}\rho\kappa a s$ $a\mathring{v}\tau\hat{\omega}\nu$). Therefore, it is obviously correct that most modern scholars assume the phrase "as fire" ($\acute{\omega}s$ $\pi\hat{v}\rho$) to be connected with this clause and not with the next,[39] for the use of the word "to eat" ($\acute{\epsilon}\sigma\theta\acute{\iota}\epsilon\iota\nu$) suggests the comparison with fire.[40] But if "as fire" does go with this clause, it is also obvious that v 3c represents a unit which is complete in itself, and it is perhaps even an independent saying which has been taken over and introduced into this context.[41] *1 En.* 94ff, in particular, offers parallels to such a threat.

■ **3d** The difficulty in the text tradition is reflected also in v 3d. Not only have there been various attempts to connect this last abrupt clause with the preceding words,[42] but those who have rejected such a connection have even created an object for the verb "to treasure up" ($\theta\eta\sigma a\upsilon\rho\acute{\iota}\zeta\epsilon\iota\nu$). By analogy with Rom 2:5, various interpreters have tacitly inserted "wrath" ($\dot{o}\rho\gamma\acute{\eta}\nu$), or have made other conjectures.[43] But the different improvizations mutually discredit one another. $\theta\eta\sigma a\upsilon\rho\acute{\iota}\zeta\epsilon\iota\nu$ needs no object, at least not here, where all the emphasis lies upon the second part of the clause: Even in the Last Days, the Eschaton, the rich have collected treasure. The accusation found in *1 En.* 94.8: "You have not remembered the Most High in the days of your riches" (trans. Charles, *APOT*), is strengthened here in Jas because of the certainty that the Eschaton has already dawned.

To be sure, the clause stands quite isolated in the present context, but formally it belongs with vv 5, 6, where the perspective which looks back from a position at the time of the end is maintained. Since v 4, which stands in between, has its formal parallels in *Hermas* (see below), it can be conjectured that vv 3d, 5, 6 really belong together. They would then have been separated from one another by an example (v 4) for the first accusation. This explanation is naturally only a hypothesis, but it is one which has several points in its favor given the mosaic character of the whole piece.

---

36 $\dot{v}\mu\hat{\iota}\nu$ is the dative of disadvantage (*dativus incommodi*).

37 See above in the Introduction, section 6. Cf. *1 En.* 96.7: "Woe to you who work unrighteousness and deceit and blasphemy: It shall be a memorial against you for evil" (trans. Charles, *APOT*).

38 E.g., Beyschlag, Windisch-Preisker.

39 An example of the attempt to connect it with what follows is the interpretation of Oec: "Your riches, which you have treasured up as fire, will devour your flesh" ($\dot{o}$ $\pi\lambda o\hat{v}\tau o s$ $\dot{v}\mu\hat{\omega}\nu$, $\dot{o}\nu$ $\dot{\omega}s$ $\pi\hat{v}\rho$ $\dot{\epsilon}\theta\eta\sigma a\upsilon\rho\acute{\iota}\sigma a\tau\epsilon$, $\kappa a\tau a\phi\acute{a}\gamma\epsilon\tau a\iota$ $\tau\grave{a}s$ $\sigma\acute{a}\rho\kappa a s$ $\dot{v}\mu\hat{\omega}\nu$); cf. the similar translations in sy^{vg} aeth m: "Your gold and silver which you have stored up in the last days has rusted, and its rust will be a testimony against you and devour your flesh as fire" (aurum et argentum vestrum quod reposuistis in novissimis diebus aeruginavit et aerugo eorum in testimonium vobis erit et comedit carnes vestras sicut ignis) [Trans.]. Also, the reading $\tau\epsilon\theta\eta\sigma a\acute{v}\rho\iota\sigma\tau a\iota$ ("it has been stored up") in Ψ has in mind a connection of v 3c with v 3d.

40 Cf. Isa 30:27: "His passionate wrath devours like fire" ($\dot{\eta}$ $\dot{o}\rho\gamma\grave{\eta}$ $\tau o\hat{v}$ $\theta\upsilon\mu o\hat{v}$ $\dot{\omega}s$ $\pi\hat{v}\rho$ $\ddot{\epsilon}\delta\epsilon\tau a\iota$). Cf. further, Amos 5:6; Isa 10:16f; Ezek 15:7; Ps 21:9; Rev 11:5; 20:9. On the future form $\phi\acute{a}\gamma o\mu a\iota$ instead of $\ddot{\epsilon}\delta o\mu a\iota$, see Blass-Debrunner, § 74.2.

41 Recognizing this might help to explain a text-critical question in this verse: the reading which has "rust" ($\dot{o}$ $\dot{\iota}\acute{o}s$) inserted again before "as fire" ($\dot{\omega}s$ $\pi\hat{v}\rho$) would be the original reading for this saying. These words were later omitted, since the second mention of the subject seemed superfluous in its present context. Von Soden (*Schriften*, part 2, *ad loc.*) believes that recension *H* included this reading. It is found in $\aleph^c$ A P 33 1175 81 sy^{hl}. It is omitted in the Koine text and in B $\aleph^*$ Ψ and all the Latin versions. O. Kirn, "Noch einmal Jakobus 4, 5," *ThStKr* 77 (1904): 595, n. 1, would like to solve the difficulty which is undoubtedly present here by omitting $\dot{\omega}s$ $\pi\hat{v}\rho$ as a gloss which would originally have read $\dot{o}$ $\dot{\iota}\acute{o}s$ $\pi\hat{v}\rho$.

42 See above, n. 39.

43 Windisch–Preisker suggests "treasures" ($\theta\eta\sigma a\upsilon\rho o\acute{v}s$). Part of the vulg text tradition (Amiatinus, but not

■ **4** This verse is then an amplification on the phrase "you have stored up treasure" (ἐθησαυρίσατε). This kind of expanded paraenesis was discussed with regard to 4:11.[44] Here the accusation, which in itself is directed toward the efforts of the rich in general, is particularized against those who hold back the wages from their employees. My hypothesis that this verse is an expansion of the speech stating the indictment in vv 3d, 5, 6, can be supported by the observation that the form and the content here are thoroughly traditional. Just such motifs from the tradition were natural favorites for the expansion of paraenesis by Jewish and Christian teachers.

The form is traditional: An Old Testament solemnity overlies the words. The expression "unto the ears of the Lord Sabaoth" (εἰς τὰ ὦτα κυρίου σαβαώθ) also is probably to be explained from traditional style (see Isa 5:9) rather than from the notion that the "heavenly hosts" of the Lord carry up such prayers to his ears. The parallelism of the clause shows that in v 4a "the wages of the workers cry out"[45] is only a more elevated expression for the idea which v 4b presupposes: "The workers cry out." Traditional phraseology is perhaps at work here. One is reminded most of all of Abel's spilled blood which cries out to God according to Gen 4:10 and *1 En.* 22.5ff. Compare also *1 En.* 47.1: "And in those days shall have ascended the prayer of the right-

eous, and the blood of the righteous from the earth before the Lord of Spirits" (trans. Charles, *APOT*).

The content is also traditional: In legal, prophetic, and paraenetic texts there is repeatedly the warning against the sin of withholding the wages of the workers. Sometimes the warning is that the wages should not remain with the employer,[46] at other times, that the workers must not be robbed.[47] The cries to God of those who have been cheated is also a traditional theme.[48] This motif is encountered in the small paraenesis in *Herm. vis.* 3.9. There, however, it is applied to the relationship between the rich and the poor in general, and to good deeds which have been omitted:[49] "Watch out then, you who rejoice in your wealth, lest the destitute groan, and their groans go up to the Lord" (βλέπετε οὖν ὑμεῖς οἱ γαυρούμενοι ἐν τῷ πλούτῳ ὑμῶν, μήποτε στενάξουσιν οἱ ὑστερούμενοι καὶ ὁ στεναγμὸς αὐτῶν ἀναβήσεται πρὸς τὸν κύριον *Herm. vis.* 3.9.6) [Loeb modified]. Both the similarities as well as the differences between this text and that in Jas are evidence that the motif of our text was familiar elsewhere in early Christianity.[50]

■ **5** Now the author continues the accusation begun in v 3d. Also because of their content these verses belong together.[51] The rich are not reproached here for a specific act of injustice as in v 4, but simply for the fact that they have gathered treasure and have lived riot-

---

Fuldensis) inserts an object: "you treasure up wrath" (thesaurizastis iram).

44 See the Analysis preceding that section.

45 The verb "to cry out" (κράζειν) can be explained from the tradition, and does not need to be completed here by ἀφ' ὑμῶν. ἀπό does not mean "because of" here, but rather is used in the agential sense of ὑπό (Blass-Debrunner, § 210.2).

46 Lev 19:13: "The wages of the worker shall not remain with you until morning" (οὐ μὴ κοιμηθήσεται ὁ μισθὸς τοῦ μισθωτοῦ παρὰ σοὶ ἕως πρωΐ); Tob 4:14: "Do not hold over till the next day the wages of any man who works for you, but pay him at once" (μισθὸς παντὸς ἀνθρώπου ὃς ἐὰν ἐργάσηται παρὰ σοὶ μὴ αὐλισθήτω, ἀλλὰ ἀπόδος αὐτῷ παραυτίκα); *Test. Job* 12.4 (text in J. Armitage Robinson, *Apocrypha anecdota*, vol. 2, TS 5, 1 [Cambridge: University Press, 1897], 111): "I did not allow the worker's wages to remain with me" (οὐκ ἔων μισθὸν μισθωτοῦ ἀπομεῖναι παρ' ἐμοί another manuscript has a similar version with οὐκ ὑστέρησα) [Trans.]; probably dependent upon Leviticus, if not in form at least in content, is

Pseudo-Phocylides 19: "Provide the wages to him who has toiled" (μισθὸν μοχθήσαντι δίδου) [Trans.].

47 Mal 3:5: "... and upon those who steal the wages of the worker" (καὶ ἐπὶ τοὺς ἀποστεροῦντας μισθὸν μισθωτοῦ); Sir 34:22: "To take away a neighbour's living is to murder him; to deprive an employee of his wages is to shed blood" (φονεύων τὸν πλησίον ὁ ἀφαιρούμενος συμβίωσιν καὶ ἐκχέων αἷμα ὁ ἀποστερῶν μισθὸν μισθίου).

48 Deut 24:14f: "You shall not withhold wrongfully the wages of the poor . . . you shall pay him that very day . . . because he is poor and depends upon his pay, and he will cry out against you to the Lord, and you will be guilty of sin" (οὐκ ἀπαδικήσεις μισθὸν πένητος . . . αὐθημερὸν ἀποδώσεις τὸν μισθὸν αὐτοῦ . . . ὅτι πένης ἐστὶν καὶ ἐν αὐτῷ ἔχει τὴν ἐλπίδα, καὶ καταβοήσεται κατὰ σοῦ πρὸς Κύριον, καὶ ἔσται ἐν σοὶ ἁμαρτία).

49 See above, on v 3b.

50 The position of Jas 5:4 in the tradition is not without significance for the text-critical questions in this verse. Only B* ℵ have "withheld" (ἀφυστερημένος),

238

ously—"on earth," i.e., the words are spoken from the viewpoint of an eschatological position at the End of the time.

The expression "day of slaughter" (ἡμέρα σφαγῆς) raises some questions. Certainly it, too, comes from the tradition, but the parallel passages in Jer 12:3 and *1 En.* 16.1 (Greek) are not entirely clear. If the Day of Judgment is intended,[52] then it is best interpreted in accordance with v 3: You have dared to fatten yourselves at the Last Time, indeed, on the very Day of Judgment itself.[53] But every solemnly mentioned day does not have to be the Day of Judgment. In the context of this ardor of the pietism of the Poor, "the day of slaughter" could also mean any day of disaster upon which things turned out terribly only for the poor, or upon which the poor had to suffer precisely from the rich. Cf. *1 En.* 100.7: "Woe to you, Sinners, on the day of strong anguish, you who afflict the righteous and burn them with fire: you shall be requited according

to your works" (trans. Charles, *APOT*). Thus, the sense in Jas could be: You can live riotously while it goes badly for the pious.[54] A certain confirmation of this meaning is provided by the following verse.[55]

■ **6** The rich are now accused of the most severe of transgressions, the unrighteous judgment and murder of the righteous. This is intended to be a general accusation (Cassiodorus and Oec apply it to Christ) and not a reference to a specific instance. For such accusations run down through the centuries through the literature of the Poor.[56] Joined to the accusation here is the comment, "He offers you no resistance"—i.e., he cannot defend himself. The lack of a conjunction and the change of tense is not surprising in this style, which is modeled after Old Testament parallelism.[57]

In content, the best parallels are offered by Wisd 2:10, 12, where the rich reveller devises a plan against the righteous: "Let us oppress the righteous poor; let us not spare the widow nor regard the gray hairs of the

while all the others have "stolen" (ἀπεστερημένος or ἀποστερημένος). Therefore, if one considers the group evidence and not that of individual witnesses, the latter reading will be accepted. Yet the possibility exists that the widespread reading has only occurred because of adjustment of the text to the tradition (see n. 47) by ancient editors, and that B* and ℵ have retained the original text.

This verse is instructive from a methodological point of view. The modern textual critics prior to von Soden, in accordance with their high regard for the oldest manuscripts, had placed the B* ℵ reading in the text. Von Soden, however, understood B ℵ as representatives of one recension, and a recension of which the other representatives were all opposed to B ℵ in this instance. Therefore, von Soden had no basis for accepting the reading "withheld" (ἀφυστερημένος) which could appeal to no recension for its support (von Soden, *Schriften*, part 2, *ad loc.*).

The other variants in this verse are neither methodologically nor materially as significant: εἰσελήλυθαν B P 1175 81; εἰσεληλύθασιν ℵ and most others (A *et al.* have εἰσελήλυθεν). On the frequency of the first form of the perfect, cf. Blass-Debrunner, § 83.1. For "who have mowed" (ἀμησάντων) and "who have harvested" (θερισάντων), *ff* has "who have ploughed" (qui araverunt) and "who have harvested" (qui messi sunt), perhaps merely to fulfill the need for variety. Two different terms have not been found by *s* and vulg, but rather, "who harvested" (qui messuerunt) is written first, and then after that, "their cry" (clamor ipsorum).

51   Cf. above, on v 3d.
52   So Spitta and Beyschlag.
53   For σφαγή used of judgment, cf. Isa 34:2; cf. also *1 En.* 94.9: "You have . . . become ready for the day of slaughter, and the day of darkness and the day of great judgment" (trans. Charles, *APOT*). The idea that ἐν here = εἰς: "just for the Day of Judgment," reads too much into the text.
54   So Windisch-Preisker. The reading "on the day of slaughter" (ἐν ἡμέρα σφαγῆς) is supported by B ℵ* P 33 and all the Latin versions (A has the plural ἡμέραις, by analogy with v 3). All the others have "*as* on the day of slaughter" (ὡς ἐν ἡμέρα σφαγῆς). As a result, von Soden again (see above, n. 50) preferred the second reading. However, I still believe it to be an emendation which gives the difficult text a metaphorical character and wishes to interpret it: as beasts which glut themselves even on the day of their slaughter. Cf. aeth: "as one who fattens the ox on the day of *its* slaughter."
55   If, with Aland, "Der Herrenbruder," 103, one brings into consideration the ancient church's interpretation of "the righteous man" (δίκαιος) in v 6 as Christ, then "the day of slaughter" must be the crucifixion. The objection of Hauck, 222f, that nowhere in the Gospels is the death of Jesus blamed upon the rich, is countered by Aland with a reference to Jas 2:6.
56   See above in the Introduction, section 6.
57   It is also not surprising that various manuscripts, none of which can be seriously considered for the determination of the text here, attempt to improve

aged. . . . Let us lie in wait for the righteous person, because he is inconvenient to us" (καταδυναστεύσωμεν πένητα δίκαιον, μὴ φεισώμεθα χήρας, μηδὲ πρεσβύτου ἐντραπῶμεν πολιὰς πολυχρονίους . . . ἐνεδρεύσωμεν δὲ τὸν δίκαιον, ὅτι δύσχρηστος ἡμῖν ἐστιν). Cf. Wisd 2:19: "Let us test him with insult and torture" (ὕβρει καὶ βασάνῳ ἐτάσωμεν αὐτόν); 2:20 "Let us condemn him to a shameful death" (θανάτῳ ἀσχήμονι καταδικάσωμεν αὐτόν). But this passage is an echo of a complaint which had been resounding for a long time: LXX Isa 3:10 (the scheming of the wicked): "Let us bind the righteous, because he is inconvenient to us" (δήσωμεν τὸν δίκαιον, ὅτι δύσχρηστος ἡμῖν ἐστιν); Prov 1:11: "Let us hide the righteous man in the earth unjustly; let us swallow him alive just as Hades" (κρύψωμεν δὲ εἰς γῆν ἄνδρα δίκαιον ἀδίκως, καταπίωμεν δὲ αὐτὸν ὥσπερ ᾅδης ζῶντα).[58]

Consideration of these parallels provides the proper standpoint for determining the question of the significance of the whole section 5:1–6 within the letter of Jas. In the interpretation of this section, I have emphasized from the outset that here, in contrast with 4:13–16, Jas is traveling on traditional pathways. The same view of the ungodly rich as in 1:10f and also 2:6, 7 is presupposed by Jas here. But predominant in 5:1–6 is a temperament quite different from that in 1:10f. Instead of the teacher who is passing on the treasures of inherited wisdom, we hear in 5:1–6 the prophet who passionately revives again the ancient threats against the rich. Therefore, in spite of the traditional form of the verse, we may ask about the personal occasion for it.

The passage in 2:6f permits the conjecture that Jas has in mind rich enemies of the Christians. Their behavior gives him the opportunity to revive anew all the accusations which the pietism of the Poor had for centuries raised against "the Rich." As a Christian, Jas had an even more particular reason, because the poor Christian could anticipate the longed–for compensation with even greater certainty than the poor Jew had previously because the Christian was convinced of the imminent parousia of the Lord. Therefore, Weep you rich! Jas is no more addressing his Christian audience here than the author of *1 Enoch* is addressing his Jewish audience in the section of woes in *1 En.* 94.6ff. However, the threat against the rich is also a warning for the Christians. The danger exists that with the entrance of the more affluent into the Christian community, an "affluent" attitude might gain entrance as well: Therefore, let it be said to you that this whole world of the rich is doomed to perdition!

Again we observe, as in 4:16, the characteristic difference from the *Shepherd of Hermas*. As *Herm. sim.* 2 shows, many rich people are presupposed as members of the community. Consequently, the warning to the well-to-do in *Hermas* is more moderate. In *Herm. vis.* 3.9.4, only excess is mentioned, not cruel injustice as in Jas 5:4, 6. The admonition is also more specialized: a more just use of riches for the benefit of the poor saves the rich in the coming judgment (*Herm. vis.* 3.9; *Herm. sim.* 1.8f and 2). On the other hand, in our passage it is the old unbroken, one-sided spirit of the traditional literature of the Poor which speaks. Specific urgent objectives are also present here, but they have not been transformed into various particular admonitions, as has been done in *Hermas*. The difference has already been characterized in the comments on 4:16: applied paraenesis in *Hermas*, general (i.e., traditional) paraenesis here.

---

the asyndeton by the insertion of a καί, or by using participial forms such as ἀντιτάσσοντα or ἀντιτασσόμενοι. The conjecture of Richard Bentley (*Bentleii critica sacra*, ed. Arthur Ayres Ellis [Cambridge: Deighton, Bell, 1862], 79) of ὁ κύριος for οὐκ (*OKΣ* for *OYK*) is a similar attempt. If one is convinced of the traditional character of this section, however, the misgivings which lead to such attempts seem unnecessary.

58   Cf. also Amos 5:12 and Isa 53. [Without taking anything away from Dibelius' derivation of the motifs in Jas 5:1–6 from traditional polemic, perhaps one may still ask whether the fiction that the letter is written by the brother of the Lord does not allow there to be in the words "you have murdered the just man" (ἐφονεύσατε τὸν δίκαιον) a veiled, melancholy allusion to the death of James. Isa 3:10 (LXX: "Let us bind the just man" [δήσωμεν τὸν δίκαιον], Masoretic text corrupt?) is applied by Hegesippus to the death of James, in the following form: "Let us take the just man for he is inconvenient, etc." (ἄρωμεν τὸν δίκαιον, ὅτι δύσχρηστος κτλ. in Eus., *Hist. eccl.* 2.23.15); cf. above in the Introduction, section 2—Greeven.]

5

A Series of Sayings on Various Themes

7 Be patient, therefore, brothers and sisters, until the coming of the Lord. Behold, the farmer waits for the precious fruit of the earth, being patient with it until it receives the early and late (rains). 8/ You also be patient. Establish your hearts, for the coming of the Lord is at hand. 9/ Do not grumble against one another, brothers and sisters, lest you be judged; behold the Judge is standing at the doors. 10/ As an example of patience amidst affliction, brothers and sisters, take the prophets who spoke in the name of the Lord. 11/ Behold, we consider those who were steadfast to be blessed. You have heard of the steadfastness of Job, and you have seen the outcome (of the story of Job) which the Lord brought about, for the Lord is compassionate and merciful.

12 Above all, my brothers and sisters, do not swear, either by heaven or by earth nor with any other oath. Let your yes be true and your no be true, so that you may not fall under condemnation.

13 Someone among you is suffering; let him pray. Someone is cheerful; let him sing psalms. 14/ Someone among you is sick; let him call for the elders of the church and let them pray over him, anointing him with oil in the name of the Lord. 15/ And the prayer of faith will heal the sick person and the Lord will restore him to health, and if he has committed sins, he will be forgiven. 16/ Therefore, confess your sins to one another, and pray for one another, that you may be healed. The energetic prayer of a righteous person has great power. 17/ Elijah was just a human like ourselves, and yet he prayed fervently that it might not rain, and it did not rain upon the earth for three years and six months. 18/ Then he prayed again and the heaven gave rain, and the earth brought forth its fruit. 19/ My brothers and sisters, if any one among you wanders from the truth and someone brings him back, 20/ let him know that whoever brings back a sinner from the error of his way will save a soul from death and will cover a multitude of sins.

Analysis

This section does not hold together as a unit, for 5:12 stands in the middle as a totally isolated saying, and 5:7–11 and 5:13–20 have no relation in thought either to this saying or to one another.[1] 5:12 treats the subject of swearing. The following verses contain various

---

1 The isolation of v 12 is recognized by both Beyschlag and Windisch. Spitta assigns the motivation of the saying to circumstances of the period, an assumption which is at least unnecessary. There are no grounds for the hypothesis of von Soden that the sufferings (cf. v 10) could have "achieved the form of legal proceedings" in which the taking of oaths was involved. Belser and Gaugusch read into the text another motive, of which there is again no trace: that it is a matter of an oath spoken as a result of a bad temper or impatience, and therefore the very opposite of the "patience" ($\mu\alpha\kappa\rho\sigma\theta\nu\mu\iota\alpha$) demanded in the preceding passage. Bede's assertion that there is a connection with 3:1ff is scarcely even considered nowadays.

precepts which cannot be traced back to any common underlying theme. 5:7, 8, 10, 11, to be sure, do have something in common, for all these sayings stress patience. However, in the midst of these verses stands the warning in v 9 not to grumble against one another. This warning noticeably disrupts the continuity, since it has scarcely any material connection with the admonition to patience.[2] Vv 7, 8, two verses which no doubt belonged together from the very beginning, have been combined with v 9 probably upon the basis of their common eschatological motivation: The coming of the Lord is near (v 8) = The Judge stands at the door (v 9). Similar reasons are behind the association of v 12 with v 9, for "in order that you might not be judged" ($\ddot{\iota}\nu\alpha$ $\mu\dot{\eta}$ $\kappa\rho\iota\theta\hat{\eta}\tau\epsilon$) is equivalent to "in order that you might not fall under judgment" ($\ddot{\iota}\nu\alpha$ $\mu\dot{\eta}$ $\dot{\upsilon}\pi\dot{o}$ $\kappa\rho\dot{\iota}\sigma\iota\nu$ $\pi\acute{\epsilon}\sigma\eta\tau\epsilon$).

Therefore, it can be accepted as probable that originally 5:7, 8, 9, 12 formed a paraenesis made up solely of sayings. This would then have been expanded in the usual manner by adding a supporting argument to the motif of patience, and perhaps this expansion was first introduced by our author himself. Since 5:7, 8, 9 already constituted a unit, and since the phrase "above all" ($\pi\rho\dot{o}$ $\pi\acute{\alpha}\nu\tau\omega\nu$) in 5:12 perhaps appeared to mark a new paragraph, the expansion would be inserted only after v 9. Such a procedure is not without example in the history of paraenesis. There is also the possibility that 5:12 was added only at a later stage. In any event, it appears to me that vv 7, 8 + 9, and 9 + 12, are connected on the basis of formal association.

Vv 13–20 can also be broken down into individual sayings. Vv 13–15 certainly belong together; they are precepts for particular situations of which the occasion of illness is treated last and in most detail. On the other hand, vv 16–18 deal with the subject of prayer, and only at the beginning is this a matter of prayer for the sick: "in order that you might be healed" ($\ddot{o}\pi\omega\varsigma$ $\dot{\iota}\alpha\theta\hat{\eta}\tau\epsilon$). After that, the subject is simply prayer in general, for otherwise the example of Elijah would not be appropriate. Finally, vv 19, 20 treat the subject of the correction of a brother who has sinned, and therefore a completely different theme is again introduced.

Also in this section, it can only be a question of a connection on the basis of formal association. It can be found in the occurrence of the words "sin" and "sinner" ($\dot{\alpha}\mu\alpha\rho\tau\dot{\iota}\alpha$—$\dot{\alpha}\mu\alpha\rho\tau\omega\lambda\acute{o}\varsigma$). This is a purely external connection by means of catchwords,[3] and it has nothing to do with any connection in thought. For the remark about sins in v 15 forms only an appendix and the mention of sin at the beginning of v 16 is only a prelude, so to speak, for what follows. It is only in the last saying, in vv 19, 20, that the thought about the sins of the brother is really the main subject. If then these sayings really have nothing to do with one another— even the first two (13–15 and 16–18)—then the words "in order that you might be healed" ($\ddot{o}\pi\omega\varsigma$ $\dot{\iota}\alpha\theta\hat{\eta}\tau\epsilon$) must be considered a connecting phrase probably inserted by Jas. The second saying dealt with confession of sins and prayer. The initial specialized application of this to illness, a specialization which is not maintained afterwards, provided the transition between the first and second saying.

Interpretation
■ **5:7–11** *Sayings On Patience.*
■ **7a** This saying urges the audience to await patiently the great change of fortune which will take place at the parousia. Those who believe hat Jas is a Christian document, will see in the expression "the coming of the Lord" ($\pi\alpha\rho\upsilon\sigma\dot{\iota}\alpha$ $\tau\upsilon\hat{\upsilon}$ $\kappa\upsilon\rho\dot{\iota}\upsilon\upsilon$) a reference to the messianic coming of Jesus Christ.

The possibility that this expression could have been used in a Jewish (non-Christian) context has been raised by Spitta[4] in support of his thesis that Jas was originally a Jewish document. In fact, this possibility cannot be totally excluded. "Lord" would then refer to God, as in 3:9 and 5:4, and the parousia would mean the coming of God at the Judgment (cf. *1 En.* 92–105). Jas would then be adopting a Jewish saying here, as he frequently does elsewhere. Yet this hypothesis is by no means necessary. We do not have enough evidence to determine the possibility of a technical use of the term "parousia" among Greek–speaking Jews.[5] The LXX offers no examples of such a usage, and the witnesses which do exist are isolated and sometimes

---

found in passages where the reading of the text is not absolutely certain.[6]

■ **7b, 8** As a model of patience, Jas presents the farmer who calmly awaits the ripening of the "precious fruit of the field." This image is so natural in the context of an eschatological faith that there is no need to suppose any literary dependence between this text and the parable of Jesus in Mk 4:26–29. In the latter text the thought is somewhat more profound: "You have absolutely nothing to do with the (mysterious) process." In Jas the idea is simply, "Do not lose patience."

The image itself contains a peculiar feature the significance of which is disputed: "early and late" (πρόϊμον καὶ ὄψιμον). Most manuscripts add "rain" (ὑετόν) as the obvious interpretation of these terms, but others read "fruit" (καρπόν).[7] The origin of both readings is best explained upon the basis of the text tradition which has the adjectives "early and late" (πρόϊμον καὶ ὄψιμον) without any noun.[8] This text presupposes that these adjectives are technical terms which do not need an explanation. In that case, they are designations for early and late rain. πρόϊμος and ὄψιμος appear with this meaning numerous times in the LXX (Deut 11:14; Hos 6:3; Joel 2:23; Zech 10:1; Jer 5:24). To be sure, they are found there with the noun "rain" (ὑετός), but the regular use of the adjectives within the same context could have led to the omission of the noun. On the other hand, those who favour the interpretation "early and late fruit"[9] can cite only (apart from the secondary textual reading) Jer 24:2 and Hos 9:10, where "early" (πρόϊμος) is used of early figs, but without the term "late" (ὄψιμος) also being used in a parallel fashion. Therefore, this is not a technical use of these terms which could explain the later omission of the noun, and we must conclude that the meaning here is early and late rain.[10]

In Palestine, the climate of which is probably presupposed in the origin of this expression (cf. the Old Testament passages cited above), there are actually three periods of rain: early rains, winter rains, and

explain the juxtaposition of these imperatives.

3   See above in the Introduction, section 1.

4   Also by Grafe, *Stellung und Bedeutung*, 13, and Bousset, *Kyrios Christos*, 291, n. 159 (cf. 372, n. 82).

5   So also Albrecht Oepke, *TDNT* 5, p. 864. A. Feuillet, "Le sens du mot Parousie dans l'Evangile Matthieu—Comparaison entre Matth. 24 et Jac. 5, 1–11," *The Background of the New Testament and Its Eschatology*, ed. W. D. Davies and D. Daube (Cambridge: University Press, 1956), 261–80. Feuillet seeks to prove that παρουσία in Matthew and Jas does not mean the coming of Christ at the end of the world, as in Paul, but rather the appearance of Christ at the historical judgment of the people of Israel. What is to be awaited with patience (5:7) is the punishment of the rich (5:1–6) who have opposed God, mistreated the poor, and murdered Jesus. 5:6b is punctuated by Feuillet as a question. However, that Jas wished to distinguish a final coming of the Lord from this punishment in 5:1–6 is very doubtful. In addition, Feuillet is forced to assign a different meaning to the expression "the close of the age" (συντέλεια τοῦ αἰῶνος) in Matt 24:3 than in Matt 13:39, 40, 49 and 28:20. His attempt, which is defended with every conceivable argument, really only makes clear how hopeless it is to want to bring together over the common denominator of a straight-line historical calendar what is comparable or common among several intersecting conceptions.

6   *Test. Jud.* 22.2: "until the coming of the God of righteousness" (ἕως τῆς παρουσίας θεοῦ τῆς δικαιοσύνης, but these words are lacking in the Armenian version): *Test. Abr.* 13 (J. Armitage Robinson, ed., *The Testament of Abraham*, TS 2, 2 [Cambridge: University Press, 1892], 92) "until his [God's] great and glorious coming" (μέχρι τῆς μεγάλης καὶ ἐνδόξου αὐτοῦ παρουσίας but not in recension B). In *2 Bar.* 55.6, what is mentioned is not the "coming" of the Lord but of the "day of the Almighty." Finally, Josephus uses the term παρουσία for the marvelous epiphany of God, but not in the eschatological sense. Yet it is precisely the eschatological meaning of the term which is beyond doubt in Jas 5:7, 8 (For the passages in Josephus, see A. Schlatter, *Wie sprach Josephus von Gott?* BFTH 14, 1 [Gütersloh: Bertelsmann, 1910], 51).

7   E.g., ℵ_c 1175 *ff* boh sy_hl (ℵ* has καρπὸν τὸν πρόϊμον κτλ.).

8   In such respectable witnesses as P_74 B 1739 sah vulg arm *et al.*

9   Hofmann, Burger, Spitta, Belser.

10   Spitta's argument that "early and late" refer to the parousia, and therefore must be fruit and not rain, assumes that the details of the image are understood

late rains.[11] However, the term used in Jas 5:7 does not refer to this early rain, which must soak the dried-up soil in November or late October before the beginning of the cultivation of the fields, for the rains in our text are something still to come to benefit the farmer who is already waiting for the fruit. But in using these terms Jas has hardly been worried about such agricultural facts. Instead, he has simply employed proverbial expressions from the Old Testament for early and late rain. This is all the more understandable since one of the Old Testament passages mentioned above (Deut 11:14) stands in the second part of the daily confession, the Shema, and the custom of the recitation of the Shema was already established within Judaism by the time of Jas.[12]

The subject of the clause "until (it? he?) receives" ($\check{\epsilon}\omega\varsigma$ $\lambda\acute{\alpha}\beta\eta$)[13] is also disputed. If the reading "fruit" ($\kappa\alpha\rho\pi\acute{o}\nu$) is accepted, or if that is understood to be the meaning of "early and late," then naturally it is the farmer who receives the "early and late fruit." But if "early and late" refers to rain, which appears to me to be correct, then the farmer is only indirectly the recipient, while the actual subject of the verb could be the growing and ripening fruit.[14] The words "with it" ($\dot{\epsilon}\pi$' $\alpha\dot{v}\tau\hat{\omega}$) make this probable, for perhaps these words would not have been placed after the participle "being patient" ($\mu\alpha\kappa\rho o\theta\upsilon\mu\hat{\omega}\nu$) were they not intended to clarify the following clause: The farmer waits for the fruit and is patient *with it* until *it* receives the rain. The application of the metaphor then follows in v 8.

■ **9** This verse is quite isolated,[15] so there is no need to find some sort of connection between the warning not to "grumble against one another" and the preceding saying. Moreover, suppositions regarding the occasion for this warning, such as the suggestion that it alludes

to the opposition between poor and rich,[16] would only be appropriate if this were a letter dealing with concrete situations. Therefore, the saying has reference to *any* grumbling against a neighbour no matter what the reason.

Although the Analysis has shown how vv 7, 8 and v 9 are tied together by the eschatological motivation, no special eschatological significance can be read into this prohibition against grumbling. For example, we do not have here the "rule of repayment in kind" (jus talionis)—"grumble not" = "judge not"—, so that the idea found in Matt 7:1 would be present here.[17] Nor does the saying contain the thought that vengeance is the Lord's and therefore one need not grumble and thus wish for vengeance.[18] The image of the Lord standing before the door[19] is suggested by the apocalyptic imagery of watching and waiting.[20]

■ **10, 11** Now reference is made to examples, but not examples in support of v 9 as one might suppose, but rather of vv 7, 8.[21] In order to understand the terse allusions of the author one must keep in mind the fact that he, and probably many of his readers, are obviously familiar with lists taken over from Judaism which enumerate the glories of righteous people in the Old Testament. Samples of these enumerations, which are arranged either according to specific virtues or according to names, are found in Sir 44ff; Heb 11, and *1 Clem.* 4–19 (the prophets are mentioned in 17.1).[22] We have already seen in 2:21–25 (cf. 5:17) how Jas refers to such "ancient examples" ($\dot{\alpha}\rho\chi\alpha\hat{i}\alpha$ $\dot{v}\pi o\delta\epsilon\acute{i}\gamma\mu\alpha\tau\alpha$).[23]

Furthermore, one must keep in mind how common the notion of the prophets as martyrs was during this period. Evidently this notion had already developed within Judaism under the influence of certain legends (as in *Asc. Isa.* 2.8ff), and perhaps there was also the

---

allegorically—a thought that is certainly far from Jas' mind.

11 Karl Bädeker, *Palestine and Syria: Handbook for Travellers* (New York: Scribner [5]1912), pp. xlix–l. The difficulty discussed here appears to have been noticed also by Ewald, who wanted to conclude from Jas 5:7 that the early rain came only after the sowing. Cf. also Gustaf Dalman, *Arbeit und Sitte in Palästina*, vol. 1, Schriften des deutschen Palästina–Instituts 3, 1, ed. G. Dalman (Gütersloh: Bertelsmann, 1928), 122ff, 160ff, 302ff.

12 See above, on 2:19.

13 This is the reading of the Koine text and also B A Ψ. Others (e.g., $\aleph$ 33 P 1175) read $\check{\epsilon}\omega\varsigma$ $\check{\alpha}\nu$.

14 Gebser, von Soden, Mayor, Ropes.

15 Cf. above, in the Analysis.

16 So de Wette.

17 So von Soden.

18 So de Wette.

19 Whether this is Christ or God is uncertain (cf. above, on 5:7).

20 Cf. the close parallels in Rev 3:20 and 3:3; Mk 13:34; Matt 24:45ff = Lk 12:42ff; Mk 13:29 = Matt 24:33.

influence of a cult centered around the tombs of martyrs, a phenomenon which can be deduced from Matt 23:29–31.[24] But Jesus and the Christians put special emphasis upon this idea. Their own struggle with Judaism was justified by recalling the misdeeds of the Jews against the prophets (cf. Matt 5:12; 23:29–39; Mk 12:1ff). This notion was frequently held up as an accusation against the Jews, by their own fellow–believers (Dan 9:6; *Test. Levi* 16), and especially by the Christians (cf. Acts 7:52; Justin, *Dial.* 16). Allusions to prophet–martyrs are found in Heb 11:33ff and Justin, *Dial.* 120.5. These passages, which are to some extent very general in their content, prohibit us from placing too great a limitation on the category of "prophets" in Jas 5:10. It is very possible that Jas also

had in mind the heroes of the Maccabaean period, whose "suffering" (κακοπάθεια *4 Macc.* 9.8)[25] is extolled in 2 Maccabees and *4 Maccabees*, or the men in the fiery furnace (*1 Clem.* 45.7),[26] who are mentioned along with Abraham, Isaac, and Daniel in *4 Macc.* 16.20f, and between Abraham and Elijah in Justin, *Apol.* 1.46.3.

■ **11** Continuing along the lines of this martyr–eulogy is v 11, which praises people who were steadfast[27] and then mentions one of the most popular of their number,

---

21 Cf. above, in the Analysis.

22 *1 Clem.* 4–6 contains a rather detailed list of instances in which jealousy (ζῆλος) had disastrous consequences. Cf. a similar list in *P. Oxy.* XV, 1785.2–4, under the heading "because of sexual intercourse" (ἕνεκεν συνουσιασμοῦ): 1. Susanna, 2. the wife of the "chief cook" (ἀρχιμάγειρος LXX Gen 39:1) and Joseph, 3. the tribe of Benjamin (Judg 19; 20), 4. the Sodomites (Gen 19).

23 *1 Clem.* 5.1. ὑπόδειγμα occurs also in 2 Macc 6:28, 31 and *4 Macc.* 17.23 with relationship to martyrdom, and also in Sir 44:16 (of Enoch).

24 Cf. J. Wellhausen, *Das Evangelium Matthaei* (Berlin: Reimer, 1904), *ad loc.*

25 On the independence of the form κακοπαθία alongside the proparoxytonone κακοπάθεια, cf. Winer-Schmiedel, 44f. Characteristically, ℵ has put in place of this word the Hellenistic ideal of "nobleness" (καλοκἀγαθία), a word which occurs in early Christian literature only in Ign., *Eph.* 14.1.

On the words τῆς κακοπαθίας καὶ τῆς μακροθυμίας, Gudmund Björck, "Quelques cas de ἐν διὰ δυοῖν dans le Nouveau Testament et ailleurs," *Con Neot* 4 (1940): 1–4, following the lead of G. Rudberg ("Ad usum circumscribentem praepositionum graecarum adnotationes," *Eranos* 19 [1919–20]: 173ff) calls attention to the fact that a hendiadys in the genitive sometimes occurs merely for the sake of avoiding a series of dependent genitives, and therefore Björck argues that it need not be translated as a co-ordination. Consequently, he suggests that Jas 5:10 be translated, "Take the prophets as an example of patience *amidst* affliction." Other examples are Acts 14:17: "joy *for* food"; 23:6: "hope *in* the resurrection." Cf. Blass-Debrunner, § 442.16.

26 A different conclusion is not made necessary by the

relative clause "who spoke in the name of the Lord" (οἳ ἐλάλησαν ἐν τῷ ὀνόματι Κυρίου [Koine A Ψ 33 *et al.* have simply τῷ ὀνόματι. ἐν ὀνόματι and ἐπὶ τῷ ὀνόματι also occur. These expressions are all synonymous; cf. Heitmüller, "*Im Namen Jesu*," 23f, 38; Deissmann, *Bible Studies*, 197f]). For this Old Testament expression does not make a distinction between true and false prophets, but only says that the prophet calls upon "the Lord" in the sense of speaking or confessing his name (Heitmüller, "*Im Namen Jesu*," 38ff). Therefore, the martyrs mentioned above could be included in this category, since the literature attributes hymns and speeches to them, as well as a great number of other figures in the Old Testament who may be called "prophetic" in the wider sense of the term (so also Belser and Mayor). Bede calls Zechariah, Uriah, and the Maccabbees "martyrs." Significant also are the variants to Heb 11:32: after the mention of Gideon, Barak, Samson, Jephthah, David, and Samuel, a number of witnesses read "and the *other* prophets" (καὶ τῶν ἄλλων προφητῶν). On the other hand, the Latin Codex Harleianus adds after "and the prophets" the names of Ananias, Azariah, Mishael, Daniel, Elijah, and Elisha.

27 For an understanding of the relationship between this text and martyr literature some statistics are helpful: "to be steadfast" (ὑπομένειν) occurs in *4 Maccabees* fifteen times and in Job fourteen times; of the twenty-five occurrences of the noun "steadfastness" (ὑπομονή) in the LXX, eleven of them are in *4 Maccabees*. On the verb to consider blessed" (μακαρίζειν), cf. Dan (Th) 12:12: "blessed is the one who is steadfast" (μακάριος ὁ ὑπομένων); *4 Macc.* 7.22: "It is blessed to be steadfast against all affliction for the sake of virtue" (διὰ τὴν ἀρετὴν πάντα πόνον ὑπο-

Job.[28] This might seem strange if one considers the content of the canonical Book of Job, which reports the defiant arguments of its hero with God rather than his patient endurance. Yet the conception of Job as the righteous sufferer, the model of "steadfastness" (ὑπο-μονή), is older than the Book of Job and goes back to the ancient popular legend of Job, who did not sin in spite of all his misfortune (cf. Job 1; 2:1–10; 42:10–16). The proof for the antiquity of the legend is perhaps provided by Ezek 14:14, 20, where Noah, Daniel, and Job are mentioned as typical and obviously well–known examples of righteous men.

The traditional character of such "examples" must be kept in mind in order to explain the difficult words "the end of the Lord" (τὸ τέλος κυρίου). If this is the correct reading of the text,[29] then these words refer to the good outcome of the story of Job.[30] Such an outcome is called an "end" (τέλος or סוֹף) in other texts, and it is precisely Jewish reflection about the past which

is fond of perceiving in stories such as those of Job or Joseph or Daniel the admonition: "Observe the end of the matter."[31] In this context it is also stressed that it is God who brings the outcome. A particularly good example of this is *Test. Gad* 7.4: "If a man becomes wealthy by means of evil, as my father's brother Esau did, do not be jealous but instead await the end of the Lord" (ἐὰν δὲ ἐκ κακῶν τις πλουτήσει, ὡς Ἡσαῦ ὁ πατρά-δελφός μου, μὴ ζηλώσητε· ὅρον δὲ κυρίου ἐκδέξατε) [Trans.]. The sense which "the end of the Lord" has here is shown by the words just before this passage: "examine carefully the judgments of the Lord" (ἐξέτα-σον κρίματα Κυρίου).

In Jas 5:11, also, the "end of the Lord" refers to the visible judgment of God which consists in the happy outcome of a period of suffering, and not, as Spitta interprets it, to the reward in the next world (that would not at all suit the character of the ancient story of Job). Hence, most modern interpreters (but already sy^{vg})

μένειν μακάριόν ἐστιν) [Trans.]. In our text ὑπο-μείναντας is to be preferred over the Koine text which has ὑπομένοντας. Cf. the similar fluctuation of the witnesses between the present and the aorist of ὑπομένειν in Dan 12:12 (Theod) and *4 Macc.* 16.17, 19.

28 *1 Clem.* 17 also mentions Job as an example, along with Elijah, Elisha, Ezekiel, Abraham, and Moses; Clem. Alex., *Strom.* 2.103f mentions Daniel, Job, and Jonah; Abraham and Job are compared in *Test. Abr.* 15 (Rec. A).

29 However, it is debatable whether one must accept the traditional reading. Certainly the reading "mer-cy" (ἔλεος) instead of τέλος (1175 1739 *et al.*) is an emendation suggested by what follows and is not to be taken seriously. Könnecke, *Emendationen*, 17, pro-poses "his" (αὐτοῦ) instead of "of the Lord" (κυρίου). E. Preuschen, "Jac 5, 11," *ZNW* 17 (1916): 79, prefers the hypothesis that after τέλος a verb such as "behold" (θεωροῦντες) has been omitted and in-appropriately replaced by κυρίου. However, when he rejects the interpretation of κυρίου as a subjective genitive on the grounds that that is grammatically impossible, reference must be made both to the con-struction "the end of the Lord" (ὅρος κυρίου) in *Test. Gad* 7.4 (quoted below in the text), where κύριος also lacks the article, and to the explanation in the Catena (see below in n. 30), which seems to have no problem with this meaning of the genitive here. Perhaps the proper meaning of τέλος in this genitive construction is "purpose" or "aim," and it could be maintained that the readers would hear the word

this way and consequently understand the genitive correctly, also. Nevertheless, I still am not without misgivings with regard to the traditional text, due to the fact that the following portion of the verse is not entirely certain text-critically either (see below, n. 35).

30 Cf. Catena: "For from the outcome of the matter [i.e., involving Job] both the slander of the devil and the truthful testimony of God were revealed" (ἐκ γὰρ τῆς ἐκβάσεως τῶν πραγμάτων ἐδείχθη καὶ ἡ τοῦ διαβόλου συκοφαντία καὶ ἡ τοῦ θεοῦ ἀψευδὴς μαρ-τυρία).

31 *Test. Ben.* 4.1: "Therefore, my children, behold the end of the good man [Joseph]" (ἴδετε οὖν, τέκνα μου, τοῦ ἀγαθοῦ ἀνδρὸς τὸ τέλος. The variant ἔλεος occurs here also, obviously from a misunderstanding of the sense of τέλος); *Test. Asher* 6.4: "The ends of people reveal their righteousness" (τὰ τέλη τῶν ἀνθρώπων δεικνύουσι τὴν δικαιοσύνην αὐτῶν) [Trans.]; cf. the warning against a bad end in *4 Macc.* 12.3: "You see the end of your brothers' folly" (τῆς μὲν τῶν ἀδελ-φῶν σου ἀπονοίας τὸ τέλος ὁρᾷς) [Trans.]; Wisd 3:19: "For the end of an unrighteous generation is griev-ous" (γενεᾶς γὰρ ἀδίκου χαλεπὰ τὰ τέλη); *Pirke Aboth* 1:5: "and his end is that he inherits Gehenna" (וְסוֹפוֹ יוֹרֵשׁ גֵּיהִנָּם) [trans. Charles, *APOT*]. In Wisd 2:16c the ungodly say of the pious man, "He calls the last end of the righteous blessed" (μακαρίζει ἔσχατα δικαίων), and in 2:17b, "let us test what will happen at the end of his life" (πειράσωμεν τὰ ἐν ἐκ-βάσει αὐτοῦ); cf. Heb 13:7: "consider the outcome of their life, and imitate their faith" (ὧν ἀναθεω-

246

have understood the words to mean the outcome of the story of Job. Others[32] believe that "the end of the Lord" refers to the end (i.e., suffering and death) of Jesus. Yet precisely the traditional character of such examples invalidates all the arguments which are adduced in support of this interpretation. For example, one of these arguments is that it could not refer to the end of Job's life because according to Job 42:16 the hero lived another 140 years. But τέλος in the technical sense in which it is used here does not mean the end of one's life, but the outcome of the story—in this case, the outcome of the period of suffering.[33] A more weighty objection is that from the plural in v 11a ("those who were steadfast") one ought to expect more than one example; hence, the author must be including both "the steadfastness of Job" and "the suffering and death of the Lord." However, as was shown, Jas touches in v 11a upon an entire chain of thoughts which is very familiar to both him and his readers. Thus, he needs to mention only one example—Job.

Finally, the traditional nature of paraenetic material accounts for the fact that in this verse the Christian author has not referred to the example of Jesus Christ, in the manner of 1 Petr 2:21. The Christianization of paraenetic material which Christians borrowed from Judaism and popular philosophy was not such a matter of course, nor accomplished so swiftly, as is commonly thought.[34] At first—and there is no way to establish fixed chronological boundaries for this—the Jewish lists of examples were simply repeated, without using the example of Jesus. The rigidity of the tradition itself was partly responsible for this. Perhaps another factor was that the Christians thought about their Lord—and especially about his "outcome"—in a different way than they did about the righteous and martyrs in the Old Testament. Thus, the inclusion of the life of Jesus among the other "examples" (ὑποδείγματα) did not immediately suggest itself to them. Therefore, an interpretation that finds Jesus in Jas 5:11 is out of the question. The use of "Lord" in two senses within the same verse, which would be presupposed if there were such an illusion, would already make this interpretation questionable.

The problems in the remainder of v 11 are largely textual. If the imperative "behold" (ἴδετε) is read,[35] it is best to place a full stop after "Lord" and begin a new sentence with "behold": "You have heard about the patience of Job and the outcome which the Lord

---

32 From Augustine, *Ep.* 140.10.26, *De symbolo ad catechumenos* 1.3.10, and Bede, to Schmidt, *Lehrgehalt*, 76, Karl Werner, "Ueber den Brief Jacobi," *ThQ* 54 (1872): 258, and A. Bischoff, "τὸ τέλος κυρίου," *ZNW* 7 (1906): 274–9.

33 τέλος is used in this way also in the trial scene in Matt 26:58: It is not the end of Jesus' life which Peter is waiting to see, but rather "how things would turn out."

34 1 Peter is evidence for a relatively advanced stage in this process, as a comparison of its rules for the household (2:18–3:12) with those in Colossians (3:18–4:1) reveals.

ροῦντες τὴν ἔκβασιν τῆς ἀναστροφῆς μιμεῖσθε τὴν πίστιν). But also in Imperial Rome from the time of Claudius there can be demonstrated a literature which deals with "the ends of the lives of eminent men" (exitus inlustrorum virorum); see R. Reitzenstein, "Ein Stück hellenistischer Kleinliteratur," *NGG* (1904): 327–32; *idem, Hellenistische Wundererzählungen* (Stuttgart: Teubner, 1906), 37, n. 3; *idem,* "Die Nachrichten über den Tod Cyprians: Eine philologischer Beitrag zur Geschichte der Märtyrerliteratur," *SAH* 4,14 (1913): 52, n. 2.

35 B* ℵ Ψ K and many others read the aorist "you have seen" (εἴδετε) although several do have the imperative (e.g., Bᶜ A L 33); the form οἴδατε occurs in isolated cases. "The textual evidence excludes εἴδετε as the reading of [recension] *I* and probably also *H*" (von Soden, *Schriften*, part 1, p. 1888). By these criteria, it would be preferable to decide against the smoother reading εἴδετε, which more closely approximates the "you have heard" (ἠκούσατε) earlier in the verse. However, it may be that only an itacistic vowel change underlies this uncertainty in the text. In that case, neither the criterion of the textual witnesses, nor any text-critical formula, could allow a decision here. Yet the judgment to be made about the construction is dependent upon just this decision. Karl Werner, "Ueber den Brief Jacobi," *ThQ* 54 (1872), 258n, solves the problem by conjecturing that both forms were originally in the text: "and you know the end of the Lord. Behold that . . ." (καὶ τὸ τέλος κυρίου εἴδετε· ἴδετε, ὅτι κτλ.). ἴδετε would

247

provided. Behold! The Lord is compassionate . . . ."[36] With the reading "you have seen" (εἴδετε), it is possible to construe the following clause as an explanation of what precedes it: "You have seen the outcome which the Lord provided (and in that you have seen) that the Lord is . . . ." However, a causal understanding of ὅτι would then seem simpler: "*for* the Lord is . . . ." The word for "compassionate" (πολύσπλαγχνος) here is used only in this verse and *Herm. mand.* 4.3.5 (cf. *Herm. sim.* 5.7.4). In the *Hermas* passage it is also used of the "Lord," meaning God.

■ **12** Since this verse has no relationship with what precedes or follows,[37] nothing can be determined about the significance of the phrase "above all" (πρὸ πάντων). For we do not know whether these words originate from another context, or whether Jas himself has inserted them here.[38]

The Prohibition Against Swearing

In Jewish paraenesis, the way for this absolute prohibition of swearing is at least prepared by the prohibition of frivolous swearing. For example, in Sir 23:9–11 the "man who swears many oaths" (πολύορκος)

is reproached. A statement from Epictetus has the same intention.[39] A total prohibition of oaths did not prevail in Judaism, probably out of regard for the Old Testament, which contains frequent oaths.[40] Pseudo–Phocylides 16 prohibits only perjury. A prohibition of oaths is probably ascribed to Pythagoras, however,[41] and it is a well–known question whether there was Pythagorean and Cynic–Stoic influence upon certain elements within Judaism, such as the Essenes and Philo. The Essenes forbade oaths in general,[42] but were required to take a solemn oath upon initiation.[43] As is so often the case, we find in Philo instructions of the most diverse nature on this subject. Quite in the spirit of Epictetus, he urges that one should at least avoid oaths as much as possible.[44] In grandiose style, he asserts the transcendence of God above oaths, and therefore rejects swearing by God himself.[45] However, in the treatise against frivolous oaths he gives advise regarding the use of rather petty devices in order to avoid the name of God.[46] Among the substitutes for the divine name in oaths which he mentions, and which were obviously current in his environment, we encounter the practice of swearing by the parts of the

---

then be resuming the introductory ἰδού.

36 Cf. Hofmann, Beyschlag; cf. the construction in 2:22a.

37 Cf. above, in the Analysis.

38 ὀμνύετε is the Hellenistic form of the imperative here, as opposed to the classical imperative σβέννυτε in 1 Thess 5:19. However, the construction with the accusative of the god by whom the oath is taken is the classical construction (cf. Blass-Debrunner, § 149).

39 Epict., *Enchr.* 33.5: "Avoid an oath, altogether if you can, and if not, then as much as possible under the circumstances" (ὅρκον παραίτησαι, εἰ μὲν οἷόν τε, εἰς ἅπαν, εἰ δὲ μή, ἐκ τῶν ἐνόντων) [Trans.].

40 Islam also knows no prohibition of oaths, only a warning against excessive swearing and the relaxing of the obligation to an oath in the case of thoughtless swearing. Cf. Johs. Pedersen, *Der Eid bei den Semiten in seinem Verhältnis zu verwandten Erscheinungen sowie die Stellung des Eides im Islam*, Studien zur Geschichte und Kultur des islamischen Orients 3, ed. C. H. Becker (Strassburg: Trübner, 1914), 196f.

41 Diog. Laert. 8.22; Iambl., *Vit. Pyth.* 47; cf. also P. Wendland, review of Theodor Zahn, *Der Stoiker Epiktet*, in *ThLZ* 20 (1895): 494. Adolf Bonhöffer, *Die Ethik des Stoikers Epictet* (Stuttgart: Enke, 1894), 113f: "I know of no statement from the earlier Stoics

which would prohibit the use of oaths or even place a limitation upon it." For that reason he presumes that the prohibition of oaths in Epictetus (see above, n. 39) is a result of Pythagorean influence. However, in his book *Epiktet und das NT*, 30f, he has withdrawn this conjecture and suggested instead that the prohibition of oaths in the *Enchiridion* is to be understood upon the basis of the special purpose of this document: to be a handbook for the close circle of students. Cf. also Franz Mörth, "Epiktet und sein Verhältnis zum Christentum," *Festschrift der 50. Versammlung Deutscher Philologen und Schulmänner* (Graz: Selbstverlag des Festausschusses, 1909), 178–94. Cf. Karl Prächter, "Bericht über die Litteratur zu den nacharistotelischen Philosophen (mit Ausschluss der älteren Akademiker und Peripatetiker und von Lukrez, Cicero, Philon und Plutarch) für 1889–1895," *Jahresbericht über die Fortschritte der classischen Altertumswissenschaft* 96 (1898): 39f: "upon closer examination . . . this prohibition (i.e., against oaths) in Epictetus can be recognized as a part of a complex of precepts which intrinsically belong together. For the restrained and reflective Stoic, who avoids idle speech, excessive and loud laughter, as well as participation in the usual social enjoyments, the fervor and intense effort to obtain credence from another person which go with swearing are also im-

cosmos (*Spec. leg.* 2.5): "But also a person may add to his "Yes" or "No" if he wish, not indeed the highest and most venerable and primal cause, but earth, sun, stars, heaven, the whole universe" (ἀλλὰ καὶ προσπαραλαβέτω τις, εἰ βούλεται, μὴ μέντοι τὸ ἀνωτάτω καὶ πρεσβύτατον εὐθὺς αἴτιον, ἀλλὰ γῆν, ἥλιον, ἀστέρας, οὐρανόν, τὸν σύμπαντα κόσμον). Rabbinic Judaism also knows of such weakened substitute formulae.[47]

Measured against these parallels, therefore, Jas 5:12 appears to be a radicalization of an ethical tendency which is recognizable elsewhere. It is a moral admonition which is therefore prompted by circumstances such as those which Philo criticizes in *Decal.* 92: There are men who are all too accustomed to swear at every opportunity out of mere habit and without thinking. Since this admonition has to do chiefly with the morality of individuals, the question of the propriety of taking an oath in social contexts, such as in a court, recedes totally into the background. For one would not think of a Christianization of these social contexts at this point in time. However, for that very reason, it cannot be asserted that this saying licenses the taking of oaths before a court.

What must be said is that the principal intention of the saying has to do with private assertions, and thus two familiar substitute formulae for oaths are added as examples. But because it is not a question of formulae for specific occasions, but rather a question of the duty to be truthful, the second clause does not mean, "Let your affirmation be a simple 'yes,'"[48] or even, "Let your manner of affirmation be the double 'yes.'"[49] Instead, the clause must be read: "Let your 'yes' be true and your 'no' be true." Therefore, the saying has the same sense as the demand which Pythagoras is supposed to have made in connection with the prohibition of oaths (Iambl., *Vit. Pyth.* 47).[50] The con-

---

proper." A prohibition of oaths is also found in the so-called "Delphic Precept": "Do not use an oath" (ὅρκῳ μὴ χρῶ). Cf. the inscription from Melitopolis (and the parallels provided in the apparatus) in Ditt., *Syll.* III, 1268.

42 Josephus, *Bell.* 2.135; Philo, *Omn. prob. lib.* 84.

43 Josephus, *Bell.* 2.139, 142.

44 Philo, *Decal.* 84: "To swear not at all is the best course and most profitable to life, well suited to a rational nature which has been taught to speak the truth so well on each occasion that its words are regarded as oaths; to swear truly is only, as people say, a 'second-best voyage'" (κάλλιστον δὴ καὶ βιωφελέστατον καὶ ἁρμόττον λογικῇ φύσει τὸ ἀνώμοτον, οὕτως ἀληθεύειν ἐφ' ἑκάστου δεδιδαγμένη, ὡς τοὺς λόγους ὅρκους εἶναι νομίζεσθαι. δεύτερος δέ, φασί, πλοῦς τὸ εὐορκεῖν). Therefore, one should defer taking an oath as long as possible, and if finally it cannot be avoided, then one should consider carefully everything which the oath involves (*Decal.* 85).

45 Upon two occasions Philo deals with the question of why God swears in the Old Testament: *Leg. all.* 3.203ff (on Gen 22:16) and *Sacr. AC.* 91ff (on Ex 13:11). Both times Philo concludes that God can swear only by himself since there is nothing equal to him, let alone better than him. However, human beings cannot swear by God himself, since they do not know his true essence, but only by the name of God (*Leg. all.* 3.207). Humans must have recourse to oaths because of their own unreliability, but the words of God are in themselves as certain as oaths (*Sacr. AC.* 93).

46 *Spec. leg.* 2.2ff: One should swear rather by the health, welfare, or memory of his parents, or say only, "Yes, by—" (νὴ τόν) or, "No, by—" (μὰ τόν), breaking off before actually saying a name.

47 In *b. Shebu.* 35b, also, swearing by heaven and earth is mentioned in this same way, as a weakened formula. Cf. on this August Wünsche, *Neue Beiträge zur Erläuterung der Evangelien aus Talmud und Midrasch* (Göttingen: Vandenhoeck & Ruprecht, 1878), 59.

48 So de Wette, Beyschlag, Spitta, Mayor.

49 This is the interpretation in the reading ἤτω δὲ ὁ λόγος ὑμῶν (ℵ* *et al.* boh vulg [with the exception of a few witnesses]), which is a harmonization of this verse with Matt 5:37. The scholion of Cyril in the Catena (also in Theoph and Scholion [Matthäi, p. 195]) also takes ναὶ ναί, οὒ οὔ to be substitute formula for an oath (ἀντὶ τοῦ ὅρκου). Cf. also Belser: "Let yours be 'yes, yes,' 'no, no.'"

50 So Gebser; B. Weiss, *Jakobusbrief*; Hollmann; Windisch-Preisker. Cf. the interpretation in Theoph (and similarly in Oec): "Instead, let your affirmation be firm and reliable, as also your denial" (ἀντὶ τοῦ, ἡ κατάθεσις ὑμῶν βεβαία καὶ ἐπὶ βεβαίου, καὶ ἡ ἀπαγόρευσις ὑμῶν ὡσαύτως) [Trans.]. Also the reading "lest you fall into hypocrisy" (εἰς ὑπόκρισιν Koine and P), which probably originated in the first place as a misreading of the two separate words "under judgment" (ὑπὸ κρίσιν), might be a similar interpretation. Cf. Didymus on 2 Cor 1:23 (MPG 39, 1688), who cites as the content of the dominical saying: "One must not swear, but rather keep one's word above reproach, regarding his 'yes' as actually yes

clusion of the verse also agrees with this interpretation, for the judgment is not upon everyone who swears,[51] but only upon him whose "yes" does not remain firm. It suits the style of this ethical paraenesis that the prohibition is based upon a general moral concept, and then impressed upon the audience by means of an eschatological threat.

Now we turn to the literary relationships of this saying. It has a well–known parallel in Matt 5:34–37. The saying in Jas, however, cannot be considered simply a paraphrase of the words in the Matthean text, for a form of the saying similar to that in Jas is quoted by a number of early Christian writings. A quotation in Justin, *Apol.* 1.16.5 which in other respects agrees with the version in Matthew has the "Let your yes be yes"–clause in the form found in Jas.[52] This same form occurs in Clement of Alexandria, the *Pseudo–Clementine Homilies*, and Epiphanius.[53] Hence, the saying seems to have been current in two different forms. The fol-

lowing synopsis illustrates the difference in the content:

James	Matthew
Prohibition of all oaths	Prohibition of all oaths
Examples:	Examples:
Heaven	Heaven
Earth	Earth
Or any other oath	Jerusalem
	Head
	Demonstration that to swear by each of these is to swear by God[54]
Injunction of an absolute truthfulness which makes swearing superfluous:	Recommendation of a formula of affirmation to be used in place of an oath:[55]
Let your Yes be Yes	Let what you say be Yes, Yes
Threat of judgment against untruthfulness	Condemnation of anything which goes beyond this

and his 'no' as actually being such" (μὴ δεῖν ὀμνύναι, ἀλλ' ἔχειν λόγον ἀκατάγνωστον περὶ τοῦ ναὶ ὡς ὄντως ναὶ καί τοῦ οὒ ὡς οὕτως ἔχοντος) [Trans.]. The reading "into hypocrisy" (εἰς ὑπόκρισιν) seems to underlie a passage in Possidius of Calama, and therefore the evidence for it is quite old. In his *Vita Augustini* (c. 432 A.D.) we find in chapter 25 (MPL 32, 54): "And lest someone fall *into perjury* by taking a frivolous oath, Augustine both preached publicly in the church and taught privately to his own people that one should not swear—not even at table (Et ne quisquam facili juratione etiam ad perjurium decidisset, et in ecclesia populo praedicabat, et suos instituerat, ne quis juraret, ne ad mensam quidem) [The suggestion of this significance of the Possidius passage was in a correspondence from Adolf von Harnack to Dibelius, dated Jan. 29, 1930].

51 Against von Soden.

52 Justin, *Apol.* 1.16.5: "Do not swear at all, but let your yes be yes and your no be no: anything more than this comes from evil" (μὴ ὀμόσητε ὅλως· ἔστω δὲ ὑμῶν τὸ ναὶ ναί, καὶ τὸ οὒ οὔ· τὸ δὲ περισσὸν τούτων ἐκ τοῦ πονηροῦ) [Trans.]. To be sure, the final words treat the clause "let your yes . . ." as if it contained the short formula of affirmation. Therefore, this version in Justin ought to be viewed as a mixture of the two types. Since Justin otherwise shows no points of contact with Jas, his knowledge of the non-Matthean form must come from elsewhere.

53 Clem. Alex., *Strom.* 5.99.1 (with ἔστω at the beginning). Clement compares with the saying the words of Plato (*Theaet.* 151d): "It is quite out of the ques-

tion for me to agree to a lie or to suppress the truth" (ἀλλά μοι ψεῦδός τε συγχωρῆσαι καὶ ἀληθὲς ἀφανίσαι οὐδαμῶς θέμις) [Loeb modified]. Therefore, Clement understands the saying in the same way as it is interpreted above. He quotes the saying again in *Strom.* 7.67.5 in the same sense; cf. also *Strom.* 7.50.5. *Ps. Clem. Hom.* 19.2.4 offers a mixed form: "Let your yes be yes and your no be no" (ἔστω ὑμῶν τὸ ναὶ ναί, καὶ τὸ οὒ οὔ), and then the final clause from Matthew is added. *Ps. Clem. Hom.* 3.55.1 has exactly the same mixed form, but without the καί. Epiph., *Haer.* 19.6.2 agrees with Jas almost exactly. Cf. the various examples given by Alfred Resch, "Miscellen zur neutestamentlichen Schriftforschung," *ZWL* 9 (1888): 283ff, and Wilh. Bousset, *Die Evangeliencitate Justins des Märtres in ihrem Wert für die Evangelienkritik von neuem untersucht* (Göttingen: Huth, 1891), 72. The Jas form of the saying also appears in a Coptic Gnostic writing, *The Two Books of Jeu* 43: "He charged him not to swear falsely, nor even to swear at all . . . neither to slander falsely nor defame, but let their yes be yes and their no be no" [Trans.]; text in Carl Schmidt, *Gnostische Schriften in koptischer Sprache aus dem Codex Brucianus*, TU 8, 1–2 (Leipzig: Hinrichs, 1892), 102.

54 Therefore, the examples are not introduced here to elucidate the main prohibition, but rather to bring in something new: Behind this passage, but not expressly stated within it, is the Jewish presupposition that swearing by God is to be avoided at all times. It is the validity of this presupposition (and not the prohibition of Jesus in Matt 5:34a) which is brought

If this understanding of the two passages is correct, then the judgment concerning their relationship is certain. The form in Jas displays the character of a simple paraenesis: a single prohibition is reduced to a general precept, and this is reinforced with a threat. The saying in Matthew contains expanded paraenesis in the first part. It presupposes that there will be an attempt to dodge the prohibition by means of a substitute formula, and it refutes this procedure. But the second part of this saying in Matthew is a nomistic modification of the imperative which originally was addressed to the question of a person's moral attitude: now the teaching no longer says what one ought to *be* (i.e., truthful), but rather what one should *say* if one had to make an affirmation. Admittedly, the casuistry of the Jewish practice seen in the Philo examples[56] is not attained here by any means. The simpler, more unified and ethically purer form of the saying in Jas must be considered the earlier form.

But if the priority of the saying in Jas is accepted, the question arises whether this saying is really a saying of Jesus at all, or whether Matthew has placed into the mouth of Jesus a saying from Judaeo–Christian paraenesis—wrongly so, and moreover in the form of a legalistic prescription. This possibility *seems* to be recommended by three facts: 1) Jas does not quote the saying as a dominical saying; 2) it occurs in the Gospels only in Matthew, and it is precisely in Matthew that legal prescriptions of a Jewish origin occasionally appear as dominical sayings; 3) there are Jewish parallels to this saying.[57] But these arguments are only apparently valid. Because of their very nature, the last two naturally prove nothing. Regarding the first argument, the absence of a quotation formula in Jas does not qualify as evidence that the saying about swearing was not regarded as a dominical saying in the time of Jas. Other sayings of Jesus whose provenance is more assured are also used in paraenetic texts without special introductory identification.[58] This is not surprising, for all paraenesis which is delivered by teachers who are considered bearers of the Spirit stems ultimately from the Lord, and therefore it possesses an even higher authenticity than a quotation formula can provide. Probably there were also collections of dominical sayings as such (e.g., the so–called "Sayings Source" [Q]), but that is a completely different process in the history of early Christian paraenesis and not evidence which indicates that this prohibition of oaths in Jas did not originate with Jesus. Of course, if Jas was aware of such a provenance, this would not be important for him in this paraenetic context. Therefore, there is no need to attribute the introductory words "above all" (πρὸ πάντων) and the threat of judgment at the end to a special estimation of this precept as a dominical saying.[59]

■ **13** Jas 5:13–15. *A saying dealing with various life situations.* Only the third circumstance, illness, is treated in more detail. The first two life situations—bad and good circumstances—are treated very generally. But the question which is dealt with throughout is: How must the Christian, if he is devoted to the practice of religion, react to such situations in life? This is the real

---

to bear also upon the substitute oath formulae. Cf. Matt. 23:16ff.

55 This is the obvious meaning of ναὶ ναί in this passage. Cf. the commentaries of H. J. Holtzmann, *Die Synoptiker*, HCNT 1, 1 (Tübingen and Leipzig: Mohr [Siebeck], ³1901), and Erich Klostermann, *Das Matthäusevangelium*, HNT 4 (Tübingen: Mohr [Siebeck], ²1927). Evidence for this is also provided by the occurrence of such a formula in *Mekilta*, tractate *Jithro (Bachodesh)*, section 5, fol. 66b Friedmann. Cf. also below, n. 57.

56 See above, n. 46.

57 *2 En.* 49.1: "I swear to you, my children, but I swear not by any oath, neither by heaven nor by earth, nor by any other creature which God created. The Lord said: 'There is no oath in me, nor injustice, but truth.' If there is no truth in men, let them swear by the words 'yea, yea,' or else, 'nay, nay.'" (49.2 continues: "And I swear to you, yea, yea," etc.) [trans. Charles, *APOT*]. Cf. also *Baba Metzia* 49a: "But it is to teach you that your 'yes' should be just and your 'no' should be just" (trans. Epstein).

58 Cf. Rom 12:14, or the Christian interpolation in the "Two Ways" section in *Did.* 1.3ff; see Dibelius, *From Tradition to Gospel*, 240f.

59 As does Ewald.

sense of the saying, and from this viewpoint the instruction to sing psalms when one is happy is certainly not strange. The circumstance of life in each case is not introduced as a conditional clause ("If someone is . . . then let him . . ."), but rather as an independent sentence ("Someone is . . . Let him . . ."). Such asyndeta belong among the dialogical features of diatribe.[60]

■ **14** The sick person is to call the elders of the community and the latter are to pray over him[61] and anoint him with oil in the name of the Lord. That this is not a recommendation of oil as a natural medication is proven by the formula "in the name of the Lord." For that can only mean "while invoking the name."[62] Irenaeus (*Adv. haer.* 2.6.2) indicates that the Jews had employed the name of God in miraculous healings. Jas 5:14 is also dealing with such a miraculous healing, in which the demon of the disease must yield to the divine power summoned by the invocation of the name. Therefore, the healing is not effected by the oil as a medicine, but by the oil applied along with prayer and the pronouncing of the name. The question can be left open as to whether one or two acts accompany the anointing of the body—i.e., whether the invoking of the name takes place in the prayer or whether it is reserved for a special magical formula. 5:15 mentions only the prayer and therefore would tend to support the first alternative.

The whole procedure is an exorcism. A remedy from folk medicine was frequently applied in such miraculous healings, and such is the role of the oil here and in Mk 6:13.[63] The intention is not to take advantage of its alleged or actual therapeutic effectiveness as a folk medicine, but rather to apply it as a medium of the divine power which is being conjured by means of the name. The result of the entire act is, of course, not only the healing but also the forgiveness of sins.

If this passage were speaking about pneumatics in possession of a charisma, or spiritual gift, then it would be calling for the exercise of the "charismatic" gift of healing, as is mentioned in 1 Cor 12:9, 28, 30. But instead, the reference is to the elders of the church (πρεσβύτεροι τῆς ἐκκλησίας): they must be bearers of the miraculous power by virtue of the fact that they are the elders, for otherwise why would they be called upon and not others? Yet it cannot be said that only old people—perhaps having experience with rem-

---

60 Cf. Blass-Debrunner, § 494. Of more value for our text than the examples from classical literature (and also 1 Cor 7:18, 27) are instances from diatribe style given by Bultmann, *Stil*, 15, especially from Teles, p. 10.6f Hense (2nd edition): "You have become an old man. Do not seek after the things of youth" (γέρων γέγονας· μὴ ζήτει τὰ τοῦ νέου). Cf. also Philo, *Jos.* 144; M. Ant. 8.50.1.

61 This is the way in which the phrase must be understood. Obviously, Origen so interpreted it: in *Hom. in Lev.* 2.4 (9, p. 193 Lommatzsch) he sees fulfilled "in the remission of sins through penitence that which James the apostle says, 'If someone is sick, let him call the elders of the church and let them *lay their hands upon him*, anointing him with oil in the name of the Lord'" (remissio peccatorum per poenitentiam . . . quod Jacobus apostolus dicit: si quis autem infirmatur, vocet presbyteros ecclesiae et imponant ei manus, ungentes eum oleo in nomine domini) [Trans.]. That he interprets the illness as a moral one does not concern us here.

62 As has been shown especially by Heitmüller, "*Im Namen Jesu,*" 86, 168, *et passim*.

63 Philo, *Som.* 2.58: "For unguents what need was there to look for anything more than the fruit-juice pressed from the olive? For indeed it produces smoothness, and counteracts physical exhaustion, and brings about good condition. If a muscle be relaxed it braces it and renders it firm, nor is there anything surpassing it for infusing tone and vigour" (τί δὲ τοῦ ἀπὸ τῆς ἐλαίας ἐκθλιβομένου καρποῦ πλέον ἔδει ζητεῖν πρὸς ἀλείμματα; καὶ γὰρ λεαίνει καὶ κάματον σώματος λύει καὶ εὐσαρκίαν ἐμποιεῖ, κἂν εἴ τι κεχαλασμένον εἴη, σφίγγει πυκνότητι καὶ οὐδενὸς ἧττον ἑτέρου ῥώμην καὶ εὐτονίαν ἐντίθησιν). Cf. in addition Galen, *De simpl. medicam. temp. et fac.* 2.10ff (11, pp. 485ff Kühn). Cf. also Seneca, *Ep.* 53.5, "When I finally calmed my stomach [after sea-sickness] . . . and refreshed my body with an *anointing* . . . (ut primum stomachum . . . collegi, ut corpus unctione recreavi) [Loeb modified]. On the supposed origin and significance of anointing among the Mediterranean peoples, and on the magical power of anointing with animal fat, etc., cf. Clotilde Mayer, *Das Öl im Kultus der Griechen*, Diss. Heidelberg (Würzburg: Stürtz, 1917). Mayer refers on p. 14, n. 6 to Plato, *Menex.* 238a: ". . . she [i.e., the earth] brought to birth for her children the olive, which is *beneficial for aches* (ἐλαίου γένεσιν, πόνων ἀρωγήν, ἀνῆκεν τοῖς ἐκγόνοις) [Loeb modified]. The use of oil as a medication among the Israelites is proven by Isa 1:6. On the oil bath taken by Herod when he was ill, see Josephus, *Ant.* 17.172; *Bell.* 1.657. In Judaism it is sometimes used in pure form and sometimes mixed with wine (see Lk 10:34).

edies—are intended by this verse,[64] for miracle workers are required and not elderly patriarchs. Therefore, these must be official "elders" of the congregation, and their healing power must be connected with their official character.

Only in light of these considerations, which interpreters sometimes avoid because they modernize the conceptions of the healing activity, can we deal with the question of what situations within the community can be perceived through this saying. In accordance with his overall conception of Jas, Spitta imagines a Jewish community here, and there is no need to stress that the title of "Lord" as well as the office of "elders of the assembly" could indeed be understandable within a Jewish context. But that the community leaders possess gifts of healing by virtue of their office is something which is not immediately understandable within such a context. At least, we have no knowledge of a development within the Jewish community which makes an office the vehicle of strong ecstatic–pneumatic powers.[65]

But precisely within early Christianity such a development can be observed. It is not known just when this development was completed within those churches who called their leaders "elders" after the Jewish model.[66] Within these churches one can probably presuppose a certain patriarchialism which is inclined to bestow upon especially experienced members of the community the official rank as well. This would certainly favor the development mentioned above. At any rate, the power of healing was ascribed to the presbyters by the time of Jas, just as by the time of 1 Tim 4:14 the transfer of a charisma was something which derived from the laying on of the hands by the "presbytery"— although this took place with the assistance of the prophets.

Therefore, it is a Christian community of which Jas 5:14 gives us a glimpse, and the "Lord" is Jesus Christ.[67] Of course, the possibility exists that the "anointing with oil in the name of the Lord" was already a Jewish practice employed by Rabbis.[68] and that this is the origin of the practice and of the expression, though not of the precise formulation in Jas 5:14 which restricts it to the presbyters. The designation ἐκκλησία ("church") for the Christian community here does not collide with the term συναγωγή ("synagogue")

Physicians probably made use of the derivative benefits effected by certain oils when rubbed upon the skin, or they used the oil as a medium for the application of other medicines. On the other hand, the folk medicinal use of oils may have been apotropaic in character: to the oil were ascribed divine powers which warded off spirits. Cf. H. Gressmann, W. Heitmüller, and O. Scheel, the article on "Ölsalbung," *RGG*¹ 4, 874–6; E. Kutsch, G. Delling, and C. A. Bouman, "Salbung," *RGG*³ 5, 1330–4; in *Midrash Koheleth Rabbah* on Eccl 1:8, the Jew Ḥanina, who had apostatized to Christianity, is forgiven by means of oil; but cf. the interpretation of that passage by Adolf Schlatter, *Die Kirche Jerusalems vom Jahre 70–130*, BFTh 2, 3 (Gütersloh: Bertelsmann, 1898), 10f.

64 Bede; similarly, Adolf Schlatter, *Die Briefe des Petrus, Judas, Jakobus der Brief an die Hebräer* (Berlin: Evangelische Verlagsanstalt, 1953), 177f.

65 In the passage in *b. Baba Bathra* 116a which Spitta quotes, what is involved is only the practice in cases of illness of having a scribe pray for the sick. But there is neither any mention of "elders," nor is a miraculous healing depicted. In *b. Chag.* 3a, where a healing of two mutes by a "rabbi" is reported, it is not a matter of the office of teacher, but rather the glorification of the rabbi and the skill in the Law to

which the two mutes had attained. The exorcisms mentioned in Matt 12:27, Acts 19:13, Josephus, *Ant.* 8.46ff, and *Bell.* 7.185 also have nothing to do with offices within the community.

66 Cf. Hans Lietzmann, "Zur altchristlichen Verfassungsgeschichte," *ZWTh* 55 (1913): 113ff.

67 Most witnesses read "in the name of the Lord" (ἐν τῷ ὀνόματι τοῦ κυρίου. A Ψ 33 81 omit the τοῦ). The very infrequent expansion "the Lord Jesus (Christ)" (τοῦ κυρίου Ἰησοῦ [Χριστοῦ]) is worthless, and this is probably also true of the unique reading in B: "in the name" (ἐν τῷ ὀνόματι), which would change nothing materially (cf. Jas 2:7). That "Lord" (κύριος) in 5:14f (and 1:1; 2:1; 5:7), thus, has a different meaning than elsewhere in Jas is plausible, given the literary character of the work. Moreover, in all these instances the possibility remains open that there is a Christian reinterpretation of originally Jewish expressions.

68 On healing by means of prayer, cf. Sir 38:9.

used in 2:2. For as was shown, the term in 2:2 is probably simply an expression for "assembly," and one which is used in a traditional phrase at that.

Judging by the literary style of this paraenesis, there is no doubt that the saying is not intended to introduce the practice of such miraculous healings, but rather presupposes their existence.[69] This practice, which here is naturally still far from being an ecclesiastical institution, is older than Jas and was based originally upon the possession of the charisma, and only later upon the occupation of the office. From this practice the mystery in the Greek Church, called the "oil of prayer" ($\epsilon\dot{\upsilon}\chi\dot{\epsilon}\lambda\alpha\iota\sigma\nu$) or Holy Unction, developed in connection with Jas 5:14f. This anointing of the sick—practiced in most Orthodox churches—is usually performed by seven priests. The act involves accompanying prayers and scripture readings and is for the purpose of strengthening both the body and soul of the sick person.[70] Only in the Middle Ages did there develop from the practice of anointing the sick the sacrament of Extreme Unction for the person who is dying. This is a transition in which the curative intention at the very least recedes into the background.[71]

■ **15** Quite by contrast to the sacrament of Extreme Unction, the healing aspect stands in the foreground in Jas 5:15. For since in this context the word $\kappa\dot{\alpha}\mu\nu\omega\nu$ must mean "the person who is sick" (= $\dot{\alpha}\sigma\theta\epsilon\nu\hat{\omega}\nu$ in

v 14), then the words $\sigma\dot{\omega}\zeta\epsilon\iota\nu$ and $\dot{\epsilon}\gamma\epsilon\dot{\iota}\rho\epsilon\iota\nu$ here must have the technical meanings which they would normally have in this connection—i.e., "to heal" and "to restore to health." Hence, they do not refer to salvation and resurrection.[72] The elders are not called to a dying person but to a sick person, so there are no grounds for interpreting these verbs to mean anything other than what they would have to mean in a similar context elsewhere. That the sick person does not participate himself in the praying is not evidence of enfeeblement at the point of death. Rather, it is merely part of the miraculous character of the healing, for the only ones who pray are those who possess the divine power.

The absence of any further mention of oil in v 15 is only felt by one who presupposes some sort of natural healing effect of the oil. But the oil is only the medium, the power is what counts. This power is called "faith" ($\pi\dot{\iota}\sigma\tau\iota\varsigma$) here. It corresponds to the charismatic faith with which we are familiar from the stories in the Gospels, a faith which looks for an answer to prayer, expects miracles, and therefore effects miracles.[73]

Yet it is striking that there is no mention in v 15 of a limitation of this power to the circle of the elders. The words give the impression that anyone who has this charismatic power of faith (1 Cor 12:9; 13:2) could heal the sick by prayer. I suggest that this formulation,

69 A further example of this practice—perhaps an example just as old as Jas 5:14f—is the prayer over the oil of anointing in *Const. Ap.* 7.27. Carl Schmidt, "Das koptische Didache-Fragment des British Museum," *ZNW* 24 (1925): 85, 94ff, believed that underlying the appendix to *Did.* 10 found in the Coptic fragment *Br. Mus. Or.* 9271 was the Greek word for "ointment" ($\mu\dot{\upsilon}\rho\sigma\nu$). However, more recent research has proven almost beyond doubt that the Coptic word *stinoufe* corresponds to $\epsilon\dot{\upsilon}\omega\delta\dot{\iota}\alpha$ ("fragrance") and in this text means prayer. Cf. L. Th. Lefort, ed. and tr., *Les Pères Apostolique en Copte*, CSCO 136 (Louvain: Durbecq, 1952), 26, n. 13; Alfred Adam, "Erwägungen zur Herkunft der Didache," *ZKG* 68 (1957): 8–11.

70 Cf. Ferdinand Kattenbusch, *Lehrbuch der vergleichenden Confessionskunde*, vol. 1 (Freiburg: Mohr [Siebeck], 1892), 434ff; *idem*, "Ölung," *Realencyclopädie für protestantische Theologie und Kirche*, ed. Albert Hauck, vol. 14 (Leipzig: Hinrichs, ³1904), 304–11; *idem*, "Extreme Unction," in *The New Schaff-Herzog Encyclopedia of Religious Knowledge*, ed. Samuel Macauley

Jackson *et al.*, vol. 4 (New York and London: Funk & Wagnalls, 1909), 251–3. O. Scheel, "Ölung," *RGG*¹ 4, 876–7. On the Gnostic sacrament of chrism, see Wilhelm Bousset, *Hauptprobleme der Gnosis*, FRLANT 10 (Göttingen: Vandenhoeck & Ruprecht, 1907), 297ff.

71 The decrees of the Council of Trent describe the result of this "sacrament . . . insinuated indeed in Mark, but recommended and promulgated to the faithful by James the Apostle, and brother of the Lord" (Session 14, Chapter 1 on Extreme Unction), with these words: "whose anointing cleanses away sins, if there be any still to be expiated, as also the remains of sins; and raises up and strengthens the soul of the sick person." Thus the procedure allows the sick person to bear his suffering more easily, and more readily withstand temptations, "and at times obtains bodily health, when expedient for the welfare of the soul" (Session 14, Chapter 2 on Extreme Unction) [trans. J. Waterworth, *The Canons and Decrees of the Sacred and Oecumenical Council of Trent* (London: Dolman, 1848), 105f].

which is in fact peculiar, was taken over from an earlier period at which this power was ascribed only to pneumatics and not to the presbyters. If this is true, then another factor which is often observed would also be explained: the promise of healing is stated totally without qualification; the possibility of a failure is not mentioned. This is quite understandable as long as the healing depended upon the possession of the charisma. For then any disappointments could perhaps be explained as resulting from the lack of the charisma in the first place, while such explanation was no longer applicable, once the miraculous healing power had become the property of the presbyters of the community. Of such a change this saying does not yet disclose anything.

Along with the assurance of healing there is a promise of the forgiveness of sins. This half of the verse is not a reference to a special case.[74] Instead, "and if" ($\kappa\check{\alpha}\nu$)[75] evidently introduces a second promise. It does seem odd that there has been no mention of forgiveness of sins earlier. But this is no longer strange when we consider how closely already the Jews associated sins with illness. This association is stated here only as a condition: *if* the illness was a punishment for sins, then the cause as well as its effect will be removed. This has nothing to do with general sinfulness (Jas 3:2). But perhaps this is still another indication of the fact that this is a miraculous healing by divine power—only then could the forgiveness of sins be promised—, and that the bearer of the office has merely inherited what at first belonged exclusively to the pneumatics.

■ **16–18** I have already indicated in the Analysis the difficulties with which these verses are laden. It is easy to perceive that beginning in v 16b we have to do with a saying about prayer in general. Yet the words "so that you might be healed" ($\H{o}\pi\omega\varsigma\ i\alpha\theta\hat{\eta}\tau\epsilon$) in v 16a seem to point back to the previously mentioned instance of illness. Consequently, I suggest that these words in v 16a are an interpolation by the author into an older

saying, which by means of this interpolation is attached to the preceding material.

That there is something wrong with the connection between 5:15 and 5:16 can be demonstrated in detail. If such a connection is maintained, it is necessary to read into v 15 a confession of sins upon the part of the sick person,[76] for v 16 appears here as a generalization of v 15.[77] But in v 15 there is no confession of sins upon the part of the sick person, and the idea that the confession in v 16 is made to the presbyters[78] is ruled out by the expression "to one another" ($\dot{\alpha}\lambda\lambda\acute{\eta}\lambda o\iota\varsigma$). On the other hand, if one attempts to interpret v 16 independently, and yet still maintains that there is a reference to illness, then one is necessarily forced to an interpretation such as the one stated very clearly by de Wette: "If you are sick, then confess your mistakes to one or more brethren . . . and these brethren may pray for you, that you may be healed." Yet that is not a generalization of what precedes, but rather a contradiction of it. For, in the case of sickness, there is a recommendation of *either* a miraculous healing by the presbyters *or* a confession of sins upon the part of the sick person and prayer by his Christian brethren. A consciousness of these difficulties has led many interpreters[79] to explain "to be healed" ($i\hat{\alpha}\sigma\theta\alpha\iota$) as a metaphorical expression for forgiveness of sins. Certainly this meaning might be possible in itself, but surely not in the understanding of our author, who has v 16 follow v 15. Therefore, that Jas has tied together two originally heterogeneous sayings by means of the phrase "so that you might be healed" ($\H{o}\pi\omega\varsigma\ i\alpha\theta\hat{\eta}\tau\epsilon$) seems to me to be the best interpretation.

■ **16** Hence, this verse is a saying which calls for confession of sins and intercessory prayer. It contains no command for the establishment of an ecclesiastical institution, but neither is it limited to instances where someone has offended some other person. Instead, the confession of sins[80] is thought of here simply as an act in preparation for prayer, similar to the purification

---

72 So von Soden.

73 See above on 1:6, and in the second Excursus on 2:26, n. 133.

74 So Huther, Beyschlag.

75 $\kappa\check{\alpha}\nu$ must not be translated here "even if"; cf. Lk 13:9; Mk 16:18; and Blass-Debrunner, § 374.

76 So de Wette, Belser.

77 Especially since "*therefore,* confess" ($\dot{\epsilon}\xi o\mu o\lambda o\gamma\epsilon\hat{\iota}\sigma\theta\epsilon$

$o\hat{v}\nu$) is the probable reading (against Koine 33; sy^vg would require $\delta\acute{\epsilon}$).

78 So Gaugusch; also, with some caution, Belser.

79 Hofmann; David Erdmann, *Der Brief des Jakobus* (Berlin: Wiegandt and Grieben, 1881), *ad loc.*; von Soden; Gaugusch.

80 The Koine reading $\tau\grave{\alpha}\ \pi\alpha\rho\alpha\pi\tau\acute{\omega}\mu\alpha\tau\alpha$ ("transgressions"), instead of the reading $\tau\grave{\alpha}\varsigma\ \dot{\alpha}\mu\alpha\rho\tau\acute{\iota}\alpha\varsigma$ ("sins")

of the heart from all vanity in *Herm. mand.* 9.4.[81] The only theme in what follows is prayer.

The chief difficulty is the term ἐνεργουμένη. The passive rendering ("made effective") is the most obvious possibility, but it makes sense only if one has in mind here prayer which is actuated by the Spirit.[82] But is the thought of Rom 8:26 really supposed to be hidden mysteriously in this one word? The possibility that this is the middle voice does not make sense with even the simplest rendering, for the translation "by virtue of the effectiveness within it"[83] would result in a bad tautology. Therefore, certainly a proviso for success must be contained in this participle; yet construing the word as a participial condition does not give this kind of result. For with that construction one must either first add the important element: "if it (properly) becomes effective,"[84] or understand the proviso to be that the one for whom prayer is being offered cooperate with the one who is praying.[85] Neither of these ideas is present in the text.

Thus, there really remains only the possibility of interpreting ἐνεργουμένη almost as an adjective.[86] In fact, in the only LXX passage in which the verb ἐνεργεῖν is used without an object, the word must be construed as an adjective—Wisd 15:11: "inspiring him with an *active* soul" (τὸν ἐμπνεύσαντα αὐτῷ ψυχὴν ἐνεργοῦσαν); cf. also 2 Cor 4:12.[87] If in our verse a vigorous or energetic request becomes the prerequisite for success, this proviso is possibly a result of disillusionment with regard to prayer.[88]

In the case of v 16, the statement refers only to the prayer of the "righteous person." This term must be viewed simply as a designation for any devout person in the traditional Jewish sense, and it must not be burdened with any dogmatic issues. Therefore, the statement in 5:16b holds good for every believing petitioner. There is no need to understand it, in light of the reference to Elijah (vv 17, 18), to mean righteous people who have died and who assist in the prayers of humans by making intercession in heaven.[89] Elijah is not mentioned in v 16 at all, and in vv 17, 18 he is mentioned only as an example of the power of human prayer, not heavenly intercession. Also there is no need to call to mind "James the Just" and his intercession (Hegesippus, in Eusebius, *Hist. eccl.* 2.23.17). Instead, we have to recall passages such as Ps 34:15, 17; Prov 15:29, and in general the Jewish and Christian pious people who believe in the God "who hears prayer."[90]

■ **17, 18** The Elijah example also originates from Jewish tradition. The provenance and use of such examples is discussed above in the comments on 2:21, 25 and 5:10, 11. Here in vv 17, 18 Jas is again following the tradition, not the canonical account. For that it was the prayer of Elijah which shut the heavens and then reopened them is found in neither 1 Kings 17:1 nor 18:42. But presumably this story was developed out of those two verses by the Jewish tradition, for in *4 Ezra* 7.109 Elijah appears as an intercessor "for those who received rain," and in the great hymn in praise of the fathers in Sirach it is said of Elijah that "by the word of the Lord he shut up the heavens" (ἐν λόγῳ κυρίου ἀνέσχεν οὐρανόν Sir 48:3). It is possible that the tra-

---

in the better texts, constitutes no material difference. Nor does it mean that the saying is restricted to mistakes made against one's neighbour; so Erasmus: "παραπτώματα are more 'mistakes' than 'sins'; one might call them 'slips.'" Erasmus' interpretation as well as that of many others is discussed in Paul Althaus, "'Bekenne einer dem andern seine Sünden': Zur Geschichte von Jak 5, 16 seit Augustin," in *Festgabe für Theodor Zahn* (Leipzig: Deichert, 1928), 165–94.

81 Cf. above, on 1:6 and 4:3.
82 So Mayor.
83 So B. Weiss, *NT Handausgabe, ad loc.*
84 So Windisch, *Katholische Briefe* (1911).
85 So Oec.
86 This is argued by Luther and many older commentators; it is also argued by many modern scholars

(Beyschlag, von Soden, Belser), but with different variations ("earnest," "forceful," "exerted").

87 The Latin versions *ff* (frequens) and vulg (assidua) must have understood the term in Jas 5:16 in a similar way, as also an interpretation in the Catena: "the prayer must be active and vivacious, animated by behaviour in accordance with the commandments" (δέησις ἔνεργος καὶ ζῶσα τοῖς τρόποις τῶν ἐντολῶν ψυχουμένη) [Trans.].

88 Cf. above on 4:3.
89 So Spitta.
90 The address, "O Thou who hearest prayer" (שֹׁמֵעַ תְּפִלָּה Ps 65:3), has also passed over into the Jewish Eighteen Benedictions (in the 15th or 16th petition, O. Holtzmann, *Berakot*, 17, 22).

91 Dan 7:25; 12:7; Rev 11:2; 12:6, 14. On the number 3½ years = 42 months = 1260 days, cf. Hermann

dition especially emphasized the power of the prophets over heaven and earth. If that is the case, then the phrase "upon the earth" (ἐπὶ τῆς γῆς) in v 17 and the antithesis "heaven—earth" (οὐρανός—γῆ) in v 18 would be occasioned by such a tradition. There is also nothing in the Biblical text about the 3½ years. Jewish exegesis has made "the third year" mentioned in 1 Kings 18:1 into 3½ years (cf. Lk 4:25), which somehow is a typical period of time.[91]

In our passage, the majestic greatness of Elijah which is stressed by the tradition (Sir 48:1ff) is not found, but rather the interest is precisely in his humanity. For he is an example of the power of human prayer. Consequently, one can rule out more subtle distinctions in the expression "with the same nature" (ὁμοιοπαθής);

it simply means "a human like us." The first clause is used in the place of a participle with a concessive force, and therefore the conjunction καὶ expresses a contrast: He was just a man, *yet* he prayed fervently[92] that it might not rain[93] and his prayer was answered.

■ **19, 20** The writing concludes with an admonition to bring back (convert) the erring brother. For this is what the saying is intended to convey, not instruction about conversion itself. The admonition is clothed in an assurance of the success of this work of conversion. Any more subtle distinctions are avoided; the terms "to wander" (πλανᾶσθαι) and "to turn, bring back" (ἐπιστρέφειν), "truth" (ἀλήθεια), "error" (πλάνη), and "way" (ὁδός) are common in Jewish and Christian paraenesis.[94] What is involved here is someone who

---

Gunkel, "The Religio–historical Interpretation of the New Testament," *The Monist* 13 (1903): 443f; idem, *Schöpfung und Chaos in Urzeit und Endzeit: Eine religionsgeschichtliche Untersuchung über Gen. 1 und Ap. Joh. 12* (Göttingen: Vandenhoeck & Ruprecht, [2]1921), 268, n. 1; Wilhelm Bousset, *Die Offenbarung Johannis*, KEK 16 (Göttingen: Vandenhoeck & Ruprecht, [6]1906; reprint 1966), on Rev 11:9; Franz Boll, *Aus der Offenbarung Johannis* (Leipzig and Berlin: Teubner, 1914), 24f. Gerhard Kittel, *Rabbinica*, Arbeiten zur Religionsgeschichte des Urchristentums 1, 3 (Leipzig: Hinrichs, 1920), 31ff, has explained the number as a popular paraphrase to indicate one half of seven (similar to our "half-dozen"); Kittel bases this upon Rabbinic witnesses which to a certain extent constitute evidence for precisely the Elijah tradition in our passage.

92 The combination of a verbal substantive with its cognate verb, as in προσευχῇ προσηύξατο ("he prayed fervently"), is usually considered a Hebraism or at least "translation Greek," since the LXX translates the Hebrew infinitive absolute in this way: מוֹת יָמוּת ("surely die") translated with θανάτῳ θανατοῦσθαι, ἀποθνήσκειν, τελευτᾶν, etc. But since similar constructions are found also in original Greek outside of Jewish-Christian circles, the question of a Semitism is disputed in Jas 5:17, too. Radermacher, *Grammatik*, 106, denies that there is a Hebraism here; arguing for a Hebraism are Blass-Debrunner, § 198.6 and, with reservations, Moulton, *Prolegomena*, 75f. See the examples from the New Testament in Blass-Debrunner. The classical examples are well-known, e.g., Plato, *Symp.* 195b: "fleeing old age in utmost haste" (φεύγων φυγῇ τὸ γῆρας). Radermacher refers to related constructions from Old Comedy and Tragedy, such as "to be so by very nature" (φύσει

πεφυκέναι), or "to be very ill" (νόσῳ νοσεῖν). Connections in Koine with Attic poetry would not be without example. In any case, the figure in Jas 5:17 has an intensifying effect.

93 τοῦ is placed before the infinitive "to rain" (βρέξαι) here just as in many similar constructions in Acts. The LXX also provides examples of this (1 Kings 1:35, after ἐνετειλάμην, cf. Blass-Debrunner, § 400.7). A few isolated witnesses have instead of this a ἵνα–clause.

Just as in the LXX version of the Elijah story (1 Kings 18:1), the expression "to provide rain" (ὑετὸν διδόναι) is found here in Jas, except that in the LXX version God is the subject. The word order ὑετὸν ἔδωκεν, which has slightly better attestation, is reversed by such respectable witnesses as ℵ A Ψ 33 1739. Just such a rain miracle, and modeled upon Jas 5:17, is ascribed to James himself in Epiph., *Haer.* 78.14 (See above in the Introduction, p. 17).

94 On "to turn, bring back" (ἐπιστρέφειν), cf., e.g., *Test. Ben.* 4.5 (longer reading): "by admonition he brings back the one who rejects the Most High" (τὸν ἀθετοῦντα τὸν ὕψιστον νουθετῶν ἐπιστρέφει); Pol. *Phil.* 6.1: "[presbyters] bringing back those who have wandered" (ἐπιστρέφοντες τὰ ἀποπεπλανημένα). The Jewish religion is designated "truth" (ἀλήθεια) by Philo in expressions which portray the conversion of proselytes (*Spec. leg.* 1.51, 309; 4.178; *Virt.* 102). The Christian religion, also, is characterized in this way in the expression "knowledge of the truth" (ἐπίγνωσις ἀληθείας) in the Pastoral Epistles; cf. Dibelius, "*Ἐπίγνωσις ἀληθείας*," 1–13. "To wander" (πλανᾶσθαι) occurs frequently in conjunction with "way" (ὁδός): Deut 11:28; Prov 21:16; Isa 53:6; Wisd 5:6: "from the way of truth" (ἀπὸ ὁδοῦ ἀληθείας); 12:24: "the paths of error" (τῶν πλάνης ὁδῶν,

has in some way apostatized from the "truth," i.e., from the devout, righteous way of life. It is to the one who converts this apostate that the assurance is given, since the reading of most witnesses, "let him know" (γινωσκέτω, cf. on 1:3), should probably be accepted.[95] What follows gives the impression of being a quotation because of the repetition of the subject, but perhaps this is occasioned merely by an effort at clarity.

It is debatable to whom the two promises at the end of v 20 actually apply.[96] However, in the first of these promises what is probably in mind is the danger of eternal damnation at the Judgment, and in that case only a reference to the apostate would be suitable.[97] For this fate of "death" would not be a threat at all for the converter, since he has remained a Christian and true to his faith. But many commentators[98] take the second promise also to apply to the apostate: It is the sins of the apostate which will be covered. Yet then the clause lags behind insufferably, for the one who has already been rescued "from death" does not need further eradication of sins. Therefore, it is necessary to consider whether the converter is not really the one who is being assured of a reward here.

The strong expression "multitude of sins" (πλῆθος ἁμαρτιῶν) appears to speak against this possibility, and in fact this has led some exegetes to consider interpretations which might reconcile the difficulty.[99] Yet this objection is misleading, for the phrase "to hide a multitude of sins" (καλύπτειν πλῆθος ἁμαρτιῶν) turns out to be a fixed expression. The saying in Prov 10:12: "Love covers all offenses" (וְעַל כָּל־פְּשָׁעִים תְּכַסֶּה אַהֲבָה) seems to have been taken over into early Christian paraenesis in the form "love covers a multitude of sins" (ἀγάπη καλύπτει πλῆθος ἁμαρτιῶν. The LXX translates differently). It appears in exactly this form in 1 Petr 4:8, *1 Clem.* 49.5, and *2 Clem.* 16.4. Later, as can easily happen in the development of paraenesis, it is labeled as a dominical saying (Clem. Alex., *Paed.* 3.91.3; *Didasc.* 4, p. 14, 32 Achelis). As Spitta has shown with particular clarity, the underlying thought is the originally Jewish idea that good deeds and sins are recorded opposite one another in the heavenly books (Sir 3:30; cf. also Tob 4:10). This thought has also passed over into Christian paraenesis. Jas 2:13 is in harmony with it, and it is plainly expressed in *Did.* 4.6: "Give of your earnings as a ransom for your sins" (ἐὰν ἔχῃς διὰ τῶν

in Jas 5:20, on the other hand, it is not the "ways of error" but the "error of his ways"); *Did.* 6.1: "from this way of the teaching" (ἀπὸ ταύτης τῆς ὁδοῦ τῆς διδαχῆς). A treatment of these fixed terms of the missionary vocabulary is found in Grete Gillet, *Evangelium: Studien zur urchristlichen Missionssprache*, Unpub. Diss. (Heidelberg, 1924). Perhaps the frequency with which these words are associated is responsible for the reading "from the way of truth" (ἀπὸ τῆς ὁδοῦ τῆς ἀληθείας, ℵ 33 81 *et al.*) in v 19.

95 The second person plural imperative in B 69 *et al.* γινώσκετε must be understood as a revision into the style of paraenesis delivered to a community.

96 The text is uncertain:
ψυχὴν ἐκ θανάτου Ψ 1175 81 sah *et al.* Koine "a soul from death"
ψυχὴν αὐτοῦ ἐκ θανάτου ℵ A P 33 1739 *s* vulg sy boh "his soul from death"
ψυχὴν ἐκ θανάτου αὐτοῦ P[74vid] B *et al.* *ff* "a soul from death itself"

To be sure, the third reading is all but out of the question, but certainty in the case of readings one and two is impossible. Von Soden, *Schriften*, part 1, vol. 3, p. 1888, expresses doubt (contrary to his later edition of the text, with apparatus) whether the second reading listed above can be the reading of his recension *H*. If it is not, then the first reading

listed above could be claimed as the original one. This reading would subsequently have been strongly influenced by Matt 16:25 = Mk 8:35 = Lk 9:24. The αὐτοῦ making its entrance into Jas 5:20 as a result of this influence would have to be understood in the third reading as an incorrectly inserted marginal gloss (Note that B and *ff* are in agreement here! On this, cf. above in the Introduction, section 10, under the discussion of B). For the interpretation of v 20 which is set forth in this commentary, the first reading is no more unfavorable than the second reading. As far as the ambiguity regarding the person to whom the promises are made is concerned, it might be noted that even the second reading would provide no absolute solution, for the rough breathing αὐτοῦ ("his own") could be intended. The Achmimic parchment fragment (4th cent.) containing Jas 5:17, 18, 20, published by Walter Till, "Ein achmimisches Jakobusbrieffragment," *Le Muséon* 51 (1938): 69–71, unfortunately has a lacuna here.

97 So most modern commentators, against Hofmann.

98 Gebser; Beyschlag; Belser; Windisch, *Katholische Briefe* (1911); Gaugusch.

99 The expression is applied by Bede to the sins of both people; David Julius Pott, in J. B. Koppe, *Novum Testamentum Graece perpetua annotatione illustratum* 9, 1: *Epistola Jacobi* (Göttingen: Dieterich, [3]1816), *ad loc.*,

χειρῶν σου, δώσεις λύτρωσιν ἀμαρτιῶν σου, cf. *Barn.* 19.10). In all these passages, it is not stated how many sins a human being had committed, but rather how great was the power of the action in question to erase his sins. Therefore, "multitude of sins" (πλῆθος ἁμαρτιῶν) does not mean "this person's many sins," but simply "many sins." Thus, applying the last words of v 20 to the converter does not make this person appear to be an archsinner, but rather displays the very great effectiveness of his deed in erasing sins. And that is probably what the author intends to express.

That the first half of the sentence concerns the sinner and the second half his mentor ought not to pose any difficulty, for there are other examples of this. According to *2 Clem.* 15.1,[100] whoever follows the counsel of the author "shall save both himself and me his counsellor; for it is no small reward to turn to salvation a soul that is wandering and perishing" (καὶ ἑαυτὸν σώσει κἀμὲ τὸν συμβουλεύσαντα. μισθὸς γὰρ οὐκ ἔστι μικρὸς πλανωμένην ψυχὴν καὶ ἀπολλυμένην ἀποστρέψαι εἰς τὸ σωθῆναι, cf. also *2 Clem.* 19.1).[101] Jewish and Christian paraenesis[102] generally commended the admonition and conversion of erring brethren as an especially meritorious work; this also lends support to the proposed interpretation of the last words in v 20 as a reference to the converter. *Pirke Aboth* 5.18 reads: "Every one that makes the many virtuous, sin comes not by his means" (אֵין חֵטְא בָּא עַל יָדוֹ) [trans. Charles, *APOT*]. This saying is then supported with the example of Moses and then the opposite example of Jeroboam. The same idea with different supporting arguments is found in the Talmud in *b. Yoma* 87a. Among the meritorious works on behalf of the community which *Barn.* 19.10 enumerates is the following: "striving to save a soul by the word" (μελετῶν εἰς τὸ σῶσαι ψυχὴν τῷ

λόγῳ); cf. *2 Clem.* 17.2: "Let us then help one another, and bring back those that are weak in goodness, that we may all be saved, and convert and exhort one another" (συλλάβωμεν οὖν ἑαυτοῖς καὶ τοὺς ἀσθενοῦντας ἀνάγειν περὶ τὸ ἀγαθόν, ὅπως σωθῶμεν ἅπαντες καὶ ἐπιστρέψωμεν ἀλλήλους καὶ νουθετήσωμεν). Precisely this section in this very early Christian sermon reveals to us the interests which also motivate the saying in Jas 5:20.[103]

They are the interests of a developed communal life. The closeness of individuals to one another brings with it the fact that each observes and passes judgment upon what the other does. Disruptions of the community can only be avoided if criticism by one brother of another can be directed into the proper path—i.e., if it does not lead to slander or alienation (4:11; 5:9), but rather to the beneficial influence of one brother upon the other. Therefore, this admonition has an important place in paraenesis which is directed toward the religious life of a closely knit community. Consequently, it is found in the literature of Jews, and also in that of Christians at least from the time when the Christian community began to consolidate itself within the context of the world.

And it is for this reason that this paraenesis was also transmitted and developed. The nearest relative to the saying in Jas 5:20 probably is a saying in the *Epistola apostolorum* 39.10ff (p. 149 in Coptic text):[104] "Now if his neighbour [has admonished] him and he returns he will be saved; (and) he who admonished him will receive a reward" (Eth: "will obtain eternal life") [trans. Hennecke–Schneemelcher 1, p. 225]. That is exactly the two–fold promise of the saying in Jas. In Gal 6:1 there is an admonition to correct the erring brother, but there is no promise to the corrector. This

---

interprets it (with some reservations) as a reference to the future sins of the sinner; de Wette sees it as a reference to the sins of the apostate and whoever "cooperated with him."

100 The exact analogy of *2 Clem.* 15.1 is found in 1 Tim 4:16.

101 In the *Epistola apostolorum* (Carl Schmidt and Isaac Wajnberg, *Gespräche Jesu mit seinen Jüngern nach der Auferstehung*, TU 43 [Leipzig: Hinrichs, 1919]), on p. 135 of the Coptic text, it says (Jesus speaking to the disciples): "And you will have (a) great reward with my Father who is in heaven, and they [i.e.,

those who have been converted by the disciples] shall have forgiveness of sins and eternal life, and will have a part in the kingdom of heaven" (trans. Hennecke-Schneemelcher 1, p. 221).

102 Perhaps following older models (see Ezek 3:18–21).

103 Cf. further a passage from the later *Acts of Thomas* (in Montague Rhodes James, ed., *Apocrypha anecdota* II, TS 5, 1 [Cambridge: University Press, 1897], 29): "He who saves souls from idols will be great in my kingdom" (ὁ λυτρούμενος ψυχὰς ἀπὸ τῶν εἰδώλων, οὗτος ἔσται μέγας ἐν τῇ βασιλείᾳ μου) [Trans.].

104 However, there seems to be a connection with the

promise also plays a leading role in a related passage in *Pistis Sophia* 104, which must be viewed as an echo of the early Christian admonitions already cited.[105]

The little communal regulation which we read in Matt 18:15ff can be regarded as a development of the paraenesis in our passage, or a related Judaeo–Christian paraenesis, into a community rule, assuming that the text in Matthew refers to mistakes in general and not to wrongs which have been suffered by the one who is to correct the sinner.[106] In the Matthean version, there is not only the counsel to correct the sinner but also instruction about the course of action to be adopted in

case he cannot be corrected. Admittedly, there is no mention of the reward for the converter—it is no longer paraenesis, but a community regulation.

Thus the final saying in Jas reminds us again that many of his admonitions represent not something which is final, but something which is changing, which expands or contracts to suit the situation and need of the community. Only someone who has gained an insight into this process of historical transformation can understand the Letter of James within the context of the history of which it is a part.

---

preceding instruction regarding the one who from his few possessions gives to the poor: "But if [someone] should fall [under the] load because of the sins he has [committed, then let] his neighbour admonish him in exchange for [the good that] he has done to his neighbour" (39.6ff) [trans. Hennecke-Schneemelcher 1, p. 225 modified]. Then there follows the passage quoted above in the text. If the restoration of the text is correct, then the paraenesis about correcting one's fellow-Christian is applied here to the needy person and the person who has possessions. The needy person shows his gratitude for the latter's support by directing him upon the right way. That closely corresponds to the theory in *Herm. sim.* 2 (see above in the Introduction, toward the end of section 6) and in general it would be characteristic of the way in which paraenesis is specialized. But admittedly, the Ethiopic version (p. 148) has, instead of the last words restored above from the Coptic, simply: "in return for what he has done to his neighbour."

105 *Pistis Sophia* 104: "He who will vivify one soul and deliver it, besides the glory which he has in the kingdom of the Light, he will receive other glory on account of the soul which he delivered" (trans. George Horner, *Pistis Sophia* [London: S. P. C. K., 1924], 133). Adolf Harnack, *Über das gnostische Buch Pistis-Sophia*, TU 7, 2 (Leipzig: Hinrichs, 1891), 22f, conjectures that underlying this passage in *Pistis Sophia* and the saying in Jas is a dominical saying. However, the relationships in the paraenetic tradition which have been shown are probably sufficient to explain the kinship between the two texts.

106 This assumption can be made since the case of wrongs which are suffered is not treated until Matt 18:21ff. In that case, Koine reading "if he should sin *against you*" (ἁμαρτήσῃ εἰς σέ) in Matt 18:15 is incorrect and the passage cannot be interpreted according to Lk 17:3, where the thought seems to be narrowed to wrongs which are suffered. This narrowing also has its Jewish parallel in *Test. Gad* 6.3.

Bibliography
Indices

1. Commentaries

The Ancient Church:

As was discussed above in section 9 of the Introduction, Jas was recognized as a Biblical book only at a relatively late date. As a result, the early Christian literature which deals with Jas is not abundant at all. The writing apparently was not treated in the *Hypotyposeis* of Clement of Alexandra,[1] and the great Antiochene exegetes have dismissed the Catholic Epistles altogether. Other material has been preserved for us only indirectly, in collections made by later editors. In such collections, the fragments of earlier commentators are preserved—sometimes with, sometimes without identification of the author of the fragment—and quite possibly also combined with the editor's own observations. Of such *catenae and scholia*, there are four which have been published; and in fact they have been published under various names and under titles which do not reveal the close association in which these texts actually stand. For all these works, no doubt, represent in reality only one ancient collection of patristic exegesis of individual passages, and this collection has probably been abridged, supplied with additional trimmings, adapted and revised. Further research needs to be done regarding the age, provenance, and mutual relation of these texts. In this commentary I cite the four texts using the customary names, and I have made observations about the relationship of these texts to one another and to other texts only in particularly important cases.[2] Where several of the following texts are in agreement, I have usually indicated this by referring simply to the "catenae and scholia":

Catena (= the so-called "Catena of Andreas")

    J. A. Cramer, ed., *Catenae Graecorum Patrum in Novum Testamentum*, vol. 8 (Oxford: University Press,

1840). The term "catena" refers to a chain or connected series of fragments from patristic commentaries. This particular catena contains the so-called commentary of Andreas on the Catholic Epistles.[3]

Oecumenius

    Jacobi apostoli epistola catholica, MPG 119, 451–510. This work has some points of contact with the Catena, but it does not mention the names of the authors of each fragment, so that the work as a whole no longer gives the impression of being a "chain." The work has nothing to do with Oecumenius, bishop of Tricca in Thessaly (10th cent.).[4]

Theophylactus

    Epistola catholica Sancti Jacobi apostoli, MPG 125, 1131–90. Likewise, the commentary of Theophylactus is not the work of the Bulgarian archbishop whose name it bears; rather, it is very closely related to the Oecumenius commentary, and like the latter it is partially related to the Catena.[5]

Didymus Alexandrinus

    In epistulas catholicas enarratio, MPG 39, 1749–54. This work contains Latin scholia on certain passages. In support of its authenticity one could cite the report of Cassiodorus that he had had the commentary of Didymus on the Catholic Epistles translated into Latin (Cassiodorus, *Institutio divinarum litterarum* 8, MPL 70, 1120). But against its authenticity there is, above all, the relationship of this work to the Catena—and indeed, to fragments which are designated in the Catena as the work of Chrysostom, Origen, and Severus.[6]

I have used the designation "Scholion" to refer to the scholia gathered from various manuscripts by Christian Freidrich Matthäi and printed in his edition of the Catholic Epistles (*SS. Apostolorum Septem Epistolae Catholicae* [Riga, 1782]). Of these scholia, those which are found in the appendix on pp. 183ff (Codices d and

---

1   See above on p. 51.

2   Cf. above in the commentary on 4:3 (Didymus and the other catenae and scholia), on 3:6 (two letters of Isidore of Pelusium in the Catena), and above in the Introduction, n. 103 (*Hermas*—Catena, Oecumenius, Theophylactus).

3   Cf. von Soden, *Schriften*, part 1, pp. 278f, 529f, 682ff. The Chrysostom fragments which are found in MPG 64, 1039ff come from Cramer's Catena. The commentary of Euthymius Zigabenus (*Commentarius in xiv epistolas Sancti Pauli et vii catholicas*, ed. Nicephorus Calogeras [Athens: Perri, 1887]) is identical with the Catena as far as the Catholic Epistles are concerned (see Calogeras' edition, vol. 2, p. 1). On the Catena, cf. further Karl Staab, "Die griechischen Katenenkommentare zu den katholischen Briefen," *Biblica* 5 (1924): 296–353, and James Hardy Ropes,

"The Greek Catena to the Catholic Epistles," *HTR* 19 (1926): 383–8.

4   Cf. Otto Bardenhewer, "Oecumenius," in *Wetzer und Welte's Kirchenlexicon*, 2nd edition by Joseph Hergenröther and Franz Kaulen, vol. 9 (Freiburg im Breisgau: Herder, 1895), 708–11; von Soden, *Schriften*, part 1, pp. 691f; Fr. Diekamp, "Mittheilungen über den neuaufgefundenen Commentar des Oekumenius zur Apokalypse," *SAB* (1901): 1046–56.

5   Cf. von Soden, *Schriften*, part 1, pp. 689f.

6   A synoptic table of the relevant fragments from "Didymus" and the Catena is found in E. Klostermann, *Über des Didymus von Alexandrien in epistolas canonicas enarratio*, TU 28, 2 (Leipzig: Hinrichs, 1905); cf. also Friedrich Zoepfl, *Didymi Alexandrini in epistolas canonicas brevis enarratio*, NTAbh 4, 1,

h, today designated 103 and 463) are identical with interpretations from the Catena; others (Codices a and f, now 101 and 462) are printed throughout the edition beneath the text.[7]

The Middle Ages:

Flavius Magnus Aurelius Cassiodorus (6th cent.)
Complexiones canonicarum epistularum septem, MPL 70, 1377–80. This is not a commentary but rather a synopsis of the contents which is divided into eleven sections.

Bede (8th cent.)
Super divi Jacobi epistolam, MPL 93, 9–42. This work is a valuable running commentary; along with the "Catena of Andreas" (Oecumenius, Theophylactus), it is the most valuable exegetical tool which we possess from the ancient period.

Isho'dad of Merv (9th cent.)
The Commentaries of Isho'dad of Merv, Bishop of Ḥadatha (c. 850 A.D.) in Syriac and English, ed. and tr. Margaret Dunlop Gibson, vol. 4, Horae Semiticae 10 (Cambridge: University Press, 1913). This work contains commentary on three Catholic Epistles (James, 1 Peter, 1 John), including brief commentary on eight passages in Jas.

Dionysius Bar Ṣalibi (12th cent.)
In Apocalypsim, Actus et Epistulas catholicas, ed. and tr. I. Sedlacek, CSCO, Scriptores Syri, series 2, vol. 101 (Rome: de Luigi, 1909). Brief commentary (Syriac text with Latin translation) on most verses of Jas.

The 16th through 18th Centuries:

Erasmus, Desiderius
Opera omnia, vol. 6 (1516; Leiden: Vander, 1705; reprint London: Gregg, 1962), 1025–38.

de Vio, Thomas (Cajetan)
Epistulae Pauli et aliorum Apostolorum ad graecam veritatem castigate (Paris: Badius Ascensius & J. Parvus & J. Roigny, 1532).

Calvin, John
Commentaries on the Catholic Epistles, tr. John Owen (Edinburgh: Calvin Translation Society, 1855).

Grotius, Hugo
Annotationes in Novum Testamentum, ed. Christ. Ern. de Windheim, vol. 2, part 2 (Erlangen and Leipzig: Tetzschner, 1757), 948–1003.

Manton, Thomas
An Exposition on the Epistle of James (1693; reprint London: Banner of Truth Trust, 1962).

Heisen, Heinrich
Novae hypotheses interpretandae felicius epistulae Iacobi apostoli (Bremen: Rump, 1739). This commentary contains valuable citations of parallel material.

Wettstein, Johann Jakob
Novum Testamentum Graecum etc., vol. 2 (Amsterdam: Ex Officina Dommeriana, 1752). This work also contains parallel material—unsifted, but nevertheless extremely useful. But it is necessary to warn against misusing this gigantic work by simply copying Wettstein's parallel passages uncritically, retaining antiquated designations for sources, and not checking them against new editions.

Herder, Johann Gottfried
Briefe zweener Brüder Jesu in unserem Kanon (first published in 1775), in *Herders sämmtliche Werke*, ed. Bernhard Suphan, vol. 7 (Berlin: Weidmann, 1884), 471–573.

Pott, David Julius
in J. B. Koppe, *Novum Testamentum Graece perpetua annotatione illustratum* 9, 1: *Epistola Jacobi* (1786; Göttingen: Dieterich, [3]1816).

The 19th Century:

Hottinger, Jakob
Epistolae d. Iacobi atque Petri I. (Leipzig: Dyck, 1815).

Schulthess, Johannes
Epistola Iacobi (Zürich: Schulthess, 1824).

Gebser, August Rudolph
Der Brief des Jakobus (Berlin: Rücker, 1828). This commentary is especially valuable because of Gebser's copious quotation and use of the patristic commentaries.

Schneckenburger, Matthäus
Annotatio ad epistulam Iacobi perpetua cum brevi tractatione isagogica (Stuttgart: Löflund, 1832).

Kern, Friedrich Heinrich
Ber Brief Jacobi (Tübingen: Fues, 1838).

de Wette, W. M. L.
Kurze Erlärung der Briefe des Petrus, Judas und Jakobus, in his *Kurzgefasstes exegetisches Handbuch zum Neuen Testament*, vol. 3, part 1, 3rd edition by Bruno Brückner (Leipzig: Hirzel, 1847, [3]1865).

Huther, Joh. Ed.
Critical and Exegetical Handbook to the General Epistles of James, Peter, John and Jude, tr. Paton J. Gloag *et al.*, Meyer Commentary on the New Testament 10 (first German edition 1857; New York: Funk & Wagnalls, [2]1887).

Bouman, Hermann
Commentarius perpetuus in Jacobi epistolam (Utrecht: Kemink, 1865).

Ewald, H. G. A.
Das Sendschreiben an die Hebräer und Jakobus' Rundschreiben (Göttingen: Dieterich, 1870).

Hofmann, J. Chr. K.
Der Brief Jakobi, in his *Die heilige Schrift neuen Testaments*, vol. 7, part 3 (Nördlingen: Beck, 1875–6).

Diss. München (Münster i. Westf.: Aschendorff, 1914); Otto Bardenhewer, *Geschichte der altkirchlichen Literatur*, vol. 3 (Freiburg im Breisgau: Herder,

7

1912), 109f.
Cf. above in the commentary on 4:5.

Erdmann, David
Der Brief des Jakobus (Berlin: Wiegandt & Grieben, 1881).

Beyschlag, Willibald
Kritisch-exegetisches Handbuch über den Brief des Jacobus, KEK 15 (Göttingen: Vandenhoeck & Ruprecht, ⁴1882, ⁶1897). Huther (see above) produced the 1st-3rd editions of this volume of the Meyer commentary series, Beyschlag the 4th-6th editions.

Burger, Karl and G. Chr. Luthardt
Die katholischen Briefe, in Kurzgefasster Kommentar zu den heiligen Schriften Alten und Neuen Testaments sowie zu den Apokryphen, eds. Hermann Strack and Otto Zöckler, part B, vol. 4 (Nördlingen: Beck, 1888), 209–31.

von Soden, H.
Hebräerbrief, Briefe des Petrus, Jakobus, Judas, HCNT 3, 2 (Freiburg: Mohr [Siebeck], 1890, ³1899).

Carr, Arthur
The General Epistle of St. James, Cambridge Greek Testament for Schools and Colleges (Cambridge: University Press, 1896).

Spitta, Friedrich
"Der Brief des Jakobus," in his *Zur Geschichte und Litteratur des Urchristentums*, vol. 2 (Göttingen: Vandenhoeck & Ruprecht, 1896), 1–239 (also published separately, with the same pagination).

The 20th Century:

Mayor, Joseph B.
The Epistle of James (London: MacMillan, 1892, ³1910).

Schlatter, Adolf
Die Briefe des Petrus, Judas, Jakobus, der Brief an die Hebräer, in his *Erläuterungen zum Neuen Testament*, vol. 9 (1900; Stuttgart: Calwer Verlag, ³1964).

Knowling, R. J.
The Epistle of St. James, Westminster Commentaries, ed. Walter Lock (London: Methuen, 1904).

Hollmann, Georg and Wilhelm Bousset,
Der Jakobusbrief, SchrNT 3 (Göttingen: Vandenhoeck & Ruprecht, 1907, ³1917), 218–47.

Belser, Johannes Evang.
Die Epistel des heiligen Jakobus (Freiburg: Herder, 1909).

Hort, F. J. A.
The Epistle of St. James: The Greek Text with Introduction, Commentary as far as chapter IV, verse 7, and Additional Notes (London: MacMillan, 1909).

Oesterley, W. E.
The General Epistles of James, in the Expositor's Greek Testament, vol. 4 (London: Hodder & Stoughton, 1910), 383–476.

Windisch, Hans
Die katholischen Briefe, HNT 4, 2 (Tübingen, Mohr [Siebeck], 1911).

Meinertz, Max and Wilhelm Vrede
Die katholischen Briefe, Die heilige Schrift des Neuen Testaments 9 (Bonn: Hanstein, 1915, ⁴1932).

Ropes, James Hardy
A Critical and Exegetical Commentary on the Epistle of St. James, ICC (Edinburgh: Clark, 1916).

Plummer, Alfred
The General Epistles of St. James and St. Jude, The Expositor's Bible (New York: Doran, 1920).

Hauck, Fr.
Der Brief des Jakobus, Kommentar zum Neuen Testament, ed. Theodor Zahn, vol. 16 (Leipzig: Deichert, 1926).⁸

Strack, Hermann L. and Paul Billerbeck
Kommentar zum Neuen Testament aus Talmud und Midrasch, vol. 3 (München: Beck, 1926, ²1954).

Chaine, Joseph
L'épître de Saint Jacques, Études Bibliques (Paris: Gabalda, 1927).

Bardenhewer, Otto
Der Brief des heiligen Jakobus (Freiburg im Breisgau: Herder, 1928).

Moffatt, James
The General Epistles (London: Hodder & Stoughton, 1928).

Windisch, Hans
Die katholischen Briefe, 3rd edition by Herbert Preisker, HNT 15 (Tübingen: Mohr [Siebeck], ²1930, ³1951).

Schlatter, Adolf
Der Brief des Jakobus (Stuttgart: Calwer Verlag, 1932, ²1956).

Hauck, Friedrich
Die Briefe des Jakobus, Petrus, Judas und Johannes, NTD 10 (Göttingen: Vandenhoeck & Ruprecht, 1933, ⁸1957).

Marty, Jacques
L'épître de Jacques: Étude critique (Paris: Alcan, 1935).

Brun, Lyder
Jakobs Brev (Oslo: Aschenhoug [Nygaard], 1941).

de Ambroggi, Pietro
Le Epistole Cattoliche di Giacomo, Pietro, Giovannie Giuda, La Sacra Bibbia (Turin and Rome: Marietti, 1947, ²1949, reprint 1957).

Michl, Johann
Die katholischen Briefe, Regensburger Neues Testament 8, 2 (Regensburg: Pustet, 1953, ²1968).

Garcia ab Orbiso, Theophilus
Epistola Sancti Iacobi, Lateranum, Nova Series 20, 1–4 (Rome: Facultas Theologica Pontificii Athenaei Lateranensis, 1954). This work also contains all the material relating to Jas which this author published in *Verbum Domini* 1935–54.

---

8   Cf. the review by Martin Dibelius in *ThLZ* 53 (1928): 315–7.

Ross, Alexander
   The Epistles of James and John, New International
   Commentary on the New Testament (Grand Rap-
   ids, Mich.: Eerdmans, 1954).
Tasker, R. V. G.
   The General Epistle of James, The Tyndale New Test-
   ament Commentaries (London: Tyndale Press,
   1956).
Blackman, E. C.
   The Epistle of James, Torch Bible Commentaries
   (Naperville, Ill.: Allenson, 1957).
Easton, Burton Scott and Gordon Poteat
   The Epistle of James, in The Interpreter's Bible, vol.
   12 (New York and Nashville: Abingdon, 1957),
   3–74.
Barclay, William
   The Letters of James and Peter (Edinburgh: Saint
   Andrews, 1958, [2]1960).
Thurneysen, E.
   La foi et les oeuvres: Commentaire de l'Épître de Jacques
   (Neuchâtel: Delachaux, 1959).
Smelik, E. L.
   De Stiefapostel: De Brief van Jakobus (Nijkerk: Cal-
   lenbach, 1960, [2]1963).
Schneider, Joh.
   Die Briefe des Jakobus, Petrus, Judas und Johannes,
   NTD 10 (Göttingen: Vandenhoeck & Ruprecht,
   [9]1961).
Simon, Louis
   *Une Ethique de la Sagesse: Commentaire de l'Épître de
   Jacques* (Geneva: Éditions Labor et Fides, 1961).
von Speyr, Adrienne
   Die katholischen Briefe, vol. 1 (Einsiedeln: Johannes,
   1961).
Elliott-Binns, L. E.
   James, in Peake's Commentary on the Bible (Lon-
   don: Nelson, 1962), 1022–5.
Roberts, J. W.
   A Commentary on the General Epistle of James (Austin,
   Tex.: Sweet, 1963).
Mussner, F.
   Der Jakobusbrief, Herders theologischer Kommentar
   zum Neuen Testament 13, 1 (Freiburg and New
   York: Herder & Herder, 1964, [2]1967).
Reicke, Bo
   The Epistles of James, Peter, and Jude, Anchor Bible 37
   (New York: Doubleday, 1964).
Williams, R. R.
   The Letters of John and James, The Cambridge Bible
   Commentary on the New English Bible (New York
   and London: Cambridge University Press, 1965).
Mitton, C. L.
   The Epistle of James (Grand Rapids, Mich.: Eerd-
   mans, 1966).
Sidebottom, E. M., ed.
   James, Jude and 2 Peter, The New Century Bible
   (London and New York: Nelson, 1967).
Leahy, Thomas W.
   The Epistle of James, Jerome Bible Commentary,

vol. 2 (Englewood Cliffs, N. J.: Prentice-Hall,
   1968), 369–77.
Souček, Josef B.
   *Dělná víra a živá naděje: Výklad listu Jakubova a prvního
   listu Petrova* [Active Faith and Living Hope: Com-
   mentary on the Epistle of James and the First
   Epistle of Peter] (Praha: Kalich, 1968).
Haar, Johann
   Der Jakobusbrief, Praktische Schriftauslegung für
   Predigt, Bibelarbeit, Unterricht 9 (Stuttgart and
   Göttingen: Klotz, 1971).
Scheef, Richard L.
   The Letter of James, The Interpreter's One-Volume
   Commentary on the Bible (Nashville and New
   York: Abingdon, 1971), 916–23.
Songer, Harold S.
   James, The Broadman Bible Commentary 12 (Nash-
   ville: Broadman, 1972), 100–40.
Balz, H. and W. Schrage
   Die katholischen Briefe, NTD 10 (Göttingen: Van-
   denhoeck & Ruprecht, [11]1973).
Cantinat, Jean
   Les Épîtres de Saint Jacques et de Saint Jude, Sources
   Bibliques (Paris: Gabalda, 1973).
Grünzweig, F.
   Der Brief des Jakobus, Wuppertaler Studienbibel
   (Wuppertal: Brockhaus, 1973).
Schiwy, Günther
   Die katholischen Briefe (Aschaffenburg: Pattloch,
   1973).

2. Select Monographs and Articles (alphabetically)

Agourides, Savas C.
   "The Origin of the Epistle of St. James: Suggestions
   for a Fresh Approach," *Greek Orthodox Theological
   Review* 9 (1963): 67–78.
Aland, Kurt
   "Der Herrenbruder Jakobus und der Jakobusbrief:
   Zur Frage eines urchristlichen Kalifats," *ThLZ* 69
   (1944): 97–104.
Aland, Kurt
   "Jakobusbrief," in *RGG*[3] 3, 526–8.
Althaus, Paul
   " 'Bekenne einer dem andern seine Sünden': Zur
   Geschichte von Jak 5, 16 seit Augustin," in *Festgabe
   für Theodor Zahn* (Leipzig: Deichert, 1928), 165–94.
Amphoux, Christian-Bernard
   "A propos de Jacques I, 17," *RHPhR* 50 (1970):
   127–36.
Amphoux, Christian-Bernard
   "Études structurales: Langue de l'Épître de
   Jacques," *RHPhR* 53 (1973): 7–45.
Baltzer, Klaus and Helmut Köster
   "Die Bezeichnung des Jakobus als 'ΩΒΛΙΑΣ,"
   ZNW 46 (1955): 141f.
Bartmann, Bernhard
   St. Paulus und St. Jacobus über die Rechtfertigung, BSF
   2, 1 (Freiburg: Herder, 1897).

Beck, David Lawrence
　　The Composition of the Epistle of James, Unpub. Diss.
　　(Princeton Theological Seminary, 1973).
Bergauer, Paulus
　　Der Jakobusbrief bei Augustinus und die damit verbunde-
　　nen Probleme der Rechtfertigungslehre (Wien: Herder,
　　1962).
Bieder, Werner
　　"Christliche Existenz nach dem Zeugnis des Jako-
　　busbriefes," *ThZ* 5 (1949): 93–113.
Bischoff, A.
　　"τὸ τέλος κυρίου," *ZNW* 7 (1906): 274–9.
Blenker, Alfred
　　"Jakobs brevs sammenhaeng," *Dansk Teologisk*
　　Tidsskrift 30 (1967): 193–202.
Böhlig, A.
　　"Zum Martyrium des Jakobus," *Nov Test* 5 (1962):
　　207–13.
Böhmer, J.
　　"Der 'Glaube' im Jakobusbriefe," *NKZ* 9 (1898):
　　251–6.
Bonsirven, J.
　　"Jacques (Épître de S.)," in the *Supplement au Dic-*
　　tionnaire de la Bible, ed. Louis Pirot and André
　　Robert, vol. 4 (Paris: Letouzey et Ané, 1949), 783–
　　95.
Braumann, Georg
　　"Der theologische Hintergrund des Jakobus-
　　briefes," *ThZ* 18 (1962): 401–10.
Brinktrine, J.
　　"Zu Jak. 2, 1," *Biblica* 35 (1954): 40–2.
Brown, Scott Kent
　　James: A Religio-Historical Study of the Relations be-
　　tween Jewish, Gnostic, and Catholic Christianity in the
　　Early Period through an Investigation of the Traditions
　　about James the Lord's Brother, Unpub. Diss. (Brown
　　University, 1972).
Brückner, Wilhelm
　　"Die nach Petrus, Jakobus und Judas sich nen-
　　nenden Briefe," *StGGB* 5 (1879): 145–77.
Brückner, Wilhelm
　　"Zur Kritik des Jakobusbriefs," *ZWTh* 17 (1874):
　　530–41.
Cadoux, Arthur Temple
　　The Thought of St. James (London: Clarke, 1944).
von Campenhausen, Hans
　　"Die Nachfolge des Jakobus: Zur Frage eines ur-
　　christlichen 'Kalifats,'" *ZKG* 63 (1950/1): 133–44;
　　also published in his *Aus der Frühzeit des Christentums:*
　　Studien zur Kirchengeschichte des ersten und zweiten Jahr-
　　hunderts (Tübingen: Mohr [Siebeck], 1963), 135–
　　51.
Carr, Arthur
　　"The Meaning of Ὁ ΚΟΣΜΟΣ in James III.6,"
　　Expositor, ser. 7, vol. 8 (1909): 318–25.
Carroll, Kenneth L.
　　"The Place of James in the Early Church," *The*
　　Bulletin of the John Rylands Library 44 (1961): 49–67.

Charue, André-Marie
　　"La maîtrise de la langue dans l'Épître de St.
　　Jacques," *Collationes Namurcenses* 29 (1935): 393–
　　407.
Charue, André-Marie
　　"Quelques avis aux riches et aux pauvres dans
　　l'Épître de St. Jacques," *Collationes Namurcenses* 30
　　(1936): 177–87.
Cladder, H. J.
　　"Die Anlage des Jakobusbriefes," *ZKTh* 28 (1904):
　　37–57.
Cladder, H. J.
　　"Der formale Aufbau des Jakobusbriefes," *ZKTh*
　　28 (1904): 295–330.
Coppieters, H.
　　"La signification et la provenance de la citation
　　Jac. IV, 5," *Revue Biblique* 12 (1915): 35–58.
Corssen, Peter
　　Review of Bernhard Weiss, *Die katholischen Briefe:*
　　Textkritische Untersuchungen und Textherstellung, TU 8,
　　2, in *GGA* (1893): 573–602.
Cranfield, C. E. B.
　　"The Message of James," *SJT* 18 (1965): 182–93,
　　338–45.
Dibelius, Martin
　　A Fresh Approach to the New Testament and Early Chris-
　　tian Literature (ET London: Nicholson and Watson,
　　1936), 226–30.
Dibelius, Martin
　　"Jakobusbrief," in *RGG*² 3, 18–21.
Eckart, Karl-Gottfried
　　"Zur Terminologie des Jakobusbriefes," *ThLZ* 89
　　(1964): 521–6.
Edsman, Carl-Martin
　　"Schöpferwille und Geburt Jac 1, 18: Eine Studie
　　zur altchristlichen Kosmologie," *ZNW* 38 (1939):
　　11–44.
Edsman, Carl-Martin
　　"Schöpfung und Wiedergeburt: Nochmals Jac.
　　1, 18," *Spiritus et Veritas* [Festschrift Karl Kundsin]
　　(Eutin: Ozolin, 1953), 43–55.
Eichholz, Georg
　　Glaube und Werke bei Paulus und Jakobus, Theolo-
　　gische Existenz Heute, N.F. 88 (München: Kaiser,
　　1961).
Eichholz, Georg
　　"Jakobusbrief," *Evangelisches Kirchenlexikon*, ed.
　　Heinz Brunotte and Otto Weber, vol. 2 (Göttingen:
　　Vandenhoeck and Ruprecht, 1958), 234–5.
Eichholz, Georg
　　Jakobus und Paulus: Ein Beitrag zum Problem des
　　Kanons, Theologische Existenz Heute, N.F. 39
　　(München: Kaiser, 1953).
Eleder, Felix
　　Jakobusbrief und Bergpredigt, Unpub. Diss. (Wien,
　　1964).
Elliott-Binns, L. E.
　　"James I.18: Creation or Redemption?" *NTS* 3
　　(1957): 148–61.

Elliott-Binns, L. E.
"The Meaning of ὕλη in Jas. III.5," *NTS* 2 (1956): 48–50.

Endemann, K.
"Zur Frage über die Brüder des Herrn," *NKZ* 11 (1900): 833–65.

Engelhardt, Eduard
"Bemerkungen zu Jac. 4, v. 5 u. 6," *ZLThK* 30 (1869): 232–43.

van Eysinga, G. A. van den Bergh
"De Tong . . . . en Erger! Proeve van Verklaring van Jakobus 3, vs. 6," *NThT* 20 (1931): 303–20.

Feine, Paul
Der Jakobusbrief nach Lehranschauungen und Entstehungsverhältnissen (Eisenach: Wilckens, 1893).

Feine, Paul
"Über literarische Abhängigkeit und Zeitverhältnisse des Jakobusbriefes," *NJDTh* 3 (1894): 322–34.

Feuillet, A.
"Le sens du mot Parousie dans l'Evangile Matthieu —Comparaison entre Matth. 24 et Jac. 5, 1–11," in *The Background of the New Testament and Its Eschatology*, ed. W. D. Davies and D. Daube (Cambridge: University Press, 1956), 261–80.

Fischer, H.
"Ein Spruchvers im Jacobusbrief," *Philologus* 50 (1891): 377–9.

Fonjallaz, Olivier
Le problème de l'Epître de Jacques, Unpub. Diss. (Lausanne, 1965).

Forbes, P. B. R.
"The Structure of the Epistle of James," *Evangelical Quarterly* 44 (1972): 147–53.

Francis, Fred O.
"The Form and Function of the Opening and Closing Paragraphs of James and 1 John," *ZNW* 61 (1970): 110–26.

Friesenhahn, Hans
"Zur Geschichte der Überlieferung und Exegese des Textes bei Jak V, 14f," *BZ* 24 (1938/9): 185–90.

Gächter, Paul
"Jakobus von Jerusalem," *ZKTh* 76 (1954): 129–69.

Gallagher, J. Tim
"A Study of von Soden's *H*-text in the Catholic Epistles," *Andrews University Seminary Studies* 8 (1970): 97–119.

Gaugusch, Ludwig
Der Lehrgehalt der Jakobusepistel, Freiburger theologische Studien 16 (Freiburg: Herder, 1914).

Gertner, M.
"Midrashic Terms and Techniques in the New Testament: The Epistle of James, a Midrash on a Psalm," in *Studia Evangelica*, vol. 3, TU 88 (Berlin: Akademie–Verlag, 1964), 463.

Gertner, M.
"Midrashim in the New Testament," *Journal of Semitic Studies* 7 (1962): 267–92.

Grafe, Ed.
Die Stellung und Bedeutung des Jakobusbriefes in der Entwicklung des Urchristentums (Tübingen and Leipzig: Mohr [Siebeck], 1904),

Greeven, Heinrich
"Jede Gabe ist gut, Jak. 1, 17," *ThZ* 14 (1958): 1–13.

Grimm, Wilibald
"Über die Stelle Br. Jakobi IV, v. 5 und 6a," *ThStKr* 27 (1854): 934–56.

Gryglewicz, Feliks
"L'épître de St. Jacques et l'évangile de St. Matthieu," *Roczniki Teologiczno-Kanoniczne* 8, 3 (1961): 33–55.

Halson, B. R.
"The Epistle of James; 'Christian Wisdom?'" in *Studia Evangelica*, vol. 4, part 1, TU 102 (Berlin: Akademie-Verlag, 1968), 308–14.

Hartmann, Gerhard
"Der Aufbau des Jakobusbriefes," *ZKTh* 66 (1942): 63–70.

Haupt, Erich
Review of David Erdmann, *Der Brief des Jakobus*, and W. Beyschlag, *Kritisch-exegetisches Handbuch über den Brief des Jakobus*, in *ThStKr* 56 (1883): 177–94.

Haupt, Erich
Review of F. Spitta, *Der Brief des Jakobus*, and G. Wandel, *Der Brief des Jakobus*, in *ThStKr* 69 (1896): 747–77.

Hilgenfeld, A.
"Der Brief des Jakobus," *ZWTh* 16 (1873): 1–33.

Hodges, Zane C.
"Light on James Two from Textual Criticism," *Bibliotheca Sacra* 120 (1963): 341–50.

Holtzmann, H.
"Die Zeitlage des Jakobusbriefes," *ZWTh* 25 (1882), 292–310.

Hoyos, P.
"La Extreme Unción en el primer siglo: Santiago 5, 14–15 a la luz de un nuevo descubrimiento," *Revista Biblica* 25 (1963): 34–42.

Jäger, Gottfried
"Der Verfasser des Jakobusbriefes," *ZLThK* 39 (1878): 420–6.

Jeremias, Joachim
"Jac 4, 5: ἐπιποθεῖ," *ZNW* 50 (1959): 137f.

Jeremias, Joachim
"Paul and James," *ET* 66 (1955): 368–71.

Johanson, Bruce C.
"The Definition of 'Pure Religion' in James 1:27 Reconsidered," *ET* 84 (1973): 118–9.

Johnston, Charles
"The Controversy between St. Paul and St. James," *Constructive Quarterly* 3 (1915): 603–19.

Karo, G.
"Versuch über Jac. 2, 18," *PrM* 4 (1900): 159f.

Kawerau, Gustav
"Die Schicksale des Jakobusbriefes im 16. Jahrhundert," *ZWL* 10 (1889): 359–70.

Kelly, Francis Xavier
Poor and Rich in the Epistle of James, Unpub. Diss (Temple University, 1973).

Kern, F. H.
."Der Charakter und Ursprung des Briefs Jakobi," *TZTh* (1835, 2. Heft): 3–132.

Kilpatrick, George D.
"Übertreter des Gesetzes, Jak. 2, 11," *ThZ* 23 (1967): 433.

Kirk, J. A.
"The Meaning of Wisdom in James: Examination of a Hypothesis," *NTS* 16 (1969): 24–38.

Kirn, O.
"Ein Vorschlag zu Jakobus 4, 5," *ThStKr* 77 (1904): 127–33.

Kirn, O.
"Noch einmal Jakobus 4, 5," *ThStKr* 77 (1904): 593–604.

Kittel, Gerhard
"Der geschichtliche Ort des Jakobusbriefes," *ZNW* 41 (1942): 71–105.

Kittel, Gerhard
"Der Jakobusbrief und die Apostolischen Väter," *ZNW* 43 (1950/1): 54–112.

Kittel, Gerhard
Review of Martin Dibelius, *Der Brief des Jakobus*, in *ThLBl* 44 (1923): 3–7.

Kittel, Gerhard
"Die Stellung des Jakobus zu Judentum und Heidenchristentum," *ZNW* 30 (1931): 145–57.

Klöpper, Alb.
"Die Erörterung des Verhältnisses von Glauben und Werken im Jakobusbriefe (cap. 2, 14–26)," *ZWTh* 28 (1885): 280–319.

Klostermann, E.
"Zum Texte des Jakobusbriefes," in *Verbum dei manet in aeternum* (Festschrift O. Schmitz), ed. Werner Foerster (Witten: Luther-Verlag, 1953), 71f.

Knox, W. L.
"The Epistle of James," *Journal of Theological Studies* 46 (1945): 10–17.

Köhler, Albert
Glaube und Werke im Jakobusbrief, Beilage zum Jahresberichte des Gymnasiums zu Zittau, Easter 1913 (Zittau: Menzel, 1913).

Köster, Friedrich
"Ueber die Leser, an welche der Brief des Jakobus und der erste Brief des Petrus gerichtet ist," *ThStKr* 39 (1831): 581–8.

Köster, Helmut
(See above under Baltzer, Klaus)

Kübel, Robert
Über das Verhältnis von Glauben und Werken bei Jakobus (Tübingen: Fues, 1880).

Kühl, Ernst
Die Stellung des Jakobusbriefes zum alttestamentlichen Gesetz und zur paulinischen Rechtfertigungslehre (Königsberg i. Pr.: Koch, 1905).

Kürzdorfer, Klaus
Der Character des Jakobusbriefes: Eine Auseinandersetzung mit den Thesen von A. Meyer und M. Dibelius, Unpub. Diss. (Tübingen, 1966).

Kutsch, Ernst
"'Eure Rede aber sei ja ja, nein nein,'" *Evangelische Theologie* 20 (1960): 206–18.

Kuttner, Otto
"Einzelne Bemerkungen über das Verhältnis von Jac. II zu Röm. XII–XIV," *ZWTh* 31 (1888): 36–40.

Lackmann, Max
Sola Fide: Eine exegetische Studie über Jakobus 2 zur reformatorischen Rechtfertigungslehre, BFTh 50 (Gütersloh: Bertelsmann, 1949).

Laws, Sophie S.
"Does Scripture Speak in Vain? A Reconsideration of James IV.5," *NTS* 20 (1974): 210–5.

Leloir, Louis
"Traduction latine des versions syriaques et arméniennes de l'Épître de Jacques," *Le Muséon* 83 (1970): 189–208.

Lohse, Eduard
"Glaube und Werke: Zur Theologie des Jakobusbriefes," *ZNW* 48 (1957): 1–22.

Lohse, Eduard
Review of Franz Mussner, *Der Jakobusbrief*, in *ThLZ* 91 (1966): 112–4.

Luck, Ulrich
"Der Jakobusbrief und die Theologie des Paulus," *Theologie und Glaube* 61 (1971): 161–79.

Luck, Ulrich
"Weisheit und Leiden: Zum Problem Paulus und Jakobus," *ThLZ* 92 (1967): 253–8.

Lyonnet, Stanislas
"Les témoignages de Saint Jean Chrysostome et de Saint Jérôme sur Jacques le frère du Seigneur," *Recherches de Science Religieuse* 29 (1939): 335–51.

Mader, Joh.
"Apostel und Herrenbrüder," *BZ* 6 (1908): 393–406.

Massebieau, L.
"L'Épître de Jacques est-elle l'oeuvre d'un Chrétien," *RHR* 32 (1895): 249–83.

Mehlhorn, Paul
"Noch ein Erklärungsversuch zu Jac. 2, 18," *PrM* 4 (1900): 192–4.

Meinertz, Max
Der Jakobusbrief und sein Verfasser in Schrift und Überlieferung, BSF 10, 1–3 (Freiburg: Herder, 1905).

Meinertz, Max
Der Jakobusbrief und sein Verfasser nach der ältesten Überlieferung, Diss. Strassburg (Freiburg: Herder, 1905).

Meinertz, Max
"Die Krankensalbung Jak 5, 14f," *BZ* 20 (1932): 23–36.

Ménégoz, Eugène
"Étude comparative de l'enseignement de saint

Paul et de saint Jacques sur la justification par la foi," in *Études de Théologie et d'Histoire* (Paris: Fischbacher, 1901), 121–50.

Meyer, Arnold
Das Rätsel des Jacobusbriefes, BZNW 10 (Giessen: Töpelmann, 1930).[9]

Michl, Johann
"Der Spruch Jakobusbrief 4, 5," in *Neutestamentliche Aufsätze* (Festschrift Josef Schmid), ed. J. Blinzler, O. Kuss, F. Mussner (Regensburg: Pustet, 1963), 167–74.

Minear, Paul S.
"Yes or No: The Demand for Honesty in the Early Church," *Nov Test* 13 (1971): 1–13.

Morris, Kenneth F.
An Investigation of Several Linguistic Affinities Between the Epistle of James and the Book of Isaiah, Unpub. Diss. (Union Theological Seminary in Virginia, 1964).

Mussner, Franz
"'Direkte' and 'indirekte' Christologie im Jakobusbrief," *Catholica* [Münster] 24 (1970): 111–7.

Noack, Bent
"Jakobus wider die Reichen," *StTh* 18 (1964): 10–25.

Nötscher, F.
"'Gesetz der Freiheit' im NT und in der Mönchsgemeinde am Toten Meer," *Biblica* 34 (1953): 193f.

Noret, Jacques
"Une scholie de l'épître de Jacques tirée de Syméon Métaphraste," *Biblica* 55 (1974): 74f.

Obermüller, Rudolf
"Hermeneutische Themen im Jakobusbrief," *Biblica* 53 (1972): 234–44.

Paret, Eugen
"Noch ein Wort über Jac. 4, 5 nebst 1 Mos. 4, 7," *ThStKr* 36 (1863): 113–8.

Paret, Eugen
"Nochmals das Zitat in Jak. 4, 5," *ThStKr* 80 (1907): 234–46.

Parry, Reginald St. John
A Discussion of the General Epistle of St. James (London: Clay, 1903).

Patrick, William
James the Lord's Brother (Edinburgh: Clark, 1906).

Peterson, Erik
"Der Gottesfreund: Beiträge zur Geschichte eines religiösen Terminus," *ZKG* 42 (1923): 161–202.

Pfeiffer, Ernst
"Der Zusammenhang des Jakobusbriefes," *ThStKr*

23 (1850): 163–80.

Powell, Cyril H.
"'Faith' in James and its Bearing on the Problem of the Date of the Epistle," *ET* 62 (1950/1): 311–4.

Preisker, Herbert
"Die Eigenart des Jakobusbriefs in der Geschichte des Urchristentums," *Theologische Blätter* 13 (1934): 229–36.

Prentice, William K.
"James the Brother of the Lord," in *Studies in Roman Social and Economic History* (Festschrift Allan Chester Johnson), ed. P. R. Coleman-Norton (Princeton: University Press, 1951), 144–51.

Preuschen, E.
"Jac 5, 11," *ZNW* 17 (1916): 79.

Reicke, Bo
"L'onction des malades d'après Saint Jacques," *Maison-Dieu* 113 (1973): 50–6.

Rendall, Gerald H.
The Epistle of James and Judaic Christianity (Cambridge: University Press, 1927).

Rendtorff, Heinrich
Hörer und Täter, Die urchristliche Botschaft 19 (Hamburg: Furche, 1953).

Review and Expositor 66 (1969): 365–434 (contains various contributions on Jas).

Riesenfeld, Harald
"'ΑΠΛΩΣ: Zu Jak. 1, 5," *Con Neot* 9 (1944): 33–41.

Robert, David J., III
"The Definition of 'Pure Religion' in James 1:27," *ET* 83 (1972): 215f.

Robertson, A. T.
Practical and Social Aspects of Christianity: The Wisdom of James (New York: Doran, 1915).

Rönsch, Hermann
"Abraham der Freund Gottes," *ZWTh* 16 (1873): 583–90.

Ropes, James Hardy
"The Greek Catena to the Catholic Epistles," *HTR* 19 (1926): 383–8.

Ropes, James Hardy
"'Thou Hast Faith and I Have Works' (James II.18)," *Expositor*, ser. 7, vol. 5 (1908): 547–56.

Rose, Vincent
"L'Épître de Saint Jacques est-elle un écrit Chrétien," *Revue Biblique* 5 (1896): 519–34 (a response to the article by Massebieau—see above).

Rost, L.
"Archäologische Bemerkungen zu einer Stelle des

---

9   On Meyer's book, cf. Martin Dibelius, "Zur Formgeschichte des Neuen Testaments (ausserhalb der Evangelien)," *Theologische Rundschau*, N.F. 3 (1931): 216f; the review by Hans Windisch in *Gnomon* 10 (1934): 382f; Kittel, "Der geschichtliche Ort," 76f; Wilhelm Michaelis, *Einleitung in das Neue Testament* (Bern: Haller, ²1954), 276.

Jakobusbriefs (Jak. 2, 2f.)," *Palästinajahrbuch* 29 (1933): 53–66.

Rusche, Helga
"Der Erbarmer hält Gericht: Einführung in die Grundgedanken des Jakobusbriefes (2, 1–13a)," *Bibel und Leben* 5 (1964): 236–47.

Rusche, Helga
"Standhaben in Gott: Einführung in die Grundgedanken des Jakobusbriefes (1, 1–27)," *Bibel und Leben* 5 (1964): 153–63.

Rusche, Helga
"Vom lebendigen Glauben und vom rechten Beten: Einführung in die Grundgedanken des Jakobusbriefes (2, 14–26; 4, 1–10)," *Bibel und Leben* 6 (1965): 26–47.

Rustler, M.
Thema und Disposition des Jakobusbriefes: Eine formkritische Studie, Unpub. Diss. (Wien, 1952).

Sahlin, Harald
"Noch einmal Jacobus 'Oblias,'" *Biblica* 28 (1947): 152f.

Sailer, Johann
"Jak 5, 14f und die Krankensalbung," *Theologisch-praktische Quartalschrift* 113 (1965): 347–53.

Sanday, W.
"Some Further Remarks on the Corbey St. James (*ff*)," *Studia Biblica*, vol. 1 (Oxford: Clarendon, 1885), 233–63.

Schammberger, Hermann
Die Einheitlichkeit des Jacobusbriefes im antignostischen Kampf (Gotha: Klotz, 1936).

Schanz, P.
"Jakobus und Paulus," *ThQ* 62 (1880): 3–46, 247–86.

Schep, J. A.
"Een onaanvaardbare exegese van Jacobus 2:1," *GThT* 58 (1958): 54–6.

Schmidt, Woldemar Gottlob
Der Lehrgehalt des Jacobus-Briefes: Ein Beitrag zur neutestamentlichen Theologie (Leipzig: Hinrichs, 1869).

Schmidt-Clausing, Fritz
"Die unterschiedliche Stellung Luthers und Zwinglis zum Jakobusbrief," *Reformatio* 18 (1969): 568–85.

Schökel, Luis Alonso
"James 5, 6 and 4, 6," *Biblica* 54 (1973): 73–6.

Schoeps, Hans Joachim
"Jacobus ὁ δίκαιος καὶ Ὠβλίας: Neuer Lösungsvorschlag in einer schwierigen Frage," *Biblica* 24 (1943), 398–403; reprinted in his *Aus frühchristlicher Zeit: Religionsgeschichtliche Untersuchungen* (Tübingen: Mohr [Siebeck], 1950), 120–5.

Schoeps, Hans Joachim
Theologie und Geschichte des Judenchristentums (Tübingen: Mohr [Siebeck], 1949), Excursus 1: "Die Stellung des Jakobusbriefes," pp. 343–9.

Schwartz, E.
"Zu Eusebius Kirchengeschichte, I. Das Martyrium Jakobus des Gerechten," *ZNW* 4 (1903): 48–61.

Schwarz, G.
"Jak. 2, 14–26," *ThStKr* 64 (1891): 704–737

Seitz, Oscar J. F.
"Afterthoughts on the Term 'Dipsychos,'" *NTS* 4 (1957/8): 327–34.

Seitz, Oscar J. F.
"Antecedents and Signification of the Term ΔΙΨΥΧΟΣ," *JBL* 66 (1947): 211–9.

Seitz, Oscar J. F.
"James and the Law," in *Studia Evangelica*, vol. 2, TU 87 (Berlin: Akademie-Verlag, 1964), 472–86.

Seitz, Oscar J. F.
"Relationship of the Shepherd of Hermas to the Epistle of James," *JBL* 63 (1944): 131–40.

Shepherd, Massey H.
"The Epistle of James and the Gospel of Matthew," *JBL* 75 (1956): 40–51.

von Soden, H(ermann)
"Der Jacobusbrief," *JPTh* 10 (1884): 137–92.

Souček, Josef B.
"Zu den Problemen des Jakobusbriefes," *Evangelische Theologie* 18 (1958): 460–8.

Southwestern Journal of Theology 12 (1969): 9–88 (contains various contributions on Jas).

Staab, Karl
"Die griechischen Katenenkommentare zu den katholischen Briefen," *Biblica* 5 (1924): 296–353.

Stauffer, Ethelbert
"Das 'Gesetz der Freiheit' in der Ordensregel von Jericho," *ThLZ* 77 (1952): 527–32.

Stauffer, Ethelbert
"Petrus und Jakobus in Jerusalem," in *Begegnung der Christen: Studien evangelischer und katholischer Theologie* (Festschrift Otto Karrer), ed. Maximilian Roesle and Oscar Cullmann (Stuttgart: Evangelisches Verlagswerk, 1959), 361–72.

Stauffer, Ethelbert
"Zum Kalifat des Jacobus," *ZRGG* 4 (1952): 193–214.

Steck, R.
"Die Konfession des Jakobusbriefes," *Theologische Zeitschrift aus der Schweiz* 15 (1898): 169–88.

Terrinoni, Ubaldus da Fiuggi
Il cuore diviso: Studio esegetico su Giac. 1, 8; 4, 8, Unpub. Diss. (Gregorian University, Rome, 1966).

Thomas, Johannes
"Anfechtung und Vorfreude: Ein biblisches Thema nach Jakobus 1, 2–18, im Zusammenhang mit Psalm 126, Röm. 5, 3–5 und 1 Petr. 1, 5–7, formkritisch untersucht und parakletisch ausgelegt," *Kerygma und Dogma* 14 (1968): 183–206.

Tielemann, J.
"Zum Verständnis und zur Würdigung des Jakobusbriefes," *NKZ* 44 (1933): 256–70.

Tielemann, Th.
"Versuch einer neuen Auslegung und Anordnung des Jakobusbriefes," *NKZ* 5 (1894): 580–611.

Till, Walter
"Ein achmimisches Jakobusbrieffragment," *Le Muséon* 51 (1938): 69–71.

Tobac, É.
"Le problème de la justification dans saint Paul et dans saint Jacques," *Revue d'Histoire Ecclésiastique* 22 (1926): 797–805.

Torrey, Charles C.
"James the Just and his Name 'Oblias,'" *JBL* 63 (1944): 93–8.

Toxopeus, Hendrik Jan
Karakter en Herkomst van den Jacobusbrief, Diss. Amsterdam (Amsterdam: Clausen, 1906).

Trocmé, É.
"Les Eglises pauliniennes vues du dehors: Jac 2, 1 à 3, 13," in *Studia Evangelica*, vol. 2, TU 87 (Berlin: Akademie-Verlag, 1964), 660–9.

Usteri, L.
"Glaube, Werke und Rechtfertigung im Jakobusbrief," *ThStKr* 62 (1889): 211–256.

Via, Dan Otto, Jr.
"The Right Strawy Epistle Reconsidered: A Study in Biblical Ethics and Hermeneutics," *Journal of Religion* 49 (1969): 253–67.

Vowinkel, Ernst
Die Grundgedanken des Jakobusbriefes verglichen mit den ersten Briefen des Petrus und Johannes, BFTh 6 (Gütersloh: Bertelsmann, 1899).

Walker, Rolf
"Allein aus Werken: Zur Auslegung von Jakobus 2, 14–26," *ZThK* 61 (1964): 155–92.

Walther, W.
"Zu Luthers Ansicht über den Jakobusbrief," *ThStKr* 66 (1893): 595–8.

Wandel, Georg
"Zur Auslegung der Stelle Jak. 3, 1–8," *ThStKr* 66 (1893): 679–707.

Ward, Roy Bowen
The Communal Concern of the Epistle of James, Unpub. Diss. (Harvard, 1966).

Ward, Roy Bowen
"Partiality in the Assembly," *HTR* 62 (1969): 87–97.

Ward, Roy Bowen
"The Works of Abraham: James 2:14–26," *HTR* 61 (1968): 283–90.

Weiffenbach, Wilhelm
Exegetisch-theologische Studie über Jak 2, 14–26 (Giessen: Ricker, 1871).

Weiss, Bernhard
Der Jakobusbrief und die neuere Kritik (Leipzig: Deichert, 1904).

Weiss, Bernhard
Die katholischen Briefe: Textkritische Untersuchungen und Textherstellung, TU 8, 2 (Leipzig: Hinrichs, 1892).

Werner, Karl
"Ueber den Brief Jacobi," *ThQ* 54 (1872): 248–79.

White, Henry J., ed.
Portions of the Acts of the Apostles, of the Epistle of St. James, and of the First Epistle of St. Peter from the Bobbio Palimpsest (s), Old Latin Biblical Texts 4 (Oxford: Clarendon, 1897).

Wiersma, S.
"Enige opmerkingen over de betekenis van de woorden *diakrinesthai* en *pistis* in de brief van Jacobus," *GThT* 56 (1956): 177–9.

Wifstrand, Albert
"Stylistic Problems in the Epistles of James and Peter," *StTh* 1 (1948): 170–82.

Wilkinson, John
"Healing in the Epistle of James," *SJT* 24 (1971): 326–45.

Williams, A. Lukyn
"The Epistle of St. James and the Jewish-Christians of his Times," *Church Quarterly Review* 123 (1936): 24–32.

Windisch, Hans
"Zur Rahabgeschichte: Zwei Parallelen aus der klassischen Literatur," *ZAW* 37 (1918): 188–98.

Wolverton, Wallace I.
"The Double-Minded Man in the Light of Essene Psychology," *Anglican Theological Review* 38 (1956): 166–75.

Wordsworth, John
"The Corbey St. James (*ff*), and its relation to other Latin versions, and to the original language of the Epistle," *Studia Biblica*, vol. 1 (Oxford: Clarendon, 1885), 113–50.

Zahn, Theodor
"Die soziale Frage und die Innere Mission nach dem Brief des Jakobus," *ZWL* 10 (1889): 295–307.

Zeller, E.
"Ueber Jak. 1, 12," *ZWTh* 6 (1863): 93–96.

Zimmer, Michael
"Das schriftstellerische Verhältnis des Jacobusbriefes zur paulinischen Literatur," *ZWTh* 36 (1893): 481–503.

Zodhiates, Spiros
The Labor of Love: An Exposition of James 2:14–4:12 (Grand Rapids, Mich.: Eerdmans, 1960).

Zodhiates, Spiros
The Patience of Hope: An Exposition of James 4:13–5:20 (Grand Rapids, Mich.: Eerdmans, 1960).

Zodhiates, Spiros
The Work of Faith: An Exposition of James 1:1–2:13 (Grand Rapids, Mich.: Eerdmans, 1959).

Zyro, Ferd. Friedrich
"Ist es mit Jakobus 4, 5 nun im Reinen?" *ThStKr* 45 (1872): 716–29.

Zyro, Ferd. Friedrich
"Noch einmal Jakob. 4, 5.6," *ThStKr* 34 (1861): 765–74.

Zyro, Ferd. Friedrich
"Zur Erklärung von Jakob. 4, 5.6," *ThStKr* 13 (1840): 432–50.

Indices*

1. Passages

a / Old Testament and Apocrypha

---

*Numbers in parentheses following page citations for this volume refer to footnotes.

275

d / Early Christian Literature and the Ancient Church

2. Greek Words

ἀγαπᾶν
89, 138

ἄγειν (ἄγε)
231

ἁγνός
213

ἀδιάκριτος
214

ἀκατάστατος
83, 200

ἀλαζονεία
234

ἀλήθεια
105

ἀνεμίζειν
81(56)

ἀνήρ
82

ἄνθρωπος
82

ἀνυπόκριτος
214

ἀπαρχή
104, 106

ἀπείραστος
92

ἁπλῶς
77–79

ἀποκύειν
94(136), 104

ἀποσκίασμα
100–102

ἀπόστολος
12(29)

ἀργός
161(64)

ἄσπιλος
21f, 146

ἀτμίς
233

γένεσις
116

γιγνώσκειν
72

δαιμονιώδης
213

διακρίνειν
136f

διακρίνεσθαι
31

διασπορά
66(15)

δικαιοσύνη
30, 110, 162, 165

δικαιοῦν
161f

διψυχία, δίψυχος
31(102), 82, 83(65), 226

δοκίμιον
72(18), 75f

δόσις
99f

δοῦλος
65

δώρημα
100

ἐγείρειν
254

ἐκκλησία
134, 253

ἐλευθερία
116

ἔμφυτος (see also λόγος)
113f

ἐνεργεῖν
256

ἔνοχος
144(110)

ἐπιεικής
214(29)

ἐπιθυμία
93, 215(40)

ἐπιτήδειος
153

ἐργάζεσθαι
110

ἔργον
74, 122, 146, 162

ἔργον τέλειον
73f

ἐριθεία
209, 210(9)

εὐλογεῖν
202

εὐπαθής
214(30)

ἡδονή
215

ἡλίκος
191

θερμαίνειν
153

θησαυρίζειν
237f

θρησκεία, θρησκός
120–22

ἰᾶσθαι
255

ἰός
236(34)

καρπός
215

κατεργάζεσθαι
75

κατιοῦν
236

καύσων
86

κενός
161(62)

κλύδων
82

κόσμος
37(128), 121, 194, 220

κρίνειν
228(103), 229

κτίσμα
106

κύριος
65, 82, 202, 253(67)

λογίζεσθαι
164f, 172–74

λόγος
105

λόγος ἀληθείας
48(173), 104

λόγος ἔμφυτος
21, 48, 112

μάχεσθαι, μάχη
216–18

μοιχαλίς
219, 224

νεκρός
153

νόμος
122, 146

νόμος βασιλικός
142f

ὁδός
86

ὁμοιοπαθής
257

ὄνομα
140

ὁρμή
190

ὄψιμος
243

παραλλαγή
100–102

παρουσία
243(5)

πᾶς
72(11), 99(151)

πατήρ
100, 102, 202

πειρασμός
69f, 88, 90, 138

περιοχή
15

περισσεία
113

πιστεύειν
165, 174, 176

πίστις
80, 152, 161, 168, 176

πλούσιος
70, 84, 135(64)

πλοῦτος
236

πνεῦμα
224

ποιητής
114

πολεμεῖν, πόλεμος
216–18

πορεία
86

πραΰτης
112

πρόϊμος
243

προσωπολημψία
30, 126, 129

πρόσωπον
86, 116

ῥιπίζειν
81(56)

ῥυπαρία
113

σάρξ
217(47), 237

σήπειν
236

στέφανος
88

συναγωγή
134–34, 253

σφαγή
239

σῴζειν
254

ταλειπωρεῖν
227, 235(30)

ταπεινός
70, 71(6), 84

ταπείνωσις
85

τέλειος
24(70), 74, 77

τέλος
246

τροπή
100–03

τροχὸς τῆς γενέσεως
195, 197(81), 198, 212

ὕλη
191

ὑπομονή
73, 75, 88

ὑποπόδιον
132

ὕψος
84

φθονεῖν, φθόνος
217, 221f, 224

φονεύειν
147(121), 217

φύσις
200

τὰ φωτά
100, 102

χαίρειν
18, 20(55), 67f

χαλιναγωγεῖν
121

χαλινός
185(27)

χαρά
18, 68

χρή
202(104)

ψυχικός
21, 25, 210–12

3. Subjects